Recent Titles in
Studies in Penal Theory and Philosophy

R.A. Duff, General Editor

Just Sentencing
Principles and Procedures for a Workable System Richard S. Frase

Popular Punishment
On the Normative Significance of Public Opinion
Jesper Ryberg and Julian V. Roberts

Taming the Presumption of Innocence
Richard Lippke

Sentencing Multiple Crimes
Edited by Jesper Ryberg, Julian V. Roberts and Jan W. de Keijser

Playing Fair
Political Obligation and the Problems of Punishment
Richard Dagger

Hate, Politics, Law
Critical Perspectives on Combating Hate
Edited by Thomas Brudholm and Birgitte Schepelern Johansen

Criminal Law in the Age of the Administrative State
Vincent Chiao

Punishment and Citizenship
A Theory of Criminal Disenfranchisement
Milena Tripkovic

Beyond Punishment?
A Normative Account of Collateral Restrictions on Offenders
Zachary Hoskins

Neurointerventions, Crime, and Punishment Ethical Considerations
Jesper Ryberg

The Metamorphosis of Criminal Justice
A Comparative Account
Jacqueline S. Hodgson

Guilty Acts, Guilty Minds
Stephen P. Garvey

Sentencing and Artificial Intelligence
Jesper Ryberg and Julian V. Roberts

Punishment for the Greater Good
Adam J. Kolber

Punishment, Penalty, anc

Punishment, Penalty, and Incapacitation

A Dignity-Respecting Model of Targeted Restrictions of Liberty for Liberal States

ALEC WALEN, *JD, PHD*
Distinguished Professor of Law and Philosophy, Rutgers University, USA

OXFORD
UNIVERSITY PRESS

OXFORD
UNIVERSITY PRESS

Oxford University Press is a department of the University of Oxford.
It furthers the University's objective of excellence in research, scholarship,
and education by publishing worldwide. Oxford is a registered trade mark of
Oxford University Press in the UK and in certain other countries.

Published in the United States of America by Oxford University Press
198 Madison Avenue, New York, NY 10016, United States of America.

Library of Congress Cataloging-in-Publication Data
Names: Walen, Alec author
Title: Punishment, penalty, and incapacitation: a dignity-respecting model of targeted restrictions of liberty for liberal states / Alec Walen.
Description: New York : Oxford university press, 2026. |
Series: Studies in penal theory and philosophy |
Includes bibliographical references and index. |
Identifiers: LCCN 2025041931 (print) | LCCN 2025041932 (ebook) |
ISBN 9780199325795 hardback | ISBN 9780199325801 |
ISBN 9780197523117 epub | ISBN 9780197523124
Subjects: LCSH: Punishment—United States | Punishment in crime deterrence—United States | Prison sentences—United States | Sentences (Criminal procedure)—United States
Classification: LCC KF9225 .W35 2026 (print) | LCC KF9225 (ebook) |
DDC 345.73/0773—dc23/eng/20250909
LC record available at https://lccn.loc.gov/2025041931
LC ebook record available at https://lccn.loc.gov/2025041932

DOI: 10.1093/9780197523124.001.0001

Printed by Integrated Books International, United States of America

MIX
Paper
FSC FSC® C183721

Note to Readers

This publication is designed to provide accurate and authoritative information in regard to the subject matter covered. It is based upon sources believed to be accurate and reliable and is intended to be current as of the time it was written. It is sold with the understanding that the publisher is not engaged in rendering legal, accounting, or other professional services. If legal advice or other expert assistance is required, the services of a competent professional person should be sought. Also, to confirm that the information has not been affected or changed by recent developments, traditional legal research techniques should be used, including checking primary sources where appropriate.

(Based on the Declaration of Principles jointly adopted by a Committee of the American Bar Association and a Committee of Publishers and Associations.)

Contents

Preface

How can a liberal state justify restricting the liberty of specific individuals for the sake of security, and how can it do so in a way that is consistent with respect for the dignity of those whose liberty is restricted? This book seeks to answer that question by distinguishing four different types of justifications for targeted restrictions of liberty, all of which respect the dignity of the individuals restricted. These types of justifications are (1) deserved punishment, (2) forfeiture of rights, (3) enforceable duties to self-restrict, and (4) lack of accountability, which undermines a precondition for claiming liberty rights.

My central thesis is that targeted liberty restrictions must appeal to one of these justifications, and that each type of justification imposes characteristic limits on the way restrictions can operate. Targeted liberty restrictions cannot be justified simply by balancing the value of security against the value of liberty. We should be pluralists about what can justify targeted liberty restrictions, but we should be principled pluralists, not sloppy ones. That is, we should recognize and respect the need for justificatory coherence within each type of justification.

The book grows out of a paper that I published in 2010: "A Unified Theory of Detention, with Application to Preventive Detention for Suspected Terrorists." In the intervening years, my views on preventive detention, and incapacitative restrictions more broadly, have evolved somewhat, but my views on criminal law have evolved substantially. Most importantly, I no longer think we can properly account for all of the occasions when "hard treatment"—treatment meant to deter—can justifiably be imposed on people in terms of the criminal law. I think the criminal law should be understood as the branch of law defined by the aim of providing censure and punishment that are deserved for and proportional to culpable public wrongdoing. But I think that much of what a liberal state can justifiably do to sanction people for lawbreaking cannot be justified in that way. Rather than adopt a pluralist conception of the aims of criminal law, I think we would do better to distinguish criminal law proper from what I call "penal law."[1] Penal law, unlike criminal law, does not appeal to the notion of what a wrongdoer deserves for her culpable actions; rather, it justifies the imposition of hard

[1] The term is already in use in many jurisdictions, but I can find no better contrasting term, so I adopt a technical definition for it. For more on terminology, see Section 1.3.4.

treatment by appealing to the notion of fair forfeiture of the right not to suffer a penalty.[2]

Furthermore, I have come to believe that the fundamental divide for a comprehensive theory of targeted restrictions of liberty is between justifications for incapacitation—that is, a restriction on an agent's ability to act achieved by removing one or more liberty rights, where that loss is backed up by the threat of sanctions if not by direct force—and justifications aimed at other means of providing security, primarily deterrence. Earlier, I held the view that the primary divide was between the retrospectively-oriented justification inherent in a retributive conception of criminal law (a response to a past crime) and the prospectively-oriented justifications inherent in preventive detention imposed on someone who is taken to pose a threat. But I have since come to realize that some justifications for preventive restrictions on liberty are as much a reflection of past actions that forfeit the normal rights to liberty as they are a reflection of the fact that a person seems to pose a threat to others. That realization, and an independent one that the criminal law cannot properly take incapacitation as one of its defining or constitutive aims, led me to believe that the fundamental divide is between justifications that are aimed at incapacitation and those that are not.

Of course, the world does not sit still while one develops one's thoughts. Now, fifteen years after I published "A Unified Theory of Detention," the significance of the "War on Terror"[3] has faded into the background, replaced by more traditional threats, such as Russia's war against Ukraine and the domestic threats to rights-respecting, democratic forms of government from authoritarian politicians and movements. Nevertheless, the fact that the leading concerns of the day have changed does not mean that the issues raised by the "War on Terror" are no longer important. The core issue—how to pursue national security and the security of individuals in ways that respect the dignity of individuals—remains, I believe, undertheorized. Getting a clearer view of the normative bases, and attendant limits, of different kinds of law that purport to justify restricting people's liberty will not do much to help us to get at the root causes of the threats to our security. The focus on restricting liberty is admittedly primarily reactive. Nonetheless, no state can long survive without providing security. And a liberal state must figure out how to provide security in ways that respect the dignity of those under its power.

The xenophobic and autocratic politics that seem to be ascendant across much of the democratic world as I make final revisions may seem to make this project quixotic. But even if we are entering a dark age for liberal law, the project

[2] This is a theme I first developed in "Criminal Law and Penal Law: The Wrongness Constraint and a Complementary Forfeiture Model."

[3] This term was coined by George W. Bush to describe the United States's response to the attacks by al Qaeda on 9/11/2001.

of figuring out what is required to make the laws just is a project as old as philosophy itself. I hope this book will contribute to that project. And I have faith that, sooner or later, the project will again find a receptive audience among those who wield power.

This book is structured in five parts. Part I lays out an introduction to the book as a whole and in particular to the Dignity-Respecting Model of Liberty Restrictions (DR Model) (Chapter 1), my methodological commitments (Chapter 2), the conceptions of dignity and rights on which I rely (Chapter 3), and the presumption of law abidingness (POLA), without which it would be much easier to justify restrictions on liberty for the sake of security (Chapter 4). Part II develops my conception of the criminal law. It starts with a retributive account of criminal law as providing deserved, proportional responses to culpable public wrongdoing (Chapter 5) and then proceeds to provide an account of blame and guilt as the basis for censure and punishment (Chapter 6), a theory of punishment that matches the theory of blame and guilt (Chapter 7), and an exploration of the constraint of proportionality (Chapter 8). Part III discusses the value and potential limits of the criminal law. It starts by assessing, at a very general level, the costs and benefits of using the criminal law (Chapter 9). Next, it considers the potential problem unjust states have in retaining the standing to blame wrongdoers (Chapter 10) and the extent to which restorative justice might be a better alternative (Chapter 11). It wraps up by arguing that the proportionality constraint on criminal law provides a strong reason to complement the criminal law with another kind of law, based on fair forfeiture rather than retributive desert, that is, penal law (Chapter 12). Part IV then develops this notion of penal law. It starts with an overview of the penal law (Chapter 13). It then describes a theory of forfeiture (Chapter 14) and doctrinal basics for the penal law (Chapter 15). Finally, Part V develops dignity-respecting justifications for incapacitation and provides a conclusion. It starts with a discussion of how forfeiture of the POLA can justify incapacitation (Chapter 16). It then discusses the idea of an enforceable duty to accept certain types of incapacitation (Chapter 17). It applies these ideas to the difficult issue of how and when to justify pretrial detention (Chapter 18). It then covers another kind of reason why incapacitation might be justifiable: lack of accountability, both intrinsic lack of accountability (Chapter 19) and extrinsic lack of accountability, grounded in the state lacking either the duty or the capacity to adequately police some or all people and hold them accountable (Chapter 20). The book then concludes with a theoretical summary, a list of practical options for a state seeking to respond to security threats in ways that respect the DR Model, and two lists of practical implications for the law (one confirming current practices and another a list of reforms). It ends with some final thoughts on the most important lessons of the project.

Acknowledgments

First and foremost, I have to thank Antony Duff, who asked me to write a book proposal along these lines more than twelve years ago. I was to have finished the book within three or four years, but I had another iron that was hotter, and accordingly I first wrote *The Mechanics of Claims and Permissible Killing in War*. I now think that is all to the good, as it gave me more time to develop my understanding of the criminal law and the need for penal law. Nonetheless, through the long delay, Antony has remained a supporter and a mentor, and a constructive critic who has given me detailed comments on an earlier draft. I will remain ever grateful.

I am also incredibly fortunate, over the past seventeen years or so, to have been supported and befriended by two of the other leading theorists of criminal law from the generation that preceded me: Doug Husak and Michael Moore. Equally important, I've had the good fortune to exchange work with and learn from people more or less my age, most importantly Kim Ferzan. Last but not least, my younger colleague Sandra Mayson has been a most enthusiastic supporter of this project; she has helped me tremendously by helping me to see what the project was about and how I should respond to certain objections.

In addition, I would like to offer special thanks to Mitch Berman, Kim Ferzan, and Sandra Mayson for organizing a workshop at the University of Pennsylvania Carey Law School; to Ken Ehrenberg and Hrafn Asgeirsson for organizing a workshop at the University of Surrey School of Law; and to Stephen Galoob and Brenner Fissell for organizing a workshop at Villanova Law school, all while this was still a work in progress. Likewise, I'd like to thank Tatjana Hörnle for her invitation to present part of the book, while still a work in progress, at the Max Planck Institute for the Study of Crime, Security, and Law, and to Michael Moore and Leo Katz for inviting me to discuss my views on criminal law with their law school seminar.

I thank Fiona Clarke for providing a careful edit of the whole manuscript before I turned it in. I also thank Craig Agule and Findlay Stark for especially meticulous comments on earlier drafts of the book. In addition, I thank students in both a graduate and then an undergraduate class at Rutgers for their helpful comments on the book. From the graduate class, I thank Caroline Hoskins, Ethan Muse, and Cosim Sayid. From the undergraduate class, I thank the following students whose comments all caused me to make changes in the book: James Brandofino, Leah Bushra, Patrick Cahill, Leonardo Celi, Erkabay Girma, Isaiah Lederman,

Ricardo Mercado, Ana Ortega, Navindu Ralapanawe, Danny Ramadan, Samuel Reyes, Vianna Scott, Tejus Sinha, and Madeleine Yashar. And I thank the following individuals, whose comments at various workshops or in personal communication were helpful to me: Hrafn Asgeirsson, Saba Bazargan-Forward, Kristen Bell, Mitch Berman, Patrick Cahill, Charles Capps, Aaron Chipp-Miller, David Clark, Leora Dahankatz, Perry Dane, Samuel Delorme, Michelle Dempsey, Ken Ehrenberg, Kim Ferzan, Brenner Fissell, Chad Flanders, Daniel Fryer, Stephen Galoob, Stuart Green, Clair Hogg, Zachary Hoskins, Heidi Hurd, Doug Husak, Thea Johnson, Josh Kassner, Leo Katz, Kierstan Kaushal-Carter, Erin Kelly, Adam Kolber, Guha Krishnamurthi, Ambrose Lee, Youngjae Lee, Robert Leider, Sandra Mayson, Matthew Mattravers, Gabe Mendlow, Crescente Molina, Michael Moore, Dana Nelkin, John Oberdiek, Doug Portmore, Faron Ray, Sam Ridge, Alex Sarch, Sandy Steel, Sarah Swan, Rick Swedloff, Eleanor Wachtel, Amelia Wirts, and Yuan. I also want to thank the anonymous reviewer at Oxford University Press, whose comments on an earlier draft were generous and exceedingly helpful. And I would like to thank Johann Frick and Daniel Viehoff for helpful discussions of the material in this book as I was drafting it.

I am also grateful to Chuck Beitz and the people at the Princeton Center for Human Values for offering me a fellowship year (2014–2015) in which to write the book. I didn't make much progress on the book that year, but I did lay some of the groundwork for it. I would also like to thank Rutgers University for giving me a sabbatical (2022–2023) in which I was finally able to get the book fully drafted.

Finally, I want to thank my wife, Rachel, and my son, Ami, for their consistent, loving support while I brought this book to fruition.

Table of Cases and Positive Law

FICTIONAL CASES:

U.S. LEGAL CASES

FOREIGN LEGAL CASES

POSITIVE LAW, U.S.

POSITIVE LAW, OTHER

PART I

INTRODUCTION AND MORAL BACKGROUND

1
Introduction

1.1 Introduction to the Central Question of the Book

There are dangerous people in the world: murderers, robbers, and rapists; carriers of contagious diseases; mentally ill people who are a danger to themselves and others; combatants who would wage war when so ordered, whether the war is just or unjust; terrorists who aim to kill noncombatants for political or other ideological causes; and perhaps most dangerous of all, autocrats and demagogues who all too often successfully mobilize states in pursuit of their own or their people's power and glory, heedless of consequences to others or even themselves. What are we to do?

Sometimes it is permissible to kill people who pose serious threats to others. If there are no less harmful ways to neutralize the threat posed by people who lack the right to threaten, and if killing those people (and possibly innocent bystanders) is proportional to the threat posed to others, then killing may be justified.[1] But I limit my concern in this book to cases in which such killing is not necessary. More generally, I limit it to cases in which the threats are not so imminent that physically harmful force is necessary to stop them; rather, some restrictions on liberty will probably (with sufficient likelihood) suffice. I also limit it to cases in which individual self-help is not necessary. That is, I focus on cases in which the relevant issues concern state actors who are trying to provide security to individuals in their states (or possibly elsewhere), while trying to uphold respect for laws that are assumed to be basically just and legitimate.

The focus of this book is reactive: Given that certain people do or will pose threats that cannot be justified, what can be done to them? And what can be done to others who have already committed illegal acts, who may not pose an ongoing threat themselves but whose punishment or other sanctioning may play a deterrent or norm-reinforcing role? What can be done *to* such people to reduce the prevalence of unjust threats?

One might, instead, want to ask: What constructive things can a state do *for* people so that fewer of them pose threats that cannot be justified? In some sense, that is the more important question. I believe that the most impactful thing a

[1] This was the concern of my prior book: *The Mechanics of Claims and Permissible Killing in War* (henceforth *The Mechanics of Claims*).

Punishment, Penalty, and Incapacitation. Alec Walen, Oxford University Press.
DOI: 10.1093/9780197523124.003.0001

state could do to protect rights would be to reform its institutions so that fewer people are tempted to pose threats that cannot be justified. But that can't be the *only* thing it does. Just as we cannot do away with doctors and hospitals just because the marginal health care dollar would, as I understand it, be better spent on public health than treatment, so we cannot do away with the criminal law,[2] health-care-based quarantines, prisoner of war detention, and other reactive forms of restricting liberty for the sake of security. My question is: Assuming these reactive restrictions on liberty are helpful, and indeed essential, how and when can they be morally justified?

I should say that I believe that the most dangerous people in a liberal society are not criminals or terrorists or enemy soldiers; I believe the most dangerous people are demagogues and autocrats. They are the ones who can organize and motivate millions of people, who can direct them to unjustly attack the scapegoats or other victims that they pick out. They are the ones whose actions are most likely to lead to mass murder or genocide. They are also the ones who, by focusing political energy on "the enemy," distract their people from constructively addressing more pressing problems. And unfortunately, I think many politicians in normal democratic societies function in this way. Moreover, they are often supported and influenced by capitalists who care more about protecting their wealth and their access to more wealth than about the public good.

I have no good ideas about how to handle this sort of threat. Indeed, I suspect that the paradigmatic state tool for addressing small-scale threats posed by individuals who act badly, the criminal law, is morally distorting when brought to bear against bad actors whose crimes are national in scale. Consider, for example, the trial of Adolf Eichmann.[3] As Tom Hurwitz, who was present for the filming and editing of his trial, reports: "The work of studying fascism could not compete with the satisfaction of blaming a villain and imagining that the problems could be solved with his sentencing."[4] This strikes me as plausible and deeply important. Holding historically significant figures responsible for historically significant crimes can cause us to focus too much on guilty individuals and too little on the historical and systematic forces that allowed them to do the horrible things they did. It may be essential to prosecute them, as doing so reinforces

[2] Vincent Chiao argues for an approach to criminal law that seeks to deploy it only when doing so "is most likely, out of the range of possible interventions, to optimally promote everyone's basic rights and interests." *Criminal Law in the Age of the Administrative State*, 34. I am skeptical of our ability to optimize in this way. I discuss the range of options, relevant considerations, and degrees of flexibility in the system in Section 20.2. But more importantly, I am also sympathetic to a contrary position, articulated by Alon Harel, that states have a constitutional duty to criminalize wrongful behavior. See his "The Duty to Criminalize."

[3] One might also argue that the four prosecutions of Donald Trump after he lost his 2020 bid for reelection only served to strengthen and radicalize him politically.

[4] "Adolf Eichmann Was Ready for His Close-Up."

the deeply important norm that no one is above the law.[5] But the criminal law cannot be relied on to fix the problems posed by such great crimes.

The proper role of the criminal law is not to heal society of great evils; it is to help society deal with mundane, quotidian evils by holding criminal wrongdoers accountable, hoping thereby to shore up respect for the law. This is the quotidian focus of this book. Its concern is dealing with the threats posed by "normal" criminals,[6] by those with contagious diseases, by the mentally ill and dangerous, by captured prisoners of war,[7] by would-be terrorists, and by others whose relatively small-scale threats and disruptions need to be contained if life in a society is to proceed in a stable, normal way.

Despite focusing on smaller threats, I think the topic of this book is nonetheless fundamentally important. Addressing these sorts of threats is a basic function of any government; any government that failed to address them would not last long. Additionally, it is fundamentally morally important for states to address these threats in a way that respects the dignity of all. Insofar as states seek to promote security in ways that are inconsistent with respect for the dignity of all, they perpetrate injustices. This is to be avoided, first and foremost, because it is unjust. But I believe it is also to be avoided because when states act unjustly, they trigger resentment (at least among people with a sense of their own dignity) that can undermine the security they aim to provide.

This last claim is causal and empirical in nature, and there are reasons to doubt its truth, so I'll end this section with a few quick thoughts on the matter. I'll start by saying that my belief is connected to John Rawls's hope that it is possible for just institutions to be stable, and for the right reasons.[8] But there are reasons to be skeptical about this hoped-for stability. We in the United States, and societies across much of the Western world, have surely made significant strides in addressing injustices over the past sixty years or so. Old regimes of racial oppression have been reformed, sexism is no longer as prevalent as it once was, equal rights for LGTBQ people have come a long way, and so on. Moreover, as Thomas Piketty writes, "[b]etween 1780 and 2020, we see developments tending toward greater equality of status, property, income, genders, and races within most regions and societies on the planet, and to a certain extent when we

[5] I first wrote this sentence before the U.S. Supreme Court handed down Trump v. U.S., 603 U.S. 593 (2024), which gave presidents near complete immunity for what would otherwise have been criminal actions.

[6] Corporations present the kinds of threats that this book could in principle cover, but I feel uncertain about whether it makes sense to prosecute corporations as such, rather than go after their responsible officers. Accordingly, I say nothing more about corporate criminal law.

[7] Prisoners of war are taken in war, which is normally a large-scale threat to society. But each individual prisoner poses only a small-scale threat, and they are not dealt with by violent force but by restricting their liberty.

[8] *Political Liberalism*, pp. 141–143.

compare these societies on the global scale."[9] And yet, Western societies do not seem stable at the moment.

There are many possible reasons for this. One is that technological and social change have made people feel insecure, creating a backlash to liberal governance that has been exploited by demagogues. Another is that we still have a long way to go in addressing injustices, especially economic ones. A further reason is that the process of calling out and addressing injustices has valorized victimhood, resulting in people now seeking out opportunities to be resentful. Insofar as the last of these is true, it provides reason to worry that addressing injustices cannot hope to cure the resentment of them.

Whatever the right causal story here is, the issues are obviously complex, beyond my expertise, and beyond the scope of this book. So I'll rest with this statement of faith: that in a free society in which people value their own dignity, state action that rides roughshod over the rights of some will tend to make the problem of resentment worse, and that is likely to be worse for the pursuit of security, all else equal, than an alternative in which the state promotes security in a way that respects rights. But fundamentally this is a secondary concern for me. The first imperative of a liberal society is simply to act justly by respecting the dignity of individuals, as expressed in their basic *moral* rights, including their right to liberty.[10]

1.2 General versus Targeted Restrictions

My concern in this book is with targeted restrictions on liberty. Targeted restrictions, as I use the term, are restrictions aimed at individuals or subsections of the population. The contrasting notion is of general restrictions, which apply to people quite generally, though they may allow for small exceptions.

The law is full of general restrictions on our liberty for the sake of security. For example, prohibitions on performing wrongful acts, such as unjustifiably causing death or bodily harm to others, are general restrictions on our liberty for the sake of security. But we feel the law's restrictions more as *restrictions* when they do not simply mirror prior moral prohibitions but are instead grounded in pursuit of the common welfare. Consider, for example, the regulation of controlled substances. Whatever one thinks about the details of the Controlled Substances Act,[11] the aim of pursuing the general welfare by regulating the production,

[9] *A Brief History of Equality*, 1.

[10] When I speak of rights without qualification, I mean *moral* rights. Legal rights inform moral rights in important ways. See Section 3.7.2. But legal rights are largely creatures of positive law, and they may be substantially unjust. My concern is with moral rights, which provide much of the content of justice.

[11] See 21 U.S.C. § 801 (2).

distribution, and consumption of substances ranging from over-the-counter medications to heroin is surely a proper function of government. Yet it limits our freedom quite generally. No agent can simply decide to start manufacturing and selling, for example, ephedrine, a central nervous system stimulant; he[12] must first register and get a license.[13]

Many of us do not deal with that sort of specialized licensing, but most of us are used to dealing with licenses of some sort, which again are general regulatory structures meant, at least in substantial part, to protect others. To drive, an agent needs to get a driver's license, which requires him to show that he has the basic skills and knowledge required to drive with at least a minimal level of safety. To own or purchase a gun, many states require that an agent get a license to possess or a permit to purchase the gun, and most of those states also require safety training or an exam to get that license or permit.[14] And to practice law, an agent needs to pass the bar, demonstrating that he was, for at least two days in his life, capable of holding a vast quantity of information about the law in his head, and that he possesses at least minimal competence in legal analysis. In truth, some of these licenses are also about protecting those who are in the "guild" from competition. But there's at least some other-regarding, general-welfare-promoting, security-protecting justification for requiring people to get these licenses before engaging in certain activities.

Another context in which general restrictions apply is in high-risk locations. As anyone who has been on a flight in the past fifty years knows, most people cannot bring weapons onto an airplane. Similar rules limit access to courthouses and other sensitive locations. In all of these cases, there are exceptions to the general rules. Security personnel may be licensed to carry weapons on airplanes, just as emergency vehicles like ambulances may be permitted to exceed the speed limit. Nonetheless, these regulations impose quite general restrictions on how individuals within a jurisdiction can live.

Some have suggested that this sort of restriction is in some sense inconsistent with the presumption of law abidingness (POLA)—a presumption that is core to a state respecting the dignity of those who live in it.[15] For example, Andrew Ashworth and Lucia Zedner treat "mass screening of airline passengers" as "dispens[ing] with 'the presumption of harmlessness.'"[16] Indeed, it does. But my point in distinguishing general from targeted restrictions is that the justification for general restrictions is much less in tension with the respect we owe to individuals, including respecting the POLA. We should accept the basic truth

12 To be inclusive, I alternate the gender of the generic agent by section.
13 21 U.S.C. § 822.
14 See Giffords Law Center, "Owner Responsibility."
15 I argue for the POLA in Ch. 4.
16 *Preventive Justice*, 147.

that in the general population there will be people who abuse their freedom. Restrictions on all of our liberty that are meant to prevent or at least limit that abuse do not impugn anyone in particular. They do not mark anyone as less worthy of freedom and respect than others. Thus, they are not as difficult to reconcile with respect for dignity as targeted restrictions. The POLA rests fundamentally not on the thought that we should be free from restrictions that presuppose that some among us will act badly; it rests fundamentally on the thought that we are all fundamentally equal and that unless special circumstances apply, we should be presumed to be as law abiding as anyone else.

That's not to imply that general restrictions are always just. They can go too far in limiting basic freedoms (of speech, of association, of movement, and so on), they can be too invasive of privacy, and they can be too intrusive for the good they achieve. But those sorts of overreach are a different matter from targeting individuals or subgroups of the population for special treatment because they pose a danger to others. It is this latter targeting that is my concern in this book.

One might object that general licensing schemes undermine this distinction. If the state can restrict the right to engage in certain activities to those who can pass certain tests, it can simply design the tests so that they effectively impose restrictions on particular groups of people, be they doctors, lawyers, or drivers. Thus, general restrictions are no different from targeted ones.

My response to this objection is twofold. First, insofar as a licensing scheme marks out a group as being different from others in virtue of some immutable or nearly immutable characteristic, such as age, it becomes a targeted restriction, and has to be justified as such. That's quite different from a licensing scheme simply requiring people in general to do certain things to get a license before engaging in certain kinds of activity. Second, characteristics that a license might require, characteristics that might mark someone as dangerous or not, such as prior criminal convictions, are problematic bases for treating individuals differently. They may track statistically relevant predictors of dangerousness, but invoking them as such flies directly in the face of the POLA and requires special justification as a form of targeted restriction.

I want to say two more things about this distinction between general and targeted restrictions. First, it is particularly relevant to *state-based* restrictions, which is my concern in this book. I say this because I think individuals have and should have much greater freedom than states to limit, in targeted ways, those with whom they interact. Of course, what individuals do can add up across a society to impose unjust restrictions on certain groups. If, for example, many people fear Black men as unsafe and choose to exclude them from their private spaces, that could put Black men at a distinct social disadvantage. The state may have good reason to step in to ensure that at least certain kinds of private transactions, especially economic and cultural ones, are not affected by racial fears (whether based on unfounded prejudice or sound statistics).[17] But the need for this sort of corrective is not my concern here; my concern is with state-based limitations on liberty.

Second, the idea of targeted restrictions of liberty covers two fundamentally different kinds of state activity. Restrictions aiming at incapacitating are straightforwardly responses to the fear that certain kinds of people are distinctly dangerous. But I will argue that the criminal law is not fundamentally designed to incapacitate. Neither is a related kind of law that I will argue we should distinguish from criminal law, which I call penal law. In brief, criminal law is defined by the aim of giving wrongdoers the censure and punishment they deserve; penal law is based on the idea that lawbreaking can cause an agent to forfeit the right not to suffer a penalty. But both criminal law and penal law share the ends of deterring unjust lawbreaking and in that way reinforcing respect for the law, and they both aim to achieve those ends by imposing hard treatment on those who unjustifiably and without excuse break the law.[18] Hard treatment may include restrictions on liberty, but those restrictions are only indirectly related to providing security. Despite this indirectness, I will count them as targeted restrictions because they are imposed by the state in a targeted way only on certain individuals who comprise a small subset of the population, and the full justification for imposing these restrictions refers to the contribution they are believed to make to overall security.

1.3 The Dignity-Respecting Model for Targeted Restriction of Liberty

The aim of this book is to describe the conditions under which the state can impose targeted restrictions on liberty that are consistent with respect for the dignity of individuals. To clarify what that means, I need to explain what I mean by dignity and how the imperative to respect it imposes limits on what the state may do to people; and then I need to explain how certain forms of targeted liberty restrictions are nonetheless consistent with respect for people's dignity. I start here with a brief overview of the main ideas, including the Dignity-Respecting

[17] It is worth noting that with the advancement of technology, things are getting more complicated. For example, the threat to privacy from private corporations—not only internet companies but shops and theaters too—is growing. See A. Satariano and K. Hill, "Barred from Grocery Stores by Facial Recognition."

[18] The phrase "hard treatment" is commonly used in punishment theory. See, e.g., J. Feinberg, "The Expressive Function of Punishment," 397; A. Duff, *Punishment, Communication, and Community*, 83. But it sometimes is confused with "hard labor" or "harsh treatment." It should not be taken to carry those meanings; it merely means treatment that is sufficiently undesirable that threat of its imposition can effectively deter.

(DR) Model for targeted restrictions of liberty. I then explain how this model expresses what I call "principled pluralism." I end the chapter with an introductory explanation of two novel arguments in this book: that criminal law needs to be complemented with penal law, and that directly pursuing the aim of incapacitation requires different legal tools than either criminal law or penal law provide. I also include a short discussion of terminology.

1.3.1 The DR Model

Dignity, as I understand it, is the status held by agents who can navigate what I call the space of rights. A paradigmatic being with dignity not only has rights[19] but has what Wesley Hohfeld calls second-order powers to change her rights.[20] She can change those rights by such acts as trading, giving, promising, claiming, waiving, forfeiting,[21] and, importantly, by voting as a citizen to affect the way her government shapes the rights that people have. Most rights that can be held can also be lost, including rights not to suffer punishments, penalties, or various forms of incapacitation; but one cannot waive, trade away, or forfeit one's dignity.

Having the status of "a being with dignity" does depend, however, on having attained a certain threshold capacity as an autonomous moral agent. We may have good moral reason to treat all humans, even those who fall below that threshold of autonomous capacity, as having the same basic dignity; not to do so is to open them up to morally abhorrent treatment. But as an intrinsic matter, dignity belongs first and fundamentally to fully autonomous moral agents.

Respect for dignity is not a psychological state; it's a way of treating others. It is achieved by respecting, that is, not violating, their rights.[22] The imperative to respect the dignity of individuals who have it applies both to states and to other individuals.

For fully autonomous moral agents, the right to liberty is a core right. It follows directly from the autonomous capacity to set and pursue their own ends. But that right also comes with responsibilities, including the responsibility to respect the rights of others and to obey just laws. If fully autonomous moral agents do not respect the rights of others, or if they violate just laws, that failure affects their rights, and the law can then take action against them that would otherwise be a violation of their rights.

[19] I think animals lack dignity but can be rights holders.

[20] See "Some Fundamental Legal Conceptions as Applied in Judicial Reasoning."

[21] Forfeiting, I will argue, is not best conceived of as a "power." See Section 15.1.1.

[22] One may wonder why I don't include the thought that no disrespect is implied when rights are justifiably infringed. I explain why I don't use that language in Ch. 3.

This raises a basic question: must the state presume that people will respect the rights of others and laws that are just, or may it make predictions about how people will act and treat them accordingly? I argue in Chapter 4, when it comes to targeted restrictions, for the former view, the POLA. I argue that this presumption applies to limit what the law may do to target people with restrictions on their liberty unless and until one of a short list of conditions applies. These conditions constitute the DR Model,[23] which can be formulated in one long sentence: An individual agent can be subjected to targeted restrictions of her liberty only if (1) those limits are part of a just and proportional punishment or penalty,[24] or (2) they aim at incapacitation—that is, a restriction of her ability to act that works by removing one or more liberty rights, where that loss is backed up by the threat of sanctions if not by direct force—which is justified in one of three ways:

a) She has forfeited the POLA,
b) She has an enforceable duty to limit herself to a similar degree, or
c) She cannot be held accountable either because
    i. she lacks full autonomous capacity (intrinsic unaccountability), or
    ii. the state lacks the duty or the ability to adequately police her and hold her accountable (extrinsic unaccountability).[25]

I admit that there is a sense in which the last condition, (2)(c)(ii) on extrinsic failure of accountability, could be read to say that when the state cannot be expected to do its job normally, then respect for individual dignity can be put aside. But I reject that reading. It is not that the demands of dignity can be simply disregarded under that condition; rather, the demands of dignity in that situation are different, allowing the state to treat people as not benefiting from the POLA. The state can treat people as not benefiting from the POLA

[23] In "A Unified Theory of Detention," I called this the Autonomy-Respecting Model of detention. I have substituted "dignity" for "autonomy" because I've come to see dignity as more fundamental than autonomy.

[24] There is another theoretical alternative worth mentioning, though I will discuss it only here in this note: self-defense taken to be a justification for punishment. See W. Quinn, "The Right to Threaten and the Right to Punish." I reject this theory for two reasons. First, it does not account for "punishment," because it does not connect properly to culpability. Second, it begs the question in terms of the DR Model. It does so by arguing that the state can permissibly threaten punishment to deter wrongs, and that it can (generally) permissibly follow through on the threats that it is permitted to make. I think the permissibility of threatening (generally) goes the other way: it is permissible to threaten only what one is permitted to do (nuclear war threats being an interesting counterexample). For this critique, see R. Brook, "Threats and Promises." For Quinn's reply, see "Reply to Brook." For an interesting general discussion of the right to threaten, see D. Gauthier, "Assure and Threaten."

[25] This is a modification of the formula presented in "A Unified Theory of Detention," 879.

because a precondition for demanding the liberty that comes with the POLA is accountability for failure to live up to the presumption. If accountability is missing, whether for intrinsic or extrinsic reasons, then the claim to enjoy liberty must be taken into account in a different way. Indeed, condition (2)(c), in both forms, is also deeply connected to condition (2)(a), forfeiture of the POLA. Both operate by appealing to the thought that the POLA is a precondition for having a right to avoid targeted restrictions of liberty. If the precondition is missing, the right does not apply. In other words, this last exception fits the moral logic of the DR Model; it is not merely an instance of threshold deontology, in which the moral logic of the DR Model is overridden.

I want to end this subsection with two observations about the DR Model. First, the DR Model is a more pluralistic account than is normally given. Its two-part basic structure more or less tracks the canonical idea that the state can justifiably lock up only two sorts of people: the mad and the bad.[26] The mad are those who are "suffering from a disease (especially a mental disorder)" on the basis of which they cannot justly be held accountable, but on the basis of which they can be locked up as dangerous.[27] The bad are those who are taken "seriously" as agents, but who can be locked up because they have engaged in blameworthy criminal activity.[28] But the differences between the DR Model and this mad-bad dichotomy are as important as the similarities. The first condition involves more than judgments of culpability that ground punishment; it also involves the penal law, which focuses on forfeiture of the right not to be subjected to penalties. In addition, the second condition adds two other bases for targeted liberty restrictions.[29]

Second, the DR Model provides a complete account of the justifiable conditions for targeted restrictions of liberty. It holds even in war.[30] It is based on the thought that one set of liberal, dignity-respecting principles can cover everything we want to say about what the state has a right to do to people.[31]

[26] See, e.g., S. Morse "Neither Desert nor Disease," 277. Sandra Mayson discusses this dichotomy extensively in "A Consequentialist Framework for Prevention." See also Foucha v. Louisiana, 504 U.S. 71 (1992).

[27] "Neither Desert nor Disease," 269.

[28] Ibid., 268.

[29] Others have recognized that the mad-bad dichotomy is inadequate. Kimberly Ferzan, for example, seeks to fill the gap that it leaves by emphasizing forfeiture as another basis for preventive action. See "Beyond Crime and Commitment." I discuss her views in Section 17.1

[30] This draws on the revisionist program in just war theory that I embraced in *The Mechanics of Claims*. If there are exceptions, they arise only in the most extreme situations covered by threshold deontology. I touch on the idea of threshold deontology a few more times, especially in Section 21.1.

[31] For more on its completeness, see Section 17.1.

1.3.2 Principled Pluralism

The DR Model presents us with what I call "principled pluralism." It is clearly a pluralistic model, insofar as it provides a plurality of bases for restricting liberty. But it's worth being clear about two distinctive features of this kind of pluralism. First, the DR Model is an instance of *deontic* pluralism, not *value* pluralism. Value pluralism holds that there are fundamentally different kinds of value. I am a value pluralist; I think many things are valuable in themselves, not just instrumentally: social connections, meaningful activity, understanding the world, beauty, justice, pleasure, and so on. But deontic pluralism is different. It holds that there are fundamentally different ways to justify actions as permissible.

Second, the DR Model calls for *principled* pluralism as opposed to *sloppy* pluralism. Sloppy pluralism treats the different deontic justifications as if their component parts can be mixed and matched, as if they are not types of justifications, but tools to be used to achieve an end.[32] This is an appropriate way for a lawyer, who has a task to accomplish, to think, but it is an inappropriate way for a philosopher, legal theorist, judge, or legislator—a designer or critic of legal systems—to think. A designer or critic of legal systems ought to think about what each type of justification for an action can justify, and about how legal systems can be designed to ensure that what cannot be justified cannot be done.

One might want to push back and ask: Why think there is a single core function of anything as complicated as, say, the criminal law? It is an institution that carries the baggage of its evolution, which is surely as complex as that of any living creature.[33] My answer is not that I claim to be discerning some metaphysically true core of the criminal law; it is that by separating what is normally done with the criminal law into different kinds of law, we can design better law. The law evolves by splitting in this way from time to time. There was a time when tort law and criminal law were not distinguished; now they are, and they have grown quite distinct.[34] My suggestion is that it is time to develop other cleavages in the law. Doing so will help us to avoid some of the injustices that our current law perpetuates.

Admittedly, I do suggest that one possible function of the criminal law—that it responds to culpable public wrongs with proportional censure and punishment—should be treated as *the core* of criminal law, around which to

[32] For a similar criticism of forms of deontic pluralism that fail to reckon with how different kinds of justifications are incompatible, see L. Zaibert, "Rethinking Mixed Justifications," 232–234. (I disagree with some of the substantive claims Zaibert makes about retributivists and consequentialists, but support his criticism of sloppy pluralism.)

[33] Nietzsche is explicit about thinking about punishment and the criminal law in this sort of way. See *On the Genealogy of Morals*, Second Essay, sections 12–14.

[34] See F. Sayre, "Mens Rea," 976, 989. Punitive damages in tort law are a vestige of that earlier fusion.

build a purer criminal law. That suggestion, however, is not arbitrary. I pick that as the core of criminal law because I think that function explains and gives coherence to the majority of criminal law doctrine. In this regard, as in many others, I take my lead from Antony Duff: "We begin to theorize not with nothing . . . , but with what we have: with a contingent, historically formed, set of practices and institutions—in the present case, with the practices and institutions that make up 'our' criminal law."[35] But, as he goes on to say:

> [T]hat is not to say that we cannot hope to transcend those local beginnings, to engage with a wider 'we', with interlocutors from different traditions and different starting points, with whom we find that we can converse and from whom we can learn. . . Nor is it to say that we must take for granted as an unchangeable given the particular institutions and practices with which we begin. . . [W]e can hope to engage in a process of 'rational reconstruction' of those institutions and practices: to excavate, or (re-)construct, the goals and values by which they purport to be structured; to construct on that basis a theoretical account of what 'our' criminal law claims to aspire to be . . . [36]

In accordance with Duff's vision, my aim here is to set out an ideal of the criminal law that will capture one coherent justificatory reason for targeted restrictions of liberty. This is not a matter of conceptual analysis; it is a matter of moral tool design, seeking to create a better criminal law.

To be clear, I am not suggesting that different kinds of law cannot be combined to achieve social goals. Quite the opposite. This book aims to draw on a range of different kinds of law to achieve the social goal of security. And certain aspects of the DR Model naturally work together. For example, one basis for forfeiting the POLA is a conviction for a serious criminal offense, or a series of less serious criminal or penal offenses. My point in emphasizing principled pluralism is that we can better respect the dignity of individuals if we are clear about what can be done with different sorts of legal tools first, before we seek to use them in combination.

1.3.3 Criminal Law as a Blaming Institution

I now offer a preview of my account of criminal law, spelled out in Part II, in order to make it clear why this book is committed to developing the distinction between criminal law and penal law.

[35] *The Realm of Criminal Law*, 4.
[36] Ibid.

I approach the criminal law from a broadly retributive perspective: if a person commits a criminal act—a culpable public wrong—then he deserves, morally and legally, censure and punishment. Censure is straightforwardly a blaming practice, one aimed at communicating blame for crimes to the wrongdoers themselves, to their victims, and to society as a whole. Punishment involves the intentional extraction of material amends or the infliction of hard treatment on wrongdoers. But that trait does not suffice to distinguish punishments from what I call a penalty. To count as punishment, the extraction of amends or the infliction of hard treatment has to be delivered at least in part to reinforce the message of censure.[37] This integrated function is what Andrew Simester highlights when he refers to the criminal law as "a blaming institution."[38]

This commitment to the fundamental importance of culpability for the criminal law is widespread.[39] In the common law tradition, it traces back to the Latin maxim *actus non facit reum nisi mens sit rea* (an act does not make one guilty unless one's mind is guilty). Likewise, German law is structured around finding not only that the defendant has committed the elements of a crime (the *Tatbestand*) but also that he lacked a justification (*Rechtswidrigkeit*) and that he lacked an excuse and thus could be found culpable (*Schuld*).[40]

Why have a blaming institution? The answer refers to the function of blame and the reasons the state should care about that function. Starting with the former, I argue that blame is a judgment: the thought that the person blamed (it could be oneself) should own his guilt. The communication of blame serves to call a wrongdoer to do just that, that is, to own his guilt. Owning his guilt involves more than admitting that he was wrong and repenting of his wrongdoing. It involves appreciating, intellectually and emotionally, the significance of his act being wrongful, and making amends.

Blame is something that need not be communicated—an agent can blame the target of his blame privately, in his mind. And it certainly need not be communicated by the state. It might be left a merely personal (interpersonal and intrapersonal) affair. Why, then, should the state have an institution for blaming? My answer is that the state is a creature of a shared moral and political community, centrally tasked with developing and protecting our rights. In placing blame

37 My views on this matter are strongly influenced by the work of Antony Duff, and in particular by his *Punishment, Communication, and Community* and *The Realm of Criminal Law*.

38 *Fundamentals of Criminal Law*, 493.

39 Many theorists, from Blackstone to the present, embrace this connection between punishment and culpable action. See W. Blackstone, *2 Commentaries on the Laws of England*, 20–22. For modern views, see, e.g., H. Hart, "The Aims of the Criminal Law," 405; M. Moore, *Placing Blame*, 168; S. Morse, "Neither Desert nor Disease," 879; D. Husak, *Ignorance of Law*, 8; A. Duff, *The Realm of Criminal Law*, 18–19, and A. Simester, *Fundamentals of Criminal Law*, 11. See also Holloway v. U.S., 148 F.2d 665, 666–667 ("Our collective conscience does not allow punishment where it cannot impose blame.")

40 See M. Dubber and T. Hörnle, *Criminal Law*, 173.

through censure and punishment, the state is carrying out its pro tanto duty to speak up for and defend the rights of its members, rights which it articulated. In other words, the state's duty to provide security is complemented by a duty to provide accountability.

At a more granular level, punishment can play four complementary roles: (1) reinforcing censure; (2) providing an occasion for a wrongdoer to engage in serious reflection about her guilt; (3) helping to ensure that she is not happy about her wrongdoing; and (4) collecting the amends that she owes either as material compensation or in the form of contribution to deterrence. In all these ways, it seeks to make the wrongdoer own her guilt, which is important in particular for reconciling the wrongdoer to her political community and to the broader moral community.

It is important to be clear: censure and punishment cannot simply *make* wrongdoers own their guilt because they cannot make wrongdoers *feel* guilty.[41] Often, they work at cross-purposes to that end (though care should be taken that they do not overly interfere with wrongdoers coming to feel their guilt). Alternatives to punishment, such as restorative justice,[42] may be more apt to bring wrongdoers to accept their guilt and to *feel* guilty. That gives restorative justice an advantage over censure and punishment in terms of reconciliation. But restorative justice also has shortcomings relative to censure and punishment, and I argue that there is good reason to think we should retain the latter practices. Most importantly, censure and punishment are expressions of the political community, and as such they reinforce not just the importance of not wronging individuals, but also the importance of publicly recognizing the rights of individuals and the importance of the law.[43]

This point about the significance of censure and punishment leads me to offer a few quick thoughts about abolitionism in the context of the criminal law. Narrowly understood, abolitionism is concerned only with imprisonment. As Angela Davis once wrote, its "ultimate aim [is] dismantling the prison system as the dominant mode of punishment."[44] But in more recent work she and others embrace a broader aim: "Abolition is a political vision with the goal of eliminating imprisonment, policing, and surveillance and creating lasting alternatives to punishment and imprisonment."[45] I am not an abolitionist in either sense. I think the criminal law, and even prisons, perform important roles, even if their current operation calls out for substantial reform. Whether criminal

[41] And if combined with drugs or other techniques that could *make* them feel guilty, they would violate the autonomy of those so affected.

[42] See Ch. 11.

[43] For a similar view, see Harel, "The Duty to Criminalize."

[44] *Are Prisons Obsolete?* 110. For an essay in support of abolitionism, understood in this first way, in the very limited context of the United States, see E. Kelly, "The Problem with Prisons."

[45] A. Davis et al., *Abolition, Feminism, Now*, 50.

law and prisons can be sufficiently reformed, or whether alternative sorts of systems should be put in place is a question I address to some extent when I consider the consequentialist case for and against the criminal law,[46] and again when I consider the alternative of restorative justice.[47] But my fundamental aim in those discussions is not to resolve any empirical questions; it is to highlight what is at issue: both the values that the criminal law addresses beyond simply locking up "the bad guys," and what would go missing if the state did not use it.

Some revisionists think that tools like policing and imprisonment cannot be justified as part of criminal law, understood as a blaming institution; but they think they are justifiable nonetheless because they are too important for community safety to do without.[48] But one of my main points in this book is that we must not simply pursue this sort of utilitarian thinking.[49] Rather, if offenders cannot be blamed, we must ask whether they can at least be taken to have forfeited their right not to be imprisoned, or whether the conditions for holding them accountable might not hold.

1.3.4 Penal Law as a Distinct Way to Reinforce Respect for the Law

At the end of Part III, I explore the problem that I think creates the need for carving out the penal law as a complementary avenue for reinforcing respect for the law. Before saying why the state might need the penal law, I should say a few words about what I mean by "respect for the law." One might take the phrase to mean holding the law in high esteem or taking it as an authority to be obeyed. But creating respect in that sense is a job for pundits, politicians, teachers of various sorts, religious and community leaders, and so on, not for people working to provide security. People who work with the security apparatus of the state are generally not in the business of extolling the law's virtues and authority—though judges at sentencing can take on that role. For the most part, these people can support respect for the law only in two other ways. First, they can promote respect in the sense that they try to ensure that people generally abide by the law. They can promote this by seeking to impose sanctions on lawbreakers, thereby deterring further law breaking,[50] and by seeking to incapacitate people

[46] See Ch. 9.
[47] See Ch. 10.
[48] See, e.g., Tommie Shelby, *The Idea of Prison Abolition*, 52-53, and *Dark Ghettos*, 248.
[49] It is not clear whether Shelby is being strictly utilitarian or is instead relying to some extent on forfeiture of the right not to be imprisoned. I return to this issue in Section 10.4.1.
[50] When I speak of deterrence, I am talking primarily about general deterrence, not specific deterrence. Even if sanctions, especially incarceration, have *some* tendency to specifically deter, that effect seems to be washed out, as a general matter, at least in the United States, by the criminogenic effects of incarceration. See B. van Rooij and A. Fine, *The Behavioral Code*, 21 (noting that the latest review article "concluded that incarceration raises the rate of re-offending to somewhere between 5 and 14 percent.").

who are likely to be law breakers.[51] Second, they can promote respect for the law by holding people accountable for breaking the law, thereby conveying the social message that the law breaking is unacceptable. The criminal law aims at promoting respect for the law in both ways. And it is important that it be seen to be just when it does so, otherwise it will undermine respect for the law at the same time as it seeks to promote it.

The problem the criminal law runs into in its efforts to promote respect for the law arises from the intersection of the proportionality restriction—which is necessary for the criminal law to be just—and the need to provide sanctions that are adequate to the task of deterrence. This is a problem in particular for the sanctioning of proxy crimes—crimes that target acts that are not in themselves particularly wrongful but that are correlated with serious wrongs. Proxy crimes serve an important function.[52] They allow the state to target actions that are easier to detect, or easier to prove, or performed before a danger is too proximate. Examples range from various activities performed without the required license to statutory rape[53] and drug possession. The problem arises because there is reason to think that proxy crimes can serve their purpose only if they are, at least sometimes, enforced with penalties that are harsher than what would count as proportional punishments.[54]

The solution to this problem that I argue for in Part IV is that the justification for these harsh sanctions rests not on retributive desert but on fair forfeiture.[55] Marking this distinction is a core innovation in this book. Accordingly, I will take some extra space here to introduce the distinction and explain why it is significant.

Proxy crimes often involve little to no culpability, and thus the sanctions associated with them, which often are not trivial, seem problematically to constitute disproportionate punishments. People have proposed three primary responses to this problem. Some think we need to be more pluralistic about criminal law theory, complementing the commitment to responding to culpable action using proportional punishment with consequentialist considerations in a way that

[51] The effect of incapacitation on general patterns of law-abiding behavior is largely indirect, by removing models of disrespect.

[52] For a detailed discussion of the evolution of proxy crimes in England, see M. Dyson *Explaining Tort and Crime*, ch. 3. For an overview in France, Spain, Scotland, and the United States, see ibid., ch. 5.

[53] This is the term used in the United States to cover a person having sex with another who is usually at least four years younger and usually under age sixteen.

[54] This presupposes that magnitude of sanctions is relevant to their capacity to deter. I believe this is true, though weakly so. I develop this position in Sections 8.2 and 12.2.

[55] This distinction can have application outside the state. A parent, for example, might punish his child with the sense that she deserves blame and punishment for a wrong done, or might impose a sanction on his child, appealing to the notion of forfeiture, simply to convey that his rules are to be respected. But I focus in the book on the development of these ideas in the law.

makes sense of the full range of criminal law.[56] Some think we can do more to understand the culpability of committing mala prohibita offenses[57]—offenses that are grounded in essentially consequentialist considerations.[58] And some think we should substantively revise the criminal law so that it only ever punishes people in proportion to their culpable wrongdoing.[59]

I reject all three of these responses. I reject the pluralist response primarily because the appeal to consequentialism threatens respect for the dignity of the individual.[60] I reject the expansive approach, which seeks to show how broadly the notion of culpable wrongdoing sweeps, because it fails to capture the commitment to providing only a *proportional* response.[61] And I reject the substantive revisionist approach insofar as it not only seeks to clean up the criminal law but throws out the residue.

I suggest a fourth way. It accepts the purist, revisionist approach to criminal law theory but offers an alternative account of the justification for the sanctions that cannot be justified by appeal to the criminal law. In other words, it accepts pluralism, but rejects the sloppy pluralism involved in complementing retributive justice with consequentialism. The resulting picture is of a criminal justice system that operates with two independent justifications—retributivism and fair forfeiture—that can be harmonized to provide a set of practices that respect human dignity as consequentialism does not, and that fits the law reasonably well, though retaining some revisionist force.[62]

Before going further, I should say something about my terminology. The phrase "penal law" is often used as a synonym for criminal law, just as penalties are often used as a synonym for punishments. But I want to introduce a technical distinction, according to which penal law, unlike criminal law, does not presuppose that the offender acted culpably. Most agents who can justifiably be penalized will also have acted culpably, but establishing culpability is not essential to imposing penalties, and penalties

[56] See, e.g., J. Gardner, "Crime: in Proportion and in Perspective," 214–215; D. Husak, "Pluralistic Theory."

[57] See, e.g., A. Duff, *The Realm of Criminal Law*, ch. 7, § 5. In a very different way, see D. Husak, "Preventive Detention as Punishment?"

[58] I say "*essentially* consequentialist considerations" because I reject the relevance of naked consequentialism. See especially Sections 3.2 and 3.3. Note, not all mala prohibita offenses are proxy crimes. Consider tax evasion. See Section 8.3.1.

[59] See, e.g., M. Moore, *Placing Blame*, 784.

[60] I say more about how I think of consequentialism in Section 2.3.

[61] I cover this problem with Duff's approach to this issue in Ch. 13. I hereby endorse Sandra Mayson's response to Husak's attempt to extend culpability to cover what is normally taken to be a matter of preventive restrictions on liberty in "A Consequentialist Framework for Prevention," 224.

[62] Matt Matravers embraces a model of the criminal law that is very much what I have in mind for the penal law. See "De-Moralising Retributivism." My main objection to his view is that he sees this as a better model for *the criminal law*, rather than a complement to the criminal law.

do not have to respect the criminal law's commitment to culpability-based proportionality.[63]

To accompany the distinction between criminal law and penal law, I use the term "wrongdoer," rather than the more common "offender," when writing about criminal law and punishments. I do so to emphasize that the criminal law ought to be strictly limited in its application to culpable wrongdoing.[64] I use the term "offender" for people who violate the law in ways that ground penalties and as the generic term that covers both. I also reserve the word "crime"—with the exception of "proxy crimes"—for violations of the criminal law. I use the term "offense" as the relevant word for the penal law and as the generic. I use the term "sanction" as the generic to cover the hard treatment that might be imposed as a punishment or a penalty.

One might object that "sanction" implies a level of censure, but I think it can instead be understood to imply only that the act in question was *not to be done*. That does not fit one common use of the notion of a penalty. As Joel Feinberg points out, the term "penalty" can be used to label responses that can "be treated as retroactive license fees,"[65] that is, as the functional equivalent of taxes meant to make certain kinds of behavior less frequent but not to mark them as *not to be done*. But as I use the terms, penalties and punishments both respond to acts that are not to be done; they just respond in different ways. Given that narrow, technical use of "penalty," I think the word "sanction" fits well enough.

One might think that there is nothing novel in this use of penalties; many countries have a notion of offenses that can be penalized without establishing culpability. The Model Penal Code (highly influential in the United States) proposes that below the level of felonies, misdemeanors, and petty misdemeanors, there should be a level of mere violations. An offense "constitutes a violation . . . if no other sentence than a fine, or fine and forfeiture or other civil penalty is authorized upon conviction . . . "[66] Canada requires some form of fault, even if it is the defendant's burden to establish that she lacks fault, for any serious crime (a crime for which imprisonment might be imposed),[67] but it allows liability without fault for non-serious crimes, for which imprisonment cannot be imposed. And German law distinguishes regulatory infractions (*Ordnungswidrigkeiten*) from

[63] This distinction between punishments and penalties tracks, though not exactly, Joel Feinberg's in "The Expressive Function of Punishment," 397–400 (his use of "penalty" is broader than mine). See also A. Duff and T. Hörnle, "Crimes of Endangerment," p. 160; Sheras v. De Rutzen [1895] 1 QB 918, 922 (Wright J.).

[64] I deviate from this practice when necessary to track how others use the relevant terms.

[65] "Expressive Function of Punishment," 399.

[66] Model Penal Code, § 1.04 (5).

[67] See Lévis (City) v. Tétreault, 2006 SCC 12, ¶ 18.

criminal violations (*Straftaten*) on the ground that criminal violations require culpability.[68]

What I have in mind for penal law, however, is different from a regime of merely regulatory penalties. As just observed, those are normally conceived of as being qualitatively minor, and as excluding imprisonment,[69] whereas my conception of penal law includes the sanction of imprisonment. Indeed, its raison d'être is to provide harsher sanctions than the criminal law would provide for the same act. Penal law, as I use the term, could offer penalties as minor as mere regulatory penalties; I propose no hard line to distinguish between them in terms of the sanctions offered. But the high end goes well beyond what is available from mere regulatory penalties.

There are two other important differences. Penal law always uses the procedures of criminal law. This is not the case for mere regulatory law, although some regulatory law, sometimes referred to as quasi-criminal law, uses the procedures of criminal law. More importantly, as noted above, penal law offenses are not to be done. By contrast, mere regulatory offenses often do not imply that it was *wrong* to act as an agent acted.

In sum, penal law is a new suggestion, a suggestion for an analog to criminal law that is different not in terms of the nature of the sanctions, the processes used in court, or the marking out of offenses as wrong, but in what justifies the sanction. Punishments are justified by retributive desert; penalties are justified by fair forfeiture. The state can exploit that difference to use the penal law to do more to deter lawbreaking and to reinforce respect for the law than it could do with proportional punishments alone. By theorizing *when* it is justifiable to use the penal law, we can also develop a sense for the constraints that apply when the state can go beyond proportional punishment for culpable wrongdoing, a critical perspective that otherwise goes missing.

1.3.5 Three Routes to Incapacitation

There is one thing that I think punishment and penalties cannot aim to do: incapacitate. Both can impose sanctions that have the effect of incapacitation, but that cannot be their defining aim. It also cannot be a constitutive aim, in the sense that incapacitation is part of what punishments or penalties aim to produce. The state cannot punish or penalize *in order* to incapacitate. Penal law

[68] On the distinction between *Ordnungswidrigkeiten* and *Straftaten*, see A. Duff and T. Hörnle, "Crimes of Endangerment," 160–162, and "Principles of Criminalization." On the German use of the "culpability principle," see M. Dubber and T. Hörnle, *Criminal Law*, 250.

[69] Re the exclusion of imprisonment from *Ordnungswidrigkeitenrecht*, see Duff and Hörnle, "Principles of Criminalization," draft 4–5.

cannot aim to incapacitate for the straightforward reason that I've defined it as aimed at deterring lawbreaking and thereby reinforcing respect for the law. The more controversial claim is that the criminal law cannot aim to incapacitate. Incapacitation is often offered as one of the main consequentialist reasons to have criminal punishment. The controversial claim I defend here is that this is a mistake.

My reason is straightforward: Incapacitation presupposes distrust, and distrust is inconsistent with the idea of reconciliation between the wrongdoer and the larger political community.[70] Indeed, such reconciliation is the ultimate aim of censure and punishment. Even as a wrongdoer is being punished, the message being sent should be inclusive: that she is respected as an autonomous agent, with dignity, who is being held responsible for what she has done. She can owe the community amends, and those can be extracted through punishment, but she cannot owe the community being distrusted. She can earn distrust—that's what POLA forfeiture represents—but she cannot owe it. And thus owning her guilt-debt should be consistent with being respected as a person who still benefits from the POLA as a general matter, even though she violated that trust on the occasion that grounds her punishment. She may *also* have forfeited the POLA, but that is a separate matter from owing a guilt-debt.

To be clear, there is an element of distrust in *forcing* her to make amends.[71] This may be justified on the ground that a wrongdoer who has been convicted of a crime for which the punishment is a serious sanction may be presumed, at least in many cases, to have forfeited the POLA with regard to her voluntarily submitting to the punishment. But her forfeiture of the POLA should remain minimal, as forfeiture of the POLA is always in tension with the goal of reconciliation. The idea of incapacitating her quite generally, so that she does not commit future crimes, is a much bigger step. That is not to say that it cannot be justified. But the justification for the requisite forfeiture has to be given in those terms: forfeiture of the POLA. It cannot be grounded in the very notion of punishment because it is, in fact, in tension with the goal of punishment.

Saying that incapacitation cannot be a goal of punishment does not imply that punishment cannot be valued in part for its incapacitating effect. But the

[70] This justification for denying that incapacitation can be a reason for punishment is different from the main reason Zachary Hoskins gives for not treating it as a reason for punishment. For him, the primary reason is that incapacitation is not inherently burdensome, but punishment must be intended to be burdensome. See *Beyond Punishment?* 58. This is a conceptual point about punishment for Hoskins. For me, it is a moral point. Hoskins elsewhere emphasizes that punishment addresses the punished with reasons, while incapacitation does not. See his "Against Incapacitative Punishment." That comes closer to my reason for denying that incapacitation can provide a reason to punish.

[71] This is not present in all punishments. For example, "honor farms" assume that the inmates will not leave without permission; they don't hold the inmates behind bars. See the classic treatment of these in S. Bates, "Honor System for Inmates of Prisons and Reformatories."

justification for the loss of liberty has to be that it is a form of hard treatment that serves the legitimate ends of punishment. The benefits of incapacitation may give the state reason to adopt incapacitating *forms* of punishment, as long as they are deployed proportionately. In addition, when considering individual cases, the state may consider the benefits of incapacitating a dangerous person to offset the costs of incarceration that might otherwise make that form of punishment too costly to carry out.[72] What may not be done is punishing *in order* to incapacitate. Insofar as incapacitation is the aim of a policy, it has to be justified in other ways.

The question is, what are those ways? I have already mentioned them briefly when I introduced the DR Model[73]: an agent having forfeited the POLA, having enforceable duties to restrict herself, or being unaccountable, either intrinsically or extrinsically. There is much to be said about each of these; the details are provided in Part V of this book.

[72] This justification, however, requires finding forfeiture of the POLA.

[73] See § 1.3.1.

2
Methodological Commitments and Foundational Ideas

2.1 Substantive Commitments Rather than Thin Ones

I want to start this chapter by flagging the distinctive and somewhat unusual way I argue in this book. I argue from a robust set of commitments: a particular conception of dignity, of rights, and of blame, as well as the rejection of consequentialism. I rely on a contestable conception of liberalism, one that contrasts, for example, with John Stuart Mill's view, according to which respect for autonomy matters only insofar as it promotes the welfare of individuals.[1]

Why argue from a set of thick moral commitments, rather than seek whatever overlapping consensus can be found among the family of liberal authors? Why not argue as, for example, Zach Hoskins does when he concludes that punishment must be burdensome by appealing to four different views of punishment—those based on deterrence, retribution, communication of social censure, and education—showing that they all agree on that point?[2] I don't think there is anything *wrong* with starting from a wide overlapping consensus (I too sometimes start from widely accepted practices or premises), but I try not to rest on wide acceptance alone. I try always to ground my argument in basic assumptions about the nature of dignity, rights, and blame. I proceed this way because I believe we can make valuable progress in moral philosophy, and by extension in legal theory, by seeing where substantive commitments take us.

The particular advantage of proceeding in this way, in my view, is that it allows me to make certain arguments that I would not otherwise be able to make. My aim is not just to argue for a particular set of policies, but to see what can be justified if one takes seriously particular conceptions of dignity, rights, blame, and so on, the stuff of the dignity-respecting model (DR Model). I am also skeptical of claims that different starting points in moral philosophy converge, as if we are, to use Derek Parfit's phrase, climbing the same mountain from different sides, converging at the peak.[3] I think the underlying theoretical differences

[1] See *On Liberty*.
[2] *Beyond Punishment?* 47.
[3] See *On What Matters*, 419. For a defense of my skepticism, see my "Separate Peaks."

Punishment, Penalty, and Incapacitation. Alec Walen, Oxford University Press. © Oxford University Press 2026.
DOI: 10.1093/9780197523124.003.0002

often matter more than some of us would like to admit, and that we should therefore be willing, when we think it might make a difference, to own particular commitments, even if they are not widely shared, just to see how they work out.

What if you don't accept my account of dignity, rights, and blame? There may still be value in reading this book, as it will explain what is implied if one does accept this plausible (or so I believe) set of commitments. In addition, if the whole hangs together well, that provides some extra reason to trust the premises. That is part of the method of reflective equilibrium, which is the only method we moral philosophers have to use.[4] One has reason to reject a theory if one thinks the deep commitments are wrong, the implications of them for practice are implausible, or the whole thing just does not hang together well (it seems to be gappy, or beset by unnecessary and implausible tensions, or jury rigged and contrived). If, however, a theory seems to offer an attractive vision of how a range of practices should be organized, one that seems to rest on plausible deep premises, to have mostly plausible practical conclusions, and to be fairly coherent overall, then that set of virtues should make the theory seem sound. It is my hope that the DR Model that I offer will seem sound in that way, and that that virtue will offset the cost of not seeking to build on premises supported by a wide overlapping consensus.

One might object that my methodology is inconsistent with political liberalism, and that political liberalism is important for making policy in a pluralistic society. One might think that Rawls was right to emphasize the importance of a commitment to public reason, which seeks to appeal only to values that all liberals can accept, rather than appeal to contested "comprehensive doctrines."[5]

In response I want to register a general sympathy with the thought that those engaging in arguments about public policy should strive to provide reasons that all liberals can recognize as the right sorts of reasons, reasons that are consistent with basic liberal commitments. But at the same time, I don't think one should fetishize that goal. Disagreement cannot be avoided, even if arguments are framed in terms of public reasons. And sometimes, an honest discussion of disagreements has to dig deeper than public reason can go. I'm not suggesting that the law should seek to embody contested comprehensive doctrines as such. Insofar as people who accept different comprehensive doctrines can come together to embrace a set of laws, that is all to the good in terms of the perceived legitimacy of those laws. Legislatures should generally not seek to offer reasons that most people cannot accept as true. And while courts have to be more explicit about their reasoning than legislatures, they generally can and should avoid

[4] The notion of reflective equilibrium traces back at least to John Rawls. For his mature statement on it, see *Political Liberalism*, 28.

[5] See "The Idea of Public Reason Revisited."

engaging in deep philosophical arguments. But a philosophical project aiming to improve our understanding of and inspire reform of the law can profitably engage with issues in ways that legislators and judges should not. Philosophical exploration and persuasion are different tasks from law making and law interpreting. If I manage to persuade some people of the moral importance of certain reforms that I think follow from the DR Model, it will then be a separate task to see if those reforms can be democratically enacted.

2.2 A Multidimensional Problem with No Priority for Prosecution

Trade-offs between security and liberty are inevitable. When thinking about how to make such trade-offs, it is natural to imagine scales, like the proverbial scales of justice, with the value of liberty weighing on the one pan and the value of security weighing on the other. That model suggests a consequentialist framework. But such a model is too simple in several ways. I mention two here: first, it fails to make sense of deontological limits on consequentialist trade-offs; second, it fails to make sense of the rich set of trade-offs that are possible when seeking to find an optimal or even a decent solution. I cover the deontological limits in the next section and in Chapter 3. Here I focus on two themes: first, that there are trade-offs to be made between different values, but the trade-offs are too complex to be modeled on a simple scale. Second, there is no natural priority that should be assigned to one way of achieving security, such as prosecution, over others.

On the multidimensional point, security itself is, of course, a complex idea. It concerns, among other things, the ability to protect against unjust attacks, both foreign and domestic, on a range of targets: the individuals in the state; the government's democratic capacity; clean air and water; safe, nutritious, and affordable food; electricity, roads, and other forms of infrastructure; economic productivity; and public health. It also concerns the ability to protect against natural and man-made disasters and, of course, the ability to suppress criminal activity. This book focuses on the last, but other security concerns emerge from time to time.

The more important source of multidimensionality for my purposes is what can be done to achieve security in terms of targeted restrictions. There may be trade-offs between the different ways of justifiably targeting liberty to achieve security. For example, governments can try more or less hard to make criminal punishments effective as deterrents (mostly by making them more certain with better policing,[6] and by communicating clearly what the penalties are,[7] but also,

[6] See D. Nagin, "Deterrence in the Twenty-First Century," 201.
[7] See B. van Rooij and A. Fine, *The Behavioral Code*, 38–40.

to some extent, by raising the level of the punishments in ways that are consistent with proportionality); but they might also seek to do less with punishments and more with penalties. Doing more with penal law might be more effective at preventing crime and reinforcing the law, but it might also undermine the meaningfulness of the criminal law as the more fundamental institution, and that might change the character of society in alienating and dangerous ways.[8] Or the government might seek to do more with forfeiture of the presumption of law abidingness (POLA). This is fairly constrained by proportionality concerns, but some latitude remains, and insofar as more is done with forfeiture of the POLA, there may be less need to use punishments or penalties. On the other hand, as an empirical matter, it may turn out that doing more with forfeiture of the POLA alienates people in a way that creates more of a problem for the criminal law and the penal law.

The government also has choices to make about how best to handle the trilemma regarding those with limited autonomous capacity: it can (1) allow them normal individual freedom and hold them responsible for their wrongful behavior, (2) allow them normal individual freedom and give them more excuses for wrongful behavior and thereby put more burden on those who would be wronged by them, or (3) restrict them more than most individuals are restricted.[9] Pressures that result from those policy choices could affect the way the criminal law, the penal law, and forfeiture of the POLA work. The government can also put more resources into policing. Doing so may have costs both in economic and privacy terms, but it may alleviate pressure along all the other dimensions just discussed. Or the government can emphasize general restrictions, rather than targeted restrictions, or seek to do more to address the causes of insecurity. Or, finally, the government can be fairly laissez-faire, tolerant of insecurity, leaving individuals to deal with it as they see fit within their own means (or, the means of others that they wrongly appropriate).

I have a few things to say about some of these choices. For example, I argue that there are good reasons to give the criminal law priority over the penal law when choosing the means for deterring law breaking and reinforcing respect for the law.[10] But for the most part, I limit my ambitions in this book to laying out what can justifiably be done, leaving the trade-offs to others. My point here is that these trade-offs cannot be well modeled with a simple balance between liberty and security. The state may decide that it needs more security, or it may decide that individual liberties have been overly restricted in one way or another. But such a decision is merely the first step toward

[8] I explore this trade-off in Section 15.1.3.

[9] I explore this trade-off in Section 19.3.

[10] Again, see Section 15.1.3. But note, the argument there is subject to empirical questions about the consequences of both types of law.

action. The government must then decide whether it will respect the DR Model (as it is morally obliged to do), and if so, which trade-offs to make within that model.

Finally, I want to make one negative observation about priorities: prosecution should not be treated as a moral priority relative to other justifiable targeted modes of addressing security risks. That is to say that the DR Model does not require that all options for prosecution (whether aiming at punishment or penalty) be exhausted before options for incapacitation are explored. It is common to think otherwise. Sandra Mayson, for example, writes: "The state is [] prohibited from preventively detaining people if it can adequately manage whatever risk they present through legitimate punishment."[11] And Christopher Slobogin writes: "If government chooses to preventively detain an individual rather than punish him, it must show the person is not eligible for the right to punishment."[12] This view is incorrect. Consider the detention of prisoners of war (POWs). Even if the military has reason to believe a POW has committed war crimes, it is not obliged to prosecute him before detaining him preventively. Or consider quarantine. It would be bizarrely inappropriate to seek to prosecute those with contagious diseases as far as possible before simply ensuring that they are quarantined. Or consider someone who has committed a crime and thereby forfeited the POLA in a substantial way: if, after serving time for his crime, he is found to be an ongoing danger, he can be preventively detained. It would be perverse to insist that the state first ensure that there are no other crimes he has committed for which detention would be a suitable punishment. Finally, consider the wide range of limitations that target juveniles, such as not being free to drink or to drive, even if the two are not combined. Clearly, the state should not first seek to prosecute and punish every juvenile it can and then impose incapacitative restrictions on the rest.

This widely endorsed mistake has at least two roots. First, it reflects an appropriate concern with the thought that the need for and the effectiveness of incapacitation is hard to establish. It is hard to know what a person would have done if he had not had his liberty restricted. To fill the epistemic void, we may be tempted to rely on "stereotypes and prejudices as proxies for dangerousness."[13] One way to resist that temptation is to restrict people only when they have done something that could serve as the basis for a prosecution. But that's not the only way to resist the temptation. We can instead be assiduous in trying to use scientific data as the basis for predictions of dangerousness.

[11] "A Consequentialist Framework for Prevention," 235.

[12] "A Jurisprudence of Dangerousness," 5. See also D. Cole, "Rights Over Borders," 104–105; S. Schulhofer, "Two Systems of Social Protection," 93.

[13] D. Cole, "Rights Over Borders," 104.

That's often very difficult, and our ability to predict will remain limited.[14] But it need not be reduced to reliance on stereotypes and prejudices.

Another source of the error is the fear that the state will reach for incapacitative measures even if they are unjustifiable. This fear has been pronounced, especially since the "War on Terror" was launched. The United States has held people who were not POWs as if they were for decades. The United Kingdom has used Control Orders and their replacement, Terrorism Prevention and Investigation Measures, in a similar effort to prevent terrorist attacks for decades as well.[15] These are dubious practices, and insisting on exhausting the criminal law first is one way to push back on them. But putting too much pressure on the criminal justice system can lead to its distortion, causing it to rely on a great number of proxy crimes with punishments that are disproportionate to the culpability of the offenses.[16] The better solution is simply to respect the DR Model. That will not allow incapacitative restrictions when they are unjustified, but it will not put too much pressure on the criminal justice system when other dignity-respecting bases for providing security are a more natural fit.

2.3 Deontology: The Basic Idea

Deontology is the morality of right or permissible actions and wrong or impermissible actions. Even utilitarians and consequentialists take deontological positions insofar as they say things like "actions are right insofar as they produce the most happiness or the best consequences." But most people who use the term "deontology" these days have in mind "commonsense deontology," which departs from the maximizing answers found in traditional utilitarianism and act consequentialism. And what *I* mean by "deontology" is a version of commonsense deontology, one that is grounded in respect for rights and for justice more broadly. My conception of rights, which I sketch out in the next chapter, is grounded in respect for the dignity of individuals. From here on, when I use the term "deontology," I mean to refer to my rights-based, dignity-respecting conception of it.

The space of rights, as I understand it, is grounded not only on rights, as they are normally understood, but also on the aim of promoting welfare. As a result, my conception of deontology allows for the aggregation of rights claims. This is a conception that many "deontologists"—people committed to a deontology based

[14] As Mayson points out: though "[t]oday's actuarial tools . . . are rapidly improving in sophistication and predictive power," the ability of these tools to predict rearrest for a six-month period remains remarkably low. "Dangerous Defendants," 496. Of the tools she surveys, the highest risk for rearrest for "high risk" defendants was only 16 percent. Ibid., 495.

[15] For a brief history, see A. Ashworth and L. Zedner, *Preventive Justice*, 184–187.

[16] The distorting effects on the criminal law are central concerns of, among others, Paul Robinson in "Punishing Dangerousness," and Kimberly Ferzan in "Beyond Crime and Commitment."

on respect for the individual—reject. On one common alternative conception of deontology, deontological restrictions operate as what Robert Nozick called "side-constraints."[17] The image is of a steel barrier that will not yield unless hit with truly massive (moral) force—the massive force accounting for "threshold deontology."[18] But, as I argue in the next chapter, that is not how rights-based deontology works. I illustrate the point with an example of a deontologically-informed trade-off that is neither what an act consequentialist would endorse, nor what can be explained by a mere side-constraint on action. Consider this classic example of a choice between (a) saving some people's lives at the cost of killing another person as a side effect of doing so, and (b) allowing the larger number of people to die but also not killing anyone:

> *Trolley Switch*: Betty, a bystander at a switch, can throw a switch and thereby turn a trolley that is hurtling down a hill, out of control, away from five innocent people and toward one innocent person on a sidetrack (the "sidetrack man"), thereby killing the sidetrack man and saving the five.[19]

Most people think Betty may kill the sidetrack man to save the five. But at the same time, almost no one thinks that Betty may turn the trolley from one stranger onto another. This combination of judgments is most plausibly understood by appealing, on the one hand, to the principle that it is harder to justify killing than it is to justify failing to save, and, on the other hand, to the thought that numbers matter. Or, putting this in terms that invoke the language of rights and help disentangle the moral interests of patients from agents: negative patient claims (claims not to be harmed) are stronger, all else equal, than positive patient claims (claims to be saved), but they are not categorically stronger, regardless of the strength of the interest protected or the numbers involved. If Betty can save one person from dying only by turning the trolley toward another who would suffer a broken arm, then I think she may justifiably turn the trolley. And if she can save five only by turning the trolley onto the sidetrack man, then again I think she may turn the trolley. The different strengths we accord positive and negative claims is a deontologically significant feature of how rights work. But the priority of negative over positive patient claims is not an absolute side-constraint; rather, it is a matter of weighing and counting.

[17] *Anarchy, State, and Utopia*, 32.

[18] For a classic statement, see Larry Alexander, "Deontology at the Threshold." For my critique and my own views on the topic, see "Deontology in Graphs," § VII.

[19] The first person to frame that example was Philippa Foot in "The Problem of Abortion and the Doctrine of the Double Effect." But the first person to point out that the case is best understood by making the trolley turner a bystander, rather than the driver, was Judith Jarvis Thomson in "Killing, Letting Die, and the Trolley Problem."

This is not to say that there are no absolute side-constraints in deontology. I think there is only so much harm that one can justifiably impose on one person whom one would use as a means of saving others, at least if the person to be used has not consented to being so used and is not especially liable to bearing costs as a means of helping those others. Regardless of whether that is correct or not, the important points are (1) that we can understand the deontological issues in *Trolley Switch* by paying attention to how different kinds of claims on an agent who has to make a choice weigh against each other, and (2) that claims concerning the same set of outcomes (life or death) can come in different strengths, with negative claims being stronger than positive claims, and claims not to be used as a means being stronger still, again, all else equal.

There have been some consequentialists who have sought to track these distinctions by attaching value to *how* outcomes are achieved. For example, a consequentialist can say that it is worse to kill than to fail to save, and that it is *much* worse to impose a substantial harm on someone who is used as a means. The problem with this move is that the consequentialist who counts value from an evaluator-neutral perspective cannot make proper sense of deontological restrictions. From their point of view, such restrictions are inherently "paradoxical."[20] The paradox arises when one thinks about a case in which A would have to use B as a means, killing B, to prevent C from using five others as a means, killing them. Even if killing as a means is *very* bad, it would seem to be *better* (less bad) for A to kill B than for A to allow C to kill five others. The deontology I defend disallows such a sacrifice, but from a value-maximizing consequentialist point of view, that seems unreasonable.[21]

The sense that deontology is paradoxical is an artifact of starting with a value-maximizing consequentialist model of morality, and assuming that deontology must respect that way of thinking. There is no reason, however, for deontology to respect that starting point. Deontology is agent centered; it looks at the claims of individual patients on an agent.[22] B has a claim on A not to be killed as a means; the five have claims on C not to be killed as a means; the five do *not* have the same sort of claims on A; their claims on A are to be saved from C. There is nothing paradoxical in saying that A has to respect the strongest set of claims on her, which in this case is B's claim.

A consequentialist can reach the same result by letting value add up from an agent-relative point of view.[23] But as far as I can tell, this is just an exercise in

[20] See *Anarchy, State, and Utopia*, 30.

[21] Matthew Oliver, in "The Means and the Good," has a clever account of how consequentialist could agree with the deontologist that Amy should not kill Ben. I argue that his solution is overall implausible in "Separate Peaks."

[22] The ground for taking deontology to be taken to be agent centered is explored in Section 3.3.2.

[23] See A. Sen, "Rights and Agency"; D. Portmore, *Opting for the Best*.

mapping from one set of ideas (a dignity-respecting model of rights) onto another (consequentialism). The moral reasoning that grounds this sort of agent-relative reasoning is fundamentally about claims, and it is worked out with reference to what it takes for people to operate in a space of rights that respects their dignity. Therefore, for the sake of simplicity and clarity, I talk about consequentialism from here on in its classic, evaluator-neutral form, the form that does not track agent centered rights-based reasoning.

2.4 The Importance of Justifications

A central theme of this book is that we need to be careful to trace which justifications are in play in different situations, to understand just what may be done. But if restrictions on liberty are justified, one might ask: why focus on *how* they are justified? If detaining someone in a prison-like facility, for example, is justified, why worry about whether it is justified as punishment or as incapacitation? Isn't it enough to know that it is justified one way or another?

The answer is that the justifications invoked determine how it is permissible to carry out that sort of act. I illustrate the point with two examples. Consider, first, imprisonment, and consider two competing justifications: punishment and incapacitation grounded in forfeiture of the POLA. If the state tries to justify the act of imprisoning someone on the grounds that it is a punishment, then it has to determine whether it is a proportional punishment, one that fits the crime. If, however, the state tries to justify it through forfeiture of the POLA, then it has to ask different questions. First, there's a different kind of proportionality question: Did the potential prisoner do something serious enough to have forfeited the POLA in a way that could justify imprisonment? Even if the answer is yes, it has to ask a second question: Is imprisonment the least restrictive alternative for protecting others from him? That is, would imprisonment provide a fair balance between his interest in freedom and the interests others have in safety?

These are different sorts of questions. Suppose a proportional punishment would be five years in prison. Then that is the maximum prison sentence that could be imposed. The maximum incarceration time might be longer, however, if the justification is that the agent forfeited the POLA, she forfeited it for longer than five years, and she remains such a serious threat that only imprisonment will provide adequate protection for others. In addition, the nature of the institution holding the person would presumably be different. Punitive imprisonment can presumably be in a harsher setting than imprisonment aimed only at incapacitation, as the aim of the former, but not of the latter, is to provide hard treatment that deters lawbreaking.

For a second example, consider the requirement that sexual offenders register as such, in a public way which the neighbors can access, whenever they move into a new residence.[24] While registration would be an unwanted burden on most people, the degree to which it would be burdensome would presumably vary substantially from person to person and from community to community. If the state wants to impose hard treatment on sexual offenders to deter such behavior, this would be a peculiar element to add to the mix. But if the state's concern is with limiting the liberty of sexual offenders—in this case, the liberty to move into a neighborhood while keeping an important feature of their past private—in such a way as to provide safety to others, then this might seem like a sensible policy, at least in theory.[25] But that would require us to assess the policy as a matter of forfeiture of the POLA rather than as a punishment.

If a legislature is clear about which justification it is using, then a court assessing whether the action is justifiable would, I believe, have reason to apply the relevant set of criteria to see if the act is actually justified in that way. For example, if the legislature is clearly proposing sexual registration as a part of the punishment, then it would have to be proportional and adhere to other requirements of criminal law, such as avoidance of ex post facto legislation. Arguably, a court could consider alternative justifications if they would work better, especially if asked to do so by counsel for the state. I won't take a position on that here. But that would just lead such cases to be decided like those cases in which the legislature does not make it clear what justification it is relying on for its action, it simply adopts a new law—which seems to be the common practice. In those cases, the state, in defending the law, would have to make a choice regarding how it wants the law to be defended, and accept the restrictions that come with that.

In sum, justifications are a structuring device. When considering whether an action is justified, we should not look merely at the "weight" or "strength" of reasons for or against. We need to first assess what kinds of reasons count for a particular kind of justification. The fundamental choice about whether an act is a punishment, a penalty, or an incapacitation based on forfeiture of the POLA or some other ground will determine how then to assess the reasons. For example, if a punishment is justified in its own terms as deserved, but it would have costs that weigh against imposing it, the state may consider the benefits of incapacitation as relevant to offsetting those costs. However, the benefits of incapacitation

[24] For the seminal example of such a law, see New Jersey Code at 2C:7-12 to -19 (Meagan's law). Registration laws do not work the same in all countries. In England, for example, a sex offender has to register her new address with the police, but the public cannot access the register.

[25] For a trenchant critique of the policy in practice, see A. McLeod, "Regulating Sexual Harm."

cannot be considered as a reason to punish in the first place, nor as a reason to treat a crime as more serious than it is, so as to allow for more incapacitation.[26] And to the extent that incapacitation is invoked to offset costs in particular cases, the permissibility of doing so must first be established by forfeiture of the POLA that would cover that sort of use of incapacitation.[27]

[26] Frances Kamm's doctrine of triple effect may be helpful here. The goal of imposing just deserts is the "in order to" reason to punish; positive effects like incapacitation can, given conditions I discuss in the text immediately below, be "because of" reasons; the unintended harms or costs of punishment are the side effects that need to be outweighed. See *Intricate Ethics*, 92–93.

[27] See Section 1.3.5.

3

A Dignity-Respecting Model of Rights for Liberal States

3.1 Why Bother with a New Account of Rights?

The basic function of rights, *moral* rights,[1] as I understand them, is to provide a normative space in which (paradigmatically) individual persons can each pursue their own ends while treating each other respectfully as free and responsible agents, with fundamentally equal status, whose welfare morally matters. I call this normative space the "space of rights," and the agents who construct it with their choices are citizens in the "republic of rights." Dignity, as I conceive it, consists in having the status of an equal citizen in the republic of rights. And a liberal state is one that is committed first and foremost to respecting the rights of the people on whom it exercises its power. Thus, to understand how a liberal state can pursue the security of its people, we need to have a basic understanding of the rights a liberal state must respect.

My understanding of rights is, admittedly, idiosyncratic. I have developed a distinctive theory of rights, which I call the Mechanics of Claims (MOC)[2] and which I will articulate in this chapter. One might wonder: "Why should I bother learning a new theory of rights in order to discuss the permissibility of targeted restrictions of liberty?" I offer here four reasons.

First, the MOC provides a complete framework for discussing how to respect the dignity of all individuals while protecting the welfare of those who are threatened. It is a complete framework because all interests that are relevant to determining what may be done are picked up by claims (pro tanto rights), which are put into a structured balance that determines who has a right to do what or to receive what from others. The framework does not itself provide sufficiently determinate answers to determine who has a right to what; the state has a crucial role to play in creating legal rights that provide determinate content to many moral rights.[3] The sense in which the MOC is complete is that naked interests do

[1] See Section 1.1, n. 10.
[2] I first published the basic idea in "Agents, Impartiality, and the Priority of Claims over Duties" (with David Wasserman). The most well-developed and complete version is in *The Mechanics of Claims*, ch. 3.
[3] See Section 3.7 below.

Punishment, Penalty, and Incapacitation. Alec Walen, Oxford University Press. © Oxford University Press 2026.
DOI: 10.1093/9780197523124.003.0003

not have to be appealed to in order to determine who has a right to what. This sort of completeness allows for a more coherent and principled accounting of rights than the common alternative framework, which treats people as having a mix of rights that protect some interests and naked interests that somehow weigh against rights to determine what may be done.[4]

Second, and relatedly, I use the MOC to provide insights into many phenomena that otherwise seem morally mysterious. Most fundamentally, I use it to explain the means principle—the principle that it is hard to justify using people as a means if they have neither consented to being so used nor done something to make such using permissible, and they lack a special duty that would make such using permissible. This principle has proven hard to justify. There are two ways to frame it, and both are problematic. On one framing, picked up by the Doctrine of Double Effect (DDE), the means principle is concerned with whether an agent has the intention to use another as a means of achieving some end of his. The DDE has been criticized in multiple ways, but the most significant criticism, in my opinion, is that the DDE wrongly directs agents to focus inwardly on their mental states, rather than on the rights of others.[5] On the other framing, the means principle is concerned with the causal role of the person used to achieve some good that might justify causing or allowing some harm. With regard to this idea, Thomas Scanlon declared: "being a means in this sense—being causally necessary—has no intrinsic moral significance . . . "[6] I use the MOC to explain why, Scanlon's claim notwithstanding, being causally necessary *does* have profound moral significance.[7]

I also find the MOC helpful for describing how forfeiture—another fundamental normative principle in this book—works in a way that is more nuanced than one finds in other forfeiture theories. Standard forfeiture theories take rights to be completely forfeited or not, leaving the relevant questions to be things like which rights are forfeited, for what reasons, and for how long.[8] I think rights forfeiture is better understood by distinguishing the different kinds of claim that can be weakened or shifted around. For example, forfeiture can affect who counts as having a property right over some property, and it might also swap who counts as having a claim for aid and who has a claim not to be made

[4] See Judith Jarvis Thomson's *The Realm of Rights* for a classic account of the alternative.

[5] See J. Bennett, "The Tanner Lectures on Human Values," 97, and J. J. Thomson, "Self-Defense," 293. For a detailed follow up on those criticisms, see K. Ramakrishnan, "Treating People as Tools," §§ 1.A, C, D, and F.

[6] *Moral Dimensions*, 118.

[7] See Section 3.5 below. There are others who have developed accounts similar to my first attempt to use the MOC to justify the means principle. See G. Øverland, "Moral Obstacles"; L. Alexander, "The Means Principle," and K. Ramakrishnan, "Treating People as Tools." None of these accounts rely on anything like my MOC, nor do any of them pick up my revised and improved account, which, as far as I can tell, can only be spelled out using the MOC.

[8] See C. Wellman's discussion in "The Rights Forfeiture Theory of Punishment," 380–391.

worse off, but neither of these changes by itself need imply that the person who forfeited some claims loses his right not to be harmed. One has to think through how the claims balance after forfeiture has played its role.[9] Those ideas make sense only if one uses a theory of rights like the MOC.

Third, the foundations for the space of rights that I spell out in this chapter are also important for two basic theses that I defend in the book: that the state must grant people the presumption of law abidingness (POLA) unless they have forfeited it or they are unaccountable for what they do, and that punishment must aim at reconciliation. I ground the POLA on the same principles that ground my account of rights. And my belief that punishment must aim at reconciliation between the wrongdoer and the political community whose state punishes him rests on two ideas that I argue for in this chapter: that the state has a fundamental role in shaping rights, and that this role extends to a concern with promoting rightful relations between people, which includes reconciling wrongdoers with their local political communities and with the broader republic of rights.

Fourth, as a matter of theoretical aesthetics, I like the MOC because it avoids a concept common to contemporary rights discussions that I have always disliked, the idea that people can be permissibly wronged. This view rests on the thought that rights are an input into moral deliberations, and as such they come into conflict with other rights and with naked interests in ways that make it morally appropriate to *disrespect* some rights. The idea is not that it is ever acceptable to *violate* rights; rather, a distinction is drawn between impermissible violations and permissible infringements. The suggestion is that sometimes we may, sometimes we should, and sometimes we must infringe the rights of some to give proper moral consideration to the interests or rights of others. People seem tempted by some such account in part because they like the idea of rights as inputs into our moral deliberations, and in part because they believe that some such account is necessary to explain why compensation is often owed to people when they are permissibly harmed: it is owed them because they had a right that was infringed.

I find the idea of merely infringing rights, and thereby permissibly wronging, unhelpfully paradoxical and unnecessary.[10] It is unhelpfully paradoxical for the straightforward reason that wronging should be wrong, not permissible. The idea of an "infringement" is meant to lessen the sense of paradoxicality. The idea is that infringements are permissible because they do not go to the heart of a right but only nibble away at the fringes. But that's a misleading suggestion. To put the

[9] See Section 14.2.

[10] In "Deontology in Graphs," 246–249, I explore in graphical form some reasons why we should not use the idea of permissible wronging, except in the context of threshold deontology, which should be reserved for extreme cases that rarely occur.

point more honestly, those who embrace rightful wronging should say that when other moral considerations, whether conflicting interests or conflicting rights, justify contravening a right, then a person can rightfully be wronged because his rights are weaker than competing considerations. That lays out, in plain language, what is at stake, but I think we have no good reason to engage in such talk.

I want to reserve the concept of wronging for impermissible action, and I want to reserve the concept of rights (patient rights, to be precise) for a normative status that must be respected *as a matter of right*. The way to do that, as I will explain, is to treat *claims* as inputs in a rights-based balancing framework, and to treat *rights* as the output.[11] Not all claims need to be respected, but all rights do. And as for compensation, that can be explained as well if not better by appealing to the idea of shifting the bad luck of one party onto another.[12]

I don't provide a complete discussion of the MOC here.[13] But I spell out the basics so that the reader can follow the argument, understanding why I use this idiosyncratic conceptual framework for rights. What if you, the reader, think my conception of rights is wrongheaded? As I said in Chapter 2, there may still be value in seeing where it leads. And if the whole seems coherent, that may give you reason to reconsider whether this account of rights is sound after all.[14]

3.2 The Foundations of Rights

Rights are relevant to us both as agents and patients. As agents, we want rights to do certain things and not to do others, and we want the power to trade and waive our rights as suits our plans. The flip side of the power to shape our rights, the flip side that reflects our status as *responsible* agents, is the liability to losing rights. We can lose them as a matter of desert, through forfeiture, through the

[11] Specificationists also speak about rights as absolute, but their conception of rights is conclusory; they engage in no distinctive rights-structured reasoning. See *The Mechanics of Claims*, 45–46.

[12] See ibid., 101–103. In that context, I focused on patient claims, the thought being that when negative claims (not to be harmed) are outweighed by competing positive claims (to be helped), then the bad luck of those with positive claims can permissibly be shifted onto those with negative claims. This negative-positive distinction can be extended to agents as well. When agents have a positive claim to be free to act, but it is limited by some patient's negative claim, the agent is due no compensation. But when the agent has a negative claim not to have to act, and it is overridden by a patient's positive claim for aid, then the agent has a claim for compensation. As with harming some for the sake of others, the patients with the bad luck to have positive claims shift their bad luck onto someone else, only in these cases, it is an agent. Note, however, that the agent's claim for compensation may not ground a right, especially if the patient is too poor to provide compensation.

I take this opportunity to acknowledge an error in my earlier account. My argument that the standard account of the right to compensation falls victim to a "normative gulf" was unsound. Ibid., 111–113. See J. Bowen's review of *The Mechanics of Claims*.

[13] This chapter is already the longest in the book, and a longer, more complete exposition can be found in *The Mechanics of Claims*, ch. 3.

[14] See Section 2.1.

acquisition of duties, and due to changes in our capacity to be held accountable. As patients, we want rights to protect us from agents who mean us harm and we want rights to secure us aid in times of need. We also want our rights to have a certain stability, or immunity, in the face of others who might seek to change them.[15]

The space of rights, as I conceive it, presents itself to us in two ways. On the one hand, it presents as a space structured so that agents can tell who has a right to what. With regard to first-order rights—patient rights against agents and agent rights to liberty—it works by allowing us to weigh competing patient claims and agent claims against each other to determine who, in the end, has a right to what. We can think of that weighing as providing a substantive reading of the space of rights. On the other hand, it presents as a space that can be navigated by agents. For an agent to navigate the space of rights, she needs to be aware of her own rights and the rights of others, and she needs to be aware of how she can use her powers to seek changes to her rights and the rights of others, while relying on the immunities she and others enjoy that protect them from unwanted changes to their rights. We can think of this as the dynamic reading of the space of rights. But a better way to frame it, one reflecting our status as building this space together, is as a republic of rights, in which all the fully competent agents are equal citizens.

The space of rights rests on three basic liberal principles. These principles should be understood not as values—though the third does concern the integration of value into the space of rights—but as axioms, analogous to those in geometry.

1. *Autonomy Principle:* Agents all have their own lives to lead; the space of rights must give them substantial freedom to do so, while also holding them accountable for their choices and the effects they have on others.
2. *Equality Principle:* All fully autonomous agents are fundamentally equal as citizens in the republic of rights.
3. *Welfare Principle:* The welfare of agents has value, and that value affects the rights agents have.

These are clearly *liberal* principles, taken from the Lockean tradition that Thomas Jefferson quoted in the *Declaration of Independence*: "that all men are created equal, that they are endowed by their Creator with certain unalienable Rights, that among these are Life, Liberty and the pursuit of Happiness." I also think of this as a distinctly Kantian conception of the function of rights. As he

[15] This is a broadly Hohfeldian conception of rights. See W. Hohfeld, "Some Fundamental Legal Conceptions as Applied in Judicial Reasoning."

wrote: "Right is . . . the sum of the conditions under which the choice of one can be united with the choice of another in accordance with a universal law of freedom."[16] I depart from Kant, however, insofar as I incorporate welfare into the foundational principles.[17] In my view, all three of these principles must be respected for a space of rights to count as a liberal space of rights.

Before saying how these principles ground and structure the space of rights, I offer a few more words on what each of the principles means. Autonomy has moral significance in three fundamentally different senses, and it is important to be clear about the sense that is meant in the Autonomy Principle. Autonomy can be considered a capacity, a value, and a status. Autonomous capacity is the ability to make decisions and be self-governing. In a weak sense, it is possessed by any self-directing organism that has its own subjective point of view. A computer (at least as of the date of this writing) is not autonomous, but a normal fish or chicken is. In a stronger sense, it is a capacity to make decisions in such a way that the agent is prudentially competent. In this sense, a dog or a young child is not autonomous, but most adults are. More substantively, for an agent to have autonomous capacity in this stronger sense is for her to be capable of (1) setting ends for herself that correspond to a conception of a good life; (2) changing her mind about her ends and her conception of a good life only in a fairly coherent, reason-guided manner (not shifting goals whimsically); (3) foreseeing, reasonably well, the effects of her behavior and taking those effects into account in making her choices; and (4) conforming her choices (at least for the most part) to pursuit of her ends using suitable means. In short, prudential autonomy requires the rational, self-governing abilities we associate with sane, adult self-governance. But full moral autonomy, the sort that is implied by the Autonomy Principle, requires agents to govern themselves so that they generally respect the rights others have against them, recognizing that if they violate the rights of others or just laws, they may owe compensation and may be liable to punishment.[18]

Having autonomy, even in the weak sense, confers value on the welfare of those who have it. That is one sense in which autonomy is morally significant. Even fish and chickens have a kind of welfare that merits concern that is not owed to a river or a tree. This value-conferring function of autonomy is even stronger for beings who are autonomous in the strong sense. Moreover, there is a special value in helping a person achieve and maintain both her prudential and her full moral autonomy—a point with both first-person and third-person significance.

[16] "The Doctrine of Right," Academy page 230.

[17] For a similar departure, see Rawls, *A Theory of Justice*, 4 (discussing the way "the rules [of a society] specify a system of cooperation designed to advance the good of those taking part in it").

[18] This conception of full moral autonomy is modeled on Rawls's conception of full autonomy. *Political Liberalism*, 77.

As a status, autonomy can be understood as the normative claim that an agent who is autonomous in the full moral sense should be treated as such. That means that the space of rights must be structured so that she can order her life primarily around her own ends. But her liberty to do so will also depend on her being accountable for her choices and the effects she has on others. Conversely, if she lacks full moral or prudential autonomous capacity, and if therefore she cannot be held fully responsible for her choices, then the state may have sufficient reason to limit her liberty to pursue her own ends.

The Autonomy Principle is fundamentally concerned with the last of these three: status. It says, in essence, that the space of rights must recognize that people who are autonomous, in the full moral sense, have the status of beings who may rightfully pursue their own ends as long as they do so within the bounds set by the space of rights, and that they can be held accountable for what they do.[19]

For the Equality Principle, the idea that we who are fully autonomous are *fundamentally* equal is key. We do not all share the same rights: my property is *mine*; yours is *yours*. Even if they are worth the same in the marketplace, which they probably are not, they are distinct and distinctly connected to each of us. Nevertheless, all who have crossed the threshold of full moral autonomous capacity have fundamentally equal status as "citizens" in the republic of rights. And even when people (or other beings with rights: animals or corporations) have different statuses, those who have the same sorts of claims for the same sorts of interests must have their claims counted the same. Equal claims must be treated equally. This is basic fairness. And the converse is true too: when there are relevant differences between people and their claims, those differences should be reflected in who has a right to what. Doing otherwise would also be unfair.

Again, it is important to be clear that equality in this sense is a principle, not a value. This is not to deny the importance of equality or distributive justice as a value. It is only to say that for the purposes of the MOC, equality is not a state to be achieved, it is a principle to be respected. It is a principle affecting how people's interests register in the space of rights and how their claims get balanced against one another.

It is important to note that it is not obvious how to understand interests: Are they the subjective value a person has for a thing or for her liberty, or should they be measured more objectively, to reflect the way that sort of thing or liberty is normally valued by relevantly similar beings in relevantly similar circumstances?[20]

[19] I return in Section 19.6 to the question of the status of people—paradigmatically psychopaths—who have reached threshold capacity in terms of prudential autonomy, but who lack moral autonomous capacity.

[20] For the latter position, see G. Fornaroli, "Rights, Wronging, and Equality of Status," 69–70 (citing work by Leif Wenar and Julian Jonker, and R. Jay Wallace).

Without some sort of objective measure, those who do not value something as others do might simply lose their right to it, and that seems wrong. Likewise, if a person values some object much more than others do, but the state has reason to exercise eminent domain over that object and take possession of it for a public purpose, it seems that there should be some limit to her ability to demand whatever she considers fair compensation. One might think that this second limit reflects only the need to avoid fraudulent claims of subjective value, but even if the state had perfectly reliable evidence of how much an agent values her property, it seems that there should be an objective limit to what she can demand by way of compensation for a public taking of that property. On the other hand, a purely objective measure of value seems too strong. If a person does not care about a liberty in the way others do, and the question is whether to impose on her an obligation to act that takes away that liberty, there is reason to think that her subjective valuation should matter. And something similar applies to compensation for the state's exercise of eminent domain. Perhaps a person should always at least be able to demand market value, but if she can show that she valued it substantially above the market rate, some rise above the market rate might be called for. I won't try to resolve this issue here. I'll simply say that interests should be understood in a hybrid way: objectively grounded, but with some room for the significance of subjective valuation.

Finally, the Welfare Principle introduces value into the space of rights.[21] It straightforwardly explains why claims add up.[22] Each person's welfare matters, and it matters as a good thing, such that, all else equal, we have reason to ensure that it is protected or, if possible, enhanced. This should not be taken to mean that we should create more people so that there is more value in the world.[23] It implies only that insofar as people exist (now or in the future), their interests are picked up by claims that add up. What makes rights-based deontology different from consequentialism is not the rejection of the significance of welfare and aggregation; what distinguishes rights-based deontology is that welfare interests are taken into account only through the filter of claims that get weighed in the distinctive way that the MOC weighs claims.[24]

[21] I cover this topic in significantly greater depth in *The Mechanics of Claims*, 50–55.

[22] John Taurek influentially argued that it is a mistake to aggregate in this way, in "Should the Numbers Count?" I take his argument to be decisively refuted by Derek Parfit's "Innumerate Ethics."

[23] I believe that we should not create miserable people, and that except insofar as creating happy people helps promote the welfare of those who exist or will exist, we should be neutral on creating happy people. See J. Frick, "Conditional Reasons and the Procreation Asymmetry."

[24] For a graphical representation of the difference, see my "Deontology in Graphs."

3.3 Autonomy and Structure in the Mechanics of Claims

It is time now to explain how the MOC works. In short, it holds that rights arise as the output of a two-step balancing process. In step one, we balance competing *basic* patient claims on an agent, and then we weigh the agent's claim not to have to respond to the balance of basic patient claims on him; in step two, if the agent has some liberty to act after step one, we ask whether there are any patients with *special* claims on that liberty. I now unpack that and explain why we need such a structure if we are to respect the Autonomy Principle.

3.3.1 The Structure of the Mechanics of Claims

Let's start with the idea of balancing basic patient claims against each other. A *basic* patient claim is a claim that presupposes no special relationship between agent and patient. It is a claim that arises simply from the fact that the patient has interests picked up by claims. The claim of a promisee on a promisor to keep his promise is *not* a basic claim; the claim of one person not to be killed by another, a stranger to him, *is* a basic claim. Unless I specify otherwise, my default notion of patient claims is basic patient claims.

Patient claims on an agent often compete. Some patients have claims that push an agent to do one thing, and other patients have claims that push him to do something else, something incompatible. Assuming one set of patient claims is stronger than all competing sets, the net balance of claims sets what the patient claims on him would have him do. If those claims are also stronger than his claim not to have to respond to the balance of patient claims on him, then those patients have corresponding rights. If, however, the agent's claim is stronger than the balance of patient claims on him, then she has a right *not* to do what they would have him do.

A few illustrations should help. Suppose, first, that the agent comes across two sets of drowning people, a group of five to his left and single person to his right. Suppose he could jump in a rowboat and rescue the members of either set, but not both—by the time he got to the one set, the member(s) of the other would have drowned. The five have the stronger set of claims; they could object if he chooses to rescue the one instead. He has a claim not to have to rescue them, and if the cost to him were great, he would have a right not to. But if the cost is only that it will take ten minutes of his time, minutes that he does not need to use for some other *very* important end of his own, then his agent claim not to have to serve their interests is outweighed and they have a right against him that he rescue them.

Let's change the example to make it more costly to the agent. Suppose the boat has an outboard motor, but to reach the boat, he would have to jump off a bridge into the boat, where he would certainly sustain serious injuries (at least a broken leg). He might be confident that he would survive the injuries well enough to operate the boat and save one party. Nonetheless, he would have the right to decline to save them when the costs are that high.[25]

Now let's suppose that the strongest patient claim is a negative claim, not to be killed. Suppose the agent could save five people from drowning, but to get to the boat, he would have to push someone else off a bridge into the water, where she would drown. I'll assume that the negative claim not to be killed *in that way* (which is not merely as a side effect) is stronger than the positive claims to be saved.[26] Thus, the balance of patient claims on the agent pushes to prevent him from saving the five. Suppose that he nonetheless really *wants* to save the five—he would gladly break a leg to do it. Does he have the same freedom to prioritize his agent claim to do so as he has to avoid breaking a leg to save them if he doesn't want to? No. In my view, his positive agent claim to be free to do what he wants has no significant weight qua *agent* claim; his interest in *doing* things is best understood as picked up by his *patient* claim to enjoy the benefits he would receive from doing them, and weighing that against the claims of others not to be harmed.[27] It is only his negative agent claims, claims to be free *not* to serve others for their benefit, that have significant weight.[28] They have significant weight because an agent's freedom not to have to serve as a means by which to maximize the satisfaction of patient claims on him is fundamental to having his own life to lead. Negative agent claims do not always outweigh the competing balance of patient claims on the agent—as seen in the first rescue case—but they protect agents from having to make large sacrifices for others with basic claims on him, whether those sacrifices are large one-time costs or large costs that would add up over a series of demands.

I want to offer one more illustration, to help make sense of how an agent can have the right to choose either of two options, even though they are very different from a utilitarian point of view. Consider again *Trolley Switch*.[29] Most people

[25] Some extremists disagree; they think that those in need have a right to be rescued even at the cost of a broken leg. I think almost no one lives by such a demanding understanding, and I reject it as inconsistent with the Autonomy Principle. The law agrees. Consider the criminal law regarding good Samaritan duties. See, e.g., Vermont Title 12, § 519; German Criminal Code, § 323c.

[26] This has been the dominant view of such cases going back to Philippa Foot's "Killing and Letting Die" and Warren Quinn's "Actions, Intentions, and Consequences."

[27] I think you have a small claim to freedom to act as such, but it is easily swamped by serious welfare concerns that others, and you as the agent, have. See *The Mechanics of Claims*, 71–73.

[28] I argue for this position in *The Mechanics of Claims*, 73–76. In those pages, I argue against the view taken by Jonathan Quong, who emphasizes a general freedom agents have to give priority to their own interests (except when using others as a means). See *The Morality of Defensive Force*, 69–70 (my response was to an earlier presentation of his ideas).

[29] See Section 2.3.

think it is permissible for Betty to turn the trolley, and that it is permissible for her not to do so. But one might think: given what is at stake, she should either be required to turn it for the sake of the five or required not to turn it for the sake of the one. How could she be at liberty to choose between these options?

My explanation is that the balance of patient claims on her weighs in favor of the five with claims to be saved (the sidetrack man would be killed as a mere side effect). This makes it at least permissible for her to turn it. But the balance is not overwhelming; the negative claim of the sidetrack man is almost on a par with the five claims. In addition, she has an agent claim not to have to make large sacrifices on their behalf. By turning the trolley, she would kill the one. Most people would find killing very traumatizing—substantially more traumatizing than allowing people to die. Her claim not to have to take on that trauma gives her a right not to turn the trolley.[30] She is free to waive that claim, but she is also free not to.[31]

Helen Frowe objects that the interest in not being a killer is too weak to give the bystander a right not to turn the trolley.[32] I think, however, that she underestimates the cost to an agent of killing.[33] More recently, Kerah Gordon-Solmon and Theron Pummer offer a different account of why it is permissible to turn the trolley or not: the moral reasons to turn and not to turn are on a par.[34] But this fails to explain why, if the agent were a police officer or other official who waived his agent claim not to have to take on substantial burdens for the sake of others while on the job, he would be obliged, while on the job, to turn the trolley.

Now, let's incorporate special patient claims. Suppose that after the stage 1 analysis, Betty has the liberty to act or not in *Trolley Switch*. But suppose her child is one of the five whom she could save. He has a special claim on her based on his special relationship to her. Given that special claim, she has no right not to turn the trolley. But her child's special claim can restrict her liberty only if she has it, given the balance of basic claims on her and her own agent claim to be free to act. His claim can't restrict her right to use a freedom she does not have. To appreciate why this is important, consider this variation on *Trolley Switch*:

[30] Trauma alone does not explain her right not to turn the trolley. If she would feel equally traumatized by killing a cat, she would still be obliged to turn the trolley, as the balance of patient claims would be much more strongly in favor of the five.

[31] I first offered this explanation in "Agents, Impartiality, and the Priority of Claims over Duties" (coauthored with David Wasserman).

[32] See "Lesser-Evil Justifications for Harming."

[33] What if the agent would not be traumatized by killing? Then it depends how the hybrid nature of interests registers. See Section 3.2. If the claim reflects the objective value people normally put on not being a killer, then the agent would have a right not to kill; if it reflects the subjective value he puts on not being a killer, then he might lack the right not to turn the trolley. The law, however, would be hard-pressed to track this moral possibility; it would presumably reflect the objective value people normally put on not being a killer.

[34] See "Lesser-Evil Justifications."

> *Massive Man*: Bertha, a bystander at a switch, can throw the switch and thereby cause a massive man to topple into the path of a trolley that is hurtling down a hill out of control, thereby killing him and saving five people whom the trolley would otherwise kill.[35]

We might understand why it would be tempting for Bertha to use the massive man to save the five. But it would still violate the massive man's right not to be used as a means of saving others.[36] She may not use him at the cost of his life, even if doing so would save her child.

These examples illustrate the basic structure of the MOC, in both stages. But there is one more important point to make about its structure: the *kind* of claim that picks up an interest matters for how that interest gets weighed in the final balance. This was implicit in the idea that the positive claims of the five can justify killing the sidetrack man by outweighing his negative claim not to be killed, but they cannot justify killing the massive man who would have to be toppled into the path of the trolley to save the five. The explanation of the difference is that he has a different kind of negative claim not to be killed. It was also implicit in my claim that negative agent claims (claims not to have to do things *for* others) are quite strong, whereas positive agent claims (claims to be free to do things *to* others) have no significant weight. This is key to understanding why the MOC is helpful: it allows us to weigh competing claims, understanding that how they compete is a function not only of the interests represented by each claim but also of the kinds of claims that pick them up.

3.3.2 Why Autonomy Requires this Structure

So far, I have simply asserted that patient claims compete with each other to control what an agent may do, and that an agent has his own agent claim to resist having to serve as the means for promoting the balance of patient claims on him. But one might wonder: Why should we think of rights as relational in this way at all? Why not think of claims not to be harmed in certain ways (say, as a means) as having a particularly high value in comparison with claims not to be harmed in other ways (say, as a side effect)—holding the level of harm constant? Why not say that an agent should simply maximize the value of claims in such cases? Or, if he needs some sort of agent prerogative to avoid having to live as a servant to the overall good, why not say that he may always maximize value in

[35] *The Mechanics of Claims*, 85.

[36] I explain why this kind of claim is stronger in Section 3.5 below.

this sort of consequentialism of rights, but he is permitted to give some priority to himself?[37]

The answer is that this sort of consequentialism of rights fails to make sense of the Autonomy Principle and the idea that agents have their own lives to lead. For an agent to have his own life to lead, he needs not only to be free to make his own choices but also to live with them and with the way that luck inevitably filters into them.[38] This does not mean that the space of rights should treat his bad luck as something that others have no duty to address; the Welfare Principle is inconsistent with that. It does mean, however, that his claims to be helped to overcome harms already inflicted or already heading his way have to be weaker, all else equal, than competing claims not to be harmed. And to make sense of that notion, rights have to be relational.

The need for a relational topology in the space of rights is a point that I already made while discussing the "paradox" of deontology.[39] As I noted, the paradox arises when one thinks about a case like the one in which A has to use B as a means, killing B, to prevent C from using five others as a means, killing them. The reason A may not kill B is that claims are relational. B has a claim *on A* not to be killed as a means; the five have claims *on* C not to be killed as a means; the five do *not* have the same sort of claims on A; their claims on A are to be saved from C. They may not demand that A treat their luck as pooled with B's in such a way that she can treat them as all making equivalent claims on her. As far as A is concerned, it is their bad luck to have been threatened by C. The only way to make sense of that notion—that they each have to own their own luck—is for the topology of the space of rights to be relational.

3.4 Dignity, Inalienability, and Inviolability

Dignity is in a way like autonomy: it can be understood as a capacity (to act with dignity), a value (it is better if people have the capacity to act with dignity, and better still if they exercise it), and a status (people with a certain capacity as moral agents *have* it). Dignity is also like autonomy insofar as what matters for rights is the status notion.[40] To have dignity is to have the status of equal citizens in the republic of rights. As Joel Feinberg put it, "what is called 'human dignity' may simply be the recognizable capacity to assert claims."[41] And as he

[37] This is essentially the view of morality put forward in S. Scheffler, *The Rejection of Consequentialism*.

[38] See *The Mechanics of Claims*, 60–65.

[39] See Section 2.3.

[40] See Section 1.3.1.

[41] J. Feinberg "The Nature and Value of Rights," 252.

also wrote: "Having rights enables us . . . to look others in the eye, and to feel in some fundamental way the equal of anyone."[42] To be clear, dignity is not in the asserting itself; it is not to be found in the act of looking another in the eye rather than glancing furtively at the ground. That may be part of what it is to *act* with dignity. But the status of *having* dignity is to be found in one's status as a rights holder, as a citizen in the republic of rights who has the *right* to look anyone in the eye.[43]

Inalienability is crucial to dignity. Normal rights can be waived, traded, or forfeited. An agent can trade her car for some money; she can waive her right not to be punched in the boxing ring; she can forfeit her right to life by unjustly attacking another. What she cannot do is waive, trade, or forfeit her status as a being with dignity. All of those other changes in her specific rights are moves *in* the space of rights. They do not affect her status as a being with dignity. Once an agent is a citizen in the republic of rights, she is a citizen for as long as she retains her autonomous moral capacity. Even the worst of criminals who deserves the harshest of punishments has a right not to be gratuitously or disproportionately punished. And even those who fall short of full autonomous moral capacity should be treated as beings with dignity, even if the rights they enjoy are not the same as the rights of those who have full autonomous moral capacity.[44]

This idea that we possess a status that cannot be lost may seem particularly plausible only to people who come from a certain kind of cultural background. Ryan Brown writes of the difference between an "honor culture" and a "dignity culture."[45] Dignity cannot be alienated, but honor can. And if an agent lacks honor, she can be shamed and shunned, and life itself may seem not to be worth living.[46]

Is there anything to say against taking honor, rather than dignity, as the fundamental norm for life? One thing to say is that honor culture seems to be born of failures of the rule of law; it is born of living in precarious circumstances in which agents have to stand up for themselves because they cannot rely on the law to stand up for them.[47] It is born, that is, of failure to provide the psychological space in which agents can appreciate the dignity of all. Honor culture is, in that way, not on an equal footing with dignity culture.

Arguing for the priority of dignity by reference to the etiology of honor culture flirts with committing the genetic fallacy, the fallacy of inferring that a set of beliefs is false or faulty because it was adopted for bad reasons. In truth, this

[42] Ibid.
[43] See Section 1.3.1.
[44] Ibid.
[45] See *Honor Bound.*
[46] Ibid., 68.
[47] Ibid., 9.

etiology, even if accurate, provides merely a reason to be suspicious of honor culture. But I can do no better here; properly defending the priority of dignity is a project beyond the scope of this book. Accordingly, I state the following as an article of moral faith: honor culture rests on a moral mistake insofar as it goes beyond merely valuing honor. In raising honor to the status of the fundamental value, it loses sight of the dignity of all. It makes it too easy to disdain, to shame, and to condemn those who seem to make choices that do not conform to particular notions of honor. I am not suggesting that we should disparage the idea of honor; I too value the idea of living an honorable life. My point is that honor should be considered a secondary value, on a par with living with dignity. It should not be allowed to displace the commitment to the dignity of all as a matter of fundamental status.[48]

Returning to the content of the concept of dignity, some people think of dignity as conferring the status of inviolability on us.[49] For example, Thomas Nagel writes: "we identify... the possession of rights" with a "status... that of a certain kind of *inviolability*".[50] He elaborates:

> Being inviolable is not a *condition* like being happy or free... To be inviolable does not mean that one *will not be violated*. It is a moral *status:* It means that one *may not* be violated in certain ways. Such treatment is inadmissible, if it occurs, the person has been wronged.[51]

While I accept this reference to our status, I think we need to be careful with the notion that we are inviolable. People who accept that rights can sometimes permissibly be infringed accept that wronging is sometimes "admissible." Once that is said, then it is hard to make sense of the thought that we have the status of inviolability, except in the tautological sense that we are violated whenever our rights are violated. As noted above,[52] I reject the understanding of rights which allows for permissible wronging (outside of the extreme context of threshold deontology). Thus, I am happy to say that we are "inviolable" insofar as we possess rights. But I'm not sure Nagel or others who use that term are clear about how to connect that thought with the prospect of rights infringements. For the sake of clarity, then, I think it is better to say only (a) that all people possess dignity insofar as they are full citizens in the republic of rights, (b) that other people have dignity as a derivative matter, (c) that dignity is inalienable, and (d) that proper

[48] One way the rejection of honor culture is relevant to the details of this book is in the rejection of shaming (dishonoring) punishments. See Section 7.3.1.

[49] This idea can first be found in F. Kamm, "Harming Some to Save Others," and W. Quinn, "Actions, Intentions, and Consequences."

[50] "Personal Rights and Public Space," 37 (emphasis in the original).

[51] Ibid. (emphases in the original).

[52] See Section 3.1 in this chapter.

reasoning about rights is fundamental to determining what treatment of us is "admissible" or not.

3.5 The Claim Not to be Used as a Means

Using another as a means, at some non-trivial cost to him—as is done by punishments and penalties that sanction people to deter lawbreaking—is morally difficult to justify. It may be justifiable if the gain for others is great enough and the cost to the person used small enough, or if some exception to the means principle applies. But the default assumption is that some such justificatory hurdle must be overcome. In this section, I explain how the means principle is grounded in the MOC, and why it is sometimes nonetheless justifiable to use people.

3.5.1 Grounding the Means Principle

As noted above,[53] some have tried to defend the means principle in terms of intentions, appealing to the DDE, but this seems to wrongly direct agents to focus inwardly on their mental states, rather than on the rights of others. Others think it has to be framed in terms of the causal role that patients occupy, but this gives rise to Scanlon's objection that "being a means in this sense—being causally necessary—has no intrinsic moral significance."[54] Here I want to use the MOC to explain why Scanlon is mistaken. That is, I want to explain why occupying a causal role in a potential justification for an action has profound moral significance.

To explain the moral significance of a patient's causal role, I distinguish two kinds of patient claims: property claims and restricting claims.[55] This distinction is independent of the distinction between positive and negative patient claims. It reflects the different relationships patients have to the baseline freedom of agents.

Starting with restricting claims, they normatively push to restrict agents from acting on their baseline freedom. Positive restricting claims (claims for help) weigh against negative agent claims (claims not to have to act) by pushing

[53] See Section 3.1.

[54] *Moral Dimensions*, 118.

[55] A full account requires the introduction as well of empowering claims, whose job is to shift around property claims from one or more patients to an agent who could use that property. For a discussion of that sort of detail, see *The Mechanics of Claims*, section 4.4. I will discuss these claims in Section 14.2.

to require agents to act for the sake of the patient. Negative restricting claims (claims not to be harmed) weigh against positive agent claims (claims to be free to act), by pushing to require agents *not* to do something harmful to the patient. We have already seen these illustrated in the discussions above of rescue and trolley switch cases.

Property claims function to set the baseline freedom of agents. This idea of a baseline freedom is fundamentally important for the space of rights as a normative space in which persons can each pursue their own ends while treating each other respectfully. Property notions set the baseline freedom because they control what an agent can take to be available to him for acting. An agent can't act by will alone, he can act only by using the means available to him. The means available to an agent include, first, his body, and then objects in the world around him that he can use. His baseline freedom to act is set by the things he is free to use. To live in the world together, agents have to normatively divide the world into that which is available to each agent for [his] own use, that which is reserved for others, and that which is available for all (or none). This is, obviously, a division along property lines.[56] This agent–agent division of the world sets each agent's "toolkit" for acting and thereby sets his baseline freedom to act. It is that freedom that restricting claims then seek to affect.

The claim of a massive man not to have his body used to stop a trolley, even if doing so would save others, is a property claim. It's a claim to deny whoever would use him in this way the baseline freedom to do so. It's a claim that his body is not to be considered part of the other's toolkit. In pushing to deny that Bertha has a right to use him, it explains why causal role *is* relevant to permissibility. It is relevant because agents need to know what they can use to act, and causal role concerns what they can use.[57] The ability of agents to justify their actions is limited by the things they have in their toolkits.

Completing the picture, the means principle flows from the thought that property claims do not restrict an agent relative to his baseline freedom, but restricting claims do. This is particularly relevant for understanding why negative restricting claims, like those of the sidetrack man, should be weaker than property claims that serve the same interest, such as the claim of the massive

[56] See *The Mechanics of Claims*, 87.

[57] The way property claims protect interests depends on how tightly the interest in question is connected to the use someone else would make of the tool. For example, if the sidetrack man owned a tool that Betty could use to turn the trolley, but that he did not need to use himself at the moment Betty would use it, then the empowering claims of the five may put it in her toolkit. The connection between his ownership interest and his life is loose. But if a drug owner needed to consume his drugs to stay alive, and someone wanted to take them and give them to another, the drug owner's property claim would outweigh the competing empowering claims. That's because of the tight connection between the drug owner's interest in staying alive and his property right over the drugs. For my most recent treatment of that issue, see my "In Defense of Patient-Centered Theories of Deontology,"631–634.

man not to be used as a means of stopping the trolley. The thought is this: while a claim not to be killed seems as if it should be a very strong claim either way, if it is a restricting claim, it imposes something like a negative externality on the five. It threatens to make others worse off than they would be if that claim did not register as it does. In this case, if the sidetrack man's claim had to be respected as a right, Betty could not permissibly turn the trolley away from the five as she has the baseline freedom to do.[58] The claim of the sidetrack man thus pushes to restrict Betty in a way that would make the five worse off, relative to her baseline freedom. Even though the sidetrack man is not *doing* anything, his presence with his restricting claim pushes to make the five worse off. To register the moral significance of this "externality," and to ensure that it does not cause undue damage to the five, the strength of negative restricting claims has to be taken to be not that much stronger than positive restricting claims with which they compete, all else equal. Property claims, by contrast, pose no such externality. They merely mark where an agent's baseline freedom lies. Thus, they retain whatever strength we think they should carry to reflect the idea that each person has his own life to lead.

3.5.2 Exceptions to the Means Principle

Property rights have a dual role: they function as agent rights by giving agents with those rights their baseline freedom to act; they also serve as patient rights by limiting the rights of other agents to use what is not in their toolkit. They are grounded in the Autonomy Principle, which gives agents substantial freedom to pursue their own ends—at least as long as they are using what is theirs to use and no restricting claim outweighs their claim to be free to act. But the Autonomy Principle also presupposes that agents can be held accountable for their choices and the effects they have on others. The accountability face of the Autonomy Principle explains why it is sometimes permissible to use another as a means, even at great cost to him.

First, he may have waived or traded his right not to be used. Just as he may use his body or time to save others—say by working in a hospital—so he may waive or trade his right not to be used (as in an employment contract) and thereby empower others to use him. It is natural and appropriate that we have qualms about allowing one person to use another in irreversible ways, ways that lead to death or permanent physical damage. But I think those qualms reflect concerns

[58] This assertion *assumes* that she can treat the switch as in her toolkit. To make that plausible, we need to include empowering claims, which would give her the freedom to use a switch that is presumably not hers.

about whether the consent was knowing and uncoerced, and whether such usings set a precedent that will lead to social pressure on others to make similar sacrifices.[59] Those are perfectly legitimate worries. But in an emergency, when someone needs to suffer permanent harm to save a greater number, we should be open to the thought that waiver permits one person to use another in irreversibly harmful ways.

Second, an agent may have forfeited his claim not to be used. Suppose the massive man unleashed the trolley at five innocent people below, and the only way of saving them is to use him as a means of stopping the trolley. That using seems morally justifiable, even if he would die. This may not be true if he were *merely* a cause of the trolley being unleashed, without being in any appreciable way responsible for that fact. Imagine someone pushed him, for no good reason, into the trolley and it then started to roll down the hill and became a threat to the five. It would then be unjust to lethally use him as a means of stopping the trolley. But if he is meaningfully morally responsible for the trolley rolling out of control down the hill—whether through negligent action, advertent risk taking, or the purpose of killing the five—it seems fair to say that another could trade his life for theirs.

The idea of penal law will draw on this notion of forfeiture—forfeiting the right not to be used to deter future lawbreaking.[60] And the criminal law draws on something stronger than forfeiture: desert. In both cases, using one to deter others can be justified.

3.6 Targeting Threats with Incapacitating Action

Much of what will be covered in this book is *not* justified with reference to deterrence. Much of it is about incapacitation. To incapacitate a person because she is a threat is not to use her as a means. Indeed, I have argued that if we assume that a person is a threat who lacks the right to threaten (a qualification I leave implicit from hereon), then it is *easier* to justify imposing costs on her than it is to impose costs on a person harmed as a mere side effect.[61] Merely being a threat weakens an agent's claim not to be harmed. And the more responsible and the more culpable she is for posing a threat, the weaker her claim not to be harmed.

I flag here two issues I address later about threats. First, we need to know what the baseline presumption is with regard to whether people should be thought of

[59] I return to this theme in Section 15.1.2.

[60] The bases of forfeiture overlap substantially with culpable mental states, and culpability is relevant to the degree to which rights are forfeited. But forfeiture does not presuppose culpability. See Section 14.5.

[61] See *The Mechanics of Claims*, ch. 6.

as threats or not. I argue in Chapter 4 for the default being the POLA. Second, we need to know what the standard of proof (SOP) should be for determining that a person *is* a threat.[62] This will vary, depending on whether the POLA applies or not, and on the nature of the restriction. For example, the SOP for an arrest in the United States is probable cause to believe the person "had committed or was committing an offense."[63] But the standard for detaining a person because she is mentally ill and dangerous is a higher standard: "clear and convincing" evidence.[64]

3.7 The Two-Way Relationship Between the State and Rights

States are both bound by the rights I have been discussing and are important shapers of the rights agents have. To understand the project of this book, it is important to get a sense for both roles.

3.7.1 States as Bound by Rights

States are artificial persons. They have a kind of agency that in many ways tracks that of normal adult humans. Given that they have an internal decision-making structure, it makes sense to ascribe to them beliefs, goals, and actions. And many of them, as Christian List and Philip Pettit point out, are "capable of operating in the space of obligations"[65]: they are capable of taking into account normative statements about morality and law and "have the necessary control to make choices based on those judgments."[66] As such, they can be bound by rights as much as any other agent operating in the space of rights.[67]

[62] A third issue, that I don't discuss here, is what to make of mistakes. Some find it tempting to say that restricting people's liberty while acting on the notion that there is an acceptable risk of error amounts to using those whose liberty is wrongly limited as a means of achieving the overall social welfare. See, e.g., Laurence Tribe, who wrote that failing to insist on "the greatest certainty that seems reasonably attainable" amounts to choosing to "sacrifice" the wrongly convicted for "the interests of others." "Trial by Mathematics," 1374. I argue that this is a mistake. Those who are wronged are collateral damage of the pursuit of security using what one can hope are just but imperfect tools. See my "Proof Beyond a Reasonable Doubt," 380–382.

[63] Beck v. Ohio, 379 U.S. 89, 91 (1964). I return to what this means, and why it might be appropriate, in Section 17.2.

[64] Addington v. Texas, 441 U.S. 418 (1979). I return to what this means, and why it might be appropriate, in Section 15.3.

[65] *Group Agency*, 176.

[66] Ibid.

[67] For a helpful discussion of artificial persons as rights holders, see T. Isiksel, "Corporate Human Rights Claims under the ECHR." Her discussion concerns rights in the European Court of Human Rights, but it is sensitive to the ways in which these might be grounded in more fundamental notions of moral rights.

Nonetheless, artificial persons are not equal citizens in the space of rights. They are not ends in themselves; they exist to serve other purposes. They therefore lack the normal basis for agent claims. They still have agent claims insofar as they have a chartering purpose: to make profits for the owners, as for-profit companies aim to do; to achieve some other-related end, as non-profits aim to do; or to govern a territory justly and well, as states are charged with doing. To achieve any of those purposes, they need to be able to control their property much as a natural person does. But they don't claim those property rights as part of what they need to pursue their own lives; they don't have their own lives; they exist to serve.[68]

But states are not like other artificial persons; they have powers over rights holders that other artificial persons don't have, for example, the power to levy taxes, to regulate behavior, and to impose serious punishments and penalties, such as imprisonment. That might tempt some to adopt the view that we cannot look to the moral rights between agents to understand the limits on state power. But I believe we can. I adopt here a variation on a view common in just war theory: reductive individualism. Reductive individualism is the view that we can understand what states may do by appeal to the rights natural persons generally have against other natural persons. Unqualified, the view is false; states have special powers, powers that no natural person acting on his own behalf, in or outside of a state, has. But I think a weak form of reductive individualism is correct.

There are three reasons why the unique powers of the state do not undermine weak reductive individualism.[69] First, the special authority that states have is immanent in the rights and duties natural persons have to come together to solve collective action problems.[70] Second, the state's authority is limited by the rights of natural persons that states must respect, as well as by other norms of justice. Third, the residual difference between the state's authority to use force and to interfere with the liberty of others and any other agent's authority to do the same reflects the way agents in a state relinquish their right of self-help, rather than the state having some right to use force and interfere with liberty that other agents fundamentally lack. I take these points in turn.

We accept states as at least potentially legitimate primarily because they help natural persons to form communities in which behavior can be coordinated for

[68] It is also notoriously hard to make sense of punishing them as there is no one to feel guilt. But that topic is beyond the scope of this book.

[69] This and the next three paragraphs are taken, with some modifications, from *The Mechanics of Claims*, 31–33.

[70] I should add that individuals also have duties to respect what their own states direct them to do or direct others to do to them. I did not properly appreciate that when I wrote *The Mechanics of Claims*. Among the authors who convinced me to change my mind are D. Viehoff in "Legitimate Injustice and Acting for Others," Y. Yuan in "The Exclusionary Power of Political Directives," and M. Skerker in *The Moral Status of Combatants*, especially ch. 7. I engage that issue in the next subsection.

the common good, resources can be gathered through taxation and spent on public goods, rights such as property rights and rights of contract can be made determinate and protected, other social norms can be set, and disputes can be settled in a fair and impartial way.[71] In line with those functions, other activities, such as punishment, take on a special meaning in the state: punishment becomes a public act of holding a wrongdoer to account.[72] One might say that none of these are activities that natural persons have a right to perform on their own. For example, agents may not tax each other for the common good. Thus, in some sense, the state clearly has authority that cannot be reduced to the authority of agents. But I think this departure from reductive individualism is a minimal one because, as I said, I think the authority of the state is immanent in the rights and duties of natural persons to come together to solve collective action problems. That is to say that the state's authority reflects (a) the claims agents have on each other to come together and form a state that will enable them to live in a well-organized way in a social setting, and (b) their power to create a state to meet their duty to respond to those claims. Indeed, the space of rights is ultimately problematically indeterminate unless and until the state sets rules and procedures fixing the contours of certain terms, like property rights dealing with external objects.[73] Thus, while the state does have authority that natural persons lack, it has that authority only because it is given particular powers so that it can serve a set of basic social and political ends of natural persons.

Regarding the second reason not to reject reductive individualism, the rights of natural persons limit the state's authority. For example, no liberal thinks the state is free to punish at will. It may punish only to a proportionate degree and only after providing criminal defendants with due process. Liberals also agree that the state, with limited exceptions, must respect the same limits that individual agents must respect on harmfully using people as a means, harming them as a side effect, or killing them to prevent them from threatening others. Even the authority to tax is fundamentally limited. It arises from the need to provide for public goods and is limited by that purpose. The state may not simply take property; it may take property only as part of a just punishment or penalty, as part of a civil action to compensate itself or others for damages, as part of a general tax scheme that applies to all (although allowing for progressive taxation), or as a means of achieving a public good, with just compensation provided. And even insofar as the state taxes its residents to promote the common good, the

[71] See M. Renzo, "Political Authority and Unjust Wars," 343 (discussing how states have authority because of how they "enable us to discharge some of our most important duties of justice").

[72] See A. Duff, *The Realm of Criminal Law*, 78–79. In that sense, I think theorists like John Locke are wrong to suggest that punishment in the state simply takes over what an individual could do in the state of nature. See *Second Treatise of Government*, §§ 8 and 123–127.

[73] See L.-P. Hodgson, "Kant on Property Rights and the State," 64.

Autonomy Principle implies that it cannot do so at such a high rate that people are effectively working *for* the common good and not for themselves. These matters of fundamental justice constrain the state and show the deep truth of reductive individualism.

Regarding the third reason, the residual difference between the authority of the state to use force and to interfere with the liberty of others, on the one hand, and the authority of natural persons to do the same, on the other, is to be explained by the fact that agents in a state generally relinquish their right to use self-help. Returning to the example of punishment, there may be a core Lockean right to punish that agents possess in the state of nature that they mostly give up in civil society in order to avoid bias in judging, excessive punishment based on emotion or bias, and the inequities that would result if only the strong could punish. Likewise, agents give up self-help in settling disputes and avoiding threats in order to avoid bias, cycles of violence, and the inequities that would result if only the strong could engage in self-help. But that does not imply that the state has some power that natural persons *fundamentally* lack. It implies only that, when there is a better way to meet certain ends, agents are morally obliged to use it. When this way is unavailable—as happens in self-defense cases when the threat is imminent and the state cannot respond in time to protect a victim—the right of self-help is recovered. Thus, I conclude that weak reductive individualism is morally sound, and that we can refer to general reasoning about rights to understand the basic limits on justifiable state action.

3.7.2 States as Shapers of Rights

In the previous section, I mentioned a number of ways in which states are crucial shapers of our rights: They can tell agents how property can be acquired by mixing their labor with unowned objects (as opposed to simply pouring away their labor);[74] how much of their income and property they get to keep by setting tax rates; how property can be passed on; how contracts can be formed so as to be enforceable, and so on. Given the importance of property rights, these are important functions. In addition, they tell agents what sorts of positive duties of aid they have, and when acts that are not inherently wrongful will still be impermissible because they undermine important regulatory schemes. They also set punishment and penalty schedules for doing impermissible things, and they mark when agents will be taken to forfeit rights and what exactly they forfeit

[74] As Robert Nozick asked, with characteristic rhetorical flair: "If I own a can of tomato juice and spill it in the sea so that its molecules ... mingle evenly throughout the sea, do I thereby come to own the sea, or have I foolishly dissipated my tomato juice?" *Anarchy, State, and Utopia*, 175.

when they act in certain ways. It's not that we have no idea how to draw any of these lines in certain cases. We are generally in no doubt about the ownership of our own bodies and actions. Likewise, if an agent picks up a stick in a public forest and carves it into the shape of a cat, it is clear that the cat-stick belongs to him—he left enough and as good for others.[75] Nonetheless, many cases are not so clear. What I want to emphasize here is that the state's role as a shaper of rights is fundamentally important in a way that undergirds the significance of, in particular, punishment.

The theory I will articulate here is related to Kantian versions of the authority of the state. As indicated in Section 3.2, I depart from Kant's view of rights insofar as I think we should incorporate the significance of welfare in rights.[76] But I think there is something deeply right about the Kantian idea that the state has a fundamentally important role to play in overcoming the problem of unilateral enforcement of rights. The thought, as I embrace it, is that many of our rights cannot be determined with a sufficient degree of precision by the MOC alone. As a result, for people to use the space of rights as a guide to pursue their own ends while treating each other respectfully as free and responsible agents, with fundamentally equal status, whose welfare morally matters, they need to turn to the state to resolve reasonable conflicts about how the balance of claims should be understood.

The alternative has individuals simply using force to defend their own interpretation of how the balance of claims should be held to work. That is problematic for two reasons. First, even when there is a single best interpretation of the right balance of claims, there are classic Lockean vices in letting individuals enforce their understanding of that balance: unnecessary violence, self-serving bias, lack of due process, and abuse of the weak. But there's another level of problem when there is no truth about which balance is right because of the vagueness inherent in the notion that different kinds of competing claims are more or less strong. Many cases have that feature. Here's just one example:

> [S]uppose that you plant an apple tree on your side of [a] fence, and that some of its branches come to grow over my land. . . . It seems at least arguable that we both have a claim to them – you because you planted the tree, and I because they are over my land.[77]

In such cases, one agent's unilateral enforcement of one interpretation is simply the unjust arrogation to himself of authority over others. People need an

[75] That's the Lockean proviso. *Second Treatise of Government*, Chapter V, paragraph 33.

[76] In this regard, I also depart from the sort of project carried out by Arthur Ripstein in *Force and Freedom*.

[77] L.P. Hodgson, "Kant on Property Rights and the State," 64.

impartial state to set laws that will give them a framework within which they can work.

The more hardcore Kantians want a stronger thesis than this. The best discussion that I have read of the hardcore Kantian position, by Yuan Yuan, argues that our fundamental right not to be governed by the unilateral will of others obliges us to accept *any* rules or individual judgments the state makes, as long as it is not unreasonable in doing so.[78] If it used reasonable procedures to determine the facts, and reasonably engaged in balancing the conflicting claims to make normative judgments, then we are obliged to respect its directives.[79] They function as exclusionary reasons that exclude any reconsideration of the issues that the state has already taken into account.[80]

I think there is much to be said for this view. When there is no single right answer regarding how to balance competing claims, then I think Yuan is correct to say that when the state provides a reasonable interpretation of that balance, then its answer must be taken to set *the right answer* in its jurisdiction. I am also willing to grant the state a margin of appreciation for cases in which it is not so clear whether there is a right answer or whether its answer is at least close to the right answer. In such cases, the state's determination should simply govern. But I reject the dichotomous thought that either the state must govern, or we must declare its law to be unreasonable and hence illegitimate. I think there is a middle category in which the state may have spoken reasonably (in the sense that reasonable people, committed to respecting the dignity of all, can defend that view), and its determinations are due a certain amount of deference, but not absolute deference. If an agent reasonably thinks the state's balance of claims, while reasonable, is nonetheless mistaken, and if he thinks that a sufficiently great injustice would result from accepting such a law or judgment, then he may take unilateral action to oppose the state.

The right to take unilateral action arises for a combination of two reasons. First, there are some prelegal rights that the state is bound to respect. Second, while it may be hoped that reasonable people will mostly agree on what those are, it cannot be assumed that they will always agree. It may sometimes happen that reasonable people will disagree about the right balance, and some might reasonably conclude that the state got it wrong, and that resistance to the law is justified.

[78] "The Exclusionary Power of Political Directives."

[79] If it failed to be reasonable in these ways, then its laws and judgments would be illegitimate and not automatically binding; individual agents would have to use their moral judgment to decide what they can permissibly do.

[80] The importance of this qualification on the scope of exclusionary reasons is that it allows the necessity defense to come into play when certain kinds of reasons were not considered in the making of a legal rule.

This disagreement can occur for two reasons. One is that there are issues on which people differ profoundly because they reasonably apply moral or metaphysical concepts in fundamentally different ways. If these produce different judgments on important matters of justice, then some agents may reasonably decide to take unilateral action. The other is that people have different access to facts, and some may conclude that the law reasonably disbelieved them but is nonetheless making a mistake that warrants responding with unilateral force. I give examples to illustrate each kind of case.

The first example is one I first discussed decades ago when I argued that John Rawls was mistaken to argue that reasonable people would never use illegal force to oppose legitimate law: abortion.[81] I argued then and still believe that reasonable people can disagree substantially about the permissibility of abortion regulations. If one thinks (a) that fetuses have the moral status of persons, and (b) that when a woman has consensual sexual intercourse with a man and gets pregnant, she forfeits her right to control her body, as against the claim a fetus might have to use it for life support, then one can justify highly restrictive views on abortion. But if one holds the opposite view on either of those issues, then one should take women to have much greater rights to choose to have an abortion. I think there is a best answer amongst these competing views, but I also think that reasonable people can disagree about what it is. Moreover, I think that one can reasonably believe that if the state adopts the wrong view, then a certain amount of illegal force may be justified. There are considerations having to do with respect for one's fellow citizens, concern with setting a bad precedent, and so on, that may weigh against using illegal force. But those are only pro tanto forceful moral considerations. In the overall balance, one might reasonably judge that the injustice is great enough to justify using some degree of illegal force.

The second example concerns a person who has been wrongfully convicted of a serious crime. Suppose there were no glaring procedural flaws in the trial. Some witnesses were merely mistaken, and evidence that the defendant knew exonerated him was reasonably disbelieved by the finder of fact. Suppose that he has then been sentenced to decades in prison, and he has exhausted his legal options for getting his conviction overturned.[82] Yuan admits that she has "discomfort" when she entertains the thought that he is "obligated to serve his prison sentence."[83] But she bites the bullet and argues that this is the right conclusion because, in her view, the alternative is to give in too readily to unilateralism. I say, however, that she is too reluctant to admit that his superior knowledge of the truth matters in this context. I say this in part because even she admits that

[81] See "Reasonable Illegal Force."
[82] See "The Exclusionary Power of Political Directives," 230.
[83] Ibid., 259.

unilateralism is appropriate when the state's actions are unreasonable. Our dispute really concerns only where to draw the line about when unilateral action is permissible. I believe the better place to draw it allows its use in this case because the state's action, while not unreasonable, is sufficiently unjust that the pro tanto reasons to respect it are outweighed. One who is wrongly sentenced to prison for decades is a prime candidate for using illegal force to rectify the injustice he is suffering. That does not mean that he can harm guards who believe they are acting justly.[84] But he can certainly take non-violent, or minimally violent, illegal actions to free himself.[85]

This disagreement with the hardcore Kantians notwithstanding, I think they are right to turn to the state to provide essential content to our rights. And this has deep significance for the criminal law in particular because it sets the state up as a fundamentally important moral actor. It not only facilitates our ability to get along peacefully, and hopefully justly, it also determines to some extent what it means to get along justly. And this role in creating and upholding the republic of rights makes it important for *it*, and not just for private individuals, to level blame (censure) on culpable wrongdoers. This is why the state has an irreplaceable role in the criminal law.

Expanding on that idea a little more here,[86] the basic idea is this: the state has a special responsibility to flesh out and support the space of rights. But at an even deeper level, the state has that responsibility because individual members of the republic of rights have an obligation to come together to form the state, so that they can relate to each other as fellow citizens in that republic. The state has a positive obligation to support their ability to relate to each other as co-citizens both in their state and in the broader republic of rights.

Before concluding, it is worth saying a few words about different levels of states and their relationship to the republic of rights. Most of us are members of many nested states. In the United States, we are political members of local communities like towns, cities, or counties; states; and the federal government. Some Europeans would add another level, that of the European Union. There are different ways of prioritizing those, with richer or thinner sorts of political activity possible at different levels. Those are differences that won't concern me here. What does concern me is establishing a political level in which we are citizens in the universal republic of rights, not just in the sense that we have powers to adjust our rights with respect to others, but in the *political* sense that we are responsible for how the law treats us. How can we be citizens in it if there is no universal state? My answer is that we must still take seriously the claims of

[84] See D. Viehoff, "Legitimate Injustice and Acting for Others."
[85] Who does not cheer for the escape of Dufresne in "Shawshank Redemption" (and not just because the warden was himself a criminally oppressive monster)?
[86] I develop it further below, starting in Chs. 5 and 6.

non-citizens, even those living abroad, who are affected by the choices we are entitled to make by our state law and that our states make. States can negotiate the respect others are due in treaties such as the Fourth Geneva Convention, the Convention Relative to the Protection of Civilian Persons in Time of War. But even outside of such international treaties, we have a political obligation within our states to ensure that our laws do not lead to the unjust treatment of others. The politics of responsibility for non-citizens is the thin form of political citizenship possessed by citizens in the republic of rights. This too will have some bearing on the scope of the criminal law, especially when applied extra-territorially.[87]

Taking stock: the primordial political obligation on individuals is to do what it takes to relate to each other as fellow citizens in the universal republic of rights.[88] One facet of that obligation is to form a state to fix what our rights are and to adjudicate disputes where individual cases of uncertainty remain. Another is to use the state to ensure that people are treated with dignity. A related use of the state is to stand for and speak up for the importance of the republic of rights and for justice more generally. And an important aspect of those last two uses for the state is holding people accountable in ways that promote rightful relations between, on the one hand, those who have culpably violated the rights of others or the law more generally and, on the other hand, the political communities that flesh out the rights we have.[89] This is more than a matter of restoring rightful relations between private individuals, as is done in tort and contract law. This is a matter of restoring rightful relations between individuals and the moral community of fellow citizens in their states and in the republic of rights more broadly. This is the function of state-based blame (censure).

[87] For brief treatment of universal jurisdiction of the criminal law, see Section 5.5.2.

[88] Ultimately, people have to come together not just within a state but within an international framework that allows them to relate rightfully to *all* citizens of the republic of rights. But states play, and for the foreseeable future will play, a crucial role in setting up that framework. These ideas were first, as far as I know, developed by Kant in "To Perpetual Peace," Academy page 379. I introduced this point in Section 1.3.3, and I return to it in Ch. 5, in the context of discussing universal jurisdiction.

[89] For a related view, see M. Thorburn, "Criminal Punishment and the Right to Rule." Thorburn's emphasis is different from mine, however, as he focuses on remedies that reinforce the state's right to rule without connecting that to fixing rightful relations between the wrongdoer and the community broadly.

4

In Defense of the Presumption of Law Abidingness

4.1 Introduction to the Presumption of Law Abidingness

A fundamental premise of the dignity-respecting model (DR Model) is that agents who have crossed the threshold of full moral autonomous capacity deserve the benefit of the presumption of law abidingness (POLA) unless they have forfeited it to some greater or lesser degree or the external conditions for holding them accountable don't exist. Those who benefit from the POLA must be presumed to respect the rights of others and thus should be left free to govern themselves without any targeted restrictions designed to protect others from their potentially dangerous choices. The POLA is not the same as the presumption of innocence, which implies that one is to be considered innocent of past offenses unless and until one is convicted at a fair trial or one pleads guilty. The POLA is, by contrast, a forward-looking presumption that an agent will be law abiding. But they are principles with a kindred spirit: we assume that people have been and will be law-abiding citizens unless specific defeating conditions apply.

It is worth pausing for a moment on the word "presumption" in the POLA. One might think that a presumption can be outweighed, but that is not how the POLA operates. It is a presumption that may apply in certain contexts and not in others, but insofar as it applies, it must be respected.

One might also think it is an epistemic claim, which can be epistemically canceled by evidence that it is statistically unlikely to hold true. In that case, the refusal to relinquish it when such evidence is present might be thought irrational. But it is not a belief about how others will behave. It's a way of approaching each other. It's a way of giving force to a moral commitment to treat each other as trustworthy unless one of three conditions that negate it are met: an agent has forfeited it; she lacks full autonomous capacity and cannot be expected to be able to control, as a normal adult can, whether she is a threat to others;[1] or the

[1] An agent may benefit from a shrunken presumption if she has some degree of autonomous capacity but not enough to cross the threshold to full autonomous capacity, if her forfeiture of the presumption is only partial, or if such a presumption is consistent with the state's policing capacity being limited but not altogether absent.

Punishment, Penalty, and Incapacitation. Alec Walen, Oxford University Press. © Oxford University Press 2026.
DOI: 10.1093/9780197523124.003.0004

state cannot be expected to provide adequate policing.[2] If none of these three conditions provides an exception, then the DR Model presumes that the POLA applies.

Given how central the POLA is to the DR Model, I devote this chapter to arguing that it ought to be accepted. I start by quoting recent leading thinkers in criminal law and human rights to demonstrate the appeal of the POLA. I then explain how it is grounded in the principles that ground the space of rights. Finally, I respond to two objections.[3] The essence of the objections is that targeted preventive restrictions of the liberty of fully autonomous individuals are permissible much as general restrictions are: because there is, in fact, no reason to presume that people will be law abiding. According to these objections, we need only to make reasonable predictions and then act as reasonable consequentialists would act. Understanding why this form of criticism fails illuminates what is really at stake in accepting the POLA.

4.2 Authorities Who Accept the Presumption of Law Abidingness

The POLA—or something very close to what I mean by the POLA—is a widely shared assumption. For example, Stephen Schulhofer writes: "In the absence of mental illness sufficiently serious to preclude criminal responsibility, predictive confinement violates the first principle of limited government—to treat every mentally competent adult as a free and autonomous person responsible for his chosen actions—and only for his chosen actions."[4]

Stephen Morse writes: "In the interest of liberty, we leave potentially dangerous people free to pursue their projects until they actually offend, even if their future wrongdoing is quite certain. Indeed, we are willing to take great risks in the name of liberty."[5]

David Cole writes: "To lock up a human being on the prediction that he will undertake dangerous and illegal action if left free is, in an important sense, to deny his autonomy."[6]

[2] I have left out the duty prong of the DR Model because it does not presume loss of the POLA, except in a marginal sense that explains why the duty is *enforced*. See Section 1.3.5.

[3] A third objection to the DR Model does not challenge the POLA but rather challenges the idea that preventive restrictions are needed to provide the security we need. Douglas Husak, in "Preventive Detention as Punishment?" argues that the criminal law can be extended to cover our worries about future behavior. I do not discuss this proposal because Sandra Mayson provides a compelling explanation of why Husak's proposal fails. Her most important point is this: "[C]ulpability does not necessarily track risk; there might be a need for preventive incapacitation beyond what culpability allows." "A Consequentialist Framework for Prevention," 224.

[4] "Two Systems of Social Protection," 96.

[5] "Preventive Confinement of Dangerous Offenders," 58.

[6] "Out of the Shadows," 696.

And Antony Duff writes: "[I]t is plausible to see the [presumption of innocence] as it operates in the criminal trial not as a separate demand of justice peculiar to the criminal trial, but as an implication of a wider demand that the state should treat us (as we should treat each other in our civic lives) as both prospectively and retrospectively innocent until proven guilty."[7]

4.3 A Foundation for the Presumption of Law Abidingness

The spirit of the POLA is not only widely shared among liberal authors, it is also well supported by the liberal principles that ground the space of rights.[8] The natural place to start in explaining why that is so is with the Autonomy Principle, which says that "agents all have their own lives to lead" and that "the space of rights must give them substantial freedom to do so, while also holding them accountable for their choices and the effects they have on others." The POLA reflects this commitment to autonomy: agents start with liberty unless and until either they do something to lose it, they cannot exercise normal autonomous control over themselves, or they cannot be held accountable for what they might do that would not respect the rights of others or the law more broadly. In addition, the Equality Principle says that "all fully autonomous agents are fundamentally equal as citizens in the republic of rights." This implies, again, that unless they do something to lose their autonomy-grounded right to freedom or the conditions for holding them accountable do not apply, they should be presumed as law abiding as anyone else.[9]

The Welfare Principle can pull in the other direction. It says that "the welfare of agents has value, and that value affects the rights agents have." But the Welfare Principle should work in ways that harmonize with the other two principles. The mere fact that more welfare could be achieved by restricting another's freedom should not suffice to deny that person freedom, if doing so would disrespect her equal status. It can ground *general* restrictions.[10] And insofar as an agent has a special duty to accept limitations for the security of others, *some* targeted restrictions of her liberty might be justifiable even if she has done nothing to lose her right to be presumed law abiding. But the priority of the Autonomy Principle in a liberal society implies that the demands imposed by such special duties must be relatively small. And beyond that limited range of duties, the state cannot justify specific targeted restrictions unless the person has done something to make

[7] "Pre-Trial Detention and the Presumption of Innocence," 120.
[8] See Section 3.2 for the statement of these principles.
[9] See Section 1.2.
[10] Ibid.

herself susceptible to them, or, again, the conditions for holding her accountable do not obtain.

One might wonder whether it really makes sense to be so protective of the freedom to act. I claimed in Chapter 3 that negative agent claims (claims not to have to act for the sake of others with positive restricting claims) are very strong, but that positive agent claims (claims to be free to act, despite the negative restricting claims against doing so) have no significant strength. Is not freedom from targeted liberty restrictions a positive agent claim to be free to act? Should it not, therefore, be relatively easy to justify, in the same way as it is relatively easy to justify restricting agents from harming others?

The answer to this objection is that freedom from targeted liberty restrictions is not a matter of positive agent claims. What determines whether an agent's claim is positive or negative is not whether she is acting or refraining from acting. Rather, it depends on the nature of the patient claim that it opposes. If it corresponds to a positive claim for aid, it is a negative agent claim; if it corresponds to a negative patient claim not to be harmed, then a further question has to be asked: What is the relationship between the agent and the potential harm of the patient? There are cases in which the patient claim not to be harmed is better seen as a positive claim for aid. Those are cases in which the patient needs to use the agent's body or property to protect herself. Consider this case:

> *Cart Avoidance*: David is on a crowded sidewalk, and he sees a heavy cart rolling down a steep hill toward him. He can tell that if he stays where he is, he will be knocked down and seriously injured by the cart. He can also tell that if he jumps out of harm's way, two people behind him, strangers to him, will be knocked down and seriously injured by the cart. Moreover, he can tell that if he takes the blow, they will be unharmed.[11]

The people behind David have positive claims on him, claims for aid, claims that fail. They fail to impose a duty on him that he serve as their means of not being hit. Accordingly, when he acts to avoid being hit, he is not acting on a positive agent claim with regard to them; he is acting on a negative agent claim: to refuse to serve as the means by which they are saved.[12]

I think something similar is going on with claims not to be subject to targeted restrictions when the agent has done nothing to lose the POLA. The relevant claims of others are not negative restricting claims that the agent avoid harming them. Of course, the agent may not harm them in any way that violates their rights, but that's not what is at stake. Rather, the patient claims are claims for

[11] See *The Mechanics of Claims*, 172.
[12] In *The Mechanics of Claims*, I refer to this as the "right of non-sacrifice."

reassurance; they are claims that the agent lose a freedom that others have because of a fear that she will act as she has no right to act. Removing her freedom as a way of reassuring others is morally equivalent to using her as a means to help others.[13] We should treat her as having a very strong negative agent claim not to have to make such sacrifices.

Finally, it is worth adding that it is normally quite harmful to a person to be denied the POLA. It stigmatically sets her apart.[14] That partly explains why forfeiture of the POLA should be difficult to establish—a theme I explore in Chapter 17.

4.4 Objections and Replies

The objections that I want to address here both build on the thought that the state can know that an agent poses an unjust threat to others, which is a sufficient basis for denying him the POLA. It does not need to wait until he does something to forfeit the POLA, nor does it need to assume that he lacks autonomous capacity or that the state lacks adequate policing capacity. Even with normal policing capacity, the state cannot always respond in time to people who pose threats to others. If the state knows that a person poses a threat to others, one that they have a right not to suffer, that should be reason enough to impose targeted restrictions on him.

I handle this objection in two steps. In the first, I assume the kinds of technology for prediction we now have. In the second, I examine the argument in light of possible future technology, thereby showing how deep the argument for the POLA goes.

4.4.1 Anticipated Aggressors with Modern Technology

Consider the following case:

> *Anticipated Culpable Aggressor*: Adam carries a loaded gun. Tom knows that Adam is a murderously jealous man, and knows that Adam's wife, Eve, has sent Adam a letter to his office, confessing an affair with Victor. Tom also knows that Adam is about to meet Victor in his office, and that he will open his mail before meeting Victor. In sum, Tom knows that Adam does not now harbor the

[13] I return to this point in Section 17.2.

[14] Stigma's tendency to set people apart is also why punishment—or so I will argue in the next Part—must aim at reconciliation, not at stigma.

intention to murder Victor, but he will, if not stopped, come to form such an intention, and at that time he will also have the means for carrying it out.[15]

It seems clear that Tom can interfere with Adam's liberty to protect Victor. Indeed, if there were no way to protect Victor other than by shooting Adam, even that might be justifiable. That's not because Adam has yet done anything to forfeit his rights. It is because it is fundamentally Adam's burden to bear, his *fault*, that he has the disposition to murder if made jealous. As an adult, he should have brought that predisposition to culpable behavior under control. Not having done so, it seems that Tom should, if necessary, choose Victor over Adam. It might be different if Adam had been drugged and this is what gave him the disposition. In that case, he would be an anticipated innocent aggressor, and Tom, assuming he knew about the drug, should be more inclined to be neutral between him and Victor.[16] But in either case, if Tom could impose a targeted restriction on Adam's liberty, for the sake of Victor's life, he should do so. And this seems inconsistent with the POLA.[17]

I acknowledge that the POLA should not block Tom, or a state agent in Tom's shoes, from applying a targeted liberty restriction on Adam. And I agree that this restriction could, if necessary to save Victor, be very costly to Adam. But I don't think that tells us much about the POLA. The reason is that this case calls for other-defense, and that is not the sort of interference with another that I am considering in this book. As I wrote in Chapter 1, in this book, I limit my attention to cases in which the threats are not so imminent that physically harmful force is necessary to stop them; rather, some restrictions on liberty will probably (with sufficient likelihood) suffice.

The relevant question for the POLA is not whether we can justify the state limiting Adam's liberty in this very special context, where if it is not limited an innocent person will almost certainly die in the near future;[18] the question is whether the state can justify limiting the freedom of people like Adam when they pose a more open-ended risk. It can be open ended either because Adam poses a general risk to others—for example, that he might harm women because of his sexist beliefs; or that even if he poses a threat to a particular person, like Victor, it is an open-ended risk, a threat that the state has reason to think he might realize sooner or later. In these more open-ended contexts, I think we need to be more careful about how the state might come to form the belief that some agent poses a

[15] I take this case from L. Alexander, "Self-Defense," 223.

[16] For my treatment of innocent aggressors, see *The Mechanics of Claims*, ch. 6.

[17] For a similar example and argument, see V. Tadros, "Controlling Risk," 145–146. Tadros there targets my earlier work—"A Unified Theory of Detention," 881. I offer no comment here on that exchange; rather, I offer a new kind of response in the text here.

[18] These sorts of limits are short term, and I presume that one has a duty to submit to them. See Section 17.2.

threat.[19] To make it concrete, let's stick with Adam, but let's make it the case that the state has reason to fear that he will kill his ex-wife, Victoria sooner or later. May it deny him the POLA in order to protect her?

Let's consider various grounds upon which the state might have concluded that it needs to impose targeted restrictions on Adam. Here are seven possibilities:

1. Naked statistics about his demographic group (for example, he's a member of an ethnic minority the males of which generally believe that men may use force against their wives, even ex-wives, if they disobey or dishonor them).
2. Information about some impulse he's going to have or is likely to have, based on a pattern he has of putting himself in situations in which he has that impulse (for example, he drinks, and when he gets drunk, he tends to become jealous and violent).
3. Information about some impulse he's going to have or is likely to have, based on his character (for example, that he is prone to violent jealousy).
4. His past behavior in relevantly similar circumstances (for example, he has been stalking and threatening Victoria, or he has engaged in such behavior with past partners).
5. His expressed intentions.
6. His expressed values.
7. His association with people who engage in or valorize unjust violence, along with evidence that he is especially susceptible to peer pressure.

Before proceeding to evaluate these possible grounds for denying Adam the benefits of the POLA, we should also distinguish two ways in which Adam might lose his liberty: specifically or generally. A specific limit on Adam, such as a restraining order requiring him to stay away from Victoria—the violation of which would trigger possibly serious sanctions as well as a more general POLA forfeiture—is naturally much easier to justify than a general restriction on his liberty, such as house arrest. And these different restrictions could reflect different kinds of POLA loss: a specific loss that implies that he might be willing to unjustly harm Victoria; or a broader one that implies that he might be so committed to unjustly harming her that he would also defy a restraining order to do so; or a broader one still implying that he would willingly commit unlawful and unjust actions across a range of situations. It is the more general losses of the

[19] The line between self-defense cases and open-ended cases is admittedly vague. But that vagueness is less of a problem when the agent has no known intention to harm. If he has a known intention to harm, that can serve as the basis for POLA forfeiture. See Section 16.2.2. If he has no known intention to harm, then the self-defense cases seem appropriate only in tightly temporally constrained window when the risk seems especially acute.

POLA that are particularly concerning. If those can be justified without appeal to the DR Model, then the DR Model must be wrong.

With that spectrum of losses in mind, let's review whether it seems justifiable for the state to deprive Adam of the POLA given these different bases for thinking that he poses an open-ended threat to Victoria. Starting with naked statistics based on demographic data, I think it is hard to justify denying him the POLA. In a well-functioning liberal state, where "honor killings" are rare, such group affiliation must correlate only weakly with posing a serious threat to his ex-wife. It is, moreover, exactly the sort of evidence of threat status that those who support the POLA find most objectionable as a basis for liberty restrictions. The problem is not only that it might target people because of their ethnicity or cultural background—a problem in societies that are already excessively prone to such "profiling"—but that naked statistical evidence, based on that sort of group membership, gives a person no chance to establish that he is *not* a threat to others.[20] I'm not saying that such evidence can give the state no reason to act. It might offer Victoria some extra protections and provide extra resources to keep an eye on Adam. But it is hard to see withdrawing the POLA in any way on this sort of ground.

Turning to the second possibility: suppose that the state knows that Adam is prone to excessive drinking and that when he drinks too much he becomes violent. If the odds of him becoming violent are high enough, the state might impose some targeted restrictions on him. Perhaps it would limit his access to alcohol or impose a restraining order on him. But these restrictions would depend not *only* on his statistical dangerousness; they would depend on him having *done* something—engaged in prior violent behavior—that caused him to forfeit the POLA more or less generally.

For a variation on that theme: suppose he was known to be a violent drunk years ago, but he no longer drinks. But now add that it is known that others have an interest in getting him involuntarily intoxicated, either because they want to get him in trouble or because they want him to harm Victoria. Now the forfeiture line works less well. It seems in this context that the state should warn him to be on his guard about the others who might try to get him involuntarily drunk. Perhaps it should help him by providing him a way to test if he is drunk, and so that he can be restricted only in that brief time when he is out of control. Or perhaps, if it has specific information about those others, it ought to impose targeted restrictions on them. But it does not seem that it should deny him the POLA.

Turning to the third possibility: suppose the state claims to know about his character: that he is a jealous man with a violent streak. Now we need to know how it knows that. That brings us to possibilities 4–6. If his past behavior

[20] See K. Ferzan, "Beyond Crime and Commitment," 157.

is the basis for that knowledge, then, again, the state could invoke forfeiture of the POLA. The same is true if he expresses his intention to harm Victoria if she triggers his jealousy.[21] Mere expression of values—for example, support for "honor killing"—is more problematic as a basis for loss of the POLA. Free speech rights privilege expressions of value.[22] In addition, values themselves seem to be an inadequate basis for stripping a person of the POLA. There may be a correlation between expressed values and intentions consistent with those values. But when the act in question is a serious crime, such a correlation is not only insufficient to justify punishment, it is also insufficient for overcoming the POLA. It may, like demographic data, be a basis for providing Victoria with some extra protection, or for keeping a close eye on Adam. But it should not be sufficient for general loss of the POLA.

I qualify that last statement because Victoria might reasonably feel quite threatened if she finds out that Adam has been espousing the virtues of "honor killing." And the state may reasonably share her concern. It might seem obtuse to insist that it can take no action other than providing her with some extra resources to help with her safety and surveilling him a bit more closely. But this is where the idea of a small duty to accept sacrifices for the sake of others can come into play. A narrowly tailored restriction of his liberty, imposing a restraining order on him with regard to Victoria, could be justified on that ground. What cannot be justified, I believe, is a broader loss of the POLA, and with it a more serious loss of his liberty.

That leaves the last category of evidence that the state might cite to strip Adam of the POLA: his associations. I'm not talking about joining a criminal gang or terrorist group. An affiliation with a criminal enterprise as such can be a crime and a basis for loss of the POLA. But what I have in mind is merely associating with people who might be a bad influence on him. On the one hand, association is a protected freedom, akin to speech. On the other hand, if he is particularly susceptible to influence, that might give the state reason to restrict his freedom. To determine whether it does or not, we need to inquire into why the state might believe that he is particularly susceptible to their bad influence. If the state takes him to be particularly susceptible because of his limited autonomous capacity, that would provide a basis for limiting the POLA for him. But that basis fits a DR Model category. If it's because of cultural generalizations—that people from a particular culture tend to be very deferential to group norms—then I think

[21] That is a significant theme in K. Ferzan, "Beyond Crime and Commitment." I also have argued that such expressions can be the basis for criminal prosecutions. See "Criminalizing Statements of Terrorist Intent." For more on this, see Section 16.1.

[22] The line between expression of values and making threats may be hard to draw in practice. But the state would need solid evidence of the latter before acting on it as a basis for punishment or POLA forfeiture.

we're back to the first reason and the POLA seems to survive the supposed counterexample. If it's his own behavior that makes him seem particularly susceptible to peer pressure, but he has only ever done imprudent things, not immoral things, because of peer pressure in the past, then again, this seems to be too thin a basis for limiting the POLA. But, if he's shown himself to be susceptible to peer pressure that has led him to do morally unjustifiable things in the past, then he might be held to have lost the POLA to some degree. But again, this fits the DR Model, as it would be a basis for forfeiting the POLA.

In sum, if we delve into the example, looking at the various bases upon which the state might claim to know that Adam poses an open-ended danger to Victoria, there is nothing about it that seems to make my account of the POLA implausible. The risk he poses may call for the state to take extra precautions where Adam is concerned. It may even call for imposing on him the duty to accept a restraining order, reflecting a specific loss of the POLA. But nothing about the case suggests a general loss of the POLA except when the DR Model would license it.

4.4.2 Anticipated Aggressors with Future Technology

Stephen Morse, as the quote from Section 4.2 indicates, is one of the people committed to the POLA. But it turns out that his commitment to the POLA is contingent. As he puts it, his commitment to liberty "hangs by a technological thread."[23] The foundation for his commitment to the POLA seems to be his "fear that our predictions of future violence are likely to be inaccurate because predictive technology is insufficient and bias will intrude."[24] He might then respond to the argument I just gave by saying that it neglects the possibility that we could have more direct information that a person will pose a danger to others. Such a person could be "innocent of any wrong-doing, [and] not suffering from mental disorder" and yet we might know that he will pose a threat that would be great enough to justify "an intrusion on liberty that rivals and even exceeds criminal punishment or civil commitment."[25] If that is right, then the POLA is not a fundamental principle of political morality; it is just the expression of our current, limited epistemic possibilities.

There are two ways to view this challenge. One is radical and the other is more limited. The radical challenge comes from the possibility that we might get technology that allowed the state to "correctly predict[] all or most future behavior."[26]

[23] "Neither Desert nor Disease," 294.
[24] Ibid., 295.
[25] Ibid., 299.
[26] Ibid., 297.

As Morse points out, if that world were possible and we were to find ourselves in it, "our view of ourselves and many of our moral and legal arrangements would be quite different from those at present."[27]

I think we can dispense with this as a real possibility. I don't deny that we could have the technology to predict what a person will do a few seconds hence. But I think that both we and the world we live in are far too complex, with too many feedback loops, for predictions based on brain scans or some equivalent technology to be, as a general matter, significantly more accurate than the ones we now make based on folk psychology, referring to a person's beliefs, desires, and character traits, assessed in contexts that it is predicted he will encounter in the world.

The more limited challenge is that we might be able to detect things about a person's brain that would allow limited but highly accurate predictions that would surprise even the person whose behavior is predicted. For example, it might be possible to detect a disease that would evolve over the coming months in such a way as to make the person much more prone to violence than he now is. Alternatively, it might be possible to implant chips in a person's brain that would read the development of certain behavioral impulses that allow the prediction of an intention before the person acts on it, indeed before the person has formed the intention himself.[28] I now explore each of these possibilities.

Suppose the general restrictions on our liberty included having to submit to medical scanners on a regular basis (say, monthly) that would allow detection of changes that would lead, in some months' time, to experiencing a new strong desire, in certain kinds of circumstances, to unjustifiably attack others. Would that justify negating the POLA for such individuals? The answer surely depends on how well people who are informed of such a pending change in their psychology can adjust to handle the change. Suppose that people who receive that diagnosis find that they can avoid violent acts by some combination of therapy, self-monitoring, and care with regard to the circumstances they let themselves encounter. It would seem unjust to simply strip them of the POLA. It would seem fairer to offer them therapy and help them avoid circumstances that would trigger their new desires for violence. Given that they know that they will come to feel a new, strong desire to unjustly attack others, they have an enforceable duty to take extra care around others.[29] They could be taken to forfeit the POLA

[27] Ibid.

[28] Research by Benjamin Libet in the 1980s showed that at least when it comes to the intention to perform simple physical tasks like moving a finger, the brain shows a "readiness potential" some 200 milliseconds before the person was aware of forming the intention to move their finger. See M. Moore, *Mechanical Choices*, 217–218.

[29] I explore this kind of duty of self-restriction in Section 17.1.

only if they choose not to take advantage of these forms of aid. This is not inconsistent with the DR Model. Rather, it is an invocation of one prong of it.

What about those who are unable to control their violent impulses? Those people would also be handled properly under the DR Model. They could be held to have a duty to submit to more extreme restrictions on their liberty, or they could be held to have lost their autonomous capacity. Either way, the exceptions to the POLA in the DR Model cover their cases.

What if we assume that some people would be able to control themselves and others would not, and that no one can tell in advance who falls into which category? This would be the equivalent of a diagnosis that one is more or less likely to lose control of oneself at some point in the future, but one won't know in advance if one will lose control or not. How are we to handle that prospect? I think the sensible thing to say is that if the odds are high enough that an agent is going to be unable to control himself, then the state would have reason to treat him as, to some extent, not autonomous. Permissible restrictions should be proportional to the risk that he will engage in wrongful and harmful behavior. But they would still be grounded in the fact that he cannot know that he can control himself.

Turning now to the second possibility, suppose the general restrictions on our liberty included having to submit to the implantation of chips in our brains that would detect the impulse to commit violent acts—chips that, in effect, have an "off switch."[30] Would these chips not function to impose justifiable, targeted—targeting those people who are "switched off"—exceptions to the POLA?

There are two things to say here. First, insofar as the chips would prevent us from committing particular wrongful actions, we are, once again, not dealing with the kind of open-ended threat that the POLA is meant to address. Rather, we're back in the realm of other-defense where targeted force may be justifiable even against innocent threats. If the chips could detect impulses that would lead to violence, then we have to weigh the importance of retaining control over ourselves as against the importance of preventing violence. If the chips were sufficiently effective, and they didn't have bad side effects, then we might want to accept a duty to have such chips implanted.

But—and this is the second point—we can learn something about the POLA by seeing why we might not want to embrace such chips. Even if such chips could reduce violence, they would have a cost in terms of the value of autonomy. And the real question is, do we need such help?

To answer that question, note that there are two ways such chips might work. Chip type 1 can see a violent intention forming before the agent can see it, and it

[30] This is a cleaner, more scientifically plausible version of the thought experiment contained in Philip K. Dick's *Minority Report*. One might worry that such an off switch would make people vulnerable to the unjust attacks of others. But if *everyone* had such a chip, then there would be no aggression, just or unjust, to respond to. So, I think we can put that worry aside.

heads off the intention formation by performing a kind of brain reboot in which the recent brain activity that was leading toward forming a violent intention is erased. Chip type 2 intercedes later, only after the agent has formed a violent intention. I think we can say that agents who form the intention to perform a wrongful violent action have forfeited their right not to be rebooted—intentions are mental states that we choose to form.[31] Now, suppose that chip type 1 is much more effective than chip type 2. Does that give us reason to choose to use chip type 1?

I think there are two reasons to deny that it does. First, I think the idea that we could have chips that would detect what we would intend before we have any clue that we are heading there is not a real possibility for autonomous people. I say this not because I doubt the possibility of building sophisticated brain-reading chips, but because I think rather a lot of the ability of autonomous people to know themselves. Part of the maturation process involved in becoming an autonomous person is coming to realize that there are many precursors to our intentions. We can learn to avoid temptation. We can learn to detect early signs that we are getting emotionally engaged in ways that distort our reasoning, and we can learn how to pull ourselves out of those emotional ruts. Thus, the practical predicate for thinking that chip type 1 would add a lot of value is unrealistic.

Second, it's not as if we have no means of dealing with violent intentions. That's what the general regulations on our freedom help to contain. That's what adequate policing helps to contain. The choice that concerns me is not between having our autonomous capacity short-circuited and living autonomously in a Hobbesian state of nature. It's a choice between having our autonomous capacity short-circuited and living autonomously in a well-structured state. If that were the choice, I would choose the latter.

In the end, then, I think the sort of thought experiments suggested by Morse do not show that our commitment to the POLA hangs by a thread. Moreover, the deepest threat does not concern the POLA as I care about it in this book, the POLA with regard to open-ended threats based on mere dispositions to act wrongly. But even if we put that restriction aside and focus on cases of specific threats to identifiable victims, I think our respect for autonomy should give us reason not to adopt highly reliable "off switches" in our brains. We should, rather, offer each other the respect of the POLA, and control risk only with general liberty restrictions, effective policing, and the use of the exceptions to the POLA that are built into the DR Model.

[31] See my "Criminalizing Statements of Terrorist Intent," 835–838. It would be important that the chip could detect the difference between merely entertaining the fantasy of violence and actually intending violence. But we can assume the chip could do that. See also Section 16.2.2.

PART II
CRIMINAL LAW

5

Criminal Law and the Retributive Idea of Deserved Punishment

5.1 Criminal Law's Core Functions

I approach the criminal law from a broadly retributive perspective: if a person commits a criminal act—properly understood as a culpable public wrong—then she deserves, morally speaking, to be held accountable with censure and punishment that is proportional to the magnitude of her culpable wrongdoing. Censure is straightforwardly a blaming practice, one aimed at communicating blame for crimes to the wrongdoers themselves, to their victims, and to society as a whole. Punishment is not so straightforwardly a blaming practice. Understood simply as the intentional infliction of hard treatment on wrongdoers, it could serve other social functions as well. Indeed, I will argue in Part IV that penal law, which should be carved off from criminal law, involves the intentional infliction of hard treatment on wrongdoers and it is *not* a blaming practice. To count as punishment, in my view, the infliction of hard treatment must be delivered at least in part to reinforce the message of censure. In that way the criminal law, which aims to deliver deserved censure and punishment, is "a blaming institution."[1]

I argue that punishment is a blaming institution in another way as well: it is properly designed to collect on the guilt-debt wrongdoers have, a debt they owe to the political community and to their fellow citizens in the republic of rights more broadly.

The idea that the criminal law's core function is to operate as a blaming institution helps to explain many of the criminal law's doctrines—from the importance of mens rea to the role of defenses such as irresponsibility, justification, and excuse.[2] The premise that this blaming function is central to the criminal law is the foundational premise for much contemporary theoretical work on the criminal law.[3] Of course, there are theorists who reject this idea,[4] but I think that insofar as

[1] See Section 1.3.3, citing A. Simester, *Fundamentals of Criminal Law*, 493.

[2] Supporting this claim is the organizing principle of Simester's *Fundamentals of Criminal Law*.

[3] In addition to ibid., see M. Moore's *Placing Blame*, L. Alexander and K. Ferzan's *Crime and Culpability*, and A. Duff's *The Realm of Criminal Law*.

[4] See, e.g., V. Chiao, *Criminal Law in the Age of the Administrative State*; A. Kolber, *Punishment for the Greater Good*.

Punishment, Penalty, and Incapacitation. Alec Walen, Oxford University Press. © Oxford University Press 2026.
DOI: 10.1093/9780197523124.003.0005

they reject it but seek to stay within the bounds of the dignity-respecting model (DR Model), they should be taken to be defending the penal law, not criminal law. The criminal law is a blaming institution.

Taking the blaming function of criminal law as settled, my primary aim in the remainder of this section is to explain the connection between the blaming function and a deeper one: that of achieving reconciliation between wrongdoers and the political community broadly understood (by which I mean the various levels of state that can punish a criminal wrongdoer and the republic of rights itself).[5]

To see the connection between the blaming function and reconciliation, start by asking: Why have an institution that is a blaming institution? The answer follows from my conception of the state's role in establishing rights. As I noted in Chapter 3, the state should hold people accountable in ways that promote rightful relations between, on the one hand, those who have culpably violated the rights of others or the law more generally and, on the other hand, the state that fleshes out the rights we have. This is more than a matter of restoring rightful relations between private individuals, as is done in tort and contract law. This is a matter of restoring rightful relations between individuals and the moral community of fellow citizens in their states and in the republic of rights more broadly. This is the function of state-based blame (censure).[6]

In other words, among the basic functions of the state is not only fleshing out and making determinate the space of rights but also protecting the value of what it has done by seeking to ensure that individuals relate to each other as they should in this space. Culpable wrongdoing is inconsistent with respecting rights and the law; it alienates the wrongdoer from the political community. It is incumbent upon both the political community and the wrongdoer to seek to set things right so that the members of the community can resume recognizing each other as equal members in good standing. That means that both must seek reconciliation between the wrongdoer and the political community.[7]

It is worth pausing on the idea that the state and the wrongdoer are obliged to *seek* reconciliation. There is no right to *be* reconciled. Reconciliation is not something that can simply be chosen, especially not by the state. It takes resources to catch, prosecute, and censure and punish wrongdoers. There are many other things the state is obliged to do as well, such as protect people from future violations, promote distributive justice, protect public goods, and so on. The imperative to seek reconciliation between wrongdoer and the political community

[5] On the importance of reconciliation, see A. Duff, *Punishment, Communication, and Community*, 107.

[6] See Section 3.7.2.

[7] This account is related to the Hegelian idea of punishment as "the annulment of the crime." *Philosophy of Right*, ¶ 101. I hope my account will be, in the end, much less mysterious than Hegel's. But I hereby acknowledge my intellectual debt to him.

is only one among many duties the state has. In addition, reconciliation is not complete unless and until the wrongdoer owns her guilt. Thus, the state's duty is only to *seek* reconciliation, not to *achieve* it.

How can the state seek this sort of reconciliation? It can communicate to the culpable wrongdoer the appropriateness of owning her guilt. That is one central function of censure.[8] Others, as noted above, are communicating to other potential wrongdoers that this sort of behavior is wrongful and communicating to the victim, if there is one, that his status as a person with dignity is important, and that the community disapproves of such treatment.

The state can also seek to achieve reconciliation by extracting material amends that the culpable wrongdoer owes the community for her wrongdoing. It can do that by extracting compensation in the form of a fine or community service, or by imposing hard treatment on her to deter potential wrongdoers. Importantly, it is a mistake to think of hard treatment as somehow aimed (badly) at helping victims.[9] Tort suits or restorative justice are better tools for extracting what the wrongdoer owes the victim. And insofar as the state takes a special interest in the victim's material well-being, it can provide material care for him that in most cases would be more effective than anything the wrongdoer could provide. But, again, that is not what punishment is about. The debt payment at issue should be fundamentally responsive to the harm of a public wrong, which is to say that it should be aimed at vindicating the rule of law.[10]

I end this section with two important clarifications. First, reconciliation is not what wrongdoers deserve. What they deserve is censure and punishment.[11] Reconciliation is the ultimate goal that explains, in a justification-shaping way, why we should have an institution to mete out deserved censure and punishment.

Second, reconciliation is not a psychological state; it is not about *feeling* reconciled. It concerns a set of moral relations. Feelings are relevant; insofar as people resent each other, it is hard for them to relate to each other as equals,

[8] Of course, that is not how everyone understands censure. It is often understood as the communication of stigmatizing blame. But I will argue against that conception of blame in Section 6.4.

[9] I discuss how badly in Ch. 11, when I discuss the case for restorative justice.

[10] What about the society on the verge of dissolution, as in Kant's famous example of people leaving an island nation and deciding whether to execute a prisoner who had been on death row? Kant famously wrote: "[T]he last murderer remaining in prison would first have to be executed, so that each has done to him what his deeds deserve and blood guilt does not cling to the people for not having insisted upon this punishment; for otherwise the people can be regarded as collaborators in this public violation of justice." "Doctrine of Right," Academy page 333. Kant's position is too extreme in two ways: (1) the endorsement of the death penalty, and (2) the absolute imperative to carry out the punishment. But if we temper those two features of his position, I agree. Reconciliation is not only between the wrongdoer and a particular political community. The political community is just the voice for the republic of rights more broadly. If a particular community can carry out a just punishment on the way out of the door, it has reason to do so.

[11] I say more about desert in Section 5.4.

deserving of basic respect. That is why it is important for punishment to be designed so that it is not excessively shaming or alienating, as having those features would make it hard for wrongdoers to own their guilt and be fully reconciled with the broader political community. In other words, the psychology of reconciliation is relevant to the ultimate achievement of reconciliation. But the ultimate goal is not to achieve certain feelings (except the feelings intrinsic to an agent owning her guilt); it is about the wrongdoer owning her guilt and the community accepting her back as a member in good standing.

5.2 The Relevance of Security and Targeted Liberty Restrictions

In this section, I tie the two functions of the criminal law just discussed to the DR Model for targeted restrictions on liberty for the sake of security. I start with the observation that in reinforcing the law and deterring lawbreaking punishment also perforce promotes security. That too is part of its overall justification. Promoting security is not a part of the justification that gives punishment its character as punishment—though it can shape the way punishment is meted out. But if we ask whether to have the practice of punishment, given its costs, the provision of security is a fundamentally important part of the answer.[12]

It is also noteworthy that hard treatment can promote security directly by incapacitating those who are more likely than most to break the law. But it's important to recognize that punishment does not have to take an incapacitating form. Fines, for example, tend not to incapacitate. This raises the question: Are there any reasons to treat incapacitating restrictions of liberty as the paradigmatic form of hard treatment? I think the answer is yes. There is a positive reason, namely that people tend to value their liberty and to disvalue being incarcerated, no matter how pleasant the conditions of incarceration. There is also a negative reason, namely that the other possible modes of punishment are more problematic.

Consider, first, fines. Many do not have the resources to pay them. If the state takes what little they have, they may find it hard to live. Or, if they are left with what they need to live, then they won't suffer much of a loss, undermining it as a form of hard treatment. In addition, deciding how much property to take for a proportional punishment is tricky. It depends on how much they have, how

[12] For more on this, see Ch. 9.

much they expect to have, what sort of life plans they have, and so on. This is not to say that fines cannot be part of proportional punishment, but there are good reasons not to rely only on fines.

Bodily harm is now a disfavored form of punishment, at least in most Western countries.[13] If it is permanent, like the removal of a hand or limb, then it is hard to reconcile the permanent damage with reconciliation as a status that can be achieved. If, however, the punishment is just temporary pain or discomfort, perhaps combined with bodily damage that heals (like a beating), then it is likely to send a message not so much of extracting a debt and thereby achieving reconciliation as of domination.[14]

Consider, finally, the aim of inflicting psychic harm. Whether delivered as public shaming or private torment, this sort of punishment, punishment designed to tear down the person being punished, should be avoided. Punishment should not be pleasant, but its ultimate goal should be to help the wrongdoer become a better person, one who owns his guilt and is reconciled with the political community, broadly understood. I understand that punishment that deprives a convicted wrongdoer of liberty or property often leaves him psychologically harmed. My point is that such harm should not be the end or the means by which punishment is inflicted. It should be, at most, an unfortunate side effect that the state generally tries to avoid.

Given the competition, then, targeted and proportional deprivation of liberty should be a paradigmatic form of punishment as hard treatment. Keep in mind that not all punishment has to take the form of *hard* treatment aimed at deterrence. It is possible to extract the material debt the wrongdoer owes through fines or community service that reinforces the law in other ways (for example, speaking to community groups about what not to do).[15] But insofar as the public debt is extracted through deterrent punishment, it will often and properly take the form of targeted restrictions on liberty.[16]

[13] For a history of this change, along with a critique of imprisonment and an articulation of an Islamic view that corporal punishment is to be preferred, see A. Zulfiqar, "The Immorality of Incarceration."

[14] I admit that the meaning of such practices is almost certainly culturally contingent. I presume there are cultures where those who are beaten, whipped, or mutilated feel that that is just as punishment, and that those who are so punished have then paid their debt for their wrongdoing. But it is my educated hunch that such cultures are also not liberal, egalitarian cultures. As such, I don't think that we who live in cultures where bodily harm has been banned as cruel and unusual punishment—pace Ingraham v. Wright, 430 U.S. 651 (1977) (upholding the constitutionality of corporal punishment in schools, in part on the grounds that the 8th Amendment ban applies only to *criminal* punishment)—can resume corporal punishment without also losing our grip on our liberal commitments.

[15] See Section 7.1.2.

[16] In Section 7.2, I discuss other things punishment can aim to do, including forced rehabilitation and community service.

5.3 The Measure of Culpable Wrongdoing

I have been using the phrase "culpable wrongdoing" as though it is clear enough. But given the centrality of the notion, I should say a bit more about what I think it means for an act to be a culpable wrong, so that we can make sense of taking its measure.[17] The culpability of an action—omissions count too, but for brevity I'll refer to actions as covering both—I take to be a function of both the wrongness of the action in itself and the culpable mens rea with which it is performed. And I take the wrongness of the action to be a function of the magnitude of the harm—to individuals or to the rule of law—caused, intended, or unreasonably risked, and the degree to which that harm is unjustified.

The law normally treats a harm caused as worse than the same harm intended but not caused or merely unreasonably risked.[18] For example, the law normally treats a murder as a worse harm than an attempted murder. Some criticize that judgment;[19] I accept it, but nothing I say here depends on taking one view or another on the relevance of causing harm. The more important point is that the magnitude of harm is relevant in this straightforward sense: the worse the harm caused, intended, or unreasonably risked, the worse the wrong, all else equal.

That said, the notion of the magnitude of a harm to a person is not simple and straightforward. Do we judge it as a loss compared to a prior state, or compared to what could have been? Do we judge its magnitude in terms of what a person would give to avoid it? How do we then account for the differences in what a person could give depending on her wealth? Do we look for something like a market price—one where there is, of course, no (legal) market? These are serious problems, but I'll proceed as if we have a sufficiently clear intuitive understanding of the magnitude of harm to an individual.

More difficult still is the notion of harm to the rule of law. The rule of law seems, in truth, fairly robust. It can tolerate a fair bit of low-level lawlessness. In addition, one more lawless act will rarely make a dent in the overall health of the rule of law—it might have a noticeable effect only when a high-profile defendant gets away with a crime. Yet we need to have some way of recognizing that unlawful actions harm the rule of law and undermine the propensity of people in a political community to take the law seriously. One might try to model this harm on the idea of a large collection of people all causing a serious harm to

[17] Some theorists would not accept what I say here, but I believe it suffices to lay out a plausible position; I think it would take me too far astray to argue for it as the best account of culpable wrongdoing.

[18] In favor of harm counting, see A. Simester, *Fundamentals of Criminal Law*, ch. 14. See also K. Levy, "The Solution to the Problem of Outcome Luck"; A. Cornford, "Resultant Luck and Criminal Liability."

[19] See, e.g., J. Feinberg, "Equal Punishment for Failed Attempts"; L. Alexander and K. Ferzan, *Crime and Culpability*, 172–175.

an individual. Even if none of them make a significant difference on their own, they are normally all—with possible exceptions for those who have particularly marginal roles—held responsible for the harm they cause. The problem with this model is that truly undermining the rule of law in general would be a huge harm, dwarfing any particular crime with a victim. It would make the harm each person is responsible for risking too large.

A better approach, I suggest, distinguishes two kinds of laws that do more than just protect victims: laws that protect against unjust freeriding (for example, an agent not paying her taxes), and proxy crimes. The latter, as I understand the term, target acts that are not in themselves particularly wrongful, if they are wrongful at all, but they are correlated with serious wrongs so that blocking the one has some tendency to block the other.[20]

The magnitude of the wrong of unjust freeriding can be modeled on the unjust advantage the wrongdoer gets, the advantage functioning as the mirror image of a harm. As for proxy crimes, their magnitude can be modeled on the idea that failure to enforce them creates the risk of a more serious wrong. The risk could result from a person getting into a better position from which to complete a crime she wants to commit, in which case the risk could be quite high. Or, even if she is very unlikely to commit the target crime herself (most often because she has no intent to commit it, and is a competent agent), knowledge of her unlawful behavior could inspire others, who will then commit the target crime. The measure of the harm from such a proxy crime is taken by starting with the harm associated with the more serious target harm and then discounting its magnitude by the risk that a person who commits that act will go on, if not stopped, to commit the target crime herself or will inspire someone else to do so. In some cases, those more serious crimes will be serious indeed, and the harm of committing the proxy crime might then count as, at least, somewhat serious. Proxy crimes relating to terrorism can fit this model. In other cases, either the ultimate harm is not very great, or the risk of it occurring if the proxy crime is committed is low. In those cases, the harm of the proxy crime should be taken to be low. Many regulatory offenses fit this model. I won't try to be more precise about such issues, but I note, when discussing proportional punishments for proxy crimes, that the harm is often so low that a proportional punishment would be quite small as well.[21]

Turning now to degree of justification, it is relevant in this sense: people with stronger claims not to suffer a harm will be wronged more, all else equal, than people with weaker claims regarding the same harm. For example, people have stronger claims not to be harmed as a result of being used as a means than as a

[20] See Section 1.3.4.
[21] See Ch. 13.

side effect.[22] For illustration, assume an agent is acting to save herself from a bad injury. Her killing another who is not liable to be killed would be wrong. But her killing another as a means to avoid that injury would be further from justified than her killing another as a side effect of avoiding that injury. This point can also be framed in terms of partial justification. Suppose, for example, that an agent acted in self-defense in conditions in which lethal force was not necessary because she could have safely retreated. Such a killing is less wrong, but it is less culpable, than one that is not justified at all.

Given an action with a particular level of wrongness, the agent's mens rea, broadly understood, will affect the overall culpability of the wrong. If it is recklessly performed, it will likely be less culpable than if it is knowingly or intentionally performed. If it is negligently performed, it will likely be less culpable still. And holding constant the mens rea in that modern sense (that is, intentional, knowing, reckless, or negligent), it will likely be more culpable if it was maliciously caused than if it was reluctantly caused.[23] The details of these ideas are outside the scope of this book.[24] I say this much only to provide a basic idea of what I mean when I refer to the overall culpability of a wrongful act. The point is that censure and punishment should be proportional to this notion of the culpability of a wrongful act.

5.4 The Meaning of Desert

Desert is often analyzed into a three-way relationship between the person who deserves something, what he deserves, and that in virtue of which he deserves it. These are often cast, respectively, as the desert subject, the desert object, and the desert basis.[25] I believe a fourth relatum should be added: the person or persons who can appropriately give, or have a duty to give, the desert subject what he deserves. I call these persons "desert agents." In the context of the criminal law, the wrongdoer is the desert subject, censure and punishment are the desert objects, culpable wrongdoing is the desert basis, and the state, through the actions of the prosecutor, judge, jury, and whoever actually metes out the punishment (often referred to as "corrections") is the desert agent.

That's a formal description of the concept. More important are two substantive commitments. The first concerns the difference between *deserving* some

[22] See Section 3.5.1.

[23] This distinction normally arises at sentencing, not the stage of crime definition.

[24] For a good discussion of how the modern mens rea terms—negligence, recklessness, and intention (knowledge too if one follows the Model Penal Code)—reflect much more than concern with differential culpability, see A. Simester, *Fundamentals of Criminal Law*, 233–234, and Part III of his book, more broadly.

[25] See J. Feinberg, "Justice and Personal Desert," 61; M. Berman, "Two Kinds of Retributivism," 437.

treatment and the treatment merely being fitting. Desert, as Mitch Berman puts it "is a *favoring* concept."[26] By that he means: "[A]n agent's deservingness of a desert object entails either that realization of that object would be impersonally non-instrumentally good, or that some agent(s) have special reason or duty to bring the object about."[27] By contrast, fittingness is not necessarily a *favoring* concept. A hat may fit, but that by itself provides no reason to wear it. But it's important to realize that fittingness need not be merely neutral; it can have a positive significance. Consider the grief. Suppose someone has lost a loved one and feels grief. Others might not only understand why his grief "fits"; they would, in most cases, approve of it as a fitting reaction. They might consider it odd or worrisome if he felt no grief. Still, there is a contrast that concerns the practical significance of the different judgments. Desert provides a reason for a desert agent to act; mere fittingness does not. If the agent who lost a loved one felt no grief, it would be inappropriate to nag or in other ways pressure or force him to feel it. It would even be inappropriate for the agent to try to force himself to feel grief if that's not what he feels. The same is true for positive reactions. If someone completes an arduous task or wins an award, it would normally be fitting to feel happy. It would be somewhat odd or worrisome if someone does not feel happy in that context. But it would be inappropriate to nag or try to force him to feel happy. In either case—failure to feel grief or failure to feel happiness—another would have reason to suggest he seek therapy so that his reactions to events are more "fitting." Fittingness can be relevant to action in this indirect sense. But it does not directly call for action.[28] Desert, by contrast, does.

Now suppose someone has carelessly harmed someone he loves. Guilt would be fitting, but blame would be deserved. Guilt would not be deserved because there are no morally appropriate actions to bring it about.[29] But blame—communicating the fittingness of guilt—would be deserved. Moreover, to the extent that the agent's guilt-debt can be extracted, the extraction would be deserved. The reasons to blame or to extract guilt-debt are only pro tanto reasons; other reasons may outweigh them. But the agent's deserving blame and debt-extraction grounds these pro tanto reasons to act.

[26] "Retributivism," 46.

[27] Ibid. These two alternatives are meant to capture consequentialist and deontological approaches to desert, respectively.

[28] Dana Nelkin also takes fittingness to provide no reason to act. Her example: "[T]he fact that a racist joke is funny seems to entail a certain fittingness of laughing. But such fittingness needn't provide any reason [to laugh] at all, . . . not even a pro tanto one that is overridden." "Guilt, Grief, and the Good," 185. But I think her account makes fittingness too neutral. An agent might reasonably consult fittingness to relax certain constraints on how he reacts. And in that context, the fact that a racist joke is funny does provide reason to let oneself laugh; it's just a reason that might well be outweighed by the reasons not to laugh.

[29] I argue for this claim in Section 7.1.1.

Second, as Joel Feinberg points out, "the facts which constitute the basis of a subject's desert must be facts about the subject."[30] That means that the fact that the state has a pro tanto duty to censure and punish the subject cannot, by itself, show that he deserves it. That duty has to reflect something about what the wrongdoer did or some other relevant fact about him.

I think we can make sense of a wrongdoer's desert basis by noting that his culpable wrongdoing creates a problem for the political community: he has disrespected it and in that way is no longer well integrated into it. This is a relational fact about him and the community, but it is at least in part about him. It is to reconcile him and the community that the state has a pro tanto duty to censure and punish him. In that sense, he deserves that desert object.

One might object that desert cannot by itself license punishment because the right not to be punished must first be forfeited; only after the right is forfeited can the reason to punish come into play. David Dolinko makes an argument along these lines:[31] there is a difference between someone morally deserving something and others having a right to give it to her. In one example, he imagines a father who (perversely) gives his reprobate son almost everything in his will and leaves his loving and respectful son a pittance. We may believe that the loving son *deserves* to inherit at least half of his father's estate, but that would not entitle anyone to take property from the other son to give to him.[32] Putting the point more generally, desert by itself does not justify doing things that otherwise would violate rights.

I used to think that the right response to Dolinko's point is that "retributive desert presupposes forfeiture of the right not to be punished."[33] I now think that response is mistaken. The idea of a separate forfeiture step suggests that we have to think about forfeiture in its own terms, and then we can ask about desert. That suggests the coherence of something like negative retributivism, in which an agent simply forfeits the right not to suffer a proportional punishment. But why would he forfeit *that*? The explanation for why he would forfeit *that* must implicitly refer to the thought that he deserves *that*: *that amount* of punishment.[34] But if he deserves it, then the desert agent has a pro tanto duty to inflict it. Forfeiture just gets in the way of thinking clearly here. It's better to say that when desert agents have a pro tanto obligation to mete out proportional punishment, that obligation comes with the loss of the right not to receive such punishment from a proper desert agent. What of Dolinko's example? No one has a pro tanto obligation, much less right, to take from one son to give to the other. There are simply

30 "Justice and Personal Desert," 59.
31 The rest of this paragraph is taken from my "Retributive Justice," § 4.1.
32 "Some Thoughts About Retributivism," 544.
33 "Retributive Justice," § 4.1.
34 For more on this, see Section 14.3.2.

two kinds of desert: pro tanto obliging desert and contingently reason-giving desert. Criminal punishment involves the former.

I won't assess whether the idea of deserving punishment makes substantive sense until I have laid out my account of blame in Chapter 6. I will say only this much about the substance here: censure is a more straightforward candidate for a desert object than punishment. As Antony Duff writes: "[I]t is not puzzling—in the way that critics of retributivism find the idea of penal desert puzzling—that offenders deserve censure for their criminal wrongdoing."[35] That is not to say that it is always appropriate, all things considered, to censure those who are blameworthy. Sometimes it will be counterproductive or insensitive to blame the blameworthy (for example, if they have blamed themselves enough already); or the blamer may lack the standing to blame.[36] Nonetheless, censure, as an expression of blame, is intuitively deserved as a response to culpable wrongdoing.

The idea that punishment is deserved is more problematic. That's not to say that everyone recognizes it as problematic. Michael Moore writes: "To say that a person deserves punishment is to say that he has culpably done wrong."[37] He and other traditional retributivists seem to operate from the premise that it is intrinsically good for culpable wrongdoers to suffer, and that punishment can be justified as a mechanism for ensuring that they suffer as they should.[38] My problem with traditional retributivists is that suffering is normally a negative state. There are contexts in which states that normally are negative are fitting and positive. As Leo Zaibert points out, it is fitting and, in a way, good for people to feel grief at the loss of a loved one.[39] "What is grief, if not love persevering?"[40] Still, we need an *account* of why grief or suffering should sometimes be good. In the context of lost love and grief, the connection through the significance of ongoing love is straightforward.[41] Some think the connection between wrongdoing and suffering is straightforward too. But to others the idea is "a mysterious piece of moral alchemy in which the combination of the two evils of moral wickedness and suffering are transmuted into good."[42] I take it to be at least mysterious enough to warrant a good effort at an explanation.

Given that the idea of deserved hard treatment or suffering is more mysterious than the idea of deserved censure, it is tempting to try to justify the former

[35] *Punishment, Communication, and Community*, 27.

[36] See Ch. 10.

[37] *Placing Blame*, 168.

[38] As Berman writes, "the dominant retributivist view" is "that what wrongdoers deserve is 'to suffer.'" "Rehabilitating Retributivism," 87. See also L. Zaibert, *Rethinking Punishment*, chs. 2 & 3; L. Alexander and K. Ferzan, *Reflections on Crime and Culpability*, 184–185.

[39] *Rethinking Punishment*, 75–76 (embracing G.E. Moore's notion of "organic unities"). See also D. Moller, "Love and Death."

[40] Vision in *WandaVision*, episode 9.

[41] That said, I will revisit the point in Ch. 6.

[42] H.L.A. Hart, *Punishment and Responsibility*, 234–235.

in terms of its role in promoting the latter. There is something to be said for this justificatory relationship, but it would be a mistake to put too much weight on it. The justification that results may be—and in this case, I think it would be—impoverished and distorting. The better account, which I will offer in Chapter 7, ties punishment to the idea of owning one's guilt.[43]

5.5 Criminal Wrongs as Public Wrongs

There is one more piece of my basic understanding of the criminal law that I have yet to discuss, which is the idea that criminal wrongs are "public wrongs." There are three meanings one might give that idea: (1) that the wrongs are made wrong by the public process of lawmaking (legality); (2) that the wrongs are the proper business of the state; and (3) that the state has a special kind of concern with the wrongs. I will say something about each.

5.5.1 Legality

Legality is the prohibition on retroactive application of the criminal law. As the Latin saying goes: *nullum crimen sine lege* (no crime without law). This has been authoritatively declared "the first principle of American criminal law jurisprudence."[44] The common rationales for it are surprisingly weak. But I will argue that there is another reason, reflecting the state's essential role in fixing rights and punishments, that does justify a version of it.

Joshua Dressler mentions three common rationales for legality. First, it is supposed to prevent "the 'arbitrary and vindictive use of the law.' "[45] Second, it is supposed to "enhance[] individual autonomy by . . . negating the risk that one's lawful conduct will be punished retroactively."[46] Third, it gives each agent "a fair opportunity to conform her conduct to the law."[47]

The problem with these rationales starts with the reality of massive overcriminalization. Given the degree of overcriminalization that now exists, at least in jurisdictions like the United States, with far too many criminal laws on the books for anyone to possibly be aware of them all, it is easy to run afoul of the law in some minimally (or non-) culpable and unexpected way. The law itself thus opens people up to "arbitrary and vindictive uses of the law."[48] This

[43] See Section 7.1.2.
[44] J. Dressler, *Understanding Criminal Law*, section 5.01[A].
[45] Ibid., ch. 5.01[B] (quoting Rogers v. Tennessee, 532 U.S. 451, 460 (2001)).
[46] Ibid.
[47] Ibid.
[48] See D. Husak, *Overcriminalization*.

fact undermines the second point as well. True, legality means that one cannot be punished on the basis of a law that did not exist when one acted, but one can be punished on the basis of a law that one would only discover existed by being charged with its violation. That is surely just about as bad for one's autonomy, especially if one does not have the time and money to hire a lawyer to do careful legal research before one acts.[49]

Insofar as prosecutors are guided by an ethics of avoiding prosecution when the act is not culpable, that addresses both bases for legality, arguably better than legality itself. Moreover, there is good reason not to be overly scrupulous about the legality principle. Consider the Nuremberg prosecution of Nazis for acts that were legal under German law. As Bernard Meltzer notes:

> Where, as in the case of the Nazi aggression, there has been a grave, deliberate, and flagrant violation of widely accepted standards; where such a violation necessarily involved death and misery for millions, it is more important to condemn and punish such conduct than to follow literally the principle against retroactivity.[50]

The Nazi defendants in those trials had ample reason to believe that what they were doing would be condemned by anyone who took seriously the "widely accepted" moral standards that they flouted. Their prosecution was not arbitrary and vindictive (even if it was in a sense vindictive), nor did they lack autonomy in choosing to commit those crimes, nor did they lack a fair opportunity to avoid criminal punishment.

All that said, there *are* good reasons to hang onto legality as a guiding if not strictly necessary condition for criminal punishment, reasons that reflect the role of the political community in making the law and shaping the space of rights. First, as a matter of substance, many claims would be too contested to count as rights absent the law.[51] And while there are clear cases where we do not need the law to know that a rights violation has been performed, there is a secondary problem of determining how to draw the line in the vast gray area between moral rights that any just state must recognize and those which need to be established by the state.[52] As a matter of principle, then, it makes sense to say that the law has to demarcate what counts as a rights violation and a crime before we can say

[49] Even then, one is not protected if one's lawyer fails to discover some relevant law. See the Model Penal Code, § 2.04 on mistake of law.

[50] "A Note on Some Aspects of the Nuremberg Debate," 458. But see my earlier skepticism about the utility of criminal law in prosecuting Nazi war criminals. See Section 1.1 (discussing the prosecution of Adolf Eichmann).

[51] See Section 3.7.2.

[52] See Section 3.7.2.

that one acted wrongly and culpably and deserves punishment. The alternative would certainly invite drawing the line in the wrong place.

Second, even if a right is clear enough without the state having to recognize it in the law, the proper punishment requires the state to have set a schedule of punishment. A schedule of punishment is how a state can put flesh on the bones of ordinal proportionality and a vague sense of anchoring.[53] In a narrow sense, that does not require the state to adopt the legality principle. It could take a newly recognized crime and retroactively assign a level of punishment to it that fits it reasonably into the existing schedule of punishments. And as for those who rely on a punishment being only so large when they decide to commit a crime, we could say that the only thing they can really rely on is that the punishment will not be disproportionate. Even so, in a broader sense, the state needs to adopt a schedule of punishments before any punishment can count as proportional. Thus, the wrong has to be publicly recognized and fit into an existing legal scheme of punishment before its breach is fit for criminal punishment.[54]

5.5.2 Wrongs that Are the Proper Business of the State

Not all culpable wrongdoing should be criminalized. For example, few today would argue that a liberal society could properly criminalize adultery or betrayal of a friend. But many would take at least one of those to be presumptively morally wrong. Granted, most *liberals* in a liberal society would suggest that marital infidelity is sometimes morally justifiable, all things considered. And many would accept that there are extenuating circumstances that can justify betraying a friend. But a good liberal, in the political sense of the word, *could* reasonably hold that that these activities are at least presumptively immoral, and yet not want to criminalize them, not even with generous defenses available. The question is: if one thinks they are presumptively immoral, then why not criminalize them?

Criminalization is a big topic, beyond the scope of this book. But I offer two contrasting views and endorse one of them. The first view is Michael Moore's view that there is "*a* reason" for the law to criminalize, and for the state to punish, any moral wrong.[55] This does not mean that, all things considered, the law should criminalize, and the state should punish every moral wrong. Moore thinks there often are defeating reasons not to do so. One set of defeating reasons is that "the small good of punishing minor wrongs could be outweighed by other goods

[53] See Section 8.2.
[54] This is related to the ban on ex post facto laws. See Section 15.4.
[55] "Liberty's Constraints on What Should be Made Criminal," 199–200.

achieved by not punishing such minor wrongs."[56] There are many different ways that could be true, but here's a paradigmatic kind of reason: enforcement costs.

> These enforcement/punishment costs include not just dollars and the opportunity costs such dollars represent, but also privacy costs. These will predictably vary somewhat across different kinds of actions. Actions that are typically done with no non-participant witnesses—victimless crimes, crimes done in secrecy—will incur greater such enforcement costs. Sexual behaviors form prime examples, of course, if any of those actions were to be regarded as even somewhat immoral to start with.[57]

There are other reasons as well, such as that some wrongful actions are manifestations of constitutionally protected liberties, like free speech. The point is that these are countervailing reasons that defeat the basic assumption that wrongdoing, *all* wrongdoing, is pro tanto criminalizable.

The second view is Duff's view that certain wrongs are not "the polity's business,"[58] whereas other wrongs are. Acts like "betrayal of a friend's confidence" fall "within a realm of private conduct"; they "do not fall to be judged as either right or wrong by the polity at all."[59] That's not to say that people *in* the polity cannot judge such acts as right or wrong; it's to say that concern with such private affairs falls outside the public realm.

Importantly, there's another dimension to proper criminalization on Duff's view: even if a wrong is in the public realm, it has to be significant enough to warrant imposing the burden of a criminal conviction on the wrongdoer. Some wrongs, like speeding only a bit over the speed limit, or tossing trash on the ground, are public but also petty enough that it would be more fitting for the state to impose a civil penalty (not to be confused with a penal law penalty) rather than a criminal conviction.[60] But these are independent notions—a wrong can be public and petty, public and substantial, private and petty, or private and substantial—and the main distinction I am concerned with here is publicity of the wrong, not its magnitude.

It would be helpful if Duff could provide a straightforward account of what belongs in the public realm and what does not. But he does not and insists that he cannot. Instead, he offers this "thin" principle: "A type of conduct constitutes a public wrong if, and only if, it violates a polity's civil order."[61] The point in

[56] Ibid., 200.
[57] Ibid., 203.
[58] *The Realm of Criminal Law*, 79.
[59] Ibid., 100.
[60] See *The Realm of Criminal Law*, 284–286.
[61] Ibid., 232, 275.

being so thin or vague is that there are many things that a liberal polity could care about, and he argues at length that it's not possible to define what should be on that list in simple, reductive terms. We can say certain things without a doubt. For example, if someone commits a malum in se crime such as rape or murder, "the substantive wrong he commits [is] against his victim," but what makes it a crime is "that that wrong violates the polity's civil order."[62] Or, as he puts it elsewhere, "[W]e ought to criminalize certain types of wrong because we ought (as a matter of justice, or what we owe to each other as citizens) to respond to such wrongs by formally declaring them to be (public) wrongs."[63] Other things too, such as failing to respect reasonable regulations, can be public wrongs.[64] But not everything is properly a concern of the state. There is an important set of private decisions in a liberal society. Even some actions that violate the rights of others—such as marital infidelity—are arguably better viewed as private affairs than affairs of state concern. The reasons for setting a matter off as a private affair may match the sorts of reasons Moore discusses. But rather than saying, as Moore does, that the reason to criminalize such conduct is outweighed, Duff holds that there is simply no reason to criminalize such conduct once it is determined to be in the private sphere, or not relevant to the polity.

One might think this is a distinction without a difference. But it matters in terms of how we think about what the criminal law is fundamentally up to. For Moore, there's no deep difference between private punishment and state punishment. Both are just meting out retributive justice. That's not to say that there are *no* differences. For Lockean sorts of reasons, to ensure that the weak benefit from criminal justice as well as the strong, and to avoid bias in their own cases, people should transfer their right to punish, at least in serious ways, to the state. States also have other duties that they have to weigh against the importance of punishing. In addition, states have to respect constitutional rights in ways that individuals don't. But fundamentally, it's the same activity, done to achieve retributive justice, only done by different sorts of agents operating in different contexts.

For Duff, and for me, that's an impoverished view of the nature of the state. The state is not just another agent. A just state is the representative of a political community that did what political communities are obliged to do: establish just laws to make rights determinate and then use the laws to protect the members of the community.[65] There's a sense in which state punishment is like private punishment. Private individuals and non-state entities like churches, families, and companies can also punish for wrongs that are relevant to them. But state

[62] Ibid., 275.
[63] Ibid., 252.
[64] Ibid., 313–332.
[65] See Section 3.7.2.

punishment is grounded on the idea of calling wrongdoers to account for wrongs in which the state has a distinctive interest: public wrongs. It calls wrongdoers to *public* account.[66]

One might object that this notion of a community's censure is inconsistent with punishment of criminal acts performed outside the community. For the most extreme case, consider the idea of universal jurisdiction over crimes such as trading in enslaved people, crimes against humanity, torture, and acts of terrorism.[67] If state A wants to prosecute someone from state B for committing one of those crimes in state B, against citizens of state B, can it do so? Duff denies that it can, writing that we cannot "be held criminally (as distinct from morally) answerable to 'humanity' for any wrongs, however serious."[68] But I think that Duff mistakes what is at issue here. It is not beyond the pale for state A to say that its polity is so concerned with these wrongs that it takes a public interest in them. Saying that does not presuppose a universal state. Rather, it presupposes two separate things. First, it presupposes that discrete political communities can legitimately take an interest in what happens to *anyone* if the wrong is sufficiently serious.[69] Second, it presupposes that political communities are the means by which people in certain jurisdictions act as citizens in the republic of rights. It is through states that they make their own rights sufficiently determinate, both locally and in a universal context, and that makes it possible for *all* of us to recognize each other as citizens in the republic of rights. There will be difficult questions of how to deal with the conflict of laws between jurisdictions. But these should not lead us to think that law is completely parochial. Even if it is mostly parochial, it is still grounded in the universal project of governing a universal republic of rights.

The position I just sketched is consistent with the international law on universal jurisdiction, which holds that it applies when there is "universal condemnation of those activities and general interest in cooperating to suppress them, as reflected in widely-accepted international agreements and resolutions of international organizations."[70] State A should presumably defer to state B to prosecute the crimes—that's the "principle of complementarity."[71] But if state B

[66] One might wonder if we are still committed to calling wrongdoers to *public* account, given that punishment is no longer a public affair but tends to be done in private. See A. Davis, *Are Prisons Obsolete*, 40–41. The question conflates the publicity of the *punishment* itself with the publicity of the censure. Few may care when people with few personal connections are punished for common crimes, but the conviction and sentencing are done in public and on the public record.

[67] See J. Cabranes, "Our Imperial Criminal Procedure," 1673–1675.

[68] *The Realm of Criminal Law*, 113. (Duff is here responding to the account provided in M. Renzo, "Responsibility and Answerability in the Criminal Law.")

[69] In Section 10.2, I argue that this interest can ground a punitive response only if those held accountable in that way can also hold the state to account for its injustices. In Section 10.5, I weaken that claim somewhat.

[70] E. Podgor and R. Clark, *Understanding International Criminal Law*, 31.

[71] See Rome Statute of the International Criminal Court, art. 1.

does not rise to the challenge, there is nothing outlandish in state A saying that it is a matter of public concern to its citizens that such crimes are not tolerated anywhere.[72]

5.5.3 The State's Distinct Interest in Public Wrongs

There is yet one more way in which it is important to see the criminal law as responding to public wrongs: namely that it does so in a distinctly public way. I have already emphasized this a number of times, stating, for example, that its censure and punishment is meant to pursue reconciliation between the wrongdoer and the political community. But I want to point out here what a difference this makes for theorizing about the criminal law. There is another prominent approach to the criminal law that rejects this approach. I don't mean to argue that it is simply wrong. But I do want to argue that it is engaged in a different project, one that might seem important only insofar as one fails to understand the state's distinct interest in public wrongs.

The alternative that I have in mind seeks to build the criminal law up from a fundamentally private response to wrongdoing that the state then takes over. The most significant theory of this sort in recent years was Victor Tadros's *The Ends of Harm*.[73] Here's a potted, but I believe essentially accurate, summary of the theory. It starts with the premise that a wrongdoer who attempts to harm another owes her potential victim a substantial sacrifice to try to prevent the threat that she has unleashed from materializing. If the harm has materialized, then her duty changes into the duty to try to make up for it in some way, and one way to do that would be to absorb future threats of a similar magnitude. From there he argues that if wrongdoer A could better protect the victim of wrongdoer B, and vice versa, then they should swap so that better protection is provided. And if we generalize this suitably into a society, then we see that they owe the collection of potential victims protection by serving as deterrents for future harm.

I accept the conclusion of this argument, that wrongdoers owe amends which can be extracted by being forced to serve as a deterrent. But the rest of the picture I reject. There are many small points at which to quibble. One could try to do better, for example, with describing what one owes to one's victim.[74] But I think such corrections focus on the trees and miss the forest. The main point is that Tadros is operating as if there is no fundamentally public interest holding

[72] I return to this theme in Section 10.2.

[73] See especially, ch. 12.

[74] Richard Child, for example, argues that Tadros's mistake is to narrowly stipulate what the wrongdoer owes the victim, rather than "ask what victims can *demand* of wrongdoers." "The Unilateral Authority Theory of Punishment," 201.

wrongdoers accountable and seeking reconciliation between them and the political community. He's operating as if the only basis for criminal law is something like a collection of private wrongs, which, when properly packaged together, ground action of the state to achieve a sort of collective solution to these many private wrongs. That starting point is, I think, unnecessary and misleading.

6
An Account of Blame and Guilt as the Basis for Censure and Punishment

6.1 Blame as a Call for Guilt

I have argued that the criminal law is a blaming institution, that censure is the public expression of blame, and that one defining feature of punishment is that it reinforces censure. It is time now to provide my account of blame. I start with a theory of what it is.[1] In brief, I think of it as a judgment to the effect that it would be fitting for the person blamed to feel guilt. The judgment need not be expressed, and it can concern oneself or another. But in the context of criminal law, it is primarily a matter of expressed blame of another (though a wrongdoer's self-blame is relevant to proper punishment), blame that the state has determined the wrongdoer deserves in virtue of her unexcused wrongdoing.

Blaming someone—in a way that one would defend as appropriate—involves the belief that the following three elements are met, at least if she is still alive and functioning as a moral agent:

1. The agent is a responsible agent who behaved wrongly without a full excuse and should acknowledge as much.
2. She should make reasonable efforts, insofar as it is possible to make them, to try to make amends for her wrongful action.
3. She should suffer a two-pronged sort of psychological pain:
   a) The pain of recognizing that she has wronged others whom she should care about.
   b) The pain of recognizing that she is not as good a person as she should want to be.

[1] Contemporary writing on blame is voluminous. Among the most helpful and illuminating accounts I have read are those by M. Fricker, "What's the Point of Blame?"; A. Carlsson, "Blameworthiness as Deserved Guilt"; and D. Portmore, "A Comprehensive Account of Blame."

Punishment, Penalty, and Incapacitation. Alec Walen, Oxford University Press. © Oxford University Press 2026.
DOI: 10.1093/9780197523124.003.0006

I will now say something about each of these prongs. The first prong reflects the thought that if an agent is either not a responsible agent, or did nothing wrong, or had a full excuse for what she did, then blame is misplaced.[2] It also implies that if she is a responsible agent who did something wrong without a fully exculpating excuse, then she should acknowledge this to herself and to those who blame her and to others who might have reason to care that she recognizes her wrongdoing.

The second prong concerns the duty to make amends. Amends have three components, which vary in the degree to which they can be coercively obtained. The first component is the apology that should accompany a wrongdoer acknowledging her wrongdoing. This helps address the resentment and indignation others might feel. One might think that apologies have value only if freely given, but that is not true.[3] Being willing to offer an apology, even if under pressure, shows a certain willingness to conform to normative expectations. If an agent is determined to reject the charge of wrongdoing, or to avoid giving her accusers the satisfaction of an apology, she might instead choose to suffer the consequences that could be avoided by apologizing. Of course, there's pressure and there's pressure. If she apologizes because of excessive pressure, the wrongness of the pressure would corrupt the value of the apology. In addition, a heartfelt apology is to be preferred to a grudging one.[4] And a mocking apology—one that indicates disdain for the very idea of demanding an apology—should be taken as no apology at all.[5] But a facially sincere (non-mocking), even if grudging, apology normally helps to make amends.

The second component of amends is material aid given to make up for the wrong done. Ideally this would be offered voluntarily. And there are contexts in which, if it is not given voluntarily, it would not count as amends. For example, if A breaks a date with her friend B and disappoints him, she might have a duty to try to make it up to him. But if he pushes for compensation, any compensation he gets might come at the cost of the friendship. But in other contexts, a duty to provide material aid to compensate for a wrong done can be enforced. For example, if A has wrongly destroyed B's property, A would presumably have a duty to try to make B financially whole. If A refuses to carry out that duty voluntarily, a court might force her to do so. This may leave a bitter feeling, possibly in both parties. But their status as people who are treated justly will be improved, mending their

[2] Blame might also be misplaced if the blaming agent lacks the standing to place it. That is an agent-relative disability. What concerns me here are the more general preconditions for blaming. I return to standing in Ch. 10.

[3] See Duff, *Punishment, Communication, and Community*, 94–95.

[4] I'm indebted to Isaiah Lederman for pointing out that this is, in part, because of the third prong of blame: the *feelings* of guilt.

[5] See C. Fabre, "The Duty to Accept Apologies."

objective relationship as fellow citizens in the republic of rights. This will be important when we turn to explaining the justification for hard treatment.[6]

The third component is self-reflexive: Insofar as the wrongdoer sees that her wrongful act was a manifestation of a character flaw, she should commit to fixing that flaw so that she is less likely to commit such wrongs again. And even if it was an act that seems out of character, triggered by unusual circumstances unlikely to be repeated, the wrongdoer should at least cultivate a new-found awareness of her potential to act wrongly and commit to avoiding such wrongdoing in the future.[7] In one sense, this sort of commitment to mending herself has to be fundamentally voluntary. There is truth in the old joke about psychologists and light bulbs: "How many psychologists does it take to change a light bulb? One: but it really has to want to change." In another sense, however, one can be forced to undergo certain forms of rehabilitation in the form of things like anger management, skills training, and general education. This kind of forced rehabilitation may not work, but it's an open empirical question how often it might, if well designed.[8]

It is important to point out one more thing about amends: they need not be responsive to a concrete harm. Even if others merely feel offended by a wrong, the wrongdoer should seek to mend the hurt feelings (presumably primarily with an apology), should consider whether material compensation might also be called for, and should try to reform herself to avoid such wrongdoing in the future.

The third prong concerns suffering a two-pronged sort of psychological pain.[9] To see why this is an essential part of a conception of blame, imagine that it is missing. Consider this case:

> *Bike Theft*: Sabine notices that her neighbor [Ted] leaves his expensive bicycle unlocked on his porch when he returns home from school. When he is fast asleep at night, she sneaks onto his porch, steals his bike, and sells it. . . On a purely prudential calculus, she increases her expected utility by taking the bike.

[6] See Section 7.1.2.

[7] There is a limit to how perfectly an agent should want to mold herself. Agents should want to retain a level of passion and spontaneity, and that might sometimes lead them to behaving badly. See generally S. Wolf, "Moral Saints." If any changes to her character would be for the worse, then she should not embrace this aspect of amends, and she should not feel the second prong of guilty feelings. She should only apologize and make material amends.

[8] It is conceivable that reform could be more effective if provided in the form of brainwashing of some sort. But it is unclear how well that works in practice. More importantly, it's clearly inconsistent with respect for autonomy. For a compelling account of the ethical horrors of forced reform, see S. Kubrick's *A Clockwork Orange*.

[9] For recognition of both prongs, see H. Morris, "Guilt and Suffering," 426–427. Dana Nelkin offers a good survey of others who connect blame and guilt (Hilary Bok, Randolph Clarke, Agnieszka Jaworska, and Michael McKenna), but all of them focus only on the first of these prongs: the pain of wronging those one cares about. "Guilt, Grief, and the Good," 177–180. This is a significant oversight, as I explain in the text below.

Nonetheless, she recognizes the existence of moral reasons against her act of theft, and knows these reasons outweigh her prudential reasons to steal. But she takes the bike anyway. No excuse (e.g., duress) or justification (e.g., necessity) applies to her behavior.[10]

Now imagine that the response to her was to say this and no more: (a) that she behaved wrongly, without excuse; (b) that she should acknowledge this fact; and (c) that she should make amends by (i) apologizing to Ted, (ii) compensating him for the loss of his bike, and (iii) reforming herself, seeking to cabin her greed so that she does not steal again. What is missing is the thought that she should feel bad about what she did to Ted and that she should feel, in some way, bad about herself. It is at least consistent with these three claims that she should, instead, simply look to what she needs to do going forward to make amends and to be a better person. If someone said that this was the way to approach Sabine, I would say that she was telling me not to blame her.[11] In other words, this essentially forward-looking response to Sabine—one that does not direct her to dwell in any way on what happened—is not a blaming response.[12]

Note that the feeling prong is essential *only* for the person who is blamed, not for those who blame her. In this way, my account is distinctly *not* a Strawsonian account. It does not take reactive attitudes like anger, resentment, or indignation to be fundamental.[13] These emotions seem to bring with them the desire that the other suffer, but I think it is a mistake to take the emotional desire for suffering to be fundamental to blame.[14] I think we can say that it is normally fitting to feel these emotions when one believes another is blameworthy and has not owned her guilt by doing and feeling what a guilty person should do and feel.[15] But it is the judgment, not the emotional reaction, that should be normatively fundamental.[16] Moreover, the emotions are not essential to making that judgment.

[10] This is Doug Husak's example of a paradigmatically blameworthy act. *Ignorance of Law*, 148.

[11] It would be different if they insisted that Sabine say she is "sorry" and mean it. In that case, they'd be insisting that she have the right feelings.

[12] In support of this, see J. Prinz and S. Nichols, "Moral Emotions," 128. I am not saying that feelings are essential to blame; I am saying only that blame involves the thought that the wrongdoer *should* feel guilt, in both of its dimensions.

[13] See P. Strawson, "Freedom and Resentment." To reject this aspect of the Strawsonian project is not to reject the significance of the distinction between the participant and the objective attitude. See ibid., 9. One does not have to take an objective attitude to avoid feeling reactive attitudes.

[14] Strawsonian scholars such as Michael McKenna go wrong, I think, in exactly this way, seeking to explain why harming or inducing suffering in the blameworthy is intrinsically good. See, e.g., *Conversation and Responsibility*, esp. ch. 6.

[15] I return to that theme in Section 7.3.

[16] One source of appeal for Strawsonian accounts of blame is their naturalism and their apparent ability to respond to the threat from determinism. For a recent attempt to unpack that appeal, see P. Hieronymi, *Freedom, Resentment, and the Metaphysics of Morals*. For a convincing critique that Hieronymi's reconstruction fails, see P. Russell, "Responsibility Skepticism and Strawson's Naturalism."

Other-directed blame can be, and in the context of judges censuring wrongdoers arguably *should* be, emotionally cool.[17]

One might think that the Strawsonian focus on reactive attitudes is important because it helps us distinguish between merely judging another blame-*worthy* and actually blaming another. That is, one might think that what it means for A to withhold blame of B whom she judges blameworthy is for A not to have any blaming reactive attitudes toward B.[18] I don't think that's correct. If A normally has reactive attitudes when she blames, her not feeling them toward B in a particular case may be a reliable indication that she does not blame B. But her emotional non-reaction is not constitutive of her not blaming B. Rather, I think two other things can better explain what we mean when we say that A judges B to be blameworthy but does not blame him. First, she may be thinking about blame as something to be communicated, and she thinks that there are reasons why communication of blame would be inappropriate. Second, she may forgive B. I return to forgiveness in Section 6.5; for here, I'll just say that it has more to do with judgments about amends than reactive attitudes.

Having explained why I am not a Strawsonian about blame, I now offer two advantages of my account. First, it helps to explain why a certain sort of suffering is normatively appropriate. That, in turn, helps to explain why retributivists who seek to inflict suffering on unexcused wrongdoers are not altogether confused. I think they are confused insofar as they think that it is valuable for unexcused wrongdoers to suffer in some unqualified way,[19] and insofar as they think punishment should be used to *inflict* suffering.[20] But they are right to think that there is a sense in which wrongdoers should suffer. If a wrongdoer behaves wrongly toward others, it would be fitting for her to experience a sort of sympathetic suffering.[21] She would have no real attachment to others, no human appreciation for their moral and personal worth, if she didn't feel badly when thinking about how her wrongs have harmed, offended, or at least demeaned them.[22] And if

[17] See Lacey and Pickard, "To Blame or to Forgive?" (contrasting "detached blame" and "affective blame"). One might wonder if the right position for judges isn't some sort of cool-emotional form of blame, like disappointment. Daniel Telech and Leora Dahan Katz argue for recognizing "reactive disappointment" as a form of blame. See "Condemnatory Disappointment." But there are two reasons to reject the idea that this emotion is what judges should show. First, according to Telech and Dahan Katz, reactive disappointment is distinct from reactive anger/indignation/resentment because disappointment presupposes a special relationship based on shared values, whereas anger and its cousins respond to expectations grounded in thinner but more universal moral norms (rights and duties). Judges, however, need not share any such special relationship with those they censure. Second, it is simply not clear that judges need to feel or express *any* emotion; they need to express a *judgment*. This is not a criticism of Telech and Dahan Katz; it's a criticism of a potential application of their account of detached blame to the role of judging.

[18] See G. Watson, "Two Faces of Responsibility," 238.

[19] See Section 5.4.

[20] See Section 7.1.1.

[21] In this way, guilt is like grief. See Section 5.4.

[22] This is the position psychopaths are in. For more on that, see Section 19.6.

she sees that she not only wronged another, but did so out of a character defect, then she should feel badly about herself as well.[23] Any healthy moral agent feels some love for herself and wants to be a good person. Realizing that she not only wronged another but did so out of some personal fault hurts that love of self.[24] Neither basis for suffering is instrumental; rather, they are both natural and proper reflections of caring about others and herself.

One might think this "advantage" is actually the basis for an objection, namely, that my account embraces a peculiar asymmetry between the first-person and the second- or third-person point of view. If guilty *feelings* are essential for an agent to own her guilt, why aren't they likewise essential to properly registering the attitude of blame?[25] One might think that if an agent thinks about those who have been wronged, she should be indignant on their behalf, and she should *feel* a certain blame-based anger at the person who wronged them. Failing to have those feelings, one might think, would likewise reflect a failure to appreciate the moral worth of victims and the moral responsibility of victimizers.

My response to this objection is that it overlooks the moral significance of personal relationships. An agent who has wronged others has thereby formed a relationship with them; she owes them amends. And, of course, she has a unique relationship to herself. A second-person criticism—*you* wronged someone—seems to imply some sort of relationship. But it could be a fairly formal one, like that of a judge and a defendant. There is no reason to think a judge need have *feelings* about each defendant he censures and punishes. Likewise, when passing a third-person judgment—she wronged someone—the judgment of blame need not be tinged with emotion. It might be. But emotion is expensive, and there are too many wrongdoers and too many victims in the world to feel it in all cases. This is a practical point: the economy of emotion calls for allowing the judgment of blame without emotion for second- and third-person blaming. But when dealing with the special relationships a wrongdoer has to her victims and herself, there is no reason to cut her slack; she should have the feelings of guilt, at least sometimes.

The second advantage of my account highlights how the self-directed feeling helps to explain how excuses work. To see this, consider what an excuse does, and does not, allow an agent to say to herself. If she says to herself, "It wasn't my fault," that should not free her from the conclusion that the act was wrong, that she should try to prevent herself from acting that way again, that she should make amends to anyone who was harmed, or that she should feel badly that she harmed others. All but the first of these elements may be modified somewhat by

[23] This is more than the kind of agent-regret Bernard Williams had in mind. *Moral Luck*, 27–30.

[24] This self-reflected pain should not be confused with shame, which concerns how one feels one is viewed by others. For more on shame, see Section 7.3.1.

[25] I'm grateful to Yuan Yuan and Saba Bazargan-Forward for pushing me on this point.

her excuse. She may reasonably feel as if the material amends she owes are less if she was excused—perhaps then the burden can be shared.[26] She may properly feel a different level of sorrow when she says, "I'm sorry," because now her sorrow concerns only the harm caused, and not her fault. But the last feeling, the self-reflective sorrow, is different; it is the one part that should disappear completely.[27]

6.2 Objection and Reply

One might object that I am mistaking a set of statistically normal reactions for normative reactions. That is, one might object that an agent could be properly committed to showing others the moral respect they deserve without *feeling guilty* if he happens to wrong them. One might then embrace what I said would be a non-blaming response to Sabine as the best one: that she should acknowledge that she behaved wrongly, with no excuse, and that she should make amends. And Sabine, one might say, should wish for no more for herself. Guilt is just a negative feeling which she would be better off without if she could follow through on fixing her behavior. As Victor Tadros puts it: "Negative feelings may be an inevitable consequence of [these appropriate judgments about what is permissible], but that is not to say that they *are* good."[28] Indeed, he thinks "we ought to regret the fact that the world is set up in the way that it is: that one cannot have the appropriate set of judgments about one's wrongdoing and be motivated by those judgments without those negative feelings."[29]

I think there are two reasons to reject Tadros's claim that we should wish for a world in which wrongdoers can simply become better people without having to endure the pain of guilt. First, I think he misdiagnoses where the negative feelings come from. He thinks they come from the "frustration" an agent feels at not being able to turn the clock back to undo the wrong he has done, and "anxiety" about how others will treat him.[30] Without denying that people do often experience these feelings upon realizing that they have wronged others, I think this is a misdiagnosis of the proper source of the suffering of guilt. As I just indicated, I think the proper source is sympathetic pain that a morally well-grounded agent

[26] In the criminal context, there will be *no* amends owed to the state, as amends are owed as a matter of punishment only for *culpable* wrongdoing.

[27] In the same spirit, some things that are called guilt should not be confused with true guilt. Agent-regret and survivor's guilt may both be experienced as guilt. But if an agent did nothing wrong to make it the case that another was harmed, or that she survived while others perished, we might want to convey that only grief is fitting, not guilt.

[28] *The Ends of Harm*, 50.

[29] Ibid. See also D. Nelkin, "Guilt, Grief, and the Good," 180–182 (expressing sympathy with the position Tadros takes).

[30] *The Ends of Harm*, 46–48.

feels for those whom he has wronged and his wounded self-love. While he might wish to do away with frustration at something he cannot change and anxiety about how others will treat him, it is altogether different to wish to do away with the pain that is essential to the experience of guilt.

Second, Tadros's view commits him to the analogous view on grief: "[I]n grief . . . , the fact that the emotion has this painful affective dimension is not something to be celebrated."[31] I think this is simply wrong. If an agent does not feel the pain of grief at the loss of a loved one, he would not *care* about the loved one as a valuable part of his life.[32] It is conceivable that a person could simply turn off his feelings of love, with the accompanying desire for contact, once he learns that the object of his love is lost. But to live that way, as though one can fully appreciate the value of the lost love by being conceptually aware of it, is not to be sought after.[33] It is to live as though what matters is merely awareness of facts and the feeling of happiness, rather than having an emotional connection to others. Real connections are a significant part of a meaningful life. To substitute propositional awareness, complemented by pleasure and the lack of pain, is to live a life with relatively little meaning. And if guilt is about connections to others and self-love, then it would be just as bad for an agent to be able to switch off that negative feeling and simply move forward with awareness of how he behaved wrongly. It would be an indication that he had no real connection to others and no real commitment to being a good person.[34]

In sum, to be a person with the sorts of connections to others that make life meaningful and to live with a proper sense of self-worth, an agent should *feel* guilt when he realizes that he has wronged others or even just acted unjustly. And other-directed blame can be understood as the thought that the other should *feel* such guilt (along with accepting the first two prongs: acknowledging his guilt and making amends).

6.3 Connecting the Basis for Blame to the Agent Blamed

Blame need not be limited to wrongful actions; we can also blame ourselves and others for our moral failings even when they are unchosen reactions to things or people.[35] But blame that has the serious implications of public censure and

[31] Ibid., 49.

[32] That's not to say the people *deserve* to feel grief; it is merely fitting. See Section 5.4.

[33] As Portmore puts it, "one one can come to believe that some painting has great aesthetic value on the basis of someone's testimony. But one doesn't fully appreciate its great aesthetic value unless one is sufficiently awed by its beauty." "Deserving to Suffer," 809.

[34] There may be high-functioning psychopaths who lack these feelings but can govern themselves well enough in society to be treated as members in good standing. I discuss that issue in Section 19.6.

[35] See A. Smith, "Responsibility for Attitudes."

punishment must be reasonably avoidable. This is a minimal fairness consideration, and it implies that criminal censure and punishment must be based on either wrongful choices or, at the very least, actions that the agent ought to have avoided taking, where the circumstances in which the action was taken provided her with reasons to act differently, reasons she could have responded to if only she cared enough to pay attention.[36] Putting it more simply, blame in the criminal context should be reserved for wrongful actions performed by responsible agents acting without a full excuse.

This much is fairly uncontroversial.[37] What is more difficult is explaining the connection between the action we blame an agent for and the agent herself.[38] The common position on the connection is that we blame an agent for a wrongful action when her wrongful action is a manifestation of some bad quality in her will.[39] But it is important to understand the connection in the right way. If we see the "manifesting" point as merely a diagnostic tool, allowing us insight into the deep problem, which is the bad quality of her will, that will undermine the point that we should censure and punish agents only for their actions.

I now unpack that problem in terms of four objections to quality of will theories of blame in the criminal law. First, as Douglas Husak puts it: "If the ultimate basis of responsibility inheres in the will, and the will enjoys this status because it represents the core of who we are as persons, [then] quality of will theories [come] dangerously close to those that ground responsibility in our *character*—in *who* we are."[40] What makes them come "dangerously close" to blaming people for their character is the very thing that makes this sort of account of blame attractive: it allows us to understand why we blame *her*. The problem is that we don't want to blame people simply for *who they are*, at least not with criminal censure and punishment. Those weighty reactions, as I noted above, should be reserved for actions.

Second, deepening the first point: if we conceive of blame as about a person's character, that feeds into a powerful but misguided criticism of retributive justice. Erin Kelly exemplifies this misreading by assuming that retributive punishment

[36] See A. Simester, *Fundamentals of Criminal Law*, 248–250.

[37] The idea of blame for negligence is controversial, but the broader idea, as articulated in the last sentence, is not.

[38] An account that I will not review here is Doug Husak's "reasons responsiveness" account, according to which the paradigmatic reason to blame a person for acting wrongly is that she saw the reason not to do so and did it anyway. See *Ignorance of Law*, 9. This account makes the paradigmatic explanation for blameworthy action weakness of will. But that seems like an excusing condition to me, and I think the account is ultimately incoherent. For that criticism, see my "On Blame and Punishment," § III. Much of this chapter was prefigured in that paper, but much has been changed; I refer the reader to that paper only for my rejection of Husak's proposal.

[39] As Alex Sarch notes in *Criminally Ignorant*, 29, it is embraced not only by him but by, among others, Larry Alexander, Kimberly Ferzan, Victor Tadros, Peter Westen, and Gideon Yaffe.

[40] *Ignorance of Law*, 167.

tracks blameworthiness, which in turn concerns making "a negative evaluation [of] a wrongdoer's personhood, character, or will, in light of her wrongful behavior."[41] Kelly is not wrong to think that this is a common understanding of what retributive justice calls for,[42] and she's not wrong to then object that retributive punishment "brand[s criminal wrongdoers] as bad people who deserve harsh treatment, stigma, and exclusion from normal life in society."[43] That conception of retributive justice is indeed to be rejected as inconsistent with the aim of reconciliation, as discussed in the last chapter.[44] But the problem is not with retributive justice per se; the problem arises from taking censure and punishment to be responsive to judgments of *personhood* or *character* or *quality of will*, because if that is what they are about, then it would be reasonable to think that this sort of branding and exclusion *is* what retributive punishment is committed to. To avoid that conclusion, we need to remember that the judgment of blame is fundamentally about the wrongful action, not the actor—although some connection to the actor has to be made.

Third, insofar as we use actions to get access to a person's quality of will, we rest our judgment on a shaky epistemic foundation. As Antony Duff argues, "one would usually expect more than one such piece of evidence as grounds for an adequately confident inference to its cause" (a character flaw).[45]

Fourth, there is often a mismatch between how bad an agent's will was and the amount of blame the criminal law assigns her.[46] Two people with equally bad wills may commit different crimes, because one has a greater opportunity to manifest her bad will than the other had. Or two people may commit equally grave crimes with different levels of bad will, the differences being hidden (not manifest) because the circumstances allow only so much wronging to be done. Alexander Sarch raises this worry and suggests that the criminal law should handle this potential mismatch by employing a principle of lenity according to which the law takes a person to manifest only as much ill will as is necessary "to explain why a rational and otherwise well-motivated person would do [what she did] in the circumstances as [she] believed them to be."[47] His suggestion accounts for the level of blame the criminal law associates with particular crimes, but it does so on a rather tenuous ground, lenity. If one were not inclined to be

[41] "From Retributive to Restorative Justice," 238.

[42] A. Lee and A. Sarch quote George Gardner to say that "the essence of punishment . . . is the expression of the community's hatred, fear, or contempt for the convict." *The Moral Prerequisites of the Criminal Law*, 28. Note the focus on *the convict*, not the convict's *actions*.

[43] Ibid., 237–238.

[44] As Duff put it in recent writing, blame should be understood as "inclusionary rather than exclusionary." "Communicative Theory," 97.

[45] "Virtue, Vice, and Criminal Liability," 153.

[46] See A. Sarch, *Criminally Ignorant*, 34–39.

[47] Ibid., 51.

lenient, one might think that the right thing for the law to do is to probe more deeply and punish according to the bad quality of will, however it manifested.

The mistake that leads to the threat of a mismatch is in Sarch's framing of the connection between the action and the agent: An agent "is culpable for an action *to the extent* that it manifests insufficient regard (or more simply, disrespect) for the legally protected interests of others or for protected values more generally."[48] This magnitude-focused idea suggests that culpability is simply a function of the degree of insufficient regard. But as I argued in the previous chapter,[49] the extent of culpable wrongdoing is a more complicated function of the magnitude of the wrongdoing and the subjective elements of modern mens rea and degree of malice. The relevance of bad quality of will should be understood, then, in two different ways: (1) as a contribution, but only a contribution, to the magnitude of the culpable wrongdoing, and (2) as an explanation for why we should bother to censure and punish. What is relevant when searching to connect the basis for blame to the person is the second point.

What we do when we look to connect the basis of blame to the person blamed is ask: Why did she behave wrongly? Was it a fault in her (that is, in the quality of her will), or was it because she blamelessly didn't know something relevant, or was under duress, or was extremely provoked, or was, at least at that time, not operating as a responsible person.[50] We blame only when the explanation ties her wrongful action to a fault in the quality of her will. This does not mean that we blame her *for* the quality of her will. Rather, when we can correctly explain her wrongdoing by reference to the quality of her will, we are then in a position to say, rightly, "You should feel guilty, as there was a failure in *you*, in how you value things and/or how you reason about what to do, that explains why you acted wrongly." This explanation explains why she should own her guilt, but it should not be confused with the thought that she should be blamed *for* her bad character.

6.4 How Can Guilt Be a Matter of Public Concern?

I turn now to a substantive challenge that could be raised to the idea that this conception of blame could be relevant to the criminal law: that it is too concerned with people's private, emotional reactions to be a proper concern of a liberal state. Spelling out the worry: if other-directed blame is aimed at communicating the

[48] *Criminally Ignorant*, 28. See also N. Arpaly, "Quality of Will and (Some) Unusual Behavior," 17–18.

[49] Section 5.3.

[50] For a clear statement of the function of moral vice along these lines, see A. Simester, *Fundamentals of Criminal Law*, ch. 11, esp. pages 243 and 261.

appropriateness of guilt, and if guilt is concerned, at least in part, with suffering a two-pronged sort of psychological pain, that seems to be a private matter. Why should the state or the political community care about such a private matter? Indeed, this seems particularly peculiar given that the criminal law doesn't care *why* people act lawfully, it cares only *that* they do.[51] Why shouldn't a liberal state just hold people responsible essentially as tortfeasors if they break the law: As long as they pay their amends, all is good?[52] Or why shouldn't it just want to ensure that they don't commit more crimes in the future? Why be particularly concerned with whether they acted *culpably*, and whether they then own their guilt for that?[53]

The answer, as I have already suggested, is that the criminal law serves as a vehicle by which the state can reinforce the idea that we should aim to relate to each other as people who live together in a mutually respectful political community.[54] As I've said before, the political community acts as the voice of the citizens in the republic of rights.[55] It fleshes out for them a workable space of rights and cares about whether those rights are respected. Insofar as they are not, it cares to reestablish the respect that was breached.

A mutually respectful political community must start by according all who are fully autonomous and accountable the presumption of law abidingness (POLA).[56] If a prosecutor can prove or the defendant admits that he has broken just laws, then the political community can take him to have negated that presumption and demonstrated that he lacked, at least on that occasion, the respect that is a precondition for being a member in good standing of a mutually respectful political community.[57] This alienating act grounds the truth in the notion that the criminal law is concerned with stigma. The traditional thought that punishment itself should stigmatize should be rejected.[58] Stigmatizing, marking as different and defective, is an undeniable and inescapable *effect* of a criminal conviction. But we should not think of that as a *goal* of the criminal law. Rather, we should see a conviction as marking a fact—that a person has culpably committed a public wrong—that should be addressed. The fact itself is stigmatizing,

[51] See H. L. A. Hart, *The Concept of Law*, 112.
[52] For such a view, see J. Bronsther, "The Corrective Justice Theory of Punishment."
[53] See J. Goldberg and B. Zipursky, *Recognizing Wrongs*, 165: "One need not be particularly culpable or blameworthy (if at all) in order to have committed a tort."
[54] See Duff, *Punishment, Communication, and Community*, esp. ch. 2.
[55] See Sections 3.7.2 and 5.1.
[56] See Ch. 4.
[57] Jurisdictional limitations are crucial here. I touch on that in Section 5.5.2.
[58] The idea that criminal convictions should stigmatize is all over criminal law theory. See, e.g., A. Simester, *Fundamentals of Criminal Law*, 292. He there describes "stigmatic crimes" as those for which a "conviction asserts publicly that she is a reprehensible wrongdoer." Note, he does not say the crime is reprehensible; it is the *wrongdoer*. See also, as noted above, E. Kelly, "From Retributive to Restorative Justice," 237–238.

but the purpose of the criminal law's blaming response is ultimately to unwind the objective alienation created by the crime.

Putting it another way, the community and the criminal law should not give up their respect for the wrongdoer as a person with dignity who *is* a member of the political community, but it can blame him to convey the importance of owning his guilt if he is to regain the status of a member in good standing. For it is through owning his guilt that he reestablishes the *mutuality* of respect.[59] The criminal law still need not care about why he obeys the law when he does; but it does have reason to care about whether he cares enough about his failure to obey the law to (a) acknowledge his mistake, (b) make amends, and (c) demonstrate that he cares enough about the community and himself to reestablish trust.

This is a theme on which Duff has written at great length. He does so in the context of explaining how culpability for public wrongs can ground both censure *and* punishment. He writes that "Punishment . . . aims at the goals of *repentance, reform*, and *reconciliation*."[60] In aiming at these three goals, punishment aims to bring to fruition the aims of censure. I'll come back to punishment in the next chapter; here my focus is on these three "r"s as expressing the core aims of censure.

Repentance, Duff notes, is "an aim internal to censure. When we censure others for their wrongdoing, our intention or hope is that they will accept that censure as justified."[61] To do that, a wrongdoer "has to recognize and own [his wrong] . . . not deny it or seek to justify or excuse it."[62] Note that this is just another way of putting the first prong in blame: the agent should come to accept and acknowledge that he "behaved wrongly without adequate excuse."

Reform, Duff writes, is "more precisely a commitment to self-reform [and] is an implication of repentance."[63] This is an implication of the second prong in blame. As I wrote in Section 6.1, the agent should make efforts to try to make up for her wrongful act. Among those efforts, I noted, was committing to addressing herself so that she is less likely to commit such wrongs again.

What about the suffering dimension of guilt? This is fundamentally tied to repentance on Duff's view. It is not enough simply to say: "Yes, I did wrong and am sorry for it."[64] The wrongdoer must "seriously" repent.[65] At this juncture, I think it is best to let Duff's words flow uninterrupted by mine:

[59] Blame is thus offered, in part, for the benefit of the person blamed, as it reinforces his status as a responsible person. For a strictly interpersonal account of this feature of blame, see A. Lichter, "Wrongdoer-Centered Reasons for Blame."

[60] *Punishment, Communication, and Community*, 107.

[61] Ibid.

[62] Ibid.

[63] Ibid., 108.

[64] Ibid., 107.

[65] Ibid.

> Repentance, at least with serious wrongs, cannot of its nature be something that is achieved and finished in a moment, however intense the feelings of guilt might be in that moment. It must go deep with the wrongdoer and must therefore occupy his attention, his thoughts, his emotions, for some considerable time. Someone who claims to have been deeply grieved by the death of a loved one, but who resumes her normal life, thoughts, and feelings after a day, thus belies her claim. Similarly, someone who claims to have repented the serious wrong he did, but who rapidly resumes his normal life and gives that wrong no further thought, thus belies his own claim.[66]

Or, as Duff puts it elsewhere, the wrongdoer "should suffer . . . the pains of remorse."[67]

This brings us back to the question with which I opened this section: Why should a *political* community care about such suffering? It should care because it has a pro tanto duty to seek reconciliation between the wrongdoer and itself. Reconciliation, according to Duff, "is what the repentant wrongdoer seeks with those [he] has wronged—and is what they must seek with [him] if they are still to see [him] as a fellow citizen"[68] (I add, in a way that Duff does not accept: if he is not a fellow *political* citizen, then as a fellow citizen in the republic of rights). This is what I meant to highlight with my claim that it is through feeling (as part of owning) his guilt that a wrongdoer reestablishes the *mutuality* of respect. If he does not engage in *sincere* repentance, the breach of mutual self-respect will remain. That's not to say that the state should continue to punish him until he sincerely repents.[69] It is to say only that the state should care about whether he fully repents.[70]

I want to end this section with three thoughts. First, the emphasis on the guilt being a matter of public concern has another important implication: the forum in which blame takes place should be public. As Duff puts it:

> A criminal trial calls a citizen to answer a charge of wrongdoing. He is called to answer by and to the community whose law he has allegedly broken, for a "public" wrong in which the community is properly interested. . . . Such a procedure makes clear that the wrong allegedly committed is the concern of the whole political community, and makes it clear to both victims and defendants that they are seen and treated as members of that community.[71]

[66] Ibid., 108.
[67] Ibid., 95.
[68] Ibid., 109.
[69] See Section 7.3.1.
[70] See Section 7.3.2.
[71] *Punishment, Communication, and Community*, 72.

That's not to say that all convictions must be the result of a trial; plea bargains can be struck. But they too must be accepted at a public hearing at which the defendant pleads guilty.

The point of contrast here is a kind of communicative blame that is private, between two people, the blamer and the blamee, or even between a small group of people, but not the public as a whole. There is nothing wrong with private individual A blaming private individual B for some wrong B performed, nor is there anything wrong with A conveying to C that B is to blame for some wrong. That's just not what the criminal law is meant to do. It is a *public* sort of blame.[72]

Second, one might worry that this focus on the state emphasizing the importance of guilt, guilt which is not easily absolved, reflects a peculiarly Protestant approach to life. Catholics, by contrast, one might think, believe in guilt, but also in the possibility of shedding guilt through confession, Jesus having taken on our sins for us.[73] Why should the state treat those who have made confession and had their guilt lifted as though they still need to own their guilt?

My answer is that a wrongdoer must "Render to Caesar the things that are Caesar's, and to God the things that are God's."[74] In other words, one may clear one's conscience with God (assuming there is a God), but that does not clear one's conscience with the political community.[75] The political community is not thereby assuming a Protestant view of guilt. It is simply assuming that a culpable wrongdoer must relate to his fellow citizens as equals, people whose standing to blame and thereby seek reconciliation is not to be displaced by his relationship to God.

Third, one might also worry that the political community is epistemically barred from this sort of engagement. Erin Kelly argues that criminal proceedings do not provide the state with the kind of insight into a wrongdoer's circumstances and mind to make a proper judgment of blameworthiness. She concludes that, "skeptical modesty about our ability to make these judgments calls into question appraisals of blameworthiness and desert closely associated with criminal punishment."[76]

This is an important worry, but it is also important not to exaggerate it. There are two reasons why I am less bothered by it than Kelly is. First, I think Kelly's worry is grounded in part in her embrace of a misguided interpretation of the quality of will approach to blame, an approach tied to the thought that blame

[72] This point is relevant to both Ch. 10, which discusses the state's standing to blame, and Ch. 11, which deals with restorative justice, which eschews the idea of state-based blaming.

[73] I write this paragraph with some trepidation, as a non-Catholic. But I am grateful to Kristen Bell for pointing out that I need to address the point.

[74] Mark 12:17.

[75] For a similar view, see M. Schmitz, "Why Do I Still Feel Badly About my Sins After I've Confessed?"

[76] *The Limits of Blame*, 13.

targets a culpable wrongdoer's character. But as I argued in Section 6.3, that is not the right conception of blame for the criminal law. The criminal law should be concerned only with blame for particular actions. For that, the inquiries available in a trial and its aftermath, inquiries into agential competence and aggravating as well as mitigating circumstances, should suffice.

Second, part of Kelly's worry is grounded in the thought that the state is not in a position to know the details of the excuses that could mitigate guilt. But, in my view, there is good reason for the criminal law to presume that a defendant is a morally competent agent, able to rise to the occasion even when the circumstances are challenging: the alternative involves stripping him of the rights that come only with full autonomous competence.[77] This is not to deny that the law is sometimes too reluctant to afford defendants the benefit of morally relevant mitigation. But being somewhat insensitive should not be confused with being fundamentally incompetent.[78] The state has competence enough, I believe, to carry out its pro tanto duty to blame and thereby seek reconciliation.

6.5 Reconciliation and Forgiveness

I close out this chapter with a discussion of what it could mean to achieve reconciliation, recognizing that reconciliation is tied up with the notion of forgiveness. Forgiveness is the act by which those who blame give it up. I argue here for two relevant features of forgiveness. First, I argue that forgiveness normally leaves a residue that has deep implications for the way in which reconciliation can take place. Second, I argue that forgiveness can be given without punishment, but that there are nonetheless good general reasons to punish. Before making those arguments, I start by saying something about forgiveness itself.

6.5.1 The Meaning of Forgiveness

First, forgiveness is not mercy. Mercy, as Nicola Lacey and Hanna Pickard put it, is "exercised necessarily *de haut en bas*" (from on high to those below).[79] It can also be exercised while continuing to blame the person granted mercy; mercy involves only withholding sanctions that are tightly connected to suffering: punishment in the form of hard treatment meant to deter or fines or community

[77] I return to this theme in Section 19.3.

[78] For a different set of responses to Kelly on this point, see D. J. Coates, "Extending the Limits of Blame," 208–211.

[79] "To Blame or to Forgive?" 9.

service meant to materially compensate for the wrong done. Forgiveness is different along both dimensions.

First, an agent need not have power over a wrongdoer to forgive. She only needs to hold some sort of debt.[80] Holding debt, with the power to forgive it, is, admittedly, a *kind* of power over the wrongdoer. But it is not the power to give orders nor to impose sanctions. It is a power only in the thin Hohfeldian sense in which all autonomous citizens in the republic of rights have powers over each other, the power to alter another's first-order claims and duties by taking a range of actions, from giving gifts to making promises to relieving promise makers of their duty to keep their promises made.

Many parties may hold debts incurred by a wrongdoer for a culpable act or set of acts. There may be multiple victims, in the sense of individuals whose interests have been harmed. In addition, the state as the party concerned with the space of rights and the law generally has its own status as a debt holder. Assuming a wrongful action has more than one individual victim, one or more of them may forgive the person who wronged them, and the others will still hold their debt. And even if all individual victims forgive the wrongdoer, the state may nonetheless have reason to punish her. This is not to imply that victim forgiveness should be irrelevant to punishment. Insofar as the state has reason to care about the magnitude of the harm inflicted by wrongdoing when it punishes, it has reason to care about the subjective dimension of the harm inflicted. And insofar as the state should take victims to have the authority to waive the significance of their subjective harm, then the state should take their forgiving a wrongdoer to imply that the state should not count that harm. Thus, victim forgiveness should affect sentencing. But the state retains its status as a debt holder with the power to forgive, or not, the debt owed it in a way that is fundamentally independent of the actions of any individual victims.

Second, forgiveness is not just about withdrawing sanctions; it must come with relinquishing two aspects of blame: the debt collection aspect and the endorsement of reacting attitudes as fitting.[81] To relinquish blame is not to judge that blame was never appropriate; it is to judge that it was appropriate and then to relinquish these two dimensions of it. To appreciate the difference, suppose that A harmed B and B then blamed A for the harm. Suppose that B then realized that A was acting under duress in a way that fully excused her action. It may be tempting to say that B should forgive A. But I think the better thing to say is that

[80] I say that one needs to hold some sort of debt because I think it would be inappropriate for a third party to forgive the wrongdoer. It is not for *them* to forgive, at least not in the first instance.

[81] Not all forgiveness needs be premised on blame; it can be premised simply on having been hurt and having then come to feel resentment. For example, A might forgive a former romantic partner, B, for the pain B caused her in a break up, even if B did no wrong in ending their relationship. In *that* kind of case, only one dimension of forgiveness is in play. My concern here is limited to blaming cases.

B should simply withdraw the blame she directed at A on the grounds that A was not blameworthy in the first place. Forgiveness is a response to acts that an agent believes really are blameworthy.

There are two ways to relinquish blame. One is proactive: even without the guilt-debt having been paid, those to whom it is owed can forgive it and forswear any negative reactive attitudes they may have. Even if they never had any reactive attitudes, this is meaningful as they can come to the judgment that the wrongdoer owes them nothing more by way of amends, and that they no longer care whether she admits to her unexcused wrongdoing, has apologized, sought to reform herself, or feel the pangs of guilt. Often, it's easier, all else equal, to forgive a wrongdoer if she has taken at least some of these steps: For example, she has accepted that she acted wrongly and apologized.[82] But proactive forgiveness does not presuppose that she has taken any of these steps.

The other way to relinquish blame is through a recognition that the debt has been paid. In the fullest sense, this requires the wrongdoer to have not only made amends to those who are to forgive her, but also to have adequately worked on self-reform and had the appropriate feelings of guilt.[83] An agent who has fully owned her guilt and paid her debts might want to say that there is nothing to be forgiven. And in a sense, she would be right. In a simple case of a debtor-creditor relationship, a debt that is paid is not forgiven; it is simply discharged. But in the context of blame, I think things are different for two reasons.

First, even if reactive attitudes are not essential to blame, they do often mark it. The wrongdoer can say that she has paid her debt, but because the guilt makes certain reactive attitudes fitting, more is required of the "creditor" than in a simple financial arrangement. Even if the "creditor" recognizes that the other has owned her guilt and paid her debt, he might still feel a lingering resentment. To forgive in this second sense is to commit to rejecting this lingering resentment as normatively inappropriate.[84] Insofar as an agent feels resentment and does not reject it, I think the fair thing to say is that he has not actually forgiven the person he blamed.[85]

[82] It is not always easier to forgive if another accepts that she acted wrongly and apologizes; unfortunately, sometimes those acts reinforce the victim's sense that he is entitled to claim the status of a victim, making it harder to forgive. Victims should seek to overcome this reaction.

[83] On the connection between wrongdoers feeling guilt and others letting go of resentment or indignation, see B. Dill and S. Darwall, "Moral Psychology as Accountability," 40.

[84] One might have to do the same work if one recognizes that the person one blames was not blameworthy in the first instance. But then the work is not the work of forgiving; it is simply the work of recognizing that one's emotional response was never well grounded.

[85] The impact of forgiveness on third parties who might feel indignation seems to me more complicated. They don't have the right to forgive, but it's not clear if their feelings of indignation ought to follow the lead of those who forgave. Perhaps the best thing to say is that it then becomes an option for them to forgive as well, where their forgiveness is of a secondary nature: not forgiving the debt but agreeing that they should seek to overcome any lingering indignation.

Second, the feelings of the guilty party, which are essential to self-blame, matter too. And they are complicated. While a person may be able to fully make amends, there is no reason to think that the feelings of guilt should be assuaged at the same time. The feeling of sorrow toward others may properly linger even after she has done all she can do or should do to make them whole. And the feeling of sorrow about her own failure may properly linger even after she has made whatever amends were (properly) deemed proportional. Indeed, I will argue that proportional punishment should be capped at a few decades of imprisonment, no matter how heinous the crime.[86] But I also think that it may be appropriate for an agent who has committed a particularly heinous crime to carry a sense of guilt for having done so to her grave.[87] I'm not saying she should be wracked by guilt ever after; I am saying that a certain willingness to own it as hers, to admit that it cannot simply be associated with the failures of a young person long outgrown, is often appropriate. She may forgive herself, concluding that she has made the amends that she should make and owned her wrongdoing as much as she should own it. But the fittingness of some ongoing feelings of guilt imply that self-forgiveness sometimes must remain incomplete.[88]

6.5.2 The Incompleteness of Forgiveness

If what I just wrote about the limits of self-forgiveness is correct, it may set a model for the limits of other-forgiveness as well. Forgiveness from others normally has a long, reluctant tail, and it is important to distinguish its body from its tail. The tail is manifested in the expression: "Fool me once, shame on you; fool me twice, shame on me." After having been wronged, it is natural to remain somewhat distrustful, somewhat wary. If A has broken the trust of B, it is natural for A to want to reach a point where trust is fully restored, as if it had never been broken. And sometimes this happens. But the expression "to forgive and forget" has two parts; sometimes an agent gets only one of the two. Sometimes, she must live with the burden of a certain wariness, a certain change in the baseline trust or mistrust from the other, even though she has been "forgiven."

How can we make sense of this? I think the answer refers to the gap between blame and wariness. An agent's guilt-debt can be fully repaid, and if it is fully repaid, those she wronged should now forgive her, and they should recognize that

[86] See Section 8.5.

[87] In this regard, I agree with Michael Moore, who imagines that he has committed some horrible violent crime and then says that he hopes his response "would be that I would feel guilty unto death." *Placing Blame*, 145.

[88] The model of grief as a slowly shrinking ball in a box that bangs on a pain button as it bounces around seems apt for guilt too. The ball may hit the button less often as it shrinks over time, but when it hits, the pain may be just as intense.

any ongoing resentment they have of her for whatever created that guilt-debt is now inappropriate. The recognition of that transition is the body of forgiveness. But her wrongdoing may still leave others with a lingering wariness or simply a desire to keep more distance than they would normally want to keep. This wariness or distance is different from ongoing blame or resentment. They can recognize that the wrongdoer need do nothing else to make up for the wrong done, and yet they can justifiably feel wary or distant.

This feature of guilt and reconciliation, of forgiveness having a body and a tail, has its place in the criminal justice system as well. Punishment properly responds to the guilt-debt. Wrongdoers should normally be able to "pay their debt to society." At that point the main body of reconciliation should be accomplished. But there may be a lingering wariness that is not an expression of an ongoing guilt-debt. It is just an expression of the fact that the wrong still changed the way the wrongdoer is viewed by the community. She is welcomed back as a member in good standing, but the fact of the wrong is not simply forgotten.

There are two ways that lingering tail can manifest in the law. One is the recidivist premium. If a convicted wrongdoer has done her time, one might think that a subsequent crime should be punished like a first crime. But liberal states don't treat it that way. It is a universally accepted practice that a second punishment may be and often is harsher than the first, all else equal.[89] I think the best defense of this is to say that the second crime's recidivist premium "punishes an ex-offender's omission—the omission being his failure to take steps to prevent himself from committing another crime."[90] Of course, the failure is not itself criminal and it does not itself warrant punishment. It is, however, blameworthy—the wrongdoer should have taken the prior occasion of censure and punishment as a call to have reformed herself.[91] And just as a worse mens rea can justify a harsher punishment, even though attitudes by themselves are no basis for punishment, so this sort of failure can make the wrongful act to which it is attached more blameworthy.[92] Someone who has already been convicted should retain a

[89] "In general, people with prior convictions are treated more harshly in all criminal justice systems, civil and common law." J. Roberts and S. Harrendorf, "Criminal History Enhancements at Sentencing," 261. See also G. Krishnamurthi, "Against the Recidivist Premium," 418: "every jurisdiction in the United States employs the recidivist premium in some way."

[90] Y. Lee, "Recidivism as Omission," 610. For an alternative account, see A. von Hirsch and A. Ashworth, *Proportionate Sentencing*, 148–155. For a skeptical response to this account, see "Criminal History Enhancements at Sentencing," 276–281. For others who are critical of the idea, on the ground that it amounts to double punishment of the original crime see, R. Singer, *Just Deserts*; G. Fletcher, *Rethinking Criminal Law*, 462.

[91] Why not say that the duty of self-reform should extend the sentence for her prior crimes until she has reformed herself? First, that would violate the limits on proportional punishment. See Ch. 8. Second, it is also impossible to tell if she has reformed herself unless the failure to do so manifests in future wrongdoing. Thus, holding her accountable for the failure if she commits a future crime is a better option.

[92] Krishnamurthi raises an interesting question: Suppose someone takes all reasonable steps to prevent herself from re-offending, but then, "in a moment of weakness," reoffends anyway? "Against

heightened awareness of her own tendency to engage in wrongdoing.[93] If it turns out she has not done enough to check that tendency, that failure augments the culpability of further wrongful actions that are tied to it.[94]

The other way this lingering tail can manifest is in the (partial or full) forfeiture of the POLA. This will be further explored in Parts IV and V. For now, I'll say only that I think this sort of forfeiture of the POLA is consistent with the thought that the wrongdoer is no longer being "punished." But at the same time, there is an undeniable tension between saying that the wrongdoer has been forgiven and saying that she has forfeited the POLA in some way even after her punishment is complete. This tension gives us reason to use forfeiture of the POLA sparingly.[95]

6.5.3 Why Punish to Forgive?

Before turning to punishment as a blaming response, I turn to one last issue with regard to forgiveness: Given that it can be done proactively, without requiring repayment of the debt, why require repayment of the debt? Why should the state punish rather than proactively forgive?

There are at least two good reasons for the state to proactively forgive.[96] First, it produces less suffering, at least among wrongdoers, and as I noted above, suffering is normally negative.[97] One might think that if punishment is deserved, then the suffering of punishment must be, like the feeling of guilt, a rare instance in which suffering is intrinsically positive, something to be valued in itself and

the Recidivist Premium," 441–442. He takes this to be a reductio of this defense of the recidivist premium. It could, however, be taken to be an indication that a person deserves to be moved into a different category: that of a non-responsible agent, who cannot control herself and who therefore does not benefit from the POLA. See Ch. 19.

93 Recidivist premiums do more than provide an extra penalty for a second-time wrongdoer; they provide a ladder of higher penalties for each additional conviction, at least until the person has the status of habitual or career offender. Richard Lippke rightly asks what could justify that sort of ladder. See "The Ethics of Recidivist Premiums," 19. I leave it an open question whether the justification in the text could meet that challenge. If not, the practice would presumably need reform.

94 In some countries, if a conviction is sufficiently old, it will not ground a recidivist premium. "Courts in England and Wales, for example, often exercise their discretion to ignore prior convictions when they seem too old... [And in] Germany, criminal records held at the Federal Central Register are deleted after certain periods of time [5 to 20 years, depending on the nature of the crime] without reconviction." J. Roberts and S. Harrendorf, "Criminal History Enhancements at Sentencing," 289. This strikes me as a reasonable accommodation of the thought we gradually become different people from the ones who committed earlier wrongs.

95 See Sections 7.2 and 16.3.1.

96 In addition, if the law (or customary legal practice) is overly punitive, a version of proactive partial forgiveness—what Kristen Bell calls "critical mercy"—may be called for. See her "Critical Mercy in Criminal Law." But I assume in this book that the punishments (and penalties) imposed are proportional and just.

97 See Section 5.4.

not for the goods it might bring about. If that were true, then this would *not* be a good reason to proactively forgive. But I think the only thing we have reason to accept, based on the preceding discussion of guilt, is that the suffering of guilt is inherently positive. The suffering of punishment may be instrumentally valuable, but I see no reason to think it is intrinsically valuable.

Second, it may sometimes help to promote law-abiding, rights-respecting behavior to proactively forgive people. This is true for four reasons. Proactive forgiveness may directly contribute to their mending their ways.[98] On the flip side, punishment may embitter them and make them less prone to own their guilt. It may also expose them to criminogenic conditions. Finally, proactive forgiveness may even set a model for them of how they may forgive others, and that may help them to become more generous, socially constructive people.

That said, I think there are three reasons for the state to think that it is at least often the case that forgiveness should be given only *after* punishment has been meted out. First, and most obviously, forgiving culpable wrongdoers undermines the prospect for deterrence. The degree of deterrence for wrongdoing is correlated with the certainty that hard treatment will be meted out.[99] The more proactive forgiveness is on offer, the harder it will be to achieve deterrence. And that will also undermine that state's ability to convey the message that the law must be respected and that rights are not to be violated.

Second, the idea that the state should simply forgive wrongdoers, without requiring them to own their guilt, may suggest the ideal of magnanimity. The idea is that the state should be the greater party, willing to let debts go, rather than a petty party insisting on the repayment of debts. But this suggests the idea of mercy, rather than simple forgiveness. And mercy reinforces a notion that is problematic for a liberal state, namely that of hierarchy. That notion has the potential to interfere with reconciliation between the political community and the wrongdoer, one in which all are equal in status. This is not to say that proactive forgiveness by the state is always wrong. But the state should be careful to avoid using it in a way that reinforces the sense that mercy is being dispensed.

Third, and relatedly, there is reason to think that proactive forgiveness would make it less likely, in many cases, that wrongdoers would own their guilt, and that that would undermine their capacity to operate as responsible agents who *are* in good standing with the political community. This possibility contradicts

[98] The classic model for this latter effect, at least in Western literature, is Victor Hugo's character of Jean Valjean, who becomes a paragon of a responsible citizen after being forgiven, and even treated generously, by a priest from whom he had stolen. See *Les Misérables*, Book II, ch. 12. See also D. Ariely, *The (Honest) Truth About Dishonesty*, 250–253 (discussing "resetting" or "secular repentance" to increase "moral adherence"). I am aware of the irony that Ariely's reputation has been tainted by charges of dishonesty. See G. Lewis-Kraus, "They Studied Dishonesty. Was their Work a Lie?" Nonetheless, this claim remains, I think, at least plausible.

[99] See D. Nagin, "Deterrence in the Twenty-First Century," 201.

the second reason in favor of proactive forgiveness. But it seems likely to me that some people would respond better to proactive forgiveness, and some would respond better to being punished first. I lack the empirical expertise to know who falls into which category, and I'm not sure that anyone has the relevant expertise. But if a substantial number of people would be more likely to own their guilt if they are first held accountable, as opposed to being proactively forgiven, then there is a reason to retain the institutions of accountability and to try to use them in the cases where they seem likely to work better than proactive forgiveness. This is not to say that punishment is the best means of holding wrongdoers accountable.[100] My point here is only that proactive forgiveness by the political community may make it less likely that wrongdoers will own their guilt and operate as responsible fellow citizens in the republic of rights.

One might object that this idea that *holding* people responsible will make them more responsible for themselves is just confused nonsense. Their agency is not engaged in *being punished*, so how can it help them to become more responsible agents? My answer is that even if the material amends are taken from them involuntarily, they will nonetheless have paid what they were required to pay. If they can come to own that as normatively appropriate, then they will have made progress in understanding what responsible agency requires of them. In addition, if they can own their guilt, then that should affect the way they are punished. This distinction between those wrongdoers who own their guilt and those who do not is central to my discussion of how a practice of punishment should respond to wrongdoers, which is the topic of the next chapter.

[100] See Ch. 11, where I discuss restorative justice, which is arguably better at holding people accountable and getting them to own their guilt.

7
A Theory of Punishment as a Blaming Response to Culpable Wrongdoing

7.1 From Blame to Punishment

7.1.1 Punishment is Not a Tool by Which to Inflict Guilt

Before saying anything positive about the connection between blame and punishment, I want to be clear that punishment should not be thought of primarily as a tool by which to create guilty feelings and thereby inflict guilt. Those who support state punishment can hope that it will foster having such feelings. And it's crucial to ensure that punishment does not excessively interfere with having such feelings. But the aim of punishment cannot be to *cause* guilty feelings.

We can imagine, in a science fiction way, forms of treatment that would simply induce guilty feelings. But we want people to come to those feelings because they recognize the truth that undergirds them. It might be possible, again in a science fiction way, to induce not just feelings of guilt but a "recognition" that it is appropriate. But if that recognition is induced artificially, from the outside, it would be a deep violation of their autonomy, and hence of their dignity. The only dignity-respecting way to bring people to own their guilt is by presenting them with reasons or opportunities to see the reasons that have already been there for them to see. Thus, the connection between punishment and an agent owning his guilt has to be at best one of hopefully fostering guilt ownership and at worse not being too much of an obstacle to guilt ownership; it cannot be using punishment as a tool by which to instill it.

7.1.2 How Punishment Responds to Blameworthiness

Joel Feinberg famously framed punishment as "a conventional device for the expression of attitudes of resentment and indignation, and of judgments of disapproval and reprobation."[1] As Antony Duff puts it, "We can more forcefully

[1] "The Expressive Function of Punishment," 400.

Punishment, Penalty, and Incapacitation. Alec Walen, Oxford University Press. © Oxford University Press 2026.
DOI: 10.1093/9780197523124.003.0007

communicate censure by giving it such material expression."[2] That is the first reason to move from mere words of censure to punishment. But as Duff also notes, this reason does not do much to answer the question: "Why *should* we communicate the censure in this way, rather than merely by some formal public declaration . . . or by some purely symbolic punishment?"[3]

Duff has something else to offer, however. He claims that repentance "must go deep with the wrongdoer and must therefore occupy his attention, his thoughts, his emotions, for some considerable time."[4] To ensure that, Duff claims that censure must also, at least for serious crimes, be accompanied by "hard treatment" which aims to "focus [the wrongdoer's] attention on his crime."[5] This may seem redundant if the wrongdoer has already fully and *deeply* repented, as some will have done. But Duff responds that even in those cases there is value in submitting to the punishment rather than protesting or seeking to escape it. Enduring the hard treatment that proportionately symbolizes the crime's magnitude is a way for the wrongdoer to "make clear to the victim and to the community as a whole that [he] really does repent [his] crime."[6]

Duff's supplemental answer gives the state a second reason to *punish*. But it too leaves us with an incomplete account. There are two reasons it remains incomplete. First, it is unclear that the goal of providing hard treatment sufficient to "focus [the wrongdoer's] attention on his crime" could justify a sentence of any substantial length. A few months (or maybe even just weeks) in prison would suffice to cause most people—at least those who have not yet been seriously punished—to think seriously about what they have done. And if a few weeks or months will not suffice, then it seems likely that insight won't come, if it ever comes, until they have slowly matured out of a combative approach to dealing with others. Proportionality might cap what can be done to the unrepentant, but it is not clear that time for repentance provides a sufficient reason to impose proportionately large punishments on most wrongdoers.

Second, the idea that a repentant wrongdoer should accept a long punishment as a way of reassuring others of the sincerity of his repentance seems flawed. Yes, he might choose not to protest or escape, but that need not convey to others repentance so much as his discomfort with protesting or his reluctance to be caught and punished even more for an escape.[7] And insofar as he thinks his punishment is excessive or unjustified, he may be fully repentant and yet take himself to be entitled to protest the punishment or seek to escape it.

[2] *Punishment, Communication, and Community*, 107.

[3] Ibid.

[4] Ibid., 108.

[5] Ibid.

[6] Ibid., 121.

[7] For a similar thought, emphasizing the importance of voluntary submission to punishment if it is to convey repentance, see V. Tadros, *The Ends of Harm*, 101.

I don't want to dismiss Duff's explanation of the moral significance of punishment. I insist only that it is an incomplete account, one that explains only why a certain minimum of hard treatment might be thought important in some cases.

A similar but distinct and complementary reason for hard treatment refers to the fact that someone who owns his guilt is not happy about his wrongdoing; he regrets it; he feels sorrow on account of it (hence "I'm sorry"). Conversely, being content or happy about having engaged in wrongdoing is positively antithetical to guilt. Punishment can respond to this fact by seeking to ensure that wrongdoers do not feel happy or content to have committed their wrongs. Hard treatment may not tend to foster a sense of guilt, but it nonetheless has some relevance to the broader political community. A wrongdoer's happiness about his guilt is a kind of rebuke to the political community. The community has an interest in rejecting this rebuke. Hard treatment can be understood to target this sort of morally offensive happiness.[8]

Of course, many people who commit crimes are perfectly miserable. They are often poor, socially marginalized, addicted to drugs, and driven to crime by economic reasons. Insofar as they are miserable, this third reason for hard treatment does not kick in. The mere fact that they find crime "pays," in the sense that they take themselves to have reason to engage in it, does not mean that they experience morally offensive happiness. But insofar as they take satisfaction in having committed a crime—perhaps because it gave them a sense of power, even if immorally taken at the expense of others—this third reason has relevance even if they are generally among life's less fortunate.[9]

I think this third reason plays a substantial role in the retributive intuition that wrongdoers deserve to be punished. I think the idea of "acting with impunity" is particularly offensive when one thinks about wrongdoers who feel good about the crimes they have committed. The retributive emotions of resentment and indignation seem particularly responsive to this sort of offensive happiness. And they can be seen as reflecting the morally sound judgment that the state has a reason to strip the wrongdoer of this morally offensive happiness.[10]

[8] I here retract my claim that retributive justice is not concerned with whether wrongdoers live happily. See "Retributive Justice," § 4.3.2.

[9] What should we say about a wrongdoer who is not happy about his wrongdoing per se, but seems generally content? This is an issue Victor Tadros raised when proposing the case of "Hitler's Island: Although Hitler appeared dead at the end of WWII, he in fact escaped and lived the remainder of his life in isolation on a desert island. He never came to recognise that he had acted wrongly." "Responses," 256. Tadros thinks that "Hitler's life was already going disastrously." Ibid., 259. There is therefore no reason to wish that it go any worse. My view is that the objective failures of his life are not all that matter; if he's generally content, then we can presume that some of that contentment reflects at least indifference to the incredible harms he caused. That is morally offensive contentment. Punishment can justifiably be aimed at least in part at undermining that contentment.

[10] It is well known that admitting guilt can *also* induce feelings of resentment and indignation. But this is caused, I believe, by confirmation of the belief that the wrongdoer was indeed blameworthy. That epistemic phenomenon should be distinguished from the moral reaction caused when someone seems to be "getting away with it."

I am not saying here that suffering, outside of the suffering of guilt, is intrinsically valuable.[11] And I am not saying that inflicting suffering that may "wipe the smile off the face" of wrongdoers is strongly correlated with making them feel guilty. I am suggesting only that the suffering that can be induced by hard treatment can be instrumentally valuable as a tool to prevent morally offensive happiness, and that morally offensive happiness is itself an obstacle to reconciliation.

But this reason too leaves us with an incomplete picture of the justification for punishment, as it does not apply to those who are already regretful. Moreover, it might seem to be, ultimately, a secondary, if not a petty, reason for action. But there is a fourth reason that I think completes the justification: the capacity of punishment to extract the material amends that the wrongdoer owes as part of his guilt-debt.[12]

The most obvious way to make material amends is through community service or fines. As Michael Tonry writes: "Both fines and community service are in principle ideal community punishments . . . . Both can easily be scaled in proportion to the seriousness of the crimes for which they are imposed."[13] Neither need to be particularly onerous; they don't have to be "hard treatment." Rather, they can both be used to make amends in the sense of providing material benefits to the community. As a matter of fact, community punishment typically serves multiple purposes. As the U.K. Sentencing Council puts it: "Community orders can fulfil all of the purposes of sentencing. In particular, they can have the effect of restricting the offender's liberty while providing punishment in the community, rehabilitation for the offender, and/or ensuring that the offender engages in reparative activities."[14] My point is only that community service has the potential to make amends in a direct, material way.

Another way convicted wrongdoers can make material amends, however, is by enduring hard treatment that can be expected to deter future potential criminals.[15] By serving as a means of deterring crime (and reinforcing norms, more generally), wrongdoers help the community reduce the incidence of crime, and that help serves to "pay their debt."

These are complementary possibilities. A wrongdoer may owe one quantum of money or time in community service to compensate for the wrong he has done, and another quantum of money or time in either community service or prison to make his punishment sufficiently onerous that it serves as a deterrent for future potential wrongdoers. Providing material compensation and serving as a means of deterrence can both help make amends for the

[11] See Section 6.5.3.
[12] See Section 6.1.
[13] "Community Punishments," 201.
[14] "Imposition of Community and Custodial Sentences."
[15] For a similar thought, see Tadros, *The Ends of Harm*, 283.

wrong. Insofar as punishment comprises both, however, they ought not to be combined in a way that is disproportionately burdensome, given the culpability of the wrongdoer.

The idea of using both might suggest that wealthy people should be able to provide sufficient material benefits to the political community to buy their way out of hard treatment. But there are two reasons why I reject that suggestion. First, insofar as deterrence is important, it is also important to signal that criminal acts do not merely have a price. Rather, they are *not to be done*. Allowing the rich to buy off hard treatment would undermine that idea. Second, even if the price could be adjusted to a wrongdoer's wealth level, so that the fine would be something that a rich person would normally not want to incur, there's an equity problem in allowing the rich to pick a preferred mode of paying their debt, while the poor simply have to endure hard treatment such as imprisonment. That's not to say that fines cannot be used in some cases to help make a community that has been wronged whole (even if only by helping to pay for the criminal justice system's costs or the costs of helping any victims that might have suffered from the wrong done). Nor is it to suggest that fines should not be tailored to wealth. It is only to suggest that when crimes are serious, and deterrence becomes a significant concern, then the rich should have to face the same hard treatment as the poor.

In sum, as noted in Chapter 1: punishment, understood as hard treatment, plays four complementary roles as a blaming institution: (1) reinforcing censure; (2) providing an occasion for a wrongdoer to engage in serious reflection about his guilt; (3) helping to ensure that he is not happy about his wrongdoing; and (4) collecting the amends that he owes in the form of contribution to deterrence.[16] All of these help explain how punishment as hard treatment can be deserved in virtue of an agent's culpable wrongdoing.[17] They help to reconcile him with the political community. This is not just a good effect that the state might want to achieve; it is the state's pro tanto duty to perform.[18]

7.2 The Role of Utilitarian Features of Punishment

Deterrence is one of the four possible goals of hard treatment, but it is important to highlight that my account of the role of deterrence is different from the

[16] Section 1.3.3. I dropped here the reference to material compensation, which need not be hard treatment.

[17] For minor crimes, hard treatment may be disproportionate; censure plus amends in the form of material compensation, or perhaps censure alone, may be all that is called for. But for serious crimes, a proportional amount of hard treatment may be deserved.

[18] I return to the theme of punishment being deserved in Section 7.4 below.

standard utilitarian account.[19] It's not that hard treatment is justified directly by its deterrent function. Rather, punishment in the form of hard treatment is a way in which the political community can extract the guilt-debt the wrongdoer owes in terms of his duty to make amends. Hard treatment that uses another for some social good would normally be inconsistent with the dignity-respecting model (DR Model).[20] But insofar as it extracts a debt already owed, it is consistent with the DR Model.

One might wonder whether the state can justify using individuals to deter crime when in almost all cases letting an individual go will do nothing to affect overall deterrence. The answer is that what must be justified is a practice. Ceasing to punish, in general, would certainly undermine deterrence. The justification for punishing each individual is then that each person with a guilt-debt can be expected to contribute her share to making the practice work.

One might also wonder whether something similar can be said for the other classic utilitarian justifications for punishment: rehabilitation and incapacitation. I start with rehabilitation. Should the state *punish* a wrongdoer with the aim of making it more likely that she is thereby reformed? The answer is yes, it may do so based on her guilt-based duty to engage in self-reform. People are often poor judges of their own capacity to reform themselves. Insofar as a wrongdoer has a duty to reform herself as part of her duty to make amends, the state could require her to undergo certain kinds of training programs, especially those that might help her deal with problems that might lead her back onto the criminal path. For example, if she has a history of drug or alcohol abuse, then it might make sense to require her to attend addiction counseling; if she has a problem with anger, then it might make sense to require her to attend anger-management counseling; and insofar as she lacks the skills necessary to obtain a steady job, it might make sense to require her to attend an educational program that aims to provide her with a marketable skill.[21] The point is not to force these things upon her simply to make her less of a danger to society. If she is a person with full autonomous capacity, that sort of liberty restriction would be inconsistent with the DR Model. The point is that these sorts of programs might be part of her punishment package because they help

[19] For an extended and convincing explanation of why consequentialist accounts of punishment, broadly construed, should be rejected, see Duff, *Punishment, Communication, and Community*, 3–19.

[20] See Section 3.5 on the means principle.

[21] Matt Sheridan, a convict criminologist, insists in personal communication that the most constructive thing punishment can do is educate, and he means it not just in sense of marketable skill, but in the classical sense of a liberal education and exposure to a range of role models. Not all convicted criminals have the skills and mental health to take advantage of a liberal education, and it is unclear that it could work well if made into a state-imposed duty. But it is worth exploring the possibility.

her to carry out her duty of reform, a duty she acquired in virtue of her culpable wrongdoing.[22]

What about incapacitation? As I noted in Chapter 1, the value of providing incapacitation cannot provide a justification for punishment.[23] Assuming the wrongdoer in question has full autonomous capacity, then she should be given the benefit of the presumption of law abidingness (POLA) except insofar as she has forfeited it. Benefiting from the POLA means that she should not have her liberty restricted as if she is simply a danger—which is what incapacitation aims to do. One might suggest that culpable wrongdoing forfeits the POLA, and that would license the state then to refer to statistical information about dangerousness to incapacitate anyone who it reasonably projects to be a danger. But there is nothing about blame itself that calls for POLA forfeiture. In other words, if we treat punishment as a blaming institution, then incapacitation based on POLA forfeiture cannot be a defining or constitutive aim of punishment.

This is a key thought for the book, so it bears repeating and clarifying. Blameworthiness does not ground forfeiture of the POLA. Such forfeiture might foster recognition that she wronged another and that she was not as good a person as she wanted to be, and it might constitute a form of hard treatment that serves to pay her amends. In other words, it could be used as a form of punishment. But it is unnecessary to use POLA forfeiture as punishment; there are adequate alternatives. Moreover, it is, in fact, antithetical to punishment because it is inherently demeaning, implying that she may not resume her place in the community as one among equals.

That said, it's important to see that incapacitation has justificatory value in two senses that are relevant to the overall justifiability of punishment. First, insofar as punishment incapacitates, the value provided by incapacitation can help offset the costs of punishment.[24] Second, insofar as punishment that provides *less* incapacitation is less valuable, in terms of providing security, than punishment that provides *more* incapacitation, and insofar as the costs of greater incapacitation are less than these benefits, *and* insofar as adopting a more incapacitative form of punishment is proportional, then the value of incapacitation could impact the shape justifiable punishments take. These conditions may often apply, and that

[22] Note, this is a potentially revisionist framing of rehabilitation. Many think of punishment as limited to the imposition of hard treatment; for them, rehabilitation isn't punishment. But I am framing punishment as the extraction of guilt-debt, and in that regard, *enforced* rehabilitation *is* an aspect of punishment. Merely providing a convicted wrongdoer with resources with which she can seek to rehabilitate herself is a different matter. She may be obliged to engage such resources, but insofar as she does so voluntarily, it cannot be considered "punishment."

[23] See Section 1.3.5.

[24] See Moore, "A Tale of Two Theories," 43–44, for a discussion of the difference between being directly relevant to justification and merely offsetting costs.

gives incapacitation a potentially significant role not only in the overall justifiability of punishment but in the form in which it is meted out. In addition, it may be that many of those who commit serious crimes *also* forfeit the POLA, making it relatively easy to justify incapacitation of them. Still, it bears repeating that the value of incapacitation cannot justify choosing to punish in the first place, and it cannot justify raising the limits on how much suffering a wrongdoer can be expected to endure to make proportional amends for culpable actions. Simply put, being incapacitated is not something that the wrongdoer owes as part of her guilt-debt. And the mere fact that she deserves censure and punishment does not imply that she forfeits the POLA and is therefore subject to incapacitation simply because she is deemed dangerous.

There is one other limit on aiming for more incapacitative forms of punishment that I want to repeat here:[25] To aim at incapacitation, even merely by selecting between competing forms of proportional punishment, it must be the case that those who are punished in that more incapacitative way can justly be held to have forfeited the POLA in the narrow sense relevant to how they might behave while being punished. It may be perfectly reasonable to assume that many wrongdoers who have committed serious crimes have forfeited the POLA to the degree necessary to select incapacitative forms of punishment. But we cannot simply assume that wrongdoing that justifies punishment also justifies taking the wrongdoer to have forfeited the POLA, not even narrowly, during the time of her punishment. Indeed, given that there is a tension between reconciliation and forfeiture of the POLA, there is reason to treat wrongdoers as retaining the POLA, even during the time of their punishment. This can be done by requiring them to report for punishment, but also giving them the chance to comply before imposing incapacitative conditions as a backup in case they do not comply.[26] To deny them the opportunity to voluntarily submit to punishment from the start, it must be fair to take them to have forfeited the POLA, at least with regard to the act of submitting to punishment.

To be clear, I am not saying that wrongdoing cannot license incapacitation. My point is that the duty to repay guilt-debt does not imply forfeiture of the POLA. Culpable wrongdoing may justify forfeiture of the POLA, which may then open up prospects for incapacitation that would not otherwise be available. But wrongdoing will lead to forfeiture of the POLA via a different justificatory route, one that is not concerned with blame as a response to culpability.

[25] I first mentioned it in Section 1.3.5.

[26] See the discussion of honor farms, Ch. 1, n. 70.

7.3 Punishing Those Who Do Not Accept Their Guilt

I have been framing punishment as helping to bring about reconciliation by providing an occasion for wrongdoers to reconsider their behavior and own their guilt, by helping to ensure that they are not happy about their wrongdoing, and by extracting material amends that they owe the polity, either in the form of compensation or in the form of contributing to deterrence and the reinforcement of the law. But what should the state do with people who do not own their guilt and show no signs of doing so? If reconciliation seems sufficiently unlikely, is the whole project pointless and misguided? I will address this question in three stages: First, should wrongdoers be punished until they repent? Second, if not, should they at least be punished more insofar as they remain unrepentant? Third, how should we understand the point of punishing them insofar as we expect them to remain unrepentant?

7.3.1 Should the State Punish Until Wrongdoers Repent?

The answer to the first question is no. Punishment must aim to restore a community of mutual respect, not undermine it. As pointed out above, it is simply a mistake to think that punishment can aim at inflicting guilt or causing people to have guilty feelings.[27] But even if it had some tendency to induce guilt, and the state was tempted to use it as a tool to achieve that end, the limits of proportionality restrict what can be done. The amends a wrongdoer owes as the extractable part of his guilt-debt are limited, by the proportionality principle, by the magnitude of his culpable wrongdoing.[28] It follows that the magnitude of hard treatment that can be imposed on him to extract his guilt-debt must be limited to a proportional punishment as well.

It can be argued that the failure to own his guilt is a moral failure not unlike that which grounds the recidivist premium.[29] In both cases, the wrongdoer does not commit a new crime by his failure to do what he ought, but his ongoing failures are moral failures that could be taken to augment the punishment he deserves for the crime he has committed. But even though the analogy can be drawn, there's also a disanalogy. The recidivist premium raises the culpability of a new crime; the claim here is that the culpability of the crime already committed goes up because of the wrongdoer's failure to own his guilt. This sort of retroactive boost to culpability seems to me less justifiable than the forward-looking

[27] See Section 1.1.
[28] See Ch. 8.
[29] See Section 6.5.2.

one. For wrongs already committed, the culpability was set at the time the wrong was committed. Future moral failures should have little to no impact on the culpability of that past action. But even if I am mistaken and failure to own his guilt should function like the recidivist premium, that will license only a limited boost to his punishment, not punishment that lasts until he repents.

In addition, and equally importantly, punishment should be consistent with the wrongdoer coming to own his guilt, which is the goal of reconciliation. If he comes to feel guilty, he should not feel that he has now suffered too much. Rather, he should be able to accept his hard treatment as his paying his guilt-debt. That is, he should be able to see it as amends extracted from him for his initial wrongdoing. If the hard treatment was excessive given the extent of his wrongdoing, then he will rightly view himself as having suffered too much. He may then rightly resent those who imposed that excess suffering on him, and that resentment would rightly reflect a failure with regard to reconciliation.

Reinforcing that second point: If the wrongdoer experiences punishment as domination—that is, the exercise of raw power—rather than justified extraction of a debt owed, then he is likely to experience shame, not guilt. The essence of shame is the sense an agent has that he is disrespected by others, and the reaction it produces is not responsibility for himself but either withdrawal or deception or, in many cases, the desire to use violence to establish a kind of respect: fear.[30] Moreover, it is important to keep in mind that most of those who commit crimes come from a background of unjust deprivation in which they already struggle with shame. If punishment is felt as an exercise of raw power over them, it will only increase their sense of shame and undermine any potential feeling of guilt.[31] To avoid this trap, it is necessary for censure and punishment to carefully uphold the message that the wrongdoer is still respected as a morally significant member of the community, and that what is sought is not shame but a recognition of his own obligation to respect others and to engage in self-blame for, and proportional to, his culpability for any wrongs done.[32] This puts a proportionality cap on punishing even the unrepentant.

One might still object that those who do not repent cannot really be treated as members in good standing of the political community. So what is the state to do? One answer is that it just has to content itself with doing what it can do, hoping that the wrongdoer will eventually come around. Another answer is that insofar as the wrongdoing was sufficient to forfeit the POLA, the state can take failure

[30] See J. Gilligan, *Preventing Violence*, 35–36, 56.

[31] For the claim that guilt and shame are inversely related, see J. Gilligan, "Shame, Guilt, and Violence," 1173.

[32] To avoid punishment being interpreted as shaming, it may also be necessary for the state to overcome a local honor culture. And it may need to make extra efforts to help wrongdoers overcome their attachment to an honor culture. See Section 3.4.

to repent as relevant to which restrictions meet the least restrictive alternative (LRA) requirement.[33]

7.3.2 Should the State Punish the Unrepentant More?

Should the failure to accept guilt at least lead to *more* punishment than would be fitting for those who own their guilt? I think the answer here is a qualified yes. There are two reasons to offer this qualified yes. First, there is a reason to punish the unrepentant that does not apply to the repentant, namely the third reason to impose hard treatment: the goal of undermining morally objectionable happiness. But we have to be careful with this reason. It applies only to those who are happy about their wrongdoing; a wrongdoer can be unrepentant but not *happy* about his wrongdoing.

In addition, while it is tempting to see the problem as concerning the distribution of negative emotions, I think that thought should be rejected.[34] The tempting but misleading thought goes like this: an unrepentant wrongdoer who feels self-satisfied with his wrongdoing, as though he got away with it, can cause others to rightfully feel indignant and resentful. Feeling indignant or resentful is taxing, and that sort of tax should fall on the wrongdoer, not on others. Thus, we have reason to punish the wrongdoer more in order to better distribute the experience of taxing subjective states.

The problems with this argument are twofold. First, I don't think we should put a lot of weight on the idea that feeling resentment or indignation is taxing. Yes, some don't like feeling indignant or resentful. But people experience related sorts of frustration in many ways: over their jobs, the political culture in which they live, the behavior of friends and family, and so on. It seems unlikely that most people carry a noticeably heavier emotional load because some wrongdoer feels happy about his crime. Yes, they may feel that this fact is regrettable; they may be agitated while this fact is front and center in their minds. But in most cases, it won't make their lives go distinctly worse.[35] The right way to take those feelings into account is not as a tax on those who feel them; it is as a judgment that the wrongdoer should not feel that way and that reconciliation with a wrongdoer who feels that way is problematic.

Second, if the wrongdoer is censured and punished proportionately, having amends that reflect the magnitude of his culpability extracted from him, then he has not simply got away with his crime. If he still feels self-satisfied, some small

[33] I discuss the LRA requirement most directly in Section 16.3.2.
[34] This is a change. For my earlier view, see "On Blame and Punishment," 298.
[35] I'm grateful to Victor Tadros for pushing me to recognize this.

extra quantum of punishment is unlikely to make a difference. And if there is a punishment large enough to "wipe that smile off his face" it is likely to violate the proportionality limits just discussed. Thus, I think the state cannot take his non-repentance as providing a reason to impose *more* punishment.

But there is a second reason to think that the unrepentant should be punished more than the repentant, all else equal. The reason does not rely on the thought that the unrepentant should suffer *extra* punishment;[36] rather, the thought is that an agent who owns his guilt in a clear and convincing manner deserves a discount with regard to the punishment he would otherwise get.[37] This discount would not indicate that he does not owe the amends that would otherwise be extracted from him. It would instead reflect a gesture of appreciation and welcome from the community to him. Reconciliation is a two-way street, and this would reflect earned appreciation—not mere mercy—from the other side.

One might challenge the thought that the default sentence should be for non-repentant wrongdoers.[38] One thing to say in response is that in the current world, that's the norm. Thus, in the current world, we have reason to give a bonus gesture of appreciation to those wrongdoers who own their guilt. But the challenger could come back and say: we should assume, consistent with the POLA, that people will act as they should unless and until they forfeit that assumption. Insofar as that is right, then it might seem that the point should be reframed in terms of a small additional punishment for *not* owning one's guilt. But we are not forced to frame it that way. Rather, we can say that the state's appreciation for those who own their guilt is withheld from those who do not. The appreciation still takes the form of a discount, and that still leaves us with the point, argued for in Section 7.3.1, that the unrepentant should not face *extra* punishment beyond that which is proportionate for the crime itself.

It is worth adding that this fits the way the criminal justice system tends to work. Judges tend to sentence repentant wrongdoers more lightly than unrepentant ones, all else equal, and parole boards tend to accept that one reason to release prisoners early is that they have accepted blame for what they have done. This sort of discounting is problematic. As Duff points out, it "provide[s] an incentive to a dishonest pretense of repentance" and it "can bear harshly on the innocent, who may be pressured into pleading guilty to avoid a harsher sentence if they are mistakenly convicted or who may, if wrongly convicted, be denied parole if they continue to assert their innocence."[39] Nonetheless, I think what

[36] I wrongly implied that unrepentant wrongdoers should get *extra* punishment in "On Blame and Punishment," 298.

[37] For a similar view, see P. Robinson and M. Sarahne, "The Opposite of Punishment."

[38] Duff pressed this challenge in a marginal comment on an earlier draft.

[39] *Punishment, Communication, and Community*, 120.

is called for, to avoid these problems, is care to discern honest repentance from dishonest pretense of repentance, and more importantly, to offer a discount sufficiently small that it does not tend to coerce people into false confessions.

7.3.3 What is the Point of Punishing the Intransigently Unrepentant?

I have argued that punishment should not be so harsh that it would impede the prospects of the wrongdoer owning his guilt. But what if it is quite clear at the time of conviction that he will never repent? Why bother then with punishment?

There are people who will never repent because they fall short of even threshold level autonomous capacity; they should not be punished.[40] Psychopaths may be autonomous enough to be justly held accountable, but they should be given what I call "punishment-light": punishment minus the censure.[41] But I don't have that kind of person in mind. Rather, I'm thinking of the kind of person who is deeply committed to a morally misguided set of beliefs, such as a committed racist, sexist, homophobe, or anti-Semite. If we have good reason to believe, on the basis of social science, that a particular person who holds such misguided moral views will never see the error of his ways, why bother to punish him? Why not just penalize him or even excommunicate him (either by ostracism or by locking him up and throwing away the key)?

My answer is that dignity is inalienable.[42] It cannot be lost by being intransigently mistaken about moral matters. Even those who would treat others as though they have no rights do not themselves give up their status as equal citizens in the republic of rights. They may have become alienated from the political community by their actions. But the proper community response to them is to call them back. It is to address them as responsible people who are blameworthy and who deserve punishment. If by serious or repeated offenses they forfeit the POLA, then they can be incapacitated after the period of their punishment is over. But as autonomous agents with mistaken, even monstrous, moral views, they still have the dignity of citizens in the republic of rights. The call to own their guilt stands as a call not only to them but to all culpable wrongdoers, and it reaffirms the dignity of all even if those who are directly addressed will almost certainly never heed the call.

[40] See Section 19.2.
[41] See Section 19.6.
[42] See Section 3.4.

7.4 A Retributive Account of Punishment

I close out this chapter by returning to my claim that I am offering a retributive account of punishment. I say it is retributive because I hold that punishment is deserved in virtue of a wrongdoer's culpable wrongdoing.[43] Whether punishment is deserved turns on facts about the desert subject: that *she* is a culpable wrongdoer whose culpability for a public wrong is great enough to merit not just censure but also punishment. Finally, culpable wrongdoing provides a desert basis for punishment because it creates a problem for the political community: the wrongdoer has disrespected it and in that way is no longer well integrated into it.[44] I think I have said enough about why these concepts apply, so I will not belabor the point. What I want to do here is to defend a complementary point, that penal law is different in part because penalties are not deserved.[45] Defending that claim will make it clearer, I think, what it means to say that punishments are deserved.

Here is why there is a puzzle. Penalties too can be imposed only if the agent committed an offense. Thus, in both cases, there's a fact about the agent, the "desert subject," that grounds the action. And one might say that a penal violation too creates a problem for the political community: it shows disrespect for the law and, in that way, it contributes to undermining respect for the law. This is a problem that the state has reason to respond to with a penalty. Moreover, there is a reason to impose penalties that does not depend on the contingent utility of applying a penalty in a particular case: fairness across cases. Thus, it seems that penalties too are deserved. Or, if they are not deserved, then maybe punishment is not deserved either.

I think the right thing to say here is that fairness across cases is not the right sort of favoring reason.[46] There needs to be a nexus between the desert basis, the desert subject, and the favoring reason. In the case of punishment, the act of punishing does various things to solve the problem that exists between the wrongdoer and the political community. It helps reinforce the message to her that she should own her guilt; it gives her a distinct occasion to reconsider what she has done; it helps ensure that she does not take a satisfaction in her wrongdoing that further alienates her from the community; and it extracts amends from her that she owes, making it easier for her to be reconciled with the community. In all of these ways it is deserved.

By contrast, the favoring reason in penal law is merely fairness. There is nothing about the "desert subject" herself that calls for imposing a penalty. It is

[43] See Section 5.4.
[44] Ibid.
[45] See Section 3.5.2.
[46] See ibid.

merely that her case is like other cases, and so as a matter of applying the rule of law, there is a reason to treat it like other cases.

What about the fact that a penal offense undermines respect for the law; does that not create a debt that the offender owes, making penalties "deserved"? I think that's not the best way to understand it. Consider a tort case in which a tortfeasor has wrecked someone's car. Should we say that she deserves to have the damages taken from her? I think that's too strong. If the owner of the car can get compensation from her insurance company and neither she nor the company wants to go after the tortfeasor, there is no favoring reason for them to do so. The tortfeasor is liable to pay damages, but she does not *deserve* to have the damages taken from her. Putting aside the reason to treat like cases alike in penal law, that is how I think we should conceive of penal law. It is merely a matter of liability. But criminal law is a matter of desert. Even if the state is willing to proactively forgive, there are favoring reasons of the right kind, grounded in facts about the wrongdoer, to punish—in particular, that proactive forgiveness would make it less likely, in many cases, that wrongdoers would own their guilt.[47]

[47] See Section 6.5.3.

8
Proportionality's Constraint

8.1 The Importance and Puzzle of Proportionality

Many arguments in this book rely on the premise that the punishment ought to be proportional to the culpability of the crime, and that it must not be disproportionately large.[1] That was the basis for my claim that Antony Duff's defense of hard treatment is incomplete. As I put it in Chapter 7, it is not clear that time for repentance provides a sufficient reason to impose proportionately large punishments on most wrongdoers.[2] Two sections later, I also argued that disproportionate punishment would prevent proper reconciliation and therefore must be avoided. In Chapter 9, I argue that disproportionate punishments are a potential cost of errors in punishment. And in Chapter 10, I argue that the failure to explain why punishment should be proportional to culpable wrongdoing is a reason to reject Tommie Shelby's idea of punishment as deterrence. Most importantly, I argue in Chapter 12 that we need the penal law, in addition to criminal law, because the proportionality limit on *punishments* would prevent the state from effectively deterring many offenses that it has strong reason to deter.

This list raises the question: Why should we give so much weight to the proportionality requirement? Why not say, simply: If someone commits a criminal act, then he deserves censure and punishment, and the form and amount is completely up to the state to determine, depending on its needs? If people want to avoid censure and punishment, then they should avoid committing crimes.

In a way, the question is hard to take seriously. Of course, it would be unjust to censure someone harshly for a low-level crime, such as littering. As censure for a crime involves communication regarding how serious the crime was, distortion along that dimension is simply a lie, a slander. And one can argue that it's equally obvious that the degree of punishment has to "fit the crime" insofar as punishment should reinforce the communicative content of censure.[3] But I have argued that punishment does more than reinforce the communicative content of censure; it also provides an occasion for a wrongdoer to reflect on his guilt,

[1] The discussion in this chapter focuses only on the impact on the punished wrongdoer, not his family or community. The issues raised by that concern are handled in the next chapter.
[2] Section 7.1.2.
[3] See A. Duff, *Punishment, Communication, and Community*, 132.

Punishment, Penalty, and Incapacitation. Alec Walen, Oxford University Press. © Oxford University Press 2026.
DOI: 10.1093/9780197523124.003.0008

helps ensure that he is not happy with his wrongdoing, and extracts his guilt-debt in the form of amends. Must these too be limited by proportionality? The relevance of the proportionality constraint for providing occasions for reflection and undermining morally offensive happiness is not obvious. But it seems clear that these goals cannot provide justifications for unlimited punishment; the pursuit of these goals must be restrained by a general restriction on proportional punishment. And that restriction is grounded not only in the thought that punishment should reinforce censure but also in the punitive goal of extracting a wrongdoer's guilt-debt in terms of amends. Just as any other debt has a measure, so does guilt-debt. No creditor is allowed to extract what he wants from another just because she is in his debt. The same holds true for a political community extracting amends as guilt-debt from a wrongdoer. The extraction must be limited by the magnitude of the culpable wrong.

But that does not mean that the measure of proportionality is simple. I gave a measure of culpable wrongdoing in Chapter 5. As I put it, "The culpability of an action . . . is a function of both the wrongness of the action in itself and the culpable mens rea with which it is performed."[4] And "[t]he wrongness of the action is a function of the magnitude of the harm—to individuals or to the rule of law—caused, intended, or unreasonably risked, and the degree to which that harm is unjustified."[5] This raises the question: Can we really put a measure on that?[6] And even if we can, can we put a measure on the punishment that is imposed, especially given the wide range of possible punishments, from fines, to community service (of different types), to imprisonment (in different conditions)?[7] We also have to ask: How responsive should we be to the different sensitivities to punishment of different wrongdoers, and, insofar as deterrence is the goal, how sensitive should we be to their indifference to conditions that might generally deter but might not deter them? These sorts of questions threaten to show that the retributive idea of proportional punishment is "radically indeterminate . . . and possibly incoherent."[8]

Nonetheless, I will defend the thought that we can make sense of proportional punishment. My defense has two components. First, I distinguish different senses of proportionality and argue that we need to defend only a fairly weak notion. Following Duff, I will argue that we can do well enough with what he calls a "negative" conception of proportionality.[9] The point is that we do not have

[4] Section 5.3.

[5] Ibid.

[6] For critical comments on our ability to do so, see J. Ryberg, "Proportionality and the Seriousness of Crimes," 54–56.

[7] For a discussion of the difficulties along this dimension, see D. Husak, "The Metric of Punishment Severity."

[8] See, e.g., A. Kolber, *Punishment for the Greater Good*, 129.

[9] *Punishment, Communication, and Community*, 138.

to find *the* punishment that fits *the* crime. Rather, we must avoid punishments that are clearly disproportionately large, and we have reason to avoid imposing punishments that are clearly disproportionately small. Second, I argue that this sort of problem—moving from complex inputs to unidimensional outputs or moving in the reverse direction from unidimensional inputs to complex outputs—is a quite general problem that we generally navigate tolerably well.

8.2 Negative Proportionality in Practice

To understand how we could rightly judge that some punishment *is* clearly disproportionate to a particular crime, it is essential to distinguish two basic senses of proportionality: cardinal and ordinal.[10] Cardinal proportionality sets an absolute, even if vague, measure for the punishment that is proportional to a given crime; ordinal proportionality requires only that more serious crimes be punished more severely than less serious crimes. I will argue that we have a vague sense for both, and that by combining them in a scheme of punishment we end up with a functionally usable notion of proportional punishment.

The problem with cardinal proportionality is that there is no precise and plausible basis for a cardinal measure for a proportional punishment to a particular crime. The idea of lex talionis—an eye for an eye, a tooth for a tooth—might be offered as a solution to the problem. But it is a hopelessly inadequate solution. It is either too lenient when it comes to crimes like theft—a $100 for $100—or far too harsh; as Kant put it: the thief "deprives himself . . . of security in any possible property. He has nothing and can also acquire nothing."[11] And it's far too crude to handle things like the difference between negligent homicide and murder. But without lex talionis we have, at best, a very vague idea that the most serious crimes should be met with serious punishments, and that the least serious crimes should be met with only very mild punishments.

The idea of an ordinal ranking may seem more useful. There is, in fact, empirical evidence that people across a wide range of demographics can rank order even subtle variations of "core wrongs . . . —physical aggression, takings without consent, and deception in exchanges—" with a great deal of consistency.[12] These subtle variations involve, for example, two thefts differing only in that one involved sneaking into an open garage while the other involved breaking into a locked house.[13] It could be that this consistency is nothing more than a

[10] Much of the next few paragraphs is taken from the Supplement to my 2021 entry in the *Stanford Encyclopedia of Philosophy* on "Retributive Justice."
[11] "The Doctrine of Right," Academy page 333.
[12] P. Robinson and R. Kurzban, "Concordance and Conflict in Intuitions of Justice," 1892.
[13] Ibid., 1895.

consistency in reaction, not reflecting any underlying reality that people can consistently judge correctly. But I believe the better explanation for the consistency is that it reflects a consistent ability to judge underlying facts correctly,[14] and therefore that extreme concerns about arbitrariness in rankings, at least of mala in se crimes, are somewhat alleviated by these studies.[15]

A purely ordinal approach also has problems, however. First, we still have the problem mentioned in the last section: balancing different dimensions of input. One manifestation of that problem is that even if we can rank "core wrongs" with high interpersonal consistency, it's not clear how we can compare these core wrongs to other wrongs, ranging from cheating on taxes to dealing illegal drugs. Second, even within the realm of "core wrongs," if all that a state was required to do was rank order wrongs by their gravity and then provide a mapping onto a range of punishments that likewise went from light to serious—respecting the norms of rank-ordering and parity—then neither the range of punishments from a fine of $1 up to a fine of $100, nor prison sentences from 40 years to 60 years, would provide disproportionate punishment, no matter what the crimes. This seems wrong. Murder should not be punished with a $100 fine, and littering should not be punished with 40 years in prison.

This second problem seems to call for some measure of cardinality, punishing the wrongs that are gravest and most culpable with objectively severe punishments, punishing the wrongs that are just barely serious and culpable enough to warrant the attention of the criminal law with objectively mild punishments, and punishing intermediate wrongs in a way that reflects how close their culpability is to either pole. The possibility of anchoring a punishment scheme in this way, and distributing punishments along the course of it, could provide an appropriate blend of the ordinal and the cardinal. That would allow states to construct plausible and complete schedules of proportional punishment, at least for "core wrongs."[16]

It is worth noting that this kind of schedule should also reflect the balance of two other considerations. On the one hand, the principle of parsimony should add downward normative pressure to the range of anchoring points. The idea is that since punishment involves inflicting suffering distinct from the intrinsically valuable suffering of guilt, it should be inflicted as minimally as possible, consistent with the vague, symbolic limits of cardinal desert and any other goals, such

[14] I say more about why in the next section.

[15] What about H.L.A. Hart's challenge: "Is negligently causing the destruction of a city worse than the intentional wounding of a single policeman?" *Punishment and Responsibility*, 162. I think this challenge is easy to meet: It's worse to negligently cause the destruction of the city. I say this because I believe the wrongs aggregate; each negligent homicide contributes to the overall wrongness of destroying a city, and that makes doing so worse than intentionally wounding a policeman. What Hart was really pressing on was the problem of balancing different kinds of inputs. I consider that in the next section.

[16] A. von Hirsh and A. Ashworth, *Proportionate Sentencing*, § 9.3. See also J. Kleinig, *Punishment and Desert*, 123–124.

as deterrence, that should be cited in a full justification for punishment. On the other hand, these other goals normally would provide a counter-pressure. The goal of deterrence requires that punishments be severe enough to make criminal acts seem generally imprudent, and the goal of norm reinforcement requires that they be serious enough to express sincere disapproval of their violation.[17] In addition, though incapacitation cannot be a means by which punishment extracts a wrongdoer's guilt-debt, its value can produce upward pressure on prison sentences and other forms of liberty deprivation insofar as those sentenced can fairly be taken to have forfeited the presumption of law abidingness (POLA) in a way that licenses those longer sentences and insofar as those longer sentences would not be considered disproportionate.[18]

It is worth pausing to note, regarding deterrence, that certainty of punishment has a much greater deterrent effect than severity of punishment, so deterrence will not provide much pressure toward draconian punishments.[19] Indeed, Daniel Nagin writes that "it is clear that lengthy prison sentences cannot be justified on a deterrence-based, crime prevention basis."[20] But punishments must be serious enough that they amount to more than a regime of "catch and release." If the punishments meted out are not generally perceived as serious enough for people to want to avoid them, then even providing more certainty of apprehension would do little to deter crime.

What about the first problem with ordinal punishments, that of different dimensions of input into an ordinal ranking? The answer has two parts. The first, which I will flesh out in the next section, is that while these sorts of comparisons do raise the problem of incommensurability, that problem need not swamp our sense that in some cases the mismatch between crime and punishment amounts to a disproportionately great punishment. In other words, the key to addressing this first problem is to keep in mind that we are concerned with *negative* proportionality, which tolerates incommensurable comparisons.

The second part of the answer is that we are dealing with a legal domain that can address the problem of vagueness.[21] A state must have a schedule of punishments. The schedule must respect negative proportionality. But it must also give concrete meaning to the anchored cardinal notions of more and less severe punishments. And it can fill in plausible ordered relations when the

[17] It is worth noting that there is evidence that "sanctions which are so mild that they cannot act as a deterrent... [nonetheless can] foster norm adherence." J. Roberts and S. Harrendorf, "Criminal History Enhancements at Sentencing," 274.

[18] See Section 7.2.

[19] A third parameter, swiftness, also matters. See B. van Rooij and A. Fine, *The Behavioral Code*, 19. In addition, all three of these parameters have to be known to be effective, so government investment in communication, especially to the communities most likely to engage in crime, is key as well. See ibid., 38–40.

[20] "Deterrence in the Twenty-First Century," 202.

[21] See Section 3.7.2.

ordering is not itself determined by clear prelegal intuitions. It is by adopting a schedule that does not violate proportionality that a set of punishments can be meaningfully and justly imposed on culpable wrongdoers.[22]

8.3 Our Tolerable Ability to Move Between Pluralism and Monism

8.3.1 Handling the Plural Inputs into Overall Culpability

A presupposition in the previous section is that we can generally agree on ordinal proportionality. But even that was brought into question by the problem of moving from many dimensions into one. I cited empirical research that there is intersubjective consistency in the ranking of the culpability of a range of core wrongs. But one might think that such judgments are fundamentally arbitrary. If so, if they reflect nothing more than widely shared prejudices, then it would seem to be wrong to put much normative weight on them.[23]

But I want to suggest that such rankings are not fundamentally arbitrary. They are, indeed, a commonplace in our thinking, and they generally serve us well enough.[24] Consider the analogy of ranking athletes in particular sports. Let's take basketball. There are different positions: guard, center, forward. There are different skills: shooting, dunking, dribbling, passing, rebounding, defending against the dribble, blocking, moving without the ball and getting open, setting screens, and so on. One might also want to add the ability to play well with others, expected longevity, and "basketball IQ" (the ability to understand what will happen and make the best move in that context). Over time, basketball aficionados can come to recognize that certain players were drafted too high,[25]

[22] N. Lacey and H. Pickard think that "lack of any comparable consensus [comparable to that for ordinal proportionality] about cardinal proportionality implies that appeals to proportionality are, under current conditions, unlikely to be a successful basis for institutionalising substantive criteria of a punishment's 'fitness' . . . rendering the appeal to proportionality chimerical as a basis for limiting punishment." "The Chimera of Proportionality," 227. My response is that they are asking too much of cardinal proportionality.

[23] Michael Tonry argues that "proportionality theory [cannot] provide satisfactory answers to core questions about crime seriousness, punishment severity, and links between them." "Is Proportionality in Punishment Possible, and Achievable?" But if the argument in this subsection is sound, then he is looking for more substance and precision than is reasonable to seek. This reply applies as well to the skeptical criticism made by J. Ryberg, "Proportionality and the Seriousness of Crimes," 62–63.

[24] This sort of suggestion has been made before. See, e.g., C. L. Ten, *Crime, Guilt, and Punishment*, 155.

[25] For those who don't follow American sports: The top professional leagues seek to distribute talent by allowing teams to select (or "draft") players once a year in an order which gives priority to those teams that fared worst in the last season's play. (To avoid giving teams a strong incentive to lose games, the National Basketball Association, gives teams that have especially bad records nothing more than an advantage in a lottery to determine who gets to draft in what order.)

because, say, height was given too much weight (as it were); others were drafted too low because court vision was given too little weight.[26] How do aficionados know these things? It helps that one can measure results. But even there, judgment is called for. Should one look at points per game? That might miss the ability to play well with others. Should one add assists? How do they get weighed against points? Wins during the regular season? Championships won? How can one sort out the impact of other players? There is no simple, empirical test. And yet, if we ask, who was the best player ever, some players are in contention—LeBron James, Michael Jordan, Wilt Chamberlain[27]—and almost all others are not. Putting it in other terms, there are levels of players who are on a par, and others who are better or worse, even though the metrics and their weighting are contested.[28] Some incommensurability does not undermine the ability to make clear distinctions.[29]

My suggestion is that the same holds true for proportionality in punishment. There are, as noted before,[30] a range of input values that go into determining the culpability of an action: the wrong threatened, the harm actually caused (if any), the degree to which the harm threatened or caused was unjustifiable, the mens rea for the action, the general degree of autonomous capacity of the agent, more temporally local limits on the agent's autonomous capacity that might give him a partial excuse, whether he had any prior convictions, and other aggravating and mitigating factors that might be taken into account at sentencing.[31] If we focus on variations within a particular dimension of input, holding the rest constant, there's no problem understanding how we can make reliable ordinal proportionality judgments. The problem arises when we try to combine different dimensions of input. But if we can combine input values in basketball, it's not

[26] It's a different sport, but the idea of "sabermetrics" changed the way baseball players were assessed for talent to be more statistically rigorous than the original, more intuitive indicators of baseball talent, like batting average. See M. Lewis, *Moneyball.*

[27] Of course, others might deserve to be in the running: Bill Russell, Larry Bird, Karem Abdul Jabbar, and so on.

[28] For general guidance on the idea of being on a par, see N. Hsieh and H. Andersson, "Incommensurable Values."

[29] Ralf Poscher offers a fascinating take on incommensurability, appealing to the idea of degrees of realization of different skills. He illustrates with great care how this is plausibly done in determining the winner of the decathlon, which compares the performance of athletes across ten very different competitions. And then he extends that discussion to the idea of proportionality in constitutional and criminal law. He does not suggest that arriving at proportionality judgments across different input categories is easy, but he does suggest it is at least sometimes possible to do it in a meaningful way. See his "What Would It Take?"

[30] See Section 5.3.

[31] In practice, courts will tend to start with the nature of the crime, which sets a range of sanctions, then adjust for aggravating and mitigating conditions, apply credit for assistance offered to the state, and increase the sentence if a recidivist premium applies. See, for example, the U.S. Sentencing Guidelines. But while this process is laid out in a fairly sophisticated way, limiting the range of normal disagreement, that by itself does not show that it tracks culpability in the relevant way. The list in the text is meant to make that connection.

clear why we should not be able to do the same for judgments of overall culpability. And the same goes for judgments concerning, for example, who is the better painter, composer, or philosopher. One might be tempted to look for independent measures such as popularity or citation rate, but these are obviously such problematic measures that no serious critical discussion would even refer to them. One looks to the underlying criteria and uses one's educated judgment.

If we add mala prohibita, the situation gets murkier, but it does not descend into complete arbitrariness. We can still rank certain crimes as worse than others by reference to factors such as the magnitude of the harm they threaten, and the ease of avoiding the illegal activity. For this to be a matter of *culpability* it has to be the case that mala prohibita crimes are actually wrongful. But I follow Duff on this point: we have an obligation to respect reasonable regulations that aim to achieve important social goods such as protection of the environment, collection of taxes to fund legitimate government services, and protection of others from things like car accidents and poisoning, as long as the regulations do not impose "unreasonable burdens on those who are required to obey."[32] As long as that moral obligation is present, acts that flout it can be blameworthy and subject to proportional censure and punishment. Even if there is no particular victim, the unfairness of exempting oneself from a reasonable regulation can be a wrong that can be compared, even if only roughly, with a malum in se crime.[33] In Chapter 13, I argue that proportional responses to a subset of mala prohibita crimes, proxy crimes,[34] probably do not suffice to ensure that these regulations are respected as much as they should be—this is the reason why the state might want to adopt penal law. But for now, the point is that there is a meaningful measure of a proportional *punishment* for such crimes.

8.3.2 Handling the Plural Outputs of Punishment

Let us turn now to the different output dimensions: fines versus community service versus prison, length of time versus intensity of deprivation, and subjective suffering versus objective deprivation or imposition. How can we measure these against each other to get a reasonable measure of a proportional punishment? A quick answer is: the same way. Look for ways in which punishments are

[32] *The Realm of Criminal Law*, 333.

[33] Many crimes have both malum in se and malum prohibitum components. For a good discussion of the difficulties in determining the culpability of each, see Y. Lee, "*Mala Prohibita* and Proportionality."

[34] Some mala prohibita crimes, like tax evasion, are intrinsically significantly wrongful and thus not proxy crimes.

clearly not on a par, and make sure they are ordered correctly. But that's a little too quick; there is more that ought to be said.

One output problem concerns the relevance of the subjective experience of punishment, as opposed to objective deprivation or imposition. Consider Dostoyevsky's observation: "Here is a man who is wasting away in prison, melting down like a candle; and here is another who before he came here had no idea that there was in the world to be found such a merry existence, such an agreeable club of lion-hearted companions."[35] Insofar as someone is happy to experience something, it seems peculiar to say that inflicting it on him counts as punishment; and if the state knows that he would enjoy it, then the state's attempt to punish him by inflicting it on him seems to fail even if others would find the same thing aversive. We might then conclude that subjective suffering is relevant. But the aim of inducing subjective suffering could lead to a sadistic approach to punishment, one that calls for ever more grotesque treatment, torture in effect, if necessary to exact the desired degree of suffering from someone who is unusually sanguine about what is done to him. This raises the question: Can the state avoid the one horn of this dilemma without being impaled on the other?

I think three points can adequately answer this dilemma: First, the standard features of hard treatment, such as confinement in prisons, are nearly universally disliked, Dostoyevsky's observation notwithstanding. And if someone enjoys it, then perhaps the state has to allow him to escape without being meaningfully punished. That is better than the alternative of tightening the screws until he screams. Second, we are assessing institutional responses; they don't have to be finely tailored to ensure that adequate, much less equal, suffering is experienced by all who are punished; it suffices if there is a normal response that can be calibrated to be ordinally and cardinally appropriate. Third, underpunishment is an acceptable outcome; it is overpunishment that is a problem for proportionality. But the prospect of occasional overpunishment—more precisely, punishment that leads to suffering that is greater than that which the state aims to impose—is a problem a liberal state can live with, at least as long as three conditions obtain:[36]

1. The deprivation or hard treatment that leads to it is itself deserved,
2. The importance of giving wrongdoers what they deserve is sufficiently high to outweigh the bad of excessive suffering, and
3. The problems with eliminating excessive suffering are too great to be overcome without excessive costs to other morally important ends.

[35] *The House of the Dead*, 76.

[36] The argument that follows is taken, with small modifications, from my "Retributive Justice," § 4.3.3.

These conditions call for a few comments. First, the excessive suffering in condition (2) should be incidental excessive suffering. If it is suffering that is inflicted to achieve some other end, then it will be as hard to justify as punishing the innocent. Second, there is reason to think that these conditions often obtain. Focusing only on the last condition, there are at least four reasons to think it obtains. These are that individual tailoring of punishment would:

a) Invite gaming the system;
b) Lead to extra conflict as those who claim to be extra sensitive would seem to be given undue leniency, and that would lead to resentment;
c) Undermine predictability, which would arguably be unfair to people contemplating a crime in the same way that ex post facto increases in punishment are considered unfair; and
d) Likely lead to abuse of power.

In addition, it is often less problematic to cause excessive suffering than it may at first seem because people are to some degree responsible for their own hypersensitivity.[37]

Adam Kolber has responded to an earlier version of this argument.[38] He writes: "[U]njustified resentment and conflict do not seem to be concerns that retributivists would typically use to justify knowingly causing someone harm, especially not in criminal justice contexts."[39] My response starts by pointing out that Kolber is assuming that as a retributivist I must justify excessive harm as part of the punishment, and therefore as targeted harm. But the goal of punishment is not to inflict *excess* harm; excess harm is just a side effect the state can foresee will arise in some percentage of cases and that it may be able to foresee will arise in particular cases. And even as a side effect, it may not be that hard to justify in the context of a punishment that A experiences more severely than most would. As long as A knew the kind of punishment he was risking by committing his particular crime (that is, the punishment does not violate the ban on ex post facto punishment), it is not a stretch to say that A is liable to that harm. In that case, it's not an injustice to refuse to help A avoid extra suffering when there would be costs on many others if the state were to adopt a policy of helping people like him.

Kolber also writes: "[I]f we had a reliable, cost-effective hedonimeter, Walen would seem to be committed to its use in carceral contexts."[40] My response here

[37] Compare Rawls's thought that people are responsible for their own preferences. See "A Kantian Conception of Equality," 261.

[38] He has responded multiple times, but his latest response can be found in *Punishment for the Greater Good*, 157–159. Some of his objections were anticipated in the text, and I won't engage them here.

[39] Ibid., 158.

[40] Ibid., 159.

is to say: yes and no. I think if we had such a meter, and it gave reliable interpersonal comparisons, then I agree, we would have a reason to use it. Its use would avoid the problem of imposing excessive suffering on those who would find prison unusually hard to handle. But I have two reasons to resist the use of such a device. First, such a meter would allow the rich and pampered to be punished on a par with others when they suffer what, to a normal person, would be fairly small setbacks to their welfare. Again, I think people need to be to some degree responsible for their hypersensitivity. The second reason is that this idea smacks a bit of the hyper-focus on *suffering*, the focus that I think leads all too quickly to a torture-oriented mentality. The point is not to induce graded suffering; the point is to impose graded hard treatment that is generally found to be undesirable. The fetish with suffering should be avoided.

That said, the state should accommodate people who would suffer extreme trauma from normal punishments. For example, someone who is extremely sensitive to the cold should be given extra clothing and blankets or a space heater. The person who is claustrophobic should be given a larger cell if possible. The person with severe allergies should be given allergy medication or a cell free of the relevant allergens. And given the prevalence of mental illness in prison, all prisoners should be screened for that and offered treatment so that their suffering from prison is not exacerbated by mental illness. But that does not imply that the punishers should try, in general, to tailor the subjective experience of suffering to be proportional to the crime. Rather, employing fixed levels of deprivation or hard treatment that can be objectively scaled suffices for a proportional response.

But we cannot stop there. That deals only with one dimension of the output problem. We still need to handle duration versus intensity, as well as the comparison between material compensation (fines and community service) and hard treatment. On the former, duration versus intensity, I don't think there is much we need to worry about. We don't want the intensity to become so great that punishment becomes torture. But insofar as there is a trade-off to be made, we have some reason to choose shorter and harsher treatment: people change over time and their connection to their crime diminishes.[41] In addition, we might want somewhat harsher conditions to make treatment more of a deterrent and to ensure that those who are punished are not happy with their wrongdoing. On the other hand, we have reason to seek somewhat milder conditions to provide time and a conducive environment for reflection and rehabilitation. But this extra dimension presents us with a problem no different from the input problems discussed in Section 8.3.1.[42]

[41] See P. Tomlin, "Time and Retribution."

[42] Kolber points out that "in most jurisdictions, the assignment of particular offenders to particular facilities is primarily managed by prison bureaucrats, not judges." *Punishment for the Greater*

The other trade-off is between material compensation and hard treatment. Material compensation in terms of fines should be limited by the degree of harm caused, in a tort-like sense, as well as by the wrongdoer's capacity to pay. The limits on material compensation in terms of community service are harder to articulate. On the one hand, they could reflect the same tort-like limit: compensation should be capped with reference to the harm caused. On the other hand, the normal subjective toll of community service—which should be relevantly tied to the crime; it should not simply be free labor for the state (like a chain gang)—may be substantially lower than that of serving time in prison, so it might be tempting to set the community service demands to go quite a bit longer. But I think the law in California, to pick one jurisdiction, is correct in limiting it to the maximum prison sentence for the crime.[43] The alternative involves leaving the wrongdoer living with a punishment hanging over his life for too long.

What if these are combined, as they often are? How can their common measure be taken? This is again just a mirror image of the input problem. It requires only some way of ensuring that they do not add up to be disproportionately demanding. For example, fines might increase the overall suffering, but insofar as they are disgorgement of illegally obtained profits, there is no problem in exacting them. And insofar as they are instead simply a form of hard treatment, then a reasonable conversion rate for a given wrongdoer, given his wealth, can be used. The aim of such a conversion rate would be to mimic the idea of a prison sentence of a given length, in a given facility: providing an objective measure of deprivation that is not clearly disproportionately large. This can then be added to any sentence that he serves.

8.4 Concrete Implications of Proportionality

To appreciate the concrete significance of proportionality, I want to start with the most extreme punishment meted out currently in the United States, the death penalty. I think it is unjustifiable. I say that first and foremost because it is inconsistent with the goal of reconciliation between wrongdoer and the moral

Good, 139. Insofar as this trade-off is meant to provide the right measure of punishment, that is a problem. But it is not the problem Kolber thinks it is. He notes that one reason prison bureaucrats put some prisoners in "more austere conditions" is that they are judged "more dangerous." Ibid., 140. He thinks this would require those prisoners to be given shorter sentences. But that's not true. If they have forfeited the POLA, then their more austere conditions may be something they are liable to insofar as they are correctly judged to be more dangerous. Kolber's mistake is to think that retributivists are committed to the view that punishment has to track all suffering.

[43] See C. Bacchi, "What Kind of Community Service Can a Judge Order?" Note, in the United Kingdom, the amount of unpaid work that can be required of a wrongdoer is capped at 300 hours. See U.K. Sentencing Council, "Imposition of Community and Custodial Sentences."

community. One might respond that the worst forms of wrongdoing bring in their wake the most extreme forms of guilt-debt, and those can impose on the wrongdoer the duty to endure the death penalty as the most extreme form of deterrence and norm reinforcement. Such a wrongdoer may not be reconciled with the community in a way that allows her to live reconciled with it for a protracted period of time, but if she gets the death penalty, and if that alone can carry her guilt-debt, then she can go to her death reconciled with her community.[44]

This response is, in principle, sound. But it presupposes that the death penalty would serve uniquely well to pay off a wrongdoer's guilt-debt. Without begging the question and insisting that only death will pay for certain debts, why would anyone think that? The only reason I can see is that death might be uniquely effective as a deterrent. But that is myth. As pointed out in Section 8.2: Certainty of punishment has a much greater deterrent effect than severity of punishment, so deterrence will not provide much pressure toward adopting draconian punishments. Taking the contrary position, Cass Sunstein and Adrian Vermeule report studies claiming to show that the deterrent value of the death penalty is so strong that each execution prevents "some eighteen murders on average."[45] If that were so, then one might be able to argue that it is proportional for the most heinous and culpable of crimes. But these studies are very likely incorrect. As Daniel Nagin and John Pepper write in the National Research Council report on the deterrent effect of the death penalty:

> Research to date on the effect of capital punishment on homicide is not informative about whether capital punishment decreases, increases, or has no effect on homicide rates. . . . Consequently, claims that research demonstrates that capital punishment decreases or increases the homicide rate by a specified amount or has no effect on the homicide rate should not influence policy judgments about capital punishment.[46]

Given that the death penalty lacks a clear and pronounced deterrent effect, there is no reason to think that it could be a proportional punishment for any crime. It makes it impossible to live reconciled with others. Moreover, the principle of parsimony calls for avoiding it, and it is surely unnecessary, as a matter of

[44] Avery Cardinal Dulles argues for a religious analog. He claims that traditional Catholic doctrine had four reasons for supporting the death penalty, one of which included the thought that "In cases where the criminal seems incapable of being reintegrated into human society, the death penalty may be a way of achieving the criminal's reconciliation with God." "Catholicism and Capital Punishment." If we substitute the community for God, one can see the point in the text.

[45] C. Sunstein and A. Vermeule, "Is Capital Punishment Morally Required?" 706. Other studies they cite indicate a lower but still substantial deterrent rate: "an execution deters 3 additional murders." Ibid., 712.

[46] *Deterrence and the Death Penalty*, 3.

cardinal anchoring, to represent the thought that the most serious and culpable crimes are being met with truly serious punishments.

More controversially, I want to argue against life in prison or indeed any sentence much longer than twenty years. The rationale is the same. Fundamentally, the prospect of reconciliation calls for a time in which the wrongdoer gets to resume her life in the community as a person reconciled with it.[47] The only things calling for sentences that approach life in prison are the value of deterrence and of norm reinforcement through having a punishment that conveys the thought that the most serious of crimes are being met with truly serious punishments. But twenty years in prison is surely a very serious punishment. And if the sentencing scheme tops out at twenty years in prison, it would soon enough come to carry the symbolic significance of the most serious punishment. The fact that harsher punishments have been performed elsewhere or in the past should carry no more weight than the fact that today's death penalty is not nearly as gruesome as earlier versions that involved forms of torture inflicted before the person died.

Twenty years could also deter about as effectively as a longer punishment. From the point of view of a young person, the prospect of spending the prime of her life in prison is surely about as horrible as the prospect of spending it all there. Going in at age 25 and coming out at age 45, she would be of an age so different as to seem practically a different person.[48] And even if she went in at 45, the prospect of coming out at age 65 would mean that she would only be free again as a fairly old woman. If one is willing to risk spending that much of one's life in prison, one is presumably also willing to risk spending all of it in prison. The extra period might make some difference in some cases, but surely not much and in few.[49]

[47] This was a point made by the German constitutional court, which held that respect for dignity requires that prisoners have "opportunities to resocialize themselves." D. van Zyl Smit, "Outlawing Irreducible Life Sentences," 40 (describing the position taken in *Lebach*, BVerfGE 35, 203). For a more personal appreciation of the pro tanto injustice of denying people this opportunity, see M. Kondkar et al., "They Know What They Did." See also the ECtHR, which recognizes a "right to hope" that tells against whole life sentences. See Hutchinson v. The United Kingdom, 57592/08 (2017).

[48] See again Tomlin's argument in favor of shorter but harsher sentences. See n. 38 and accompanying text.

[49] One complication with a 20-year cap in the United States is that our system, being largely dependent on plea bargaining, threatens longer sentences to induce plea bargains. If a 20-year cap were imposed, then in practice the maximum sentences would end up being much shorter; either that or the United States would have to change its reliance on plea bargains. Given that other countries with adversarial systems (like England) run criminal justice systems without such reliance on plea bargains driven by the sort of high discounts offered in the United States, and given the unfairness of imposing such extreme costs on people who choose to exercise their right to go to trial and who are then convicted, I suggest the solution should be to substantially reform the plea-bargaining system in the United States. See J. Turner and T. Weigend, "Negotiated Case Dispositions in Germany, England and the United States."

It could be argued that a life sentence with the possibility of parole allows one to have at least the hope of living reconciled with the community. But it is a hope that would be, as parole is, contingent on the unreliable judgment of a parole board. There is no need for the longer sentence in general. And if there is a need for incapacitation past twenty years, it should be addressed by appeal to forfeiture of the POLA,[50] not as ongoing punishment that might be lifted for good behavior.

Conversely, one might think that even twenty years in prison is more than necessary for the high-end anchor. Who, after all, would consider committing a murder if the punishment were ten years, but not if it were twenty? It seems likely that one is either so dedicated to committing the murder that one would do it even if the punishment were life, or one would take the punishment of ten years in prison as sufficient deterrent reason not to commit it (assuming the same odds of being caught and punished). There may be a few recidivists, for whom time in prison has a concrete meaning, for whom such a difference might make a difference, but surely there are not many people for whom it would make a significant difference. And the principle of parsimony would then call for dropping the high-end sanction even lower.

But I think there are meaningful counter-pressures. The first is symbolic; twenty years already feels, at least in the United States, like a sentence on the low side of serious; ten feels like a distinctly low sentence for the worst of crimes. This reason has only limited weight, however, as the symbolic value of a ten-year sentence could shift over time.

Second, a concern with incapacitation may make a difference. If we assume that the anchor point for the most serious crimes is up for debate, but that detaining some people, those who have committed the most serious crimes, for twenty years, as opposed to ten, would make a meaningful difference to security, then I think the concern with incapacitation can push the state in the direction of the longer prison term.[51] To be clear, this move requires us to assume that a twenty-year sentence is equally plausible as a proportional punishment. But that seems credible to me. In addition, if it is that important, for the sake of security, to be able to detain people who commit the most serious crimes for at least twenty years, there are reasons to prefer *not* to rely on a shorter sentence followed by POLA forfeiture. If we take the most serious offenders to deserve only a ten-year sentence, followed by ten more years of POLA forfeiture, then they would be entitled to the least restrictive alternative, which often would not be incarceration, but which would result, we can assume, in either more crimes being committed or in higher costs to police these individuals. Moreover, if most

[50] See Ch. 16.
[51] See § 2 and Sections 1.3.5, 2.4, and especially 7.2.

serious wrongdoers could simply be released upon serving twenty years, then we would have a situation that is symbolically better in society at large if they were sentenced to twenty years: we would have fewer people living in the alienating condition of having served their punishment but still living without the POLA. Taken together, I think these reasons provide good reason to keep a longer maximal sentence.

I want now to end this section with two final thoughts. First, I am not suggesting that twenty years is a magic number. Maybe the maximal sentence should be fifteen years, or thirty years. Empirical details such as those discussed in the previous two paragraphs should inform that choice. In addition, it could be argued that there should be some flexibility to go higher than the normal maximum punishment for extremely culpable crimes, if for no other reason than to be able to symbolically recognize that some crimes are particularly heinous.[52] My point is only that something like twenty years is more defensible than life in prison as the maximal sentence under normal conditions.

Second, I am not suggesting that those who commit the most heinous of crimes should consider their guilt fully owned and in the past after their sentences are up. As I noted before, while a person may be able to fully make amends, there is no reason to think that the feelings of guilt *should* be assuaged at the same time.[53] But it is also important to turn that point around. Even if one should, to quote Michael Moore, "feel guilty unto death,"[54] that does not mean that one should be punished unto death. Punishment addresses only what is necessary and proportional for the particular purposes it serves. The feeling of guilt is a related but nonetheless distinct matter.

8.5 An Objection Based on Universal Jurisdiction

I have argued that the state can get enough substance to apply the notion of negative proportionality if it appeals to a combination of ordinal proportionality and a schedule of punishment that is legally anchored by meting out punishments so that minor crimes get a minor punishment, and the most serious crimes get a serious punishment, and other punishments are distributed appropriately in between. But a problem might seem to arise if we allow for universal jurisdiction.[55]

[52] This is effectively the position in German law. Code § 57a (1) directs courts to suspend the remainder of life sentences after 15 years have been served, with two meaningful exceptions. The first exception is that "the particular severity of the convicted person's guilt does not require its continued enforcement." This corresponds to the idea in the text. The other exception is that suspended enforcement "can be justified having regard to public security interests." § 57(1)(2). This point is better understood, I think, in terms of POLA forfeiture.

[53] See Section 6.5.1.

[54] *Placing Blame*, 145.

[55] For my defense of universal jurisdiction within my model of punishment, see Section 5.5.2.

Consider this test case. Suppose the United States and Germany both take an interest in prosecuting an alien defendant for an act of international terrorism, and both invoke universal jurisdiction.[56] And imagine a counterfactual United States in which the maximal punishment is thirty years in prison, while Germany retains its commitment to fifteen years as a default maximal punishment, which, we can assume, it would apply in this case.[57] If Germany tried and convicted the defendant and sentenced him to fifteen years, could the United States complain that the punishment was too light? And if the United States tried and convicted him and sentenced him to thirty years, could Germany claim that the punishment was too draconian?

My response is that they should both respect the sentence of the other if the other takes jurisdiction of the defendant.[58] Each is vying to do the same thing, to express condemnation on behalf of the broader community of the republic of rights using its own schedule of punishment to collect his guilt-debt on behalf of all of humanity. As long as its schedule is defensible in terms of ordinal proportionality, and its anchor points are reasonably set with reference to its own culture and its own needs for deterrence and norm reinforcement, taking parsimony properly into account, it may use its scheme.[59] If Germany got to exercise jurisdiction and punished him with fifteen years in prison and then released him, the United States should refrain from seeking to arrest him to impose an additional fifteen years in prison. It should recognize Germany as having acceptably imposed the punishment he deserved.

I think the case comes out differently if we suppose that the United States is seeking to exercise jurisdiction based on passive personality,[60] on the ground that U.S. citizens were among those killed. The United States would then be claiming a right to impose punishment not just on behalf of the republic of rights but on behalf of its citizens.[61] For that, it might reasonably say that fifteen years

[56] According to Amnesty International, both Germany and the United States have invoked universal jurisdiction since World War II. "Universal Jurisdiction," 10, n. 23.

[57] See n. 52.

[58] This accords with international law commitment to the double jeopardy principle (*non bis in idem*). See Zolotukhin v. Russia, European Court of Human Rights, Feb. 10, 2009 (application no. 14939/03), ¶¶ 31–44.

[59] There are limits. Kolber discusses the case of Ex Parte *Crow Dog*, 109 U.S. 556 (1883), concerning a Native American who killed another Native American, and who was punished, as a matter of tribal justice, by being made to make monetary restitution to the victim's family. *Punishment for the Greater Good*, 64. The United States considered that punishment inadequate. I agree. I believe the tribal justice system was not trying to operate a regime of retributive justice of the sort I'm discussing in this book; more likely, it was operating a restorative justice process. It's a separate question whether the United States had jurisdiction to intervene. The U.S. Supreme Court found it did not.

[60] Passive personality jurisdiction allows a country to prosecute non-resident aliens who wrong its own citizens abroad.

[61] This would provide an exception to the double jeopardy rule based on the fact that the United States and Germany would be prosecuting based on different acts: the killing of their own citizens, respectively.

punishment was insufficient, and it might reasonably seek extradition to impose an additional fifteen years of punishment. But if we suppose that its interest is in exercising universal jurisdiction, then it should recognize that the debt has been collected.

One might object: How can a person owe either fifteen years or thirty years? What kind of debt is that? No contractual debt could be that open-ended in magnitude. Arguably no tort debt should be that open either. But the criminal law's guilt-debt is fundamentally a more symbolic matter. It is not completely open-ended the way symbolic representation of ideas in words is. There is a limited range of reasonable interpretations of the idea of the most serious punitive burdens that can be imposed on a wrongdoer. But within that range, any country can act on behalf of all citizens in the republic of rights. And if an agent commits a crime grave enough to ground universal jurisdiction, he is on notice—there is no ex post facto violation—that the material expression of that idea will vary from state to state, and thus the punishment he may suffer will depend on who actually takes jurisdiction over him.

PART III

THE VALUE AND LIMITS OF THE CRIMINAL LAW

9
Consequentialist Concerns about the Criminal Law

9.1 The Basic Consequentialist Challenge

I have argued that the security benefits of the criminal law contribute to its overall value.[1] But whether its benefits outweigh its costs is an empirical question. Moreover, the question cannot simply be: Does the proportional censure and punishment of culpable wrongdoing provide more benefit than cost? There are an infinite number of ways to establish punishment regimes that are at least in principle consistent with the dignity-respecting model. The question has to be: Could a legal regime that metes out censure and punishment, if run as well as we could reasonably expect, have benefits, including security against crime, that outweigh its costs? And it's important to see this question as arising in a comparative context. The question is not simply: Would it be better to have proportional censure and punishment as opposed to no institutions for holding people accountable and reinforcing respect for the law? The question is: Could a legal regime that metes out censure and punishment, if run as well as we could reasonably expect, have greater benefits than an alternative set of institutions for holding people accountable and reinforcing respect for the law that excludes censure and punishment?

The consequentialist critique of the criminal law holds that the answer to this question is: No; a set of institutions that includes censure and punishment will be worse than a set of institutions that excludes them. My aim here is to respond to that challenge. But I have to qualify my response in two ways. First, I am not an empiricist and answering the question in a substantive way is well outside my abilities and the scope of this book. All I can offer are a few brief observations about the sorts of issues that are at stake. However, I hope that in doing so I can show that the answer is quite plausibly: Yes; including censure and punishment is likely to be a net positive. Second, when I talk of a consequentialist critique, I don't really mean to engage in a pure consequentialist analysis. As I pointed out in Chapter 3, I think pure consequentialism is *never* the right approach, even for

[1] See Sections 1.3.2 and 2.4.

Punishment, Penalty, and Incapacitation. Alec Walen, Oxford University Press. © Oxford University Press 2026.
DOI: 10.1093/9780197523124.003.0009

basic policy questions.[2] That's because it does not track the way claims register on the state. Claims are always relational, and claims for help are weaker, all else equal, than claims not to be harmed; likewise, claims not to be used as a means, at least if the harm is serious, block the justification of state action *even if* it would reduce the total number of cases of people being used as a means.[3] Nonetheless, to a first approximation, a consequentialist analysis is appropriate to answer this kind of policy-choice question.

The basic consequentialist challenge rests on the thought that the costs of censure and punishment—for the rest of this chapter, I will focus on punishment—are so great that they cannot plausibly be justifiable. There are, in places like the United States, at least six significant types of cost:

1) The institutions are financially very expensive, and the money might be better spent elsewhere, such as on education, healthcare, transportation, and other forms of infrastructure.[4]
2) Errors can unjustly lead to the imposition of significant costs on the innocent or disproportionately excessive costs on the guilty.
3) The power to punish can be abused for personal or political purposes.
4) The collateral consequences of punishment on the families and communities of the punished are often very costly.[5]
5) Those who are punished often emerge from the process alienated and damaged in ways that make them *more* likely to commit future crimes and *less* likely to serve as constructive members of society.
6) If carried out unjustly, or in an already unjust society, punishment can exacerbate already strained relations between classes or races that make up the population.

9.2 Responses to the Consequentialist Challenge

Against these costs we have at least six hoped-for benefits:

1) Punishment responds to the imperative—one grounded in the very nature of a space of rights—to achieve reconciliation between culpable wrongdoers and the political community.

[2] See Sections 3.2-3.3.

[3] See Sections 2.3 and 3.3.2.

[4] This and the next two costs are taken from D. Husak, "Holistic Retributivism," 996-997.

[5] The effects on children of having incarcerated parents can be particularly damaging and long-lasting and can be criminogenic as well. For a collection of resources on this issue, see National Institute of Corrections, "Children of Incarcerated Parents."

2) Punishment can deter future wrongdoing.[6]
3) Punishment can serve to rehabilitate wrongdoers so that they are *less* likely to commit future crimes and are better able to serve as constructive members of society.
4) Punishment can pacify the resentment and indignation others would feel at the prospect of wrongdoers "getting away" with their crimes and feeling happy about having committed them.
5) Punishment can reinforce moral and legal norms in society.
6) Punishment can incapacitate the dangerous—not as a defining or constitutive aim of punishment, but as a valuable side effect and as a secondary aim that may lead a state to choose one type of punishment over others.

It seems plausible to me that the benefits, all told, outweigh the costs. My primary reason for saying that is that it is perfectly clear that a society needs some way of holding people accountable for culpable wrongdoing; a state that failed too drastically on that score would become a failed state and other powers would arise and seek to do that essential job.[7]

It may be responded that it is not clear that punishment itself has to be a large part of the criminal justice system. Some mix of restorative justice and forfeiture-based penalties might also do the trick. And if the essential job of holding people accountable and providing security can be taken care of with little or no punishment, then maybe adding punishment to the mix only makes things worse.

Again, I am not able to answer this challenge with appeals to empirical data. But I can articulate reasons for thinking that it's not clear that the combination of penal law and restorative justice could do substantially better operating alone rather than as complements to the criminal law. The institutions of penal law and restorative justice would still be very expensive and would still soak up resources that could otherwise be spent elsewhere. There's still a risk that penal law convictions would make mistakes and impose penalties on the innocent. And given that part of the purpose of penal law is to allow the state to impose sanctions that are harsher than would be proportional under the criminal law, the risks to the innocent are, in a straightforward way, even greater.[8] And while restorative justice does not seem to run the same risk of sanctioning the innocent, that is only because it presupposes that the sanctioned person owns her guilt. In contested cases, restorative justice runs into trouble.[9] In addition, restorative justice seems to have more problems with deterrence, which calls for using

[6] See D. Nagin, "Deterrence in the Twenty-First Century," 200.

[7] See Section 1.1.

[8] See Section 12.3. In another way, they are lower, as the censure dimension would be missing. I leave it to the reader to decide how those two balance against each other.

[9] See Section 11.2.1.

either the criminal law or penal law.[10] The power to impose penal sanctions or restorative justice penalties can also be abused. Collateral consequences may be taken into account better in restorative justice, but they would not be taken into account better with the penal law. The same is true for the alienating and criminogenic properties of penal law institutions, and with the problem of strained relations between classes and races in an unjust society.[11] Finally, insofar as restorative justice or penal law seem to provide useful functions that are missed by the criminal law alone, I am open to using them.

In sum, the fundamental need for *something* like the criminal law means that its costs, or related costs, almost certainly have to be borne. Sensible reforms in the criminal law may help lower them, but they cannot simply be avoided by embracing some alternative set of practices. And that suggests that the distinct goods provided by the criminal law—especially the aim of achieving reconciliation between culpable wrongdoers and the political community—provide the state with good consequentialist reason to keep the criminal law.[12] I lack the empirical data to argue that the reason is dispositive; I claim only that it is plausibly great enough to keep the criminal law in the mix, and quite likely to keep it at the center of the criminal justice system.

9.3 Confusions to Avoid

I close out this chapter with a brief discussion of three confusions to avoid. First, Erin Kelly contends that the idea of blame in the criminal justice system marks convicted criminals as "defective, tainted, and morally inferior."[13] This marking, or stigmatizing, is a cost that she takes to provide strong reason not to use the criminal law. In response I want to say that there is no doubt that stigmatizing is part of what happens in punishment as it now occurs, at least in places like the United States. But it is important to see that this is not the essence of punishment, as properly conceived.[14] Its essence is to communicate censure, extract the debt owed, and set a foundation for reconciliation. Insofar as this marking is an unfortunate side effect of punishment, even when done in an optimal manner, it is to be counted a cost.[15] In sum, this is a real concern, but it is a concern that

[10] See ibid.

[11] See also A. Lanni, "Taking Restorative Justice Seriously" (acknowledging that racial and class problems can persist for restorative justice). See also R. Delgado, "Prosecuting Violence."

[12] See Section 15.1.3. See also Duff, *The Realm of Criminal Law*, 212, 283 (emphasizing how important it is for public institutions to hold defendants to account for their public wrongdoing—something that is lost on the alternative models).

[13] E. Kelly, *The Limits of Blame*, 9; E. Kelly, "From Retributive to Restorative Justice," 244-245.

[14] See Sections 6.3-6.4.

[15] I would count it under cost (5) in the list in § 1.

should be seen as theoretically subject to minimization, as there is no reason such alienation should be seen as a goal of punishment.[16]

Second, a number of theorists charge that retributivism itself, as a theory, has contributed to overpunishment, in a way that causes more harm than good. Consider the charge as made by James Whitman. He acknowledges that "all thoughtful philosophers are careful to distinguish retribution from vindictiveness or vengeful ferocity, just as all of them insist on the principle of proportionality."[17] But then he adds that "[t]he problem . . . is that the public is not very good at understanding all the subtle stuff."[18] He continues: "to the extent retributivist philosophers are heard at all, they are heard in ways that amount to pouring gasoline on the fires of American punishment."[19] In other words, books like this one may be, for the most part, culturally and politically irrelevant, but to the extent that they influence anyone by giving support to the idea of retributive justice, I and this book are likely doing more harm than good.

I'm willing to accept the risk of being either irrelevant or dangerous. But I want to say three things in reply. First, even if retributive theory is dangerous, that does not show that *punishment* necessarily does more harm than good. Second, while retributive theory *might* do more harm than good, it also might do more good than harm. As Douglas Husak puts it:

> Desert-based arguments can be used to bring about reductions in the severity of sentences either by narrowing the number and breadth of offenses, or by increasing the scope and application of defenses. . . Thus retributivists should be encouraged to promote themselves as part of the solution rather than as a cause of the problem of mass incarceration and over-punishment.[20]

Third, there is good reason to think that retributive theory has had a negligible role in causing the United States, in particular, over the past fifty years or so, to become such a "world leader" in punishment. As John Pfaff points out, as of 2016, the United States has "the world's highest incarceration rate, one that is four to eight times higher than those in other liberal democracies . . . [even] repressive regimes like Russia and Cuba have . . . lower incarceration rates."[21] But it wasn't always so. "[I]n the 1970s, [the US] incarceration rate was one-fifth what

[16] Constanza Porro argues that criminal censure is necessarily more "stigmatizing and exclusionary" than moral blame between individuals. "Criminal Blame, Exclusion and Moral Dialogue," 226. I don't dispute the considerations she raises in support of that claim, but I insist that these problematic features are reasons for the state to take care, not problems that show that the state, in punishing, is "systematically disregard[ing] one of its core duties." Ibid., 230.

[17] "A Plea Against Retributivism," 93.

[18] Ibid.

[19] Ibid., 94.

[20] "Retributivism and Over-Punishment," 190.

[21] *Locked In*, 1.

it is today. It was comparable to that of most European countries, and it had been relatively stable all the way back to the mid- to late 1800s."[22] What happened? Part of the explanation, according to Pfaff, is that crimes rates started to climb in the 1960s. But looking carefully at the data and the politics, Pfaff concludes that "Prosecutors have been and remain the engines driving mass incarceration. Acting with wide discretion and little oversight, they are largely responsible for the staggering rise in admissions since the early 1990s."[23] Assuming this is right, the reasons for overpunishment in the United States are fundamentally structural, not a result of the promulgation of retributive theory.[24]

This brings me to the third confusion to avoid: confusing the thought that prisons as now used, at least in the United States, cause more harm than benefit with the thought that punishment as a whole should be abolished. Pushing for prison abolition has become fairly popular in recent years.[25] I remain skeptical of the abolitionist movement,[26] but like any fair-minded observer, I acknowledge that too many people, at least in the United States, are spending or have spent time, often too much time, in jail or prison. But this is not an objection to punishment per se; it is an objection to the overuse of a particular *method* of punishment.

I am not ready to join Husak when he claims: "retributivists have no basis to prefer one [method] to another on grounds of desert. Since they have no special allegiance to incarceration as the default mode of punishment, retributivists can even join the growing chorus of penal theorists who advocate prison abolitionism."[27] As I pointed out above,[28] states have good reason to want to have hard treatment as one mode of punishment, and as I also pointed out,[29] states have good reason to treat deprivation of liberty (in prisons) as the paradigmatic form of hard treatment. But saying that is consistent with saying that the use of prisons, at least in the United States, is in need of reform, so that prisons are less degrading and put people less at risk of physical abuse, so that people are sent to prison less often and for less time, and so that racial and class disparities come to play little to no role in determining who gets sent to prison, at least when controlling for the culpability of the crimes committed.

22 Ibid.
23 Ibid., 206.
24 It is also worth noting that the great rise in incarceration in the United States is not a result of the war on drugs. As Pfaff points out, "As of the end of 2015, about 15% of all people in state prisons [were] there for drugs." "Decarceration's Blindspots," 263. Moreover, that "number overstates the number who are 'truly' in prison for drugs." Ibid., 264. That is because "[p]rison data classifies an inmate by the most serious offense for which he was *convicted*, not for which he was charged or arrested." Ibid. If charges for a more serious violent offense were dropped as part of a plea bargain, the "defendant will show up in prison data as a 'non-violent' drug case, even though the conduct that brought him into contact with the police is violent." Ibid.
25 See Section 1.3.3. See also the student note, "Developments in the Law – Prison Abolition."
26 See Section 1.3.3.
27 "Retributivism and Over-Punishment," 176.
28 See Section 7.1.2.
29 See Section 5.2.

10
The Standing to Blame of an Unjust State

10.1 The Problem of Standing and the Power to Call to Account

The United States—and I presume most if not all other countries—continues to struggle with substantial injustices.[1] Over the past seventy years or so, it has improved in many regards. Most obviously, Civil Rights legislation addressed the worst forms of racism and sexism.[2] Progress has been made. But much progress remains to be made.[3] And this raises the question: Can a state that tolerates or even perpetuates substantial forms of injustice, much of which it was responsible for creating, have the standing to censure culpable wrongdoers?[4] If not, then it seems that it must also lack the standing to punish, as state punishment is a feature of the criminal law as a blaming institution.[5]

To answer the question of whether an unjust state retains the standing to blame, I start by addressing the question: What does it mean to have standing to blame? As the title of this section implies, the standing to blame is, in my view, the power to call to account, which implies more than the right to *communicate* blame; it also involves having the power to impose on those who are blamed a pro tanto duty to answer the charge of wrongdoing. This power presupposes that the blamer has the right kind of relationship (is not just a busybody) to the blamed person, that the blamed person is a responsible agent who can account for his actions, and that he has done something prima facie wrong.[6]

[1] It is, in a way, odd to focus on the United States, because it is a federal system and much of what goes wrong, in terms of injustices, happens at the level of individual states or even counties, cities, and towns. Moreover, not all local jurisdictions have the same problems. But to avoid picking on a particular state, and to acknowledge the extent to which the states are *united*, legally and culturally, in one country, I'll speak of the United States. Insofar as it is relevant, the reader should imagine that the proper focus of the discussion is an individual state or local jurisdiction.

[2] See, e.g., Title VII of the Civil Rights Act, 42 U.S.C. §§ 2000e–2000e17 (1964) (as amended), which, among other things, banned employment discrimination based on race, color, religion, sex, and national origin.

[3] And as I revise this, it looks likely that much progress will be *undone*.

[4] Among those who argue that it lacks this standing, at least insofar as punishment is meant to convey blame, are T. Shelby, *Dark Ghettos*, ch 8, and E. Kelly, *The Limits of Blame*, ch. 6.

[5] See Section 1.3.3.

[6] J. Edwards is particularly clear and helpful on these points. See "Standing to Hold Responsible," 446-452. (For a weaker conception of the power to blame, see B. Ewing, "Do Unjust States Have the Standing to Blame?" 253-254.) I disagree with Edwards, however, on one point. Edwards says that the person blamed must have committed a "pro tanto" wrong. I think that's a mistake. That implies that there was something wrongmaking about what he did, even if it was not wrong all things

Punishment, Penalty, and Incapacitation. Alec Walen, Oxford University Press. © Oxford University Press 2026.
DOI: 10.1093/9780197523124.003.0010

To illustrate: if A blames B, and B is (and was when he performed the act in question) a responsible agent (the kind who can rightly be blamed for wrongful actions), then B can offer one of three kinds of responses that take A seriously as an interlocutor.[7] First, he can deny that he did anything that was actually blameworthy, either because he did not do the act in question, or, if he did it, the act was not in fact blameworthy (because it was either justified or excused). Second, he can accept that his action was blameworthy and offer remorse and, if appropriate, make amends. Third, he can deny that A has the standing to call him to account. That is, he can deny that he has a duty to respond to her with an accounting of what he has done. Others, he might say, retain the power to call him to account, but that power is agent relative, and he might say that she lacks it. If he takes this third option, then it doesn't matter if he has done something blameworthy; the challenge to A's standing asserts that she has no power to call him to account and he has no duty to respond on the substance of the accusation that is contained in her blame.

10.2 How to Lack the Standing to Blame

The basic idea behind the thought that an agent lacks the standing to blame another is that it sometimes makes sense for someone to respond to blame with: "Who are you to blame me?" There are at least four ways that this response can arise: the busybody objection, hypocrisy, complicity, and non-reciprocity/exclusion.

The busybody objection is a way of saying that another *has* no standing to cast blame, not that he has *lost* his standing do so. It manifests in the private law as lack of standing to bring a case.[8] The court system doesn't want busybodies bringing suits; it wants suits to be brought only by those with a personal stake. If A has been injured by B, then A has standing to sue B. By contrast, if C just saw

considered. That's too strong. The blamer can have standing if she could have reasonably judged his act wrong. The better term is thus "prima facie." I add, however, that the law should distinguish two ways of accepting the facts charged but rejecting that they are blameworthy. A response that claims that the action was merely prima facie wrong is one that calls for dismissing the charges up front. This corresponds to a de minimis defense. If the action was a pro tanto wrong, then a trial might be required to determine if it was (a) *merely* pro tanto (because justified) or (b) a wrong all things considered but still excused. For similar thoughts, see A. Duff, "'De Minimis' and the Structure of the Criminal Trial."

[7] B can also not respond or respond by changing the topic in some way.

[8] I focus here on the first of the three canonical requirements for standing: "an injury in fact (i.e., a concrete and particularized invasion of a legally protected interest)." Sprint Communications Co. v. APCC Services, 554 U.S. 269, 273 (2008) (internal quotation marks omitted). The other two elements are causation and redressability.

A get injured by B, and C was not especially traumatized, then C lacks standing to sue B.

In the context of a defendant objecting to a state bringing criminal charges, the legal point is a jurisdictional one. If A wrongs B in state C, C has standing to prosecute A, but state D presumably does not. There are exceptions to this presumptive jurisdictional limit. If A or B is a citizen of D, then D has some claim to jurisdiction.[9] Or if A wronged B in a particularly egregious way, and C is doing nothing about it, then D may claim universal jurisdiction.[10] But universal jurisdiction is meant to apply only in exceptional cases. Normally, states must avoid the busybody objection by appealing to another form of jurisdiction.[11]

How can a state *lose* standing? One thought is that it can lose standing just as a private person would lose standing in an interpersonal context, by acting as a hypocrite. The question this raises is: What's so bad about hypocrisy? Why should it undermine standing to call to account?[12] There are two common answers to this question in the literature: the moral equality account[13] and the commitment account.[14] The moral equality account holds that a hypocrite "lacks standing to blame because his act of blaming, or some other fact about him [such as an unfair differential blaming disposition], clashes with the basic moral equality of persons."[15] The commitment account holds that a hypocrite "lacks standing to blame because he is not committed to the norm he is invoking."[16] Between these two, I am more inclined to follow Kasper Lippert-Rasmussen in rejecting the former and embracing the latter.[17] The important thought in the

[9] If A is a citizen of D, then the nationality principle would allow D to prosecute her. See K. Gallant, *International Criminal Jurisdiction,* ch. 5. If B is a citizen of D, then the passive personality principle would allow D to prosecute A if he commits certain heinous crimes against B. See ibid., ch. 7.

[10] See Section 5.5.2.

[11] Morality may seem to be less concerned with the busybody problem. We can often blame strangers for what they do to strangers. But not always. Duff offers the example of someone who fails to buy rounds of drinks when going out with their friends. The friends have a reason to complain; strangers don't. See "Responsibility, Citizenship and Criminal Law," 133.

[12] There's a separate question of whether and in what sense hypocrisy wrongs others. That is mostly beyond the scope of my concern here, which focuses only on why the power to blame might be lost.

[13] Supporters include R. J. Wallace, "Hypocrisy, Moral Address, and the Equal Standing of Persons"; and G. Fritz and D. Miller, "Hypocrisy and the Standing to Blame."

[14] Supporters include K. Lippert-Rasmussen, "Why the Moral Equality Account of the Hypocrite's Lack of Standing to Blame Fails," and "Lesser Transgressions and Loss of Standing to Blame"; S. Riedener. "The Standing to Blame, or Why Moral Disapproval is What It Is"; and P. Todd, "A Unified Account of the Standing to Blame."

[15] Lippert-Rasmussen, "Lesser Transgressions and Loss of Standing to Blame," 7.

[16] Ibid., 9.

[17] See ibid. Fleshing out the reasons here would take too much space. For a critical response, see J. Snegegar's review of Lippert-Rasmussen's *The Beam and the Mote.* I agree with his criticism that one can be a hypocrite and think one is committed to the norm in question, despite not applying it to oneself in a plausible way, because one engages in ad hoc rationalizations or simply does not critically self-reflect. Nevertheless, I think that Lippert-Rasmussen's account is in the right ballpark.

latter is that if one is not suitably committed to the norm in question—a lot gets packed into "suitably"—then one forfeits the power to call to account.

Another thought about how the state can lose standing is through what has been called complicity in the wrongdoing of the other.[18] If one party bears responsibility for the other one acting unjustly, then the first party's standing to complain is seriously compromised. Imagine A coerced B into stealing from C, and then A blames B for doing so. Given A's coercive pressure, B can say to A: "You, of all people, have no business blaming me for that theft." States are unlikely to engage in this sort of intentional coercion to commit a wrong, but they are likely to "create[] or fail[] to eradicate conditions of criminogenic injustice" that could make it hard for individuals to avoid committing certain kinds of crimes.[19] If the state is culpable for the creation of or failure to eradicate these conditions, then it might seem that those who are subject to those conditions, whose wrongful actions are prompted by them, can rightly reject the state's standing to blame them.

A third and final thought about how the state might lose its standing to blame appeals to non-reciprocity/exclusion. At an individual level, this manifests as a failure of reciprocity: if A refuses to hear blame from B for wrongs she may commit against B, then B can refuse to accept blame from A. At the state level, this failure can manifest as exclusion. In its paradigmatic form, it appears as unjust exclusion from the status of fellow citizen with a right to criticize the state and hold it accountable. And in a theory, like mine, in which the point of punishment is reconciliation, it's obvious why this is important. Reconciliation is a two-way street. It is therefore no surprise that in Antony Duff's work on state standing, this idea takes center stage. As he puts it:

> [T]he question is whether [someone] is answerable as a citizen to his fellow citizens: but if their collective treatment of him has effectively excluded him from many of the rights and goods of citizenship, if they have collectively failed to treat him as a citizen, how can they now call him to account as a fellow citizen?[20]

In other words, unjust exclusion undermines reciprocity, but reciprocity is a precondition of blame playing its proper function in pursuit of reconciliation.[21]

[18] The problem of complicity seems to have been raised first by G. Cohen in "Casting the First Stone: Who Can, and Who Can't, Condemn the Terrorists?" See also Victor Tadros in "Poverty and Criminal Responsibility." As Gary Watson notes, however, the "claim of the law's complicity is a moral, not a legal claim." "A Moral Predicament in the Criminal Law." It does not require the same mens rea as the crime and is not itself a crime, just a basis for lost standing.

[19] B. Ewing, "Do Unjust States Have the Standing to Blame?" 258.

[20] *Punishment, Communication, and Community*, 188.

[21] See Sections 5.1, 6.4, and 7.3.

10.3 Assessing These Bases for Loss of State Standing to Blame

I want now to assess how plausible it is that these three bases for loss of standing to blame might impact an unjust state.[22] Before proceeding, I want to emphasize that there are two different ways the state's injustice might block it from punishing people who commit what would ordinarily be crimes. The state's injustice might cost it the standing to blame, but it might also change what counts as justified or excused behavior.[23] Consider, for example, economic injustices that might leave people without adequate legal means to provide for food, clothing, shelter, or a life with social dignity. That sort of injustice might justify people violating a range of laws as a matter of necessity. For example, a homeless person might be justified in squatting in a building to find shelter, or in selling illegal drugs if there is no other work available to him.[24] Economic injustice might also contribute to excuses. Extreme poverty is known to make rational decision-making difficult.[25] But my concern is different; it is with cases in which the person is still morally blameworthy, but the state lacks the standing to blame him.

10.3.1 State Hypocrisy

I start with hypocrisy, understood as failed commitment to norms. What might that look like? There are complete and partial versions, and the latter is much more likely to be a problem—it is very unlikely that a state will completely fail to respect the values that undergird important sets of criminal laws, such as the value of life or property. States are substantially more likely to fail to respect the lives or property of members of some marginalized or politically unpopular groups, as opposed to failing to respect those goods altogether. But one might find hypocrisy in the state blaming the well-connected as well as the marginalized and oppressed.[26] Even if the state is blaming the well-connected, its failed commitment to the relevant norms makes its blaming hypocritical.

The main question is: What kinds of failure to provide protection would forfeit the standing to blame? Focusing on the domestic setting, where the state should provide comprehensive rights protection, the easy cases are those in which the state intentionally treats certain people as undeserving

[22] I assume the jurisdictional issue is nonproblematic.

[23] For a general treatment of this possibility, see Stuart Green, "Just Deserts in Unjust Societies: A Case-specific Approach."

[24] For a similar list, see A. Duff, *Punishment, Communication, and Community*, 182.

[25] See, e.g., Sendhil Mullainathan and Eldar Shafir, *Scarcity: Why Having Too Little Means So Much*; Cara Feinberg, "The Science of Scarcity."

[26] See V. Tadros, "Poverty and Criminal Responsibility," 395; B. Ewing, "Do Unjust States Have the Standing to Blame?" 258.

of protection. These are cases in which the state essentially excludes those individuals from meaningful participation in the economic and political dimensions of their countries. Examples include the treatment of Black people in the United States living under slavery or Jim Crow, or Jews living in Nazi Germany.[27]

The more difficult cases are the ones in which the state may offer unequal and inadequate protection, but the reasons for doing so are complicated and arguably involve negligence as much as intentional exclusionary disregard. Consider the problems of inadequate policing in poor or racial minority communities in the United States.[28] This is complicated terrain. Sometimes what looks like state failure to invest is as much a reflection of the well-earned community distrust of the police, which makes it harder for the police to provide protection.[29] The existence of racial bias in policing may substantially explain the mistrust, but bias, at least implicit bias, is hard to overcome.[30] And insofar as the problem is that the police have the unenviable job of enforcing the law on communities that suffer from structural injustices, there may be no way of doing so that will not engender distrust at the same time as it does what needs to be done.

It's not my place here to wade into these sorts of problems and disputes. I will, however, say this: I think the state can lose the standing to blame based on hypocrisy only if its failure to take care of the welfare of those it blames is itself a culpable failure, a failure that shows inadequate commitment to the relevant norms. I'm not saying that the United States's failure is or is not culpable. But I do want to say that insofar as problems result from intractable difficulties dealing with complex problems, then the state's acts and omissions, relying on reasonable even if mistaken opinions on how best to deal with them, are not culpable. Insofar as the state's failure is based on negligence, it might be culpable, but it is culpable only if it is really a matter of negligence, not mere mistake. Finally, we should be fairly generous with regard to the state's claims to have standing to blame, for reasons that will become clearer when I address the idea of exclusion.

[27] I return to those cases in Section 3.3.

[28] On inadequate policing and the possibility of doing better, see J. Leovy, *Ghettoside*.

[29] See M. Bell, "Police Reform and the Dismantling of Legal Estrangement" (discussing illegitimacy of police, the efforts to address that with procedural changes, and the need for more substantive changes when minority communities are estranged based on a belief that the law exists to oppress them). See also See M. Alexander, *The New Jim Crow* (articulating the view that American policing of poor, minority communities as essentially the continuation of Jim Crow in another form).

[30] See C. Lai et al, "Reducing Implicit Racial Preferences" (examining eight interventions meant to reduce implicit racial biases and finding that none were effective after a delay of more than several days). But see R. Fryer, "An Empirical Analysis of Racial Differences in Police Use of Force" (arguing that police use of force shows no racial bias when they use lethal force, though acknowledging that it shows racial bias when they use nonlethal force); C. Epp et al., "Beyond Profiling" (distinguishing the bias that shows up in discretionary but not in non-discretionary investigatory stops).

10.3.2 State Complicity in Criminal Behavior

What about complicity? There is reason to think that states at the very least tolerate conditions that are criminogenic. As Corina Graif and her collaborators write: "[S]tudies find that neighborhood poverty and associated structural factors continue to predict multiple crime-related outcomes, including: . . . adolescent violent crime; aggression; . . . domestic violence; . . . and recidivism. With few exceptions, these patterns tend to hold in multiple cities and in nationally representative studies."[31] And Ta-Nehisi Coates reports that "When . . . Robert J. Sampson examined incarceration rates in Chicago in his 2012 book, *Great American City*, he found that a Black neighborhood with one of the highest incarceration rates (West Garfield Park) had a rate more than 40 times as high as the white neighborhood with the highest rate (Clearing)." Whether this reflects higher criminal activity, a higher prosecution rate, or both, the state seems to be complicit in a disproportionately high rate of Black people being incarcerated. Citing this statistic is not meant to remove agency from those Black people who commit crimes—though some may be committing crimes that are, in the circumstances, justified or excused. The point is that the state, through action and inaction that seems to have unjustly contributed to that criminality, may have lost the standing to condemn people for it.

The question is: Is such *causal* complicity, when it is not the *aim* of the state to induce criminality, sufficient to cause the state to lose the standing to blame? Perhaps such complicity reinforces the sense of hypocrisy that comes with claiming to care about property and human welfare. But then we need not introduce a separate basis for lost standing; hypocrisy will do. Or perhaps the problem is that the state cannot be held properly accountable by those whom it harms with its criminogenic failures. But in that case the problem seems to be not just that the state is complicit, but that the state has set up a non-reciprocal relationship with marginalized people. I'm not suggesting the complicity is not an exacerbator along both dimensions; I am suggesting, however, that its relevance to standing is secondary to these other dimensions.

10.3.3 Non-Reciprocity/Exclusion

What if a person is politically excluded in a way that prevents her from holding the state that blames her accountable for its own failures toward her? As I noted in Section 10.2, blame aims at reconciliation, and reconciliation is a two-way street.

[31] "Urban Poverty and Neighborhood Effects on Crime," 1140.

A state that cannot be held accountable by certain people loses the standing to blame those people.

Though my ultimate concern is domestic law enforcement, I need to take a detour to discuss international prosecution, because it suggests that this idea that exclusion blocks blame must be wrong. Gary Watson raises this objection against Duff, arguing:

> [A]s Duff of course realizes, it is false that citizenship is a precondition for answerablity [sic] to the laws of a particular community. The criminal law is often entitled to prosecute lawbreakers who are not "bound [by its law] as citizens," and to hold someone criminally liable is therefore often not "to treat her as a citizen."[32]

Duff responds to Watson by acknowledging that the criminal law "claims authority over non-citizens as well as citizens."[33] But he suggests that he can handle that by saying "that non-citizens should be seen as having the distinctive normative status of guests, and that it is therefore as guests, rather than as members, that they are answerable under the criminal law of a polity whose jurisdiction they have entered."[34] In one way, this may seem like a non sequitur: guests *are* excluded from political participation; they can't vote. But Duff could respond that they can sue. They benefit from most of the rights of citizens, and they can sue if those rights are violated.[35]

The real problem for Duff is that his response is inadequate to account for the extra-territorial jurisdiction to punish non-resident aliens that many states claim. Duff seems committed to rejecting this kind of jurisdiction. He worries that it commits us to a conception of the criminal law according to which people are answerable "to 'humanity.'"[36] But as I argued in Chapter 5,[37] that is a mistake. Extra-territorial jurisdiction presupposes only that political communities can legitimately take an interest in what non-resident aliens do, and that sometimes, if the crime is sufficiently serious, that interest extends to what they do to other non-resident aliens. What Duff should have said is that if the state wants to hold non-resident aliens criminally responsible, it must accept that it can be blamed and held accountable by them.

[32] "A Moral Predicament in the Criminal Law," 180.

[33] "Moral and Criminal Responsibility: Answering and Refusing to Answer," 185.

[34] Ibid.

[35] See U.S. v. Verdugo-Urquidez, 494 U.S. 259, 271 (1990) (listing cases holding that resident aliens, or aliens with "previous significant voluntary connection[s] to the United States" benefited from constitutional rights under which they could sue).

[36] *The Realm of Criminal Law*, 113.

[37] Specifically, Section 5.5.2.

What could that mean? I think the answer is that state accountability depends on being subject to moral blame and to some form of legal accountability. I have argued that even non-resident aliens have the protection of basic legal rights that could form the basis for lawsuits.[38] The United States currently rejects this possibility, at least with regard to constitutional rights,[39] though it does grant non-resident aliens limited statutory rights to sue.[40] Whether the right of non-resident aliens to sue for damages is adequate to retain standing to prosecute is an issue that, to my knowledge, has not been addressed by a court. But I think it's an argument that ought to be justiciable, as this sort of reciprocity is a basic legal presupposition for universal jurisdiction, if not also for passive personality jurisdiction.[41] However, such cases might come out as a matter of positive law, my point is that there is a way of preserving the justifiability of universal jurisdiction for states that are willing to be held accountable by non-resident aliens.

At this point, I leave the issue of extra-territorial jurisdiction, assuming that it can be made consistent with Duff's appeal to non-reciprocity/exclusion as a basis for holding that a state has lost the standing to blame. Returning to the domestic context, one problem with state standing to censure and punish citizens and resident aliens turns on whether, as Duff puts it, the state "effectively excluded [them] from many of the rights and goods of citizenship" or respected guest status. If their fellow citizens, acting through the state, "have collectively failed to treat [them] as a citizen [or respected guest], how can they now call [them] to account...?"[42]

Arguably, if the state tolerates sufficiently grave economic injustices, that could leave those people with little to no time to do anything but struggle to live and that could effectively exclude them from participation in civic life. Likewise, if the state unjustly bars people from political participation (speaking, organizing, or voting), then it excludes them straightforwardly from participation in civic life. Either way, it could lose the standing to censure and punish them for their crimes. I do not want to take a stand on whether any particular state at the present moment has lost the standing to blame in that way. Suffice it to say that the United States formerly crossed that line with regard to racial oppression, and there are some who argue that it still does with regard to economic marginalization of at least some people.

38 See "Constitutional Rights for Nonresident Aliens."

39 The most recent case holding that was Hernandez v. Mesa, 589 U.S. 93 (2020).

40 See ibid., 112–113 (discussing the Foreign Claims Act, 10 U.S.C. § 2734).

41 Passive personality jurisdiction, which allows a country to prosecute non-resident aliens who wrong its own citizens abroad, might be justified in a more indirect fashion: if each country can use it to prosecute aliens, then there is a measure of reciprocity.

42 *Punishment, Communication, and Community*, 188.

10.4 Inadequate Responses to the Problems with State Standing to Punish

10.4.1 Contra a Direct Appeal to the Importance of Punishing

There are many who have argued that the state should punish, whether it has standing or not, simply because it's valuable to do so. Gerald Cohen, framing the point in terms of blame, not punishment, put it this way: "I believe that there is something wrong with condemning unless certain presuppositions are fulfilled, but if dodgy condemning is going to save the children, then I say: 'Condemn away!' "[43] This is not a response I can offer, however; it treats blame or condemnation as a mere speech act with consequences. It fails to reckon with the idea that it is a power that involves putting another under a pro tanto duty to respond.

But one might think punishment is different; it need not be concerned with putting another under a duty to respond; it need only deter and incapacitate. Tommie Shelby seems to take this line. He thinks that even an unjust state has the right to punish crimes that are violations of natural duties (crimes that are mala in se)[44] as a matter of other-defense, to deter and contain crime.[45] The preconditions for state punishment, on his view, don't include the standing to blame, which he thinks that the United States lacks with regard to at least some economically and racially marginalized people.[46] The preconditions for state punishment, on his view, are merely that the state can provide fair procedures and that "penalties are generally proportionate to offenses."[47]

I reject Shelby's response because I don't think we should treat what he has in mind as *punishment*. This is not merely a verbal dispute; it's a matter of tracking the implications of the justifications we each have in mind. He thinks that what justifies what he calls punishment is "prevent[ing] unjust and harmful aggression."[48] How can taking action *after* the crime has been committed count as "*prevent[ing]* unjust and harmful aggression"? The answer must appeal to the standard utilitarian ideas that punishing uses the punished to deter future crime and often incapacitates them. It may be that Shelby is simply appealing to these utilitarian ideas here. If so, my objection to him is that naked utilitarian justifications never work, as they show no commitment to the dignity-respecting model (DR Model).[49] But it could be that he is instead thinking implicitly of a

[43] "Casting the First Stone," 119, n. 10. See also J. Edwards, "Standing to Hold Responsible," 455.

[44] His examples include not being cruel, not causing unnecessary suffering, and avoiding "gender-based violence and sexual harassment." *Dark Ghettos*, 219-220.

[45] Ibid., 248.

[46] Shelby's ideas for how a state might lose the standing to blame refer to complicity and hypocrisy, not exclusion. Ibid., 245.

[47] Ibid., 245.

[48] Ibid., 249.

[49] See Section 2.3.

kind of forfeiture model. In fact, he uses language related to the language I will develop for the penal law. He writes:

> If we separate *condemnation* of lawbreaking from *penalties* for lawbreaking . . ., then we can explain how punishment can be justified even when authority to punish disobedience to law and moral standing to condemn crime have both been lost.[50]

That said, the difference between us is not trivial. The problem can be brought out by thinking about the notion of proportionality.[51] The criminal law's notion of proportionality is connected to culpability on both an ordinal and an anchored cardinal basis.[52] It is hard to see how it can do so if "punishment" is just what is picked up by forfeiture of the right not to be penalized. Indeed, I will argue in Chapter 16 that the notion of proportionality in the penal law is quite different from that of the criminal law. Thus, if Shelby is appealing to forfeiture, he has no basis for insisting that punishment respect the criminal law's notion of proportionality. And if he insists that punishment must nonetheless respect the criminal law's notion of proportionality, then he would have the state send quite the mixed message: "This punishment is proportional to your culpability, but the state is not blaming you." Those who are punished should find this puzzling at best.

Shelby may want to give up on proportionality, but that too has its costs. First, it could create a two-tier system: one for people for whom the state lacks the standing to punish, who get the penal law, and another for people for whom the state retains the standing to punish. One way to avoid that is to scrap proportional punishment altogether and adopt the penal law for all. But I argue in Chapter 16 that there are good normative reasons to resist giving up on criminal law as a blaming institution.[53] Alternatively, he (or we) can seek to hang onto proportional punishment for all, as Duff tries to do.

10.4.2 Duff's Limited Proposal

Duff would agree, I'm fairly certain, with the criticism I just made of Shelby's position. He once took the same sort of position as Shelby, substituting "a qualified

[50] *Dark Ghettos*, 248.

[51] This argument goes beyond the criticism Ewing levels against Shelby: "that punishment, properly speaking, is inherently condemnatory." "Do Unjust States Have the Standing to Blame?" 263, n.1. See also J. Howard and A. Pasternak, "Criminal Wrongdoing, Restorative Justice, and the Moral Standing of the United States," 50.

[52] See Section 8.2.

[53] See Section 15.1.3.

deterrent theory" of punishment for blame-based punishment, at least in the substantially unjust world in which we live.[54] But he came to think that there were better reasons to retain punishment, in the sense of a blame-based response to culpable wrongdoing, even for those who have "been unjustly disadvantaged and excluded by the polity whose law" is cited as the legal basis for punishment.[55] I think his reasons are good, as far as they go, but also ultimately inadequate.

Specifically, Duff argues two points. First, he argues that failing to hold criminals accountable means that their victims "cannot look to the law to help them gain satisfaction for the wrongs they have suffered."[56] That would be unjust because "the political community owes it to victims of crime to bring offenders to answer for those crimes. To refuse to do this would be to that extent to exclude those victims from the normative community."[57] When the victims are also unjustly excluded and disadvantaged, that would make their exclusion worse.

Second, he claims that "punishment itself, as an exercise in moral communication, can contribute to that social and political restructuring that is needed if punishment is to be justified."[58] The justification for calling the unjustly excluded and disadvantaged to account would be "morally tainted"; it would require the "community's institutions and government" to recognize that the criminal wrongdoer has been wronged by the community, and it would require a "collective commitment to correcting" those wrongs.[59] But "it can be (imperfectly) justified as a part of that very commitment to include them as fully recognized members of the polity."[60] As such, he "suspect[s] . . . that it is the best way forward."[61]

Again, I think these are good reasons, as far as they go. But I'm afraid they don't go the distance. Let's start with Duff's offender-focused argument. The cure for unjust exclusion is presumably inclusion, but it's hard to see how punishment will do much to reestablish political *inclusion*. I agree with Duff that blame is a communicative act that signals, when it is done well, that the political community, speaking through the state, considers the target of blame to be a full member of the *moral* community and in most cases also of the political community. But if in other ways the state is unjustly excluding the defendant, that signal

[54] *Punishment, Communication, and Community*, 198 (referring back to his earlier works: *Trials and Punishments* and "Retributive Punishment—Ideals and Actualities").

[55] *Punishment, Communication, and Community*, 184. Shelby misreads Duff on this point, asserting that "Duff argues that when the state fails to treat persons in accord with its professed fundamental values, it doesn't have the right to hold them accountable for their alleged failure to abide by those values." *Dark Ghettos*, 245-246.

[56] *Punishment, Communication, and Community*, 198-199.

[57] Ibid., 199.

[58] Ibid.

[59] Ibid.

[60] Ibid.

[61] Ibid., 200.

could just as well sow cynicism as reconciliation. Ultimately, what the state needs to do is to cease unjustly excluding the defendant. Courts that are in a position to impose censure and punishment might call upon the state to do that, but they cannot *make* the state do that.

In his most recent writings on standing, Duff argues that:

> what is required is that the polity now be ready, and display such readiness in action, to answer to the defendants, and to the disadvantaged group to which they belong[], for the wrongs they have suffered—and thus show that they will now treat them fully, not selectively or partially, as citizens.[62]

But it seems to me that courts, the arm of the state in the business of calling defendants to account for their crimes, cannot speak for and act for the polity that way. As Duff himself goes on to note: "Clearly courts cannot deal with, or start to remedy, those social injustices themselves."[63] He thinks this shortcoming can be overcome "[s]o long as the court can hear, [and] can be seen to hear, the defendant's argument, and so long as it can point to another forum in which the defendant can genuinely pursue that argument."[64] I accept the point in one sense: if such a forum exists, and if it offers defendants who *think* they are excluded a meaningful chance to make their claims on the state, then the court can play a constructive role in achieving inclusion. But if these alternatives do not exist, then what is the court to do?

Turning now to the victim-focused argument, there are two reasons why I think that Duff's response on this score comes up short. First, if the state lacks the standing to punish members of a certain group of people who are unjustly excluded from participation in the state, then even their victims, victims who may be equally excluded and disadvantaged, should recognize that the state lacks the standing to blame them. That doesn't mean that they should consider their victimizers beyond blame. Loss of standing is an agent-relative loss. The victims themselves can level blame, and others too who are not as tainted as the state can back them up. But they should take the state to lack that standing to blame.

Second, even if those victims have a right to seek help from the state, they need not seek help in the form of the *state* engaging in blame and punishment. They may want help only in the sense that they would like state funding for things like community-based restorative justice approaches to holding their victimizers accountable.[65] The state can fund such activities without itself laying blame. In

[62] "Doing Justice to Injustice," draft, 11.
[63] Ibid.
[64] Ibid.
[65] Howard and Pasternak embrace this restorative justice option in "Criminal Wrongdoing, Restorative Justice, and the Moral Standing of the United States," 51-59. I have my doubts about how well it can substitute for state punishment, which I explore in next chapter.

addition, the state could use the penal law to deter people from harming them. These institutions may not be up to the job in a state, in which case victims would be left in the lurch. But it's not clear that the right solution is to blame those who are wrongfully excluded from the community. Perhaps victims just have to give up the satisfaction of states blaming those who wronged them until the state can either be more inclusive toward those wrongdoers or provide other forms of satisfaction to the victims. This is not a radical suggestion: consider the exclusion of evidence from trials when the state has gathered it in illegal ways; that may lead to the acquittal of clearly guilty defendants, but accepting such acquittals may be necessary to put pressure on the police to respect the legal limits on their evidence gathering. Something similar could be said about the limits of standing.

10.5 Other Arguments that Help Close the Gap

There are two more arguments that I think help close the gap that Duff's arguments aimed to close. The first of these is the thought I mentioned when responding to Shelby: we have good reason to avoid a two-tiered system of justice: one for defendants whom the state has the standing to blame, another for defendants whom the state has lost the standing to blame. In criticizing Duff's appeal to victim rights, I focused on their having reason to understand why the state might lack the standing to punish those who have wronged them. But I didn't address the thought that this might set up two tiers of justice. And such a two-tiered system would be particularly problematic as poor, marginalized victims would tend to be the ones who get second-class justice, justice in which those who wrong them are not publicly condemned. Even if they should understand why the state lacks the standing to blame those who wronged them, this second-class justice would seem to reinforce their second-class status.

The importance of avoiding this two-tiered system of justice provides a reason to think that the state can, in the name of the victims, recover its standing to blame. The reason is that the higher the cost to victims of *not* accepting the state's power to call them to account, the more those who are confronted with blame have reason to recognize a duty to respond to it. That is to say that the duty to respond may be sensitive not only to the hypocrisy of the blamer, or the extent to which the blamer fails to accept blame in a reciprocal way, but also to the general moral importance of responding to that party. The state may have pro tanto lost the standing to blame, but if others—the victim, or even the citizenry in general—are counting on the state to be able to hold certain categories of criminal wrongdoers accountable, their moral claims may outweigh the agent-relative loss of standing by the state. Their claims are particularly strong if the state lacks some other mechanism to hold wrongdoers accountable, because the institutions of restorative justice or the penal law are not well developed. But they are also strong if the use of these institutions, rather than the criminal law, signals to marginalized victims that they are going to get only second-class justice. These claims may functionally restore the standing of the state to lay blame and punish, not in its own name but as a conduit for these others. A criminal wrongdoer may have to accept the hypocrisy of and exclusion by the state for the sake of showing due respect to these other parties.[66]

To understand why a criminal wrongdoer may have to accept blame even if the blaming party would otherwise have lost the standing to blame, we need to pull the lens back a bit. What is at stake in *denying* another the standing to blame? The answer, I think, is a kind of dignity. It's demeaning, a sacrifice of an agent's self-respect and dignity to have to answer to another who lacks the standing to impose blame. I'm not talking about dignity here in the sense picked up as inalienable by the DR Model. I'm talking about dignity as a value.[67] Still, it is an important value and having to answer one who has lost the standing to blame is a sacrifice. It's a sacrifice we may reasonably expect wrongdoers to make if the costs to others of not making it are high and the costs to them are relatively low. It's a sacrifice we may want to acknowledge that they have a right not to make if one of those factors does not hold.

I'll end with two more thoughts. First, the importance of accepting blame for the sake of others provides just a pro tanto justification for a wrongdoer having to accept the power of the state to hold him criminally accountable if it would otherwise have lost the standing to blame him. Pro tanto justifications must not be confused with all-things-considered justifications. If the state's hypocrisy or exclusionary policies are great enough, then it may have lost the standing to hold the defendant criminally accountable no matter who else depends on that. The sacrifice of dignity may be too great to expect anyone, even a culpable wrongdoer, to make it.

Second, there may, of course, be no one in a position to fairly pass judgment on that matter. States can be expected, in a purely descriptive sense of that word, to find that they have the standing to lay blame no matter their hypocrisy (or perhaps even more, the more hypocritical they are), and no matter how egregious their exclusionary policies. But defendants can hold their head up and refuse to answer the charges. And citizens of good conscience can determine for themselves if they think defendants who act that way are justified in doing so. If enough citizens recognize that the state lacks the standing to blame, they may be able to bring political pressure to bear to make the changes to restore the state's standing to blame.

[66] I'm grateful to Daniel Viehoff for helping me see the need for this move.
[67] See Section 3.4.

In the end, citizens of good conscience ought to be ready to recognize that a sufficiently unjust state does not have the standing to censure and punish wrongdoers toward whom its censure and punishment is a particularly egregious exercise in hypocrisy, or toward whom its practices of exclusion have been particularly unjust. But the mere fact of injustice will not undermine the state's standing to use the criminal law, even against those who suffer from it.

11
The Restorative Justice Alternative to Punishment

11.1 The Basic Idea of and Appeal of Restorative Justice

Restorative justice refers to a set of practices that provides an important alternative to criminal censure and punishment.[1] Though different, these practices are not fundamentally incompatible with those of the criminal law; they can be, and have been, integrated into criminal law practices.[2] But as Paul Robinson points out, there are two conceptions of restorative justice: (1) a program for dealing with (some) crimes with different processes that would take the place of or supplement state censure and punishment, and (2) a program for replacing censure and punishment with a different set of processes.[3] Following Robinson, I want to embrace restorative justice as an important alternative or supplement to traditional state punishments, one that might be appropriate for certain kinds of cases, while also rejecting the idea that restorative justice should be thought of as a complete replacement for censure and punishment.[4]

Adriaan Lanni explains the basic idea of restorative justice this way:

> [T]he proper response to an offense should focus not on punishment, but on meeting the needs of the victim, holding the offender accountable for the harm caused, taking steps to repair as much as possible the harm suffered by the victim and the community, and addressing the offender's needs to prevent reoffending and promote reintegration.[5]

[1] I'm indebted to Adriaan Lanni and Kirstin Drenkhahn for their guidance on this topic at a meeting of the Virtual Comparative Criminal Law (VCCL) seminar on Nov. 15, 2024.

[2] As the Code for Crown Prosecutors in the United Kingdom puts it: "RJ can take place at any stage of the criminal justice process including after conviction and it can also form an integral part of any sentencing disposal, especially with children and young people. Currently it is more common for the RJ process to be used before a case comes to court, i.e., as part of a diversionary process."

[3] "The Virtues of Restorative Processes, The Vices of 'Restorative Justice'" [henceforth "Virtues and Vices"].

[4] It's a separate question whether the combination of restorative justice and penal law would be an improvement over the combination of restorative justice and criminal law. I don't think so, but I'll hold off on making that argument until Section 15.1.3.

[5] "Taking Restorative Justice Seriously," 640.

Punishment, Penalty, and Incapacitation. Alec Walen, Oxford University Press. © Oxford University Press 2026.
DOI: 10.1093/9780197523124.003.0011

Before proceeding, it is important to flag that Lanni here is talking about harms, not culpable wrongs, and that is prima facie problematic. Sometimes causing harm is justified or excused, and then a label like "offender" does not apply. At most, tort law compensation would be called for. But a generous interpretation of the reluctance of restorative justice practitioners and theorists to use terms like "wrongdoing" and "guilt" is not that they deny the relevance of justification and excuse; rather, their rhetorical shift to "harm" is meant to focus on what the offender or "responsible party"[6] is responsible for; questions of justification or excuse naturally arise in discussion of *how* the responsible party is to be held accountable: for *merely* causing a harm or for doing so in a way that is morally disrespectful. Shifting to "harm" may also help to open up an engaged dialogue between the responsible party and the impacted party. It allows the discussion to start with the more neutral fact that the responsible party harmed the impacted party, rather than starting with an accusation of culpable wrongdoing, which is more apt to make a person who caused harm defensive (a "defendant") and to close him off to assuming responsibility. Insofar as this explains the term, I have no deep objection to its use.[7]

My reasons for being open to speaking of "harm" rather than "culpable wrongdoing"—at least at the start of a proceeding—get at the core of what is important and attractive about the processes of restorative justice, and relate to why restorative justice may function better, at least in some contexts, than the standard forms of prosecution and punishment, at least in the United States: it allows the defendant to be less *defensive*. To see why, consider these observations from Danielle Sered:

> [T]he criminal justice system is like kryptonite to accountability. If you are among the people who get caught for what you do, the one person who is formally on your side is your defense attorney, and the first thing that lawyer tells you to say . . . is "not guilty." . . . And then the process continues until, almost invariably in our system, you take a plea. Almost invariably, this plea will be to something other than what you did—usually something less. . . And then you go to prison, where virtually no one talks to you about your crime. . . You may choose, in that context, to maintain your innocence. At the very least, you may deny or minimize or just obscure your guilt. And then you come home.[8]

Insofar as we want the criminal law to convey the message that guilt should be owned, and insofar as Sered presents an accurate reading of the law in action

[6] Lanni indicated in her VCCL presentation that "responsible party" is now the preferred term.
[7] Some abolitionist thinkers seem to want to do away with talk of culpability altogether. See, e.g., L. Hulsman, "The Abolitionist Case." I do object to that.
[8] *Until We Reckon*, 92–93.

in a typical criminal case,[9] this is a damning criticism. By way of contrast, Sered thinks that restorative justice can help achieve the "five key elements" of accountability:

> (1) acknowledging responsibility for one's actions; (2) acknowledging the impact of one's actions on others; (3) expressing genuine remorse; (4) taking action to repair the harm to the degree possible, and guided when feasible by the people harmed . . . ; and (5) no longer committing similar harm.[10]

How does restorative justice propose to put together these five elements of accountability? Here's how Lanni puts it:

> Restorative justice takes many forms, but in the criminal context it typically involves a meeting between the [impacted party], the [responsible party], and other members of the community. In this meeting, the [responsible party] expresses remorse for the harm caused and the group agrees on actions the [responsible party] can take to repair the harm and prevent re-offending.[11]

According to supporters of restorative justice, this not only holds the responsible party, often a culpable wrongdoer, accountable, it is also better for the impacted parties. As Lanni writes, empirical research "found that [impacted parties] who participated in a restorative conference felt more secure, less anxious, less afraid of the [responsible party], and had a greater sense of closure than those whose cases were resolved in the criminal process."[12]

It's worth pointing out that restorative justice also seems to get better results in terms of recidivism. Lanni writes that "rigorous studies of restorative processes involving encounters between [impacted parties] and [responsible parties] tend to show a reduction in reoffending compared to typical court processes."[13] One might wonder how well these studies can control for the fact that only certain kinds of offenders get to participate in restorative justice programs, at least at this point in history. But I will give her the benefit of the doubt that her claim is true

[9] It is not, in fact, representative. Even in the United States, which relies more heavily on incarceration than many other countries, there are alternatives, including simple probation, that avoid prison time, which are used more often than incarceration. M. Tonry, "Community Punishments," 200 ("In 2015, American prisons and jails held 2.17 million people. Another 4.65 million were under community supervision.").

[10] Ibid., 96.

[11] "Taking Restorative Justice Seriously," 637.

[12] Ibid., 644.

[13] Ibid., 648.

as regards the kinds of offenders who might be good candidates for restorative justice as it is now practiced.[14]

Clearly, insofar as restorative justice can operate as Lanni claims it does, the state has reason to use its processes. The question is how these reasons to use its processes weigh against the drawbacks and against what would be lost if restorative justice completely supplanted censure and punishment.

11.2 Limitations of Restorative Justice

I turn now to point out the limitations of restorative justice, both in practice and in theory. I start with six practical problems and then turn to a theoretical one.

11.2.1 Practical Problems

1) It can't stand on its own. Restorative justice presupposes that the responsible parties in question are ready to accept responsibility. But many are not, and many others who profess to be ready are not able to follow through or simply fail to do so.[15] What are we to do with these people? Presumably, the state would need to screen defendants to try to sort out who is a good candidate for restorative justice and who not.[16] More importantly, the state will have to retain something like the existing punishment system. As Lanni puts it: "Restorative justice is inappropriate for offenders who do not accept responsibility or who persist in wrongdoing and cannot be deterred through restorative processes. Offenders who pose a continuing and serious danger to others may need to be incapacitated for some period."[17] Or, as she also said, "[t]he case is returned to the police or prosecutor if the restorative process is not successful for any reason."[18]

It is important to point out at this juncture that the dignity-respecting model (DR Model) will not tolerate Lanni's suggestion that "[o]ffenders who pose a

[14] It is worth noting that Lanni also reports that "restorative encounters seem to be more effective at reducing recidivism in cases involving violent crimes than property crimes, and slightly more effective for adult serious offenders than for juveniles." Ibid.

[15] Consider Huck's father in *The Adventures of Huckleberry Finn*. "When caught stealing money from his son to buy alcohol, [he] swears that he is a changed man who will never do it again. When he is found later that evening doing precisely the same thing, the common-sense judge recognizes just how silly he had been to put trust in the father's promise to mend his ways." M. Thorburn, "The Impossible Dreams and Modest Reality of Restorative Justice" [henceforth "Impossible Dreams"], 877.

[16] That will raise its own problems of explicit and implicit biases in the screeners. A. Lanni, "Taking Restorative Justice Seriously," 669-671.

[17] Ibid., 677. See also Sered, *Until We Reckon*, 148 ("The most legitimate function of prisons in our society is to hold people we cannot safely hold in our communities.").

[18] Ibid., 649.

continuing and serious danger to others may need to be incapacitated for some period." This treats them as though they can simply be treated as dangerous. The legitimacy of incapacitation presupposes some particular finding beyond dangerousness. It is plausible that someone who is judged to be a continuing threat, especially after undergoing one or more rounds of restorative justice, either must have forfeited to some extent the presumption of law abidingness (POLA) or must be lacking in autonomous capacity. Either way, the state can supplement restorative justice processes with something incapacitative and consistent with the DR Model. But the state would need to supplement it *either* with punishment as it is now generally meted out, with forfeiture, or with a finding of lack of autonomous status. If the criminal law is to be replaced by restorative justice, it will have to be replaced by restorative justice *plus* other institutions designed to deter lawbreaking and to incapacitate recalcitrant offenders.

2) Due process problems. As Benjamin Ewing points out:

> To call for restorative justice before an authoritative finding of guilt would be to put the cart before the horse. And to leave prosecution and fact-finding to victims and communities themselves would compromise the rights of actual and potential victims by saddling them with a heavy burden of self-help—one which would be not only unfair, but arguably also impossible for them to discharge adequately.[19]

Supporters of restorative justice may want to suggest that those who plead guilty before trial should be sent to a restorative justice setting, and that those who want to exercise their right to trial can do so. If those who choose trial are found guilty, they can then be sent for restorative justice processes rather than sent for censure and punishment. That may be right, but those who are convicted after pleading not guilty may be particularly reluctant to accept responsibility and partake in a restorative justice process.[20] That reluctance may funnel them into a punishment stream, but there's then a danger that those who contest their guilt would be seen as non-cooperative. This may exacerbate the already problematic tendency to treat more harshly those who contest their guilt than those who plead guilty.

3) Undermining deterrence. As a practical matter, it seems likely that using restorative justice processes would undermine deterrence. As Malcolm Thorburn points out, it could be that would-be criminals are "encouraged to commit crimes because of what they see as more lenient sentences."[21] Robinson also claims that

[19] "Do Unjust States Have the Standing to Blame?" 272, n. 77.

[20] The impact on plea bargaining of defaulting to restorative justice is also likely to require many more trials.

[21] "Impossible Dreams," 871 n. 30. Arguably he should have written that they are "less deterred from committing crimes."

supporters of restorative justice propose "that restorative justice should be used first, and repeatedly, until it is clear that it cannot work, and only then should the system resort to deterrence."[22] His complaint is that "by turning first to restorative justice, repeatedly, deterrence has already been sacrificed."[23]

Restorative justice supporters have a response to these worries about deterrence. Lanni suggests that "any reduction in general deterrence due to a decrease in punishment severity can be at least partially offset by gains in compliance generated by enhanced legitimacy and transformative approaches to community safety."[24] She may be right, but it is an empirical question whether restorative justice would be seen as more legitimate and accompanied by transformative and effective approaches to community safety. Focusing just on the legitimacy point, if the restorative terms are seen to be insufficiently onerous,[25] or overly arbitrary, would tend to undermine its legitimacy.[26]

4) Problems with impacted party participation. Restorative justice presupposes that impacted parties are willing to participate and to seek only reasonable terms for reconciliation. But impacted parties may not be willing to participate or may be unreasonable. If so, there are options, such as surrogate impacted parties.[27] But even if such surrogates are better than nothing, it's unclear how to scale that up to handle the large run of cases. It would seem to require something like "professional impacted parties," which seems like a recipe for insincerity and corruption of the process.

In addition, many crimes, from a person cheating on her taxes to reckless endangerment, don't have identifiable impacted parties, and some, like certain forms of fraud, have many impacted parties who suffer only a little bit. When dealing with crimes without clearly identifiable impacted parties, surrogates could again be used to indicate how the risk could materialize. But this raises two problems. First, that state would have to confront, again, the problem of scaling up and maintaining a sense of sincerity. Second, for cases in which there are many impacted parties who suffer only a little bit, it's unclear how to represent them. Consider a case of tax evasion. If someone cheats on his taxes and fails to pay $5,000 to the federal government, I don't think the state can even identify a harm. The harm comes only in the aggregate from many people cheating. Is a particular tax cheat on the hook for the collective problems, or for only his share?

22 "Virtues and Vices," 379.
23 Ibid.
24 "Taking Restorative Justice Seriously," 677.
25 See "Virtues and Vices," 382-383.
26 It is also unclear that punishment is the part of the criminal justice system that does the most to undermine its legitimacy. It could be the use of biased, discretionary investigatory stops that is the biggest problem—for a discussion of that problem, see C. Epp et al., "Beyond Profiling"—, in which case the shift to restorative justice may have relatively little impact.
27 See "Taking Restorative Justice Seriously," 664-666.

If it's the former, that seems to impose an unfair excessive burden; if it's the latter, it seems to let the tax cheat off too easily.

5) Problems with proportionality. This last problem can be generalized as a problem of proportionality when there is no clear victim. Consider a case in which someone carries a gun where he is not permitted to do so. How is he to be treated? Should he have to engage in a restorative process with someone whose relative was shot and killed, or who was herself shot and injured? That's quite a distance from merely carrying a gun where he is not permitted to do so. But it's unclear what else would adequately represent the ultimate harm that grounds gun restrictions. One might suggest that the gun law offender would only have to confront such a person and acknowledge that this is the sort of harm that ultimately grounds gun restrictions; he would not have to take responsibility for anyone actually being shot. But then it's unclear what sort of restorative action would be fitting and whether it would do much to reinforce the law. Even if he sincerely acknowledges the risk, he might in good conscience say, "but I would never wrongly use my gun." That may be right in his case, but it is also irrelevant insofar as the state has a legitimate interest in ensuring that such laws are generally respected.[28]

6) Equity concerns. If the same sorts of cases are handled in idiosyncratic ways, that would raise equity concerns.[29] This was already mentioned when discussing legitimacy at the end of the deterrence point, but it's worth highlighting the problem directly. It might be possible to address that concern with official guidelines and professional facilitators. But that raises a concern with the process being well-tuned to the feelings and beliefs of the individuals involved.[30] If it is not, then it is less likely to work well as a *restorative* process.[31]

None of these six concerns should be taken to show that restorative justice processes should not be used as an alternative or complement to the forms of punishment already in standard use. But they collectively reinforce the first point, that restorative justice processes cannot stand on their own. Perhaps they can work well enough if complemented by penal law, rather than criminal law. But then a lot of the discussion needs to focus on how well penal law can be expected to substitute for criminal law—a topic to which I turn in Chapter 15.[32]

[28] A similar problem arises for the criminal law, insofar as it is committed to proportional punishment. That is the primary basis for invoking penal law. See Ch. 13.

[29] See D. Dolinko, "Restorative Justice and the Justification of Punishment," 331-334; "Impossible Dreams," 870.

[30] See "Taking Restorative Justice Seriously," 661.

[31] Adam Gopnik also observes that insofar as restorative justice emphasizes *restoration* (i.e., tort-like damages), then "[t]hose with more resources could buy more justice. . . One reason to promote the modern rule of law is that it aims to reserve retribution for the state, diminishing the crevasse between the people who can pay restitution and those who can't." "Overcorrection," 66.

[32] See Section 15.1.3.

11.2.2 Theoretical Problem

In addition to these practical problems, there is a deep theoretical problem, namely that the focus on victim-offender-community resolution has a distinctly anarchist flavor to it. The notion of community, as far as I can tell, is never well defined; it always refers to something more amorphous than the people of a particular jurisdiction, as represented by democratically elected or appointed officials. And often it refers only to the "micro-community" of the people very closely connected to the impacted party.[33]

But the criminal law is different from tort law in part because it speaks not just for the victims but for the *political* community.[34] As Robinson puts it: "All crimes have society as their victim, not merely a single person."[35] Lanni acknowledges that in passing: "What distinguishes criminal harm from other types of physical and material harm is . . . [that] the offender has shown contempt for the rights of the victim *and* for society's rules."[36] Even so, she mostly emphasizes the role of some ill-defined "community," along with the victim and the offender, in setting the terms of the agreement. Moreover, she channels the standard view in restorative justice discussions, that the government is a "danger" to the process.[37] A normatively acceptable theory of punishment, however, should be a *political* theory, not an anarchist one. And it should be concerned ultimately not just with harms, and not just with wrongs, but with public wrongs that are violations of the law. Addressing those wrongs with censure and fitting punishment is an important public function for the state. Restorative justice as currently conceived simply does not serve this function.

11.3 Restorative Justice in Perspective

In sum, I think it is important for the state to continue to explore restorative justice processes, to see how well they can be used as a diversion from or complement to normal censure and punishment. Doing so may help the state to do a better job of bringing culpable wrongdoers to own their guilt. But the advocates for restorative justice should move away from the idea that state punishment can be replaced by restorative justice. Yes, criminal wrongdoers should seek to reconcile with their victims, if there are any, and with the broader "community" of

[33] Lanni described this in the VCCL discussion as the normal position in restorative justice discussions in the United States.

[34] See Section 5.5.

[35] "Virtues and Vices," 383.

[36] "Taking Restorative Justice Seriously," 646 (emphasis added).

[37] Ibid., 659. See also Sered, *Until We Reckon*, 138 (asserting that "restorative justice's primary concern [is] with harm rather than with broken rules.").

more or less directly affected people. But they should also reconcile with the political community, represented by the state and its laws.[38] Achieving that reconciliation requires the involvement of state agents: prosecutors and courts. This is true for two reasons. First, these institutions can ensure that the actions agreed to in a restorative justice process are both fair to the wrongdoer and yet serious enough to carry her guilt-debt. Second, prosecutors and courts should *also* be involved for the more fundamental reason that they speak for the political community. It is only a court, as a representative of the state, that can provide public censure, in the name of the political community, for public wrongs. Failing to provide that sort of public condemnation, when the wrongdoer can be identified as such, would be to fail to provide a fundamental good that a just state should strive to provide.

Saying that the provision of censure and punishment for public wrongs is an important public good does not imply it must always be used. Sometimes, for the sake of bringing a defendant to reconcile with his victim, it might be worth it to let go of that public good. But doing so involves a loss.

[38] See Duff, *The Realm of Criminal Law*, 212-213, 282-283.

12
The Straitjacket of Proportional Punishment

12.1 The Aim of the Chapter

So far, in this part of the book, I have canvassed three arguments for the proposition that we might want to do without the criminal law—consequentialist objections, state injustice undermining the state's standing to blame, and the superiority of restorative justice in terms of promoting reconciliation—and found that there still seems to be good reason to retain the criminal law as a dignity-respecting, blaming institution. I have also gestured in many places in the book to the possibility that restorative justice and penal law might be adopted instead of the criminal law. But these gestures have left it open that we might be able to get by without the penal law when it comes to providing deterrent sanctions that would serve to reinforce respect for the law. In this chapter, I make the case that the criminal law alone (and implicitly the criminal law complemented by restorative justice) is inadequate to the task of providing the security modern law should offer. The problem, in a nutshell, is that criminal punishments (and implicitly restorative justice sanctions) are limited by the idea of proportionality, but when it comes to proxy crimes the level of culpability is sometimes so low that a proportional punishment would carry insufficient deterrent effect.

Current criminal law theorists of a non-consequentialist stripe, when they recognize this problem, tend either to be purists and to reject proxy crimes, or to adopt sloppy pluralism: "we're deeply committed to a proportionality cap on punishments, except when we're not."[1] My contrary proposal is that the state should carve off a distinct branch of law that is like criminal law in being responsive to prior lawbreaking and in aiming to reinforce respect for the law with serious sanctions, but it is not grounded in blaming and the retributive idea of deserved punishment. It is instead grounded in fair forfeiture. And it is freed from the proportionality caps that limit the criminal law, though it must respect its own conception of proportional sanction. I develop these positive ideas about

[1] See Section 1.3.2 for the idea of sloppy pluralism, and Section 1.3.4 for the options for responding to the problem.

Punishment, Penalty, and Incapacitation. Alec Walen, Oxford University Press. © Oxford University Press 2026.
DOI: 10.1093/9780197523124.003.0012

the penal law in the next part; here my goal is to motivate that project by showing where the criminal law comes up short.

12.2 Proxy Crimes that the Criminal Law Cannot Properly Handle

Proxy crimes are crimes that target acts that need not be wrong (except as mala prohibita), but that are correlated with committing serious, culpable wrongs. Engaging in certain businesses or dangerous activities without a license or a proper form count as proxy crimes.[2] Actions that are criminalized because they are strongly correlated with another act that is intrinsically wrong are also proxy crimes. For example, an adult having sex with a fifteen-year-old often commits the serious moral wrong of sexual exploitation, but not always. Such acts are merely strongly correlated with acts of sexual exploitation. Likewise, driving with a blood-alcohol level over a certain amount often constitutes the serious wrong of endangering others, but not always. Again, such acts are merely correlated with the act of driving with insufficient ability to be aware of and respond appropriately to dangerous situations that may arise.

Proxy crimes will be over- and under-inclusive with regard to the serious wrong with which they are correlated. Some fifteen-year-olds are mature enough to choose whether to have sex with an adult and some sixteen-year-olds are not; some people with a blood-alcohol level over a specified threshold are safer drivers than others who drive with less alcohol in their veins. Nevertheless, categorizing such acts as crimes allows the state to keep dangerous activity in check. It allows the state to ensure that agents who engage in potentially dangerous activities are properly trained, vetted, and tracked. It also allows the state simply to draw lines around certain activities that, from the state's point of view, are too likely to be harmful to be tolerated, in contexts in which the option of providing a more nuanced analysis of who is acting harmfully or excessively dangerously is too costly to pursue.[3] In a complicated, modern society, these are important functions.

The problem with simply saying that those who commit proxy crimes commit serious wrongs is that sometimes the people who commit those crimes do not themselves pose a significant risk. They have no intention to harm others, they can perfectly well avoid imposing unjustifiable risks on others, and they have

[2] See Section 1.3.4.

[3] I discuss the blood-alcohol issue in Section 13.4. For a good discussion of the reasons to have the proxy crime of statutory rape, rather than the proper crime of sex with a minor who is in fact incapable of consent in this context, see A. Cornford, "Rethinking the Wrongness Constraint on Criminalisation."

every intention of acting safely. There is always a risk that they would inspire others who would be less careful to break these regulatory laws themselves. But even then, they might know that they can break the law quietly, under the radar, in ways that inspire no copy-cat crimes by less scrupulous people. The pro tanto wrong they commit need be no greater than, as Antony Duff puts it, breaching their duty "to provide the assurance of [their] trustworthiness that [their] fellow citizens are entitled to require."[4] As pro tanto wrongs go, that's pretty thin. A proportional punishment would also, therefore, be relatively small.[5]

Let's consider a concrete case, a case involving possession of a gun without a license.[6]

Felon with a Gun: Patty has a prior conviction for a violent felony and has lost her legal right to own a gun.[7] Patty lives in the country, far from police, but she has recently started to receive death threats. She might have the option to go into hiding, but that option would be very costly to her. She appeals for an exception to the law barring her from possessing a gun, but she fails to establish to the relevant official that she is facing a serious threat.[8] So, she decides to get a gun illegally. She is caught with the gun and prosecuted for illegal possession of a gun by a felon.[9]

One reading of this case is that she has a moral right to own a gun, and the state is simply ignorant of that fact. Perhaps the state cannot be blamed for its ignorance, but then it is simply making an excusable mistake.[10] I want to put that reading aside. I want rather to stipulate three things. First, Patty has a morally

[4] *The Realm of Criminal Law*, 329.

[5] For a good treatment of the puzzle of proxy crimes, if one tries to handle them as a retributivist, see Y. Lee, "Proxy Crimes and Overcriminalization." His treatment is largely a Duff-like response to the more or less complete dismissal of proxy crimes by Larry Alexander and Kimberly Ferzan in *Reflections on Crime and Culpability*, ch. 5. He concludes that they are too quick to dismiss proxy crimes—i.e., real *crimes* that are based on the duty not to free ride and to support the state's efforts to pursue legitimate ends through law. "Proxy Crimes and Overcriminalization," 484. But he does not address the problem that drives my critique of Duff: that these proxy crimes are likely to be minor wrongs.

[6] I focus on this case in part because it was extensively discussed by Duff in *The Realm of Criminal Law* and by Victor Tadros in *Wrongs and Crimes*, 329-336.

[7] See 18 U.S.C. § 922(g): "It shall be unlawful for any person (1) who has been convicted in any court of a crime punishable by imprisonment for a term exceeding one year... to ... possess ... any firearm or ammunition; or to receive any firearm or ammunition."

[8] 18 U.S.C. § 925 allows a person in Patty's situation to apply "for relief from the disabilities imposed by Federal laws," and relief may be granted "if it is established to his satisfaction that the circumstances regarding the disability, and the applicant's record and reputation, are such that the applicant will not be likely to act in a manner dangerous to public safety and that the granting of the relief would not be contrary to the public interest."

[9] For readers outside the United States, who may find it hard to imagine a right to carry a gun, it may help to keep in mind that the reason to carry a gun may be much stronger when many others are carrying guns as well. Context matters.

[10] This is the reading I pushed in my "Criminal Law and Penal Law."

respectable reason to own a gun, but she also has a moral reason to respect the state's procedures. Second, given her failure to establish the need for an exception to the law that bars her from owning a gun, she has a moral reason to take on the burden of finding some way to live with the risk or the cost of avoiding it. Third, on balance, she has a moral duty to respect the law and live with the risk or the cost of avoiding it.

Even if we assume that, on balance, Patty should respect the law and live with the risk or the cost of avoiding it, her moral failure if she gets a gun is not highly culpable. She does not intend to use the gun in any unjust violence; she would use it only in lawful (but for her illegal possession of a gun) self-defense. She will not use it recklessly. She will not encourage other felons to illegally own a gun. In terms of the bases for finding culpability discussed in Chapter 5, her act is a minor crime. This is because, though she knowingly violates the law, the substantive magnitude of the unjust harm she risks is negligible. Nor is she taking a step toward committing a more serious crime. And in terms of undermining the rule of law, it is also negligible.[11] A proportional punishment would be a proverbial slap on the wrist; it would not be years in prison. Yet that is what the law prescribes for this kind of violation. The sentence for illegal possession of a gun by a felon under federal law is up to fifteen years in prison.[12]

To be sure, fifteen years is far from the normal sentence. Statistics from 2021 show that the "average sentence length for offenders convicted of violating only [the law governing illegal ownership of a firearm and] who were not sentenced under [the Armed Career Criminal Act] was 55 months" (that is, about 4.5 years).[13] But even that is not a minor sanction, and it is disproportionate to the culpability of someone like Patty. Assuming that it is reasonable for the state to claim that some such serious sanction is necessary to achieve a reasonable level of deterrence,[14] then the need for reasonable deterrence would push the law to run afoul of the proportionality constraint.

Lest one think that this kind of case is an outlier, something peculiar to America and its peculiar fascination with guns, consider this classic public welfare case: *U.S. v. Balint*.[15] The defendants in that case were charged with selling

[11] See the discussion in Section 5.3.

[12] 18 U.S.C. § 924 (a)(8).

[13] U.S. Sentencing Commission, "Quick Facts, Felon in Possession of a Firearm." The gap between this number and the fifteen-year maximum prison sentence presumably reflects the fact that maximum sentences in the United States are normally set not to guide actual sentences, but to induce plea bargaining. This 3 to 1 disparity is arguably indefensible, as it provides a strong incentive to plead guilty even if one is innocent. But I don't want to get distracted by the problematic nature of plea bargaining in the United States.

[14] The claim that a substantial sanction is viewed as necessary is supported by the fact that "96.9% of felon in possession of a firearm offenders were sentenced to prison." U.S. Sentencing Commission, "Quick Facts, Felon in Possession of a Firearm."

[15] 258 U.S. 250 (1922).

derivatives of opium and coca leaves without a form required by the Narcotics Act of 1914. I raise this case not to endorse the Court's holding that strict liability in such cases makes sense; I think it does *not*.[16] I raise the case as a model modern case of a proxy crime. The culpability that attaches to failure to respect the law is at most the sort of weak culpability that Duff highlights: that of failing to reassure their fellow citizens that they were properly qualified to sell narcotics. Yet Congress found, and the Court concurred, that a mere administrative fine would not suffice to control the trade in narcotics. The sanction was set at up to five years in prison. I assume that that sort of sanction was deemed necessary to provide a meaningful deterrent to breaking this sort of law. Moreover, I assume that similar cases exist in all developed countries.

One might still object that such high sanctions are not required. Most people, one might think, would find simply being convicted and censured deterrent enough, and even a sanction as weak as community service or a month in jail would suffice to back that up well enough for most people to avoid committing proxy crimes. What matters more, one might think, are the certainty and swiftness of the sanctions, along with knowledge of what they are.[17] The state could do more good, one might reasonably argue, by investing more in policing and publicizing what the law is than by creating harsher penalties.[18]

My response is: yes, given the relative investment in policing versus imprisoning, at least in the United States at the time I write this, the state would do better to invest more in policing and publicizing than in having harsher penalties. But even with optimal levels of policing, the penalties may sometimes need to be harsher than a proportional punishment. Even if it is true that most people would be sufficiently deterred by a reasonably certain small punishment, the law seeks to deter more than "most people" from violating it. There are two reasons for this. First, in the context in which substantial profits are at stake, people may be tempted to cut corners to get the profit, and many who do so may be tempted to impose the risk that proxy crimes are meant to prevent. A substantial sanction may be required to ensure that very few do that. Second, many cases are like Patty's case, addressed to people who have already had run-ins with the criminal law. These people are unlikely to be easily deterred. The point of having a penal law is to intervene earlier in the process, before real harms are caused. And when dealing with serious criminal activity as the ultimate target, serious sanctions may be required to prevent it at the earlier stage.

One might now ask: Could Patty not get her sentence reduced to a proportionate one, based on her not posing a serious risk? The problem is that

[16] See Section 15.2.
[17] See Section 8.2.
[18] See B. van Rooij and A. Fine, *The Behavioral Code*, 32–40.

making such a reduction available would undermine the effectiveness of the law. Everyone would claim it, and the state would be hard pressed to distinguish the Pattys of the world from the real threats. Perhaps, in certain cases, prosecutors or judges can tell the difference and can ask for or provide a low penalty for people like Patty. But we cannot expect that to be true in all cases. To make proxy crimes effective, people like Patty have to face the threat of serious sanctions just like others whose behavior really is dangerous. The state cannot be expected to reliably distinguish between the Pattys of the world and the real threats.[19]

In sum, the essential feature of proxy crimes is that the moral wrong done by the defendant is often small, but the legislature has determined that effective protection of the population from serious wrongful behavior requires high sanctions. The ultimate harm, the one justifying the use of a proxy crime, in cases like *Felon with a Gun* is that people get unjustly shot; the ultimate harm in *Balint* is that people consume narcotics to their detriment. But prosecuting only the acts that lead fairly directly to the harm that the state seeks to avoid will often provide too little protection against such harms. Given the choice, it's preferable to prevent significant risks of serious unjust harms rather than limiting law enforcement to prosecuting people after serious harms have befallen their victims. To require agents to stay further away from the ultimate harms, the law has to ban activities that may be innocent in themselves except for the disrespect inherent in violating the law. The inherent culpability of violating such laws is often low. But the need to penalize them seriously, to keep people from performing them, is nonetheless high. Hence the problem for the proportionality principle.

12.3 The Solution Highlights the Need for Penal Law

As noted at the start of this chapter, there are multiple ways of responding to this problem. States could give up proxy crimes. Or they could give up punishing proxy crimes more than would be proportional *as crimes*. But I think a better solution is to recognize that proxy crimes serve an important purpose and that the best way to make sense of them is with penal law. They may have a criminal

[19] Relatedly, one could appeal to the de minimis principle, as Antony Duff does. The idea is that police should not arrest, prosecutors should not prosecute, and courts should not convict defendants whose "conduct did not actually cause or threaten the harm or evil sought to be prevented by the law defining the office or did so only to an extent too trivial to warrant the condemnation of conviction." *The Realm of Criminal Law*, 320 (quoting from the Model Penal Code, § 2.12). See also A. Duff, "'De Minimis' and the Structure of the Criminal Trial." The problem with this solution is essentially the same as for reducing her sentence to a proportionate one. That's not to say that the law should do away with the de minimis principle; it is to say there may be barriers that make it too hard to tell when it should be invoked.

law core, but the bulk of their sanction has to be justified, if it can be justified, through the penal law.

Responding to these proxy crime offenses as violations of penal law means that they will be responded to with sanctions that are harsher than would be permissible if they were treated as crimes. This can only be justifiable within the dignity-respecting model if the penal law appeals to a separate basis for imposing sanctions. That is what I will argue it does in the next part of the book.

PART IV

PENAL LAW

13
Overview of the Penal Law

13.1 Contrasting Penal Law with Criminal Law

The penal law, unlike the criminal law, is based on fair forfeiture of the right not to be intentionally hit with hard treatment. It is not the only law based on forfeiture discussed in this book. Forfeiture of the presumption of law abidingness (POLA) is also important. For efficiency of exposition, I will sometimes discuss both in this part of the book. But I will focus this part primarily on the penal law, and my discussion of the implications of forfeiture of the POLA will be reserved for the next and last part of the book.

It is important to be clear about the contrast between penal law and criminal law, in large part to protect the integrity of the criminal law. The penal law, unlike the criminal law, is fundamentally non-condemning. If we don't draw the distinction well, we risk corrupting the criminal law's distinctive quality as a blaming institution.[1]

Penal law's nature as non-condemning flows from its distinctive justification. The criminal law is based on the retributive idea that the wrongdoer deserves to be punished, and the defining justificatory aim of punishment is collecting the wrongdoer's guilt-debt as a move toward reconciliation between the wrongdoer and the political community. The penal law, by contrast, is not based on the idea of deserved punishment and is not concerned with collecting a guilt-debt or with reconciliation per se. The normative issue for the penal law is only this: Can the state justify imposing hard treatment on the offender as a means of deterring offenders (herself and others) and thereby reinforcing respect for the law? It finds an affirmative answer in the idea of fair forfeiture of the right not to be so used.

This justificatory difference has implications for the functions each kind of law can play. As I've pointed out before, punishment can be added to censure to play four complementary roles: (1) reinforcing censure; (2) providing an occasion for a wrongdoer to engage in serious reflection about her guilt;

[1] As Andrew Simester writes, "[I]t is not at all obvious that extending criminal liability to non-stigmatic offenses is good for the criminal law." *Fundamentals of Criminal Law*, 311. To be clear, Simester is referring to *offenses* that are non-stigmatic, rather than offenses that are *treated as* non-stigmatic.

Punishment, Penalty, and Incapacitation. Alec Walen, Oxford University Press. © Oxford University Press 2026.
DOI: 10.1093/9780197523124.003.0013

(3) helping to ensure that the wrongdoer is not happy about her wrongdoing; and (4) collecting the amends that the wrongdoer owes either as material compensation or in the form of contribution to deterrence.[2] The penal law serves none of these functions. The only one it comes close to serving is the fourth, though it cannot be framed as amends that are owed as a matter of guilt-debt; it has to be framed simply in terms of liability to being used to contribute to deterrence, which also contributes to respect for the law.

Indeed, even when it comes to the incapacitative function of punishment, there is a basic difference. As noted earlier,[3] we could treat punishment as something to which a person has a duty to submit herself—as is done on honor farms, where security guards and fences are not used to keep people in the prison.[4] We therefore need an explanation for incapacitating people so that they have no choice about whether to endure their punishment. I noted that an explanation for such incapacitation is that they have forfeited the POLA in that regard.[5] If we are dealing with someone who has not already forfeited the presumption that she will respect her duty to submit herself to punishment by having already sought to escape it, then the forfeiture in question reflects a somewhat generalized distrust. As such, it should be presumed to apply only to people who have committed serious criminal offenses, as more general forfeiture of the POLA is hard to justify.[6] Given the low culpability of many acts that constitute violations of penal laws, we cannot assume that anyone who commits a penal offense has forfeited the POLA in any way. If we are not to make the inference that they must therefore be offered time on honor farms—and perhaps we should make that inference, but I'm not here committed to doing so—it must be because the explanation of their being forced into incapacitating detention is different. It must be that what they forfeit is the right not to be imprisoned (or hit with other hard treatment) as a means of deterring themselves or others from committing similar offenses and thereby reinforcing respect for the law.

Admittedly, there is an overlap between the criminal and the penal law, given that penal violations have a kernel of a criminal offense at their core.[7] It might seem that this would allow a judge at sentencing to mete out a modicum of censure and impose a small punishment, complemented by a larger penalty. But there are two reasons why that seems unwise. First, as I will argue below,[8] there are cases in which the culpability necessary for a crime cannot be established beyond a reasonable doubt, but a penalty would still

[2] This is the formulation from Sections 1.3.3 and 7.1.2.
[3] Section 1.3.5.
[4] See Ch. 1, n. 70.
[5] See Section 1.3.5.
[6] See Section 4.4.1, and for a more thorough discussion Section 16.2.1.
[7] See Section 13.5.
[8] See Section 13.4.

be in order. Even if that is not right, however, the point of moving to penal law is that in many cases it is too hard to tell whether a person has acted with only the low-level culpability of disregarding a law or the higher-level culpability of imposing the risk of or actually committing a substantive wrong. If the state is going to adopt the penal law, it should put aside that inquiry and treat the offense as one in which the degree of culpability is not what matters. Second, and relatedly, keeping both systems engaged in responding to individual charges would be administratively complex and might lead more to confusion than to clarity about the differences between criminal and penal laws. Thus, even if there is a criminal kernel at the heart of all penal violations, when the penal law is invoked, it should take over the case for that particular charge.

Before closing out this section, it is important to look (again) in the other direction, distinguishing penal law from existing administrative law with regulatory penalties. As noted in Chapter 1, regulatory penalties are normally conceived of as being qualitatively less serious than criminal punishments, and they exclude imprisonment.[9] I also noted there that penal law shades into the space of mere regulatory penalties. That is because penal law violations need not *always* be met with prison terms, probation backed up by the threat of a prison sentence, or community service (traditional criminal punishments); fines could also be imposed. But the penal law functions fundamentally in the space of criminal law because it uses the same range of sanctions as the criminal law, criminal procedure, criminal defenses, an analog of criminal law's mens rea, and the criminal law's standard of proof.[10] In that way, it is more like "quasi-criminal law" than regulatory law.[11]

13.2 Objections to the Penal Law

The first objection is that the penal law imposes penalties on the "undeserving."[12] That certainly sounds bad, as though it involves imposing penalties on the innocent. But that's a confusion. Those who commit penal offenses have done something, without a justification or excuse, which the state can justly take to be the basis for forfeiture of the right not to suffer hard treatment. They are liable to suffer such treatment. The complaint that they are undeserving and therefore may not be penalized is akin to saying that forcing someone who committed a tort to pay

[9] See Section 1.3.4.
[10] See Ch. 15.
[11] On quasi-criminal law, see A. Simester, *Fundamentals of Criminal Law*, 311.
[12] I owe this objection to Heidi Hurd.

damages, when he does not *deserve* to suffer for the sake of the victim, wrongs the tortfeasor.[13] Desert is not necessary to impose penalties.

The second objection is that blame has motivational force. If society does not blame people for penal offenses, that would undermine the effectiveness of the penal law.[14] I accept that this is true. But undermining is not the same as completely negating. The threat of a substantial penalty, even if it comes with no official censure, should have *some* deterrent effect, and that in turn should have some tendency to reinforce respect for the law. There are, however, two practical implications of accepting this point. First, it may increase the level of hard treatment called for in order to have a deterrent effect. Second, as that is inherently undesirable, this creates a kind of pincer, making the penal law more undesirable as a tool for a liberal state to use. That, in turn, should help reinforce the primacy of the criminal law and the secondary or complementary status of penal law.[15]

The flip-side objection is that we cannot, in fact, use the penal law as a non-blaming institution because imprisonment by itself conveys the message of blame. As Joel Feinberg wrote:

> It is not always the case that the convicted prisoner is first solemnly condemned and then subjected to unpleasant physical treatment. It would be more accurate in many cases to say that the unpleasant treatment itself expresses the condemnation, and that this expressive aspect of his incarceration is precisely the element by reason of which it is properly characterized as punishment and not mere penalty. The administrator who regretfully suspends the license of a conscientious but accident-prone driver can inflict a deprivation without any scolding, express or implied; but the reckless motorist who is sent to prison for six months is thereby inevitably subject to shame and ignominy—the very walls of his cell condemn him and his record becomes a stigma.[16]

Andrew Simester echoes the point. Concerning strict liability—not penal law but related insofar as culpability is missing—he writes: "[I]t is arguable that imprisonment is inherently a punitive sanction; as such, its imposition is always illegitimate unless deserved."[17]

To a substantial degree, I agree with both Feinberg and Simester: Imprisonment normally implies condemnation. Normally does not, however, imply inevitably; the connection is, I suggest, not so strong that it cannot be overcome.[18] There

13 Outside of torts with punitive damages, no one should object if a third party pays damages for the tortfeasor. This shows that tortfeasors do not *deserve* to have damages extracted from them.

14 I owe this objection to Crescente Molina.

15 The possibility of going the other way and substituting penal law for the criminal law will be revisited in Section 15.1.3.

16 "The Expressive Function of Punishment," 402.

17 *Fundamentals of Criminal Law*, 308.

18 I do not want to trivialize the problem, which Simester handles with some care. Ibid., 310–312.

are two reasons to say that. First, detention in an institutional facility does not always carry that meaning. In the context of prisoner of war detention or the involuntary civil commitment of the mentally ill and dangerous, it does not carry that meaning. Granted, in both of those contexts, the goal of detention is incapacitation, not deterrence. But the point stands: The mere fact that a person is forced into a detention facility does not, by itself, imply censure. Moreover, the mere fact that a person is sanctioned does not imply culpability, as is demonstrated by strict liability civil sanctions. The issue is only whether the sanction can include imprisonment without also implying that it is a punitive response to culpability.

Second, the association between imprisonment and censure is conventional. Feinberg recognized that explicitly, writing: "[I]mprisonment *in modern times* has taken on the symbolism of public reprobation. In the words of Justice Brandeis, 'It is . . . imprisonment in a penitentiary, which *now* renders a crime infamous.'"[19] But this meaning reflects the use to which we have put prisons. We need not continue to use them only for punishment. We might have two sorts of institutions: "penitentiaries" for punishment (where the goal is for culpable wrongdoers to repent and own their guilt) and "penal detention centers" for penal imprisonment.[20] The latter would presumably be different in some obvious ways to help signify that they *are* different. For example, they could be less harsh, more like a secure motel and less like rows of stacked cages, signifying that they do not presuppose that the offender *culpably* offended. If the state adopted two such clearly distinct imprisoning practices, the meaning of *penal* imprisonment could be distinguished from that of *criminal* imprisonment. And then the very walls of a penal detention center might not condemn those who are incarcerated for penal offenses.

One might object that while there might be a future in which the penal law has been established and accepted as a parallel sort of law for reinforcing respect for the law, we live in a world in which incarceration still conveys the message of condemnation. I accept that this is true, but I also think that it does not imply that the state should not start the process of separating the two kinds of sanctions. The state can start by having judges articulating clearly different messages to go with the two types of sanctions, and by segregating the incarcerated population into those who are merely serving penalties and those who are being punished. People may inevitably take incarceration in penal detention centers as a form of punishment at first. But if the idea of a separate form of law starts to take hold,

[19] "The Expressive Theory of Punishment." (quoting Brandeis from U.S. v. Moreland, 258 U.S. 433, 447 (1922)) (emphasis added).

[20] One reason Simester seems less qualified than Feinberg is that he is thinking of non-stigmatic offenses as strict liability offenses. Strict liability, when it comes to serious sanctions, is generally unfair; too often, it does not provide people a fair opportunity to avoid them. That's a point I'll return to in Section 15.2.

that association may fade. The transition period would be problematic, but it would still represent a form of progress.

It is also important to be clear: An agent's being convicted of a penal offense does not imply that he is *blameless*. In almost all cases, the offense is blameworthy. The point of using the penal law, as opposed to the criminal law, is to create space for the state to say that it is not *focused on* the degree of the offender's blameworthiness, and that it is neither aiming to express proportional condemnation nor to impose proportional punishment to collect on the offender's guilt-debt. But creating that space does not require the state to disclaim blame, as though the violation was blameless. If some echoes and associations with blame persist, that is not by itself deeply problematic. The state should avoid, to the extent possible, playing into those associations, but it need not go to extreme lengths to negate them either.

I close this subsection with two last observations. First, it may be difficult to treat particular statutes as criminal or penal; some seem mixed. This is relevant to the idea that the two systems of law should be clearly distinguished. How can such a distinction be maintained if the statutes, the violations of which ground sanctions, are themselves mixed in their nature?

To appreciate the problem, consider the statute banning the provision of material support to designated foreign terrorist organizations.[21] On the one hand, knowingly providing material support that helps organizations commit terrorist acts is a very serious public wrong. There is good reason to treat it as a serious crime worthy of serious punishment. On the other hand, the law is over-broad, and violations in cases like *Holder v. Humanitarian Law Project*[22]—providing training on how to use humanitarian and international law to peacefully resolve disputes—seem to be at best proxy crimes.[23] There are two ways to handle such statutes. One is to read them as covering both crimes and penal offenses, and to let the court sort out whether a particular defendant deserves censure and punishment or merely a penalty. The other is to read such statutes as one or the other, and if they are part penal law, as this one is, then they should be read as penal statutes as a whole. In that case, other crimes would have to be charged in cases in which the state wants to censure and punish defendants for culpably helping in the commission of terrorist acts.

It would be cleaner and less confusing if the state were to insist on clearly distinct sets of laws. But the state should not let perfection be the enemy of the

21 18 U.S.C. § 2339B.

22 561 U.S. 1 (2010).

23 For a similar point about British law, see A. Lee and A. Sarch, *The Moral Prerequisites of the Criminal Law*, 7 (discussing the overly broad UK Terrorism Act of 2000 and pointing out that many acts that it targets are "either not culpable wrongs or at least not sufficiently so to merit such severe punishment (potentially up to fifteen years in prison)").

good. In certain cases, it may make more sense to work with existing statutes to try to distinguish when it is being applied in a penal law way and when in a criminal law way. For example, in the material support context, training that is directly connected to terrorist activities, such as weapons training, could be the subject of criminal prosecutions, while training that is only at best indirectly connected to terrorist activities, such as legal training, could be the subject of penal prosecutions.

A similar choice arises for more mundane offenses such as drunk driving or statutory rape. It might be that most of the acts that get prosecuted under such laws are serious culpable wrongs: The driver was unsafely intoxicated, or the adult was having sex with a young teenager who could not meaningfully offer her consent due to the power differential. But some cases will be *mere* proxy crimes—the driver was over the legal limit for blood alcohol, but nonetheless was driving safely; the adult was having sex with a consenting partner. The problem with following the suggestion just made for material support of terrorism—let the details of the prosecution guide the determination of which kind of violation is in play—is that the state is normally not in a position to determine which cases are which. That's *why* it invokes a proxy crime, to avoid having to prove real culpable wrongdoing. But if that is the case, then there may be good reason to treat these sorts of violations as *merely* penal offenses, requiring the government to prove the actual crimes—dangerous driving or rape—if it wants to condemn the defendant for culpable wrongdoing. That does not mean that separate prosecutions would be required when a defendant is charged with multiple offenses. Prosecutors could bring charges, some of which are criminal and some of which are penal. But they should realize that insofar as they get convictions only for the proxy crimes, the judge must refrain from censure at sentencing, as culpability will not have been proved for those offenses.

To be clear, I am not suggesting that "infamous" crimes can be read as mere penal offenses, thereby escaping the criminal law's proportionality limits.[24] There can be no penal violation for dangerous driving, for rape, for selling adulterated drugs, or for recklessly handling a gun. Or, to be more precise, I suggest that such a substitution can be made only if we get rid of the criminal law altogether. As long as we retain the criminal law, we should keep the notion of crime distinct. That means that if an action is of a type that is seriously wrongful if not justified or excused, then it would undermine the distinctness of criminal law to allow it to be treated as a mere penal offense. The need for deterrence might exceed culpability even in such cases, especially when certain crimes are hard to detect or hard to prevent. But rather than treat the crime as a mere penal law violation, seeking thereby to escape the constraints of proportional punishment, the state

24 See the distinction in Morissette v. U.S., 342 U.S. 246 (1952).

should create a proxy crime that is correlated with, but easier to detect than the real crime, and sanction instances of it with harsher penalties if that is necessary to provide sufficient deterrence.

My second and final observation for this section is based on a point I turn to next, namely that the penal law should not be a pricing scheme. It should be taken to indicate that certain actions are *not to be performed*. If that is right, then I must admit that there *is* something peculiar about the state claiming that it's wrong to do X and yet not blaming people for doing X, especially if they knowingly do X, knowing there's a law against doing so. The idea of a substantial penalty seems to occupy an unstable position between a criminal response and a mere pricing scheme. But this is a bullet I think we should bite. The position of penal law would be more stable if there were no criminal law, but I will argue that there are good reasons to keep the criminal law.[25] The position would be more stable if penalties were read to reflect only the operation of a pricing scheme. But as I will argue in the next section, that's a bad reading of penal law. The position would be more stable if there were no penal law. But I argued in the last chapter that there's good reason to have the penal law. And the state doesn't *have* to blame people, even if there is a good basis for blame. It can use a non-blaming practice if a blaming practice would limit the response, on the basis of proportionality, to one that is too small to be effective. In sum, it's an instability we can and have good reason to live with.

13.3 Penal Law Is Not a Pricing Scheme

If the penalties do not come with blame, then it's tempting to think of them as merely a pricing scheme: If you're willing to pay the penalty (or, more accurately, to run the risk of being forced to pay the penalty), then there's nothing wrong with your choosing to commit the offense. If there were something truly wrong with these sorts of "offenses," then the offender would presumably be a legitimate target for blame.[26] But I've said blame does not apply.

This notion of penalties as a pricing scheme, meant only to discourage certain kinds of behavior, fits certain kinds of penalties, from fouls called in basketball games to parking tickets.[27] But I think it's a mistake to treat the penal law as a mere pricing scheme. First, it does not follow from the fact that blame is withheld that the behavior is not blameworthy. It could be that the blamer simply has reason not to blame. In the case of the penal law, I argued at the end

[25] Section 15.1.3.

[26] I'm grateful to Gabe Mendlow for raising this issue to my attention and for helping me to think about it in the right way.

[27] See Feinberg, "The Expressive Theory of Punishment," 398–399.

of the first section that it would help to avoid confusion about the distinction between the criminal law and the penal law for judges not to engage in any blaming in cases in which the penal law is invoked. Thus, the reason blame is not involved in imposing penalties in most cases is grounded in the desire to avoid confusion, not the blamelessness of the offender. Second, penal law cases have a kernel of a criminal law offense in them. Thus, the behavior *is* normally wrongful and not to be done. The issue that gives rise to the need for penal law is proportionality, not permissibility.

Now, I've hedged both points with a "most cases" or "normally" qualification. That's because I think the penal law can apply not only when the act is, all things considered, wrong and unexcused, but also when it is merely pro tanto wrong. In such cases, the agent can justifiably treat it as a mere pricing scheme. If the state concurs that the wrong is merely pro tanto, then it should withhold the penalty altogether.[28] But I think there are times when the epistemic perspective of the state and the agent come apart, and in such cases, the state can think of itself as doing no wrong, and the agent should think of herself as paying a price. I explain this in more detail in the next section.

13.4 Pro Tanto Wrongs and the Penal Law

In this section, I argue that there are cases in which the penal law can justifiably penalize actions that are merely pro tanto wrong. The example I use to illustrate the point is drunk driving. I don't mean driving dangerously while inebriated—dangerous driving, whatever the cause, should be a crime. I mean driving with a blood alcohol level over the threshold legally set as too high to drive. As noted in the previous chapter,[29] any such threshold is bound to be over- and under-inclusive. That is, some people are dangerously inebriated even at a level below that legal limit, and some people can drive safely—imposing a risk lower than whatever the relevant threshold is for safe driving—with a blood alcohol content above that limit. Suppose, then, that we have a defendant from the latter category. In some versions of that sort of case, I suggest that the defendant performs only a pro tanto wrong, not an all-things-considered wrong. And in such cases,

[28] There are also cases in which the agent has no strong reason to break the law, but the state should recognize that the law is over-broad and refrain from enforcing it. For example, if an agent drives through a red light in a quiet town, with clear visibility, at midnight, the state should not enforce a penalty. The traffic light at such an intersection should be a flashing light, not a red light. But in a town that lacks the money for such a refinement, or that has not got around to installing it, it should refuse to prosecute on the grounds that the infraction was a de minimis infraction. See Section 12.2, n. 19.

[29] See Section 12.2.

the defendant who recognizes this possibility can rightly treat the penal law's impact on her as a mere pricing scheme.

What makes it even a pro tanto wrong? The answer is that it's at least pro tanto wrong to disobey reasonable regulations,[30] and setting blood alcohol limits is a reasonable regulation. It is easy to see why. It is reasonable to suppose that it would be too expensive for the law to allow individualized certification for those who can drive safely with a relatively high blood alcohol level, and the burden on individuals not to drink and drive is relatively light. Given these two suppositions, driving with a blood alcohol level that is over the legal limit is at least a pro tanto wrong, even for a person who knows she can do so safely. Moreover, such a person is a perfect candidate for the penal law. She commits what seems to be a small wrong, all things considered, by not obeying a just rule, and yet it may be important for the state to come down reasonably hard on such violations to keep them in check.

Now suppose that on a particular occasion, D has been drinking and she gets a call from her child's school that her child has had an accident and needs to be taken to a doctor's office. D knows she's had enough alcohol at lunch to be over the legal limit. She could call for a cab or other car service, but that would take a while (there are not many such cars in her town). She could ask a co-worker to drive her, but all of them are busy. And D's spouse is out of town. D knows she can safely drive to get her child, and she knows that her child's distress would only grow by the minute if she waited for a cab, so she decides to drive to get her child and take her to the doctor herself. As it turns out, however, D gets in an accident on her way to pick up her child—one which was not her fault; the other driver ran a red light and hit her—but when the police arrive, they determine that her blood alcohol was over the legal limit. She is prosecuted for drunk driving. The question is, should the state let her use an emergency exception for her drunk driving?

I believe the state should allow her to argue that she had an emergency (necessity) justification for her drunk driving. But I also think the state could justly put the burden of establishing that justification, by a preponderance of the evidence, on D.[31] And in this case, given the stakes for her child and the judgment that was involved, I can see why the state might decide that the justification failed. Even if, in truth, she had a good justification, the basis for it—just how good a driver she is, even with a high blood alcohol level, and just how distressed her child would be if she delayed—might be something that only D knows. It might be something that she cannot convincingly convey to the judge or prosecutor.

[30] Ibid.

[31] This is the same as the "balance of probabilities" standard in English law.

One might now wonder: Is this sort of mistaken failure by the judge or prosecutor to recognize what is, in fact, a morally sufficient justification in any way interesting, or is it just another mistake that the state might make? The state might convict an innocent person, despite properly using the beyond a reasonable doubt standard as the standard of proof for a conviction. So too here, one might think, the state has merely made a mistake.

I believe this case is different. I think that in criminal cases, where the state bears the burden of proving culpable wrongdoing beyond a reasonable doubt, a mistake counts as a wronging. But in this case, where the burden is properly on D, the state's mistake does not count as a wronging. Rather, D's failure to carry her burden simply leaves her liable to the penalty. From her point of view, the risk of the penalty is simply a cost she might have to carry when deciding whether to drive with a blood alcohol level over the legal limit. It turns the penal law into a pricing scheme for her. The state has reason to know that this can happen, but it has no reason to know it has happened in this case. If it thinks, or should think given the evidence available to it, that it has happened in this case, then it would be obliged to recognize that D does, in fact, have a sufficient justification. In that case, it must not follow through with the penalty. But that need not be the case. Conflicting epistemic points of view are a fundamental part of the world in which we live. If the epistemic points of view of the state and the agent come apart like this, then the penal law would be a pricing scheme for D, who believes (rightly, I am assuming) that she is, all things considered, justified in acting as she does, but who may anticipate that she won't be able to demonstrate as much to the state. The important point is that D should not feel wronged if, in the end, she has to pay the price. The burden of proof for the necessity defense was on her, and if the state reasonably concluded that she failed to carry it, then it acted properly.

It is important to distinguish this use of putting the burden on the defendant from the way it is done in the criminal law. In the United States, the Supreme Court has determined that states can put the burden of establishing affirmative defenses like provocation and self-defense on defendants, and that defendants can have the burden of establishing affirmative defenses by a preponderance of the evidence.[32] It can therefore happen that a defendant establishes a reasonable doubt about whether she benefits from a defense, but she does not establish that she benefits from it by a preponderance of the evidence. As a result, a state can convict a defendant recognizing that it does not know, beyond a reasonable doubt, that she is guilty. Other countries, like England, agree that the burden of raising an affirmative defense can be put on a defendant, but they take it that if the defendant establishes a reasonable

[32] See Patterson v. New York, 432 U.S. 197 (1977).

doubt about whether that defense undermines her culpability, then the state has to dispel that reasonable doubt to convict.[33] In other words, the state cannot convict in such countries, believing that there is a reasonable doubt about guilt.

I think the English are right to hold that censure and punishment should be meted out only if the state can establish guilt, all things considered, beyond a reasonable doubt. My point is that the penal law is different in that way. In general, when the state deploys it, it should be careful not to impose penalties on those whose actions are justified.[34] But it *can* justifiably put the burden of establishing defenses on the defendant. If she fails to carry that burden, the state need not worry if there is a reasonable doubt about whether the justification actually works. The risks of a failed justification are on her because she can treat the penal law, in her case, as a pricing scheme.[35]

Why is the penal law different in this way? The reason is that a penal law defendant should understand that the basis for the penalty is not that she engaged in culpable wrongdoing; it is that she forfeited her right not to be penalized. The justification for penalties rests on fair forfeiture of the right not to be penalized. The standards for fair forfeiture are laxer than for censure and punishment. As long as putting the burden on the defendant to avoid the conditions that trigger a penalty is fair, then it can be applied. I'll discuss what those are in some detail in the next chapter. For now, I think it's enough to rely on the intuitive idea that D in this scenario can be supposed to know the law on drunk driving, and even if she knows she can safely drive with a blood alcohol level over the legal limit, she also knew (or should have known) that there was a chance that she would be caught so driving. It was her choices, as well as bad luck, that put her in a bind. The state gave her a fair chance to argue for an emergency exception. If she failed to persuade the state that the exception applied, the burden again falls on her.

[33] On the English view, see A. Duff, "Strict Liability and Strict Responsibility," 486. For further comparison, in Germany, the burden to establish affirmative defenses is not even put on the defendant, though it may be tactically wise for defendants to raise them. Whoever raises them, however, the court must determine their absence with the same certainty as it determines that the elements have been met. See K. Ambos and S. Bock, "Germany," 228. For a more realist take, see M. Damaška, "Evidentiary Barriers to Conviction and Two Models of Criminal Procedure," 450 (arguing that "continental legal folklore notwithstanding, the prosecutorial burden with respect to proving guilt-exemption grounds is somewhat relaxed.")

[34] I argue for this position in Section 14.6.

[35] There's a subtle argument in Patterson v. New York that the state should be free to put the burden on the defendant because that might be the political precondition for providing a more generous affirmative defense. I reject that argument, however, on the ground that it undermines the general principle that *guilt* has to be established beyond a reasonable doubt. It's this simple: If the state thinks there is doubt about a defendant's guilt, it has no business censuring and punishing him.

13.5 Is Penal Law Limited to Proxy Crimes?

I argued in Chapter 12 that a liberal state could have reason to employ the penal law because proportional penalties for proxy crimes would often be too slight to provide the deterrence a state has reason to seek. But one might think that is only *one* possible basis for having penal laws; there are probably others. I can think of no proof of why there could not be others, but I have tried to think of other reasons for adopting the penal law, and the three prima-facie plausible categories that I have thought of do not work. I present here a brief survey of why, as far as I can see, the penal law should be limited to proxy crimes, *unless*, that is, the state were to decide to get rid of the criminal law altogether and fill the gap with the penal law.[36]

The first category concerns crimes in contexts in which it is exceedingly important not to have such crimes. Consider, for example, the enforcement of discipline in war, particularly in the military, but perhaps also for populations under military rule. Arguably, petty offenses can justifiably be met with more severe sanctions in wartime than in times of peace. This might suggest that the state needs to deploy the penal law in that context. But I think there is an easier way to defend more severe sanctions in time of war: The harms done or at least threatened by petty crimes such as theft can be greater in wartime than they would be in normal peacetime life. The limits of proportional punishment can be relaxed to track the greater danger posed by what would *normally* be a petty crime.

A second category concerns the use of imprisonment to reinforce laws against drug abuse. This is a complicated topic, which I'll return to in Chapter 19. For now, I want to say that I think it may well be justifiable, in limited circumstances, to lock people up, depriving them of their liberty, to prevent them from continuing to abuse drugs. And I think such liberty deprivation should not come with condemnation. This superficially resembles a penal law sanction. But I don't think we should understand the justification of such laws as deterrence. The justification is that certain drug addicts lack the autonomous capacity to avoid using drugs in ways that pose an unjustifiable burden on others. Insofar as these laws also have a deterrent effect, that is a secondary feature of them, not a plausible justification for them. Thus, these laws do not provide a different category of action for the penal law.

The third category is civil disobedience. Following David Lefkowitz, I define civil disobedience as "deliberate disobedience to one or more laws of a state for the purpose of advocating a change to that state's laws or policies."[37] Lefkowitz

[36] A possibility I discuss in Section 15.1.3.

[37] "In Defense of Penalizing (but not Punishing) Civil Disobedience," 3.

argues that "a liberal-democratic state must make a good faith effort to ensure that the general public understands its treatment of public disobedients as the imposition of a penalty, rather than as punishment."[38] The question is: If he is right, is this another category for penal law as *I* am using the term? The answer, I believe, is no.

Lefkowitz's argument for merely penalizing civil disobedience is that such acts are grounded in the moral right to political participation, which should be understood so that it "reduces as much as possible the degree to which it is a matter of luck whether one attracts majority support for one's views regarding what justice requires, consistent with the ability of the state to achieve those ends that provide a moral justification for its existence and authority."[39] To give proper scope to the right, so that it is not used too frequently with insufficient consideration for the importance of respecting legitimate law, Lefkowitz thinks that the state should "impos[e] some costs on those who engage in public disobedience."[40] But those costs should not imply that those who engaged in civil disobedience acted culpably and deserved punishment; they were acting on a right.

This conception of a penalty conforms, as Lefkowitz notes, to Feinberg's conception of penal law. But it does not conform to the one I defended in Section 13.3, as applying to acts that are not to be done. Lefkowitz is defending, instead, a pricing scheme, one that he limits to fines that are to be set "high enough to impose a genuine sacrifice for those who carry out acts of public disobedience . . . [but not] so high that they discourage almost any protest at all."[41]

I take no position here on whether Lefkowitz is correct about civil disobedience. It seems plausible to me that as long as there are meaningful legal opportunities to challenge a law that one considers unjust, then any use of civil disobedience should be treated by the law as a culpable form of democratic cheating, and then a proportional punishment could be meted out. The law might be wrong about what is just, but those charged with enforcing the law might be epistemically reasonable in taking themselves to have a moral duty, as well as a pro tanto legal duty, to punish those who engage in illegal acts motivated by the belief that the law is unjust. This could be true even if those who are punished are epistemically reasonable in believing that the law is unjust. It could be true even if they are *right* to believe that the law is, in this way, unjust. It could, indeed, be true even if they are morally justified, all things considered, in using illegal force.[42] As I pointed out in the last section, our epistemic condition

[38] Ibid., 4.
[39] Ibid. See also Lefkowitz, "On a Moral Right to Civil Disobedience."
[40] "In Defense of Penalizing (but not Punishing) Civil Disobedience," 5.
[41] Ibid. Lefkowitz adds that the fines should be calibrated to be fair, given the income and wealth of those who engage in civil disobedience. Ibid., n. 9.
[42] See my "Reasonable Illegal Force."

does not guarantee agreement in practice on all important issues; some practical conflicts are inevitable.

These strike me as two reasonable views on the existence of a political right to engage in civil disobedience, and it is beyond the scope of this book to argue for one over the other. My point is simply this: If one believes it is culpable to engage in civil disobedience in a context in which there are meaningful opportunities to challenge a law legally, then one can support punishing civil disobedience. If, however, one believes that one has a political right to engage in civil disobedience, then one should conclude that a liberal state can justifiably impose only a weak penalty, a pricing scheme, on the exercise of that right.

Might there still be a case for imposing serious sanctions on those who engage in civil disobedience, even while avoiding condemnation (censure) of their action? I have not ruled that out. And if such a case could be made, then we would have an example of a penal law violation that is not grounded in a proxy crime. But even though this seems like a logically open possibility, I don't see the moral appeal of it. I tentatively conclude, therefore, that all justified instances of the penal law are grounded in proxy crimes, at least as long as the criminal law is generally available.

13.6 How to Get Started

I end this chapter by considering one more skeptical thought: The penal law would be too expensive to set up and too cumbersome to operate alongside criminal law. If it requires separate detention facilities and distinct laws, one might think that there is not a state in the world that will bother setting it up. It is therefore just pie-in-the-sky academic fantasizing.

My response to this objection is that distinguishing penal law from criminal law is a process. The result won't be built in a day, but it's still important to start the process. The current system has its own costs, and they should not be ignored. The criminal law as it now operates condemns and punishes people out of proportion to their culpability. This undermines the idea that the criminal law is a morally defensible institution. It reinforces morally bankrupt ideas about punishment as merely a means of incapacitating the dangerous or a way of properly stigmatizing bad people. This needlessly destroys lives. We can do better.

How could it get started? Perhaps reform commissions could take up the idea and propose changes to the legislature. The Model Penal Code started as an academic project of the American Law Institute, and it was eventually widely adopted across the United States. Many other jurisdictions have ongoing reform commissions.[43] In addition, lawyers whose clients are convicted of proxy crimes,

[43] For a survey, see S. Green and A. Walen, "Introduction to the *Rutgers Law Review* Symposium on 'Theorizing Criminal Law Reform,'" 1083.

who insist that they are not *guilty* of wrongdoing, could and should push judges to withhold condemnation at sentencing. And judges could and should take up the charge of trying to articulate the difference. If they start to embrace the difference, then that may provide the prompt for commissions to examine whether more systematic changes should be adopted. And legislatures may then take up the project.

14
A Theory of Forfeiture

14.1 Forfeiture as One Way to Lose Some Rights

The justification for the penal law rests on the premise that the right not to be subjected to harsh treatment can be forfeited. This chapter explores the idea of forfeiture to explain how such forfeiture, as well as forfeiture of the presumption of law abidingness (POLA), can be consistent with respecting dignity. The basic idea is that certain acts are sufficiently problematic, if not outright wrong, that the state can fairly impose on autonomous individuals this choice: Avoid those acts and retain the right not to be hit with a serious sanction (and retain the POLA), or perform one or more of those acts and forfeit the right not to be hit with a serious sanction (and possibly forfeit the POLA). As long as individuals have a fair opportunity to avoid the acts that would forfeit these rights, and the forfeiture would not be disproportionate if incurred, then this kind of forfeiture should be consistent with respect for dignity. It forces agents to internalize the costs of their actions, at least to a degree that is fair given the costs to them of internalizing those costs and the costs to others, either in particular cases or as a matter of general practice, of their performing the relevant actions.

To flesh out those ideas, I start by noting that forfeiture would only cause an agent to lose a right, or a set of rights; it would not cause him to lose *all* of his rights. This follows from the fact that an agent cannot forfeit his dignity,[1] the ground of his rights. Even if he forfeits the right to life in a particular situation, he retains other rights, such as the right not to be killed unnecessarily. Nevertheless, it is a way to lose some rights, and contrasting it with other ways to lose some rights—waiver and transfer in particular—will help clarify how it works.

14.1.1 The Role of Autonomous Choice in Losing Rights

Waiver and transfer are expressions of the autonomous capacity agents have to use their second-order rights to achieve their ends. If A wants B to have access to her apartment, A can give B permission to enter; if B wants a book that A has,

[1] See Section 3.4. Relatedly, contra Christopher Morris, one cannot forfeit, even in part, one's "membership in the moral community." See "Punishment and Loss of Moral Standing," 69.

Punishment, Penalty, and Incapacitation. Alec Walen, Oxford University Press. © Oxford University Press 2026.
DOI: 10.1093/9780197523124.003.0014

B can pay A for it and get ownership of the book. Forfeiture also depends on making autonomous choices, but it is not fundamentally concerned with the exercise of second-order rights. Rather, it is an expression of the need to hold people responsible for their choices so that they do not impose unfair burdens on or gain unfair advantages over others.[2]

To be clear, forfeiture does depend on the exercise of autonomous agency. Dogs, for example, cannot forfeit anything by their actions. One may be tempted to say of a dog who chews up the furniture: "That's it; you've lost your right to be in *this* kind of space." But that's just an analogical extension of the idea. The dog never had a "right" to be in that space; it was granted access to the space by the grace of the owner of the space, on the assumption that it would behave a certain way; if that expectation has been overturned, then the owner is free to revoke its access.[3] By contrast, if a person is caught driving drunk, among the things that may follow is that he *forfeits* his right to drive, at least for a while. He had a right to drive, and now, because of his autonomously chosen actions, he has lost it.

It is also important to be clear that an agent *could* forfeit a right by acting with that very goal in mind. A person with a driver's license could, for example, think that forfeiting his right to drive would prevent him from being asked to do certain tasks that he does not want to do. He might then decide to drive drunk, where he knows he's likely to be pulled over, so that he'll forfeit his right to drive.[4] Thus, it is a mistake to say that an agent who forfeits a right "does not will the end result."[5] But willing the end result is not what makes forfeiture tick. He loses his right because that loss reflects a fair balancing of the interests protected by that right and the interests others have in not being harmed or put at risk of harm by him retaining his right, a balance that is struck not in utilitarian terms but in terms that fairly hold him responsible for his choice.

It is worth noting that the interests in question are not to be measured by the subjective value a person places on a right. The driver in the previous example negatively values the right. That isn't what matters for forfeiture. What matters is an at least partially "objective" measure of the interest people normally have in retaining a right.[6]

[2] For an earlier discussion of forfeiture based on fairness, see A.J. Simmons, "Locke and the Right to Punish," 335–336. See also Kimberly Ferzan's notion of forfeiture as functioning to "restore the normative balance." "Forfeiture and Self-Defense," 240.

[3] This is not to imply that animals lack rights. See Sections 1.31 and 3.2. But their rights are limited to humane treatment. These are not subject to being forfeited or in any other way lost.

[4] For another, more gruesome example of willing the result, consider "suicide by cop," in which a person seeks to die by being shot to death and decides to attack the police, who will rightly take her as having forfeited her right not to be shot.

[5] Ferzan, "Forfeiture and Self-Defense," 235. Ferzan relies on the assumption that the person does not will the result to justify her introduction of the label "a negative normative power." Both because forfeiture is not a direct exercise of a second-order right and because a person may indeed will the result, I think this is not a helpful label.

[6] See Section 3.2.

It is also important to say that the forfeiture happens when the agent performs the forfeiting act. It is tempting to say, of the driver example, that he does not forfeit his right to drive until his license is taken from him by some court. But that's not how other instances of forfeiture work. Consider the case of an aggressor who forfeits his right to life, making it permissible for others to kill him in self- or other-defense. His moral and legal rights are forfeited as soon as he commences his wrongful aggression. I think the same should be said of the drunk driver: He forfeits his right to drive as soon as he commences to drive drunk. The state may offer him various procedural protections before stripping him of his legal right to drive. But the stripping should be understood as a legal judgment that the forfeiture has already occurred. This also keeps a parallel with the idea that when the state imposes a punishment, it does so by reference to the claim that the wrongdoer deserved the punishment for his wrongful past action. Desert and forfeiture both attach to actions; the legal judgment comes later.

14.1.2 Proportionality's Role in Limiting the Loss of Rights

In the context of waiver and transfer, proportionality has little grip in most cases. If A wants to sell B her car, worth $50,000 on the open market, for $1, she may do so. Or she may simply give it to B.[7] By contrast, forfeiture is clearly governed by concerns with proportionality. This comes out clearly in the context of self-defense, and I argue that it is a significant feature in the penal law as well.[8] But sticking with self-defense, for illustrative purposes: If we assume that an attacker is culpable, then his right not to be killed can be forfeited based on his threatening a lesser harm than death, such as rape or grievous bodily harm. The proportionality calculus is presumably different if the attacker or threat is nonculpable. Consider, for example, someone who reasonably but mistakenly thinks he faces a deadly threat and who decides to use significant force to defend himself. Given that his mistake was reasonable, his wrongful attack is not culpable. This would, I assume, make it harder to justify killing him to save someone from grievous bodily harm (but not death).[9]

The reason proportionality is relevant to forfeiture is that we need to strike a fair balance between the interests of the person whose action forfeits some of his rights and the interests of the victim or victims who will or might suffer if the acting agent does not forfeit some of his rights. This kind of balancing isn't

[7] See R. Hyland, *Gifts: A Study in Comparative Law*.
[8] Proportionality's significance for penal law is the concern of Section 15.1.1.
[9] I return to this theme in Section 14.5.

normally relevant in the context of waiver or transfer, where the other normally suffers no losses, neither as an agent nor as a patient.

That said, one can imagine cases in which proportionality would restrict the power to waive or transfer rights too. The cases that come readily to mind involve limits on the power to waive or transfer rights concerning suicide.[10] Many liberal states allow active, voluntary euthanasia; many others allow physician-assisted suicide; many do not allow either.[11] States that recognize the right to physician-assisted suicide or euthanasia do so only if the person who seeks that sort of help is sane and facing a terminal illness, or in some jurisdictions, is suffering intensely from an incurable disease. These limits reflect a paternalistic concern with protecting people from irreversible harm, except when there is good reason to agree with them that the objective value of continuing to live is quite limited.[12] Indeed, in most cases, the fundamental restriction may not be on the second-order right to empower others to help them end their lives; it may be on the right to end their own lives. Many liberal states will allow others to interfere with a suicide attempt under most circumstances (all except those in which physician-assisted suicide or euthanasia are often permitted), implying that the state does not take people to have a generally applicable moral right to commit suicide.[13] If an agent lacks the right to kill himself, it follows that he cannot transfer the right, and it's also no surprise if he cannot waive the right not to be killed.

This sort of paternalistic limit can be understood in terms of proportionality this way: The agent's interest in controlling his destiny normally loses out to the value of his life, but it is strong enough to ground his having a right to choose to die if the value of his life is objectively limited by unavoidable suffering or a terminal illness.[14]

Here is another kind of case that illustrates how proportionality could be relevant to limits on the power to transfer the right to kill oneself:[15]

[10] These come most readily to mind at least if one has lived through debates about whether people ought to have the right to end their lives.

[11] According to Wikipedia, active euthanasia is currently legal in Belgium, Canada, Colombia, Ecuador, Luxembourg, the Netherlands, New Zealand, Portugal, Spain, and most of Australia.

[12] There are also paternalistic limits on the procedures needed to waive or transfer important rights, such as home ownership. But there are also procedural limits on a state establishing forfeiture of certain rights. I leave the procedural distinction aside as a secondary complication.

[13] See D. Wang and E. Colucci, "Should Compulsory Admission to Hospital Be Part of Suicide Prevention Strategies?"

[14] One could argue that there is also a proportionality comparison between the autonomy interest of the person who wants to die and the interests of those who might be endangered by allowing practices of physician-assisted suicide and euthanasia—practices that might lead to morally problematic pressure being applied. See E. Emanuel, "What Is the Great Benefit of Legalizing Euthanasia or Physician-Assisted Suicide?"

[15] This discussion picks up a theme from Section 3.5.2.

> *Jim and the Volunteer*: Jim finds himself in the central square of a small South American town. Tied up against the wall are a row of twenty villagers and in front of them are several armed men in uniform. The villagers are a random group of the inhabitants who, after a recent act of protest against the government, are just about to be killed to remind other possible protestors of the advantages of not protesting. However, the captain of the armed men offers Jim a guest's privilege of killing another villager, one who would not otherwise be killed. If Jim accepts, then the other villagers will be set free. Jim initially declines to use one to save the others, but then the one says, "Please go ahead, shoot *me*; I forgive you in advance."[16]

I think the volunteer has the right to sacrifice himself to save the others, and that he also has the right to transfer to Jim the right to shoot him. Moreover, I believe that any liberal state should take the situation as described as providing a valid legal defense for his killing. It is not merely a necessity defense; it is a defense based on the valid transfer of the right to take his life. That difference should make a difference to how we think about Jim's act. It would be wrong of Jim to shoot the other if he did not volunteer; it is permissible to shoot him if he does.[17]

Here is where the proportionality analysis enters the situation. I doubt whether the defense would or should work if killing the volunteer would save only one life.[18] Indeed, I'm not sure it would work if the volunteer wanted to save two lives. It seems to me that it might take a significantly greater number of lives. Why should that be? I think it is because killing is harder to justify than saving. That difference, I believe, limits the volunteer's power to transfer to Jim the right to kill him, and it likewise limits his power to waive his right not to be killed. If that is right, then we see that even where proportionality does enter the space of considerations about waiver and transfer, it does so differently from the way it regulates forfeiture. In waiver and transfer, the underlying strength of the

[16] This case is based on one from Bernard Williams's "A Critique of Utilitarianism," 98, but the volunteer dimension comes from Christine Korsgaard's discussion of Williams's cases in her article "The Reasons We Can Share," 296. The idea that he is not already slated to die, getting rid of the Pareto superior feature of the case as discussed by both Williams and Korsgaard, is my variation.

[17] The role of the evil captain and his troops is actually a distraction in the case. I keep it in honor of Williams and Korsgaard, but the same situation would apply if the threat to the others was natural. It is worth noting that Iskra Fileva makes the point that voluntary acts of live-organ donation would be rejected in "Impermissible Altruism: A Response to Pummer," 162–165. She thinks that is because we should be skeptical of the motives of anyone who would volunteer in that way. I agree we should be skeptical. But I think the state should accept the rationale if clearly and sanely defended, and it should then allow the act if there is no risk that it would become a practice that would put undue pressure on others to do the same.

[18] What if a parent said this about saving her child? We could understand the impulse to make the sacrifice and might agree that she has a right to make it, but it is still not clear to me that she should be taken to have the power to transfer to another the right to kill her.

claims—not to be killed, not to be used as a means—still plays a role limiting the power to waive or transfer. In the volunteer case, the claim not to be killed remains weightier, in the proportionality balance, than competing claims to be saved. In the forfeiture case, by contrast, the claim of an aggressor not to be killed is weaker than competing claims to live.[19] Why? Forfeiture *weakens* claims.

14.2 Forfeiture and the Mechanics of Claims

I just claimed that forfeiture weakens claims, but that's not the common view. The common view is that an agent who forfeits a right simply loses it. An agent might forfeit, for example, the right to drive, or the right not to be killed, or the right not to be locked up for so many years as a deterrent to others. But I think that's not the right way to think about forfeiture. We should think of forfeiture in terms of how it affects claims. It does so in two ways: by weakening different kinds of claims and by shifting who carries the normative burden of a harm, thereby shifting which patient claims count as positive and which as negative. I consider these in turn.

14.2.1 Claim Weakening

To see claim weakening in action, consider an aggressor who threatens only an unwanted arm touching. She does not forfeit her right to life, but she does forfeit the right not to be met with a lesser degree of force. We might think that she has a number of rights on her "rights-shelf" and that proportionality determines which ones she loses. But I think we get a better insight into the nature of forfeiture if we think about it in terms of the Mechanics of Claims (MOC), as spelled out in Chapter 3. This allows us to think about rights as the output of the balance of claims, and that allows us to frame forfeiture in terms of the way an agent's actions can change the weight her claims have in the balance of claims, in a way that fairly holds her responsible for her actions.

To explain forfeiture in this way, I'll start with a reminder about the operation of the MOC.[20] The core thought in the MOC is that the first step in figuring out who has a right to what is to attend to the basic patient claims that compete against each other to influence what agents can do and then consider the claims agents have to be free not to do what the balance of patient claims on

[19] The same would be true of innocent threats, even if they do not "forfeit" their rights. See Section 14.5.
[20] For more detail, see Section 3.3.

them would have them do. Within basic patient claims, there's a fundamental divide between property claims, on the one hand, and restricting and empowering claims, on the other. Property claims establish how the world of resources, which agents need to use to act, is divided up. That sets the baseline freedom of each agent: Her baseline freedom is set by what she can count as hers to use. Her baseline freedom can be restricted by restricting claims, the normative force of which is to require her to act in ways she is free to act or not act, given her baseline freedom. And her baseline freedom can be augmented by empowering claims, the normative force of which is to give her the right to use something she normally would not be free to use.[21]

To illustrate, suppose that A has some drugs that B would need to save C. B's baseline freedom of action does not include those drugs.[22] B would use A as a means if he just took A's property to save C. This may sound wrong; we're used to thinking that using as a means requires using another's *body* as a means. But I think one's body is just one's "first property"; I think we should take *all* use of another's property as morally equivalent to using the person.[23] Now, it could be that C's interest in the drugs is *much* stronger than A's. Suppose, for example, that C will die if she does not get the drugs in the next hour or so but is expected to live for years if she does; and suppose that A could, without suffering any serious harm, wait for a fresh supply of drugs to be delivered in the coming days. Then C would have an empowering claim on A and B, one that pushes to empower B by putting A's drugs in his "toolkit" so that he can use them to save C.[24] But C's having an empowering claim does not, by itself, entail that B gets to count A's property as part of his toolkit. If we assume no forfeiture, then A's property claim loses out to C's empowering claim only if the latter claim serves a very strong interest, and only if A's claim serves a fairly weak interest. If A would suffer real hardship if B took her drugs, then B is not free to take them, no matter that C would die as a result. Property is fundamental to what agents are free to do.

Figure 14.1 depicts the claims in motion, as it were, assuming that C's empowering claim succeeds.

[21] In Section 3.5.1, I introduced both restricting and empowering claims, but I mentioned the latter only in n. 54, 56, and 57.

[22] If B needed the drug to help himself, the same basic analysis would apply. I separate B and C only for ease of tracking who has what kind of claim.

[23] See Section 3.5.1, n. 56 for an important caveat.

[24] One might object that if need empowered agents to take from the rich and give to the needy, that would license too much redistribution. See Y. Yuan, "The Mechanics of Claims in a Statist Theory of Rights." But I think this objection fails to take into account the cumulative impact of the claims of the needy. I think the needy have a right to help only when their needs present as emergencies, which can be identified as such in part on the ground that the demands they impose on agents are unlikely to repeat. See my "Welfare's Role in the Mechanics of Claims: Reply to Yuan and Sinclair." Without that restriction, we would all be living as Peter Singer once imagined we should: as servants to the overall welfare, without our own lives to lead. That is inconsistent with the Autonomy Principle. I assume here an emergency situation.

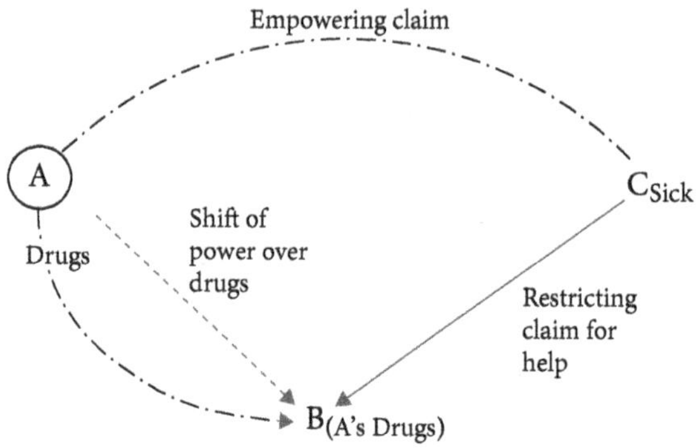

Figure 14.1 Effect of an empowering claim

C's empowering claim operates on A and B to transfer power over A's drugs from A to B.[25] C's restricting claim then operates on B, pushing to give B a duty to use A's drugs to help C. In a case like this, in which an agent is free to act because he has the right to use the resources he needs to act, then three other questions arise. First, do the competing restricting claims on him leave him free to act? A also has an interest in taking her drugs, which gives her a restricting claim on B too—a claim to leave them in her possession (for the sake of visual simplicity, I left A's competing restricting claim out of the figure). Clearly, if C's empowering claim outweighs A's property claim, then that balance would favor C. But A still has a claim. Second, does B's agent claim to be free not to act on the balance of restricting claims, which favors C, give him the freedom not to act on C's behalf? C's interest might be so strong that B has a duty to get the drugs from A and give them to C. Or the effort it might cost B to do so might give B the right not to help C. Third, does anyone have a special claim on B that limits his freedom? If B is C's father, B would have a duty to make special efforts to help C that he would not have if C were just a stranger.

Against that background, we can see that forfeiture can affect the strength of different kinds of claims and thereby have multiple effects on the balance of claims in this sort of situation.[26] Suppose A needs her drugs to such a degree that B is not free to take them for C's sake unless A does something to forfeit her claim to her drugs. In that case, if we assume no forfeiture, then A's property claim

[25] B could presumably take A's drugs even if A refused. But if A were to put up physical resistance, that would complicate things. Then we need to know whether B is not only entitled to take the drugs, but also to use self-help to take them despite the costs of doing so on him, A, or possibly bystanders.

[26] Waiver would work much the same way; transfer is presumably limited to agent claims, property claims, and special claims (i.e., excluding restricting claims).

limits B's freedom to satisfy C's claim for help.[27] But now suppose A has done something to harm C, causing C to need the drugs. It need not be culpable,[28] but suppose for the moment that it was. Suppose A negligently cut C with a knife that had a toxin on it, and that A's drug would counteract the effect of that toxin. Then we might say that A has forfeited her property claim on her drugs, at least vis-à-vis C's competing empowering claim. What that really means is that the strength of A's property claim is greatly weakened, so that B could take A's drugs as part of his toolkit to help C. But A would not simply lose her property claims over her drugs. If B has some other way to help C, then A could retain her drugs as hers.[29] The point is that the kind of priority A's property claim had to set B's baseline freedom is lost in this context, in which it comes into conflict with C's competing empowering claim to give B property-like control over it, so that B can then give it to C.

What about A's interest in her drugs, an interest that gives rise to a restricting claim? Even if we assume that B can treat her drugs as in his toolkit for saving C, that does not imply that A has lost her restricting claim to enjoy the benefit of her drugs. If A's need were much stronger than C's, we might still think that B must leave the drug with A. Suppose A would die if B took the drugs to help C, but C could wait another day in mild discomfort to get her own supply. Then B would wrong A if he took her drugs to help C, not because they were *A's* drugs but because A's restricting claim not to be harmed is still stronger than C's restricting claim to be helped. That said, A's action would affect the strength of her restricting claim to enjoy her drugs. It would be weaker than if she hadn't harmed C. Normally, a claim not to be harmed is stronger, all else equal, than a claim to be saved. But in this case, A's action has forfeited the strength not only of her property claim but also the strength of her negative restricting claim not to be harmed. As a result, if A and C would suffer the same harm if B does not give A's drugs to C, B should favor C. He should favor A only if her interest is substantially stronger than C's.

Ultimately, whether A has or has not forfeited her right to keep her drugs is a function of what would constitute a fair distribution of the burden of *someone* not having access to the drugs. A would suffer some amount if the drugs were taken by B and given to C; C would suffer some amount if B did not take the drugs and give them to her. Normally, if A would suffer even moderately, her property claim would govern as a right. But if A has culpably created C's need, then it would be fair for B to give her drugs to C unless A's need is much greater.

[27] To be clear, C has two claims that operate in stages. First, C's empowering claim pushes to put A's property in B's toolkit; second, if but only if that works, then her restricting claim pushes to require B to help her.

[28] I return to this theme in Section 14.5.

[29] I return to this point in Section 14.4.

So far, I've focused the discussion of forfeiture in this section on patient claims, and in particular on property and restricting claims. We could also discuss C's potential forfeiture of her empowering claims. For example, if she caused her own state of need in a way that would make it fair to weaken her claims for aid, then she could forfeit those patient claims. But rather than turn to a discussion of those patient claims, I want to turn now to agent claims.

Agents can have agent claims to be free to do something (positive agent claims) and agent claims to be free not to do something (negative agent claims). Both can be forfeited. For a positive agent claim, consider, again, the claim to be free to drive a car. If A is caught driving drunk or committing a certain number of moving (driving) violations, she could forfeit her license and with it her legal freedom to drive. For a negative agent claim, consider B's freedom *not* to help others, strangers to him, when the costs to him are substantial. Suppose B has harmed someone: He's pushed C off a dock and into a lake, and she's having trouble swimming to shore. It might seem that B would have a duty to save C anyway, regardless of whether he pushed her in. But suppose it's cold, and B is not feeling well. Saving C would tax his health. Arguably, B would not have a duty to save just anyone who had fallen into the water, at least not by swimming out to save her. B's negative agent claim not to have to help a stranger would give him a right not to do so. But having pushed C in, B forfeits his negative agent claim and acquires a duty to save her.

14.2.2 Shifting the Normative Baseline for Patients

Another important feature of forfeiture can be explained by this emphasis on fair distribution: It can explain why there is no moral residue when a person forfeits her right not to be harmed. This is an important difference between forfeiture cases and cases in which the positive restricting claims of some outweigh the negative restricting claims of others (classic "lesser-evil" cases). The standard explanation is that when a person forfeits some right of hers, then she is not wronged if the interest formerly protected by that right is set back; without the relevant right, she can't be wronged in that way. That explanation can't work inside the MOC, however, because while forfeiture affects claim strength, it does not eliminate claims. But there is a different, I think better, explanation that falls out of the fairness model.

To illustrate, recall the *Trolley Switch* case, and consider a modified version in which the sidetrack man has done something unjustifiable to put the five in harm's way—he recklessly damaged the brakes on the trolley. If he had not damaged the brakes, it would still be permissible for Betty to turn the trolley onto him, but he (or his heirs) would have a claim for compensation if Betty shifted the bad luck of the five onto him.[30] But given that he has recklessly damaged the brakes and caused this conflict of interest, it would be fair to treat his restricting claim not to be hit to be significantly weaker than it would otherwise be. In addition, the default position should be that it is fair to turn the trolley onto him. That does not mean that the balance of restricting claims favors the five on the track straight ahead, regardless of the strength of their competing interests. If they would suffer only bruises if Betty does not turn the trolley, and the sidetrack man would be killed if Betty turns it, she might be obliged *not* to turn it. But the fairness considerations shift which restricting claims count as positive, and which as negative. The sidetrack man's claim would normally be negative, but once he forfeits it, it effectively turns into a positive claim: to be freed from carrying the burden of his forfeiting behavior. Meanwhile, the five effectively have negative claims: not to have to suffer for his sake, given that he is responsible for the situation in which their interests conflict. If Betty refrains from turning the trolley because of the sidetrack man's claim, leaving the five to suffer bruises, the sidetrack man would presumably owe them compensation for their injury.[31]

This analysis of forfeiture in terms of the MOC lays open its inner logic.[32] Doing so provides, I think, sufficient reason to reject a sort of skepticism about forfeiture. Christián Rettig has recently expressed this skepticism, arguing that we don't need to appeal to forfeiture at all. He argues for embracing a specificationist notion, according to which "we may replace [the appeal to forfeiture] with an exception clause in the very content of the right not to be subject to some [normally impermissible] treatment."[33] I acknowledge that this is a logically coherent way of discussing rights, and Rettig argues that it has the virtue of simplicity. But I think that virtue is outweighed by the loss of explanatory function. We want to be able to think about which rights people have in different situations. Specificationism allows one to do that, but not by thinking in terms of rights; rather, it derives conclusions about rights from a set of non-rights-based reasons (usually a rather unsystematic set of non-rights-based reasons). This approach fails to appreciate the coherence and principled functioning that is characteristic of the space of rights. The MOC, by contrast, appeals to an underlying structure of claims (pro tanto rights), which allows us to make sense of the content and structure of rights in a systematic way. And

30 See Section 3.1.

31 This qualitative change is related to the loss of control over property, which occurs when forfeiture weakens property claims so that empowering claims move it from the original property owner to an agent who can use it to help those whose interest conflicts with that of the forfeiting agent.

32 For another recent analysis of forfeiture that seeks to unpack it into component parts, see D. Clark, "Mistaken Defense and the Unbundling of Rights."

33 "Let's Forget About Forfeiture," 2–3.

the idea of forfeiture, along with waiver and transfer, is a necessary element in an accounting of the dynamic way autonomous choice impacts the rights we have.[34]

14.3 More on the Mechanics of Forfeiture

In this section, I want to say something about two different questions: (1) the connection between the forfeiting action and the right that is forfeited, as well as factors that control how and when forfeiture ends; and (2) the fact that not all rights can be forfeited, not in the sense that some rights are inalienable, but in the sense that forfeiture cannot be the means by which they are alienated.

14.3.1 Symbolic Connections and Restorative Conditions

Starting with the connection between the forfeiting action and the forfeited right, sometimes it will have a direct substantive connection, sometimes not. For a direct connection, consider again driving drunk or committing one too many moving violations. Either can be the basis for forfeiting one's right to drive. But sometimes the connection will be less direct. A stalker who threatens his ex-wife may lose access to his guns, not because he threatened her with his guns, but simply because his stalking marks him as a danger to her, and the danger is greater if he has a gun.

Turning to how and when forfeiture ends, the answer is that it depends on the context. If A unjustly attacks B, A forfeits her patient-right not to be attacked and her agent-right to fight back for as long as she is acting unjustly. But once A ceases acting unjustly—really ceasing to do so, as opposed to simply taking a break for tactical reasons before resuming the attack—A recovers both rights.[35] But it's not so simple with the loss of the right to drive. If B lost his driver's license because he's been caught driving drunk in New Jersey, where I live, B would automatically lose his license for a time period determined by the court. To get it back, B would need more than the passage of time; he would need to participate in an Intoxicated Driving Program, with alcohol and highway safety classes.[36] Other instances of forfeiture may be permanent. For example, any federal officer who is successfully impeached and removed from office can also

[34] See also my earlier discussion of specificationism in *The Mechanics of Claims*, 45.

[35] For the United States's criminal law on this, see J. Dressler, *Understanding Criminal Law*, § 18.02[B][2][a].

[36] See "New Jersey's Intoxicated Driver Resource Center (IDRC) Program."

be barred forever from holding "any Office of honor, Trust or Profit under the United States."[37]

Fundamentally, however, forfeiture should be no broader nor longer lasting than necessary to properly balance the competing welfare interests, as judged after fairly weighing the moral significance of what the forfeiting agent has done. The reason attacking another does not cause A to lose her right to defend herself over a prolonged period of time is that a long-term forfeiture would not be necessary to achieve the goal of ensuring that A does not have rights that support her unjustly harming another. When the attack is over, whether A has won or lost, the right to use force against her is no longer justified by reference to her posing an unjust threat to others. That does not mean that A forfeits no other rights. She might, for example, forfeit the POLA in some way, including, for example, forfeiting the right to carry certain weapons in the future. These other forms of forfeiture would respond to the fact that A might pose an unjust threat again, and having done so once, it might be fairest, for the sake of the safety of others, to disarm her. Each particular right A forfeits, and the conditions of its possible restoration, have to be justified as necessary to achieving a distribution of burdens that is fair in light of what A has done.

14.3.2 The Right Not to Be Punished Cannot Be Forfeited

Now it might seem that any right that can be alienated can be forfeited. But I reject that claim. There is at least one category of rights that cannot be forfeited: rights agents have not to be treated in ways that make sense only if they deserve to be so treated. Forfeiture cannot, without more, ground desert. Obviously, the relevant right here is the right not to be punished.[38]

Here, I disagree with the views of Christopher Wellman, who argues that forfeiture is the right way to understand punishment.[39] He asserts that "[o]ne necessarily loses one's moral immunity to (proportionate) punishment whenever one culpably violates a moral right."[40] And he asserts that a forfeiture theorist can capture the proportionality constraint on punishment by "insist[ing]" that this is *all* that a wrongdoer forfeits.[41] He adds that his view is compatible with the kind of duty view of punishment that Victor Tadros endorses and that he finds "quite promising."[42] On Wellman's view, Tadros's argument that wrongdoers acquire an

[37] U.S. Constitution, art. 1, § 3, ¶ 7. Contrast the 14th Amendment, §3, which describes a similar forfeiture for anyone who engages in acts of insurrection or rebellion, but which contemplates lifting that disability by "a vote of two-thirds of each House" of Congress.
[38] See Section 5.4.
[39] *Rights Forfeiture and Punishment.*
[40] Ibid., 6.
[41] Ibid., 34.
[42] Ibid., 26.

enforceable duty to submit to punishment can be recast as forfeiting their liberty right—in my terms, their negative agent claim—not to submit to punishment.[43]

I think this is wrong on many levels.[44] First, as demonstrated at the end of Chapter 12, punishment that is limited to that which is proportional to culpability often would *not* suffice to achieve a fair distribution of the burdens. But I think forfeiture of the right not to suffer equivalent sanctions is not so limited.[45] Thus, we have a reason to treat forfeiture as different from deserved punishment.

Second, punishment requires a specific justification. It's punishment only if it is part of an overall blaming response to culpable action.[46] Forfeiture alone cannot supply that justification. Even if we adopt the duty view, all that we have established is that wrongdoers have a duty to make amends. That does nothing to imply that the enforcement of that duty is based on guilt that justifies blame.[47]

Third, if punishment is justified as deserved, then an appeal to forfeiture is otiose; the justificatory work is already taken care of.[48] The right not to suffer hard treatment as a penalty can be forfeited, but punishment is more than that; it can only be justified via desert, not forfeiture.[49]

14.4 Necessity and Forfeiture

I noted above that A could forfeit her right to her drugs in the sense that her property claim would be weaker than it otherwise would be, but that she might still retain her property right to them. As I put it, "If B has some other way to help C, then A could retain her drugs as hers." We could also see the point by thinking about how many of her drugs A must lose. Suppose B could help C by taking only one of A's pills, leaving A with most of her supply. The fact that she has forfeited her right to her drugs does not mean that B could take all of them. It implies only

43 Ibid.

44 In "Retributive Justice," I wrote of deserved punishment as though it might presuppose forfeiture of the right not to be punished first (section 4.1.3). I now think that was a mistake.

45 I argue this point in Section 15.1.1.

46 See Ch. 7.

47 See Section 7.4.

48 Massimo Renzo argues that the notion of forfeiture is either "incomplete or redundant." "Rights Forfeiture and Liability to Harm," 325. His redundancy argument is that it operates as an intermediate conclusion in normative arguments establishing that certain actions are permissible and that deeper principles, like my fair distribution of burdens principle, have to be appealed to in order to provide a substantive explanation for the explanandum. But my point about forfeiture being redundant in the context of punishment operates at a different level. My point is that desert operates at the same level of explanation as forfeiture. Once desert has been appealed to, then forfeiture is redundant.

49 Wellman might agree if he accepted the notion of deserved punishment. See *Rights Forfeiture and Punishment*, 21.

that he may take those that it is necessary to take from her in order to restore a fair balance of burdens.

The general lesson is this: Forfeiture is a necessary but not a sufficient condition for a patient losing out in a material way; there also has to be some positive reason to impose a cost on her. The positive reason to impose a cost on a patient may be contingent, so that it operates in a case-by-case way, or it may be a standing matter of policy, expressed in a rule that dictates handling specific kinds of cases in specific ways. The case of A who harms C provides an example of case-by-case forfeiture. The amount B would be allowed to take from A would vary according to C's need. But other cases will appeal to a rule. If the concern is deterrence and norm reinforcement, as it is in the penal law, then a rule will determine what is to be done. The rule will capture the necessity of the practice. It will convey the message to other law breakers: If you do X, then you can expect to suffer Y. That's not to say that case-specific features will not matter. A court may determine that the need for deterrence in a particular time and place is not so great, or that the harm to the defendant of being sanctioned would be especially great. Such considerations could give the court a reason to impose a lesser sanction on him. But such deviations will be with respect to a baseline schedule for default forfeitures of the right not to be sanctioned, given the particular offense performed.

It is also important to mention here how different the forfeiture of the POLA would be, as its material application will always be deeply case specific. At one level, it should operate like the penal law: For the sake of legality, the potential loss of the POLA should generally be set ex ante in law, so that one can know what one might lose if one commits certain crimes or penal violations.[50] But in application, the state will be limited, on a case-by-case basis, to using the least restrictive alternative. This means that different people, who pose different risks, can justifiably be treated quite differently, despite having committed the same crime or penal violation.[51]

Finally, to close out this section, I should say a word about necessity in the context of forfeiture of agent claims. They don't require a reason for anyone else to act; forfeiture simply applies if it's a fair way to distribute burdens. But necessity can be relevant in these cases too, in both case-specific and rule-based ways. Consider, first, the case of B harming A, who is then in need of B's help. B would forfeit his right not to help, at least up to a certain level of sacrifice; but if his help were not needed, he would not have a moral duty to act. By contrast, if B forfeited his right, say, to drive, then he would lose the right unconditionally, unless and

[50] I argue that the rigid ex post facto limits on punishment do not have to apply to forfeiture of the POLA, though they generally should respect that idea. See Section 15.4.

[51] I return to this theme in Ch. 16.

until he somehow regained it, or some emergency made his residual claim to be free to drive strong enough to overcome the forfeiture.

14.5 Culpability, Action, and Forfeiture

My view is that actions that would cause an unfair distribution of burdens if they did not trigger a forfeiture are the grounds for forfeiture.[52] This is a middle-of-the-road position. There are some scholars who have taken a narrower view, writing that forfeiture depends on having acted culpably. Wellman, for example, writes: "[O]ne does not forfeit a right unless one culpably violates (or at least attempts to violate) someone else's right."[53] And Helen Frowe writes that "a person can be liable to defensive harm only if she is morally responsible for posing an unjust threat. . . [A] person is morally responsible for posing an unjust threat if she had a reasonable opportunity to avoid posing the unjust threat and she intentionally failed to avail herself of that opportunity."[54] Her standard too requires culpability: the recklessness mens rea of knowingly imposing an unjust risk.[55] And there are reasons to take a broader position, according to which forfeiture can result from a mere causal role in a situation, without even having taken responsible action. I think the first position is too strong and the second too weak.

To appreciate why forfeiture does not require culpable wrongdoing, consider Jeff McMahan's example:

> *Conscientious Driver:* she "always keeps her car well maintained and always drives carefully and alertly [and she] decides to drive to the cinema. On the way, a freak event that she could not have anticipated occurs that causes her car to veer out of control in the direction of a pedestrian."[56]

As McMahan observes, she has done nothing culpably wrong.[57] But if one had to choose whether to allow her to kill the pedestrian or to do something to her

[52] Recall that I include omissions implicitly in "actions." See Section 5.3.
[53] *Rights Forfeiture and Punishment*, 6.
[54] *Defensive Killing*, 73.
[55] For my earlier criticism of Frowe, see my *Mechanics of Claims*, 170, 200–203.
[56] *Killing in War*, 165.
[57] One could argue that she wrongs the pedestrian in the sense that by driving her car into him she violates his right not to be hit. I would agree that if she could do something to avoid hitting him, she would be obliged to do it, even if it imposed a substantial cost on her. But if she has no ability to foresee the accident, and if she cannot avoid it once it has started to happen, I'm not sure it makes much sense to say that she "wrongs" him. At that moment, she lacks the relevant agency. She can still be liable to defensive force, and failing that, to a duty to compensate the pedestrian, in virtue of threatening him or harming him without having had a right to do so. But I think we can bypass this dispute by focusing on *culpable* wrongdoing, which she does not perform.

car that would kill her but save the pedestrian—we are to suppose that one just happens to be present with the right military-grade hardware—there's good reason to think we should take her to have forfeited her right to life in a way that makes killing her permissible. As McMahan explains, the driver presumably knew "that her action carrie[d] a small risk of causing great though unintended harm."[58] Moreover, "because she knowingly imposed this risk for the sake of her own interests[,] she is morally liable to defensive action to prevent her from killing an innocent bystander."[59] In other words, it is because she imposed the risk on the pedestrian that it is fair to say that she forfeits her right to life in this situation: her negative claim not to be harmed is weakened to such a degree that it is outweighed by the pedestrian's claim to be saved.

Seth Lazar points out that the "[p]edestrian's voluntary choices also contribute to the forced choice between their lives."[60] This leads him to conclude that it is not so clear that the driver should be taken to have forfeited her right not to be killed. In support of Lazar's point, I think it's clear that if the pedestrian was a jaywalker, then we should say that he forfeited his right to use lethal self-defense against the driver—assuming she did nothing irresponsible that led to her also being out of control and unable to avoid hitting him—and she would retain her right not to be killed in defense of him. But if he was not doing anything irresponsible to contribute to the problematic situation, then it seems fair to say that she carries more of the burden if a forced choice situation arises. Despite her having done nothing culpably wrong when she set out to attend the cinema, it is fair to hold her to have forfeited her right to life once her car is careening out of control at the pedestrian.

There are also plenty of other examples of forfeiture where culpable wrongdoing is not implicated.
Consider these three examples:

- One team fails to show up for a basketball game for reasons that are not covered by a limited set of recognized excuses (for example, severe weather)—they forfeit the game (the burden to be divided is the traveling of some teams to play others in an organized sports league).
- A gets a check and fails to cash it within 180 days—she forfeits the right to the money from the check writer's bank account (the burden to be divided is providing time to cash a check, on the one hand, and the check writer's ability to know what she has in her checking account after having written a check, on the other).

58 Ibid., 166.
59 Ibid.
60 "Responsibility, Risk, and Killing in Self-Defense," 717.

- A fails to follow through on a contract to buy a house—she forfeits her deposit (the burden to be divided is helping buyers avoid making a major financial mistake by giving them time to get the property inspected, on the one hand, and helping sellers avoid wasting time with flaky buyers, on the other).

Clearly, forfeiture does not generally require culpable wrongdoing. It requires only that the forfeiting agent has not done what she needed to do to avoid forfeiting some right, the forfeiture of which makes the final distribution of burdens fairer.

That said, while culpable wrongdoing is not necessary for forfeiture, it can play a role in determining what constitutes a proportional forfeiture. Consider again the example of self-defense against a range of threats and aggressors. Start with the non-culpable conscientious driver. Even if it's true that one such driver forfeits her life if it is necessary to blow up the car she is in to save a responsible (non-jaywalking) pedestrian, it seems unlikely that the car could justifiably be blown up if *two* people were in it, even if it was their joint decision to go to the cinema that led to their being where they are, threatening, through no fault of their own, a responsible pedestrian. But now suppose the driver was not so conscientious. Suppose she was negligent about keeping her car in good shape. Her tires have bald spots, and any reasonable person would know that they are unsafe; simply hitting a small pothole could cause them to blow, which could cause the car to lurch to the side. The driver and her friend are both aware of the sad shape of the tires, and they take the car out anyway. Arguably, they both forfeit their right against defensive force. The case for forfeiture would be even stronger if *they* (not just any reasonable person) knew not only that the tires were in bad shape, but that they could blow, leading to an accident, and they agreed to go out anyway. It would then be all the clearer that they forfeit their right against defensive force. And finally, we could imagine a busload full of people who all agree to take a bus across town with the intention of murdering an innocent person. Their high level of culpability seems sufficient to imply that they could *all* be killed if necessary to save just one innocent life.

The underlying rationale for taking the level of culpability to have significance is that it would be fair to impose an even greater burden on one who acted with a higher level of culpability. The reason is that as the level of culpability goes up, it is easier to demand that the person avoid doing what she did. This is not obviously true in terms of such contributors to culpability as malice, as opposed to indifference. But it does seem to track the Model Penal Code's concern with the four mens rea states of purpose (intent), knowledge, recklessness, and negligence.[61]

[61] M.P.C. § 2.02(2).

Those who intend to kill an innocent person without sufficient justification should simply stop; it is fair to put a very lopsided burden on them if they don't. Those who knowingly kill or recklessly put others at risk of death also should simply stop if their acts of killing or risking are not justified, but their aim may not itself be ruled out, and thus they may have some basis for claiming that the burden should not be so lopsidedly imposed on them. Those who are negligent about how they expose others to risk of death would have had a harder time avoiding what they did (they were not, after all, aware of the risk they imposed), so a fair burden sharing would put still less of the burden on them. And those who were not even negligent, those who, like the conscientious driver, were merely responsible for their choices, deserve to carry the burden only by the slightest margin (given that it's a single, indivisible burden that would fall on one or the other). Still, it's important to see that this reasoning is all about fairness, not about blameworthiness.

Coming to the other side of the issue, one might say that forfeiture does not even require action. Consider the case introduced by Robert Nozick:

> *Falling Man*: Albert was out for a walk in the woods when he was picked up—in a way he could not have foreseen was possible and that reflected no fault of his own—on the horns of a moose. The moose then tossed him down a well where he will fall upon and kill Vicky (and survive himself) unless she blows him up to save her life (Vicky cannot get out of the way). If Vicky were not present, the falling man would not die; thus, his life does not depend on his using her as a means of saving him.[62]

I have argued that it's not clear whether Vicky may kill the falling man to save herself. But at the same time, I've argued that it is clear that his claim not to be killed is weaker than the claim of a bystander onto whom a threat might be deflected to save a potential victim like Vicky. That is, I've argued that the falling man's claim not to be killed is weaker than the claim of a mere bystander.[63] This is exactly the kind of weakening that is involved in forfeiture, so it might seem that there is nothing particularly significant about responsible *action* as the basis of forfeiture.

Although claim weakening does not depend on responsible action, I think it is still worth limiting *forfeiture* to cases that involve, at the very least, responsible action. I admit that the argument in the falling man case goes via the thought that people have to be responsible for, and their patient claims have to reflect, the causal impact they have on others. That too is grounded in fairness.

[62] For the original case, see *Anarchy, State, and Utopia*, 34.
[63] See *The Mechanics of Claims*, ch. 6.

But there is something distinctly important about agents being responsible for their choices in situations in which they could at least foresee that they were imposing distinct risks on others, or at least that they were actively engaging with a situation in which burdens have to be shared in a fair way. Choices are how we navigate the world. They give us the opportunity to exercise control over which burdens we take on or risk taking on. This is where we can be actively sensitive to the claims of others. Thus, I think it makes sense to highlight responsible actions as the basis for a distinctive category of claim losing and weakening: forfeiture.[64]

14.6 Forfeiture in the Penal Law

Having argued that wrongdoing is not essential to forfeiture in general, I will now argue that wronging, or, more accurately, pro tanto wrongdoing, *is* essential to forfeiture in the penal law. Wrongdoing is not essential to forfeiture in the context in which an agent is simply trying to cooperate with others to achieve some common goal, like running a basketball league, transferring money, or selling/buying a house. It is also not essential in the context of fairly deciding who should carry the burden of an indivisible harm that has to fall on someone, as in *Conscientious Driver*. But in the context of penal law, the aim is to deter lawbreaking and reinforce respect for the law. There is no concrete good or harm that needs to be distributed on each occasion. It is not as if someone will necessarily be unfairly inconvenienced or harmed if someone else breaks the law. The problem that needs to be fairly solved is ensuring that laws that exist for a legitimate purpose are generally respected, because if they are not *generally* respected, then some group of people will suffer harms that could otherwise have been avoided, harms that it was reasonable for the state to seek to avoid.

The balance of burdens for the penal law, then, is avoiding the undermining of respect for reasonable laws, on the one hand, and avoiding imposing serious sanctions on people, on the other. If people are justified in doing what they do, despite the pro tanto duty to respect reasonable regulations (laws),[65] then it is pro tanto unjustifiable to impose sanctions on them for doing so. But, as I argued in the previous chapter,[66] the penal law can fairly put the burden of showing a

[64] There is another kind of intermediate case: the non-responsible actor, e.g., someone who is sleepwalking. I think that if such people pose threats to others, their claims are weaker than the claims of bystanders, just as the falling man's claim is. I would also frame the right to use force against them as self-defense. German law seems to reach the same result, framing cases involving non-responsible attackers as "emergency" cases, rather than self-defense cases. See A. Walen and I. Zerbes, "Self-Defense."

[65] See Section 12.2.

[66] Section 13.4.

justification defense on a defendant. It follows that penalties should not be imposed unless the action is pro tanto wrong, but it does not have to be wrong all things considered.

What about culpability? If wrongness is not necessary, then it follows that culpability is not necessary. Moreover, the nature of penal law is that it is not concerned with culpability; it is not a blaming institution. Nevertheless, the discussion in the previous section on the relevance of mens rea terms shows that something like mens rea can be relevant to penal law. The seriousness of the sanctions here matters. If what was at stake was just a small fine—the negative equivalent of failing to win a prize[67]—then we might be less concerned about how penalties are triggered. It might be justifiable to impose them on people on a strict liability basis. But that would be inappropriate for serious penalties.[68]

Relatedly, states should allow certain kinds of excuses, not because they defeat culpability, but because excuses would make it unfair to hold the defendant to have forfeited her right not to be penalized.[69] To see this, let's start with a non-penal example: forfeiting a game of basketball. When I introduced the example, I included the proviso that the reason for missing the game was not covered by a limited set of recognized excuses (for example, hurricane). The thought is that if, say, a flash flood blocked access to the roads needed to get to the game site, it would be unfair to hold the team that did not show up responsible for their failure. There was nothing they could have been expected to have done differently; moreover, there is no need to place the burden on someone. Likewise, in the penal context, if an agent failed to obey a law because she was under duress or temporarily incapacitated by involuntary intoxication, she should be excused because it would be unfair to have expected her to have acted differently, and there is no need to place the burden on someone. This parallels the point already made about justification, showing that much of the doctrinal content of penal law will carry over from the criminal law, even if the reasons why they operate—fairness versus negation of culpability—are different.

[67] I am grateful to Daniel Fryer, who pressed this question: Consider the distinction between desert and entitlement. The fastest runner might deserve to win the prize in a running race, but if she trips and falls, that's her bad luck; the person entitled to the prize is the actual winner (assuming she did not cheat to win). Why not say the penalties are the equivalent of tripping? The answer given in the text is that it's not just losing out on a prize.

[68] This is a theme I explore in Section 15.2.

[69] See H.L.A. Hart, *Punishment and Responsibility*, 52, 181; A.P. Simester, *Fundamentals of Criminal Law*, 284–285. The issue raised in these texts is whether excuses should be relativized to a defendant's mental capacities. I cover that issue in Section 19.1. See also *Fundamentals of Criminal Law*, ch. 19. Here Simester considers whether excuses have to be reasonable and concludes that some, those that apply when the defendant is on notice that he might be committing a crime, do. I think his points apply as well to penal law defenses, and thus do not presuppose, as he thinks, focus on criminal law as a blaming institution. Fleshing out this point is outside the scope of this book.

15
Doctrinal Basics for the Penal Law

15.1 Proportionality Limits on Penalties

We come now to a core difficulty for the penal law: determining what could make a penalty proportional. I've used the phrase "a fair distribution of the burdens." But what makes a distribution "fair"? Is it enough that a person has done *something* to forfeit the right not to be penalized for the state to impose *whatever* burden would maximize the overall welfare? That could be fair in this sense: As long as the law is reasonably knowable, a reasonable person could tell if she was about to violate it, and if it would not be unreasonably burdensome to avoid doing so, then any reasonably competent agent who did violate the law would have had a reasonable opportunity to avoid doing so; if he suffers a penalty, he brought it upon himself. But I think that's inadequate as an account of fairness for the penal law. Even if a reasonable person *could* have avoided the penalty if he wanted to, the penalty still must be substantively fair, given the state's goals. Moreover, there's reason to think that substantive fairness in the penal law must be in some way related to proportionality in the criminal law. It can't be responsive to culpability, but it should at least avoid undermining the significance of proportionality in the criminal law. That comment presupposes that a state will retain the criminal law; I have suggested that it need not do so, and I explore the implications of that thought for proportionality at the end of this section. To start with, however, I assume both justifications are in play in a state's criminal justice system, and I address these two points: substantive fairness and compatibility with the criminal law.

15.1.1 Substantive Fairness in Penalties

What could make penalties substantively fair and therefore at least presumptively proportional? It is tempting to model this sort of proportionality on proportionality in the criminal law. That is, it is tempting to say things like: the graver the harm the state is trying to prevent, the stronger the penalty can be, and the easier it is to avoid violating the regulation in question, the stronger the penalty can be. But these sorts of thoughts import intuitions from the criminal law,

Punishment, Penalty, and Incapacitation. Alec Walen, Oxford University Press. © Oxford University Press 2026.
DOI: 10.1093/9780197523124.003.0015

intuitions that track notions of culpability, that do not belong in the penal law. We need a notion of fairness that is properly framed for penal law. I propose that it turns on these three considerations:

- Avoidability: It must be easy enough for a person to avoid incurring it, so that no one who makes reasonable efforts to avoid penalties is hit with them;
- Necessity: Penalties must not impose unnecessary suffering on persons who incur them for the sake of whatever good the state is trying to achieve by using them; and
- Quasi-Defensive Proportionality: Penalties must not be so large that the good the state is trying to achieve through deterrence is too small to justify imposing a burden of that size on someone, even if that person could have chosen not to incur it.

Avoidability is a fairly straightforward notion with two main implications. First, certain sorts of excuses, such as duress or serious mental illness, must be recognized in the penal law just as in the criminal law.[1] Second, mens-rea-like terms must apply; strict liability is as unfair in the penal law context as in the criminal, and negligence is a more problematic basis for forfeiture than knowledge.[2]

Necessity draws on the fact that forfeiture of the right not to suffer a harm does not, by itself, provide a reason to impose the harm; the reason must come from some instrumental good. The necessity principle applies to both ends of that instrumental link. It implies that the penalties should be large enough to do the deterrent work they are meant to do—otherwise they pointlessly inflict suffering. But at the same time, they may not be larger than is necessary to do that work—otherwise they, again, pointlessly inflict suffering.

There is ample empirical support for the claim that increasing the size of sanctions has little deterrent effect once they are already big enough to deter.[3] This might imply that there should be a single penal sanction. But it's not that simple. As the incentive to violate the law grows—whether because the personal advantage of doing so grows or because the odds of getting caught are peculiarly small—the magnitude of the penalty might have to grow as well, so that it does not become simply prudent to run the risk of incurring a penalty.[4] Nonetheless,

[1] I already argued that point in Section 14.6.

[2] I say more about penal law mens rea in Section 15.2.

[3] See Section 8.2, citing D. Nagin, "Deterrence in the Twenty-First Century," 202.

[4] One might also want to have a recidivist premium, but that might be better understood as a matter of incapacitation for the undeterrable, rather than a justifiably bigger sanction that might have more deterrent force.

it may be that penal sanctions in general can best operate in a relatively narrow band: not too small to be effective and not unnecessarily large.[5]

I argued earlier that the criminal law might justifiably impose punishments of up to twenty years or so for the worst crimes, and I argued that this was plausibly required, at least in current circumstances, for deterrence.[6] One might think that the same would be true for the penal law at the high end. But I believe there are two reasons why the limit for the penal law must be lower. First, nothing as dire as deterring acts that unjustly cause death or grievous bodily harm is at stake. Rather, since the penal law reinforces only proxy crimes,[7] the deterrent goals are only reinforcing respect for reasonable legal regulations. Though the regulations may be aimed at protecting human lives and health, the threat to those is only indirect; otherwise, the criminal law would be called for. And though reinforcing respect for reasonable legal regulations is an important goal, it is not important enough to justify using penalties of up to twenty years. Second, I think the penal law should retain a kind of secondary status, relative to the criminal law, at least in a criminal justice system that uses both. Thus, the highest sanctions should be lower than those used in the criminal law. This first basis for a limit brings us to the issue of quasi-defensive proportionality, which is the third element of fairness; the second basis brings us to the independent issue of the compatibility of penal law and criminal law sanctions in the same criminal justice system. I take these now in turn.

The idea of quasi-defensive proportionality captures the thought that the state is limited in the harm it may impose, even on an agent who knowingly chooses to violate a just regulation without any good reason for doing so, in the same way that an agent who engages in self-defense is limited in the harm that she may inflict on a culpable aggressor. Even if an aggressor is fully culpable and has maximally forfeited his right not to be harmed if necessary to protect his intended victim, he has not forfeited *all* claim not to be harmed. Deadly force may not be used to prevent a culpable slapping in the face, nor may it be used if less harmful force would be equally effective and not substantially more costly to use.[8] This second point, about the possibility of using less harmful means, concerns necessity, but the first one, comparing the harms, concerns proportionality.

[5] Insofar as the temptation to break the law is economic, forfeiture of illegally obtained economic gains would presumably be an essential element to a proper penalty. But that would presumably be only an element, as the odds of not being caught and prosecuted might make it prudent to engage in illegal activity unless there is an additional penalty beyond forfeiture of illegally gotten gains.

[6] See Section 8.5.

[7] See Section 13.5.

[8] In the context of penal sanctions, it's worth noting that spending more on sanctions is probably not as cost efficient as spending more on policing, at least in the United States, at the moment. See A. Scott, "Prison and Crime."

The same sort of thought applies in the context of considering how the state may use penalties to defend its law. If the good in question is sufficiently significant, then a harsh penalty could be imposed if the first two conditions (avoidability and necessity) are met. But if the harm is insignificant (like a slap in the face), then harsh penalties would be disproportionate, even if the person could easily have avoided incurring them. As in self-defense, proportionality is not to be understood in purely utilitarian terms; the unexcused, unjustified offender, like a culpable aggressor, has forfeited his right not to be penalized, which means that his claim not to suffer the harm that would result from the penalty is weaker than it otherwise would be. Even so, proportionality imposes limits on what may be done for the sake of the good in question. And if the good is not the kind of serious good that protecting people from serious assault is, if it is the abstract good of reinforcing the law, then only a lesser sanction can be proportional.

To be clear, reinforcing respect for the law is important, and if respect for the law is tightly correlated with respect for possible victims of wrongdoing, then the necessity prong might push for high penal sanctions. This is true of both the criminal law and the penal law. Proportionality in the criminal law is to be judged in terms of a whole schedule of punishment, a schedule that should be set with an eye to necessity.[9] The high-end anchor could be set higher than twenty years if a higher sanction would have more deterrent effect. The same point can be made for the penal law. The fact that a lesser good is at stake suggests that penal law sanctions should be lower. But the necessity of higher sanctions for effectiveness could push the other way. Indeed, the reason we need the penal law in the first place is that proportional punishments are sometimes inadequate to provide effective deterrence. So we need to be careful about what we infer regarding the magnitude of penalties from the fact that maximal punishments should be capped at something like twenty years. But the comparative issue is not limited to comparing the goods that are being protected. We also need to consider the relationship between the penal law and the criminal law, given the assumption that the former should not undermine the latter.

15.1.2 Compatibility with the Criminal Law

How should we think of the relationship between proportionality in the criminal law and penal law? Putting a sharper point on it: What would make it permissible to impose penalties more severe than whatever would be a proportional punishment for a proxy crime? My answer is that penalties that impose a more serious

[9] See Section 8.2.

hardship than could be justified for a proportional punishment can nonetheless be consistent with respect for proportionality in the criminal law if we can establish two things: first, that the justifications for penalties and punishments are distinct; second, that the sanctions do not undermine the significance of proportionality in the criminal law within the wider criminal justice system.

The first point has been made already: Penalties are based on fair forfeiture, not desert. As long as the state is clear that these are not the same thing, it should be able to avoid the implication that the proportional limitations on punishment are just a paper barrier, overridable whenever it is inconvenient to respect them. Punishment would remain a distinct system, and proportionality in the system of punishment would remain sacrosanct.

I should say that insofar as the concern is with respecting the integrity of the criminal law as a matter of human psychology—ensuring that people *feel* that imposing penalties that are more serious than proportional punishments is consistent with respecting the importance of proportional punishment—then this point about separate justifications trades on an empirical assumption. The assumption is that people care not only about whether the state is going to impose hard treatment on them, but why.[10] This is an assumption in which I have a great deal of confidence. As I put it when I introduced the idea of the penal law: Loss of liberty because one is a prisoner of war (POW) is just as dire as loss of liberty because one is sentenced to prison for a crime; in some ways, the former is even worse, as its duration is indefinite. But POWs know that they are not being condemned; they are merely being detained because the detaining power is trying to limit [its] enemy's fighting ability. Likewise, I think people distinguish civil penalties from criminal fines. In the same spirit, I think they would care about whether the judge at sentencing finds them guilty and sentences them with a punishment or merely finds them to have committed a penal offense and imposes a penalty.[11]

[10] A particularly astonishing example of this concerns torture. Majid Khan, who was held and tortured first by the CIA and then later by the guards in Guantanamo, said the following: "We [he and his fellow detainees in Guantanamo's Camp Seven] actually had a lot of respect for CIA. And we understood why they're torturing us. We understood they want intelligence. It's part of the business. It comes with the job." He later said: "There's a reason behind it." By contrast, "there was no justification what they did in Camp Seven. Zero. . . . It's just the nature, sadistic nature, that I could not understand in Camp Seven. I try not to think about it, honestly. It was the lowest point in my life." See *Serial*, Season 4, Episode "Two Ledgers," minutes 20:00–20:46, 21:55–22:24. This is not meant to condone CIA torture; it is meant only to say that understanding the reason why something is done makes a big difference to how it is experienced.

[11] The second half of this paragraph is taken from "Criminal Law and Penal Law," 446. I removed parts of the text because the original had the option of a mixed sentence, part punishment, and part penalty. I still think that option could exist, but the point is more cleanly made if there are two distinct options. Indeed, as I argued in Section 13.2, I think courts may want to avoid mixed sentences to reinforce the point that penalties are a differently justified sort of sanction.

This brings us to the *other* basis for limiting penal sanctions, namely that penal sanctions must not undermine the significance of proportionality in the criminal law. To meet that criterion, I believe we should recognize two limits on the penal law. First, it should operate *only* in the realm of proxy crimes.[12] Second, the maximal penal sanctions should clearly be *less* severe than maximal criminal sanctions.[13] This signals that penal law is meant to be a secondary system that can be appealed to only when the criminal law's proportionality restriction would prevent it from operating effectively to deter significant but lesser crimes.

This is, in fact, what we find for the penalties for proxy crimes. To illustrate the point, consider again the sanction for illegal possession of a gun under federal law.[14] One can be sentenced for up to fifteen years in prison for that offense. That is a very serious sanction; indeed, it is as high as I have seen for an offense that is arguably just a penal offense. But that is the point. This high-end penalty is substantially lower than high-end criminal punishments in the U.S. federal code: life in prison, and in rare and extreme cases, the death penalty. Moreover, in practice, it is normally substantially smaller. "The average sentence for offenders convicted of violating" the felon-in-possession law, who were not also sentenced under the armed career criminal act, was only "55 months."[15] This sanction is meant to be taken seriously, but it is not meant to signal that this sort of violation of the law, which may well reflect little to no culpability, is on a par with a serious crime. And I think that is not an accident; I think it reflects an intuitive grasp of the fact that proxy crimes are operating in a different way, one that should be seen as secondary or ancillary.[16]

15.1.3 Penal Law Without the Criminal Law

I have mentioned a few times before the possibility of doing away with the criminal law and relying only on the penal law, perhaps supplemented by restorative justice practices.[17] I turn now to examine what the penal law would look like

[12] See Section 13.5.

[13] This is a weaker condition than I used in "Criminal Law and Penal Law," 444. There I tried to compare individual penal offenses and crimes that were related by the good they sought to protect. Duff took me to task for that account, writing: "[I]f the penalties regime is not to 'undermine the overall fairness of the criminal justice system,' it must therefore not involve imposing penalties notably harsher than the punishments imposed for other kinds of minor crime; but this seems to bring a requirement of retrospective proportionality back into the story in a way that would seriously limit the level of penalties that could be imposed." "Defending the Realm of Criminal Law," 495. I avoid that criticism now with this weaker system-to-system comparison.

[14] See Section 12.2.

[15] U.S. Sentencing Commission, "Felon in Possession."

[16] The same point was made in Morissette v. U.S., 342 U.S. 246, 256 (1952) (noting that "penalties commonly are relatively small" for "public welfare offenses").

[17] See Sections 9.2, 10.4, and 13.2.

if the criminal law were abandoned and what the normative costs of that shift would be.

As a general matter, there would have to be *more* use of the penal law. The penal law would no longer be restricted to application to proxy crimes. It would have to cover all acts that are now covered by the criminal law, from theft to murder. And since there would be no criminal law, the priority of which it has to respect, it would be free to expand the sort of deterrent penalties deployed as necessary.

This may all seem unproblematic, even beneficial, insofar as it gets the state out of the blame game.[18] But it's worth highlighting what I think would be some, at best, peculiar features of taking the penal law seriously as a stand-alone justification for deterrent sanctions. First, the band of penalties might remain fairly narrow, primarily because the sanctions for lower-level crimes, no longer punished but penalized, could rise. The punishment for minor crimes is low because the culpability is low, and proportionality requires the punishment to correspond to the overall level of culpability. If culpability drops out and those crimes have to be picked up by the penal law, criminal law's proportionality restriction would drop out, and we should expect the sanctions to rise. Only the loose demands of quasi-defensive proportionality would serve as a cap to those penalties, but those demands are too loose to have much bite.

There might be some pressure not to make penalties for what would have been low-level crimes too high. The deterrent function of the penal law should include norm reinforcement. The norms recognized by penal law include differences in the level of the wrong committed, even if not differences in the culpability. Tracking differences in the level of wrong committed would provide *some* reason to have something like a criminal law schedule of punishments. But it would be a looser ordering than in the criminal law because this sort of norm reinforcement is just one among many consequentialist desiderata for the penal law, not a condition of its just proportionality. Indeed, the requirements of proportionality in the penal law would remain the same: avoidability, necessity, and quasi-defensive proportionality. The fact that sanction severity does not have a large impact on deterrence would, in combination with the necessity restriction, limit high-end penal law sanctions. But the low end would likely float up in ways that would seem counterintuitive to anyone with intuitions shaped by the criminal law.

Another peculiar feature is related to the first: There would almost certainly be some inversions in the sanction schedule, ones that would be indefensible in

[18] See Section 6.4 (discussing Erin Kelly's argument that the state should not be involved in laying blame).

the criminal law. That's because certain offenses may be harder to detect or more tempting than others in ways that have nothing to do with their severity. As long as sanction severity has *some* relevance to deterrent strength, that could provide sufficient reason to treat what would otherwise be a less serious crime as a more sanctionable penal law offense. I won't speculate on how exactly this could work out in practice. But just to illustrate the idea, one might find that certain forms of reckless behavior would reasonably be penalized more severely than certain forms of equally harmful intentional behavior. This would not arise in the criminal law, as long as the reckless behavior was deemed less culpable than the intentional behavior, all else equal.

I want to supplement these peculiarities of the penal law operating without the criminal law with another point about what would be lost normatively. As Benjamin Ewing puts it, "I doubt that it is possible adequately to recognise the wrongful nature of paradigmatic crimes—for example, murder, rape, assault, theft, arson—without forming and expressing the judgment that those who perpetrate them without a justification or excuse are culpable and merit condemnation."[19] One could look to restorative justice to do that.[20] But as I pointed out in Chapter 11, it is one thing for some individuals to cast blame; it is another for the state to do so, speaking on behalf of the whole political community. Something important is lost if we rely only on private statements of blame to make that point. It's not that the penal law would not also speak for the community, by reinforcing respect for the law. It simply gives up the idea of holding people to have a *guilt-debt* if they have culpably broken the law; it gives up the idea of saying, formally, that they should own their guilt for having acted wrongly; it substitutes the idea that they have forfeited their right not to be penalized, given that such penalties generally reinforce respect for the law.

I'm not arguing here that these features of the penal law, as a stand-alone system, are so serious that such a system could not reasonably be adopted.[21] I think that jettisoning the criminal law would weaken what it means for a political community to come together to establish and protect rights.[22] But it need not do so to an unacceptable degree, all things considered.[23] My aim here is simply to flag, for purposes of imagining the abandonment of the criminal law, just how

[19] "Do Unjust States Have the Standing to Blame," 268.

[20] See J. Howard and A. Pasternak, "Criminal Wrongdoing, Restorative Justice, and the Moral Standing of the United States."

[21] Note, it's unclear how theorists like Alon Harel, who take the state to have a duty to criminalize wrongdoing, would respond to the idea of replacing the criminal law with penal law. He equates barring the violation of rights with the existence of a criminal prohibition on violating them. "The Duty to Criminalize," 7. But the penal law can equally operationalize "barring" the violation of rights.

[22] See Sections 3.7.2 and 5.5.

[23] See Section 9 on how to weigh the costs and benefits of criminal law.

odd a stand-alone system of penal law would be. I think it is all too easy to think culpability and blame could be dropped from the system, leaving everything else the same. I think that's a failure of imagination.

15.2 The Mental State Element

The penal law needs to articulate suitable mental states for penalties, but these should not be confused with mentes reae or guilty states of mind. They are needed not to capture culpability but to acknowledge that the fairness of imposing penalties on a defendant depends in part on what she knew or should have known at the time she broke the law. If she *knew*, for example, that she was providing material support to a designated foreign terrorist organization (FTO), then she has less ground to complain that it is unfair to penalize her than if she had no idea that it was a designated FTO. If she had no idea, then the state should find out whether it was unreasonable to expect her to know. If it was unreasonable to expect her to know, then it would be unfair to penalize her for offering such support. None of these questions concern *blame*. They are simply questions of fairness when it comes to holding a defendant responsible.

Implicit in the above is a rejection of strict liability as the basis for a penalty. This cuts against the grain of much of public welfare law.[24] Thus, it is worth pausing to see if there is some reason to think that strict liability might be acceptable in the context of penal law.

One reason to think that it might be acceptable is the thought that what makes strict liability particularly *unjustifiable* in the realm of the criminal law is that criminal punishment presupposes the legitimacy of censure.[25] If the defendant did not have a culpable mental state, if she was not at least negligent in committing whatever wrong she committed, then the state cannot rightly say that she was culpable. Punishment and censure based on strict liability, then, to quote Andrew Simester, "amounts to a systematic moral defamation by the state."[26] This problem would not arise in the context of penal law, as the state would not then be in the business of punishing or censuring.

Further support for the use of strict liability in penal law could come from the observation that the use of strict liability does not imply that one could do

[24] This is the name given in the United States, in the context of early 20th-century criminal case law, to modern regulatory law aimed at things such as improving the safety of food and drugs, ensuring safe water, and so on.

[25] I agree with Simester that strict liability is acceptable in the criminal law if the strict liability element is used merely to identify which of a set of culpable actions the state is choosing to punish. See *Fundamentals of Criminal Law*, Sections 13.4 and 13.5. The same would apply to the penal law.

[26] Ibid., 305.

nothing to avoid trouble. As the Court pointed out in *Balint*, a seller of narcotics has "the opportunity . . . to find out the fact" that he is selling regulated drugs.[27] That is to say that the law does not merely lay a trap; it puts people in a position where they can "ascertain at [their] peril whether that which [they] sell[] comes within the inhibition of the statute."[28] The question is: Is such a warning of potential penal liability sufficient?

There are two sorts of arguments that can be raised against relying on such warnings: efficient legal design and fundamental fairness. I'll say a few quick words about the former, but will put most of the weight of my argument on the latter.

With regard to efficient legal design, there are good reasons to doubt the wisdom of using strict liability in public welfare offenses. As Stephen Schulhofer points out, such penalties may befall those who use all due care, and thus such penalties are likely to suppress productive activity and to drive the careful out of businesses regulated in that way, leaving only the reckless behind.[29] On the other hand, the use of strict liability makes prosecution easier. Even a negligence standard requires a prosecutor to establish how much care a reasonable person would have used in a particular situation. Strict liability makes it easier to simply enforce the law with penalties.[30]

The stronger case against strict liability penalties is that it is unfair to impose serious sanctions on people who do not take unreasonable risks. To see the strength of this point, suppose one was told that if one walked home after dark, one might be mugged. Suppose the mugger, echoing *Balint*, said: "I didn't spring a trap on my victim; she was forewarned, and she chose to walk home after dark anyway." No one would accept this as an adequate defense. The choice to impose the burden on the victim/defendant must be substantively fair. To be fair, it must be reasonable to expect the person not to have done what brings on a penalty. That requires the state to ban the activity in question and punish or penalize agents who engaged in it only if they at least should have known they were engaging in it.

Remember, the issue here is not, as it is in strict liability torts, whether the agent can be held to have assumed the duty to make others whole, or compensate them for any harm that befalls them, if she engages in risky action for her own profit. Strict liability profit stripping may be fair; strict liability for deterrence

[27] 258 U.S. 250, 254 (1922).
[28] Ibid. Simester emphasizes that the same point is made in English law. *Fundamentals of Criminal Law*, 309.
[29] "Harm and Punishment," 1587. Simester makes a related point in *Fundamentals of Criminal Law*, 300.
[30] For a longer discussion of the possibility of efficiency benefits, see *Fundamentals of Criminal Law*, 294–303.

purposes, where no one needs to suffer if deterrence is not used, is not. For that purpose, a minimal fairness condition is that a defendant should at least have known that she was violating the law.

This argument has its limits. If the penalty for a violation is merely a relatively small fine, of the sort handed out for many violations of regulatory law, then it might be reasonable to apply the fine on a strict liability basis. Even if the purpose of the fine is just to deter violations of the regulatory regime, and the offender had no reasonable way of knowing in advance that she was violating the regulations, it may nonetheless be justifiable to impose the fine as a fair distribution of burdens. If she is engaging in an activity that needs to be regulated—whether parking her car or selling a product—and she occasionally incurs a fine, demanding that she pay it may be effectively like demanding that she pay a user's fee.[31] She should not have to run an unreasonable gauntlet of secret traps to avoid such fees. The state should make it reasonably clear how to avoid the unwanted behavior. But for the sake of efficiency, it may be fair to allow the state to impose fines without having to prove at least negligence in every case. However, this exception presupposes that the fine is *relatively small*, as a fair user's fee would be. No one should have to pay for the right to engage in any regulated activity with time in a prison-like system. That sort of penalty should be reserved for instances in which the person at least should have known they were doing something that they should not have done.

Finally, I want to close out this section with a brief discussion of mental states as relevant to forfeiture of the presumption of law abidingness (POLA). In my view, that too should require a fitting level of awareness. If a person was reasonably careful not to break the law and did so anyway, by a stroke of bad luck, that would in no way indicate that she should be denied the POLA. Indeed, as I will argue in Chapter 16, forfeiture of the POLA—at least when it grounds a possible general loss of liberty[32]—should be imposed only in a limited range of cases: The offender has committed a highly culpable crime; she is a recidivist who has demonstrated a consistent disrespect for the law; or she has adopted the intention to commit a serious crime but has not yet come close enough to acting on that intention for criminal liability to attach.[33] None of the relevant offenses would be strict liability offenses, and having an intention to commit a serious crime requires the agent to have a mental state: intending.

[31] For a similar position, see Simester, ibid., 309–310.
[32] See Section 16.2.1.
[33] See Section 16.2.2.

15.3 Standard of Proof

The standard of proof (SOP) in the criminal law, as everyone knows, is proof beyond a reasonable doubt (PBRD). What exactly that means is up for debate, but everyone agrees that it is the highest SOP the law can require. It does not require certainty, but if we approach it in probabilistic terms, we should say that it requires something like a very high probability of guilt, presumably well over 90 percent. High probability of guilt is not enough for a conviction. The evidence also has to be individualized in the right way. For example, if we knew that twenty-four out of a group of twenty-five people were guilty of murder, and we knew nothing else, we could say for each person that the odds of his being guilty are 96 percent. Yet that would not suffice for conviction. We should also insist that an inquiry be made into individual histories and traits of all involved to try to determine who in that group are least likely to be murderers, and we should refrain from punishing them.[34] But assuming proper individualization of the evidence, then the ultimate question is: Does it give the factfinder very high confidence that guilt has been established?

The question I address here is: Must penal law use the same SOP, or might a lower standard be acceptable? I will argue that essentially the same standard must be used. It might seem that this is an easy case to make: Penal violations are based on proxy crimes; to prove the former, the state has to prove the latter. So it might seem that the SOP would, for trivial reasons, have to be the same. But it is not that simple. One might ask why we may not view the situation like this: The state has a choice, it can either prosecute the proxy crime as a crime, and prove it beyond a reasonable doubt, or it can prosecute it as a penal offense, in which case the SOP might be quite different, as no culpability or blame is involved.

Given that penal offenses might be tried alongside criminal law offenses in a single trial, there might be pragmatic reasons to keep the same SOP. Doing so would keep the criminal justice system simpler and more coherent. But that is not a strong reason for using PBRD in all penal cases. In cases where a penalty is all that a prosecutor is seeking, we can easily imagine the court instructing a jury to use a different standard.[35] There is no practical barrier to using, say, clear and convincing evidence—the lower standard for civil commitment hearings in the United States—or even preponderance of the evidence in pure penal law cases. To decide what standard to use in pure penal law cases, we need to examine the reasons for using one standard or another.

[34] I discuss the need for individualization in "Proof Beyond a Reasonable Doubt," 382–384.

[35] I assume penal law would require a jury, at least in the United States. But that's primarily a question of constitutional interpretation, and not a question I pursue here.

In my discussion of PBRD in the criminal law, I conclude that none of the standardly offered deontological reasons for having a high SOP work. I examine and reject arguments that appeal to the means principle, to fairness and equality, to social contract theory, to the distinction between causing and allowing harm, and to the expressive value of condemnation.[36] I conclude that the only sensible way to approach the SOP is by invoking the consequentialist notion that the SOP should reflect the norm of efficiency: One should not prefer to shift the ratio of convictions to acquittals; the right balance has been struck.[37] In practice, that means that the system should use that SOP that results in the net value of convictions (including true and false convictions) being equal to the net value of acquittals (including true and false acquittals).

This equation of net values allows for the derivation of a formula for the SOP. Assuming that the value of convicting the guilty is the same as the negation of the disvalue of acquitting the guilty and that the value of acquitting the innocent is the negation of the disvalue of convicting the innocent, one can derive the formula:

$$SOP = 1/[1 + V_{AG}/V_{CI}].$$ [38]

In this formula, V_{AG} is the disvalue of acquitting the guilty, and V_{CI} is the disvalue of convicting the innocent. If one thinks that the former is much less than the latter—say by a ratio of 10:1, the Blackstone ratio—then that implies that the SOP = 1/[1 + 1/10] = 1/1.1 = 91 percent. If, on the other hand, the disvalue of acquitting the guilty is taken to be just about as large as the disvalue of convicting the innocent, then that implies that the SOP = 1/[1 + 49/50] = 1/1.98 = 51 percent.

The question then is: How should one think about the ratio of these values? I argue that if one sets the SOP as a consequentialist would, then, given the value of incapacitating the dangerous, one could reasonably conclude that the SOP should, at least in certain kinds of cases, be fairly low. Especially if different standards could be used for different kinds of cases, then the SOP could dip below 50 percent for certain kinds of cases, and a reasonably strong case could be made that it would be significantly lower than 90 percent for violent felonies in general.[39] The reason is that the disvalue of letting a guilty and dangerous person go free could be quite great, greater even than the disvalue of convicting the innocent.

One could take that argument as a revisionist call for a lower SOP in criminal law.[40] But I take it as a sign that it is a mistake to take all the consequences

[36] "Proof Beyond a Reasonable Doubt," Part II.
[37] Ibid., 406.
[38] See ibid., 407–408 for the derivation of this formula.
[39] Ibid., 411–416.
[40] That's what Larry Laudan does in "The Rules of Trial, Political Morality, and the Costs of Error."

that might flow from convictions and acquittals into account in setting the SOP. I argue that when it comes to the reasons to punish, desert functions like a gate in the normative equivalent of a transistor: Until it is switched on, the potentially greater normative force of the instrumental reasons is switched off.[41] Likewise, when it comes to setting the SOP, I argue that using a consequentialist balance to set the SOP would allow a low SOP to function as an end-run around the need to establish guilt as a precondition of punishment. In effect, by relying on the value of incapacitation to lower the SOP, the state would declare that certain people deserve punishment simply because society would benefit if the state acted *as if* their guilt had been established. A retributivist cannot condone that sort of end-run around establishing guilt as a necessary precondition for punishment.[42]

To avoid that problem, I argue that the instrumental benefits of punishment must be screened off until the prosecution has established guilt. The intrinsic value of giving those who are guilty of wrongdoing the punishment they deserve is not likewise screened off. It is the retributive value of punishing the guilty, and only that value, that should weigh in the balance against the harm of punishing the innocent, thereby setting the SOP.[43]

If we assume that the intrinsic positive value of giving culpable wrongdoers the punishment they deserve is substantially lower than the disvalue of punishing the innocent, then we get, as a result, a high SOP for a criminal conviction. And this ratio of values seems reasonable. First, we readily accept many reasons for *not* seeking to punish the guilty, from the difficulty of obtaining a conviction to the value of obtaining their help in solving other crimes. Second, no one has a right to their punishment. Their victims may have a right to an apology and tort-like amends, but punishment cannot guarantee that. Punishment, as carried out by the state, aims to hold them *publicly* accountable for the sake of ultimate reconciliation between the political community and the wrongdoers. But if any particular defendant does not suffer it, it does not cost the state significantly. Failure to impose punishment in particular cases is not a great failure of justice. By contrast, punishing the innocent *is* a great miscarriage of justice. This, I believe, is how PBRD can be vindicated by a retributivist.

Now the question is: How does this argument apply to the context of penal law? There is no desert in penal law, and forfeiture does not carry its own reason

[41] "Proof Beyond a Reasonable Doubt," 427.

[42] Ibid. In the original text, I included the value of deterrence along with the value of incapacitation. I now think that was a mistake. Contributing to deterrence is part of the guilt-debt that a wrongdoer owes; its value is part of the intrinsic value of punishment. But as I argued in "Proof Beyond a Reasonable Doubt," most of the instrumental value from a particular person's punishment comes from incapacitation, not deterrence. Ibid., 440.

[43] Ibid., 427.

to act. The reason to inflict penalties, at least insofar as they are used for deterrence, *is* that they deter and thereby reinforce the law in a fair way. Does that mean that in the penal law context, the state is dealing with a simple balance of consequences? No, I think we still need to have a two-stage assessment of what is at stake. First, we need an SOP for determining whether someone is a penal offender who has forfeited his right not to be penalized, and then we get to consider the full range of benefits that flow from inflicting a penalty, which include not only the deterrence but the incapacitation that follows from imposing certain penalties.

The value of deterrence that justifies a deterrent penalty is, like the value of retributive justice, a rather abstract value: the value of reinforcing respect for the law. And it is important to keep in mind that we are not dealing with laws that forbid malum in se wrongs. We are not dealing with laws that ban murder, rape, assault, robbery, arson, torture, or terrorism. We are dealing with laws that set up proxy crimes, laws that try to keep people from doing things that generally contribute to socially unacceptable harms or injustices. So, there's a double indirectness in the value of deterrence. First, there's the indirectness of relying on a penalty against one to deter (mostly) others in a context in which failure to sanction one person won't greatly change the percentage of lawbreakers who get sanctioned; second, there's the indirectness of the connection between the proxy crimes and the ultimate harms or wrongs that the state is trying to prevent. Given this double attenuation, I think it is reasonable to say that the disvalue of failing to deter in a given case is substantially less than the disvalue of inflicting a serious penalty on a person who did not forfeit his right not to suffer such a penalty. This implies that for the penal law, as for criminal law, the SOP should be quite lopsided in favor of protecting the "innocent" (that is, those who are not really offenders).

I am not suggesting that the SOP for penal law should be fully as high as for criminal law. Holding the sanction constant, the harm to the innocent is not as great because there is no false message of condemnation in a penalty. But at the same time, we don't have a very precise grasp of just how high PBRD is. It would be foolish to put a precise number on it, both because we don't know exactly how to weigh the moral values at stake and because those who would apply the number don't have any scientific basis for making precise estimates of the probabilities of guilt, given the evidence. The best we can do is to say that the factfinder, after carefully weighing the evidence, should be *very* confident in the defendant's guilt; he should be confident enough to consider the possibility that the defendant is actually innocent to be essentially fanciful. And I think the same qualitative guides should be applied to penal convictions.

A contrast here is, I think, helpful. Consider the standard of "clear and convincing" evidence, as required in the United States for the civil commitment of those who are found to be mentally ill and a danger to themselves or others.[44] That is meant to be an intermediate SOP, falling between simple preponderance of the evidence and PBRD.[45] Its justification in that context is multifaceted, but it is based at least in part on what is at stake.[46] On the one hand, there's a clear harm to a person who is mistakenly committed: The loss of liberty is profound, as is the stigma, and both may end up being protracted.[47] On the other hand, the harms such a person might do to himself or others are also clear and concrete, ranging from emotional harm to physical harm to death.[48] Weighing two clear concrete harms against each other, one might think that the standard should be preponderance of the evidence. But harm to the individual who is wrongly committed is a certainty; harm to himself or others if he is wrongly released is speculative. This calls for raising the level of proof beyond mere preponderance.[49] But the concreteness of the harm that might occur if the person is wrongly released and *is* a danger to himself or others contrasts with the *double* attenuation in penal law. That explains why the penal law should use a yet higher SOP.

In saying that penal law should use PBRD, I'm not denying that PBRD could be interpreted more or less strictly, depending on the issue. In fact, there is evidence that it *is* interpreted differently in different kinds of criminal cases—the death penalty seems to call for a heightened version of it;[50] penal law might call for a slightly relaxed version of it.[51] And if the penalty is not particularly serious, if it might be experienced as a mere tax, then the SOP could drop below the PBRD level, perhaps to clear and convincing evidence. But if the penalty is serious, then it should fit somewhere in the PBRD ballpark.

[44] See Addington v. Texas, 441 U.S. 418 (1979). It is also used in cases involving fraud, deportation, denaturalization, termination of parental rights, decisions to terminate life, and freedom of speech. See M. Pardo, "Second-Order Proof Rules," 1090.

[45] In the United Kingdom, the standard is formulated differently. Relevant professionals must *believe* that the person is a danger to themselves or others. But this is still an intermediate standard between *knowing* and believing it more likely than not.

[46] It was also based on the concern that it helps the jury to pay more attention to the significance of the loss of liberty than a preponderance of the evidence test (*Addington*, 427), and that it might be impossible to meet the PBRD standard in that context (Ibid., 429–430). The *Addington* case cited other, less plausible reasons as well.

[47] Ibid., 425–426.

[48] The Court mishandles this fact, writing that "the possible injury to the individual is significantly greater than any possible harm to the state." Ibid., 427. The issue is not harm to the *state*; it is harm to other individuals that the state is trying to protect. *That* harm is comparable to the harm to the individual.

[49] One might think the difference between positive claims (of potential victims to be kept safe) and negative claims (of the person whose liberty might be taken from him) also calls for a higher SOP. But it's not clear that that difference calls for more than a preponderance of the evidence. Compare a tort or contract suit where the competition between positive and negative claims is also to be found.

[50] "Proof Beyond a Reasonable Doubt," 418.

[51] I discuss the possibility of variations in the PBRD standard in ibid., 437–438.

15.4 Ex Post Facto Restriction

In this section, I discuss whether it makes sense to hold penalties to the same ex post facto restriction as punishments.[52] The U.S. Supreme Court has interpreted the restriction narrowly. The holding of *Rogers v. Tennessee* was that courts are not bound by the clause; they can retroactively make changes to the criminal law that legislatures cannot make, as long as they respect "the right to fair warning."[53] And the holding of *Smith v. Doe*[54] is that the ex post facto clause applies only to *punishments*, not to restrictions on liberty that are civil in nature, even when they attach to a person in virtue of a criminal conviction. I don't mean to rely on the authority of those holdings for the question at issue here. Rather, my point is that the text of the Constitution does not say anything about penal law per se, so we need to approach the issue as the court in *Rogers* did, by asking whether retroactive changes would violate deeper principles of fair warning.

With regard to deterrent penalties, it would seem that the same rules should apply as they do to punishments.[55] This follows from the idea that deterrence functions through a *published* schedule of sanctions. The functional mechanism of deterrence in the criminal law is: If you are convicted of having committed crime X, you can expect to receive punishment Y (normally defined in terms of some range of sentences). It is a system based on the idea of fair warning. A person who is punished for violating the law repays his debt in substantial part by enduring the punishment that was set out as the proper punishment for that crime and thereby helping to deter others. Changing the rules that apply to a wrongdoer after the fact only sends the signal that agents cannot rely on the law to provide fair warning.

The same rationale would hold for deterrent penalties. The basic idea that the system operates to deter works in the same way. Fairness calls for imposing only those sanctions that were announced as part of the general schedule of penalties. And forfeiture is limited to a *fair* distribution of the burdens. Increasing the deterrent penalty after the offense was committed and applying the change retroactively would be using the offender to deter others, when she had no fair warning that she would forfeit the right to suffer *that* particular form of using.

One might object that fairness requires only announcing in advance that those who commit proxy crimes might be hit with deterrent sanctions; the magnitude of the penalties can then be set by the court, at the time of sentencing, in

[52] There are, of course, other punishment-related restrictions that I could examine, e.g., the double-jeopardy clause. But I think examining this one clause will suffice to set the model for the sort of inquiry that is required.

[53] 532 U.S. 451, 459 (2001).

[54] 538 U.S. 84 (2003).

[55] I argue that different rules apply to forfeiture of the POLA. See Section 16.2.6.

whatever way the court thinks will best balance the interests of the defendant and the interests of society in deterring lawbreaking. This sort of flexibility provides sufficient advanced warning, one might think, and it might well allow *more* deterrence. Potential lawbreakers might be more deterred by uncertainty with regard to their penalties, and courts could ratchet up penalties for proxy crimes that seem inadequately deterred, while reducing penalties for crimes that seem sufficiently deterred. As long as the penalties respect the limits of proportionality articulated in Section 15.1, this would be fair enough. Indeed, one might argue that since proportionality in the penal law is not restricted by the ideas of ordinal and anchoring cardinal proportionality that are relevant to the criminal law—ideas that call for a schedule of punishment to be developed[56]—there is no need for legislatures to pass a schedule of penalties in the first place, except perhaps as a set of guidelines to be departed from as reason and circumstances suggest.[57]

In response, I want to concede that the case for a binding schedule of punishments is weaker when it comes to penal sanctions than for criminal punishments. But I think it is still strong enough to bind. Discretionary sentencing—even if guided by legal norms that set the relevant considerations—would make the consequences of illegal behavior too unpredictable. This is not an absolutist statement about the consequences of forfeiture in general; I take a different position when it comes to POLA forfeiture.[58] It is a point about the balance between the interest an agent has in facing predictable consequences of her actions and the state's interest in retaining flexibility. On the one side, predictability is very valuable for rational agency. On the other side, the deterrent benefit of a penalty imposed on particular offenders is small; insofar as penalties have a substantial deterrent effect, it is because they are believed to apply predictably and systematically. Of course, dramatic, unexpected penalties might make a statement that would get the attention of people who otherwise would not notice the penalties imposed on others. But the more dramatic and unexpected the penalty, the more likely it will be unfair to impose it on an offender.

It is important to keep in mind that schedules of punishments and penalties are not set in stone; they should be malleable to adapt to determinations either that certain crimes are more or less serious than they once seemed, or that more or less deterrence is called for. People should be able to rely on the law not sanctioning acts that were permissible at the time they were performed and on not being sanctioned more harshly than was allowed when they acted.[59] If it is

[56] See Section 8.2.

[57] This paragraph develops an objection Antony Duff made on an earlier draft of the book.

[58] Again, see Section 16.2.6.

[59] The original interpretation of the clause was: "1st. Every law that makes an action done before the passing of the law, and which was innocent when done, criminal; and punishes such action. 2d. Every law that aggravates a crime, or makes it greater than it was, when committed. 3d. Every law that changes the punishment, and inflicts a greater punishment, than the law annexed to the crime, when committed. 4th. Every law that alters the legal rules of evidence, and receives less, or different,

determined that the law needs to be harsher, the proper response is to institute prospective changes to the schedule of punishments or penalties, or perhaps to create new proxy crimes with associated penal law penalties that will make detection, prosecution, and sanction easier to achieve. Either way, that change can be fairly applied only to future wrongdoers or pro tanto wrongdoers.

15.5 Extra-Territorial Application

I conclude this chapter with a brief discussion of the possibility of extra-territorial application of the penal law. I have argued that the criminal law *can* justifiably be applied extra-territorially. As I argued in Chapter 5, universal jurisdiction can be defended on the ground that discrete political communities can legitimately take an interest in what happens to *anyone* if the wrong is sufficiently serious.[60] It follows that states should be able to exercise passive personality jurisdiction, in which a country prosecutes non-resident aliens who wrong its own citizens abroad.[61] It also makes sense for countries to be able to exercise active personality jurisdiction, in which a country prosecutes its own citizens who commit what it considers crimes while abroad.[62] The precondition for that sort of jurisdiction is only that a country should take a legitimate interest in holding its citizens accountable for certain forms of behavior, even if they are acting beyond its borders.[63] And it is common practice under international law for countries to apply the territoriality principle in a way that allows them to prosecute actions by aliens, performed outside the territory, if the effects are domestic.[64] The question I mean to ask is whether these forms of jurisdiction should be extended to the penal law.

Clearly, universal jurisdiction should not be extended to the penal law. It applies only to the worst of crimes, not to proxy crimes. In addition, it is unclear how the actions of aliens, against aliens, in an alien land can be relevant except in the most attenuated way to a state ensuring that its reasonable regulations are respected.

testimony, than the law required at the time of the commission of the offense, in order to convict the offender." Calder v. Bull, 3 Dall. 386, 390 (1798).

[60] See Section 5.5.2.
[61] See Section 8.5.
[62] See Amnesty International, "Universal Jurisdiction," 8.
[63] It may be especially important for a state to do that if it does not intend to extradite the defendant to be tried in the country where he is accused of committing a crime.
[64] See C. Ryngaert, *Jurisdiction in International Law*, ch. 3.4. Assuming universal and passive personality jurisdiction are morally justifiable, then surely this form is as well.

It is almost as clear that passive personality cannot apply to the penal law. The reason is that penal law violations do not involve victims in any core way. One might argue about crimes such as driving while intoxicated or having sex with an underaged person. Both are strongly correlated with at least the risk of harm to a victim. But even if countries have a clear interest in protecting their citizens abroad, it seems that the division of labor and jurisdiction between states should allow the state in which risky behavior is performed to prosecute those who perform acts that it finds too risky to tolerate, and which it approaches with its own proxy crimes. If country A thinks that country B will not do enough to protect its citizens in this way, it should warn its citizens of this risk. It's a different matter if its citizens are actually wronged. But then it should prosecute for the crime that corresponds to the wrong, such as injury caused by a reckless driver or one person having sex with another who did not give valid consent.

Active personality may be different. A country might reasonably think that at least some of its legal norms should govern its citizens wherever they go, even if they are only enforced with penal law. Presumably, its citizens should be free to engage in businesses using local licensing schemes. But, for example, it might want to enforce the prohibition on bribery even in foreign countries.[65] Bribery is one of those mixed offenses that sometimes seems to register as a real crime, where the harm is essentially the corrupting of the system for the provision of services, and that sometimes seems like a penal offense, where the core of the offense is violating a regulation and not the corruption of anything concrete. If we assume that such mixed offenses should be treated like penal offenses, and the criminal component carved out and treated differently,[66] then this would be a case for the extra-territorial application of a penal offense as a matter of active personality. Another example would be a country's insistence that its adult citizens refrain from having sex with fourteen-year-olds, even if the local country permits it. Putting the thought more generally: If proxy crimes closely track real crimes, and the real crimes are serious, then a state may want to insist that its citizens respect those limits wherever they go. This willingness to prosecute proxy crimes on the basis of active personality jurisdiction would signal serious moral concern with the behavior of its citizens and a level of respect for the universally relevant bases for regulations that would be reasonable wherever they applied.

Finally, when it comes to appealing to domestic effects as a basis for extending the idea of territorial jurisdiction, it is hard to see why the state could not apply the penal law. One of the classic applications of this sort of jurisdiction occurs in the context of antitrust violations.[67] Such violations are clearly mala prohibita.

[65] See the U.S. Foreign Corrupt Practices Act.

[66] Compare the discussion of the provision of material support to designated foreign terrorist organizations in Section 13.2.

[67] See C. Ryngaert, *Jurisdiction in International Law*, ch. 3.5.

Whether they should be treated as criminal law, in which the level of culpability for violations matches the punishment, seems debatable. Prison sentences in the United States for individuals convicted of violating the Sherman Antitrust Act, from 1999 to 2008, ranged from two weeks to four years, with the median sentence being six months; and only 30.5 percent were sentenced to prison at all.[68] That suggests a proxy crime to me. On the other hand, the U.S. Sentencing Commission defended increasing the sanctions in the sentencing guidelines in 2005 on the grounds of "the similarity of antitrust offenses to sophisticated frauds."[69] Insofar as the analogy with fraud is good, antitrust violations seem like traditional crimes. But jurisdiction should not turn on whether antitrust violations are best seen as penal or criminal offenses. Jurisdiction for the penal law based on domestic effects therefore seems justifiable.

[68] B. Howell, "Sentencing of Antitrust Offenders," 8.
[69] Ibid., 9 (quoting the U.S. Sentencing Guidelines, App. C, Amendment 678).

PART V
INCAPACITATION

16
Forfeiture of the Presumption of Law Abidingness

16.1 Two and Only Two Categories of Restriction

The restrictions on liberty discussed in this chapter, as well as the next two chapters, assume that we are dealing with autonomous agents who are fully accountable as such. They also assume that the agents in question are not being punished or penalized with a deterrent penalty. This leaves two categories of restriction that can be defended as consistent with the dignity-respecting model (DR Model).[1] The first category concerns restrictions that presuppose that agents have forfeited the presumption of law abidingness (POLA). The second concerns restrictions that correspond to duties agents have to restrict themselves.

Before discussing these two categories, I want to explain why I think this is a complete set of categories. I do so because one might think that there's a third category: Agents can be restricted because the state has sufficient reason to believe they actively intend to wrong others. Those with such an intent may not yet have committed an offense that would justify punishing them or penalizing them. That might seem to imply that the predicate for POLA forfeiture is missing.[2] Moreover, having the intent to wrong others does not make them dangerous in a way that would give them a duty to artificially restrict themselves or to submit to incapacitation from others. The reason is that whether they are dangerous or not remains up to them. They could simply change their minds. Thus, there seems to be a gap; a third category seems to be needed. Kimberly Ferzan once argued that there was such a gap and argued for filling the gap with restrictions on liberty that were grounded on and responsive to having this sort of intention.[3] I want to argue here, before moving forward, that it is a mistake to see this as a separate category.

Ferzan rightly seeks a third way between the mad-bad dichotomy that I discussed in Chapter 1.[4] She thinks that the extra basis for restrictions is a form

[1] The model can be found in Section 1.3.1.

[2] I argue in the next section that this inference is mistaken; merely intending to commit serious wrongful acts can ground forfeiture of the POLA.

[3] "Beyond Crime and Commitment."

[4] See Section 1.3.1.

Punishment, Penalty, and Incapacitation. Alec Walen, Oxford University Press. © Oxford University Press 2026.
DOI: 10.1093/9780197523124.003.0016

of liability modeled on self-defense. Just as we can use force in self- and other-defense against people whose behavior indicates that they presently intend to impose serious wrongful harms on others, so she thinks we can deprive others of their liberty if we discover a similar intention. Such an intention makes them liable to liberty restrictions. But, she thinks, it does not make them liable to *punishment*. Indeed, she rightly takes me to task for my earlier view "that forming an intention [to act wrongfully] can be itself a wrongful act of '[f]louting the law.' "[5] She puts her critique in the form of a rhetorical question: "[H]ow much punishment does 'flouting the law' deserve?"[6] Touché. I was wrong to think that mere intentions to perform serious wrongful actions, like terrorism—evidentially supported by statements of terrorist intent—are sufficiently culpable to ground the sorts of punishments that would license the level of incapacitation that we have reason to impose on those who make such statements.

But my mistake was that I—like Ferzan and all other theorists I know of who take culpability seriously—was trying to do too much with the criminal law. We need the notion of forfeiture of the POLA. That would allow us to then determine if those who make terrorist threats, or who otherwise seem to intend to wrong others, can justifiably be incapacitated.

Moreover, Ferzan's analogy with self-defense is not as useful as it seems at first blush. The problem is not that the analogy fails; it works. As she notes, restrictions and "supervision would [have to] cease once the State could no longer meet the burden of demonstrating that the defendant continued to harbor an illicit mental state."[7] That fits her model: If the basis for restricting an agent's liberty is her intention to act wrongly, she can cancel that basis by changing her intention in much the way one who is attacking another can cancel the right to use force against her by ceasing to attack. Once the change in intention is made, the question is only how she could communicate that change. In principle, she would have the key to her release. The problem is in the practical implementation of the model. It would be too difficult to determine whether an agent harbors an ongoing intent to act wrongfully.

If we assume that the state would have the burden to show that she continues to intend to wrongfully harm others, then all a detainee would have to do to regain her freedom is cease to indicate that she harbors an ongoing intent to act wrongfully. She doesn't have to change her intentions; she only has to change her manifestation of them. Given that, the only people who would be detained beyond the initial period when they were picked up for threatening to act in a wrongful way are those who are too impulsive to control themselves, too committed to

[5] "Beyond Crime and Commitment," 166 (quoting from "Criminalizing Statements of Terrorist Intent," 841).
[6] Ibid.
[7] Ibid., 170.

continuing (for ideological reasons) to threaten others, or too dumb to realize that they could more effectively succeed in wronging others if they would just cease to manifest their intentions. Most would just do their best to indicate a change of mind, whether they have changed their minds or not. Reliable data on a restricted person's intentions would, in most cases, be nearly impossible to find.

In other words, Ferzan's suggestion creates a dilemma. The state would either have to assume that people continue to intend to do harm, which seems too harsh, or let any half-way intelligent person who can fake a change of heart go free, which seems too permissive. Or it could just split the difference, but that might just make both errors worse.[8]

There is also a more principled objection to Ferzan's suggestion: Treating a person as though she has the key to her release in this way fails to take into account the moral significance of the choice to intend to act wrongfully. If an agent sincerely intends to commit sufficiently serious wrongs, then she should forfeit the POLA, at least for a substantial period of time.[9] If we treat her this way, then the question is not whether she continues to harbor that very intention. The questions are rather whether she is likely to act on it in the circumstances she would likely face if not subjected to some form of incapacitating treatment; if so, how likely it is that she would be able to cause unacceptable levels of harm; and if some form of incapacitation is called for, what exactly is called for so that it does not impose excessive risks on others. Ferzan was right to stress that "supervision would [need to] be reconsidered at specific [regular] times."[10] But that's only because the least restrictive alternative (LRA) needs to be used.[11] It is not because the POLA is itself recovered as soon as a person ceases to intend to act wrongly.

In sum, Ferzan's idea of liability to restriction based on a wrongful intention should be rejected in favor of forfeiture of the POLA. Thus, I proceed on the assumption that there are only two categories of restriction to be dealt with in this chapter and the next.

16.2 Ways to Forfeit the Presumption of Law Abidingness

There are two ways people can forfeit their rights that are relevant to targeted restrictions on their liberty. Part IV focused on forfeiture of the right not to suffer

[8] Ferzan suggests that the burden of showing that "he no longer harbors that intention" could be placed on the person who was once found to have a threatening intention. Ibid., 191. But this doesn't help if reliable data is almost impossible to find. At best, it indicates that the state would most likely never cease to restrict a person's liberty once it detains him as intending to commit wrongful harm.

[9] I argue this in the next section.

[10] "Beyond Crime and Commitment," 170.

[11] I argue for this, and describe what it means, in the next section.

penalties, which grounds penal law. Here I turn to the other: forfeiture of the POLA, which can lead to various forms of incapacitation.

It is important to keep in mind that the significance of choices (or, in the case of negligence, actions) in setting up forfeiture of the POLA is not fundamentally epistemic. It is not that an agent *shows* himself to be dangerous. It is that he acts in a way that forfeits the right to be presumed to be law abiding.[12] Except in cases in which a person has a duty to self-restrict—discussed in the next chapter—it is only *after* that forfeiture is registered that the epistemic questions should be engaged: just how dangerous is the person, and what would it take to effectively neutralize that danger? This is a core principle of the DR Model. Mere dangerousness will not justify loss of liberty; some deontologically relevant category must first determine that dangerousness can be a basis for restricted liberty. It is forfeiture of the POLA, as a fair reflection of the significance of autonomous choice to act wrongly, that licenses the state to consider the agent's dangerousness.[13]

In this section, I will explore six aspects of POLA forfeiture: (1) two basic types of POLA forfeiture; (2) the ways forfeiture of the POLA can be grounded in criminal acts, penal violations, and even merely intending to commit certain criminal acts; (3) a paradigm case of POLA forfeiture; (4) the distinction between POLA forfeiture and punishment; (5) how the idea of POLA forfeiture differs from an older "double track" idea; and (6) a quick note on procedures.

16.2.1 Two Basic Types of Forfeiture of the Presumption of Law Abidingness

Incapacitation based on loss of the POLA can take two basic forms. First, insofar as an agent has shown himself unreliable in the enjoyment of certain privileges, he can lose the presumption that he should still enjoy them. The concern here is not that he is generally dangerous; it is that he is unworthy of the trust on which a privilege rests. I call this "specific POLA forfeiture."[14]

The sorts of privileges I have in mind are privileges such as a driver's license or a professional license (to practice law or medicine, for example). These privileges are not generally available because the state has reason to ensure that people have the knowledge and skills necessary to engage in these activities without exposing

[12] See Section 4.1.

[13] It is worth noting that civil contempt detentions superficially fit the pattern of POLA forfeiture, as the detention results from an autonomous choice. But such a detainee has not forfeited the POLA. He has simply forfeited his freedom for as long as he does not do what he is obliged to do. He has the key to his freedom in a way that a person who has forfeited the POLA does not.

[14] I first raised the idea of narrow, as opposed to general, forfeiture of the POLA in Section 4.4.1.

others to undue risk. The assumption is that if an agent passes certain tests, perhaps after having also operated well during a probationary period with limited privileges and supervision, then he has established that he can be relied upon to exercise those privileges safely. But if he demonstrates, through misuse of a privilege, that he cannot be so relied upon, then forfeiture of that license or privilege is fair. It represents a kind of loss of the POLA: the presumption that he will use the privilege without exposing others to the sort of risk that the law is trying to avoid.

The main questions for this kind of sanction concern how long the forfeited privileges are lost, and if not permanently, what the agent has to do to reestablish them. A limited-term loss might be justified on the ground that the forfeiture is likely to protect others in part by teaching the agent to be more careful to avoid the forfeiting behavior. A permanent loss could be justified if his behavior was so inconsistent with the basis of his privilege that it implies that he has no respect for that foundation. Multiple violations of a less serious nature could carry that same meaning. But it might often also make sense to allow an agent to take extra steps to re-earn the trust necessary to regain the privilege. Importantly, in cases of specific POLA forfeiture, an LRA analysis need not be done. If the privilege is abused, the privilege is lost. Only durational proportionality analysis must be performed.

I flag here one type of loss that is of particular significance for general security that could nonetheless fall under this heading: the privilege a person may have to remain in, return to, or do business with a country not his own. I assume that countries generally are not free to strip their citizens of citizenship,[15] but that they grant non-citizens the right to live in, travel through, or do business in their territory as a revocable privilege. That is, I assume that non-citizens who violate the law of the country where they are living, traveling, or doing business can forfeit the right to continue doing so. The trigger for this loss should be proportional, and the stronger a person's ties to a country, the higher the threshold for loss of the right to remain in, visit, or do business in that country. But it is a reasonable form of forfeiture by which a country can protect itself from aliens it no longer deems trustworthy.

The second form of incapacitation involves the loss of liberty or the imposition of obligations, as deemed necessary to provide more general security, rather than as linked to the abuse of a particular privilege. These can involve

[15] This assumption is in accord with the UN Universal Declaration of Human Rights, Article 15: "everyone has the right to a nationality." The bar for stripping citizenship is not, however, absolute. The United States, for example, recognizes seven types of expatriating acts, including naturalizing in another state after age 18, entering the armed forces of a hostile state, and treason. See 8 U.S.C. § 1481(a). There is also the possibility of denaturalization, which can occur if the government shows that a defendant's naturalization was "illegally procured" or "procured by concealment of a material fact or by willful misrepresentation... ." 8 U.S.C. § 1451.

restrictions on movement and association, loss of other rights, and duties such as duties to register. These forms of forfeiture are meant to allow the state to flexibly address the need for incapacitation. I call this "general POLA forfeiture."

If an agent has forfeited the POLA in this way and seems dangerous, an LRA analysis should be performed to see which form of incapacitation, along the spectrum from least to most restrictive, would adequately provide security without imposing excessive costs on the state.[16]

General POLA forfeiture need not be fully distinct from specific POLA forfeiture. Consider, for example, forfeiture of the right to own a firearm. This could result from abuse of firearms, and thus be an instance of specific POLA forfeiture, or it could result from other forms of unsafe or threatening behavior and constitute a measure directed at general security. It is likewise unclear how to categorize that right: as a privilege depending on a license or as a basic right normally available in a society. In the United States, despite needing a license to own a handgun in certain states, the right is taken to be a basic one that is generally available.[17] That is not the way that right is understood in other countries.[18] But most rights that fall in this category are universally recognized (at least within liberal states), rights such as the freedom from geographical confinement within the state, freedom of speech, and freedom to associate with others.[19]

The focus of my concern in this book, and in this chapter, is on general POLA forfeiture, however vague the boundaries of it might be. If I discuss POLA forfeiture without qualification, I mean the general form of it. But there are instances of general POLA forfeiture that result in the loss of only a specific right—for example, an agent's right to come near to a particular person who has obtained a restraining order against him. In those cases, even if the right is not a privilege, it will make sense to treat it, for most purposes, as the normative equivalent of specific POLA forfeiture.

16.2.2 Bases for Forfeiture of the Presumption of Law Abidingness

The paradigmatic basis for POLA forfeiture is as a collateral consequence of a serious criminal offense or a series of smaller offenses. The thought is that serious offenses show that the wrongdoer does not have respect for important

[16] See P. Robinson, "Punishing Dangerousness," 1447. I say more about this in the next section.

[17] See District of Columbia v. Heller, 554 U.S. 570 (2008) (holding that the 2nd Amendment provides people with a private right to bear arms).

[18] See Directive (EU) 2021/555 (setting minimum standards EU states must impose on firearm acquisition).

[19] The British may have paved the way for geographical and associational limitations with their Anti-Social Behaviour Orders. For a comparison of these with U.S. law, see J. Pinkney-Baird, "Don't Tread on Me."

legal norms, and as a result, it is fair to take him to have forfeited the POLA in some general way. The same thought is vindicated by a pattern of disregard for less serious norms. Proportionality is crucial for this form of forfeiture to be fair, and I return to that theme in the next section. First, I want to explore here two ideas: that penal violations can also have this kind of consequence and that a criminal or penal law violation might not be necessary.[20]

Before extending the bases, let's focus more on the paradigmatic basis. Consider someone convicted of murder. His willingness to commit such a serious offense indicates a deep disregard for the rights of others. His punishment should be the primary response to his crime. But the state need not treat him as trustworthy enough to be punished on an honor farm; it might justifiably take him to have forfeited the POLA with regard to submitting to his punishment and forcibly take him and hold him in prison.[21] Moreover, it might take him to pose an ongoing danger even after he has finished serving his prison term and impose some limits on his freedom that others do not have to face. These limits must be necessary and proportional, as with forfeiture in general.[22] But one cannot say ex ante that they must be temporally coterminous with his punishment.[23]

Something similar follows from a pattern of violations.[24] Consider the notorious three-strikes laws in the United States. They indefensibly assume that a third minor crime, such as theft of valuable items, becomes serious on a par with a much more serious crime, such as murder. But there is a kernel of insight in them: A person who is a recidivist thief, who does not seem capable of reforming himself after being punished twice before, can fairly be taken to have forfeited the presumption that he will respect the law going forward. That does not mean that he should be punished with a twenty-five-year prison sentence. But it could reasonably be taken to mean that after his third prison sentence, it is fair to impose upon him certain general restrictions on his freedom designed to provide security to others.

It is more difficult to justify the thought that penal law violations could ground forfeiture of the POLA. These are, after all, *just* proxy crimes. But if a

[20] I first developed these sorts of bases for targeted incapacitation in "A Punitive Precondition for Preventive Detention," 1230. I have since distinguished criminal, penal law, and POLA forfeiture, so the bases I recognize have changed.

[21] This point was made before in Sections 1.3.5 and 13.1.

[22] See Sections 14.1.2 and 14.4.

[23] Conditions on probation and parole follow a similar logic: They can be imposed because the person could be forced to submit to even greater restrictions to ensure that they receive their punishment. If the punishment is lifted, then some sort of LRA analysis may still be justifiable to ensure that they behave well.

[24] Both common law and civil jurisdictions treat persistent offending, even of acts too petty to warrant imprisonment on their own, as a basis for imprisonment (the practice of "push in"). See J. Roberts and S. Harrendorf, "Criminal History Enhancements at Sentencing," p. 280. This can best be explained not as a criminal matter, but as a matter of POLA forfeiture and incapacitation once it is clear that deterrence has failed.

string of minor criminal offenses can ground POLA forfeiture, then there is no reason why a string of proxy crimes could not do the same. What about an individual proxy crime? Some proxy crimes are very close to real and important crimes. Consider statutory rape. Someone convicted of that proxy crime might reasonably be taken to have shown disrespect for an important legal device meant to protect the young and vulnerable. But insofar as the state is unwilling to prosecute him for a *crime*, unwilling to prove that he was culpable, I think a single penal law offense should not be taken to ground general POLA forfeiture. But this is where a narrow interpretation of general POLA forfeiture may be crucial. Perhaps certain extra security measures, apart from his penalty, might be appropriate in regard to his access to younger potential sexual partners. A similar point could be true for proxy crimes such as providing material support to foreign terrorist organizations. This kind of crime could be best viewed as a proxy crime if the link to culpable behavior is loose enough.[25] Nonetheless, such a person could reasonably be taken to be a security threat in ways that justify imposing narrow limits on his freedom. But to limit his freedom as a more general threat, I think the state must establish that he culpably supported a terrorist organization.

Finally, it is worth following up on a point made in the last section, that merely intending to commit a serious crime might be a reasonable basis for POLA forfeiture. The thought here is that intentions are choices in their own right, and the choice to try to commit a serious crime is itself a seriously culpable act.[26] There might be good reason to require a certain degree of proximity to causing the harm that the criminal law is concerned to prevent—or in cases like tax evasion, proximity to fully failing to do one's duty—before attaching serious criminal liability to particular actions. The law governing criminal attempts, for example, always draws a line between mere preparation and crossing the line to committing an attempt.[27] But if an agent has clearly formed the intention to commit a serious crime, that itself indicates that he has decided to flout serious moral and legal norms, and as such it should be a sufficient basis for POLA forfeiture, even if not for serious punishment. Consider, for example, threatening behavior that forms the basis for a restraining order but that is not sufficient for a prosecution. The restraining order itself is a justifiable expression of narrowly targeted yet general POLA forfeiture.

[25] See Section 13.2.

[26] I have argued these points in "The Doctrine of Illicit Intentions" and "Wrongdoing Without Motives." See also "Criminalizing Statements of Terrorist Intent."

[27] I favor distinguishing three levels: mere preparation, substantial step attempt, and full or completed attempt, where the substantial step attempt is a substantially lesser crime. On counting only completed attempts as full attempts, see L. Alexander and K. Ferzan, *Crime and Culpability*, 212.

16.2.3 A Paradigmatic Case

I discuss here one paradigmatic manifestation of POLA forfeiture,[28] the detention of people who seem to pose a serious ongoing danger to the public if released.[29] Consider the case of Leroy Hendricks. Prior to his last conviction, in 1984, he had a decades-long record of exposing himself to and sexually molesting young children. After serving ten years of his sentence for his last conviction, which was for "taking 'indecent liberties' with two 13-year-old boys,"[30] he was set to be released to a halfway house, but then the state of Kansas intervened and sought to civilly confine him as a "sexually violent predator." He admitted, at a jury trial on that issue, "that when he 'get[s] stressed out,' he 'can't control the urge' to molest children."[31] He also admitted that he suffered from pedophilia and that treatment for that condition had done nothing to help him. A jury found beyond a reasonable doubt that he was a sexually violent predator, and he was then confined to a state "security hospital."[32]

Some commentators have argued that the Supreme Court's decision to uphold his detention was logically indefensible. As Stephen Morse put it:

> It is paradoxical, to say the least, to claim that a sexually violent predator is sufficiently responsible to deserve the stigma and punishment of criminal incarceration, but that the predator is not sufficiently responsible to be permitted the usual freedom from involuntary civil commitment that even very predictably dangerous but responsible agents retain. . . .[33]

Morse's paradox hinges, however, on the thought that there are only two bases for depriving someone of his liberty: that he is mad (too insane to be held

[28] Another interesting case is discipline within prison. Officials in a prison have a high degree of discretion in using administrative segregation as a tool for discipline, as long as they do not engage in unlawful, arbitrary discrimination against an inmate and do not impose "atypical and significant hardship on the inmate in relation to the ordinary incidents of prison life." Sandin v. Conner, 515 U.S. 472, 484 (1995). But, as I've noted before, I think the existence of honor farms implies that prison itself does not imply loss of the POLA. See Ch. 1, n. 70.

[29] German law too contains such detention. It now limits "life imprisonment" to fifteen years unless one of two conditions applies: "the particular severity of the convicted person's guilt" requires a continued enforcement of the sentence, or release on probation could not be justified with "regard to public security interests." German Criminal Code § 57 (2) and 57a. If we assume that a particular prisoner did not commit an especially culpable crime, then fifteen years caps the punitive period. In such cases, further detention, based on a concern with public security, must reflect POLA forfeiture.

[30] Kansas v. Hendricks, 521 U.S. 346, 353 (1997).

[31] Ibid., 355.

[32] In one way, the statute is problematically over-broad. It allows civil commitment proceedings to be initiated if a person "has been convicted of *or charged with* a sexually violent offense." Kan. Stat. Ann. Sec. 59-29a02(a) (1994) (emphasis added). Merely being charged with such an offense is no basis for forfeiture of the POLA.

[33] "Neither Desert nor Disease," 272. See also "Mental Disorder and Criminal Law," 951–959.

accountable) or bad (criminally deserving of punishment).[34] In doing so, he overlooks the possibility that Hendricks could have forfeited the POLA in such a way that, given his urges, made him too dangerous to release. This is not to deny the other possibilities. If Hendricks really could do nothing to prevent himself from acting on his urges to molest children when he got stressed out, and if he had no way of seeing these times coming and tying himself to the mast until the urge to molest passed, then he should have had an insanity excuse, and *that*, rather than POLA forfeiture, would justify targeted restrictions on his liberty.[35] If, on the other hand, he could have done something to control himself—for example, have himself voluntarily committed to a mental hospital when he felt the urge to molest coming on, or, if his urges were not too strong to resist, then simply choose not to indulge them—then his failure to take such steps could leave him responsible for his criminal action of molesting children.[36] The point is that the statute allowing his detention as a sexually violent predator does not have to be reduced to either possibility. It makes much better sense if it is interpreted as saying that he could be detained if there were a basis for saying that he was too dangerous to release, but only given that he had forfeited the POLA.[37]

Relatedly, consider the reporting requirement imposed on sex offenders that they register as such. Currently, all states in the United States have such requirements, and there is a federal law, the Sex Offender Registration and Notification Act,[38] which makes it a federal crime for a convicted sex offender not to register a change of residency within three days of that change in at least one jurisdiction in which he is required to register.[39] Some argue that these are punishments.[40] But sex offender registration requirements are particularly clear about the fact that their basis is POLA forfeiture, as they rest on the fact that sex offenders have been "adjudged to be dangerous."[41] Again, it's not simply that the people who are required to register are thought to be more dangerous than

[34] I first mentioned, and rejected, this dichotomy in Section 1.3.1.

[35] Again, I return to that possibility in Ch. 19.

[36] Morse himself should agree, having earlier defended a crime of reckless endangerment with these three elements:

(1) prior conviction of at least one serious crime of violence or at least one prior occurrence of involuntary civil commitment for actual serious violent conduct; (2) conscious awareness of an extremely high risk that the agent will in the immediate future cause substantial unjustified harm; and (3) failure to commit oneself voluntarily or to take other reasonably effective steps to avoid causing future harm.

"Blame and Danger," 152.

[37] Ferzan tries to deal with Hendricks's case by assuming that he "harbored an intention to molest a child" and "it is likely that he continues to harbor that intention." "Beyond Crime and Commitment," 192. For reasons spelled out in Section 16.1, I think that is a less plausible way to defend his detention.

[38] 34 U.S.C. § 20911 et seq.

[39] *Criminal Practice Manual*, vol. 3, § 102:47.

[40] That was the appellant's argument in Smith v. Doe, 538 U.S. 84 (2003). See also G. Yaffe's argument in "Norm Shift Theory of Punishment."

[41] *Smith*, 85.

others. In fact, they may not be.[42] What is relevant is that they have done something to forfeit the right to be treated as no more dangerous than others. In other words, they have forfeited the POLA.

16.2.4 Forfeiture of the Presumption of Law Abidingness or Punishment?

Courts in the United States generally regard restrictions such as the loss of the right to own a firearm or to hold certain jobs, or the requirement to register as a sex offender, as collateral consequences of punishment, not punishment.[43] Sandra Mayson notes, however, that scholars and commentators have "uniformly" taken the opposite position, treating these consequences as *part* of punishment.[44] This treatment of these consequences as part of punishment, as Mayson correctly notes, runs into two problems. First, not all deprivations of property or liberty count as punishment (for example, quarantine or detention of the mentally ill and dangerous),[45] and an appeal to effects will not help draw the line in the right place.[46] Second, as Mayson puts it, many collateral consequences seem to be "driven by a preventive logic."[47] In other words, the rationale, as I have been emphasizing, is to achieve incapacitation, not censure and punishment. Given that punishment (and penalties) cannot aim directly at incapacitation, it is best *not* to conceive of these consequences as punitive.[48]

It is important to be clear, however, that not all collateral consequences of a conviction can be justified by the POLA forfeiture model either. For example, Mayson notes that "[t]he Anti-Drug Abuse Act of 1988 created 'civil penalties' for drug offenders, including disqualification from federal student loans and, depending on local implementation, public housing."[49] A similar penalty was imposed by the Personal Responsibility and Work Opportunity Reconciliation (PRWOR) Act of 1996, which permanently disqualified anyone convicted of a felony drug offense from receiving welfare or food stamps. The problem with

[42] This is in part because the idea of a "sexual offender" is often far too broad, covering not just violent sexual assaults but public urination. See M. Huffman, "Moral Panic and the Politics of Fear."

[43] S. Mayson, "Collateral Consequences and the Preventive State," 313.

[44] Ibid., 314 (citing, among others, Wayne Logan, Alice Ristroph, Andrea Yang, Deborah Archer, Kele Williams, Gabriel Chin, Richard Holmes, Nora Demleitner, Ben Geiger, and the American Bar Association). Paul Robinson is clearly an exception to Mayson's "uniformly" claim. See "Punishing Dangerousness," 1446. See also Zach Hoskins, *Beyond Punishment.*

[45] Needless to say, at least in the main text, they don't count as penalties either.

[46] Gideon Yaffe tries to draw a better line in "Norm Shift Theory of Punishment." But I believe his account ends up being over- and under-inclusive. Arguing that is beyond the scope of this book.

[47] "Collateral Consequences and the Preventive State," 317.

[48] See Sections 1.3.5 and 7.2 for the premise of this sentence.

[49] "Collateral Consequences and the Preventive State," 307, n. 22.

treating these losses as POLA forfeiture is that it is hard to see how barring drug offenders from getting federal student loans, welfare, or food stamps could be justified as a means of protecting anyone.

This issue was raised, with respect to the 1996 law, in the case of *Turner v. Glickman*.[50] The court found that the sanctions in the PRWOR Act might help combat fraud, given Congressional testimony "that food stamps were being traded for drugs."[51] *Maybe*. Indeed, the court explicitly recognized that this law might have a deterrent effect: "[I]ndividuals who are currently eligible for such assistance would undoubtedly consider potential disqualification from federal benefits before engaging in crimes involving illegal drugs."[52] The problem is that if these sanctions are taken to be punishments, they seem disproportionate. And even if taken as penal sanctions, issues of avoidability and quasi-defensive proportionality make it doubtful that they count as proportionate. If so, they fail to be justified either as instances of deterrent sanctions or as POLA forfeiture. They simply fail to be justified.

Housing forfeiture, however, is different. As Mayson notes, 42 U.S.C. § 13661 (2012) "authorizes local housing authorities to exclude persons who 'may interfere with the health, safety, or right to peaceful enjoyment of the premises by other residents,' and to 'deny admission to criminal offenders.'"[53] This is overly broad, but it at least has an incapacitating rationale that is plausibly grounded in specific forfeiture of the POLA.

Cases like *Turner* raise the question: Must a penalty be either a deterrent penalty or an incapacitating penalty? Could it not serve both functions? The answer is that it could serve both functions, but not well. POLA forfeiture is not bound by a fixed form; it should be adjusted to provide the LRA. By contrast, the deterrent penalties should be fixed in advance *in order to deter*. That's not to say that the judge should lack discretion at sentencing for a deterrent sanction. It is rather to say that it would not fit the deterrence justification to assess, on a regular basis, whether some lesser penalty might not deter just as well.[54] These two aims function in quite different ways, so it would make for a more coherent law to be clear about which aim is justifying a particular government action.

Another interesting case concerns the right to vote. Voting is not a *mere* privilege granted to citizens; it is a fundamental incident of citizenship.[55] Thus, it should be very difficult to justify stripping this right as a matter of either punishment or POLA forfeiture. Arguably, the right to vote may be suspended for as

[50] 207 F.3d 419 (7th Cir. 2000).
[51] Ibid., 425.
[52] Ibid. As such, they function as part of a punitive or penalizing response.
[53] "Collateral Consequences and the Preventive State," 336, n. 178.
[54] For a similar thought, see P. Robinson, "Punishing Dangerousness," 1447.
[55] This view has become the dominant view in U.S. law since the late 1960s. See J. Fishkin, "Equal Citizenship and the Individual Right to Vote," 1349.

long as a person is being punished;[56] arguably, that is a fair complement to other forms of punishment, given that the person's culpable behavior indicates that he did not take his duties to respect the law sufficiently seriously. But once a citizen's punishment has been served, *full* citizenship should be restored. That is, after all, a central goal of punishment: to reconcile culpable wrongdoers with the political community that is punishing them.[57] Forfeiture of the right to equal *citizenship* is inconsistent with that goal. Moreover, the right to vote is not even tenuously connected to security. The idea that former felons would collectively align politically to undermine state security is a complete fantasy. The only exception I could see to this rule, allowing forfeiture of the right to vote, would apply if someone engaged in repeated acts of voter fraud.[58] But then it would fall under the specific POLA forfeiture that responds to abuse of a "privilege."[59]

16.2.5 Differences from the Double-Track System

The necessity of using the LRA standard for incapacitation—a point I explore in more depth in the next section—helps to explain why POLA forfeiture is not just a reintroduction of what used to be called the "double-track" system in Europe. This was a system in which, to quote H.L.A. Hart:

> The habitual offender who satisfied the requirements for this form of treatment was to receive two sentences: one was the punishment fixed on conventional lines for his offense; the other was the special individualized measure. So his crime had two aspects: one was that of a responsible piece of wickedness deserving as such a certain punishment; the other was that of a symptom of disposition or character and an index of appropriate preventive treatment.[60]

[56] This is a common position. As Zach Hoskins notes, "Felons serving prison terms in 48 U.S. states, the United Kingdom, and other jurisdictions are denied the legal right to vote." *Beyond Punishment*, 143. It is, however, noteworthy that the European Court of Human Rights has found the United Kingdom's blanket ban on voting by the imprisoned to be in violation of art. 3 of Protocol No. 1 to the European Convention on Human Rights. See Hirst v. The United Kingdom (No. 2) (2005).

[57] See Section 6.4.

[58] The court in Shepherd v. Trevino, 575 F.2d 1110, 1115 (5th Cir. 1978), took the position that the state has a legitimate interest in excluding people with felony convictions from the franchise because they, "like insane persons, have raised questions about their ability to vote responsibly." This is literally and figuratively a crazy analogy. Insanity is a condition that one might overcome. And as the Supreme Court in Foucha v. Louisiana, 504 U.S. 71 (1992), held, a state may not continue to detain someone who no longer suffers from a mental illness simply because it deems him dangerous. Likewise, it cannot continue to deprive citizens of the right to vote just because they once acted irresponsibly.

[59] It would not be a privilege in this case, but it would otherwise fit the form of a specific response to a particular form of abuse, not incapacitation aimed at preventing more general forms of dangerous activity. For support of this limited exception, see Hirst v. The United Kingdom, ¶ 71.

[60] *Punishment and Responsibility*, 166.

This may seem to be very much what I have in mind, but it seems that the old double-track model involved simply sentencing offenders to a two-part sentence. As Hart mockingly put it:

> Certainly the prisoner who after serving a three-year sentence is told that his punishment is over but that a seven-year period of preventive detention awaits him and that that this is a "measure" of social protection, not a punishment, might think he was being tormented by a barren piece of conceptualism.[61]

The real problem with such a two-part sentence is that it fails to take into account that preventive measures cannot be laid out as a sentence ex ante; they have to be responsive to the ongoing need for prevention and have to use an LRA. The sentence may involve demarcating a fixed period, longer than that of the punitive incarceration, in which a person is subject to incapacitative measures. But the measures themselves generally should not be fixed as part of the sentence—the only exception would be measures that can't really come in degrees, except temporally, such as registration requirements.[62] Fixing them would indeed, as Hart suggests, put the lie to the thought that this is not just more punishment.

16.2.6 Procedures to Establish Forfeiture

I conclude this section by noting that while POLA forfeiture should be thought of as distinct from criminal law and penal law, that difference should not be taken to license a wholly different set of procedures. I touch on three matters here: a right to counsel, the standard of proof, and the ex post facto restriction.

Regarding the right to counsel, it is important to keep in mind what is at stake. POLA forfeiture can ground incapacitation from a few years to a lifetime. As the Court in Gideon v. Wainwright wrote:

> Lawyers to prosecute are everywhere deemed essential to protect the public's interest in an orderly society. Similarly, there are few defendants charged with crime, few indeed, who fail to hire the best lawyers they can get to prepare and present their defenses. That government hires lawyers to prosecute and defendants who have the money hire lawyers to defend are the strongest

[61] Ibid., 166–167.

[62] Those are sometimes temporally variable, depending on what the offender has done. In Alaska, for example (that state with the laws at issue in *Smith*), if "the offender was convicted of a single, nonaggravated sex crime, he must provide annual verification of the submitted information for 15 years. . . . If he was convicted of an aggravated sex offense or of two or more sex offenses, he must register for life and verify the information quarterly." *Smith*, 90.

> indications of the wide-spread belief that lawyers in criminal courts are necessities, not luxuries.[63]

These points apply just as well to the POLA forfeiture context. The cases will still be brought by prosecutors. And defendants would be well advised to hire counsel if they could. Thus, even if a case were brought solely as a matter of POLA forfeiture, a poor defendant should still be given the right to counsel.[64]

Turning to the standard of proof, POLA forfeiture presupposes independent proof of crimes or penal offenses, or proof of the intention to commit a serious crime. For those cases that presuppose independent proof of crimes or penal offenses, there is no question that the predicate for POLA forfeiture must be established beyond a reasonable doubt.[65] One might think that proof of the intention to commit a serious crime could be lower. But given the serious consequences that follow and that this is an *expanded* basis for liability to incapacitation, there is no reason to think that this option should allow a shortcut. Any such shortcut would be an invitation to governmental abuse. Thus, I conclude that the bases for POLA forfeiture must all be established beyond a reasonable doubt. But it is important to note that this is true *only* for general POLA forfeiture. Specific POLA forfeiture is qualitatively less significant in terms of second-class status in a society, and it is standardly, and I think rightly, secured with a lower standard of proof.[66]

Lastly, turning to the ban on ex post facto punishments, I argued in the previous chapter that it should apply to penalties as well.[67] But POLA forfeiture functions differently. Its function is not to deter; its function is to register the thought that it is fair to say that the person can no longer be trusted to obey the law, at least in certain ways and for a certain time. Because that judgment of trustworthiness is not meant to affect the person's actions at the time he acts—it is not a deterrent sanction—but rather is meant to affect his ability to cause harm in the future, it is less important that it be laid out for him at the time he acts for the penalty to be fairly imposed. If the legislature, or even a court or executive agency, were to determine that a certain form of trust is unwise, and if

[63] 372 U.S. 335, 344 (1963).

[64] This is not to say that every civil matter that might result in a significant loss (e.g., an eviction) commits the state to providing counsel.

[65] See Section 15.3.

[66] For example, loss of a medical license, in the United States, is most often based on a preponderance of the evidence standard, though often a clear and convincing evidence standard is used, and often the standard varies depending on the nature of the violation. See A. Smith, "Standard of Proof; Board-by-Board Overview." Similarly, disbarment of lawyers generally relies on a preponderance of the evidence, but sometimes a clear and convincing standard is used. See The Committee on Professional Discipline, "Survey of Attorney Disciplinary Rules in the State and Federal Courts of New York."

[67] See Section 15.4.

the case can be made that it is fair to say that a person who does a certain kind of action has broken a certain kind of trust, then the penalty can be applied retroactively.

Admittedly, there is some connection between fairness and retroactivity. Severe losses of freedom that can follow from POLA forfeiture should not be sprung on a person who could say that he had no idea that such losses could follow from what he did. But the sorts of losses that are fitting should not count as a great surprise to anyone. This is particularly true for specific POLA forfeiture. Someone convicted of reckless driving should not be surprised if he loses his driving license, at least for a while. This is true even if such a loss was not listed as a sanction that would follow from such driving at the time he so drove. But it is also true for general POLA forfeiture. Someone convicted of a violent felony should not be surprised if he loses his right to own a gun; someone convicted of a crime of sexual predation should not be surprised if he is required to register when he moves to a new town; someone who is convicted of having taken military-style training at a terrorist training camp should not be surprised if he is put on a no-fly list or even required to submit to various sorts of intrusive monitoring; and a career criminal should not be surprised if at the end of the sentence for his most recent crimes he faces some form of ongoing limitations on his basic freedom of movement. Thus, I conclude that the Supreme Court in *Smith v. Doe* was correct to conclude that many collateral consequences of a conviction should *not* be governed by the ex post facto limitation.

One might worry, as Paul Robinson did when he called for the separation of future-oriented incapacitation from retrospectively justified punishment back in 2001, that a model that embraces incapacitation as distinct from the criminal law would license governmental abuse akin to the *Gulag Archipelago*.[68] Of course, the government might abuse any power it has. And there is good reason to think that the collateral consequences of criminal convictions in the United States go way too far, expressing distrust without concern for the principle that once a wrongdoer-citizen has paid his debt, the goal should be complete reconciliation.[69] But the fact that abuse is prevalent does not change its status as abuse. My point is that no *Gulag*-style abuse is *licensed* by the forfeiture of the POLA.[70]

[68] "Punishing Dangerousness," 1455.

[69] For a survey of the excessive and punitive nature of collateral consequences in the United States, see D. Jones, "When the Fallout of a Criminal Conviction Goes too Far."

[70] Robinson himself concluded, I think correctly, that the alternative of "cloaked preventive detention"—cloaked in the guise of punishment—was worse. My argument throughout the book is that it is not only worse, but it is also literally unjustifiable.

16.3 Proportionality Limits on Using Forfeiture to Incapacitate

The acceptability of POLA forfeiture within the DR Model depends on agents who forfeit the POLA having autonomously chosen to act wrongly. But that is only a necessary condition. To be sufficient, POLA forfeiture must also be proportional. This is particularly important because POLA forfeiture is deeply in tension with a central goal of the criminal law: reconciliation between the political community and the wrongdoer. How can an agent pay her debt to society and achieve reconciliation, and at the same time be treated as someone who is not presumed to be law abiding like everyone else from that point forward? If POLA forfeiture is to be justifiable, we must, first, show that this question has an answer, and then examine how proportionality affects that answer.

16.3.1 Resolving the Tension Between Forfeiture of the Presumption of Law Abidingness and Reconciliation

The resolution of the tension between reconciliation and POLA forfeiture depends on a point I made about forgiveness when introducing my conception of blame. As I wrote in Chapter 6, forgiveness of others normally has a long, reluctant tail.[71] When an agent has been wronged, it is natural to retain a certain wariness toward the other, even if the agent forgives the other. She can both forgive and remain wary, because even while she thinks that nothing else is owed by way of amends, and that resentment or indignation are no longer fitting responses, she can also take the relationship to be changed. She need not trust the other as she did before.

The same tail can be retained in the criminal justice system, where the distrust manifests through POLA forfeiture. Formally, this is fully consistent with the thought that the wrongdoer has paid her debt to society and that any further extraction of amends from her would be inappropriate. Forfeiture in this regard is simply a separate matter. It can be justified in its own terms, as a fair response to the trust that was ruptured, even if the punishment has been meted out and the defendant has owned her guilt, much as the state wants her to.[72]

The problem is that this account of POLA forfeiture as a distinct response does not address the tension between such forfeiture and reconciliation. In

[71] See Section 6.5.2.

[72] Zach Hoskins argues that "punishment should restore offenders to full standing in their political community. If this is right, it follows that [collateral legal consequences] on offenders are at least presumptively unjustified." *Beyond Punishment*, 142. However, in the chapter in which he writes that, ch. 5, he does not consider forfeiture. In the next chapter, where he does consider forfeiture, he does not consider the specific sort of forfeiture discussed in this chapter: POLA forfeiture.

personal life, if A wrongs B and then seeks to reconcile with B, B can forgive A and still seek to have as little to do with her as possible.[73] By contrast, in the state, separation is hard to achieve. It may be possible in cases in which a polity is dealing with someone who is not a citizen. But if the polity is dealing with a citizen, they normally can't go their separate ways. Can the polity nonetheless say to the citizen that she must accept that she has forfeited the POLA? I think the answer is a qualified yes.

The tension between reconciliation and POLA forfeiture is acceptable because a wrongdoer ought to be able to recognize and respect the point of view of others, and thus respect that there are things she might have done that would forfeit future trust in her as a law-abiding person, even if she has served her punishment. But she should also expect that this would be a condition that the state seeks to minimize in order to reconcile with her. This balance calls for using forfeiture only when the grounds for doing so are compelling and only in ways that respect the LRA requirement.[74] The grounds have been discussed already,[75] but this now leads us to discuss the LRA requirement as the basis for proportionality in this context.

16.3.2 The Least Restrictive Alternative to Address the Tension

The LRA requirement has three dimensions: the scope of the loss of freedom, the material loss involved, and the duration. The minimization called for along these dimensions has to be sensitive to both effectiveness and the costs to the state of providing equal or even more effective security. Security measures typically do not come for free, and if the costs impose too much of a burden on others, then the person who forfeited the POLA may instead have to bear the burden of a heavier restriction on her freedom.

Starting with the scope of the forfeiture, it should be as narrow as possible, given the nature of the reason for distrust of the individual. For example, if someone has sexually molested children, that would provide a reason to keep that person away from unsupervised interactions with children; it would not provide a reason to prevent her from teaching in a university or working as a car mechanic. If someone has repeatedly driven in an unsafe manner, that would provide a reason to restrict her right to drive; it would not provide a reason to

[73] This is inconsistent with T.M. Scanlon's views on blame, according to which seeking such separation is what blame is fundamentally about. See *Moral Dimensions*, ch. 4. So much the worse for Scanlon's view of blame.

[74] See P. Robinson, "Punishing Dangerousness," 1447.

[75] See Section 16.2.2.

restrict her access to food stamps or public housing. And if someone has shown a tendency to cheat in financial matters, that would provide a reason to restrict her ability to work in accounting or related fields; it would not provide a reason to restrict her right to drive or to work with children.

These examples involve specific POLA forfeiture, not general POLA forfeiture. But there's a reason to bring them up: General POLA forfeiture should come as close to specific POLA forfeitures as possible while still being effective. For example, to restrict a person more broadly, as a potential violent felon rather than as a child molester, it would have to be the case that she has shown a sufficiently serious tendency toward violence. And even then, if her violence has been narrowly directed—say toward a former romantic partner—then restrictions that keep her away from that partner may suffice. If they do, then no broader restrictions may be imposed on her.

For any particular scope of forfeiture, it is a separate question what should actually be taken away—that is, what material loss should be imposed. For example, merely taking a driver's license away may suffice as a first step for those who drive recklessly. That won't physically prevent a reckless driver from driving, but it will set up a greater penalty if she drives again, and that may be sufficient deterrence to protect the public. A more intrusive step would be to take away her car while also making it a crime or penal law violation to lend or sell a car to her, more or less as gun sales can be restricted.[76]

Or consider restrictions on one who has forfeited the POLA with regard to violent behavior generally. Even in such a case, there may be a number of levels of restriction. It might start with a requirement to report to a parole officer who monitors the person for engagement in activities that could lead to violence. A still greater restriction would involve something like a tracking device, perhaps combined with geographical restrictions, perhaps in tandem with some sort of curfew. Greater still would be home arrest. And greater still would be institutional incarceration. The last option should be reserved for those rarest of cases in which a lesser option would provide insufficient security at a reasonable cost to the state. And even then, the conditions should be as non-punitive as possible, consistent with security, and avoiding excessive costs.

Only those who show either the greatest propensity to continue to commit serious crimes or some propensity to commit the most serious crimes (such as terrorist attacks) should face incarceration.[77] Outside of those who have gone

[76] Lists are notoriously imperfect, and this could be a great encumbrance on a person wrongly stripped of the right to drive; any list must allow a person ready access to challenge it for inaccuracy.

[77] The existence of such people should be acknowledged. See A. Rubin and A. Nossiter, "French Ask Whether Priest's Killer, Listed as a Threat, Could Have Been Stopped" (discussing the case of Adel Kermiche, who had been fitted with an ankle bracelet, put on weekly parole, and permitted to

to take terrorist training, this would apply only to the most committed career criminals, strongly disposed, if not dedicated, to pursuing seriously harmful crimes, or to those who seem to have some deficit in their ability to autonomously govern themselves (for example, certain kinds of sexual predators).[78] Simply being a three-strikes felon, the sort that the Supreme Court has said could be locked up for twenty-five years to life, would *not* suffice.[79] That gives up far too quickly on the possibility of a less restrictive alternative and on the question of temporal duration.

Turning to that last point, the duration should be constrained in two ways. First, as a matter of generosity, and based on the assumption that people can learn from their mistakes and that reconciliation is possible, forfeitures should be temporally limited for most first-time offenders. A period of a few years would probably suffice. That period could start right away if the offender is serving no temporally extended deterrent sanction. Or it might be started after she is released from her deterrent sanction period, whether in a parole context or simply at the end of a sentence. This period might extend longer for more serious crimes, like rape or murder, or if the threat posed is particularly grave, like a terrorist attack. The only other reason to extend the forfeiture for longer for a first-time offender would be if she has a diagnosed mental condition, making it difficult for her to stay out of trouble.[80] But even if a longer forfeiture is called for, there should be regular assessments to determine if a less restrictive alternative might suffice after a period of time.[81]

The only basis for a lifelong forfeiture would be if the person shows a serious recidivist tendency. There are only so many times a state can be expected to offer the benefit of the doubt to a person. But even if a person has forfeited the POLA for the rest of her life, that in no way obviates the need to respect the LRA requirement in terms of material deprivation of liberty.

Turning to the cost side of the balance, it is important to recognize that costs to the state matter for an LRA analysis. The best case to make that point concerns people who traveled to war zones in Syria and Iraq and received

leave his parents' house only from 8:30 am to 12:30 pm, and who nonetheless, months after being released under these terms, killed a priest in the name of ISIS).

[78] This is what Hendricks claimed for himself in Kansas v. Hendricks, 521 U.S. 346 (1997). See the discussion in Section 16.2.3.

[79] Contra Ewing v. California, 538 U.S. 11 (2003).

[80] Even then, it is important to keep in mind that people can age out of criminal activity. D. O'Connell et al., "Violent Offending, Desistance, and Recidivism," 992 (citing evidence that "[a]ging out of crime is ... the norm—even the most serious delinquents desist.").

[81] See P. Robinson, "Punishing Dangerousness," 1447, 1453.

training in terrorist camps.[82] Receiving such training was, by 2016, criminal in many countries in Europe as well as in the United States. Assuming that banning such training is justifiable and can be enforced with criminal punishment, there is still a question of how culpable it is. A proportional punishment for *merely* receiving training would seem to be relatively light. In fact, however, the punishment such people faced in France was up to ten years in prison. One might conjecture that the right way to justify this sanction, if at all, is as a penalty for a penal law violation. But let us suppose that such a penalty would be in tension with giving proper primacy to the criminal law and its notion of proportionality.[83] France could then own up to the obvious idea that such a sentence is incapacitation, not proportional punishment. Suppose France were to agree that it was really using the conviction as a basis to say that those convicted of this crime have forfeited the POLA. Would such incapacitation be justifiable as an LRA?

To answer that, one has to know what the alternatives are. The primary alternative that would prevent an agent from engaging in terrorist acts and killing possibly a great number of innocent people is actively monitoring her. But according to Magnus Ranstorp of the National Defense College in Sweden, "[15] to 20 officers per jihadist are required for constant surveillance."[84] This is a huge cost to a state. Even if states are required to devote significant resources to policing their citizens rather than simply restricting their freedom—a point I'll return to in Chapter 20[85]—the situation is different for those who forfeit the POLA. For those people, a fair distribution of the burden of security could very well involve incarceration, rather than devoting fifteen to twenty officers to carry out surveillance on one suspect. This is a general point, not limited to suspected jihadists. The point is that the LRA is not *just* a matter of effectiveness, but effectiveness without the state having to take on excessive costs.

Ultimately, this notion of effectiveness without excessive cost requires a balancing: How much would it cost to provide similar levels of security with fewer restrictions on liberty? But as with all balances, this is not a simple utilitarian balance; it's one struck taking into account the significance of forfeiting the POLA.

[82] All the information in this paragraph comes from A. Nossiter, "He Disavowed Radical Islam. Was He Lying?"
[83] See Section 15.1.2.
[84] For confirmation of this number, see R. Callimachi, "How Do You Stop a Future Terrorist When the Only Evidence Is a Thought?" (citing Jean-Charles Brisard, the chairman of the French Center for the Analysis of Terrorism in Paris, for the proposition that "[i]t takes 20 agents per suspect for 24-hour surveillance.").
[85] See Section 20.2.

16.3.3 Forfeiture Without Compensation

Finally, I want to address the issue of compensation. In the forfeiture context, because a person who forfeits a right takes on the normative burden of her forfeiting behavior,[86] no compensation is owed to her if her liberty is limited for the sake of others. Her interests count in the proportionality balance, but if restrictions are justifiable as proportionate, the burden simply falls on her.[87]

[86] See Section 14.2.2.

[87] Louis Corrado argues that compensation must be provided if "the innocent but dangerous person is being asked, on behalf of the common good, to give up sorts of freedoms unconnected to the harming others." "Punishment and the Wild Beast of Prey," 814. I return to his view in Section 17.1. For here, I'll say only that he overlooks the significance of forfeiture.

17
The Duty to Accept Restrictions for the Sake of Others

17.1 Involuntary Threats and Quarantine

There are two fundamentally different ways that a person can owe a duty of self-restriction. First, he may simply be a threat to others; that is, he may be unable to avoid posing a threat unless he avoids certain forms of contact. I'll call that being an involuntary threat. Second, he may retain full control over whether he poses a threat to others, but he may nonetheless give them sufficient reason to be worried that they can demand that he be subject to some limited loss of freedom. I'll call that being frightening. In this section, I discuss the first of these possibilities; I discuss the second in the next section.

The paradigmatic case for involuntary threats is the person with a contagious disease.[1] He owes others a duty of care, a duty to avoid contact so that he will not infect them. This is true whether by moving among them he *will* infect them or will merely expose them to a *risk* of infection; and it's likewise true whether the infection *will* cause harm or will expose the infected to a *risk* of harm. If the risk is sufficiently high, then he has a duty to take some mitigating actions.[2]

There are two questions I want to address with regard to the enforceable duty to take mitigating actions. First, what kinds of mitigating actions must an infectious person take? Is it enough to wear a mask, or must he stay in quarantine until he is no longer contagious? That is a question of proportionality, and it is to be settled, to a first approximation, by a utilitarian standard, weighing the costs to him and to those he might harm. But the utilitarian approximation is only rough. In truth, a number of non-utilitarian considerations affect what he may owe. For example, a person's claim to liberty should be somewhat weaker than the claims of others not to be harmed. We can see this by thinking about deflection-of-threat cases. A's right to harm B for her sake depends on her interest being at least somewhat stronger than his. But deflections when the physical

[1] For an earlier discussion of this category of justification, see my "A Unified Theory of Detention," 920–922.

[2] Someone who cannot control her behavior and thus is a threat to others presents a variation on this theme. I discuss that kind of case in Ch. 19.

Punishment, Penalty, and Incapacitation. Alec Walen, Oxford University Press. © Oxford University Press 2026.
DOI: 10.1093/9780197523124.003.0017

harms at stake are on a par wrong the person harmed (assuming that he has not forfeited his right not to be harmed). This shows that A's claim to the liberty to deflect—no *mere* liberty interest, as it serves to protect A from a concrete harm—is weaker than B's claim not to be harmed.[3] The same applies if A wants to act for her own ends, knowing that he'll harm others or expose them to a risk of harm.[4] In addition, distribution of risk matters. If it is concentrated on one other person, that person has a strong claim; if it is distributed so that a great many people bear a small risk of a large harm, or a large risk of a small harm, then the aggregation of their claims may amount to *less* than if the risk and harm were concentrated on one person.[5]

Second, and relatedly, there's the question of compensation. Some think that if a person does not *deserve* to be detained, or to have his liberty restricted, then he is due compensation if his liberty is restricted for the sake of others. As Louis Corrado puts it: "[T]aking for the common good is commonly believed to require compensation."[6] But this assertion is based on overlooking the relevance of being a threat. As Kimberly Ferzan notes, compensation is not owed to "those who are liable to preventive interference."[7] By "liable to preventive interference," she means those who have forfeited their right not to suffer preventive interference. That won't cover this kind of case, as those who merely have a disease have not *forfeited* any rights.[8] Nevertheless, their claims should be treated as weaker than those of mere bystanders who might impede someone's ability to evade or deflect a threat. Even if they are not in any way at fault for being a threat, the fact that they *are* a threat means that they are not simply being harmed for the sake of others. Rather, they are being asked to bear a burden so that they do not harm others. Thus, they do not have a straightforward claim to compensation.

On the other hand, it's not clear who has to bear the greater burden: the innocent person who poses a threat to others or the innocent potential victim who wants not to be harmed. It seems reasonable to say that their positions are on a par.[9] As a result, we should expect the society that wants to be protected from those who innocently pose a risk to bear some costs in order to make those who carry the contagion comfortable. If the issue is the relatively trivial interference

[3] This follows from the general priority of negative patient claims over positive patient claims, all else equal, and from the weakness of positive agent claims. See, respectively, Sections 3.5.1 and 3.3.1.

[4] See my "Deontology in Graphs," §§ 4 and 5.

[5] See my "Risks and Weak Aggregation." Details matter, such as whether it is certain or nearly certain that someone will suffer a large harm, or it is unlikely that anyone will suffer a large harm, but if the harm befalls people, many will suffer it.

[6] "Punishment and the Wild Beast of Prey," 814. I raised this issue in n. 87 in the previous chapter.

[7] "Beyond Crime and Commitment," 188. Interestingly, Corrado acknowledges that no compensation is owed in self-defense cases. "Punishment and the Wild Beast of Prey," 813. But he fails to see that quarantine is fundamentally like self-defense.

[8] See Section 14.5.

[9] Ibid.

of having to wear a mask indoors, the rest of society may want to contribute to the possibility of having more events outdoors. If the burden is greater, like quarantine, the rest of society may be obliged to facilitate enduring quarantine by, for example, providing financial support for food delivery. And if the burden were truly great, like a lifetime of quarantine, as used to be imposed on those with leprosy, then society would be obliged to make the conditions of quarantine as comfortable as reasonably possible.[10]

17.2 Frightening People and Small Duties of Reassurance

If someone is a responsible agent who has not forfeited the presumption of law abidingness (POLA) and who can mingle with others without involuntarily posing a threat to them, then she should presumably be free to enjoy the same liberties as all others who are accountable and benefit from the POLA. But there are times when others will reasonably have fears about a particular agent. I'm not talking about fears based on generalizations that concern a person's race, sex, age, style of dress, or the like. The POLA means that we all just have to live with such fears. I'm talking about individuals with regard to whom there is evidence that their past acts provide reasons for others to be concerned about what they will do next.

The paradigmatic example is someone who has been arrested, and the criminal justice system needs a little time to sort out her situation. Arrest, based merely on probable cause to believe that the person arrested has committed an offense, should not suffice to forfeit the POLA.[11] This becomes especially clear when one realizes that the probabilities in question cannot be assumed to rise even to the level of preponderance of the evidence.[12] Rather, they are simply "the factual and practical considerations of everyday life on which reasonable and prudent [people] . . . act."[13] This vague standard is meant only to justify short-term arrest, not the long-term forfeiture of rights.

Nonetheless, the state and particular individuals may have reason to fear that a person who has been arrested *might*, if released, either flee the jurisdiction or otherwise go into hiding, thereby frustrating the state's attempt to hold

[10] The discussion in the text is not to be confused with this question: If someone suffers bad luck (e.g., is paralyzed through no fault of his own), how much support should the state offer him to help him approach the ability to enjoy life that others typically have? The duty to aid here is stronger because it reflects the fact that the person posing a threat is being made worse off for the sake of others.

[11] See Section 3.6. Note that in the United Kingdom, the standard for arrest is reasonable suspicion that the person has committed, is committing, or is about to commit a crime. This seems to be a functionally similar standard.

[12] See Illinois v. Gates, 462 U.S. 213 (1983).

[13] Ibid., 231.

her accountable, interfere in other ways with the trial process (for example, by intimidating witnesses), or commit other offenses (perhaps those related to the offense for which she has been arrested). Those who have been arrested are, in that sense, "frightening."

The case of frightening people is quite different from the first kind of case, because now the others are asking the person they are afraid of to make a sacrifice for their sake. They are not saying "You *are* a threat, and thus you can be targeted for restrictions as one." They are in no position to say that because the person whom they fear has not forfeited the POLA and is capable of mixing with them without wronging anyone. Rather, they are saying: "You scare us, and we'd like to be safer than we think we will be if you are left with the normal liberty of autonomous persons." On that basis, they are asking the frightening person to accept limits on her liberty. Such a request asks the frightening person to serve the interests of the frightened by giving up, for some period of time, something she normally has a right to.

To be clear, what is being requested is not just that the frightening person make those who are afraid of her *feel* safe. If it were just a question of feelings, the right response might be: "Look away" or "Deal with it." The point is that those who are afraid may have rational concerns either for their physical safety or for the security of things they care about, such as the ability of the state to hold accountable those who have committed offenses—I use "safety" to cover both. They may be right to think that these things are put at somewhat greater than normal risk, statistically speaking, by those whom they judge to be frightening. The problem is that they cannot rely on dangerousness in this statistical sense to justify incapacitating those who benefit from the POLA as though they *are dangerous.*[14] This means that they have to approach those frightening people as if what they, the frightened, want is a sacrifice that will help to ensure that those frightening people will not *actually* wrongfully cause harm.

One might object at this point: If frightening people do pose larger-than-normal risks, then they *are* in some sense threats. The frightened would not simply be using a threat as a means if they target her with restrictions. She owes a duty to accept such restrictions, given the reality of the threat she poses. But that logic does not work in this context, where the agent would pose a threat only in virtue of misusing her autonomous will. Given that she still benefits from the POLA, others cannot treat her as if she simply *is* a threat. Rather, they can only ask her to do them the favor of accepting restrictions for their sake.

Limitations on liberty that aim to reassure those who are afraid use those who instill fear as a means of reassuring the others.[15] Given the strength of claims not

[14] See Section 4.4.

[15] An agent who is a threat who *did* forfeit the POLA would be used as a means of providing reassurance just the same, but that would not count as using as a means in the morally relevant sense.

to be used as a means,[16] that is hard to justify. Thus, there is an asymmetry in what can justly be demanded: Only a small sacrifice can be demanded to ensure against a potentially large harm. In that way, the limits that can be imposed on her are substantially smaller than they would be if they were entitled to treat her simply as a threat, like someone with a contagious and potentially devastating disease.[17]

There are two ways in which a sacrifice can be small. It can be a moderately large sacrifice, but for only a short period of time, or it can be a small sacrifice over a relatively long period of time. A few days of detention, so that the state has time for an arraignment—to sort out the charges and decide whether pretrial detention (PTD) is necessary—strikes me as a small sacrifice.[18] That's not true if the detained person is put in danger of serious physical harm, or if the conditions are so psychologically stressful that they create lasting emotional injuries. Today's jails, at least in the United States, often fail on that score.[19] But there is no reason that jails *must* fail on that score. And a few days in detention, by itself, is a proportionately small demand to make of a distinctly frightening person.[20]

If a state turns to some sort of monitoring before trial, the intrusions on liberty that it imposes likewise might be small enough to be proportionate, even if they last for months or even a year or more. For example, being required to stay in the jurisdiction (to avoid flight risk) would often not impose a great sacrifice on a person. Of course, such a restriction might interfere with vacations, work travel, or visiting family. If it does interfere with activities that are important to the defendant, she should have a way to petition for an exception. For example, if she needs to make a work trip, perhaps the employer can put up bail to ensure that she comes back. Or if she has an important family reason to travel—say her father has died and the family is gathering for the funeral—perhaps either bail or some monitoring arrangement can be set up with the other jurisdiction where

Having forfeited the POLA, she no longer has a right to the liberty that she loses. The notion of using as a means is not just a physical concept; it is a moral one, concerned with taking a person's property or liberty for the sake of others.

[16] See Section 3.5.

[17] In the text, I focus on examples connected with arrest and the pretrial period. But red flag laws present another example of a limited loss that can be imposed on people for the sake of preventing large losses to others. These laws "allow police, family members or even doctors to petition a court to take away someone's firearms for up to a year if they feel that person is a threat to themselves or others." A. Phillips, "What Are Red Flag Laws?"

[18] It was a mistake to argue, as I did in "A Unified Theory of Detention," 913–916, that up to six months in detention could count as such a short-term interference that it could be owed to the state. I failed to consider whether the detainee might have forfeited the POLA or whether other considerations that I discuss in Ch. 19 might apply.

[19] See K. Ferzan, "The Trouble with Time Served," 2017–2019.

[20] The same point applies to the intrusions into privacy that are often required to obtain and secure evidence.

she has reason to go.[21] The wearing of a monitoring device is more intrusive, but it too may be a reasonable requirement, as long as it can be done in a way that is not *too* intrusive. For example, while such devices might be used to enforce a ban on association with people who are also suspects in a criminal enterprise, they should not generally interfere with work and normal daily activities.[22]

PTD, which can last for months or even years, is much harder to justify on this model. It may be relatively easy to justify if the detainee has forfeited the POLA. But it would be too demanding to treat it as a duty that anyone owes. I return to discuss PTD as a special case study in Chapter 18.[23]

What about compensation? I said in the prior section that compensation would *not* be owed to those who pose an involuntary threat. What about those who owe a duty to the frightened? Like quarantine, restrictions imposed on those who are frightening are imposed for the sake of helping others live with heightened risks. But unlike quarantine, the risk is one that the state cannot expect a frightening person to accept that she poses—that would violate the POLA. It must then treat the restrictions as a sacrifice *for* others, rather than a sacrifice to avoid *imposing a risk of harm* on others. This might suggest that compensation would be owed.

This suggestion needs to be counterbalanced by consideration of what it means to owe a duty. An agent who does what duty calls on her to do is not necessarily owed compensation. It might seem that there's an asymmetry between duties not to harm (for which it is obvious that no compensation is owed) and duties to aid (for which it might seem that compensation is owed). But consider the duties to aid that one assumes, often involuntarily, as a family member. Parents cannot expect compensation from their children for the efforts made to raise them. And an adult child who aids a parent or a sibling as she might be morally obliged to do cannot expect compensation from others in the family who did not make equal sacrifices. It's not that one who carries out a duty to aid is owed nothing. She is owed gratitude. Along with that, fairness may call for efforts to share the load equitably. For example, if one sibling who lives near an aging mother puts in a lot of effort taking care of her, another sibling who lives farther away may be obliged to make special efforts to carry an extra burden of care when possible. But *compensation* is the wrong idea. An agent with a positive

[21] Former Congressman George Santos received this kind of accommodation while his trial was pending; he was free to go to Washington, DC, for work, or to his home jurisdiction in New York where he was to face trial. He has since pled guilty to wire fraud and identity theft.

[22] These norms are *not* respected in current practice, at least in the United States. See K. Weisburd et al., "Electronic Prisons." For a more general discussion of the ways liberty restrictions can become overly costly to those who have not forfeited the POLA, see H. Noorda, "Exprisonment."

[23] In addition, detention for interrogation, which tends to take a while, is *not* justifiable in this way. It would be justifiable only if the detention is already justified, for example, because the detainee is a POW (see Section 20.3.1), or if adequately compensated so that the net sacrifice is small. Even then, it would be justified only if not done using coercive techniques.

duty to aid should not expect to be made whole, as though she had no duty to sacrifice at all.

Carrying that point over into the context of the state and the small duty to submit to detention for the sake of getting the criminal process underway, or to contribute in other reasonably small ways to the functioning of the criminal justice system, such as by serving on a jury or providing witness testimony, the state should seek to ensure that the exercise of these duties is not too demanding or taxing. In that way, it should share the load. But it need not *compensate* those who carry out these duties.

What about trial time? Some trials last for weeks or even months. If one wants to plead guilty, one can get it over with quickly. But if a defendant wants to exercise her right to a trial, she might have to endure a long time on trial, as the jurors might have to endure a long time attending trial. One might agree with Antony Duff that a defendant has a duty to stand trial to make an accounting of herself.[24] Even so, a long time on trial is an ordeal, and one can reasonably ask whether a defendant put through that ordeal has a right to compensation.

I think the answer depends on how long a defendant spends on trial and on whether she is ultimately found guilty. For a short trial, she may have no claim for compensation; for a long one, if she is found not guilty, then she may indeed have a claim for compensation—as would any juror who served in a long trial. But if she is convicted, then I think she would have no claim to compensation. The rationale for this distinction is that, as a guilty person, she always had it in her power to plead guilty. The burden of the trial therefore falls on her. If she is innocent, however, then the burden of putting her through a long trial should fall on the government.[25]

A worry or confusion arises, however, if compensation is made. It might seem to allow the state to impose a *greater* burden on the frightening, as the *net* imposition would still be small. This could erase the line between small sacrifices and large sacrifices. But there is a good reason to think that the line between small and large sacrifices is still significant. The provision of compensation may turn state action that otherwise would be impermissible into permissible state action. But it does so not by expanding on what can be demanded as a matter of enforceable duty. It does so by imposing a loss on a frightening person for the sake of some social good and then compensating her for the loss. It is, in effect, a taking by the state, akin to a taking when the state exercises the power of eminent domain.[26]

[24] "Pre-Trial Detention and the Presumption of Innocence," 125.

[25] This sort of variation, depending on guilt or innocence, is picked up again in the next chapter, Section 18.4, under the heading "hypothetical forfeiture."

[26] Eminent domain is the state's power of taking private property for public purposes, with compensation.

Takings with compensation may be justifiable, but they are justifiable *not* because an agent has a duty to submit to them. It is not as if she has a duty to volunteer her property and then hope for compensation. Rather, they are a *taking*. They are justifiable if and only if two conditions hold. First, there must be a substantial public good that the state is trying to pursue. This is required because those who have what is theirs taken, without their consent, by the state do not usually get what it is worth to them. Their property or liberty interest is converted into an objectively reasonable price,[27] which is normally less than what they would sell it for (if there is even a market for it). The state needs good *public* reason to impose on people the loss associated with converting a property right into a claim for reasonable compensation. Second, the compensation must be objectively reasonable.

In sum, by adding compensation to reduce the net cost to someone whose liberty is taken, the state in effect admits that they do not have a duty to sacrifice to that great an extent. There may be a kernel of a duty to sacrifice in the case of a larger sacrifice that is justifiable only with adequate compensation. But the larger sacrifice is justifiable because of the adequate compensation, not because of a duty to accept it. This point too will be revisited in the next chapter, on PTD.

[27] The reason to do that is to avoid allowing the person whose property or liberty is taken to set her own price, as she could easily exaggerate its subjective value to her. See G. Calabresi and A. Douglas Melamed, "Property Rules, Liability Rules, and Inalienability."

18
Pretrial Detention: A Case Study

18.1 Overview of Pretrial Detention Issues

People arrested based on probable cause to believe they have committed offenses, especially offenses serious enough to potentially warrant prison time ("serious offenses"), may be frightening. As noted in the previous chapter, they may have reason to flee or otherwise interfere with the trial by, for example, intimidating witnesses. In addition, qua suspected offenders, they may be thought unusually likely to commit other offenses, even ones unrelated to their trial.[1] Nonetheless, at least in times of peace, the state may not simply lock up those who still benefit from the presumption of law abidingness (POLA), not even if it has good reason to fear that they are more likely than most to interfere with their trials (or other trials) or otherwise commit offenses. Perhaps, as discussed in the last chapter, it can lock them up for a short period of time during which it sorts out essential facts. But pretrial detention (PTD) often lasts months and sometimes years.[2] The state can't justify locking people up for that long just because they are frightening, at least not as a matter of duty. The justification for PTD depends, instead, on one of two things: either those subject to it have forfeited the POLA or they will receive adequate compensation.

One natural question is: Can we treat those who have been arrested for serious offenses as different from others? Leading scholars have denied it. Laurence Tribe once wrote: "If two men appear equally likely to commit a violent crime, it is arbitrary to imprison the man who is about to be tried for a past offense while imposing no restraint on the man who is not facing trial."[3] Sandra Mayson concurs, offering what she calls "the parity principle," according to which "the state has no greater authority to preventively restrain a defendant than it does a non-defendant who poses an equal risk."[4]

One might think that there's a sense in which those who have been arrested and charged with serious offenses have been found, even if only by a low standard

[1] Some authors suggest that pretrial detention may be easier to justify on the first set of ground than the second. See, e.g., A. Duff, "Pre-Trial Detention," 117; S. Mayson, "Dangerous Defendants," 533. I think it's more complicated than that, as I try to explain in this chapter.

[2] S. Mayson, "Dangerous Defendants," 549.

[3] "An Ounce of Detention," 405.

[4] "Dangerous Defendants," 499.

Punishment, Penalty, and Incapacitation. Alec Walen, Oxford University Press. © Oxford University Press 2026.
DOI: 10.1093/9780197523124.003.0018

of proof, to have committed those offenses. Thus, one might think that the state can treat them as having, to some extent, forfeited the POLA, thereby refuting the parity principle. But probable cause, as noted in the previous chapter,[5] does not even imply more likely than not; it is a far cry from proof beyond a reasonable doubt. And as I argued in Chapter 16,[6] the standard of proof for forfeiture of the POLA, at least the *general* POLA, is the same as that for criminal law: proof beyond a reasonable doubt. So, it seems that the parity principle is sound.

Nonetheless, I argue here that there are three types of cases in which the parity principle does not apply. In the first two, defendants have forfeited the POLA; in the third, the defendants are not contesting their guilt, and their PTD can be counted as the start of their sentence—a form of compensation. Where the parity principle does apply, we must acknowledge that it requires compensation—either in terms of reduced prison time or financial compensation—if it is to be justifiable. We can also distinguish a third category of defendants, those who can be treated as having hypothetically forfeited the POLA. The idea is that the state can operate on the hypothesis that they have, by their crime, forfeited the POLA, and it can test that hypothesis at trial. If it is confirmed with a guilty verdict, then the parity principle does not apply, and they are owed no compensation for their PTD; but if it is not confirmed, then the state would owe them compensation for their PTD.

18.2 Pretrial Detention in Non-Parity Cases

There are three reasons why it might be easier to justify subjecting a particular defendant to PTD than it would be to detain other people who are equally dangerous: a prior criminal record; efforts at interfering with the trial; and cases in which the defendant admits her guilt and the issue for trial is only determining which crime she has committed.

18.2.1 Prior Criminal Record

A prior criminal record for serious offenses could suffice to forfeit the POLA and thereby open up a justification for PTD.[7] Consider, for example, someone

[5] Ch. 17, n. 12 and accompanying text.

[6] Section 16.2.6.

[7] This is a completely different forfeiture ground than one that Kimberly Ferzan considers and rejects, namely the crime itself for which a person is being tried. See "The Trouble with Time Served," 2032. I return to that conception of forfeiture in Section 18.4 when I consider hypothetical forfeiture. Ferzan also considers forfeiture based on the intent to commit a future crime. Ibid., 2033–2035. I agree with her that such an intention can forfeit the POLA. But see Section 16.1 for an important difference.

who has been convicted of and has served time for aggravated assault. She might be taken to have forfeited the POLA for a few years after the sentence, at least with regard to similar acts of assault.[8] If she is arrested within a few years of finishing her sentence on another assault charge, she might reasonably be treated as having forfeited the POLA in a way that would make it easier to justify holding her in PTD. Finding this sort of forfeiture would be even more reasonable if she is a recidivist who has been convicted multiple times before.

The function of an arrest, in cases in which the defendant has already forfeited the POLA, is to trigger a reexamination of whether *post-conviction* detention is justifiable as the least restrictive alternative (LRA) for providing security against the threats this defendant is taken to pose.[9] In other words, forfeiture of the POLA would be established not by the arrest but by the prior convictions. The arrest serves only as an indicator that more security is called for. If the defendant is later cleared of the charges, then the need for detention should be reassessed.[10]

If PTD is the LRA that fairly balances the competing interests, then the defendant can be held in PTD without compensation. That means that if she is convicted, she would get no credit for time served, and if she is acquitted, she would get no other compensation for time served. This would be appropriate because her being held would be morally no different from cases of holding someone who has forfeited the POLA *after* her prison sentence has been served on *other* grounds of ongoing dangerousness. If Leroy Hendricks deserves no compensation for being held post-conviction as a sexually violent predator,[11] then a person whose prior record suffices to forfeit the POLA and who is then detained after being arrested also deserves no compensation.

I want to emphasize that even if certain defendants have forfeited the POLA, the justification for PTD does not follow automatically. It follows only if the benefits of doing so outweigh the costs.[12] The costs are multiple, including not only lost liberty but also criminogenic effects[13] and the psychosocial "costs of branding certain people or groups as dangers to the broader community."[14] Against that, we have to weigh the value of better ensuring that the trial will

[8] See Section 16.2.2.

[9] On the need to use the LRA, see Section 16.2.1.

[10] If the charges are simply dropped, the court should presumably look into why and whether there is nonetheless reason to impose restrictions on the person's liberty.

[11] See Section 16.2.3 on Hendricks and Section 16.3.3 on compensation.

[12] See Section 16.3.2 on how this sort of balancing is to be done in general. Keep in mind that claims not to be harmed (including harm through loss of liberty) weigh more heavily, all else equal, than claims to be protected from harm. See Sections 2.3 and 3.3.2.

[13] M. Mayson, "Dangerous Defendants," 547.

[14] Ibid. Mayson also mentions "the exacerbation of race and class inequalities." But for the purposes of this discussion, I assume, contra current reality in the United States, a more idealistic society without significant classism or racism.

not be interfered with,[15] and of incapacitating someone who seems more likely than most to commit other offenses. Given the relatively low level of risk of committing another violent crime, even for those who are counted as "high risk" for doing so—currently, best estimates find a risk of about 8 percent over a six-month period[16]—it is only in cases in which evidence of dangerousness is at its highest that PTD could be justified using cost-benefit analysis.

One might challenge this conclusion on the grounds that those who are detained have *forfeited* the POLA, and therefore, one might think, their interests should count for less than the interests of other people who might be taken to be frightening. Compare cases of self-defense. If A is defending herself against B, an innocent aggressor who is in no way culpable for wrongly aggressing, A should take B's interests as significantly weightier than if A were defending herself against C, a culpable aggressor. Even a culpable aggressor's interests count for something; A may not kill C to prevent C from culpably slapping her.[17] But a culpable aggressor's interests count for much less because she has substantially forfeited her right not to be attacked insofar as such an attack is necessary for defensive purposes. One might be tempted to extend that point to the context of PTD.

The problem with the analogy is that the odds that someone with a prior record *is a threat* are still very low.[18] If someone is a threat, then the analogy holds. But in truth, it is more than 90 percent likely that someone is *not* a threat, and the liberty interest of someone who is not a threat should not be discounted. Forfeiture of the POLA allows the state to take into account the statistical likelihood that she will threaten the rights of others. But that should not be confused with saying that her liberty itself counts for less than the liberty of others if she is not actually a threat to them. Making the point in terms of basic dignity-respecting principles: The state should seek to minimize the extent to which it treats someone who has forfeited the POLA as a second-class citizen. Given the importance of reconciliation, the state should read POLA forfeiture narrowly; it should be read to imply only the permissibility of considering statistical probabilities of dangerousness that are normally blocked by the POLA.

One implication of the previous point is that this justification for PTD will work only in extreme cases in which the threat to others seems maximally likely

[15] I say only "better ensuring" because the detainee may have supporters who are also willing to interfere with the trial, and even pretrial detention may not sufficiently isolate the detainee from the outside world to prevent her from signals that will lead, for example, to intimidating witnesses.

[16] Ibid., 495.

[17] See Section 14.2.

[18] There may, however, be exceptional types of cases in which it is not so low. Fiona Clark, a magistrate judge in England, reports in personal communication that perpetrators of domestic violence are more likely to reoffend. This could make PTD easier to defend in such cases when the offender already has a record of domestic violence.

and very serious. It would not justify PTD to prevent risk of lesser harms, such as flight risk or witness tampering. Those are serious, but not as serious as violent crimes. If PTD is to be based on fears related to interfering with the trial itself, the POLA forfeiture should be specific to that. I turn to that next.

18.2.2 Efforts to Undermine the Trial and Other Misbehavior While Awaiting Trial

Another basis for PTD applies to those who fail to respect their duty to cooperate in their trial, by attempting to flee the jurisdiction,[19] by engaging in witness tampering, or by demonstrating an intention to do either or both. As Antony Duff, a noted critic of PTD, notes: "If a defendant . . . tries to abscond or to obstruct, he can be legitimately detained, to prevent him from carrying through this attempt to frustrate the criminal process."[20] Such detention would again reflect the defendant's forfeiture of the POLA, this time a specific forfeiture, and as such, it would call for no compensation, neither financial nor time served.

Of course, it may not be perfectly obvious that a defendant has tried to abscond or obstruct justice. And even if she has clearly broken some technical restrictions placed on her (for example, not to leave a certain geographical area), she may have adequate justification or excuse for having done so. A hearing must be held to determine whether she has now forfeited the POLA in this specific way. But the issue can be resolved with a lower standard of proof than proof beyond a reasonable doubt; perhaps clear and convincing evidence or even a preponderance of the evidence will do. In cases where that evidence can be provided, the specific forfeiture of the POLA, in combination with the evident failure of less restrictive means of ensuring good behavior, would justify PTD.

One might object here that I have earlier argued that forfeiture of the POLA requires proof beyond a reasonable doubt.[21] But that argument concerned only general forfeiture of the POLA, of the sort that would lead to general restrictions on freedom. Specific POLA forfeiture has a more limited significance. It does not imply that one is generally not to be trusted to respect the law; it implies only that one has lost a particular limited privilege. Of course, pretrial freedom is not a "privilege"; it's a basic right. But if the limitation of PTD is grounded in the failure to perform a special duty to respect the trial process, then it should count as grounded in specific POLA forfeiture, and it should be permissible to base it

[19] For the rest of this chapter, I use "flee the jurisdiction" to cover all efforts to evade trial, whether by flight or by going into hiding.

[20] "Pre-Trial Detention," 127.

[21] See Section 16.2.6.

on a lower standard of proof, just as it is permissible to use a lower standard of proof to revoke specific professional privileges.[22]

It is important to be clear that the basis for POLA forfeiture here is that the defendant has been caught either trying or intending to flee the jurisdiction or tamper with witnesses. This is quite different from a mere prediction that the defendant *might* or *is likely* to flee or interfere with witnesses. Unless the defendant has forfeited the POLA in the first way, those sorts of predictions cannot be used to remove her liberty.

There's also the question of whether this is really a non-parity justification for PTD. Friends, family, or unindicted co-conspirators of a defendant might also engage in witness tampering, and witnesses who have been subpoenaed to testify might also seek to flee the jurisdiction of the court. Why not treat this as a parity case, then, in which any efforts or intentions to interfere with or undermine the trial should result in PTD for anyone who has made those efforts or shown those intentions?

My answer has two dimensions. First, a defendant has a particular duty to cooperate with the criminal process in his own case. Thus, the level of tolerance for actions that might be construed as something like witness tampering should be lower for a defendant than for another party, though other parties could also be subject to PTD to prevent witness tampering.[23] Second, justice is less likely to be frustrated by a witness fleeing the jurisdiction than the defendant fleeing.[24] Often, prosecutors subpoena more witnesses than they *need* to make their case, just to make it as solid as possible. Thus, a proportionality question often arises for the PTD of witnesses that does not arise for the PTD of defendants who have been caught trying or intending to flee.

Finally, the possibility that a guilty defendant released pretrial will take her release as a sign of her impunity and resume her criminal behavior has to be taken seriously. It is a familiar complaint from police officers in jurisdictions with restrictive rules on pretrial detention that arresting low-level offenders—for example, people caught for theft—is pointless because the defendants end up right back on the street, committing the same or similar crimes. The solution to this complaint is not to make pretrial detention easy to justify in general. It is, rather, to say that a person released pretrial is on notice that a further arrest will be taken to forfeit the POLA pretrial. Obviously, a second arrest should not *automatically* lead to pretrial detention. It might be a mistake; it might even be that the police will rearrest someone to harass her, seeking to get her locked up without a conviction. Some form of hearing is required to determine if the second arrest

[22] See Section 16.2.6, n. 66.

[23] They can also be subject to prosecution for the crime of witness tampering, but PTD should not have to wait for the resolution of that case. Nor should it necessarily be linked to their own trial.

[24] This assumes that the defendant cannot be tried in absentia.

is really indicative of a sense of impunity on the part of the defendant. But the second arrest would shift the presumption away from pretrial release to pretrial detention.[25] Such a shift should address the concern that the arrest is pointless and that low-level criminals can operate with impunity.

18.2.3 Guilt Is Admitted but the Crime Is Contested

A third non-parity basis for PTD reflects the fact that not all trials are about guilt or innocence; often, they are about the *degree* of guilt: What sort of offense can the government prove? What defenses can the defendant establish? Take, for example, a homicide case in which the defendant does not contest that she culpably killed her victim; the issue for trial is whether what she did counts as murder or merely manslaughter. In that case, there is no doubt that the defendant will end up serving time in prison; the only questions are: What crime did she commit, and how much time should she serve? In such a case, the state could justifiably start counting time served in PTD as pre-payment of time that will later be served in prison. Doing so is, if anything, a mercy, allowing her to get on with serving her sentence.

It is important to flag just how different this kind of pre-payment is from forfeiture of the POLA. It differs in three ways. First, when forfeiture is involved, jail time should be exceptional, used only when it is the LRA. Jail would not normally be the LRA when the forfeiture is based on prior crime; it would more often be the LRA when POLA forfeiture is grounded in attempts or intentions to flee or tamper with witnesses. But when a person is going to serve time in prison anyway, then PTD can be traded for the prison time as a default norm.

One might object that the state ought not to punish *until* the trial is over and there is a formal statement of censure connecting the punishment (or penalty) to the offense. But this objection should be addressed with pragmatic flexibility, not rigid preconceptions of how things must be done. For example, the defendant could plead early in the process to the lower-level crime, which she claims is all she committed, and the court could sentence her for that, while simultaneously scheduling a trial to determine if her guilt is greater than that.

A second difference is that in cases based on forfeiture, no compensation is owed. By contrast, when a person is being held *because* it is already understood that she is guilty of at least a lesser charge, then, as just discussed, she should get

[25] A first arrest would then operate *like* a prior conviction. But the threshold for pretrial detention with a second arrest should be higher, as the first arrest cannot itself be held to have forfeited the POLA. Another difference: The defendant might be acquitted on all charges. If so, the state should treat her pretrial detention as unjustified and in need of compensation. See Section 18.4 on hypothetical forfeiture.

credit for her time in PTD as the start of her serving her sentence. That means that she is, in effect, getting compensation, in like coin, for her PTD.

Finally, the proper place to serve time if the defendant is not contesting her guilt should not be jail but prison. This addresses a worry I will turn to in the next section, that jails should not resemble prisons, and that time served in jail should not therefore be treated as a fair substitute for time in prison. Of course, the sanction for the low-end crime that the defendant is willing to plead to might not include time in prison. Moreover, the judge should not allow the prosecution's case to color her reading of that lower-level crime and cause her to treat it as more serious than it is. The judge should import into the case a version of the presumption of innocence, one that holds that the *only* thing the defendant can be presumed guilty of is what she has pled guilty to.

In fact, it may be best to view this sort of process as not involving PTD at all, but rather the bifurcation of a trial so that guilt can be established for a lesser crime and punishment commenced for it, while guilt is contested for the greater crime. If the defendant is found guilty of the greater crime, then a new sentencing hearing should be held, which will revisit the original sentence. If she is found not guilty, then the original sentence will simply continue to play out. The fact that the defendant at the trial is being detained ends up registering functionally as a coincidence.[26]

It should be added that it may not be unusual, in this sort of case, that the sentence for the lesser crime would not include much, if any, prison time. If that were the case, then if the state still wants the defendant held in PTD, it will have to treat it as one of the first two kinds of non-parity cases or as a parity case.

18.3 Pretrial Detention in Parity Cases

The three possibilities for PTD covered in the previous section may cover a fairly large range of cases in which PTD could justifiably be sought. But the government might want to consider a different kind of justification for PTD that would apply in cases in which there is no basis for finding forfeiture of the POLA, nor certainty that the defendant would serve time after sentencing, and yet the government has serious concerns about the defendant that it takes to warrant PTD. In these sorts of cases, the defendant would be in a position that is morally the same as someone else who is merely deemed frightening. These would be the parity cases.

[26] I'm grateful to Tejus Sinha and Vianna Scott for independently pointing out the need for this paragraph.

The first thing to say about parity cases is that if the person is held in PTD, then compensation is owed. She had a right to that liberty, and if it is taken for the sake of providing reassurance to the community, then it should be treated like any other taking for a public good: It should come with fair compensation.[27]

The form that compensation should take should depend on whether the defendant can be given it in terms of time served. If she is convicted and the sentence is at least as long as the time served pretrial, then it is likely that compensation can most effectively be made by an in-kind swap: Time after conviction can be reduced to pay for time served prior to conviction. If she is convicted of a crime for which the sentence is shorter than the period of time she spent in PTD, or if the charges are dropped or she is acquitted, then the compensation would have to take another form, presumably financial.[28]

Kimberly Ferzan notes that "[e]very state and the federal government [in the United States] provide for credit for time served."[29] But she nonetheless argues against the practice. She argues that giving credit for time served (1) harms the innocent because they get no sentence that can then be reduced by time served;[30] (2) is hard to reconcile with the claim that PTD is not punishment;[31] (3) makes PTD cheaper, which makes it more tempting for the state, even when it is not justified and causes excess harm;[32] (4) makes it more likely that the innocent will plead guilty;[33] and (5) makes us complacent about the harsh conditions in jails.[34] She argues that if the state feels the need to hold certain defendants in PTD, it ought simply to provide them with financial compensation.[35]

All of Ferzan's arguments are importantly damning of the system of PTD in the United States. But I don't find them convincing if financial compensation is also available when time served either would not suffice for compensation or the defendant for some reason would prefer financial compensation. This is most obviously true of her first objection, that time served hurts the innocent. If financial compensation is made, as it would be if their property were taken for the public welfare, then the innocent are not treated unjustly.

[27] See Section 17.2.

[28] According to Adam Kolber, "England, France, Germany, Austria, Norway, and Hong Kong, among others, have systems for compensating acquitted defendants." *Punishment for the Greater Good,* 135, n. 8. Such systems *should* apply also to those whose time held in PTD exceeds their sentence or the charges were simply dropped.

[29] "The Trouble with Time Served," 2005.

[30] Ibid., especially pp. 2048 and 2060.

[31] Ibid., 2005. To streamline the discussion in the rest of this section, I will not, with one exception, carve out penal law sanctions for separate treatment. The necessary modifications are fairly straightforward, if cumbersome to spell out.

[32] Ibid., 2007.

[33] Ibid.

[34] Ibid.

[35] Ibid., 2009–2010.

Her second argument—that credit for time served is hard to reconcile with the claim that PTD is not punishment—is harder to handle.[36] Those who do not admit their guilt—contrast those discussed at the end of the prior section—should not be pre-punished;[37] punishment must be reserved for those who have been found guilty.[38] Moreover, the use of time in jail as an in-kind swap for prison time raises a dilemma: Either jails impose punitive conditions on their inmates, in which case the swap makes substantive sense, but the conditions in jail must be unjustifiably harsh,[39] or jails do not impose punitive conditions on their inmates, in which case the swap does not make substantive sense.

My response to this set of arguments is to reject the premise that credit for time served is irresistibly read as pre-punishment. It can easily be so read, but if it is seen as just one method of providing compensation, and compensation is almost always (except in POLA forfeiture cases) provided to those who are held in PTD, I think that would tend to undermine that association.

What about the dilemma? I agree with Ferzan that jails should not resemble prisons. As she puts it, the conditions should more resemble the hotel-like conditions that a state should provide to jurors who are sequestered in certain trials.[40] But why shouldn't we allow being held in a "hotel" to offset time in a prison? It still deprives the detainee of his freedom and thus might be thought close enough in terms of deprivation to count for an in-kind swap. That answer is reinforced to the extent that the function of prisons is not to induce *suffering* per se, but just to impose a condition (lost freedom) that almost all people do not want to experience.[41] Insofar as prisons are not especially harsh places in which to be held, the comparison with jails would be easier to make. Prisons should be harsher than "hotels"; they should not be desirable places to stay. But insofar as they are not meant to inflict substantial suffering beyond the loss of freedom, the gap between prisons and jails need not be large. And finally, if the gap seems too large to allow a one-to-one trade-off, then some other ratio could be used, perhaps a steeper ratio depending on how harsh the prison is (perhaps honor farms would get a one-to-one trade-off, while the trade-off for a medium-security prison would be nine days off from the sentence for every ten days in jail, and the trade-off for a maximum-security prison would be eight days off from the prison sentence for every ten days held in jail).

[36] This argument builds on a general tendency to associate PTD with guilt and punishment. See R. Lippke, *Taming the Presumption of Innocence*, 130.

[37] "The Trouble with Time Served," 2039.

[38] See Section 5.1.

[39] Ferzan discusses how unjustifiably harsh they tend to be in "The Trouble with Time Served," 2017–2019.

[40] Ibid., 2019.

[41] On the role of suffering in punishment, see Sections 6.1, 7.1, and 8.3.2.

Ferzan's third argument is that trading time served for PTD makes punishment cheaper, which makes PTD more tempting for the state, even when it is not justified and causes excess harm. Time served makes punishment cheaper because if the state grants it, then it does not have to pay for as much punishment *post*-conviction. The question is: How distorting of state incentives is this? There are at least four reasons to think it need not be very distorting. First, if PTD is used only when it is the LRA, it will not be used that often. Second, if credit for time served can be used only when the punishment would exceed the time held in PTD, that means that the state would have to respond to many cases in which it does hold the defendant in PTD with financial compensation. Third, it might be a better policy to offer detained defendants a choice: Get financial compensation or credit for time served.[42] Insofar as that choice is offered, there will still be fewer instances of credit for time served. Fourth, if defendants are offered the option of paying bail, along with the options of getting credit for time served or getting financially compensated for time served, even fewer people may end up getting credit for time served.[43] All told, the more time served is a rare option, the less likely it is to affect overall state policy.

Ferzan's fourth argument is that credit for time served makes it more likely that the innocent will plead guilty.[44] The explanation for this argument is that if an innocent defendant pleads guilty, he will end his time in jail; by contrast, if he stays in jail until his trial is completed, he will certainly spend longer in jail. A significant reason to endure the extra time in jail is the hope of being acquitted at trial and avoiding prison time. But if that prison time would be offset by jail time, then there would be less of it to avoid. It might make more sense, then, just to plead guilty and move on.[45] This argument has less force, however, if the innocent defendant would be financially compensated for her time in jail. As long as that compensation is adequate, then she should be able to afford to stay in jail and fight the charges at trial. The compensation is less likely to be adequate the more a detained defendant would earn if not in jail. But a more financially successful defendant is likely to be able to afford to post bail and get out of jail, and a

[42] Ferzan argues against offering this choice. "The Trouble with Time Served," 2067. Her main argument is the last of the arguments I address in the text.

[43] Having bail as one option among three would give the wealthy some advantage over the poor, who would have only two options. But if the two options are adequate, this need not be the basis for a strong complaint of inequity. See ibid., 2006 (emphasizing that the problem with bail for egalitarians arises for the poor and innocent, on the assumption that they would get no compensation for their time served).

[44] See also Mayson, "Dangerous Defendants," 550, n. 270 ("approximately seventeen percent of the detained misdemeanor defendants who pled guilty would not have been convicted at all had they been released rather than detained pretrial."). See also A. Natapoff, "Misdemeanors," 1316.

[45] The innocent defendant would also run the risk of getting a longer sentence, if he is erroneously convicted, than he would have received had he made a plea deal. But this risk is inherent in any system that incentivizes plea deals with shorter sentences. It is not tied particularly to credit for time served.

less financially successful defendant is more likely to be made whole by reasonable financial compensation.[46]

Finally, Ferzan's fifth argument is that time served makes us complacent about the harsh conditions in jails. Her thought seems to be that it reinforces the thought that jails should be harsh, like prisons. But this is really just the dilemma point made in the second argument. My responses to that argument suffice here as well: Jails don't need to be as harsh as prisons to allow credit for time served, nor do prisons need to be especially harsh, and if there is a substantial gap in the difficulty of spending time in one versus the other, the credit for time served need not be one-to-one. In sum, there is nothing about credit for time served that should interfere with the thought that jail for PTD should be more like a hotel—reflecting the presumption of innocence—than prison.

Having addressed Ferzan's five arguments, there are a few other worries I want to address. First, one might worry that if states have to offer financial compensation for PTD in cases in which the prison sentence is not long enough to give credit for time served, that would put pressure on state legislators or judges to create longer prison sentences so that the state can always pay off those who serve time in PTD with time served.

This is a non-trivial worry. But if judges and the public are conscious of the limits of proportional punishment,[47] that should be a check on this sort of legislative corruption.[48] And as for judicial abuse of sentencing, exploiting the flexible power judges have over much sentencing, there are ways to address that. Here is just one suggestion: Judges could be kept in the dark about whether someone served PTD at sentencing. The sentence would then have to be appropriate even if the defendant had been out on bond pretrial and was owed no compensation. If PTD is an exceptional procedure, then the sentencing norm should be one that is uncorrupted by this sort of concern.

Adam Kolber also objects that if the state allows credit for time served, then we have to ask why it should not allow a defendant to "bank" punishment credits.[49] Suppose, for example, a defendant is held in PTD for six months, then is acquitted, and then is arrested for another crime, the punishment for which is six months. Why not allow him to say he has already paid for that crime? One answer may be that the state should want to preserve specific deterrence; it

[46] Ferzan argues that those given financial compensation for their PTD should get it regularly while in jail. As she put it, that would allow them to "provide for their families and otherwise use the funds." Ibid., 2067.

[47] See Ch. 8.

[48] Of course, the politics of punishment may be hard for politicians to resist. But this point applies across much of this book. Ultimately, one has to hope that a clear moral theory can help hold back corrupt politics.

[49] See *Punishment for the Greater Good*, 136.

should not want to give defendants a get-out-of-jail-free card. But Kolber imagines a case in which the other crime was committed before the one for which he was convicted. Why not allow him to use his time-served credit against this other crime?

I think there are two things one can say. First, the state could bite the bullet and say that the PTD credit could be used against the other punishment. This may, however, seem unacceptable to a retributivist (I find it counterintuitive). What is the alternative? I think the state has to bite another bullet and say that the time that a defendant spends in PTD for a crime is in a sense tied to punishment for *that* crime. Why say that? The thought is that imprisonment for a crime has symbolic significance as a way for a defendant to pay back his guilt-debt. PTD served while waiting for trial for that crime picks up that symbolic significance. Other PTD does not. We should therefore compensate other PTD financially, not with time served.[50]

I want to wrap up this section with one last issue: Does PTD have to be the LRA if the state provides adequate compensation? I think the answer is yes. The reason is not driven by those who would get compensation in the form of time served. I assume that would generally be considered adequate by the person so compensated. The reason is driven by the normal shortcomings of financial compensation. Such compensation inevitably substitutes an objective price for the value a person puts on his own freedom.[51] But offering an objective price is likely to harm a person, as it is unlikely to be *his* price. Such takings are, I think, justifiable if there is a sufficiently important governmental purpose. That's a proportionality point. But the justification also requires passing a necessity test. If a less restrictive alternative would do well enough, then the cost may not be unnecessarily imposed. And this applies to witness detainees as well as defendant detainees.[52] Parity is parity. And to repeat the point I made at the start of this section, occasions when this sort of PTD can be used should be relatively rare.

[50] This thought presupposes that punishment should always be tied to specific crimes and never be meted out on a "whole life" basis. That view is implicit in my discussion of the basis of blame, Section 6.3. I return more explicitly to rejecting the whole life view in Section 20.5.2.

[51] See Section 17.2.

[52] There is a U.S. federal statute that provides for the arrest and detention of material witnesses when "it is shown that it may become impracticable to secure the presence of the person by subpoena." 18 U.S.C. § 3144 (2012). This statute was abused by the federal government shortly after September 11, 2001, when the government used it to round up many Muslim men. See D. Cole, "Enemy Aliens," 961. For a more recent description of how the statute has been used to detain thousands of undocumented immigrants over the past decade, nearly 850 for over six months, see S. Cutler et al., "Jailed by the Thousands, Without Charges, to Act as a Witness." If compensation had to be offered to these detainees, the temptation to abuse this statute, by using it when it is not an LRA, would presumably be substantially reduced.

18.4 Hypothetical Forfeiture

Before ending this discussion of PTD, I want to address a hybrid idea: hypothetical forfeiture. The idea is that the state could treat arrest for a serious crime as functioning as a hypothesis that the person has done something that would in fact have forfeited the POLA pretrial. The hypothesis would then be tested at trial. If the defendant is found not guilty, then the hypothesis would be rebutted, and compensation would be owed for time served. But if the defendant is found guilty, then the hypothesis would be confirmed, and the defendant would be found to have forfeited the POLA prior to trial. This would imply that she would be owed no compensation, including no credit for time served in PTD.

This may seem objectionable for two reasons. First, it may seem as if it would undermine the rule that compensation is generally owed for PTD when the person has not already forfeited the POLA either by prior criminal convictions or by trying or intending to undermine her trial. It might seem to imply that the state would owe compensation *only* when it acquits, not when it convicts. But in truth, it would not do much to undermine the duty to provide compensation discussed in the previous section. The reason is that cases in which hypothetical forfeiture would be available are quite limited. Recall from Chapter 16 that only the most serious crimes or serious patterns of recidivism would justify general forfeiture of the POLA.[53] Thus, the notion of hypothetical forfeiture could not be used for all cases in which the defendant could be expected to be sentenced, if convicted, to a prison term at least as long as his PTD. It could be used only for the most serious cases.

The second objection is that hypothetical forfeiture would justify a perverse form of unequal treatment in those cases in which people who are taken to have hypothetically forfeited the POLA and are then convicted do not get credit for time served. Here's a set of cases that pushes that intuition as well as I think it can be pushed. Suppose we have two people, A and B, who have both committed burglary. A is a recidivist, and if she is convicted one more time, she would be taken to have forfeited the POLA. B is not a recidivist, but he is accused of having committed a more serious burglary. Given the nature of the recidivist premium A would face if convicted, they both face three years in prison. They both serve twelve months in PTD and then are convicted. A would have to serve an *additional* three years, but B would serve only two years. This seems unjust.

My response is to bite the bullet. *If* A would indeed have forfeited the POLA if convicted of one more burglary, then taking the objective point of view on her action and saying that she did, by that action, actually forfeit the POLA seems fair enough. If the state discovers that it does not have proof beyond a reasonable

[53] See Section 16.2.2.

doubt that she committed that extra burglary, then she would be owed compensation for her time in PTD. But if it can be proven that she did commit it, then she is no different from someone who has already been convicted of enough burglaries to have forfeited the POLA. None of this would apply to B, who does not have a prior record.

Finally, there are two extra reasons to think that this should not change state practice much. First, the only difference hypothetical forfeiture makes is that the state does not have to give credit for time served if A is convicted. But denying credit for time served may not be attractive, as it would cost the state more money to have to hold A for an extra year, and it might prefer not to pay it. Second, even if A could be held to have hypothetically forfeited the POLA, that does not mean that the state can simply put her in PTD. The state is entitled to hold people in PTD only if PTD is the LRA. It is likely to make a practical difference only in cases in which the LRA calls for using PTD and the defendant served more time pretrial than her sentence—cases in which, without forfeiture of the POLA, the state would owe her financial compensation even if convicted. In those cases, the state would want to invoke it. But those cases (a) should be rare and (b) would be no worse than a sliver of the current practice in which no one gets financial compensation for time served.

19
Limited Accountability: Intrinsic

19.1 Overview of Limited Accountability Issues

The previous three chapters explored the justifiability of incapacitating targeted restrictions on liberty based on either forfeiture of the presumption of law abidingness (POLA) or the duty to accept such restrictions. In this chapter and the next, I engage with the last two bases for incapacitating targeted restrictions on liberty, consistent with the dignity-respecting model. These two bases concern the two ways of having limited accountability. As I wrote in Chapter 1, accountability is a precondition for demanding the liberty that comes with the POLA.[1] In this chapter, I focus on shortcomings of intrinsic accountability; in the next, I focus on shortcomings of extrinsic accountability.

To the extent that a person lacks full autonomous capacity and is therefore unaccountable, he cannot claim as a matter of right the same freedom as those who are accountable. One way to understand this point is through the thought, grounded in the Autonomy Principle, that an agent has to own the impact he has on others. He can own it retrospectively by being accountable through punishment, penalty, and forfeiture; or, if he cannot be held accountable in those ways, then he has to own it prospectively with the ex ante loss of liberty as necessary to protect others from the harm he might impose.

Straightforward as this is at a very general level, it is worthwhile breaking the argument down into two steps: (1) identifying the implications of limited autonomy for accountability and (2) identifying the implications of limited accountability for claims to liberty. Moreover, it is important to distinguish the easy case, in which someone falls far short of the threshold for full autonomous capacity, from the more difficult case in which someone is near the fuzzy border of the threshold for full autonomous capacity. After addressing that distinction, I address four further issues. First, what sort of test for insanity as a defense to criminal or penal responsibility should be used: cognitive defect only, or should problems in control also matter? Second, how can an agent's struggles with self-control explain what should be done if he is a drug addict who poses not only a danger to himself but also is a burden on the community? Third, how should the

[1] See Section 1.3.1.

Punishment, Penalty, and Incapacitation. Alec Walen, Oxford University Press. © Oxford University Press 2026.
DOI: 10.1093/9780197523124.003.0019

state respond to psychopaths, especially those who have competent prudential abilities but who are blind to moral reasons? Fourth, what sort of compensation, if any, should those whose liberty is restricted in virtue of intrinsic lack of accountability receive?

19.2 Restricting Those Who Fall Far Short of the Threshold

In this section, I flesh out the two-step argument for restricting the liberty of those whose capacities for self-government fall far short of the threshold for full autonomous capacity.

The first step holds that if an agent lacks full moral autonomous capacity, then it would be morally unjust to hold her responsible, as fully autonomous people are held responsible. In extreme cases, this is obvious. Consider the perversity of punishing small children for things that a responsible adult may not do. Imagine a five-year-old girl who picks up a gun and shoots and kills another child. She may deserve blame in some sense, but blame for a young child should be different from blame for adults. It should not have the aim of communicating to her that it is appropriate for her to feel guilt, at least not as adults should feel it. She should not feel responsible to make serious amends, as an adult would, nor should she "suffer a two-pronged sort of psychological pain."[2]

With regard to the last point, it is helpful to take the two psychological prongs one at a time: It might be appropriate for her to feel some pain, grounded in the recognition that she has wronged others whom she should care about. But the empathic pain of recognizing that she has harmed others should be tempered by forgiveness, given that, at age five, she surely had only the most rudimentary sense that death is permanent and that others normally have a right not to be killed.

As for the "pain of recognizing that she is not as good a person as she should want to be," that should be even more tempered. The failure of a child to be as good as she should want to be is just a normal condition of childhood. Some self-directed pain and regret would be normal and desirable, a sign that the child has a conscience. But adults in her life should help her to realize that she is growing and changing and that this one failure, as monstrous as it may have been, is not an indication that she is deeply flawed as a person. Her personhood is too far from fixed at that age for the flaw to be viewed as deeply ingrained.[3]

[2] Section 6.1.

[3] Craig Agule points out that children blame each other much as adults do. "Blaming Kids." But even their blame should be tempered by the realization that they are learning and not yet fully responsible for what they do.

If she has a normal moral sensibility, she will probably carry *some* guilt for this act for the rest of her life. But as a five-year-old, she deserves primarily compassion and therapy to help her deal with the fact that she killed. She deserves no criminal censure or punishment, and as far as I know, no jurisdiction would impose censure and punishment on a five-year-old.[4] And the same point would apply to penal law. She should not be used to deter others, whether children or adults, from likewise harming others. She is not responsible enough for her actions. Additionally, she cannot forfeit the POLA because, in truth, she should not benefit from it in such a way that she could forfeit it. She should be in the care of responsible adults.

The same sort of point applies to the insane and those who are severely intellectually disabled.[5] For most adults, it is better to be treated as a responsible agent than to be treated as a dangerous animal, even if a special sort of animal with distinctly human needs. But it would be cruel to hold the insane or the severely mentally disabled responsible for significant wrongs that they cause. In both cases, the question is how best to show respect. For the autonomous, it is by treating them as accountable; for those who are far from reaching threshold autonomous capacity, it is by taking a caretaker's attitude toward them, as befitting a special animal that cannot take proper care of itself.[6]

The second step in the argument is that if an agent cannot be held responsible as a fully autonomous person, then she cannot demand the same freedoms as fully autonomous people. Recall that the Autonomy Principle holds that the space of rights must give us substantial freedom to lead our own lives, while also holding us accountable for our choices and the effects we have on others.[7] Freedom and accountability are two sides of the same coin. But I don't want to merely stipulate that point. There's a reason to accept it: If an agent cannot be constrained by an appreciation for the constraints of morality, or even just of prudence, then she will likely be a threat to others (if not also to herself).[8] If the

[4] By contrast, the adults who left the gun where a five-year-old could pick it up and fire it may deserve criminal censure if they lack a good justification or excuse.

[5] One might object that children should be treated differently, as they normally outgrow their non-autonomous status, but the insane and the severely intellectually disabled normally do not, and this creates a bigger, more stigmatizing problem for them. But what is the alternative? If they fall far short of threshold autonomous capacity, they cannot be treated as if they have forfeited, by various acts that reflect their condition, their liberty rights. Forfeiture should reflect the exercise of autonomous agency. See Section 14.1.1. Moreover, the restrictions that depend on lack of autonomous capacity should be lifted if that capacity is gained or recovered; the same is not true of forfeiture. The problem of stigma is a real social problem, but it must simply be addressed head on.

[6] See P.F. Strawson, "Freedom and Resentment," 9–10. To this extent, I am Strawsonian; I reject only the Strawsonian appeal to reactive attitudes as essential to blame. See Section 5.4. See also H. Morris, "Persons and Punishment," 483.

[7] See Section 3.2.

[8] If she does not pose a threat—perhaps because she has learned some basic life skills and reliably follows a safe routine—then she would not need to face any restrictions.

state were to accord her the full set of freedoms, despite her being a danger to others and not having autonomous self-control, that would unfairly impose on others the costs of the harms she might cause.

In the end, the permissibility of restricting those who lack full moral autonomy is, like that of restricting those with contagious diseases and those who forfeit the POLA, a matter of fairness. The Equality Principle requires fairness. Insofar as it would put an unfair burden on others to allow the unaccountable to retain the same liberty as the accountable, justice requires the state to restrict their liberty.[9]

One might object by insisting that there is an alternative: The state could either directly police the behavior of those who lack autonomous capacity or appoint guardians to do the policing. Either way, it would be up to the police/guardians to interfere and prevent those who lack autonomous capacity from unjustly harming others. But they need not restrict the behavior of those who lack autonomous capacity generally; they should wait until a threat is imminent and then restrict only as necessary to protect others from unjust harm.

There is something to this objection. It rests on the idea of using a least restrictive alternative (LRA), the same principle that I argued must be used in the forfeiture context.[10] Young children should be allowed to mingle with others, to socialize, learn, and play. Parents, teachers, and other guardians should restrict them only as necessary to preserve their own safety and the safety of others. But at the same time, we cannot suppose that parents and other guardians are obliged to *maximize* the freedom afforded to young children, while still ensuring that they do not harm themselves or unjustly harm others. For example, parents don't have to let their small children handle sharp knives to the maximal extent possible consistent with safety, hovering over them to ensure that nothing goes wrong. They can simply ensure that they don't have access to sharp knives.[11] Changing the example to adults who have been acquitted by virtue of insanity, the state does not have to allow them to live independently in their own homes with tax-funded guardians supervising them to ensure that they do not get into trouble. That is too demanding of the state and its resources. A fair allocation of burdens may permit the state to keep them in an institutional setting where they

[9] Duff commented on an earlier draft that these people cannot exercise the same liberty because "the liberty we allow the accountable is the liberty to exercise their rational capacities," which they lack. That comment reflects a complementary argument, but one I'm inclined to give less weight. It puts the weight of the argument in the strength of the liberty claims—treating those of agents with full autonomous capacity as stronger than those of agents who lack full autonomous capacity. By contrast, my argument is interpersonal, putting weight on patient claims not to be exposed to the risk of harm by the unaccountable. I think that provides a stronger, more categorical foundation for the difference.

[10] See Section 16.3.2.

[11] I made a similar point in Section 16.3.2.

can be monitored, as long as that setting is humane, stimulating, and provides therapy, if therapy holds out hope of doing some good for them.

19.3 Restricting Those with Borderline Autonomous Capacity

The interesting problems arise not with the extreme cases, but with the borderline cases. H.L.A. Hart described one set of people who fit this category: "unfortunate individuals who, through lack of intelligence, powers of concentration or memory, or through clumsiness could not" observe even the low standard of care of taking "very elementary precautions against harm."[12] Another set are normal teenagers, whose susceptibility to peer pressure, impulsiveness, lack of experience being in charge of themselves, and developing brains do not count as fully autonomous adults but are also no longer well below that threshold. If the individuals in question truly "could not" observe even the most basic standards of care, then we have the kind of case discussed in the last section, in which their liberty can be restricted in accordance with the LRA requirement. But if they could observe such standards, but doing so would be more difficult for them, maybe much more difficult, than for most adults, then we have the kind of case I'm concerned with in this section. For such cases, we confront a trilemma:

1. Allow them to exercise normal adult freedom and hold them accountable for what they do.
2. Allow them to exercise normal adult freedom but refrain from holding them accountable as normal adults—reducing their level of culpability or responsibility with full or partial excuses.
3. Impose targeted restrictions on their freedom but refrain from holding them accountable as normal adult, reducing their level of culpability or responsibility with full or partial excuses.[13]

The first option puts a larger burden on them than normal adults would have to bear if they are to avoid sanctions, but it respects them as agents. This could be seen as cruel, however, insofar as facing normal punishments and forfeiture would cause them either to have to devote more time and energy to avoiding punishment or forfeiture, or, if they exert normal levels of care, then to suffer more punishment and forfeitures than others. The second option reduces the burden on them as agents, but likely puts more costs on those whom they might

[12] *Punishment and Responsibility*, 154.

[13] Logically, there could be a fourth category, of targeted restrictions and full accountability, but there is no reason to think anyone should ever be treated in this way.

harm. The third option does more to protect others than the first two options, but often at a greater cost to the borderline agents. It is a greater cost to them than option 2, which gives them their freedom and does not make them fully responsible for its abuse. The question is whether it is a greater net cost to them than option 1. It is easier for them in the sense that they don't have to carry the extra burden of care, but in another way, it's a greater burden on them because it deprives them of the status of fully autonomous, responsible agents.

How should the state choose between these options? For teenagers—who I'll take to be young people between the ages of 10 and 17[14]—the third category generally fits best. The fact that they normally live under adult supervision implies that the default treatment for them is option 3: imposing targeted limits on their freedom. And the general philosophy of juvenile corrections is that it is not meant to punish; rather, it is meant to rehabilitate.[15] This too fits option 3. If a teenager commits a serious crime, at least in the United States, he may find himself "tried as an adult." Implausibly, this decision to try him as an adult is normally framed as a reflection of his unusual maturity. A better reframing of the decision to try a teenager "as an adult" is that if his act is especially wrongful, then his level of overall culpability must be high enough for him to deserve some level of punitive accountability. Even so, his punishment should be reduced to reflect his immaturity.[16] That too fits option 3.

This is complicated territory, however. There is no reason to think that freedom to live as an adult has to align perfectly with being held criminally responsible as an adult. Some teenagers may be granted the freedom to live, for all or almost all purposes, as an adult, and if they commit crimes, their treatment may then be properly handled with category 2 for some crimes and category 1 for others. Sorting out the details is beyond the scope of this book.

With regard to borderline adults, I think the state should start with the defeasible assumption that they are fully autonomous agents, while being ready to examine the evidence to the contrary, with an eye to balancing, on the one hand,

[14] There is nothing magical about those ages; it could be better to expand the range, contract it, shift it, or make it contingent on certain demonstrated capacities. I use that range just to help make my meaning concrete for the sake of the discussion in the text.

[15] As the U.K. Sentencing Council puts it: "For a child or young person the sentence should focus on rehabilitation where possible." "Sentencing Children and Young People," § 1.2. It continues: "[T]he primary purpose of the youth justice system is to encourage children and young people to take responsibility for their own actions and promote re-integration into society rather than to punish." § 1.4.

[16] In the United States, this reduction in punishment is enshrined in constitutional law in the most extreme cases. The death penalty may not be imposed on those who commit even the most serious crimes while less than eighteen years old (Atkins v. Va, 536 U.S. 304 (2002)), and those who do not commit a homicide crime cannot be sentenced to life in prison without the possibility of parole (Graham v. FL, 560 U.S. 48 (2010)). As I argued in Section 8.4, these are excessive punishments in any case, but the Supreme Court at least recognized that teenagers, simply in virtue of their youth, are less culpable than adults, all else equal.

the need to protect people (including the agents themselves) from these borderline autonomous agents with, on the other hand, compassion for the agents themselves. If they can take on the extra burden of being responsible for themselves, despite the greater-than-normal difficulty they have in controlling their actions or anticipating the results that might flow from them, it will normally be more respectful to take option 1 or 2, not option 3. The choice between those two options should then be determined by whether it would do much good to hold them accountable as normal adults. If it might tend to concentrate their minds and thereby protect others if they are held responsible as normal adults, then there is reason to do so. That reason then has to be weighed against the extra burden that it imposes on them. If, however, holding them accountable as normal adults would do less good than giving them a complete or partial excuse, then fairness to them calls for at least partially excusing them on the grounds of the greater difficulty they face in controlling themselves. This is a particularly appealing option if the situation they faced, which led them to act wrongly, is one that they are not likely to face often.[17] It may also be best to give those with borderline autonomous capacity a first-time partial or complete excuse, with a warning that they will have to move into option 1 or 3 if they repeat the offense.[18] Repeated offending could then be considered a basis for POLA forfeiture. But such forfeiture would not operate as it would for a person with normal autonomous capacity; it would be triggered more easily because the option of full accountability would be cruel.

Likewise, if borderline agents cannot be motivated by normal penalties to devote the extra energy it would take to control themselves, and if the situations in which they are likely to find themselves out of control are likely to recur, then it may be necessary to move from option 2 to option 3. As Hart helpfully put it, the kinds of people we have to worry about are those who are "unable to detect [and avoid], or extricate themselves... from[,] situations in which their disability may work harm."[19] Of course, the state should be willing to provide reasonable external supports—therapy, medication, education, counseling, employment opportunities—to help borderline agents operate as normal responsible agents[20]—a duty that would vary depending on the wealth of a given country.

[17] The logic here is a bit like the logic of the provocation defense, in two ways. First, there is a reason of compassion to reduce a defendant's culpability from murder to manslaughter if he chose to kill only because of a kind of provocation that he is unlikely to face again. Second, there is reason to treat the failure to resist provocation as, in a way, like the failure of a child: it is something which even a normal adult may not have confronted before in a way that would make it reasonable to say: "You should have been prepared to handle yourself better in such a situation."

[18] I'm grateful to Madeleine Yashar for making this case to me in the context of people with bipolar disorder, who commit crimes while manic.

[19] *Punishment and Responsibility*, 155.

[20] See P. Robinson, "Punishing Dangerousness," 1447 ("a detainee should be entitled to treatment if it can reduce the length or intrusiveness of the restraint").

But even if the state does a good job of providing those supports, there will be some who cannot reliably avoid wronging others. It may be fair to remove from them at least some of the freedom enjoyed by fully autonomous adults.[21]

19.4 Problems with Control and Cognition

Recall the case of Leroy Hendricks, who admitted in a jury trial "that when he 'get[s] stressed out,' he 'can't control the urge' to molest children."[22] Under Kansas law, upheld by the U.S. Supreme Court, he was sentenced to be confined in a state "security hospital." I discussed the case, in Chapter 16, under the guise of a forfeiture case, supposing that his crime of "taking 'indecent liberties' with two 13-year-old boys,"[23] sufficed to forfeit the POLA. But another way one might read his situation is as someone whose ability to control himself fell short of the threshold for autonomous capacity.[24]

This idea connects to one prong of the insanity defense proposed by the Model Penal Code: lacking "substantial capacity . . . to conform his conduct to the requirements of law."[25] But this control prong is controversial, and many jurisdictions reject it, retaining only the cognitive prong, referring to the defendant's inability to appreciate the wrongfulness of her conduct.[26] Thus, I think it is important to take a moment to review the two sides of that debate.

In defense of the control prong, Michael Corrado has argued that "the defining characteristic of a mental condition that moves its victim from the category of the sane to the category of the legally insane is that it deprives her of the ability to choose to conform her behavior to the law."[27] He thinks failures of reason and awareness of wrongfulness can do that, but he adds the idea that

[21] For a tragic illustration of what can go wrong if the state does not put a person in category 3 when it should, see the case of Jordan Neely. He "had been arrested more than three dozen times, largely for minor transgressions, though in four cases for punching people, twice in the subway. He was on a list maintained by the city of the 50 homeless people in greatest need of urgent assistance." Before his death, he was arrested, spent 15 months in jail, and then was sent "to a treatment facility, where he was to remain for 15 months and stay drug-free." But he was released after thirteen days and then ended up yelling on the subway: "I don't have food. I don't have a drink. I'm fed up. . . I don't mind going to jail and getting life in prison. I'm ready to die." He was then subdued by another passenger, who put him in a chokehold, as a result of which he died. D. French, "When the Rule of Law Fails Us."

[22] Kansas v. Hendricks, 521 U.S. 346, 355 (1997), discussed in Section 16.2.3.

[23] Ibid.

[24] If this were the right way to read his case, however, then he should not have been convicted of crimes driven by those urges.

[25] Model Penal Code, § 4.01 (1).

[26] Michael Corrado notes that by his count, "thirty states, in 1980, had two-prong insanity rules, with both cognitive and volitional prongs. . . By 2004, only fifteen states still had the two-prong test, and thirty had the one-prong, purely cognitive test." "Responsibility and Control," 61–62.

[27] "The Case for a Purely Volitional Insanity Defense," 509.

mental illness straightforwardly excuses when it deprives an agent "of the ability to act in accordance with her best judgment."[28]

In response to this sort of thought, Stephen Morse has argued two points. First, he claims that "we lack operationalized tests to accurately identify lack of capacity" for self-control.[29] Second, he adds that "for all cases in which a control test may seem required, the reason can be better characterized as a rationality defect because control difficulties flow from lack of access to the good reasons not to act in the wrong way."[30]

My own sense is that Morse's position is too extreme. Taking his second claim first, the idea that lack of control can always be understood in terms of defective rationality—"the failure to access good reasons to act"—seems to me to get the causation backward, at least in some cases. As Mark Muraven and Roy Baumeister put it: "[S]elf-control operates like a muscle or strength. More precisely, controlling one's own behavior requires the expenditure of some inner, limited resource that is depleted afterward."[31] Assuming that is right, then in at least some cases the causal arrow works the other way from the way Morse thinks: People may lose their ability to control their impulses and that may lead to a rationalization of what they have done.[32] And turning to Morse's first claim, regarding tests for lack of control, Muraven and Baumeister also claim that it is possible to make "fairly specific predictions . . . with respect to self-control failure."[33] That suggests that the measurement problem is not as serious as Morse suggests either.

One might think that the relevant test for lack of control is undeterrability. As Christopher Slobogin writes: "the core trait that normatively distinguishes the dangerous person who may be preventively detained from the dangerous person who may not be is imperviousness to criminal punishment, or what I shall call undeterrability."[34] But this is not the relevant test. An agent can be undeterrable because she is more committed to a cause than to any other good on the basis of which she might be deterred. Such a person might be a fully autonomous agent, fully in control of her actions and eligible for punishment or penalty if she acts wrongly.

With this clarification, I assert that the law should be able to use both a cognitive and a control basis for deciding that people are so lacking in autonomous capacity as to be subject to limitations on their liberty.

[28] Ibid.
[29] "Mental Disorder and Criminal Law," 893.
[30] Ibid.
[31] "Self-Regulation and Depletion of Limited Resources," 247.
[32] It is also a mistake to think that a person who can control their impulses in some contexts can do so in others. See V. Tadros, "Craving and Control."
[33] Ibid.
[34] "A Jurisprudence of Dangerousness," 4.

19.5 How to Respond to Drug Addiction

Drug addiction provides a special case of limited control that can justify incapacitating targeted restrictions on liberty not based on forfeiture, but on lack of autonomous control. I argue for this proposition with reference to the 2024 law in Oregon, which recriminalized drug possession (the RDP).[35] The argument holds, in brief, that Oregon is wrong to treat drug possession as a crime, but that it is right to impose consequences on addicts who use drugs. These should be understood as operating within a different framework, however; the framework of rewards and sanctions meant to affect the behavior of people who do not operate as fully autonomous beings.

Oregon's prior law, Measure 110, "decriminalized small amounts of hard drugs, making possession punishable only by a fine." The RDP, by contrast, creates a misdemeanor for which offenders "would initially face an 18-month probation period, with the possibility of up to 30 days in jail if they violate their probation or up to six months for [a] more serious violation. Offenders could be released from jail early to attend drug treatment." Counties would also have the option to set up a "deflection" program, which "would give law enforcement the option to refer a person to a behavioral health and treatment program instead of sending them into the court system."

The first question I want to ask about the RDP is: Could this make sense as a criminal law? For it to make sense as a criminal law, the behavior would have to be wrong.[36] I think there is a good three-pronged case for it being wrong. First, people using illegal drugs like methamphetamines, heroin, and especially fentanyl are a danger to themselves, which imposes a tax on others, as they often need to be rescued from their own actions. Second, addicts tend to slip into joblessness and homelessness, and as they do so, they become a threatening and disturbing presence for others. Third, these problems give the state a reason to ban these drugs, and once banned, people have a reason to respect this law as a reasonable regulation.[37] Together, these three reasons make for a plausible case that using these drugs is a public wrong that could be the basis for a criminal charge.[38]

The case for culpability, however, is much harder. One can make the case that the initial choice to use drugs, before addiction set in, was culpable. But experimenting with illegal substances is at best a proxy crime with low culpability. Given that the ultimate harm of addiction is often relatively low and that

[35] A. Macuk, "Gov. Kotek Signs Bill Overhauling Measure 110." All further quotes in this and the next paragraph come from the same article.

[36] See Section 5.1 on the requirement of culpability and Section 5.3 on the connection between culpability and wrongdoing.

[37] See Section 5.5.2 on the public wrong of failing to respect reasonable regulations.

[38] For a much more skeptical view of drug criminalization, see D. Husak, *Overcriminalization*, 164–170.

many people can break the law without bringing it about, the culpability is on the low end even for proxy crimes. And given how many people experiment with drugs, problems of selective enforcement are a real danger. Still, the RDP's punishments are relatively light, so it could conceivably be justified as a criminal law that targets those who are experimenting with hard drugs.

The problem is that that is not the target audience for the law. Its target audience is addicts, the ones who slip into joblessness and homelessness, and as they do so, become a threatening and disturbing presence for others. So we come then to the difficult question of how to think about addiction. I do not want to suggest that addiction deprives addicts of rational agency altogether and thus makes them fit subjects for deprivation of liberty on the ground of generally limited accountability. I think that if an addict robs or assaults someone to get the drugs he wants, or the money for the drugs he wants, he can still be blamed and criminally prosecuted. But I do want to argue that an addict is excused when it comes to taking the drugs to which he is addicted. How can I make that distinction? Ultimately, it's a question of when blame is appropriate. I think a stern moral judgment is appropriate if an addict intentionally harms others to satisfy his addiction, but I think compassion calls for treating him as non-responsible when it comes to satisfying the addiction itself.

I make this last point following the lead of Keith Humphreys, who offers the following explanation for why addicts continue to take drugs, despite the harm it causes them.[39] If you ask them why they take drugs:

> [T]he answer seems to be, "Well, I can't think of a reason why not. I might as well." "Well, you won't live as long." "Well, I don't expect to live that long." "You won't do well in your brilliant career." "I don't have a brilliant career." "You won't enjoy your fabulous house." "I don't have a fabulous house." And that's a reason I think it's easy or it should be easy to have some sympathy. We all don't have the same set of rewards to choose from. Rewards any neuroscientists would tell you are judged relative to each other. We don't just make judgments over good, bad, but we do a lot of this is better than that. So as you pull rewards out of an environment, yeah, drugs become relatively more appealing.

Add to that insight the following two claims: First, "If somebody is out on the street with an addiction, it's not believable that they are going to check in once a week for an hour with a therapist, because their lives aren't that organized." Second, "remove all pressure," and it's "a very rare person" who "will spontaneously say, 'OK, I really want to make a change, and I'll come in.'"

[39] Humphreys is a professor of Psychiatry and Behavioral Sciences at Stanford University. All quotes from Humphreys are taken from "This Is a Very Weird Moment in the History of Drug Laws."

Assuming these claims are true, they have two implications. First, they reinforce the idea that the choice of an addict, one whose life has already fallen apart, to continue to abuse drugs should be excused from criminal liability. Second, they suggest that if a state wants people who are addicted to hard drugs to stop using them, it has to provide an external incentive for them to get off the drugs. This should not be a blaming incentive. Nor should it be designed as a deterrent to others. The point is simply to provide an incentive to the individual addict. And the incentive should be accompanied by a safe and supportive environment in which to get off the drugs.

One may want to object that what addicts need is harm reduction treatment, not outside pressure in the form of an "external incentive." But I believe, following Humphreys, that this is a mistake. As he puts it: People don't tend to spontaneously seek out help getting over their addictions because addiction is not like "chronic pain or depression." Rather, "Drug use feels in the short term incredibly good." Addicts "are ambivalent about giving that up in a way no one with chronic pain is ambivalent about giving up chronic pain." To get over their addiction, they need external pressure. The problem is figuring out how to provide that pressure without unjustly holding them accountable when they are excused.

One might wonder whether the penal law could be a good tool to support the external pressure dimension of getting addicts off drugs. One might think it is an exception to the rule that penal violations are all based on proxy crimes[40]—an exception based on the thought that there should be no proxy *crime* here, at least not when dealing with the choices of addicts. But this cannot be an exceptional basis for penal law's penalties because addicts' choices to use are insufficiently free to make them liable to being used to deter other addicts. Moreover, it is not as if one addict is likely to change his behavior because of what he sees happening to another addict. If he's reached the point where his life has already substantially fallen apart, he has demonstrated a strong tendency to ignore all sorts of warning signs. He should suffer sanctions for continued use, but these should not be taken to be penal law sanctions.

What about forfeiture of the POLA? Could we take addiction to forfeit that? It will not suffice for general POLA forfeiture. It is not the kind of serious crime that would ground general POLA forfeiture. And while it often indicates recidivist lawbreaking with regard to drug laws, those are such low culpability offenses that, again, general POLA forfeiture cannot be based on it. Nor could the state justify specific forfeiture of a particular right the addict might otherwise have enjoyed. It is not as if most addicts have abused their right to legally enjoy drugs.

40 See Section 13.5.

Some may have done so, if the local law, like Oregon's Measure 110, allowed legal drug use. But that's irrelevant. Denying them that limited right won't help. They need to be held accountable for their ongoing abuse of the drug, but in a way that does not fit the model of criminal or penal law.

Some inspiration for the right model can be drawn from the idea of forfeiture, however, as it might help us to understand how to assess the finding of the lack of capacity. Lack of capacity comes in degrees. Forfeiture might make sense when confronted with an addict whose life has not (yet) fallen apart. He might not be over the threshold for loss of autonomous capacity with regard to his drug use. But his drug use might allow the state to treat him as if he has forfeited not the POLA, but the presumption of autonomous capacity when it comes to his drug use. That would allow the state to treat him as it would treat the addict whose life has already mostly fallen apart and who has thereby demonstrated a lack of autonomous capacity with regard to his drug use.

This still leaves the question: How should we understand what the state may justifiably do to addicts when it comes to applying the external pressure necessary for them to stop using drugs? The answer is that they should be treated like children in respect of their addiction. They should be given penalties for indulgence and rewards (in terms of restored independence or freedom) for ongoing abstinence. Doing so would help to recalibrate their own incentive structure. But this is to be done, again, not to make an example of them for the sake of deterrence, nor to blame them. It is to be done paternalistically, to heal them.

One might worry that this licenses too much in the way of paternalistic intervention. Could one not say the same, for example, about people struggling with morbid obesity? The answer, I think, is that morbid obesity and other forms of unhealthy behavior do not pose as great a burden on others. The intervention in the case of drug abuse is not based solely on paternalism; it is based as well on the thought that the addict is engaged in wrongdoing that tends to substantially impact others in a way that the state has an interest in regulating, but this wrongdoing occurs in a context in which the state also cannot justly use the criminal law or penal law to enforce these regulations.[41]

In sum, the RDP is misframed as re-*criminalizing* drug possession. Addicts should not face "probation" or "jail time" like those who commit legitimate misdemeanors. But the possibility of involuntary commitment, within the framework of mental health, does make sense. As Humphreys notes, "Oregon's new policy mix if implemented properly . . . would be a very good one." I would

[41] One might point out that morbid obesity also imposes a tax on others, because it leads to health problems that others will, to some extent, have to help pay for. Even so, it does not tend to be nearly as socially disruptive as addiction to hard drugs. The difference is only of degree, but it is also a large enough degree to justify drawing a line between the two.

add only this friendly amendment: If an addict can demonstrate sufficient recovery, then she should be released to lead her life, just as any person who suffered from and then recovered from a serious mental illness should be free to lead her life, without a criminal or penal law record, and without any forfeiture of the POLA.

19.6 How to Respond to Psychopaths

There is one last category of people that needs to be considered to have a fairly complete treatment of people who lack full autonomous capacity: those who lack, in particular, the capacity to engage in moral reasoning, that is, psychopaths. It's not quite right to say that they cannot engage in moral reasoning at all. They can understand the logic of moral discourse as well as they can understand any other logic. But it seems to be the case, at least for extreme psychopaths—and all scholars in the field seem to agree that psychopathy occurs on a continuum—that moral discourse is just empty talk, a kind of Jabberwocky-like manipulation of language without meaning. Insofar as that's true, the question is: What can justifiably be done to them?

I will argue that psychopaths should not be held criminally liable because blame is misdirected if directed toward them. I will argue, however, that they can reasonably be held liable in a sort of criminal-law-light way. That is, they can be held to have a debt that they owe to the rest of society for the rights they enjoy. This cannot be framed as a "guilt-debt" because they cannot feel guilt. But they still owe compensation for the non-justified, not-excused wrongs they commit. The magnitude of their wrongdoing remains relevant to the compensation they owe society. In addition, mental element terms are relevant to determining what they can be held responsible for doing, just as such terms are relevant to the fairness of penalties. This way of responding to psychopaths may seem very much like the penal law. But as it presumes that they have a debt that the state has a pro tanto duty to collect, and insofar as the proper penalty tracks the magnitude of the wrong they commit, it is better seen as a form of deserved punishment-light rather than a form of penalty.

Importantly, many psychopaths also seem to be incapable of normal prudential reasoning. Insofar as their incapacity is more general than moral blindness, they may be appropriately treated like young children.

19.6.1 Are Psychopaths Accountable?

I want to start with the last point: that psychopaths might have a more general normative incapacity. Paul Litton has argued that psychopaths have a "general[ly] diminished capacity for rational self-governance."[42] They have, he claims, "no evaluative standards, not even ones related to the pursuit of excitement and pleasure."[43] He admits that they "feel and express frustration and anger . . . when they fail to satisfy their desires. . . ."[44] But he notes that "there is a significant difference between feeling frustration and anger per se, . . . and experiencing reactive emotions, such as remorse and shame, to which we are prone in virtue of holding ourselves to evaluative standards."[45]

Reinforcing the point that their normative disability is quite general, Litton claims that they "often express that they have goals, but show that they do not understand what is entailed by having . . . a goal. . . ."[46] Rather, their lifestyle is "chronically unstable and aimless; they tend to live day-to-day and to change their plans frequently; and do not show much concern about how little they have done with their lives."[47] In sum, "much of their behavior is based on whim."[48] Or, as David Shoemaker puts it, they are "wildly imprudent."[49] And this imprudence manifests in a recidivism rate, within a year of release from jail or prison, that is three times higher than for non-psychopaths, and four times higher with regard to violent acts.[50] This collection of characteristics suggests that extreme psychopaths should be treated like young children rather than as accountable adults.

Morse, however, takes a different view of psychopaths. He believes Litton's "argument understates the psychopath's capacity for some evaluative standards and reactive emotions."[51] He believes that their distinctive feature is an inability to engage rationally "when moral concern and respect for others is in question."[52]

The breadth of psychopaths' incapacity is fundamentally an empirical question, and it is one regarding which I have no expertise. I will say, however, that I think Morse is wrong to treat the disagreement as merely a matter of "empirical quibbles."[53] Rather, I think that insofar as Litton's broader view is correct, it provides a strong basis for treating extreme psychopaths as non-responsible individuals whose liberty can be restricted much as we can restrict the liberty of young children. By contrast, insofar as Morse is correct and there are psychopaths who are generally competent at framing and pursuing goals, but

[42] "Responsibility Status of the Psychopath," 375.
[43] Ibid., 377.
[44] Ibid., 378.
[45] Ibid., 379.
[46] Ibid., 381.
[47] Ibid., 380 (internal quotation marks omitted).
[48] Ibid., 383.
[49] "Disordered, Disabled, Disregarded, Dismissed," 50.
[50] "Responsibility Status of the Psychopath," 382.
[51] "Psychopathy and Criminal Responsibility," 209.
[52] Ibid., 208.
[53] Ibid.

who simply cannot fathom moral claims as providing reasons to act, then the relevant moral issue they raise is that there seems to be something amiss in blaming, and therefore in punishing, them.

For the remainder of this section, I will assume that Morse is correct and that there are a non-trivial number of psychopaths who are extremely disabled in terms of moral reasoning, but who are competent enough with regard to prudential self-governance not to be treated as children. The question is: What follows from their being morally incompetent?

19.6.2 Can Psychopaths Be Morally Blamed?

For the sake of this discussion, I adopt an analogy that I get from Morse: that blaming a psychopath for not responding to moral reasons is like blaming a person who is color blind for failing to recognize that certain colors go well together and that others do not.[54] Putting aside the issue of the different notions of blame that are implied in the two contexts—morality and aesthetics—I think the underlying analogy is strong. Those who are color blind can learn to rely on others or on certain physical cues to tell what colors things have and what colors work well together. But if they were born color blind, the idea of colors that go well together and those that don't will never have anything other than an abstract sort of meaning to them, grounded, at best, in certain analogies. They can appreciate its normative significance as something that matters only because others will respond to different combinations in different ways. That is, I think, a strong analogy for how extreme psychopaths, who nonetheless understand normative reasoning in a more general sense, must view moral reasons. These are things that they can learn to respond to only by indirectly paying attention to contextual cues and what others tell them, and that matter to them only insofar as they care, for contingent, prudential reasons, about how these things matter to others.[55]

That said, I don't want to simply stipulate that it is morally inappropriate to blame psychopaths when they wrong others. Indeed, there are three views in the literature that support blaming psychopaths despite their moral "color blindness." First, there's T.M. Scanlon's view that they can be blamed because blame is fundamentally a matter of distancing oneself from another whose behavior has impaired the relationship.[56] My view of blame, as conveying the appropriateness

[54] As Morse puts it: "It is as if they are color blind to moral concerns." Ibid., 209.

[55] For an insightful first-person account of what it is like to be a high-functioning sociopath, with meaningful relationships, see D. Marchese, "What It's Like to Be a Sociopath." As for the difference between sociopaths and psychopaths, I won't try to mark it. Neither is a term used in the latest *Diagnostic and Statistical Manual of Mental Disorders.* The current term of art is antisocial personality disorder. See WebMD, "How Sociopaths and Psychopaths Are Different."

[56] *Moral Dimensions*, ch. 4.

of guilt,[57] is fundamentally different, however, so I put Scanlon's view to one side.[58]

Second, there's the view, taken by Matthew Talbert and Angela Smith, that blame is communicative, but not essentially aimed at communication *to* the wrongdoer. In Talbert's view, blame can be appropriate because it helps a victim to affirm and reinforce her moral standing.[59] Smith's view is fundamentally similar, except that it emphasizes that the affirmation and reinforcement are meant to communicate the moral standing of the victim to the community.[60] In both of their views, the wrongdoer's ability to understand and accept blame is not essential to the appropriateness of blaming.

I think there are two fundamental problems with their views.[61] The first problem, as emphasized by Gary Watson, is that these views seem to elide the distinction between those who almost certainly *will* not be moved by proper moral considerations (such as Nazi prison camp guards), on the one hand, and those who almost certainly *cannot* be moved by proper moral considerations (psychopaths), on the other hand.[62]

> Occasionally a Nazi or a Mafioso or white supremacist makes a genuine return to the moral point of view. I say "return" because the moral changes in question depend upon suppressed or partial or partitioned moral sensibilities that are somehow reengaged or extended—sensibilities involving an at least selective concern for some moral values, virtues and for some individuals. In contrast, I am supposing, there is nothing to which to return in psychopaths.[63]

I think Watson's distinction is a deep one. And it helps contain the threat that might otherwise be posed to the idea of criminal blame if those who predictably *will* not accept it were somehow excluded from being blameworthy. We are talking only about the relatively small percentage of the population who suffer from extreme forms of psychopathy.[64]

[57] See Section 6.1.

[58] See Section 16.3, n. 73. Susan Wolf's criticism of Scanlon's account of blame seems to be the most well known. See "Blame, Italian Style." But I reject it too, on the ground that it is too focused on the reactive emotion of anger. I think we can blame with cool judgment, but at the same time expect and demand a kind of emotional *response* from the person blamed: guilt. See Section 6.1.

[59] "Moral Competence, Moral Blame, and Protest," 18–19.

[60] "Moral Blame and Moral Protest," 56.

[61] Coleen Macnamara emphasizes another objection, having to do with the way the emotions felt by those who blame are essentially directed at the wrongdoer. "Blame, Communication, and Moral Agency." As it presupposes the kind of Strawsonian, reactive attitudes account of blame that I reject, I do not engage with this argument.

[62] The elision is clearly present in Talbert's view; its influence on Smith's thought is not clear.

[63] "The Trouble with Psychopaths," 318.

[64] According to Watson, "[a]pproximately 1 percent of the general population worldwide are thought to be psychopathic." Ibid., 307. Presumably a smaller percentage still are extreme

Second, and more fundamentally, the views of Talbert and Smith fail to take sufficiently seriously the idea of an excuse. Consider those who are excused for their wrongful actions by reason of insanity, say because they believe God is directing them to do what they do. Or consider again the case of a small child who found a gun and shot and killed another. I assume that Talber and Smith would recognize that blame is inappropriate in those sorts of cases. If psychopaths are morally color blind, and if that excuses in an analogous way, then it would be equally inappropriate to express *blame* as a way of expressing or reinforcing the moral status of their victims. One can reinforce their status without blaming anyone.

The third way to support blaming psychopaths, despite their moral color blindness, appeals to the good consequences of doing so. Marion Godman and Anneli Jefferson offer this response to Morse: blaming and punishing prudentially competent psychopaths "might affect [their] social and moral behaviour over time. . . ."[65] As a matter of causal efficacy, I take it that they are correct. The problem is not that blame and punishment would be pointless from a consequentialist point of view. The problem is that it seems morally perverse to blame and punish people who are not blameworthy, even if doing so would have good consequences. Godman and Jefferson are sensitive to this worry and offer up the thought that psychopaths might have "some level of desert" when it comes to blame and punishment for their wrongful actions: "for this it may be sufficient that psychopaths understand what the rules and the sanctions are. . . ."[66] The question is: Can being aware of the fact that the law bans what they contemplate doing, and that it declares that such acts will be punished, suffice to ground their punishment if they choose to do it anyway? My answer is yes and no.

19.6.3 Punishment-light for Psychopaths

I think knowingly choosing to flout the law cannot, by itself, make prudentially competent psychopaths blameworthy. The reason is straightforward, given my account of the function of blame. Blame functions as the normative signal that guilt is the appropriate response for the agent who acted wrongly to have. Psychopaths are incapable of feeling guilt. So it cannot be fitting to send that signal to them. It's like telling the color-blind that they should *feel* the jarring effect of certain color combinations. That's not a reasonable thing to tell such a

psychopaths with *no* moral sensibilities. And a smaller portion still are nonetheless minimally competent with prudential reasoning.

[65] "On Blaming and Punishing Psychopaths," 138. Godman and Jefferson also offer a norm-reinforcing view.
[66] Ibid., 135.

person, because, in this context at least, ought implies can. It cannot be true that one should do what one cannot do.[67]

But there's something right in what Godman and Jefferson say about the appropriateness of the law holding prudentially competent psychopaths responsible. As prudentially competent beings, it's fair to hold them responsible for their choices. Moreover, as generally competent prudential agents, they move about in the space of rights. They may not feel the pull of moral reasons to respect the rights of others, but they understand how the space of rights can be manipulated and used by agents, themselves, and others, for their ends. They know how to call in a debt, and they know how to pay debts to avoid unwanted consequences. Given that level of competence, it makes sense to say that they incur a debt to society when they unjustly break the law, without an excuse. And society can justly collect that debt from them using the same schedule of punishments that is used for autonomous moral agents. Moreover, society has a pro tanto duty to do so, just as it has a pro tanto duty to collect the guilt-debt of competent moral agents.[68]

If the state strips away the censure from punishment, but still treats it as a debt that is due, we get punishment-light.[69] And if inflicting punishment-light will achieve, as Godman and Jefferson put it, "desirable results for the individual with psychopathy and for society at large,"[70] then it seems appropriate to impose such punishment on them for their wrongful, illegal, unexcused actions. One might worry that punishment-light, differing from punishment only in that it lacks official censure, will mostly come across simply as punishment. And one might then worry that the blaming aspects of punishment will inappropriately be present. But the unintended message of blame will fall on deaf ears (or color-blind eyes) and thus will not unjustly harm psychopaths on whom it is meted out. More subtle problems may arise, for example, at the stage of parole hearings. It would be inappropriate to ask psychopaths if they accept their guilt. But an analog question could be asked without undue prejudice: "Do you understand why you have been punished and accept that you have good reason for not breaking the law in this or similarly significant ways again?"

One might still wonder if we are obliged to treat psychopaths with the sort of moral respect that comes with punishment, which is aimed at mutual reconciliation. As Watson puts it, psychopaths are unable "to engage with others

[67] As Stephen White puts it, psychopaths "are beyond the reach of *punishment* (where genuine punishment requires that guilt and remorse be *justified* even for the subjects themselves)...." *The Unity of the Self*, 204.

[68] See Section 6.4.

[69] Punishment-light should not be confused with light punishment. The magnitude of the sanction would presumably be the same as for a morally competent agent who committed the same crime, with the same mens rea, in the same circumstances.

[70] "On Blaming and Punishing Psychopaths," 138.

as individuals with the standing to object when their interests and concerns are disregarded as unimportant."[71] He concludes that "[t]heir 'disorder' therefore disqualifies them as members of the moral community."[72] If they are not members of the moral community, why treat them within a framework designed to reinforce that community?

The answer I find most compelling here has four parts, which are grounded in my discussion of rights in Chapter 3. First, even if they are not part of the moral community as agents who recognize rights as morally binding, the space of rights has room for beings who do not themselves recognize rights. If animals have rights—and I think they do[73]—then psychopaths have rights. Moreover, if they are prudentially competent, then they know how to navigate the space of rights just like citizens in the republic of rights. They can play the role of a member of the community, and they have an interest in being free to do so.

Second, their interests still matter qua interests that rights would respect.[74] Moreover, unlike animals, psychopaths with prudential planning ability have second-order interests in how their lives go. Therefore, they have interests not only in enjoying property, but in controlling it. That includes an interest in having the kinds of moral powers that moral agents have: the power to trade, to promise, to consent, to waive, and so on. They may not recognize these moves as *morally* significant; they may not see anything other than a prudential reason to respect the property of others or the promises they have made. But they may be able to bring themselves to respect the rights of others as part of a reciprocal "deal," as long as they expect that this will help ensure that others allow them to control property in ways that matter to their own plans.

Third, as noted at the beginning of this section, psychopathy comes in degrees. Some people with psychopathic tendencies may also have some ability to recognize moral reasons as reasons for them. Those people are moral agents who simply suffer a deficit of moral understanding or motivation. Still, as moral agents, they are part of the moral community. Unless the reasons to treat extreme psychopaths as outside the community, the rest of this argument notwithstanding, were strong, and the costs of including them were high, we should err on the side of treating people who might be members of the moral community as members. As Watson writes: "Given the messiness of psychopathic agency, and our limited epistemic position, it is difficult in real life to be confident that we can avoid this mistake. Therefore, a wise public policy will proceed by practical faith... attempting to err in the right direction."[75]

71 "The Trouble with Psychopaths," 308–309.
72 Ibid., 309. See also S. Morse, "Psychopathy and Criminal Responsibility," 209.
73 See Sections 1.3.1, 3.2, and 14.1.1.
74 For a subtle account of the morality of showing psychopaths respect even while they cannot reciprocate, see D. Shoemaker, "Disordered, Disabled, Disregarded, Dismissed."
75 "The Trouble with Psychopaths," 323.

Fourth, and finally, the costs of respecting psychopaths as holders of rights, even when they are not part of the moral community, are not especially high. There is reason to think that psychopathy develops early in childhood, so a society that is paying attention can try to treat and respond carefully to them before they become a great danger to others.[76] If individuals seem to be extremely psychopathic and broadly unable to understand normative reasoning, their liberty can be constrained with the LRA to keep them and others safe. If they seem to be extremely psychopathic but prudentially competent, then they can be held responsible through the use of criminal-law-light. That will allow for punishments that might specifically deter them, for collecting their social debt so that they can remain community members in good standing, and for forfeiture in case the penal law or POLA forfeiture is called for. And insofar as they seem to be merely on the spectrum of psychopathy, then they can be treated as moral agents with borderline autonomous capacity, as discussed in Section 19.1.2.

19.7 Compensation and State Blame

If an agent is deprived of the liberty that others normally enjoy because of lack of intrinsic accountability, should he receive compensation? The short answer is no. His liberty can justifiably be limited because he would otherwise be a threat to others, and he has no right to be that sort of threat. Threats ought to bear the burden of being a threat; they have no right to compensation.[77] They have a right to care in virtue of the Welfare Principle, but not compensation.

But what about people who lack intrinsic accountability because the state has caused them to lack the relevant abilities? Perhaps it has taken actions that have, for example, created toxic environmental damage that caused neurological damage. Or perhaps it stood by too passively, not providing the care it should have provided, allowing others to abuse them and damage their capacity for autonomous agency.

This is a large topic beyond the scope of this book. But I will end this chapter with a few thoughts. First, it is unclear what good "compensation" can do for someone lacking autonomous capacity. Unlike cases in which a person has been held in pretrial detention, the capacity to benefit from compensation is radically limited for someone who suffers permanent brain damage. It may be that all that can meaningfully be done for him is to provide him with good care.

Second, should the state offer care to those who are owed compensation for their lack of autonomous capacity that is much greater than it offers those whose

[76] See "On Blaming and Punishing Psychopaths," 137.
[77] See Section 17.1.

deficits seem to be less traceable to state action? Perhaps for tort-like reasons. But unless the state has either had a direct and dominant causal role in causing their problems or a more attenuated role that involved culpable action, then mere causal responsibility seems inadequate to ground a duty to offer greater care to some of those who are in need than others. All citizens of a state who cannot provide well for themselves should have a claim on the state for reasonable amounts of support necessary to lead a decent life.

Third, there will, of course, be trade-offs. Insofar as the state helps make life more comfortable for those who fall short of threshold autonomous capacities, it may be less able to provide for other goods like education, healthcare, infrastructure, and so on. It is beyond the scope of this project to figure out how to balance such considerations,[78] but an equitable balance should guide policy in this area.

[78] I do, however, return to this topic in Section 20.2.

20

Limited Accountability: Extrinsic

20.1 Why Extrinsic Accountability Matters

Accountability, as I argued in Chapter 19, is a precondition for enjoying the presumption of law abidingness (POLA). I add here that accountability is a two-way relationship: being intrinsically accountable, and being in a relationship with others who can hold one to account. If the latter can't do their job, given the resources they are obliged to apply to it, then the accountability relationship does not exist. And if accountability does not exist, then the liberties that are normally taken for granted in a liberal society can be restricted as necessary to provide for a fair balance of the interests at stake.

It might seem that this idea is structurally equivalent to threshold deontology. Threshold deontology, in my understanding of the idea, applies most straightforwardly when the welfare interests of a collection of people are so weighty that it seems morally implausible to say that the rights of others must be respected.[1] In a system of rights like mine, in which rights arise from the balance of competing claims,[2] it's not immediately clear why we should ever say that *rights* may be disrespected, as opposed to saying that in extreme conditions people who otherwise would have rights lack them. But framing threshold deontology in terms of conditions in which certain people simply lack rights loses something important. Threshold deontology is not like a normal case in which someone's claim is outweighed by competing claims. It arises when someone has a right, but the categorical imperative to respect rights gives way. How can that happen? On my view of rights, it can happen because the Autonomy Principle sets limits on what can be demanded of or done to a person. It holds that the space of rights cannot demand that an agent treat herself primarily or fundamentally as a tool for the welfare of others.[3] By extension, there are limits on the extent to which costs can be imposed on a person who is being used as a means without waiving or forfeiting her right to be so used.[4] But the demands of the Welfare Principle have no limit; as the number in need and the magnitude of their need grow, there may

[1] For a classic statement of threshold deontology, see Larry Alexander, "Deontology at the Threshold." For my critique and my own views on the topic, see "Deontology in Graphs," § VII.
[2] See Section 3.3.1.
[3] See *The Mechanics of Claims*, 47.
[4] See Section 3.5.

Punishment, Penalty, and Incapacitation. Alec Walen, Oxford University Press. © Oxford University Press 2026.
DOI: 10.1093/9780197523124.003.0020

come a point—hard to describe where—after which it seems morally implausible that the right not to be used as a means sets what is ultimately morally right to do. I believe this sort of condition is so extreme that one can reasonably hope that it will never arise, but that is just a hope, not a position one can assert as an a priori moral truth. If and when such a condition arises, an innocent person may morally be used, even though such use violates her fundamental right not to be used. That disconnect between rights and what is morally permissible describes the moral space of threshold deontology.

One might think that extrinsic unaccountability is essentially the same sort of phenomenon: Rights to liberty that otherwise must be respected can be morally disrespected because of the weight of the collection of welfare interests at stake. But I believe these are different moral phenomena. In a condition in which extrinsic accountability is missing, people who are unaccountable simply lose some of the liberty rights they otherwise would enjoy. The dignity-respecting model (DR Model) applies, but in a negative way, one analogous to cases in which accountability is missing for intrinsic reasons. Still, the analogy has some force: both appeal to a justification that applies because of a breakdown of conditions that ought normally to apply.

The question now is: Why think that no one's rights are violated if the state lacks the duty to devote, or simply cannot devote, sufficient resources to policing to hold people accountable and decides, instead, to impose targeted liberty restrictions on those it deems dangerous? Why don't those restrictions violate their liberty rights?

My answer requires us to go back to basics. The core rights for an *agent* are liberty rights, property rights (without property with which to act, an agent's liberty is radically limited), and what Wesley Hohfeld calls second-order powers to change her rights (for example, by trading some rights for others) to better meet her ends.[5] A precondition for being able to enjoy these rights is that she can be held accountable for the abuse of her liberty. If she is acting as she has a right to act, then she should expect that others will not respond to her with targeted interference (except for limited conditions in which competition is permissible).[6] But if she is acting as she has no right to act, then she should expect that certain forms of responsive, targeted interference will be permissible. Indeed, insofar as she threatens unjust harm to others, or threatens to take unjust advantage of the law for herself, she can expect that the state will seek to use proportional force to prevent her from doing so, or will hold her accountable after the fact for having done so. This is the sense in which liberty and accountability are two sides of the same coin. If she cannot

[5] See "Some Fundamental Legal Conceptions as Applied in Judicial Reasoning."
[6] See *The Mechanics of Claims*, 181-182.

be policed adequately to ensure that she is unlikely to be able to act unjustly, and/or cannot be held accountable if she does act unjustly, then that two-sided coin is unavailable. If abuse of liberty can't trigger the proper response to that very abuse, then she cannot claim the normal *right* to liberty. The context for making that claim is not present.

One might worry that this makes the notion of a liberty right too contingent, that I'm losing the normative force of having such rights. But in my view, there's really only one absolute in the space of rights: the Autonomy Principle implies that no one can be forced or required to endure significant sacrifices for the sake of others unless she has done something in virtue of which she deserves to be used as a means or to acquire a duty to sacrifice herself, she has forfeited her rights to the same effect, or she has special relationships with others that have the same effect.[7] The liberty to act is not such an absolute. It can be restricted to protect the interests of others. It can also be restricted if one forfeits the POLA and is a danger to others. And it can be restricted if one cannot be held accountable for the wrongs one would do to others.

The next question is: What is left of liberty rights if external accountability is absent? It can't be that an agent is required simply to sit still. The best answer, I believe, is that the POLA is unavailable. It isn't forfeited, because the agents who live under this condition may have done nothing to lose it.[8] Still, the state is not required to treat people as though they have the POLA if it cannot hold them accountable, given the resources it is required or able to devote to the task, for the abuse of their liberty. The result, then, parallels that in which people do forfeit the POLA: they have a claim to enjoy their liberty that functions on a par with competing patient claims to enjoy welfare. An agent's claim to be left free to enjoy her liberty should then be weighed against the patient claims of those who might be harmed if she is left free. This sort of quasi-utilitarian weighing makes it much easier to justify liberty restrictions than would be the case for people who benefit from the POLA.[9]

20.2 What Constitutes Adequate Capacity to Police

In the Section 20.1, I described a broad notion of accountability, one that has two components: being subject to responsive interference that aims to prevent agents from acting wrongly, and being held accountable after the fact if they

[7] See Section 3.3.1.

[8] Insofar as they contributed to the breakdown of the state's policing capacity, they may be thought of as having forfeited the POLA. But as the breakdown of policing capacity normally applies generally, this sort of forfeiture overdetermines why they don't benefit from the POLA.

[9] This quasi-utilitarian weighing was discussed in Section 17.1.

do act wrongly.[10] Policing is a crucial component in this broad notion of accountability. It is through policing that the state tries to monitor people, most of whom benefit from the POLA, to ensure that they don't abuse their liberty. And it is through policing that people can be arrested and brought in front of a court if there is probable cause to believe that they have already broken the law. If policing capacity is inadequate, then accountability will be inadequate. I am not suggesting that the state's inability to provide adequate policing is the only way that accountability can fail. In fact, the paradigmatic example of extrinsic *un*accountability, that of prisoners of war (POWs), in some sense turns on the fact that *courts* cannot punish or penalize most POWs, which in turn reflects the state's limited *duty* to police POWs—a point I'll explore in the next section. But inadequate policing capacity, given the state's duty to provide it, is the scalar variable that affects whether people are extrinsically accountable or not. The existence of this spectrum of policing capacity gives rise to the puzzle: How much policing capacity is required for it to be "adequate"?

There can be no simple answer to that question. The issue has to be approached as a matter of competing values. Adequate policing is policing that allows the state to do two things at once: (1) to treat its citizens and guests as benefiting from the POLA, unless they are being punished or penalized, or they lack autonomy or have forfeited the POLA, and (2) to provide adequately for the security and welfare of others. This may seem to be a place where the idea of a balance between liberty and security has to be accepted, and where it has to be worked out in quasi-utilitarian or consequentialist terms. But as ever in this book, I think the idea of a simple utilitarian balance is too simple. There are at least four broad categories of values in play, not two, and there are a variety of deontic conditions that have to be engaged to understand how these values can be balanced off against each other.

First, there are a collection of concerns that might all be gathered under the heading of ensuring that the government does not intrude too much into the liberty of autonomous people who have not forfeited the POLA. These include the police respecting the privacy of those who benefit from the POLA; the state not criminalizing or penalizing the exercise of basic liberties such as the freedom of speech and association; the state respecting other relevant general limits on criminalization;[11] and the state respecting the interest people have in keeping their money, rather than paying more taxes to support a police force (one that does not have to fund itself by preying on those who are policed).

[10] I count inchoate crimes as "acting wrongly." Ideally, policing will prevent those as well as completed crimes. But often, policing can only prevent completed crimes. In those cases, the state should be able both to prevent crime and to hold agents accountable.

[11] The theory of criminalization is beyond the scope of this book. But see A. Duff's *The Realm of Criminal Law*, especially chs. 6 and 7.

Second, there is the question: What else, other than supporting the police, courts, and prisons (and other institutions for enforcing criminal and penal law), could and should be done with tax money? Insofar as there is a limited pot of money that the government can tap into, paying for the institutions of the criminal justice system competes with spending on education, employment opportunities, health care, retirement security, physical infrastructure, and national defense, to name a few. And this is not *merely* a question of fundamentally different priorities for the government; it is also a question regarding how the government can and should address security, as providing for some of these other goods—such as education and employment opportunities—is relevant to limiting the conditions that breed threats to security in the first place.[12] Of course, insofar as the government is going to provide policing resources, it is obliged to do so equitably. That is, it may not provide good policing only to the wealthy, leaving the poor to fend for themselves and, then, add insult to injury by claiming that they cannot be adequately policed, so they lose the benefit of the POLA. Those places where policing resources are most needed, so that it is possible to say that policing is adequate, are those which should be prioritized. But the overall budget for policing still has to compete with other budgetary priorities.

Third, there are the ways in which people are held accountable when caught breaking the law and the ways their liberty can be constrained when they do not benefit from the POLA that affect the overall need for policing. These include the schedules of proportional punishments and penalties that have some capacity to deter, to reinforce norms, and to incapacitate dangerous individuals; alternative structures of state-supported accountability, such as restorative justice programs; the scope of forfeiture of the POLA for those who commit offenses; and the way in which those who do not benefit from the POLA are restricted to ensure that they do not wrong others.

Fourth, there's the interest people have in not being wrongfully harmed, whether it's bodily harm, property loss, violations of their dignity, or attacks on their ability to develop and pass on various cultural ideals. This interest is relevant for ramping up policing, punishments, penalties, forfeitures, and restrictions on those who lack the POLA, but also for policing the police, to protect against state abuse of the power granted to it in order to achieve security. In other words, the state has to worry not only about non-state actors who pose threats to the welfare of its citizens and guests, but also about avoiding becoming a police state that becomes more of a threat than a source of protection.

Of these four categories, only the last more or less straightforwardly reflects a consequentialist reason to provide security. The question is: How should this

[12] See Section 1.1.

reason be acted upon? The first category, concerned with ensuring that the government does not intrude too much into the liberty of autonomous people, allows a fair degree of flexibility in terms of tax revenue to provide for a well-trained, non-predatory, sufficiently large police force. It provides a *bit* of flexibility in terms of the norms of privacy that must be respected and the sorts of general regulations of liberty, and practices of criminalization, that can be tolerated.

The second category, concerned with budgetary priorities, provides a fair degree of flexibility in terms of how much money to raise with taxes, how to raise it, and how to spend it. But this category is not infinitely flexible; taxation should not become so extreme that it either snuffs out ambition or honest reporting of income; nor should it become so extreme that it is rightly viewed as treating people fundamentally as tools of the general welfare.

The third category, covering the ways in which people are held accountable when caught breaking the law or when they do not benefit from the POLA—which is what I've spent most of the book discussing—provides a bit of flexibility in terms of the schedules of punishments and penalties that can be meted out, when the POLA can be forfeited, and what can be done to those who lack the POLA. However, it cannot provide enough flexibility to simply make up for failure to have raised money and spent it well in the past. If new security threats arise, a wise government will review its long-term investment in the welfare of its people. But the immediate options for a government committed to respecting the DR Model have to be (a) providing more policing capacity (which can be ramped up fairly quickly, though not instantly), (b) tweaking the options in the first and third categories, and (c) declaring that extrinsic accountability has broken down.

Before coming to the last possibility—declaring that extrinsic accountability has broken down—let me wrap up the point about what constitutes adequate policing capacity. Normally, an equilibrium can be found between, on the one hand, the pressure to provide security, and, on the other hand, respecting the limits just discussed: ensuring that the government does not intrude too much into the liberty of autonomous people who have not forfeited the POLA, holding people accountable only in ways that respect the DR Model, and spending enough on policing without taking too much away from other services that the government provides. That equilibrium establishes what adequate policing looks like in that context. It is a duty of the state to provide at least adequate policing, if it can do so without treating anyone unjustly as a means of doing so.

There are, however, two sorts of reasons why that sort of policing might not be available, at least for some people. First, the state is not responsible to police all people equally. It can take a different approach to insiders and outsiders. I don't distinguish between citizens and resident aliens. I think the state is responsible to police those it lets into its territory in a way that is fundamentally equal, whether they are citizens or not. My point is that the state is not responsible to let in and police everyone who wants to enter. It should, generally, be able to rely on other states to police their own citizens. This is where problems arise, however. There are circumstances in which it cannot do that, times when other states either cannot or will not adequately police their own people. Again, the paradigmatic example concerns POWs. In those situations, there will be a gap in policing coverage, and the state that happens to have physical control over people whom it is not responsible for policing may be entitled to say that it cannot provide adequate policing for them, given the relatively weak duty it has to accept them into the country and to police them—a duty grounded in the interest these people have, as foreigners, to claim freedom in a new country that will take on the burden of policing them.[13]

Second, even when it comes to citizens of a country, there may be emergency circumstances in which the state cannot, at least for certain regions of the country, provide what would count as minimally adequate policing. The paradigmatic cases concern invasion and insurrection, when the state's ability to control territory is compromised by competing forces, when the threat level posed by those who resist the state is particularly high, and when it is at least somewhat hard to determine who poses a threat connected to the invasion or insurrection and who does not.

20.3 Examples of Extrinsic Lack of Accountability

In this section, I examine four categories of people whose liberty can be restricted because they do not benefit from the POLA, and they do not benefit from the POLA because they lack accountability for extrinsic reasons: POWs, alien suspected terrorists, other deportable illegal aliens, and frightening people in times of invasion or insurrection.

20.3.1 Prisoners of War

The idea that captured enemy soldiers, POWs, can be detained is so well established that one can overlook the fact that it calls for justification. The practice is not as old as war itself. But it does go back at least to the mid-17th century.[14]

[13] Arguably, the strongest claim to a right to be allowed in and then to be released and policed like any other person who benefits from the POLA is held by refugees, whose rights are defined quite broadly by the UN Refugee Convention, 1951 and the 1967 Protocol. But under U.S. law, even a refugee can be deported for serious crimes. See 8 U.S.C. § 1227 (a)(2).

[14] See the 1648 Treaty of Westphalia, Clause 111 (discussing the return of prisoners).

And to Montesquieu, writing 100 years later, the practice seemed self-evidently justified. He brought it up in the context of arguing against the old Roman law that allowed captured enemy soldiers to be either killed or turned into slaves. His reasoning was that "War gives no other right over prisoners than to disable them from doing any further harm by securing their persons."[15] In other words, it went without argument that they may be captured and thereby disabled.

If we press for a justification, one might think that it would be relevant only to war. That is, one might think that the DR Model is designed for times of peace, and that in times of war special measures are called for. But in my view, we want *all* human activity, even war, to be governed by reference to the rights of individuals.[16] That's not to say that the law should simply mirror the underlying moral considerations. In particular, when it comes to criminalizing the actions of soldiers who obey the law of armed conflict but fight in an unjust war, there is good reason to think that they should be given a pass. Even if they are morally culpable, the legality principle bars their prosecution.[17] As Jeff McMahan put it:

> When the legal authorities in a soldier's society order him to fight in a war, international law fails to provide him with any source of guidance that might authoritatively controvert his government's assertions about the legality of the war. If the war turns out to be unjust and illegal, the law cannot fairly hold him liable when it has failed to be clear about what it demands of him.[18]

But even if the law must sometimes depart from the underlying morality, it should not turn a blind eye to the systematic violation of individual rights. It should not allow people to be harmed *simply* because the traditional practice has allowed it. Doing so would be no more justifiable now than taking slaves was in the time of Montesquieu.

The question, then, is: Can the detention of POWs be made consistent with the DR Model? If it can be, the explanation cannot be that the state is holding them accountable, because the normal modes of holding people accountable generally will not suffice to justify their detention. First, a POW may have done nothing that can give the detaining state the right to punish or penalize her. As just noted, even if the war is unjust, fighting in it is not a crime. At least under the current law of armed conflict, all lawful combatants are legally privileged to use force against a state that is at war with the state for which they fight. Second, even

[15] *The Spirit of the Laws*, Book XV, ch. 2, ¶ 3.

[16] That assumption, common to much contemporary just war theory, was an important premise in my book, *The Mechanics of Claims and Permissible Killing in War*.

[17] See the discussion in Section 5.5.1 on legality.

[18] *Killing in War*, 192. For a critical response, see V. Tadros, *To Do, To Die, To Reason Why*, chs. 12 and 13.

those who have committed the sorts of war crimes that would justify punishing and detaining them have probably done so in a context in which it would be difficult to gather evidence and hold a trial. Third, if a POW is released[19] or escapes, she normally has a legal right, if not also a legal duty, to rejoin her country's armed forces.[20] Fourth, there is no basis for saying that she forfeits the POLA in virtue of having fought legally; doing so shows no disrespect for the law.

But the very fact that the state cannot appeal to the idea of holding POWs accountable for their fighting provides a basis for saying that they are extrinsically unaccountable. Because they are mostly unaccountable (the exception being for war crimes), the state can treat POWs as a threat and detain them as it would any other threat who does not benefit from the POLA. Indeed, given their duty to their own country, the presumption that they will not pursue harmful activities is reversed; the presumption must be that a normal POW *is* a threat, and that individualized reasons do not need to be found to justify detaining them until the cessation of hostilities.[21]

We can test this explanation for the justifiability of detaining POWs by examining the implications of the power that some states grant their captured soldiers: that of giving parole, that is, giving their word that they will not again take up arms against the detaining country.[22] By giving parole, the parolee loses her status as a privileged combatant; if she is captured again, having violated her word, she is subject to criminal punishment.[23] The prospect of giving parole thus creates the legal possibility of policing a former POW's future actions. And this provides a test for the DR Model because it seems to suggest that a detaining state is obligated to release POWs who give parole. The question is: Does the DR Model really require releasing POWs who give parole? I argue it does not.

The argument from parole to a right to release seems to suggest the need for an exception to the DR Model. This is for two reasons. First, no state can be expected to grant parole to all POWs who offer it. Doing so would be too dangerous.[24] Second, since they could now be accountable for their taking up arms again, in violation of their parole, that seems to imply that in times of war the power to detain POWs is simply independent of accountability. That is, it seems

[19] The most common basis for release before the end of hostilities is exchange of POWs between warring parties.

[20] See L. Green, *The Contemporary Law of Armed Conflict*, 240.

[21] Geneva Convention III, art. 118: "Prisoners of war shall be released and repatriated without delay after cessation of active hostilities."

[22] See Geneva Convention III, art. 21, ¶ 2 ("Prisoners of war may be partially or wholly released on parole . . . in so far as is allowed by the laws of the Power on which they depend.").

[23] Geneva Convention III Commentary, 181 ("[A] prisoner of war who is released on parole and is recaptured bearing arms may be tried and sentenced by the Detaining Power.").

[24] Note, however, that parole seems to have been used in World War II for those who might need to be released from a detention facility temporarily "for reasons of health or hygiene." Geneva Convention III Commentary, 179.

to show that the basis for detaining POWs is simply that they are dangerous, and not that they are, normally, privileged to use force against the detaining state and therefore unaccountable.

This argument fails to provide an exception for the DR Model because it is too legalistic, and too detached from the reality of war, when it comes to assessing accountability.[25] The reality of war is that even if an enemy would *allow* its soldiers to give parole, it is unlikely to *enforce* on its released soldiers their duty to refrain from fighting. I am not denying that countries who allow their soldiers to be released on parole assume this duty. The Third Geneva Convention is clear that "the Power on which [POWs released on parole] depend is bound neither to require *nor to accept* from them any service incompatible with the parole or promise given."[26] What I am suggesting is that it is unreasonable to expect any enemy nation to be scrupulous about enforcing this duty during war. The commentary to the Geneva Conventions supports this skepticism, noting that the text of the Conventions does not "specify the attitude to be taken by that Power, from the penal or disciplinary point of view, in regard to breach of parole by a member of its armed forces."[27]

Assuming a country at war cannot rely on its enemies to enforce a parolee's duty to stay out of the fight, it is then clear why it cannot allow POWs to give their word and regain their status as accountable agents. The detaining power can threaten to punish POWs whom it releases on parole and subsequently recaptures using force against it. But that is a very tenuous form of accountability, given that these former POWs would be outside of the former detaining power's jurisdiction. In reality, only a former POW's honor could truly compel her to refrain from fighting. If a former POW lacks honor, there is little that the former detaining power can do to stop her from fighting against it again after release. I am not denying that released POWs can be held accountable in one sense: It would be just and legal to punish them *if* they are caught, tried, and convicted. My point is that recapture is very unlikely. In that sense, the detaining power normally would not have *adequate* ability to police those POWs it releases on parole to return to the countries for which they were fighting. Nor could the detaining power normally rely on the state with which it is at war to provide adequate policing for those POWs.

If a detaining power somehow could trust an enemy nation, or a third-party nation, to enforce a parolee's duty to stay out of the fight, then it is plausible that the detaining power would be obligated to give that enemy's POWs the option

[25] The rest of this section repeats, almost verbatim, the text from "A Unified Theory of Detention," 928-930.

[26] Geneva Convention III, art. 21, ¶ 3 (emphasis added).

[27] Geneva Convention III Commentary, 182.

of giving parole. The detaining power cannot simply choose to treat someone as unaccountable if there is another state that will hold him accountable. POW detention is justified only if the detaining power confronts a POW who does not have a state that is willing to accept responsibility for her and hold her accountable. The reason POW detention is the default position, then, is not that a POW's claims for liberty are lost during times of war; it is that the conditions for holding paroled POWs accountable if they breach their duty are normally unlikely to exist.

20.3.2 Alien Suspected Terrorists

The practical realities that explain why POWs cannot expect to be released if only they give parole also explain why some suspected terrorists (STs) can be detained without bringing criminal charges against them. Before defending the substance of that claim, I want to acknowledge and respond to two possible criticisms. First, on terminology: In 2001, when the Bush administration declared the "war on terror" and started to capture and detain people it took to be al Qaeda and Taliban fighters, it dubbed them "unlawful combatants" or "enemy combatants." I choose to call these people STs instead. My reason is that I think the label "combatant" only confuses the moral issue.[28] We are not dealing with people who have the legal privilege to fight, as lawful combatants do.[29] In addition, the term "combatant" suggests that it is natural that they could be detained indefinitely like POWs, while at the same time, given that they were not fighting as legal combatants, allowing the U.S. administration to deny them some of the benefits of POW status and to try them for crimes if it so chose.[30] I reject all such attempts to use labels to escape substantive consideration of the issues. Thus, I call them STs.

[28] It also confuses the legal issue, as the traditional view is that there are only two categories: civilians who lack the privilege to fight and combatants who have it. See The Public Committee against Torture in Israel v. The Government of Israel, HCJ 769/02 (Israeli Supreme Court, Dec. 13, 2006) ¶ 26 ("That definition [of civilians] is 'negative' in nature. It defines the concept of 'civilian' as the opposite of 'combatant.'"); see also International Criminal Tribunal for the former Yugoslavia, Prosecutor v. Blaskic (2000) Case IT-95-14-T, ¶ 180 ("[civilians are persons] who are not, or no longer, members of the armed forces.").

[29] The Taliban fighters arguably had that privilege as long as the Taliban was the government of Afghanistan (which it is again). But the government was toppled fairly quickly, and then the Taliban were fighting as an insurgent group. Such groups can maintain the privilege to fight. The Additional Protocol I to the Geneva Conventions, art. 43, refers back to the Geneva Convention III, art. 4, listing categories of people with the privilege to fight in a war, including members of a militia or resistance movement. But the conditions for fighting are fairly strict, including "having a fixed distinctive sign recognizable at a distance" and "carrying arms openly." I am aware of no one who contends that the Taliban fought that way.

[30] See D. Cole, "Out of the Shadows."

Second, the claim that the United States may hold at least some STs in the same way that it may hold POWs will disturb many liberals. Now, more than two decades after the United States started to hold STs in Guantanamo Bay, Cuba, those who remember their fate press the charge that it is outrageous to hold people for decades on end without a criminal conviction. But the issue is not that simple. We've seen over the course of this book that a sentence for a criminal (or penal) conviction is not the only basis for long-term loss of liberty. POWs can be held for as long as a war lasts; if people have forfeited the POLA, they can lose their liberty as necessary and proportional to providing security for others for as long as their POLA forfeiture lasts; and if people lack threshold autonomous capacity and are a danger to themselves or others, they too can be held for decades on end. To assess whether holding STs for decades on end is justifiable, we must first understand why doing so might be justifiable and then assess whether the conditions that would make it justifiable apply.

My substantive claim is that the explanation for why some STs might be detainable for long stretches of time is that they, like POWs who give parole, are extrinsically unaccountable and thus do not benefit from the POLA. To make sense of that thought, we need to distinguish alien STs from citizen STs. The latter, as autonomous citizens, have a right against the state that has arrested them: it must prosecute them, establish a basis for treating them as having forfeited the POLA, or release and police them, at least as long as it has the capacity to provide adequate policing. But alien STs generally lack the right to demand that the state that has arrested them expend the resources necessary to adequately police them.[31] As aliens, they are excludable; they do not have a right to stay in the country where they are not citizens; they are essentially guests who, if thought too dangerous, can be asked to leave. And as excludable, they lack the right to demand that the state where they currently are spend the resources necessary to police them. At most, they can demand to be sent to the country where they are citizens or to some other country that will spend the resources to police them. The reason they can be detained is that sometimes no other country will take up the burden of providing adequate policing for them.

[31] One might argue that it makes a difference where they were arrested. Certainly, the law puts weight on that distinction, affording rights to aliens who were arrested domestically that it does not afford to aliens arrested outside the jurisdiction of the detaining country. (See, e.g., Johnson v. Eisentrager, 339 U.S. 763 (1950).) I have argued against these sorts of cases, insofar as they imply that non-resident aliens have no legal rights against the countries that detain them. (See "Constitutional Rights for Nonresident Aliens.") But my point here concerns the rights that aliens *lack*. For that purpose, I can see no basis for saying that aliens have special rights to be released and policed just because they were arrested while resident in the detaining country. If anything, they would have special rights if arrested outside the country and brought there involuntarily. But I think the best position is one that gives no significance to where a detainee is arrested. What matters is only where a state has a duty to adequately police her.

This last point is like the point made in the context of POWs. In that context, the country that would take a POW is presumably the enemy, which would explain why that country could not be expected to police, or even respect, a pledge to stay out of the conflict. Nothing as strong applies in the context of alien STs. Nonetheless, many STs come from countries where the policing function is inadequate, and where the arresting country could not trust that an ST would not simply proceed to resume her terrorist activities. In such a case, unless a third country is willing to offer to adequately police the STs in question, there may be no country with a duty and the capacity to provide adequate policing. That combination makes those detainees effectively extrinsically unaccountable.[32]

A number of details still need to be unpacked—I discuss four. First, it is worth pausing over the basic theoretical claim that states are generally free to exclude aliens, and that that right to exclude is all the clearer if the state has probable cause to believe they are terrorists, especially if the terrorism is believed to be directed at the excluding/detaining state. I am well aware that the right to exclude is a contested issue, and arguing for it is beyond the scope of this book.[33] But I am not pressing a particularly hard line here. For example, I think states have an obligation to admit at least their fair share of refugees.[34] My point is primarily that it can exclude most people it does not want to admit, and, again, this is an especially plausible claim if it has probable cause to believe they are terrorists who mean to commit terrorist acts against it.[35] And even then, I am willing to grant exceptions. For example, I think a state can acquire a duty, as a matter of compensatory justice, to admit people it has abused (for example, through torture), *even if* it has probable cause to believe they are terrorists. I think the assumption about the right to exclude that I rely on is, thus, sufficiently weak that I will simply rely on it for the rest of this argument.

[32] The most conspicuous example in recent history concerns STs from Yemen. In 2007, "[a]lmost 100 Yemenis remain[ed] in the detention facility [in Guantanamo Bay, Cuba], more than from any other nation." A. Al-Hajj, "Yemen Receives 4 Detainees from Guantanamo Bay Prison." This could be explained on the ground that "[o]btaining the necessary assurances from Yemen has been difficult . . . ". Ibid. Two years later, when the United States still held 97 Yemenis in Guantanamo Bay, this remained a problem: "[T]he Obama administration [was] increasingly skeptical of Yemen's ability to provide adequate rehabilitation and security to supervise returned prisoners." W. Glaberson and R. Worth, "Yemen Dispute Slows Closing of Guantánamo." Indeed, as of 2022, there were still 14 Yemeni STs held in Guantanamo Bay. U. Farooq, "Guantanamo: Yemeni Detainee Cleared for Release After 20 Years." This can be no surprise given that Yemen is still so unstable that even Yemeni art is not yet being returned. G. Bowley and T. Mashberg, "Looted Artifacts, Returned to Yemen, Will Go to the Smithsonian, for Now." Note, however, on January 6, 2025, 11 more Yemeni prisoners were released from Guantanamo, but to Oman, which has a reintegration program, not to Yemen. See C. Rosenberg, "U.S. Sends 11 Guantánamo Prisoners to Oman to Start New Lives."

[33] For a good recent overview of the issues, see A. Stilz, *Territorial Sovereignty*, ch. 7.

[34] See this ch., n. 13.

[35] The connection between the right to exclude and the duty to police is discussed by Michael Blake in "Immigration, Jurisdiction, and Exclusion." Anna Stilz offers a sympathetic yet critical response in *Territorial Sovereignty*, section 7.2.

Second, one might still object that if the detaining state is not required to release and police an ST in its own territory, and no other country is willing and able to provide adequate policing, then the detaining country has an obligation to put the ST in question on trial. If she is convicted, she can be detained as part of her punishment. If she is acquitted, then she must be released. What is unacceptable, one might think, is simply holding her. But this argument is doubly problematic. First, it ignores the special difficulties that might arise in prosecuting alien STs. As Mathew Waxman pointed out: "[T]he conditions under which some suspected terrorists are captured, especially in faraway combat zones or ungoverned regions, make it impossible to prove criminal cases using normal evidentiary rules . . . ."[36] Second, even if those rules can be relaxed for the purposes of trying STs, they pose an especially significant threat. And as Jack Goldsmith pointed out, "high-stakes terrorism trials" are problematic in part because, if the government fails to obtain a conviction, "the government [still] cannot afford to let the defendant go."[37] Of course, Goldsmith is not literally correct when he says the government "cannot afford to let the defendant go." It *could* choose to treat alien STs who cannot be safely released to another country as though they were domestic STs. A wealthy country like the United States *could* afford to release and police them domestically. But if my arguments above—the ones concerning the right to exclude alien STs and the justifiability of treating STs as though they lack the POLA if they lack extrinsic accountability—are sound, then Goldsmith's point is valid in this sense: there is no obligation to release STs if the government tries them and fails to convict them.

Third, before people are treated as STs, there must be sufficient evidence to think that they are STs. It is not enough to have a hunch, or to rely on some witness whose reliability is at best completely unknown, or at worst suspect. This issue was addressed by the U.S. Supreme Court in *Hamdi v. Rumsfeld*.[38] The Court there rejected the "some evidence" standard.[39] But it allowed "a presumption in favor of the Government's evidence, so long as that presumption remained a rebuttable one and fair opportunity for rebuttal were provided."[40] It's not perfectly clear what this standard amounts to, but it seems to be a preponderance of the evidence standard in this sense: if the defendant can rebut the government's evidence, showing that it is more likely than not that she is not an ST, then the government must let her go. Hamdi was a U.S. citizen, and the Court's ruling was based on constitutional norms. But this standard was adopted by the United States for "Combatant Status Review Tribunals" making

36 "Administrative Detention of Terrorists," 11.
37 "Don't Try Terrorists, Lock Them Up."
38 542 U.S. 507 (2004).
39 Ibid., 537.
40 Ibid., 543.

the determination of whether someone could be held as an ST in Guantanamo Bay.[41] One might argue about whether this standard of proof is the right one. Arguably, the burden should be on the government to show that it is more likely than not that an ST is an ST before subjecting her to long-term detention. But something in this ballpark seems appropriate.

Finally, we get to the nature of the liberty restriction. As in all cases that aim directly at incapacitation, the restriction should meet the least restrictive alternative (LRA) standard. STs can be assumed to be more dangerous, and more likely to need to be detained in a secure facility, than a normal deportable alien. Nonetheless, their ongoing dangerousness must be regularly assessed. If an ST seems to have had a sincere change of heart, has lost the physical or mental capacity necessary to be an effective terrorist, the political situation that provided a context for her threatened terrorism has changed, some country is willing to take her and police her, or she has simply been out of action long enough that her value as a terrorist to the groups with which she once seemed to be affiliated is now substantially eroded, then the use of detention, as opposed to a lesser restriction, should be reassessed.

20.3.3 Deportable Illegal Aliens

There are two stages at which aliens might be detained simply in virtue of having no legal right to remain in the detaining country: (1) pending completion of removal proceedings, and (2) post-removal proceedings (that is, after it has been determined that they should be removed). I will not say much about the former, which operates essentially like pretrial detention. I will say only this: insofar as it has yet to be determined whether they have a legal right to stay in the country, they should not automatically be treated as though they do not. There must be some basis for determining that they have forfeited the POLA before they are held in detention. That could be a criminal history, a pattern of flight from immigration authorities, or evidence of the intention to flee from immigration authorities. If such a basis for forfeiting the POLA does not exist, the option of hypothetical forfeiture should exist here, just as it does in the context of pretrial detention.[42] And as in pretrial detention, if aliens are found not to be removable, they should be paid compensation.[43]

The more interesting problem arises when the state has determined that an alien is removable, but it cannot find a country to accept her. Consider the case

41 Order Establishing Combatant Status Review Tribunal, ¶ g (12).
42 See Section 18.4.
43 This is not how the law, at least in the United States, works. See Demore v. Kim, 538 U.S. 510 (2003) (upholding pre-removal detention without individualized hearings regarding flight risk).

of Kestutis Zadvydas. According to the Supreme Court, he was "a resident alien who was born, apparently of Lithuanian parents, in a displaced persons camp in Germany in 1948."[44] He had a long criminal history and after serving two years of a 16-year sentence, the Immigration and Naturalization Service (INS) took him into custody, and he was ordered deported to Germany.[45] Germany, however, held that he was not a German citizen and refused to take him. The INS approached Lithuania, but it denied that he was a citizen of that country, eventually claiming that his effort to claim Lithuanian citizenship based on his parents' citizenship was "inadequately documented."[46] His wife was from the Dominican Republic, but that country too refused to accept him. It thus became clear that no other country would take him. The question his case raised was: What may the United States then do with him?

I think the Court reached what is essentially the right answer. It held that the constitutional right to due process required it to read the statute to imply that "once removal is no longer reasonably foreseeable, continued detention is no longer authorized. . . ."[47] The point was not that detainees like Zadvydas have the right to be released and policed as though they were citizens. Rather, the point was that the INS had to use the LRA.[48] "[T]he alien's release may and should be conditioned on any of the various forms of supervised release that are appropriate in the circumstances, and the alien may no doubt be returned to custody upon a violation of those conditions."[49]

20.3.4 Frightening People in Times of Invasion or Rebellion

So far, the discussion in this section has focused completely on cases in which the state is not obliged to provide adequate policing for people and thus can treat them as extrinsically unaccountable. But the state might find that it simply

[44] Zadvydas v. Davis, 533 U.S. 678, 684 (2001).

[45] The INS was dissolved in 2003 and three new agencies took over its function. The relevant one for this chapter is U.S. Immigration and Customs Enforcement.

[46] Ibid.

[47] Ibid., 699.

[48] English rulings in this area seem to miss the moral point in two ways. First, in *A and Others v. Secretary of State for the Home Department* [2004] UKHL 56, the House of Lords wrongly rejects the relevance of alien status versus citizen status (though it seems that they correctly followed the European Convention on Human Rights, art. 14). Second, in *Secretary of State for the Home Department v. JJ* [2007] UKHL 45, rather than requiring an LRA analysis, it drew a line between restrictions on liberty and deprivations of liberty, a line that will necessarily be over- and under-inclusive.

[49] Zadvydas, 533 U.S. 684. Interestingly, the Zadvydas case has been read more broadly than I think it needs to be read, to imply that detainees cannot be detained at all if no other country will take them six months after they are found removable. See R. Nixon, "Nations Hinder U.S. Effort to Deport Immigrants Convicted of Crime" (noting that between 2013 and 2016 "more than 8,000 immigrants with criminal convictions in the United States have been set free" in the United States).

cannot provide adequate policing. The two most obvious bases for the state being unable to provide adequate policing are invasion and rebellion.[50] Rebellion classically takes the form of a civil war, but it might also arise if the state's monopoly on power erodes to such a degree that the police can no longer control violent criminal gangs.[51]

There is not much of philosophical significance to say about this possibility. I will mention only four points. First, it is crucial that a state not use this possibility as an excuse to suspend the POLA for the people in its jurisdiction. It must be clear that providing adequate policing truly is not possible, because the scale of resistance to the state's power is too great to meet without restricting normal liberties. And the territory where and the time when the POLA is suspended must likewise be minimized. As the U.S. Supreme Court wrote in Ex parte *Milligan*:

> If, in foreign invasion or civil war, the courts are actually closed, and it is impossible to administer criminal justice according to law, then, on the theatre of active military operations, where war really prevails, there is a necessity to furnish a substitute for the civil authority, thus overthrown, to preserve the safety of the army and society; and as no power is left but the military, it is allowed to govern by martial rule until the laws can have their free course. As necessity creates the rule, so it limits its duration; for, if this government is continued after the courts are reinstated, it is a gross usurpation of power. Martial rule can never exist where the courts are open, and in the proper and unobstructed exercise of their jurisdiction.[52]

Second, the nature of the restriction should respect the LRA principle. For example, perhaps a curfew, limiting non-necessary travel at night, would suffice, rather than subjecting a population to an extended lockdown. This is true both for general restrictions that apply to all or nearly all people, and for targeted restrictions.

Third, the suspension of the POLA must not license behavior at odds with the Equality Principle. People should have their liberty restricted in ways that

[50] These are the conditions under which the U.S. Constitution grants Congress the right to suspend the writ of habeas corpus. International law also allows "Derogation in time of emergency." As the European Convention on Human Rights puts it: "In time of war or other public emergency threatening the life of the nation any High Contracting Party may take measures derogating from its obligations under this Convention to the extent strictly required by the exigencies of the situation, provided that such measures are not inconsistent with its other obligations under international law." ECHR, art. 15 (1).

[51] This is true in many failed or nearly failed states at the moment, including Haiti, Mexico, and, as I will discuss in a note below, El Salvador.

[52] 71 U.S. 2, 127 (1866).

respond to the threats the state faces, not in ways that respond to fears that certain members of the population might have for others who look or act differently.

Fourth, care should be used to sort out who poses a real threat from those who do not. The existence of an invasion, insurrection, or general breakdown of state power in the face of gangs should not be taken to justify an attitude akin to that which Arnaud Amaury supposedly expressed toward the people of Béziers during the Albigensian Crusade: "Kill them all; God will know his own."[53] The point is not about killing versus locking up. The point is about the need to use due care to sort out the threats from the innocents.[54]

20.4 Compensation for Failure to Provide Extrinsic Accountability

Is compensation owed to those who are restricted because of extrinsic unaccountability? Naively, looking at the question in very general terms, one might think the answer is yes. After all, it is the state that has failed to provide accountability; if it also then deprives people of their liberty, it should compensate them. But having just reviewed four types of people who can be targeted for liberty restrictions because of extrinsic unaccountability, it should be clear that the answer is generally no. POWs, alien suspected terrorists, and deportable illegal aliens who cannot find a country to take them in are extrinsically unaccountable because the state that has jurisdiction over them does not owe them policing in the first place. Perhaps their home countries owe them compensation for not taking them and policing them. But the state with jurisdiction over them does not owe them compensation.

What of states in times of rebellion or insurrection? They presumably are not providing adequate policing to their citizens because they cannot. If that is the case, then compensation may, in some sense, be owed. But one can't get blood from a stone. The obligation to provide compensation is effectively moot, at least in the short term. The same is not necessarily true in the long term, however. If the state can recover the capacity to provide adequate policing *and* the ability

[53] N. Visser, "A Church of Wolves," 26.

[54] This is very much a live issue in several countries today. Take, for example, El Salvador. The current government confronted a society overrun by gangs in which "gangsters were seldom convicted without testimony that hardly anyone was brave enough to offer." It locked up "7% of male Salvadoreans aged 14-29." The murder rate plunged "from 51 per 100,000 . . . in 2019 to . . . just eight" in 2022. But little evidence is required for detention: "a suspicious tattoo or an anonymous accusation will suffice." (All quotes in this note come from "What the World's Budding Autocrats Are Learning from El Salvador.") In an emergency, such thin evidence may have to be relied on. But serious efforts must be taken to follow up promptly with individualized hearings. So far, this is not happening in El Salvador.

to provide compensation, then it should provide it to those who were detained *merely* because they were deemed frightening.

This brings up a second relevant opportunity for compensation: sorting out those who forfeited the POLA and those who were merely frightening. If, for example, a state needs to take a great number of people into custody to break the grip of gangs in the territory, it should then try to sort out who is really a gang member, and who is not. Those who are not should receive compensation for the deprivation of their liberty, while those who are should be taken to have forfeited their right to compensation. Or, in the case of war, if a country does not offer to police its citizens who offer parole to regain their freedom, then arguably that country is using them, even if just as POWs in another country, to drain the enemy's resources. This use also calls for compensation, presumably on a par with that due to soldiers.

20.5 Objection Based on Very Dangerous People, and Reply

Before concluding that the DR Model provides a complete account of when the state can restrict the liberty of people, I want to examine two kinds of cases that might seem to break the model.

20.5.1 Anticipated Terrorist Action

Consider, first, a variation on a case I discussed in Chapter 4 when defending the POLA, the *Anticipated Culpable Aggressor* case. As a reminder, the original case goes like this:

> Adam carries a loaded gun. Tom knows that Adam is a murderously jealous man, and knows that Adam's wife, Eve, has sent Adam a letter to his office, confessing an affair with Victor. Tom also knows that Adam is about to meet Victor in his office, and that he will open his mail before meeting Victor. In sum, Tom knows that Adam does not now harbor the intention to murder Victor, but he will, if not stopped, come to form such an intention, and at that time he will also have the means for carrying it out.[55]

I said of that case that short-term targeted restrictions to protect Victor would be permissible. But I also said that what the POLA protects against is not those sorts of short-term restrictions;[56] rather, it protects against ongoing, substantial

[55] See Section 4.4.1.
[56] See Section 17.2.

restrictions that target a particular person because of ongoing threats they might be thought to pose. I argued that unless the state can cite some basis for a targeted restriction that conforms to the DR Model, then it would have to afford people like Adam the POLA.

But now consider this variation, which ups the ante:

> *Anticipated Terrorist*: Audrey is a skilled bomb maker who is likely, without government intervention, to offer her skills to a terrorist group that would use them to kill hundreds if not thousands. She learned her skills in a perfectly legal way, working for a legal arms manufacturer. She has done nothing yet to aid any terrorist group, nor does she currently intend to help them. In other words, she has done nothing to forfeit the POLA. Nonetheless, there are four things that the state knows that, taken together, make her very dangerous: (a) she has sympathies with certain groups whose interests are promoted by terrorist groups; (b) she has no principled commitment to avoiding terrorist acts if done for "a good cause"; (c) she is a relatively easy target for persuasion; and (d) undercover spies in a particular terrorist group know that members of this group have the intention of recruiting her. Nothing about her emotional or cognitive abilities suggests that she is anything but a fully autonomous individual, and she is living in her home state, the state that would restrict her liberty if restrictions were justified. Moreover, the state's general policing capacity is intact, so it cannot say that she is extrinsically unaccountable.

The DR Model suggests, one might think, that the only thing the state may do is police her, ensuring that she does not get the chance to make a bomb for this terrorist group. The worry, however, is that she might be recruited, without the police knowing it, and then go underground and offer the terrorist group her services. Surely, one might think, if the odds of that happening are in any way substantial, even 10 percent, then, given the magnitude of the threat if she does work with the terrorist group, the state should be free to act preemptively, to prevent her from meeting certain people or from disappearing from view. For example, it may monitor all of her electronic communication, and perhaps even put an electronic tracker on her. Arguably, it may also order her to avoid certain kinds of people, to help ensure that she does not meet with terrorists or go underground to support them. And it may do these sorts of things even if the DR Model says otherwise.

One possible response to Audrey's case is to say that it is a case for threshold deontology. Just as there could come a time when so many lives are at stake that it becomes permissible, all things considered, to use someone as a means, even at the cost of her life, to save the others—this despite such using violating her right not to be so used—so there could come a time when the danger someone poses is so great that the state can restrict her liberty, even though doing so is inconsistent with the DR Model.[57] And one might say that a rare and extreme case like this is just an exception that proves the rule. The rules are meant to handle *most* situations; unfortunately, we cannot guarantee that the world will always cooperate, and we should not be shocked if the rules break under extreme pressure.

I accept that solution in the abstract, but I fear that being too ready to recognize an exception will undermine the integrity of the system; the exceptions will grow to eat away too much of the rule. Moreover, I don't think we really have much reason to worry about cases like Audrey's. First, if the state has reason to think that someone poses a particularly extreme threat, and it has adequate policing capacity, it can devote the resources needed to effectively prevent the person from committing serious criminal actions. That may be expensive,[58] but if there are only a few people that call for such a heavy investment, a state should be able to afford that.[59] In addition, if there are acute reasons to worry, then the state can justify, consistent with the DR Model, short-term highly intrusive restrictions or long-term slightly intrusive restrictions on her liberty or privacy—such as monitoring her electronic communication, or requiring her to wear a tracking device.[60] The state can also design proxy crimes that should keep people like Audrey from getting close to committing a serious, destructive act.[61] It could even tailor these to certain categories of people: for example, people with special bomb-making expertise. And finally, I have argued that forfeiture of the POLA does not require strict observance of the ex post facto restriction; as long as it is fair, then anything Audrey does that makes it clear that she intends to commit a serious crime could ground her losing the benefit of the POLA.[62] These various options fit together well enough that it is hard to see how Audrey could pose an unacceptably large threat that could not be met, in a way that respects the DR Model, by a state that has adequate policing capacity.

There are, it seems to me, only three realistic reasons to worry that these options might fall short. First, there might be too many people like Audrey for the state to keep track of them all. But even then, terrorists tend to operate in networks, which allows the state to penetrate the network and monitor its activities. Of course, there is no guarantee that they would not be able to pull off a major crime. But the fact that there have been no serious terrorist attacks on

[57] See the earlier discussion in Section 20.1; see also Section 2.3.

[58] As noted in Section 16.3.2, it may take fifteen to twenty people to actively monitor someone. But that's someone who is suspected of *being* a terrorist. Audrey's case would presumably be somewhat easier to police, as she is suspected only of being vulnerable to terrorist recruitment.

[59] This option assumes that active police monitoring is less intrusive than electronic monitoring combined with wearing a tracking device and an order to avoid contact with certain kinds of people. But, of course, some police monitoring might involve, e.g., electronic monitoring.

[60] See Section 17.2.

[61] See Section 13.2.

[62] See Section 16.2.6.

the soil of the United States since the attacks of 9/11—a 23-year period as I write this—indicates that it is not beyond the ability of a normal government to prevent most terrorist attacks from coming to fruition.[63] I assume it could be as effective as it has been while respecting the limits of the DR Model.

Second, people with criminal intentions might be able to effectively take control of the state, at least in certain regions of a country. But then we have a situation in which extrinsic accountability is lacking. In that case, the DR Model allows the state—assuming that only some regions have been lost to it—to treat people in the relevant region as lacking the POLA for as long as it takes to regain adequate policing capacity.

Third, the state may simply be incompetent. The government's record when it comes to discovering nefarious activities is notoriously spotty. Consider the inability of the military to take preventive action against Major Nidal Hasan, who was known to be exchanging e-mails with radical Muslim cleric Anwar al-Awlaki; or the government's inability to put Umar Farouk Abdulmutallab on a no-fly list, despite warnings from his father that he was under "the influence of religious extremists based in Yemen"; or the FBI's inability to notice that Robert Hanssen had been spying for Russia for fifteen years from within the FBI itself; or even the Security and Exchange Commission's failure to take any actions against Bernie Madoff, despite numerous tips and indications that his investment business was a Ponzi scheme.[64]

But this sort of incompetence does not support detaining people who otherwise could not be detained under the DR Model. The problem is not that the government has its hands tied. The problem is that the government would not have any idea whom to detain.

In sum, I think it is very unlikely for the government to be in a position to identify threats like the one Audrey poses, and for it to be unable to take effective measures to handle those threats in ways that are fully consistent with the DR Model.

20.5.2 Powerful Individuals and Pretextual Prosecutions

The other sort of problematic case involves a person with a clear pattern of criminal activity who has been able to use threats to undermine the criminal justice system so that she is effectively extrinsically unaccountable unless the state

[63] It goes almost without saying that there have been way too many mass shootings in this time period, but this reflects the paranoid politics of the United States, which blocks all serious efforts at gun control.

[64] This paragraph, and the last sentence of the next paragraph, come, almost verbatim, from "A Unified Theory of Detention," 932.

engages in a pretextual prosecution. The thought is that if the state can convict her of a crime that is easy to establish, it can then use that to open the door to punishment and punish her with a much longer sentence than normal for the crime for which she has been convicted. By punishing her *as if* she has been convicted of a more serious crime, the state can effectively incapacitate her. This is a perversion of criminal law, but if the target is otherwise beyond the reach of the law, then this sort of perversion might be thought justifiable.

Consider the case of Al Capone.[65] Capone ran the Chicago mafia and was responsible for killing, directly or indirectly, many of his rivals. In 1925, his men killed five people whom they thought were members of a rival bootlegging gang, but one of them was in fact an assistant state's attorney. The government tried to bring charges against Capone for murder, but six grand juries all refused to indict. This showed how difficult it would be to prosecute him for the serious crimes he was committing. In 1929, he was successfully prosecuted on weapons charges, but he served only nine months in prison and then resumed control of the mob upon his release. This again suggested how difficult it would be to use the criminal justice system in a non-pretextual way to incapacitate him. However, in 1929 the federal government started to develop a case against Capone for tax evasion. That prosecution eventually succeeded, and he was sentenced to an 11-year term in federal prison. This was "the longest [prison] term ever handed down for tax evasion."[66] After moving him from a prison in Atlanta, from which he still exercised power over the mob, to the fairly isolated confines of the prison in Alcatraz, his influence over the mob was finally broken.[67]

Why consider this a case of pretextual prosecution? Capone did, after all, evade paying his taxes. The answer is that his punishment did not fit the crime. According to the U.S. Sentencing Commission Guidelines Manual, "Under pre-guidelines practice, roughly half of all tax evaders were sentenced to probation without imprisonment, while the other half received sentences that required them to serve an average prison term of twelve months."[68] Under current practice, which is harsher, "the average sentence imposed increased from 15 months in fiscal year 2016 to 16 months in fiscal year 2020."[69] Nonetheless, Capone's

[65] Another interesting case study is Donald Trump. The reason Trump's case does not fit my purposes is that Trump used legal means to run out the clock on, if not all of the prosecutions against him as he ran again for office in 2024, then at least the sentencing, regaining the Presidency before he could be punished for the felonies he committed, or tried for the others of which he was accused. His defenders may view the prosecutions against him as pretextual, political witch hunts. But it seems to me that they were not pretextual. Nor is it clear how pretextual prosecutions would have helped protect against the dangers he poses.

[66] D. Linder, "Al Capone Trial (1931)."

[67] For more on Capone's activities, trial, and punishment, see "On This Day: Al Capone Convicted of Income Tax Evasion."

[68] U.S. Sentencing Commission, "Federal Sentencing Guideline Manual," § 2T1.1. Commentary.

[69] U.S. Sentencing Commission, "Quick Facts: Tax Fraud Offenses".

sentence was over ten times longer than the average sentence for tax evasion in the pre-guidelines era, and over eight times longer than the current average. Perhaps his tax evasion was on a grander scale than most, but it's hard to believe that his tax evasion was eight to ten times more culpable than that of the more serious half of convicted tax cheats—again, only half of convicted tax cheats served any sentence at all. A much more plausible explanation for what the government did is that it used tax evasion as a mere pretext for locking him up long enough to get him out of harm's way.

What's wrong with that? If the prosecutors and judge were sure that Capone had been engaged in murder and racketeering, why not take any available opportunity to put him away? Why not embrace former Attorney General John Ashcroft's admiration for his predecessor, Robert Kennedy, who, according to Ashcroft, would "arrest mobsters for 'spitting on the sidewalk' if it would help in the battle against organized crime"?[70] As long as they are convicted of a crime, then why not treat them as liable to any punishment that is not legally barred as outside the range for that crime?

My answer is that pretextual prosecutions distort the function of the criminal law. The central project of this book has been to try to create clear categories for justifying state actions that impose targeted restrictions on the liberty of individuals. Punishment must be proportional to the crime.[71] Pretextual prosecutions either violate proportionality, or they cut the tie between the wrongful action for which the state could get a conviction and the punishment that is meted out. In essence, they are a fraud, a lie. And that raises the question: Why even bother lying? Why not just say: "This person is too dangerous to be allowed to remain free; therefore, we're going to lock him up."?

There are two ways to respond to this objection. The more moderate one is to question the idea that the criminal law is really limited to punishing people for the crimes for which they are convicted. Sentencing, at least in the United States, is based on any conduct, even if not part of the official charge, that is established by a preponderance of the evidence and is relevant to the crime charged.[72] This might seem to open up sentencing for tax evasion as a vehicle for punishing for murder, as long as the two are *somehow* connected. And presumably there was *some* connection in Capone's case; presumably the murders in Capone's case were relevant to his business as a mob boss, and that was relevant to the money he did not report on his taxes.

But as Gabriel Mendlow points out, "the law's official view" is that these other facts must in some way show that the guilt established at trial was itself

[70] The Office of Inspector General, *The September 11 Detainees*, 12.
[71] See Section 8.1.
[72] See G. Mendlow, "Divine Justice and the Library of Babel," 193.

worse—"more wrongful, more harmful, or more culpable"—than it might seem on the surface.[73] It is hard to see how the murders that Capone might have committed to help keep control over his criminal rivals showed that his *tax evasion* was worse than it otherwise would have been. The murders may have given prosecutors even more reason to try to go after Capone for tax evasion. As Mendlow puts it: "There's no injustice in punishing a murderer for tax evasion because he's a murderer." Nonetheless, as he then immediately points out, it is unjust to punish "a murderer for murder by convicting him of tax evasion."[74]

The more radical way to defend pretextual prosecutions is to say that the job of criminal punishment is to give wrongdoers what they deserve, and what they deserve reflects a whole-life view of their virtues and vices, their good and their bad deeds. This is what Mendlow calls the "Divine Justice model" of the criminal law, according to which a conviction is "little more than an intake valve."[75] On this view, the state can use the well-founded belief that Capone had committed murders to augment his punishment for *crime*, even if the crime for which he was convicted was merely tax evasion.

This might hold some appeal for retributivists who think that wrongdoing provides a basis for saying it is good that wrongdoers suffer.[76] But I think there are sound moral reasons *not* to go there.[77] First, punishment is not merely a tool for adjusting suffering to some deserved level; it is, I have argued, a tool with four functions that relate to the state blaming wrongdoers for public wrongs and collecting on their guilt.[78] Second, the whole life view suggests that those who have suffered a lot already get a "get-out-of-prison-free" pass to commit crime without more punishment.[79] Third, to make sense of why a person should not get a "get-out-of-prison-free" pass, we only need to assume that the incentive structure of punishment, as a deterrent, is meant to say to each person, your life will go less well if you commit *this* crime. This is an intrapersonal standard, not one that seeks to align some sort of interpersonal balance between suffering and culpable wrongdoing.[80]

But if the state is not permitted to engage in pretextual prosecutions, how should it handle a person like Al Capone? The answer is that it can be honest about the problem, which is that Capone has made himself extrinsically

[73] Ibid., 204. If they are mitigating, they might also show the conduct to be not as bad.
[74] Ibid., 203.
[75] Ibid., 202.
[76] Victor Tadros, not a retributivist, articulates this sort of thought. *Ends of Harm*, 68. Kimberley Ferzan, a retributivist of this sort, expresses some sympathy for "whole-life desert views." "The Trouble with Time Served," 2064.
[77] There is also a practical/epistemic reason: it is fundamentally unclear how the state could identify and tally up the relevant bases for punishment and reward.
[78] For the first statement of the four functions, see Section 1.3.3.
[79] See L. Alexander, "You Got What You Deserved," 318.
[80] See M. Berman, "Rehabilitating Retributivism," 104.

unaccountable for crimes like murder because of the way he threatens people in his community. The first job of the state in a case like his is to incapacitate him so that he can no longer wield such threats. It should try to do so by marshaling evidence of witness intimidation. On this basis, it could declare him to have forfeited the POLA. And it could find that the LRA for him is removal to an institution from which he could no longer give orders to other mobsters. Then, once his power is broken, once witnesses feel that it is safe to testify against him, he can be tried for his crimes.

What if his power was too great for that? What if he ran Chicago, or some part of Chicago, so thoroughly that it would be impractical to get witnesses even for a forfeiture of the POLA hearing in another jurisdiction? Then the honest thing to do is to declare Chicago an area in which extrinsic accountability, at least for certain suspected mafia figures, is unavailable. That would then allow the state to move in, arrest the suspects deemed most relevant to the problem, and reestablish order. Once it is established, then either the process just described could be used for top bosses like Capone, or perhaps they could then be sent directly to trial for their crimes.

In sum, the question is: Why not just use the criminal law pretextually as a tool for incapacitating people like Capone? The answer is that this sort of pretextual use of the criminal law corrupts the criminal law to make it do things that do not fit its basic function. And that sort of corruption prevents us from understanding, ultimately, what is justifiable and what is not. Different tools in the law should do different jobs. If lawyers are allowed to mix and match to meet the needs of the moment, the limits on what may ultimately be done and what may not will be blurred, and the dignity of all will be endangered.

21
Conclusions

21.1 Theoretical Summary

When confronted with threats to our security, it is tempting to do whatever will make "us"—those who feel threatened or those who care especially about those who feel threatened—both feel safer and live more safely. But to live with each other in a respectful community, one in which the dignity of all is respected, the state can and must follow the dictates of the dignity-respecting model (DR Model) when imposing targeted restrictions on the liberty of those who seem to pose a threat to the security of others (or themselves).

The DR Model requires the state to recognize a set of fundamental distinctions. First, there is the distinction between, on the one hand, law that holds people accountable for past violations of the law, using them to deter lawbreaking and to promote respect for the law by punishing or penalizing them, and, on the other hand, law that imposes targeted restrictions on people's liberty with the aim of incapacitating them so that they can do less (or no) harm.

The criminal law provides the mechanism by which the state can punish culpable wrongdoers, as long as it does so only in proportion to the magnitude of their overall culpability for the illegal acts of which they have been convicted. Such punishment is properly seen as deserved, as a way of collecting on their guilt-debt. And a proper part of their guilt-debt repayment often is that they are used to deter others from breaking the law. Moreover, the form of punishment often justifiably involves targeted loss of liberty, paradigmatically by being imprisoned.

But the need for deterrence may outstrip the functional capacity of the criminal law, given that it is limited to imposing proportional punishments. To fill that gap, I have argued that the state can also develop a related form of law, penal law, grounded not in deserved punishment but in forfeiture of the right not to be penalized. Such penalties are not limited by proportionality to culpable wrongdoing. They are instead limited by fair forfeiture. Fair forfeiture operates with different limits. The fundamental intrinsic limit is quasi-defensive proportionality—that is, penalties must not be so large that the good the state is trying to achieve through deterrence is too small to justify imposing a burden of that size on someone, even if that person could have chosen not to incur it.[1]

[1] See Section 15.1.1.

Punishment, Penalty, and Incapacitation. Alec Walen, Oxford University Press. © Oxford University Press 2026.
DOI: 10.1093/9780197523124.003.0021

In addition, penalties can justly be imposed only when the offense—a proxy crime—was fairly avoidable and when a penalty of that scale would be necessary to achieve the state's aim of shoring up respect for the law. And the size of penalties should be limited—the harshest penalties should be less harsh than the harshest punishments—so that penal law remains secondary to criminal law.

The secondary status of penal law assumes that the state will retain the criminal law. I have argued that there are good reasons why the state should do so, the most important of which is that it is only through the criminal law that the state can hold people publicly accountable for their culpable wrongdoing. The state might also want to support private fora for holding wrongdoers responsible, primarily by supporting some restorative justice processes. But restorative justice processes cannot alone substitute for the criminal law, and even complemented with penal law, the two would fail to provide a meaningful forum for publicly holding people accountable for culpable wrongdoing.

On the other side of the fundamental distinction, we find the imperative to incapacitate those who threaten to wrongfully harm others. Incapacitation may be achieved by both punishments and penalties, and the goal of providing incapacitation has some relevance to the shape of the schedules of punishments and penalties. But it cannot be among their defining or constitutive aims. States should treat their citizens as enjoying the presumption of law abidingness (POLA) unless they have forfeited it or special circumstances ground an exception. The state can justly pursue the aim of incapacitation only for those who do not enjoy the POLA. One might think a criminal or penal law conviction would ground forfeiture of the POLA, but that can be true only in a limited way. Criminal law should aim at reconciliation between the wrongdoer and the rest of the political community. It cannot, therefore, ground a general loss of the POLA, at least not once the punishment has been served. And penal law, as ancillary to the criminal law, should also respect the goal of reconciliation. Thus, if the state is to pursue incapacitation as a goal, then outside of special circumstances, it will be limited by the limited bases for POLA forfeiture that are compatible with the importance of reconciliation.

It is not especially hard to justify the forfeiture of specific privileges when the person has abused them; it is only somewhat harder to justify the forfeiture of a narrowly specified right that would protect against a narrowly targeted threat; but as the limits on liberty become more general, the forfeiture necessary to justify them becomes harder to justify. To justify general POLA forfeiture in a way that would permit the state to go as far as detaining a person in a prison-like setting, the state must prove that he has committed serious crimes, showing deep disrespect for the law and the values it protects, or intended to commit such crimes, or is a serious recidivist with regard to the criminal or penal law. And even then, the state must use only the least restrictive alternative (LRA) to incapacitate individuals who have generally forfeited the POLA.

Alternatively, the state can incapacitate people who have an enforceable duty to incapacitate themselves. One way a person can have such a duty is by being unable to avoid imposing a threat to others if he mingles with them—the paradigmatic example of which is a person with a serious and contagious disease. Another way is if the person is reasonably deemed by others to be frightening, and some small sacrifice of his liberty—such as short-term detention to sort out charges and pretrial rights after an arrest—would suffice to provide others with reasonable reassurance. Longer-term detentions of frightening people can be justifiable if they are compensated for the harm, but as compensation is rarely subjectively adequate, this justification should be minimally relied on.

The other way the state can justify incapacitating people who pose a threat to others that they have no right to pose is if the people being incapacitated are in one of two ways unaccountable. If they are intrinsically unaccountable due to some deficit in their capacity for autonomous self-governance, then they cannot expect the benefit of the POLA. The same is true if they are extrinsically unaccountable, either because the state has no duty to expend resources to police them or because it lacks the capacity to do so.

21.2 A List of Practical Options

These options for dealing with people who threaten the rights of others, or respect for the law more generally, can be organized into a list as follows. This list does not represent normative priorities (with the exception of a preference for criminal law over penal law); it simply represents options that the state has for imposing targeted restrictions on liberty:

1) If a person has committed a crime without a justification or excuse, she may be punished with a proportional punishment. Such punishments may sometimes include measures that include targeted restrictions on liberty, paradigmatically time in prison.
2) If she has committed a proxy crime, the proportional punishment for which would be light, the state may instead seek to penalize her with a penalty that would be harsher than a proportional punishment. The justification for doing so refers not to her culpability, but to the fact that she violated the law without justification or excuse and thereby forfeited her right not to suffer such a penalty.
3) If she has committed a serious criminal offense, or a string of less serious criminal or penal offenses, she may be held to have forfeited the POLA in

a general way for some time after she finishes serving the sanction for her offense. She may also forfeit the POLA for merely intending to commit serious crimes. This forfeiture entitles the state to impose LRA-targeted restrictions on her liberty. These may include pretrial detention if she is arrested for serious crimes in the future.

4) If she has a duty to restrict herself because she cannot safely mingle with others, the state may impose restrictions on her that track her duty to self-restrict.
5) If she is frightening to others, for good statistical reasons, reasons that cannot be taken to justify imposing serious restrictions on her liberty as long as she benefits from the POLA, the state may nonetheless impose small, targeted restrictions on her liberty to provide others with some measure of reassurance.
6) If she is arrested and the state reasonably deems her a danger pretrial, but it cannot establish that she has forfeited the POLA, it may hold her pretrial, if doing so is the LRA to prevent the feared danger. But then it owes her compensation for that time served, either in the form of reduced time in prison if she is convicted and her sentence is longer than her time in pretrial detention, or financial compensation if she is acquitted or her sentence is shorter than her time in pretrial detention. It may also seek to pursue hypothetical forfeiture of the POLA: If her crime would suffice to forfeit the POLA, then a conviction would confirm the hypothesis that she forfeited the POLA, and she could be detained accordingly with no compensation for time served. If, however, she is acquitted, then she would be owed compensation for the time served.
7) If she falls short of the threshold for full autonomous capacity, whether because of youth, insanity, or severe intellectual disability, then she may be detained with the LRA to protect herself and others.
8) If she is on the borderline of the threshold for full autonomous capacity, then the state has to ask what would be the most respectful way of responding to her (respectful to her and to those she might harm): holding her accountable as if she had met the threshold, not holding her fully accountable for her actions but also not restricting her liberty (thereby endangering her and others), or not holding her fully accountable but restricting her liberty as a consequence.
9) If she is struggling with a drug addiction that causes social problems, she may lose her liberty as a result of her ongoing choices to take drugs, but the loss should fall under the category of lack of autonomous control, not the category of criminal or penal offenses.
10) If she is a high-functioning psychopath, she may be held accountable, but due to her limited ability to understand moral reasons, she should

be sanctioned only with forfeiture of the POLA or deserved criminal-law-light punishments (punishment-like sanctions that carry her social debt but that do not imply that she should feel something she cannot feel: guilt).

11) If she is extrinsically unaccountable because the state has no duty to police her, she can be targeted with LRA restrictions on her liberty. This would apply to prisoners of war, alien suspected terrorists who come from countries that will not police them, and deportable aliens whose countries will not take them.
12) If she is extrinsically unaccountable because the state is unable to mount effective policing, due to invasion, insurrection, or the uncontrolled rise of criminal gangs, then she and all others who live under the same condition can be treated as though they do not benefit from the POLA. The state can impose targeted restrictions on her liberty if she is reasonably taken to be especially frightening. But when the state regains normal policing capacity, it should quickly sort out those whose behavior during the crisis merited criminal charges or forfeiture of the POLA from the others who were *merely* deemed frightening.

If none of these conditions applies, the state may not impose targeted restrictions on persons just because they are deemed frightening. Doing so is inconsistent with respect for the dignity of persons. In addition, the state may not target liberty using one of these listed categories in ways inconsistent with the rationale of that category. Here are two important illustrations of that limit: Punishment must be proportional to culpability, and incapacitation of those who have forfeited the POLA must use the LRA.

21.3 Practical Implications for the Law

The importance of the DR Model for targeted restrictions on liberty is both theoretical and practical. Theoretically, it allows the state to be clear about the different ways its law can justifiably impose targeted restrictions on liberty. Practically, it can be cited to defend the law as it now operates, at least in the United States, against a range of common criticisms, but it can also be cited as calling for revisions to current practices.

In defense of current practices, it supports, for example, these claims:

- That punishment can be restricted by appeal to a notion of proportionality (Chapter 8).

- That penalties for proxy crimes can justly exceed proportional punishments for those crimes (Chapter 15).
- That convicted sex offenders can be required to register as such even if that requirement was not on the books when they committed their crime, because the requirement is best seen not as a punishment or penalty, but as a matter of forfeiture of the POLA (Chapter 16).
- That pretrial detention can sometimes be imposed on people who are deemed sufficiently dangerous, even though it may not be imposed in the same way on others who are equally dangerous (Chapter 18).
- That psychopaths who are prudentially competent can be sanctioned for violating the law (Chapter 19).
- That aliens arrested for suspected terrorist activities, or convicted of normal criminal activities, can be detained without trial if the only country that will take them cannot be trusted to police them (Chapter 20).

On the other hand, the DR Model has several revisionist implications. These include:

- That incapacitation cannot be cited as a defining or constitutive aim of punishment (Chapter 7).
- That the death penalty and even life sentences are per se disproportionate punishments (Chapter 8).[2]
- That separate detention facilities should be used for, on the one hand, those who are being punished for their culpable public wrongs, and, on the other hand, those who are being penalized with a deterrent penalty (Chapter 13).
- That penalties for proxy crimes can be disproportionately large, but that they then must not be treated as "punishments," and they should therefore be meted out without censure (Chapter 15).
- That strict liability should be banned even for public welfare offenses and proxy crimes (Chapter 15).
- That putting the burden of establishing a defense on a defendant—as opposed to requiring the prosecution to negate a defense that has been successfully raised as an issue by proof beyond a reasonable doubt—is permissible only for the penal law and not for criminal law (Chapter 15).
- That those who are still a danger after serving a long sentence may have their liberty restricted thereafter, but only by using the least restrictive alternative (Chapter 16).

[2] This is reformist in the United States, not in Europe.

- That loss of the right to vote should be banned as a penalty, except perhaps for the crime of voting fraud (Chapter 16).
- That compensation is owed to anyone held in pretrial detention who has not forfeited the POLA (Chapter 18).
- That drug addicts who can be held responsible for their drug use must be held responsible in a way that gives them no record of criminal or penal law offenses (Chapter 19).
- That POWs must be released if they give parole and the detaining power could trust the enemy nation or a third-party nation to enforce the parolee's duty not to fight again for the enemy (Chapter 20).
- That deportable aliens who cannot be sent to another country that will accept them and police them may have their liberty limited, but only with the LRA restriction (Chapter 20).
- That pretextual prosecutions must not be used (Chapter 20).

21.4 Final Thoughts

The concrete implications just described are of great practical importance. But in my view, the three most important implications of this book are these: First, proportionality can and should be taken more seriously than it is normally taken in criminal law theory (Chapter 8). That can be done if and only if we separate penal law from criminal law.

Second, there is no need to reach for sloppy pluralism to account for the range of practices that the state may engage in to respond to threats. A principled pluralism, dictated by the DR Model, can instead be invoked and can provide substantive guidance on important legal issues.

Third, the state should avoid simply appealing to consequentialist balances when it comes to matters of security and liberty. It should never simply say "These people are a threat, so we need to lock them up." It is never *that* simple, not even in times of crisis. The state must always, even when promoting security, respect the dignity of all.

Bibliography

Scholarly Articles, Chapters, and Books

Agule, Craig. 2023. "Blaming Kids." In *The Palgrave Handbook on the Philosophy of Punishment.* M.C. Altman (ed.). Palgrave Macmillan.

Alexander, Larry. 2001. "Deontology at the Threshold." *San Diego Law Review* 37: 893–912.

Alexander, Larry. 2012. "Self-Defense." In *The Routledge Companion to Philosophy of Law.* Andrei Marmor (ed.). Routledge Press: 222–237.

Alexander, Larry. 2013. "You Got What You Deserved." *Criminal Law and Philosophy* 7: 309–319.

Alexander, Larry. 2016. "The Means Principle." In *Legal, Moral, and Metaphysical Truths: The Philosophy of Michael S. Moore.* Kimberly Kessler Ferzan and Stephen Morse (eds.). Cambridge University Press.

Alexander, Larry and Kimberly Kessler Ferzan (with Stephen Morse). 2009. *Crime and Culpability: A Theory of Criminal Law.* Cambridge University Press.

Alexander, Larry and Kimberly Kessler Ferzan. 2018. *Reflections on Crime and Culpability: Problems and Puzzles.* Cambridge University Press.

Alexander, Michelle. 2011. *The New Jim Crow: Mass Incarceration in the Age of Colorblindness,* revised edition. The New Press.

Ambos, Kai and Stefanie Bock. 2014. "Germany." In *General Defences in Criminal Law: Domestic and Comparative Perspectives.* Alan Reed et al (eds.). Routledge.

Ariely, Dan. 2012. *The (Honest) Truth about Dishonesty.* Harper Perennial.

Arpaly, Nomy. 2022. "Quality of Will and (Some) Unusual Behavior." In *Agency in Mental Disorder: Philosophical Dimensions.* Matt King and Joshua May (eds.). Oxford University Press.

Ashworth, Andrew and Lucia Zedner. 2014. *Preventive Justice.* Oxford University Press.

Bates, Sanford. 1922. "Honor System for Inmates of Prisons and Reformatories." *Journal of Criminal Law and Criminology* 13: 109–116.

Bell, Kristen. 2022. "Critical Mercy in Criminal Law." *Law and Philosophy* 42: 351–378.

Bell, Monica. 2017. "Police Reform and the Dismantling of Legal Estrangement." *The Yale Law Journal* 126: 2054–2150.

Bennett, Jonathan. 1981. "The Tanner Lectures on Human Values." University of Utah Press.

Berman, Mitch. 2011. "Two Kinds of Retributivism." In *Philosophical Foundations of Criminal Law.* R.A. Duff and Stuart Green (eds.). Oxford University Press.

Berman, Mitch. 2013. "Rehabilitating Retributivism." *Law and Philosophy* 32: 83–108.

Berman, Mitch. 2025. "Retributivism." In *Oxford Handbook of Punishment Theory and Philosophy.* Jesper Ryberg (ed.). Oxford University Press.

Blackstone, William. 1979. *2 Commentaries on the Laws of England (A Facsimile of the First Edition of 1765-1769).* University of Chicago Press.

Blake, Michael. 2013. "Immigration, Jurisdiction, and Exclusion." Philosophy and Public Affairs 41: 103–130.

Bowen, Joseph. 2023. "Review of Alec D. Walen *The Mechanics of Claims and Permissible Killing in War* (Oxford University Press, 2019)." *Criminal Law and Philosophy* 17: 207–214.

Bronsther, Jacob. 2021. "The Corrective Justice Theory of Punishment." *Virginian Law Review* 107: 227–279.

Brook, Richard. 1988. "Threats and Promises." *Philosophy and Public Affairs* 17: 235–239.

Brown, Ryan. 2016. *Honor Bound: How a Cultural Ideal Has Shaped the American Psyche*. Oxford University Press.

Cabranes, José. 2009. "Our Imperial Criminal Procedure: Problems in the Extraterritorial Application of U.S. Constitutional Law," *Yale Law Journal* 118: 1660–1711.

Calabresi, Guido, and A. Douglas Melamed. 1972. "Property Rules, Liability Rules, and Inalienability: One View of the Cathedral." *Harvard Law Review* 85: 1089–1128.

Carlsson, Andreas. 2017. "Blameworthiness as Deserved Guilt." *Journal of Ethics* 21: 89–115.

Chiao, Vincent. 2019. *Criminal Law in the Age of the Administrative State*. Oxford University Press.

Child, Richard. 2024. "The Unilateral Authority Theory of Punishment." *Law and Philosophy* 43: 187–213.

Clark, David. 2025. "Mistaken Defense and the Unbundling of Rights," *Ethics* 135: 428–457.

Coates, D. Justin. 2021. "Extending the Limits of Blame." *Criminal Law and Philosophy* 15: 207–215.

Cole, David. 2002. "Enemy Aliens." *Stanford Law Review* 54: 953–1005.

Cole, David. 2008. "Rights Over Borders: Transnational Constitutionalism and Guantanamo Bay." *Cato Supreme Court Review* 2007–2008: 47–61.

Cole, David. 2009. "Out of the Shadows: Preventive Detention, Suspected Terrorists, and War." *California Law Review* 97: 693–750.

Cohen, Gerald. 2006. "Casting the First Stone: Who Can, and Who Can't, Condemn the Terrorists?" *Royal Institute of Philosophy Supplement* 58: 113–136.

Cornford, Andrew. 2011. "Resultant Luck and Criminal Liability." In *The Structures of the Criminal Law*. A. Duff et al. (eds.). Oxford University Press.

Cornford, Andrew. 2017. "Rethinking the Wrongness Constraint on Criminalisation," *Law and Philosophy* 36: 615–649.

Corrado, Louis. 1996. "Punishment and the Wild Beast of Prey: The Problem of Preventive Detention." *Journal of Criminal Law & Criminology* 86: 778–814.

Corrado, Louis. 2005. "Responsibility and Control." *Hofstra Law Review* 34: 59–91.

Corrado, Louis. 2009. "The Case for a Purely Volitional Insanity Defense." *Texas Tech Law Review* 42: 481–511.

Dahan Katz, Leora. 2021. "Response Retributivism: Defending the Duty to Punish." *Law and Philosophy* 40: 585–615.

Damaška, Mirjan. 1973. "Evidentiary Barriers to Conviction and Two Models of Criminal Procedure: A Comparative Study." *University of Pennsylvania Law Review* 121: 506–589.

Davis, Angela. 2003. *Are Prisons Obsolete?* Seven Stories Press.

Davis, Angela, Gina Dent, Erica Meiners, and Beth Richie. 2022. *Abolition, Feminism, Now*. Haymarket Books.

Delgado, Richard. 2000. "Prosecuting Violence: A Colloquy on Race, Community, and Justice: Goodbye to Hammurabi: Analyzing the Atavistic Appeal of Restorative Justice." *Stanford Law Review* 52: 751–775.

Dill, Brendan and Stephen Darwall. 2014. "Moral Psychology as Accountability." In *Moral Psychology & Human Agency: Philosophical Essays on the Science of Ethics*. J. D'Arms and D. Jacobson (eds.). Oxford University Press.

Dolinko, David. 1991. "Some Thoughts About Retributivism." *Ethics* 101: 537–559.

Dolinko, David. 2003. "Restorative Justice and the Justification of Punishment." *Utah Law Review* 2003: 319–342.

Dressler, Joshua. 2018. *Understanding Criminal Law*, 8th edition. Carolina Academic Press.

Dubber, Markus and Tatjana Hörnle. 2014. *Criminal Law: A Comparative Approach*. Oxford University Press.

Duff, Antony. 1986. *Trials and Punishments*. Cambridge University Press.

Duff, Antony. 1991. "Retributive Punishment—Ideals and Actualities." *Israel Law Review* 25: 422–451.

Duff, Antony. 2001. *Punishment, Communication, and Community*. Oxford University Press.

Duff, Antony. 2002. "Virtue, Vice, and Criminal Liability: Do We Want an Aristotelian Criminal Law?" *Buffalo Law Review* 6: 147–184.
Duff, Antony. 2011. "Responsibility, Citizenship and Criminal Law." In *Philosophical Foundations of Criminal Law*. R. A. Duff and Stuart Green (eds.). Oxford University Press.
Duff, Antony. 2013. "Pre-Trial Detention and the Presumption of Innocence." In *Prevention and the Limits of the Criminal Law*. Andrew Ashworth, Lucia Zedner, and Patrick Tomlin (eds.). Oxford University Press.
Duff, Antony. 2018. *The Realm of Criminal Law*. Oxford University Press.
Duff, Antony. 2019. "Two Models of Criminal Fault." *Criminal Law and Philosophy* 13: 643–665.
Duff, Antony. 2019. "Moral and Criminal Responsibility: Answering and Refusing to Answer." In *Oxford Studies in Agency and Responsibility: Volume 5*. D Justin Coates and Neal Tognazzini (eds.). Oxford University Press.
Duff, Antony. 2020. "Defending the Realm of Criminal Law." *Criminal Law and Philosophy* 14: 465–500.
Duff, Antony. 2023. "'De Minimis' and the Structure of the Criminal Trial." *Law and Philosophy* 42: 57–86.
Duff, Antony. 2023. "Strict Liability and Strict Responsibility." In *Routledge Handbook of Philosophy of Responsibility*. M. Keiner (ed.). Routledge.
Duff, Antony. 2025. "Communicative Theory." In *The Oxford Handbook of the Philosophy of Punishment*. Jesper Ryberg (ed.). Oxford University Press.
Duff, Antony. unpublished. "Doing Justice to Injustice: Standing Lost and Regained." http://dx.doi.org/10.2139/ssrn.5270383 (posted 28 May 2025).
Duff, Antony and Tatjana Hörnle. 2022. "Crimes of Endangerment." In *Core Concepts in Criminal Law and Criminal Justice*, Vol. 2. Kai Ambos et al., (eds.). Cambridge University Press.
Duff, Antony and Tatjana Hörnle. 2025. "Principles of Criminalization." In *Core Concepts in Criminal Law and Criminal Justice*, Vol. 3. Kai Ambos et al., (eds.). Cambridge University Press.
Dyson, Matthew. 2022. *Explaining Tort and Crime: Legal Development Across Laws and Legal Systems*, 1850–2020. Cambridge University Press.
Edwards, James. 2019. "Standing to Hold Responsible." *Journal of Moral Philosophy* 16: 437–462.
Emanuel, Ezekiel. 1999. "What Is the Great Benefit of Legalizing Euthanasia or Physician-Assisted Suicide?" *Ethics* 109: 629–642.
Epp, Charles, Steven Maynard-Moody, and Donald Haider-Markel. 2017. "Beyond Profiling: The Institutional Sources of Racial Disparities in Policing." *Public Administration Review* 77: 168–178.
Ewing, Benjamin. 2023, "Do Unjust States Have the Standing to Blame? Three Reservations about Skepticism." *Oxford Journal of Legal Studies* 43: 249–272.
Fabre, Cécile. 2024. "The Duty to Accept Apologies." *Journal of Moral Philosophy* 21: 355–378.
Feinberg, Joel. 1965. "The Expressive Function of Punishment." *The Monist* 49: 397–423.
Feinberg, Joel. 1970. "The Nature and Value of Rights." *Journal of Value Inquiry* 4: 243–260.
Feinberg, Joel. 1970. "Justice and Personal Desert." In *Doing and Deserving*. Joel Feinberg (ed.). Princeton University Press: 55–87.
Feinberg, Joel. 1995. "Equal Punishment for Failed Attempts; Some Bad but Instructive Arguments Against It." *Arizona Law Review* 37: 117–133.
Ferzan, Kimberly Kessler. 2011. "Beyond Crime and Commitment: Justifying Liberty Deprivations of the Dangerous and Responsible." *Minnesota Law Review* 96: 141–193.
Ferzan, Kimberly Kessler. 2016. "Forfeiture and Self-Defense." In *The Ethics of Self-Defense*. Christian Coons and Michael Webber (eds.). Oxford University Press.
Ferzan, Kimberly Kessler. 2023. "Trouble with Time Served." *Brigham Young University Law Review* 48: 2001–2076.

Fileva, Iskra. 2004. "Impermissible Altruism: A Response to Pummer." *Ethics* 135: 151–165.
Fischer, John Martin and Mark Ravizza. 1998. *Responsibility and Control: A Theory of Moral Responsibility*. Cambridge University Press.
Fishkin, Joseph. 2011. "Equal Citizenship and the Individual Right to Vote." *Indiana Law Journal* 86: 1289–1360.
Fletcher, George. 2000. *Rethinking Criminal Law*. Oxford University Press.
Foot, Philippa. 1967. "The Problem of Abortion and the Doctrine of the Double Effect." Reprinted in *Virtues and Vices*. University of California Press, 1978.
Foot, Philippa. 1984. "Killing and Letting Die." In *Abortion: Moral and Legal Perspectives*. J. Garfield and P. Hennessey (eds.). University of Massachusetts Press.
Fornaroli, Giulio, 2025. "Rights, Wronging, and Equality of Status." *Law and Philosophy* 44: 61–88.
Frick, Johann. 2020. "Conditional Reasons and the Procreation Asymmetry." *Philosophical Perspectives: Ethics* 34: 53–87.
Fricker, Miranda. 2016. "What's the Point of Blame? A Paradigm Based Explanation." *Noûs* 50: 165–183.
Fritz, G. K., and D. Miller. 2018. "Hypocrisy and the Standing to Blame." *Pacific Philosophical Quarterly* 99: 118–139.
Frowe, Helen. 2014. *Defensive Killing*. Oxford University Press.
Frowe, Helen. 2018. "Lesser-Evil Justifications for Harming: Why We're Required to Turn the Trolley." *Philosophical Quarterly* 68: 460–480.
Fryer, Roland. 2019. "An Empirical Analysis of Racial Differences in Police Use of Force." *Journal of Political Economy* 127: 1210–1261.
Gallant, Kenneth. 2022. *International Criminal Jurisdiction: Whose Law Must We Obey?* Oxford University Press.
Gardner, John. 1998. "Crime: In Proportion and in Perspective." Reprinted in *Offenses and Defenses: Selected Essays in the Philosophy of Criminal Law*. Oxford University Press, 2007.
Gauthier, David. 1994. "Assure and Threaten." *Ethics* 104: 690–721.
Gilligan, James. 2001. *Preventing Violence*. Thames & Hudson.
Gilligan, James. 2003. "Shame, Guilt, and Violence." *Social Research* 70: 1149–1180.
Godman, Marion and Anneli Jefferson. 2017. "On Blaming and Punishing Psychopaths." *Criminal Law and Philosophy* 11: 127–142.
Goldberg, John C.P. and Benjamin C. Zipursky. 2020. *Recognizing Wrongs*. Belknap Press.
Gordon-Solmon, Kerah and Theron Pummer. 2022. "Lesser-Evil Justifications: A Reply to Frowe." *Law and Philosophy* 41: 639–646.
Green, Leslie. 2008. *The Contemporary Law of Armed Conflict*, 3rd edition. Juris Publishing.
Green, Stuart. 2011. "Just Deserts in Unjust Societies: A Case-specific Approach." In *Philosophical Foundations of Criminal Law*. R. A. Duff and Stuart Green (eds.). Oxford University Press.
Green, Stuart and Alec Walen. 2018. "Introduction to the *Rutgers Law Review* Symposium on 'Theorizing Criminal Law Reform.'" *Rutgers Law Review* 70: 1083–1092.
Graif, Corina, Andrew Gladfelter, and Stephen Matthews. 2014. "Urban Poverty and Neighborhood Effects on Crime." *Sociology Compass* 8: 1140–1155.
Harel, Alon. 2015. "The Duty to Criminalize." *Law and Philosophy* 34: 1–22.
Hart, Henry. 1958. "The Aims of the Criminal Law." *Law and Contemporary Problems* 23: 401–441.
Hart, H.L.A. 1961. *The Concept of Law*. Clarendon Press.
Hart, H.L.A. 1968. *Punishment and Responsibility: Essays in the Philosophy of Law*. Clarendon Press.
Hegel, Georg Wilhelm Friedrich. 1821. *Philosophy of Right*. Translated by T.M. Knox. Clarendon Press, 1952.
Hieronymi, Pamela. 2020. *Freedom, Resentment, and the Metaphysics of Morals*. Princeton University Press.

Hodgson, Louis-Philippe. 2010. "Kant on Property Rights and the State." *Kantian Review* 15: 57–87.
Hohfeld, Wesley. 1913. "Some Fundamental Legal Conceptions as Applied in Judicial Reasoning." *Yale Law Journal* 23: 16–59.
Hoskins, Zachary. 2019. *Beyond Punishment? A Normative Account of the Collateral Legal Consequences of Conviction*. Oxford University Press.
Hoskins, Zachary. 2019. "Against Incapacitative Punishment." In *Predictive Sentencing: Normative and Empirical Perspectives*. Jan de Keijser, Julian Roberts, and Jesper Ryberg (eds.). Hart Publishing.
Howard, Jeffrey and Avia Pasternak. 2023. "Criminal Wrongdoing, Restorative Justice, and the Moral Standing of the United States." *The Journal of Political Philosophy* 31: 42–59.
Hsieh, Nien-hê and Henrik Andersson. 2021. "Incommensurable Values." *The Stanford Encyclopedia of Philosophy*. Edward N. Zalta (ed.). https://plato.stanford.edu/archives/fall2021/entries/value-incommensurable/.
Huffman, Mary K. 2016. "Moral Panic and the Politics of Fear: The Dubious Logic Underlying Sex Offender Registration Statutes and Proposals for Restoring Measures of Judicial Discretion to Sex Offender Management." *Virginia Journal of Criminal Law* 4: 241–303.
Hulsman, Louk. 1991. "The Abolitionist Case: Alternative Crime Policies." *Israel Law Review* 25: 681–709.
Husak, Douglas. 2000. "Holistic Retributivism." *California Law Review* 88: 991–1000.
Husak, Douglas. 2008. *Overcriminalization*. Oxford University Press.
Husak, Douglas. 2013. "Preventive Detention as Punishment? Some Possible Obstacles." In *Prevention and the Limits of the Criminal Law*. Andrew Ashworth, Lucia Zedner, and Patrick Tomlin (eds.). Oxford University Press.
Husak, Douglas. 2016. *Ignorance of Law: A Philosophical Inquiry*. Oxford University Press.
Husak, Douglas. 2020. "The Metric of Punishment Severity: A Puzzle about the Principle of Proportionality." In *Of One-Eyed and Toothless Miscreants*. Michael Tonry (ed.). Oxford University Press.
Husak, Douglas. 2022. "Retributivism and Over-Punishment," *Law and Philosophy* 41: 169–191.
Husak, Douglas. 2025. "Pluralistic Theory." In *The Oxford Handbook of The Philosophy of Punishment*. Jesper Ryberg (ed.). Oxford University Press.
Hyland, Richard. 2009. *Gifts: A Study in Comparative Law*. Oxford University Press.
Isiksel, Turkuler. 2019. "Corporate Human Rights Claims under the ECHR." *Georgetown Journal of Law & Public Policy* 17 (Special Issue): 979–1006.
Jones, Danielle. 2015. "When the Fallout of a Criminal Conviction Goes Too Far: Challenging Collateral Consequences." *Stanford Journal of Civil Rights & Civil Liberties* 11: 237–268.
Kamm, Frances. 1989. "Harming Some to Save Others." *Philosophical Studies* 57: 227–260.
Kamm, Frances. 2007. *Intricate Ethics: Rights, Responsibilities, and Permissible Harm*. Oxford University Press.
Kant, Immanuel. 1795. "To Perpetual Peace: A Philosophical Sketch." In *Perpetual Peace and Other Essays*. Translated by Ted Humphrey. Hackett Publishing, 1983.
Kant, Immanuel. 1797. "The Doctrine of Right." In *The Metaphysics of Morals*. Translated by Mary Gregor. Cambridge University Press, 1991.
Kelly, Erin. 2018. *The Limits of Blame*. Harvard University Press.
Kelly, Erin. 2021. "From Retributive to Restorative Justice." *Criminal Law and Philosophy* 15: 237–247.
Kelly, Erin. 2024. "The Problem with Prisons." *Ethics* 134: 539–558.
Kleinig, John. 1973. *Punishment and Desert*. Martinus Nijhoff.
Kolber, Adam. 2024. *Punishment for the Greater Good*. Oxford University Press.
Korsgaard, Christine. 1993. "The Reasons We Can Share: An Attack on the Distinction Between Agent-Relative and Agent-Neutral Values." Reprinted in *Creating the Kingdom of Ends*. Cambridge University Press, 1996.

Krishnamurthi, Guha. 2024. "Against the Recidivist Premium." *Tulane Law Review* 98: 411–470.

Lacey, Nicola and Hanna Pickard. 2015. "To Blame or to Forgive? Reconciling Punishment and Forgiveness in Criminal Justice." *Oxford Journal of Legal Studies* 35: 665–696.

Lacey, Nicola and Hanna Pickard. 2015. "The Chimera of Proportionality: Institutionalising Limits on Punishment in Contemporary Social and Political Systems." *Modern Law Review* 78: 216–240.

Lai, Calvin, et al. 2016. "Reducing Implicit Racial Preferences: II. Intervention Effectiveness Across Time." doi.org/10.1037/xge0000179.

Lanni, Adriaan. 2021. "Taking Restorative Justice Seriously." *Buffalo Law Review* 69: 635–682.

Laudan, Larry. 2011. "The Rules of Trial, Political Morality, and the Costs of Error: Or, is Proof Beyond a Reasonable Doubt Doing More Harm than Good?" In *Oxford Studies in Philosophy of Law*, Vol 1. Leslie Green and Brian Leiter (eds.). Oxford University Press.

Lazar, Seth. 2009. "Responsibility, Risk, and Killing in Self-Defense." *Ethics* 119: 699–728.

Lee, Ambrose and Alexander Sarch. 2023. *The Moral Prerequisites of the Criminal Law.* Cambridge University Press.

Lee, Youngjae. 2009. "Recidivism as Omission: A Relational Account." *Texas Law Review* 87: 571–622.

Lee, Youngjae. 2021. "Mala Prohibita and Proportionality." *Criminal Law and Philosophy* 15: 425–446.

Lee, Youngjae. 2022. "Proxy Crimes and Overcriminalization." *Criminal Law and Philosophy* 16: 469–484.

Lefkowitz, David. 2007. "On a Moral Right to Civil Disobedience." *Ethics* 117: 202–233.

Lefkowitz, David. 2017. "In Defense of Penalizing (but not Punishing) Civil Disobedience." *Res Publica*.·DOI 10.1007/s11158-017-9362-5.

Leovy, Jill. 2015. *Ghettoside: A True Story of Murder in America.* Randomhouse.

Levy, Ken. 2005. "The Solution to the Problem of Outcome Luck: Why Harm is Just as Punishable as the Wrongful Action that Causes It." *Law and Philosophy* 24: 263–303.

Lichter, Andrew. 2025. "Wrongdoer-Centered Reasons for Blame." *Ethics* 135: 489–518.

Lippert-Rasmussen, Kasper. 2020. "Why the Moral Equality Account of the Hypocrite's Lack of Standing to Blame Fails." *Analysis* 80: 666–674.

Lippert-Rasmussen, Kasper. 2024. "Lesser Transgressions and Loss of Standing to Blame." *Ratio* DOI: 10.1111/rati.12412.

Lippke, Richard. 2016. *Taming the Presumption of Innocence.* Oxford University Press.

Lippke, Richard. 2016. "The Ethics of Recidivist Premiums." In *Routledge Handbook of Criminal Justice Ethics.* J. Jacobs and J. Jackson (eds.). Routledge.

List, Christian and Philip Pettit. 2011. *Group Agency: The Possibility, Design, And Status of Corporate Agents.* Oxford University Press.

Litton, Paul. 2008. "Responsibility Status of the Psychopath: On Moral Reasoning and Rational Self-Governance." *Rutgers Law Journal* 39: 349–392.

Locke, John. 1690. *Second Treatise of Government.* Reprint, Hackett Publishing, 1980.

Macnamara, Coleen. 2015. "Blame, Communication, and Moral Agency." In *The Nature of Moral Responsibility: New Essays.* Randolph Clarke, Michael McKenna, and Angela M. Smith (eds.). Oxford University Press.

Matravers, Matt. 2016. "De-Moralising Retributivism: Agency, Blame, and Humanity in Criminal Law Theory and Practice." In *Routledge Handbook of Criminal Justice Ethics.* J. Jacobs and J. Jackson (eds.). Routledge.

Mayson, Sandra. 2015. "Collateral Consequences and the Preventive State." *Notre Dame Law Review* 91: 301–362.

Mayson, Sandra. 2018. "Dangerous Defendants." *Yale Law Journal* 127: 490–568.

Mayson, Sandra. 2022. "A Consequentialist Framework for Prevention." *Law and Philosophy* 41: 219–241.

McLeod, Allegra. 2014. "Regulating Sexual Harm: Strangers, Intimates, and Social Institutional Reform." *California Law Review* 102: 1553–1621.
McKenna, Michael. 2012. *Conversation and Responsibility*. Oxford University Press.
McMahan, Jeff. 2009. *Killing in War*. Oxford University Press.
Meltzer, Bernard. 1947. "A Note on Some Aspects of the Nuremberg Debate." *University of Chicago Law Review* 14: 455–469.
Mendlow, Gabriel. 2018. "Divine Justice and the Library of Babel: Or, Was Al Capone Really Punished for Tax Evasion?" *Ohio State Journal of Criminal Law* 16: 181–205.
Mill, John Stuart. 1859. *On Liberty*. Reprint, W.W. Norton & Co., 1975.
Moller, Dan. 2007. "Love and Death." *Journal of Philosophy* 104: 301–16.
Montesquieu, Charles de. 1748. *The Spirit of the Laws*. Translated by Thomas Nugent. Digireads.com Publishing. 2020.
Moore, Michael. 1997. *Placing Blame: A Theory of the Criminal Law*. Oxford University Press.
Moore, Michael. 2009. "A Tale of Two Theories." *Criminal Justice Ethics* 28: 27–48.
Moore, Michael. 2014. "Liberty's Constraints on What Should be Made Criminal." In *Criminalization: The Political Morality of the Criminal Law*. A. Duff et al. (eds.). Oxford University Press.
Moore, Michael. 2020. *Mechanical Choices: The Responsibility of the Human Machine*. Oxford University Press.
Morris, Christopher. 1991. "Punishment and Loss of Moral Standing." *Canadian Journal of Moral Philosophy* 21: 53–79.
Morris, Herbert. 1968. "Persons and Punishment." *The Monist* 52: 475–501.
Morris, Herbert. 1971. "Guilt and Suffering." *Philosophy East and West* 21: 419–434.
Morse, Stephen. 1996. "Blame and Danger: An Essay on Preventive Detention." *Boston University Law Review* 76: 113–155.
Morse, Stephen. 1999. "Neither Desert nor Disease." *Legal Theory* 5: 265–309.
Morse, Stephen. 2004. "Preventive Confinement of Dangerous Offenders." *Journal of Law, Medicine & Ethics* 32: 56–72.
Morse, Stephen. 2008. "Psychopathy and Criminal Responsibility." *Neuroethics* 1: 205–212.
Morse, Stephen. 2011. "Mental Disorder and Criminal Law." *The Journal of Criminal Law and Criminology* 101: 885–968.
Mullainathan, Sendhil and Eldar Shafir. 2013. *Scarcity: Why Having Too Little Means So Much*. Times Books.
Muraven, Mark and Roy F. Baumeister. 2000. "Self-Regulation and Depletion of Limited Resources: Does Self-Control Resemble a Muscle?" *Psychological Bulletin* 126: 247–259.
Nagel, Thomas. 2002. "Personal Rights and Public Space." In *Concealment and Exposure & Other Essays*. Thomas Nagel (ed.). Oxford University Press.
Nagin, Daniel. 2013. "Deterrence in the Twenty-First Century." *Crime and Justice: A Review of Research* 42: 199–263.
Nagin, Daniel and John V. Pepper, eds.. 2012. *Deterrence and the Death Penalty*. National Academies Press.
Natapoff, Alexandra. 2012. "Misdemeanors." *Southern California Law Review* 85: 1313–1375.
Nelkin, Dana. 2019. "Guilt, Grief, and the Good." *Social Philosophy and Policy* 36: 173–191.
Nietzsche, Friedrich. 1887. *On the Genealogy of Morals: A Polemic*. Translated by Walter Kaufmann, in *Basic Writings of Nietzsche*. The Modern Library, 2000.
Noorda, Hadassa. 2023. "Exprisonment: Deprivation of Liberty on the Street and at Home." *Criminal Justice Ethics* 42: 1–19.
Nozick, Robert. 1974. *Anarchy, State, and Utopia*. Basic Books Inc.
O'Connell, Daniel, Christy Visher, and Lin Liu. 2020. "Violent Offending, Desistance, and Recidivism." *Marquette Law Review* 103: 983–1006.
Oliver, Matthew. 2021. "The Means and the Good." *Analysis* 81: 665–674.
Øverland, Gerhard. 2014. "Moral Obstacles: An Alternative to the Doctrine of Double Effect." *Ethics* 124: 481–506.

Pardo, Michael. 2009. "Second-Order Proof Rules." *Florida Law Review* 61: 1083–1113.

Parfit, Derek. 1978. "Innumerate Ethics." *Philosophy and Public Affairs* 7: 285–301.

Parfit, Derek. 2011. *On What Matters*, vol. 1. Oxford University Press.

Pfaff, John. 2017. *Locked in: The True Causes of Mass Incarceration and How to Achieve Real Reform*. Basic Books.

Pfaff, John. 2018. "Decarceration's Blindspots." *Ohio State Journal of Criminal Law* 16: 254–279.

Piketty, Thomas. 2021. *A Brief History of Equality*. The Belknap Press.

Pinkney-Baird, Jonathan. 2006. "Don't Tread on Me: Would a British Solution to Anti-Social Behavior Trample the U.S. Bill of Rights?" *Arizona Law Review* 48: 639–667.

Podgor, Ellen S. and Roger S. Clark. 2013. *Understanding International Criminal Law*, 3rd ed. Matthew Bender & Company, Inc.

Porro, Constanza. 2021. "Criminal Blame, Exclusion and Moral Dialogue," *Criminal Law and Philosophy* 15: 223–235.

Portmore, Douglas. 2019. *Opting for the Best: Oughts and Options*. Oxford University Press.

Portmore, Douglas. 2022. "A Comprehensive Account of Blame." In *Self-Blame and Moral Responsibility*. Andreas Carlsson (ed.). Cambridge University Press: 48–76.

Portmore, Douglas. 2024. "Deserving to Suffer." *The Journal of Ethics* 28: 795–813.

Poscher, Ralf. 2024. "What Would It Take? The Potential and Limits of Proportionality Analysis in Law." *Jurisprudence: An International Journal of Legal and Political Thought*. https://doi.org/10.1080/20403313.2024.2419755.

Prinz, Jesse and Shaun Nichols. 2010. "Moral Emotions." In *The Moral Psychology Handbook*. J. M. Doris (ed.). Oxford University Press.

Quinn, Warren. 1985. "The Right to Threaten and the Right to Punish." *Philosophy and Public Affairs* 14: 327–373.

Quinn, Warren. 1988. "Reply to Brook." *Philosophy and Public Affairs* 17: 240–247.

Quinn, Warren. 1989. "Actions, Intentions, and Consequences: The Doctrine of Doing and Allowing." *The Philosophical Review* 98: 287–312.

Quong, Jonathan. 2020. *The Morality of Defensive Force*. Oxford University Press.

Ramakrishnan, Ketan. 2016. "Treating People as Tools." *Philosophy and Public Affairs* 44: 133–165.

Rawls, John. 1971. *A Theory of Justice*. Oxford University Press.

Rawls, John. 1975. "A Kantian Conception of Equality", Reprinted in *John Rawls, Collected Papers*, Samuel Richard Freeman (ed.). Harvard University Press, 1999.

Rawls, John. 1993. *Political Liberalism*. Columbia University Press.

Rawls, John. 1997. "The Idea of Public Reason Revisited." Reprinted in *The Law of Peoples*. Harvard University Press, 1999.

Renzo, Massimo. 2013. "Responsibility and Answerability in the Criminal Law." In *The Constitution of the Criminal Law*. A. Duff et al. (eds.). Oxford University Press.

Renzo, Massimo. 2017. "Rights Forfeiture and Liability to Harm." *The Journal of Political Philosophy* 25: 324–342.

Renzo, Massimo. 2019. "Political Authority and Unjust Wars." *Philosophy and Phenomenological Research* 99: 336–357.

Rettig, Christián. 2024. "Let's Forget About Forfeiture." *Jurisprudence*. DOI: 10.1080/20403313.2024.2321029.

Riedener, Stefan. 2019. "The Standing to Blame, or Why Moral Disapproval is What It Is." *Dialectica* 73: 183–210.

Ripstein, Arthur. 2009. *Force and Freedom: Kant's Legal and Political Philosophy*. Harvard University Press.

Roberts, Julian and Stefan Harrendorf. 2020. "Criminal History Enhancements at Sentencing." In *Core Concepts in Criminal Law and Criminal Justice*, vol. 1. Kai Ambos et al. (eds.). Cambridge University Press.

Robinson, Paul. 2001. "Punishing Dangerousness: Cloaking Preventive Detention as Criminal Justice." *Harvard Law Review* 114: 1429–1456.
Robinson, Paul. 2003. "The Virtues of Restorative Processes, The Vices of 'Restorative Justice.'" *Utah Law Review* 2003: 375–388.
Robinson, Paul and Robert Kurzban. 2007. "Concordance and Conflict in Intuitions of Justice." *Minnesota Law Review*. 91: 1829–1907.
Robinson, Paul and Muhammad Sarahne. 2020. "The Opposite of Punishment: Imagining a Path to Public Redemption." *The Rutgers University Law Review* 73: 1–32.
Russell, Paul. 2021. "Responsibility Skepticism and Strawson's Naturalism." *Ethics* 131: 754–776.
Ryberg, Jasper. 2020. "Proportionality and the Seriousness of Crimes." In *Of One-Eyed and Toothless Miscreants*. Michael Tonry (ed.). Oxford University Press.
Ryngaert, Cedric. 2008. *Jurisdiction in International Law*. Oxford University Press.
Sarch, Alexander. 2019. *Criminally Ignorant: Why the Law Pretends We Know What We Don't*. Oxford University Press.
Sayre, Francis. 1932. "Mens Rea." *Harvard Law Review* 45: 974–1026.
Scanlon, T.M. 2008. *Moral Dimensions: Permissibility, Meaning, Blame*. Harvard University Press.
Scheffler, Samuel. 1982. *The Rejection of Consequentialism*. Clarendon Press.
Schulhofer, Stephen. 1974. "Harm and Punishment: A Critique of Emphasis on the Results of Conduct in the Criminal Law." *University of Pennsylvania Law Review* 122: 1497–1607.
Schulhofer, Stephen. 1996. "Two Systems of Social Protection: Comments on the Civil-Criminal Distinction, with Particular Reference to Sexually Violent Predator Laws." *Journal of Contemporary Legal Issues* 7: 69–96.
Sen, Amartya. 1982. "Rights and Agency." Reprinted in *Consequentialism and its Critics*. S. Scheffler (ed.). Oxford University Press, 1988.
Sered, Danielle. 2019. *Until We Reckon: Violence, Mass Incarceration, and a Road to Repair*. The New Press.
Shelby, Tommie. 2016. *Dark Ghettos: Injustice, Dissent, and Reform*. Belknap Press.
Shelby, Tommie. 2022. *The Idea of Prison Abolition*. Princeton University Press.
Shoemaker, David. 2022. "Disordered, Disabled, Disregarded, Dismissed: The Moral Costs of Exemptions from Accountability." In *Mental Disorder: Philosophical Dimensions*. Matt King and Joshua May (eds.). Oxford University Press.
Simester, A. P. 2021. *Fundamentals of Criminal Law: Responsibility, Culpability, and Wrongdoing*. Oxford University Press.
Simmons, A. John. 1991. "Locke and the Right to Punish." *Philosophy and Public Affairs* 20: 311–349.
Singer, Richard. 1979. *Just Deserts: Sentencing Based on Equality and Desert*. Ballinger.
Skerker, Michael. 2020. *The Moral Status of Combatants: A New Theory of Just War*. Routledge.
Slobogin, Christopher. 2003. "A Jurisprudence of Dangerousness." *Northwestern University Law Review* 98: 1–62.
Smith, Angela. 2005. "Responsibility for Attitudes: Activity and Passivity in Mental Life." *Ethics* 1115: 236–271.
Smith, Angela. 2013. "Moral Blame and Moral Protest." In *Blame: Its Nature and Norms*. D. Justin Coates and Neal Tognazzini (eds.). Oxford University Press.
Snegegar, Justin. 2024. "Review of Lippert-Rasmussen's *The Beam and the Mote: On Blame, Standing, and Normativity*." *Ethics* 135: 184–189.
Stilz, Anna. 2019. *Territorial Sovereignty: A Philosophical Exploration*. Oxford University Press.
Strawson, Peter. 1962. "Freedom and Resentment." Reprinted in *Freedom and Resentment and Other Essays*. Routledge, 2008.
Student Note. 2019. "Developments in the Law – Prison Abolition." *Harvard Law Review* 132: 1568–1574.

Sunstein, Cass R. and Adrian Vermeule. 2005. "Is Capital Punishment Morally Required? Acts, Omissions, and Life–Life Tradeoffs." *Stanford Law Review* 58: 703–750.

Tadros, Victor. 2009. "Poverty and Criminal Responsibility." *Journal of Value Inquiry* 43: 391–413.

Tadros, Victor. 2011. *The Ends of Harm: The Moral Foundations of Criminal Law.* Oxford University Press.

Tadros, Victor. 2013. "Controlling Risk." In *Prevention and the Limits of the Criminal Law.* Andrew Ashworth, Lucia Zedner, and Patrick Tomlin (eds.). Oxford University Press.

Tadros, Victor. 2013. "Responses." *Law and Philosophy* 32: 241–325.

Tadros, Victor. 2016. *Wrongs and Crimes.* Oxford University Press.

Tadros, Victor. 2020. *To Do, to Die, to Reason Why.* Oxford University Press.

Tadros, Victor. 2024. "Craving and Control." *Criminal Law and Philosophy* 18: 167–184.

Talbert, Matthew. 2012. "Moral Competence, Moral Blame, and Protest." *Journal of Ethics* 16: 89–109.

Taurek, John. 1977. "Should the Numbers Count?" *Philosophy and Public Affairs* 6: 293–316.

Telech, Daniel and Leora Dahan Katz. 2022. "Condemnatory Disappointment." *Ethics* 132: 851–880.

Ten, C. L. 1987. *Crime, Guilt, and Punishment.* Clarendon Press.

Thomson, Judith Jarvis. 1976. "Killing, Letting Die, and the Trolley Problem." *The Monist* 59: 204–17.

Thomson, Judith Jarvis. 1990. *The Realm of Rights.* Harvard University Press.

Thomson, Judith Jarvis. 1991. "Self-Defense." *Philosophy and Public Affairs* 20: 283–310.

Thorburn, Malcolm. 2005. "The Impossible Dreams and Modest Reality of Restorative Justice." *Queen's Law Journal* 30: 863–882.

Thorburn, Malcolm. 2020. "Criminal Punishment and the Right to Rule." *The University of Toronto Law Journal* 70: 44–63.

Todd, Patrick. 2019. "A Unified Account of the Standing to Blame." Noûs 53: 347–372.

Tomlin, Patrick. 2014. "Time and Retribution." *Law and Philosophy* 33: 655–682.

Tonry, Michael. 2017. "Community Punishments." In *Reforming Criminal Justice: Vol. 4.* Eric Luna (ed.). A Report by the Academy for Justice.

Tonry, Michael. 2020. "Is Proportionality in Punishment Possible, and Achievable?" In *Of One-Eyed and Toothless Miscreants.* Michael Tonry (ed.). Oxford University Press.

Tribe, Laurence. 1970. "An Ounce of Detention: Preventive Justice in the World of John Mitchell." *Virginia Law Review* 56: 371–407.

Tribe, Laurence. 1971. "Trial by Mathematics: Precision and Ritual in the Legal Process." *Harvard Law Review* 84: 1329–1394.

Turner, Jenia and Thomas Weigend. 2020. "Negotiated Case Dispositions in Germany, England and the United States." In *Core Concepts in Criminal Law and Criminal Justice,* Vol. 1. Kai Ambos et al., (eds.). Cambridge University Press.

van Rooij, Benjamin and Adam Fine. 2021. *The Behavioral Code: The Hidden Ways the Law Makes us Better... or Worse.* Beacon Press.

van Zyl Smit, Dirk. 2010. "Outlawing Irreducible Life Sentences: Europe on the Brink?" *Federal Sentencing Reporter* 23: 39–46.

Viehoff, Daniel. 2022. "Legitimate Injustice and Acting for Others." *Philosophy and Public Affairs* 50: 301–374.

von Hirsch, Andrew and Andrew Ashworth. 2005. *Proportionate Sentencing: Exploring the Principles.* Oxford University Press.

Visser, Nils. 2013. "A Church of Wolves." *Medieval Warfare* 3: 26–33.

Wallace, R. J. 2010. "Hypocrisy, Moral Address, and the Equal Standing of Persons." *Philosophy and Public Affairs* 38: 307–341.

Walen, Alec. 2001. "Reasonable Illegal Force: Justice and Legitimacy in a Pluralistic, Liberal Society," *Ethics* 111: 344–373.

Walen, Alec. 2006. "The Doctrine of Illicit Intentions." *Philosophy and Public Affairs* 34: 39–67.

Walen, Alec. 2011. "A Unified Theory of Detention, with Application to Preventive Detention for Suspected Terrorists." *Maryland Law Review* 70: 871–938.

Walen, Alec. 2011. "A Punitive Precondition for Preventive Detention: Lost Status as an Element of a Just Punishment." *San Diego Law Review* 48: 1229–1272.

Walen, Alec. 2011. "Criminalizing Statements of Terrorist Intent: How to Understand the Law Governing Terrorist Threats, and Why It Should be Used Instead of Long-Term Preventive Detention." *Journal of Criminal Law and Criminology* 101: 803–854.

Walen, Alec. 2013. "Wrongdoing Without Motives: Why Tadros is Wrong About Wrongdoing and Motivation." *Law and Philosophy* 32: 217–240.

Walen, Alec. 2015. "Constitutional Rights for Nonresident Aliens: A Doctrinal and Normative Argument." *Drexel Law Review* 8: 53–112.

Walen, Alec. 2015. "Proof Beyond a Reasonable Doubt: A Balanced Retributive Account." *Louisiana Law Review* 76: 355–446.

Walen, Alec. 2019. *The Mechanics of Claims and Permissible Killing in War*. Oxford University Press.

Walen, Alec. 2020. "Criminal Law and Penal Law: The Wrongness Constraint and a Complementary Forfeiture Model." *Criminal Law and Philosophy* 14: 431–446.

Walen, Alec. 2020. "Risks and Weak Aggregation: Why Different Models of Risk Suit Different Types of Cases." *Ethics* 131: 62–86.

Walen, Alec. 2021. "Retributive Justice." *The Stanford Encyclopedia of Philosophy* (Summer 2021 edition), Edward N. Zalta (ed.). https://plato.stanford.edu/archives/sum2021/entries/justice-retributive/.

Walen, Alec. 2022. "In Defense of Patient-Centered Theories of Deontology: A Response to Liao and Barry," *Law and Philosophy* 41: 627–638.

Walen, Alec. 2022. "On Blame and Punishment: Self-Blame, Other-Blame, and Normative Negligence." *Law and Philosophy* 41: 283–304.

Walen, Alec. 2023. "Deontology in Graphs: An Elucidation." *Journal of Contemporary Legal Issues* 24: 233–260.

Walen, Alec. 2025. "Separate Peaks: Reasons to Reject Derek Parfit's Views About Theoretical Moral Convergence." *Journal of Moral Philosophy* 22: 22–42.

Walen, Alec. forthcoming. "Welfare's Role in the Mechanics of Claims: Reply to Yuan and Sinclair." *Journal of Moral Philosophy*.

Walen, Alec and David Wasserman. 2012. "Agents, Impartiality, and the Priority of Claims over Duties: Diagnosing Why Thomson Still Gets the Trolley Problem Wrong by Appeal to the 'Mechanics of Claims.'" *Journal of Moral Philosophy* 9: 545–571.

Walen, Alec and Ingeborg Zerbes. forthcoming. "Self Defense," in *Fundamentals of Criminal Law and Criminal Justice*, vol 1.

Wang, Daniel and Erminia Colucci. 2017. "Should Compulsory Admission to Hospital Be Part of Suicide Prevention Strategies?" *BJPsych Bulletin* 41: 169–171.

Watson, Gary. 1996. "Two Faces of Responsibility." *Philosophical Topics* 24: 227–248.

Watson, Gary. 2011. "The Trouble with Psychopaths." In *Reasons and Recognition: Essays on the Philosophy of T.M. Scanlon*. R. Jay Wallace, Rahul Kumar, and Samuel Freeman (eds.). Oxford University Press.

Watson, Gary. 2015. "A Moral Predicament in the Criminal Law." *Inquiry* 58: 168–188.

Waxman, Matthew. 2009. "Administrative Detention of Terrorists: *Why* Detain, and Detain *Whom*?" *Journal of National Security Law & Policy* 3: 1–37.

Wellman, Christopher. 2012. "The Rights Forfeiture Theory of Punishment." *Ethics* 122: 371–393.

Wellman, Christopher. 2017. *Rights Forfeiture and Punishment*. Oxford University Press.

Weisburd, Kate, Kate Weisburd, Varun Bhadha, et al. 2021. "Electronic Prisons: The Operation of Ankle Monitoring in the Criminal Legal System." George Washington Law School. https://issuu.com/gwlawpubs/docs/electronic-prisons-report?fr = sOGI5NDcxODg3.

White, Stephen. 1991. *The Unity of the Self*. MIT Press.

Whitman, James. 2003. "A Plea Against Retributivism." *Buffalo Criminal Law Review* 7: 85–107.
Williams, Bernard. 1973. "A Critique of Utilitarianism." In *Utilitarianism: For and Against.* J. J. C. Smart and Bernard Williams (eds.). Cambridge University Press.
Williams, Bernard. 1981. *Moral Luck.* Cambridge University Press.
Wolf, Susan. 1982. "Moral Saints." *The Journal of Philosophy* 79: 419–439.
Wolf, Susan. 2011. "Blame, Italian Style." In *Reasons and Recognition: Essays on the Philosophy of T.M. Scanlon.* R. Jay Wallace, Rahul Kumar, and Samuel Freeman (eds.). Oxford University Press.
Yaffe, Gideon. 2022. "Norm Shift Theory of Punishment." *Ethics* 132: 478–507.
Yuan, Yuan. 2023. "The Exclusionary Power of Political Directives." *Legal Theory* 29: 229–256.
Yuan, Yuan. forthcoming. "Mechanics of Claims in a Statist Theory of Rights." *Journal of Moral Philosophy.*
Zaibert, Leo. 2018. *Rethinking Punishment.* Cambridge University Press.
Zaibert, Leo. 2023. "Rethinking Mixed Justifications." In *The Palgrave Handbook on the Philosophy of Punishment.* M.C. Altman (ed.). Palgrave Macmillan.
Zulfiqar, Adnan. 2022. "The Immorality of Incarceration: Between Javed Ahmad Ghamidi and Angela Y. Davis." *Journal of Islamic Law* 3. doi:10.53484/jil.v3.zulfiqar2.

Non-Academic Sources

Al-Hajj, Ahmed. "Yemen Receives 4 Detainees from Guantanamo Bay Prison." http://news.findlaw.com, June 21, 2007.
Amnesty International. 2012. "Universal Jurisdiction: A Preliminary Survey of Legislation Around the World – 2012 Update."
Bacchi, Celeste. "What Kind of Community Service Can a Judge Order?" https://www.nolo.com/legal-encyclopedia/what-kind-community-service-can-judge-order.html. Accessed July 19, 2024.
Cutler, Sarah, Steve Eder and Robert Gebelhoff. "Jailed by the Thousands, Without Charges, to Act as a Witness." *New York Times*, Oct. 3, 2023.
Bowley, Graham and Tom Mashberg. "Looted Artifacts, Returned to Yemen, Will Go to the Smithsonian, for Now." *New York Times*, Feb. 21, 2023.
Callimachi, Rukmini. "How Do You Stop a Future Terrorist When the Only Evidence Is a Thought?" *New York Times*, June 21, 2016.
Code for Crown Prosecutors. 2025. "Restorative Justice." https://www.cps.gov.uk/legal-guidance/restorative-justice.
Committee on Professional Discipline, The. 2005. "Survey of Attorney Disciplinary Rules in the State and Federal Courts of New York with Comments." https://www.nycla.org/resource/committee-report/survey-of-attorney-disciplinary-rules-in-the-state-and-federal-courts-of-new-york/.
Dick, Philip K. 1956. *Minority Report.* Reprint, Pantheon, 2002.
Dostoyevsky, Fyodor. 1860. *The House of the Dead.* David McDuff (trans.). Penguin Classics, 1985.
Dulles, Avery Cardinal. 2001. "Catholicism and Capital Punishment." *First Things.* https://www.firstthings.com/article/2001/04/catholicism-capital-punishment.
Farooq, Umar. "Guantanamo: Yemeni Detainee Cleared for Release After 20 Years." *Middle East Eye*, July 20, 2022.
Feinberg, Cara. 2015. "The Science of Scarcity," *Harvard Magazine*, May-June 2015.
French, David. 2023. "When the Rule of Law Fails Us." *New York Times*, May 15, 2023.
Giffords Law Center. 2025. "Owner Responsibility: Licensing." https://giffords.org/lawcenter/gun-laws/policy-areas/owner-responsibilities/licensing/.
Glaberson, William and Robert Worth. 2009. "Yemen Dispute Slows Closing of Guantánamo." *New York Times*, April 24, 2009.
Goldsmith, Jack. "Don't Try Terrorists, Lock Them Up," *New York Times*, Oct. 9, 2010.
Gopnik, Adam. "Overcorrection: On the Abolition of Prisons." *The New Yorker*, July 29, 2024.

Howell, Beryl A. 2009 (date uncertain). "Sentencing of Antitrust Offenders: What Does the Data Show?" https://www.ussc.gov/sites/default/files/pdf/about/commissioners/selected-articles/Howell_Review_of_Antitrust_Sentencing_Data.pdf.

Hugo, Victor. 1862. *Les Misérables*. Digital ed. Bookbyte, 2017. ISBN 978-1-61306-053-7.

Hurwitz, Tom. "Adolf Eichmann Was Ready for His Close-Up. My Father Gave It to Him". *New York Times*, April 18, 2023.

Klein, Ezra. "This Is a Very Weird Moment in the History of Drug Laws." *The Ezra Klein Show* (podcast). *The New York Times*, May 5, 2024.

Koenig, Sarah and Dana Chivvis. 2024. *Serial, Season 4*, episode 8, "Two Ledgers." https://www.nytimes.com/interactive/2024/podcasts/serial-season-four-guantanamo.html#about.

Kondkar, Marcus, Calvin Duncan and Alexander Stockton. 2023. "They Know What They Did. They'd Like You to Know Who They've Become." *New York Times*, April 1, 2023 (video).

Kubrick, Stanley. 1971. *A Clockwork Orange*. Warner Brothers.

Levow DWI Law. 2021. "New Jersey's Intoxicated Driver Resource Center (IDRC) Program." https://www.nj-dmv-dwi.com/new-jersey-dwi-penalties-and-consequences/new-jersey-idrc-intoxicated-driver-resource-center-program/.

Lewis, Michael. 2003. *Moneyball: The Art of Winning an Unfair Game*. W. W. Norton & Co.

Lewis-Kraus, Gideon. "They Studied Dishonesty. Was Their Work a Lie?" *New Yorker*, September 30, 2023.

Linder, Douglas. 2011. "Al Capone Trial (1931): An Account." http://law2.umkc.edu/faculty/projects/ftrials/capone/caponeaccount.html.

Macuk, Anthony. "Gov. Kotek Signs Bill Overhauling Measure 110." *KGW8*, April 1, 2024. https://www.kgw.com/article/news/politics/kotek-signs-bill-overhaul-measure-110-recriminalize-drugs/283-041a6791-4441-4e30-a435-14707256544b.

Marchese, David. "What It's Like to Be a Sociopath." *The New York Times Magazine*. Feb. 23, 2024.

National Institute of Corrections. 2023. "Children of Incarcerated Parents." https://nicic.gov/projects/children-of-incarcerated-parents.

Nixon, Ron. "Nations Hinder U.S. Effort to Deport Immigrants Convicted of Crime." *New York Times*, July 1, 2016.

Nossiter, Adam. "He Disavowed Radical Islam. Was He Lying?" *New York Times*, April 26, 2016.

Office of Inspector General, U.S. Department of Justice. 2003. *The September 11 Detainees: A Review of the Treatment of Aliens Held on Immigration Charges in Connection with the Investigation of the September 11 Attacks*. https://oig.justice.gov/sites/default/files/legacy/special/0306/full.pdf. Accessed November 24, 2025.

Phillips, Amber. "What Are Red Flag Laws?" *The Washington Post*, June 14, 2022.

Rosenberg, Carol. "U.S. Sends 11 Guantánamo Prisoners to Oman to Start New Lives." *New York Times*, January 6, 2025.

Rubin, Alissa and Adam Nossiter. "French Ask Whether Priest's Killer, Listed as a Threat, Could Have Been Stopped." *New York Times*, July 27, 2016.

Satariano, Adam and Kashmir Hill. "Barred from Grocery Stores by Facial Recognition." *New York Times*, June 28, 2023.

Schmitz, Mike. "Why Do I Still Feel Badly About My Sins After I've Confessed?" *The Catholic Spirit*, May 18, 2023. https://thecatholicspirit.com/faith/focus-on-faith/ask-father-mike/why-do-i-still-feel-badly-about-my-sins-after-ive-confessed/.

Scott, Alexander. "Prison and Crime: Much More than You Wanted to Know." *Astral Codex*, Nov. 27, 2024.

Shaeffer, Jac. 2021. *WandaVision*, episode 9, "The Series Finale." https://www.marvel.com/tv-shows/wandavision/1/episode-9.

Smith, Andrew. 2024. "Standard of Proof; Board-by-Board Overview." Federation of State Medical Boards. https://www.fsmb.org/siteassets/advocacy/key-issues/standard-of-proof-by-state.pdf.

United Kingdom Sentencing Council. "Imposition of Community and Custodial Sentences" (effective Feb. 1, 2017). https://www.sentencingcouncil.org.uk/overarching-guides/magistrates-court/item/imposition-of-community-and-custodial-sentences/.

U.K. Sentencing Council. "Sentencing Children and Young People: Overarching Principles and Offence Specific Guidelines for Sexual Offences and Robbery, Definitive Guideline" (effective June 1, 2017). https://www.sentencingcouncil.org.uk/wp-content/uploads/Sentencing-Children-and-young-people-Definitive-Guide_FINAL_WEB.pdf.

U.S. Sentencing Commission. "Federal Sentencing Guideline Manual." https://www.ussc.gov/guidelines/guidelines-archive/2001-2t11, 2001.

U.S. Sentencing Commission. "Quick Facts, Felon in Possession of a Firearm." https://www.ussc.gov/sites/default/files/pdf/research-and-publications/quick-facts/Felon_In_Possession_FY21.pdf, 2021.

U.S. Sentencing Commission. "Quick Facts: Tax Fraud Offenses." https://www.ussc.gov/sites/default/files/pdf/research-and-publications/quick-facts/Tax_Fraud_FY20.pdf, 2020.

Unknown Author. "On This Day: Al Capone Convicted of Income Tax Evasion" (October 17, 2011). http://www.findingdulcinea.com/news/on-this-day/September-October-08/On-this-Day--Al-Capone-Is-Convicted-of-Income-Tax-Evasion.html, 2011.

Unknown author. "What the World's Budding Autocrats Are Learning from El Salvador." *The Economist* 448. July 20, 2023.

Unknown author. 2023. *Criminal Practice Manual*, vol 3. Thomson Reuters.

WebMD. "How Sociopaths and Psychopaths Are Different." https://www.webmd.com/mental-health/psychopath-sociopath-differences, 2023.

Index

For the benefit of digital users, indexed terms that span two pages (e.g., 52–53) may, on occasion, appear on only one of those pages.

The manufacturer's authorized representative in the EU for product safety is
Oxford University Press España S.A. of Parque Empresarial San Fernando de Henares,
Avenida de Castilla, 2–28830 Madrid (www.oup.es/en or product.safety@oup.com).
OUP España S.A. also acts as importer into Spain of products made by the manufacturer.

Community Quality-of-Life and Well-Being

Series editor

Rhonda Phillips, Purdue University, West Lafayette, IN, USA

The Community Quality of Life and Well-being book series is a collection of volumes related to community level research, providing community planners and quality of life researchers involved in community and regional well-being innovative research and application. Formerly entitled, Community Quality of Life Indicators: Best Practices, the series reflects a broad scope of well-being. Next to best practices of community quality-of-life indicators projects the series welcomes a variety of research and practice topics as related to overall community well-being and quality of life dimensions, whether relating to policy, application, research, and/or practice. Research on issues such as societal happiness, quality of life domains in the policy construct, measuring and gauging progress, dimensions of planning and community development, and related topics are anticipated. This series is published by Springer in partnership with the International Society for Quality-of-Life Studies, a global society with the purpose of promoting and encouraging research and collaboration in quality of life and well-being theory and applications.

More information about this series at http://www.springer.com/series/13761

Meg Holden · Rhonda Phillips
Chantal Stevens
Editors

Community Quality-of-Life Indicators: Best Cases VII

Springer

Editors
Meg Holden
Urban Studies Program
Simon Fraser University
Vancouver, BC
Canada

Chantal Stevens
King County Auditor's Office
Seattle
USA

Rhonda Phillips
Honors College
Purdue University
West Lafayette, IN
USA

ISSN 2520-1093 ISSN 2520-1107 (electronic)
Community Quality-of-Life and Well-Being
ISBN 978-3-319-54617-9 ISBN 978-3-319-54618-6 (eBook)
DOI 10.1007/978-3-319-54618-6

Library of Congress Control Number: 2017934215

Printed on acid-free paper

This Springer imprint is published by Springer Nature
The registered company is Springer International Publishing AG
The registered company address is: Gewerbestrasse 11, 6330 Cham, Switzerland

Contents

About the Editors

Meg Holden (Ph.D., New School for Social Research) is a social scientist whose research investigates the promises and results of sustainability planning in cities around the world. She is an Associate Professor of urban studies and geography at Simon Fraser University in Vancouver, Canada. Meg served as a board member of the Community Indicators Consortium from 2011 to 2016 and she currently serves as editorial board member of the journal *Applied Research in Quality of Life* as well as the Springer book series on Community Quality of Life and Wellbeing. Meg is the author of *Pragmatic Justifications for the Sustainable City: Acting in the common place* (Routledge, 2017).

Rhonda Phillips Ph.D., FACIP, has research and outreach efforts that focus on the quality of life and well-being related to community and economic development. At Purdue University, she serves as inaugural Dean of the Honors College and Professor in the Agricultural Economics Department. She is author or editor of over 20 books, including *Sustainable Communities: Creating a Durable Local Economy*, and *Introduction to Community Development*. Formerly a Senior Sustainability Scientist with the Wrigley Global Institute of Sustainability, Rhonda also served as Director and Professor in the School of Community Resources and Development at Arizona State University. She is a member of the College of Fellows of the American Institute of Certified Planners, and immediate past president of the International Society for Quality-of-Life Studies.

Chantal Stevens is the Executive Director of the Community Indicators Consortium, an open learning network and global community of practice among persons interested or engaged in the field of indicators development and application. Her interests and expertise in sustainability, community indicators, public engagement and performance management were honed over a 25-year career as the Executive Director of Sustainable Seattle, a pioneer in the field of community-generated indicators, and People for Salmon, a state-wide public engagement initiative, as well as Performance Management Analyst and Legislative Auditor with King County, Environmental Division Manager with the Muckleshoot Indian Tribe, and several terms on the Issaquah Planning Commission and many position and diverse boards or commissions. She holds a Master's Degree in Marine Affairs from the University of Washington.

Chapter 1
The History, Status and Future of the Community Indicators Movement

Lyle Wray, Chantal Stevens and Meg Holden

Abstract This introductory chapter to the volume provides an overview of the history of community indicators, beginning with a grant provided by the Russell Sage Foundation in 1910 to the Charity Organization Society (of New York) to survey industrial conditions in Pittsburgh, and moving to present day. As a social movement, we present community indicators efforts as being grounded in challenges and innovations within the distinct but overlapping domains of public administration, social work and philanthropy, community development, sustainable communities and environmental justice, happiness and wellbeing studies, and data analytics. Each frames and pursues the task of crafting and disseminating indicators of community conditions in a different way, resulting in a richly diverse field of practice and theory, that the Community Indicators Consortium seeks to serve and promote. In so doing, the Community Indicators Consortium recognizes that uniting these diverse approaches in community indicators provides a forum in which to pursue common themes of work, including the need to amplify the voice of disadvantaged communities, to seriously explore the increasing use of information technology, to produce positive community change and to sustain these efforts over time. Each chapter in this volume is also summarized here.

Keywords Community indicators · Community indicators consortium · Public administration · Wellbeing indicators · Philanthropy · Community development · Sustainable development · Data analytics · Happiness studies

---

L. Wray
Capitol Region Council of Governments, Hartford, CT, USA

C. Stevens
Community Indicators Consortium, Issaquah, WA, USA

M. Holden (✉)
Simon Fraser University, Vancouver, Canada
e-mail: mholden@sfu.ca

M. Holden et al. (eds.), *Community Quality-of-Life Indicators: Best Cases VII*, Community Quality-of-Life and Well-Being,
DOI 10.1007/978-3-319-54618-6_1

1.1 History of the Community Indicators Movement

While data and statistics have been used for centuries by governments and businesses, the origin of community indicators is associated with a grant provided by the Russell Sage Foundation in 1910 to the Charity Organization Society of New York to survey industrial conditions in Pittsburgh (Smith 1991, 40–41). After the study was released in 1914, the Russell Sage Foundation provided technical advice to many other cities to complete similar work. Partly because of this initiative, over two thousand local surveys were taken on education, recreation, public health, crime, and general social conditions.

In the second half of the 20th century, the evolution of the indicators field paralleled, and sometimes triggered, the evolution of consciousness about what constitutes quality of life in community. The 1960s and 1970s saw the rise of the social indicators movement. In 1974, the academic journal *Social Indicators Research* was founded and started publishing research results dealing with measurement of the quality of life that encompassed the whole spectrum of society at scales ranging from the individual to international systems.

In 1985, the charitable organization JCCI in Jacksonville, Florida initiated a set of quality-of-life indicators that tracked a variety of issues to understand progress. With Sustainable Seattle in 1992 and others, sustainability indicators came into existence at about the same time as sustainability became a concept in public discourse, often associated with the work of the Brundtland Commission (the World Commission on Environment and Development) in 1987 and affirmed by the 1992 Rio Earth Summit in Rio de Janeiro, Brazil. Along with their focus on sustainability, this approach to indicators, in contrast with previous efforts, was grassroots and bottom-up. As such, they established a new base for social indicators, where the community is the originator, the guardian and the audience of the project. The community indicators movement was born.

With precedent-setting work by the Reno, Nevada-based indicators initiative Truckee Meadows Tomorrow, modern indicator projects are leading movements in their communities based on a commitment not merely to measure trends but to act on trends of concern, via cross-sector collaboration. SA2020, in San Antonio, Texas, along with many contemporary projects, took to heart the criticisms directed at their predecessors that indicators initiatives were investing the bulk of their time to establish strong and defensible measurement systems, leaving far too little time for considerations of either how to publicize and generate an audience for their work, or how to act to change undesirable trends. SA2020 now outsources data collection and analysis to a third party. Instead of assembling data, the indicators initiative focuses on communicating information and engaging the community in steps toward positive change.

Building on the "Beyond GDP" approaches of the 1990s, the well-being movement emerged explicitly in this century. Recent years have seen community indicator projects evolve with greater focus on the importance of the individual, happiness and well-being, within community change. This has meant a concomitant expansion of the measures taken to include the realm of individuals' subjective experiences within community and the impact these experiences have on their assessment of life in their community. The measurement frontier of community indicators work now engages the particular challenge of identifying valid, comparable measures of happiness, mental health, and the experience of equity and fairness.

Barrington-Leigh and Escande (2016) constructed a database of well-being and progress indicators with the key elements being: material living standards, health, education, governance and civic participation, social connections, relationships and community, environment, culture, accounts of time-use, and various types of security. This list overlaps a good deal with the earlier commissioned work of Stiglitz et al. (2009) who proposed eight indicators for well-being and progress.

1.2 Evolution of the Community Indicators Consortium

The Community Indicators Consortium (CIC) started as an umbrella of nine organizations producing indicators, that came together to help provide some overall coherence, coordination, and mutual support within the burgeoning international community indicators movement. The idea for the Consortium germinated at the 2003 International Society for Quality-of-Life Studies (ISQOLS) conference on community indicators in Williamsburg, Virginia and led to the first CIC conference in 2004 in Reno, Nevada on the theme "Advancing the Science and Practice of Community Indicators." The 2004 conference in Reno drew together an unexpectedly large group of participants, who brought their diverse perspectives, skills, knowledge, and experience in community indicators work. The conference buzzed with the shared passion of attendees to improve the quality of life in communities through approaches that utilize measurable indicators of progress.

Due in part to the success of the conference and the positive interest it generated, CIC incorporated with the goal of becoming a "learning community" and offering resources and connections necessary to any group aiming to develop and implement a community indicators project that is aimed at "making a difference" in community. Now in its thirteenth year, CIC is led by a 15-member board and an executive director and counts about 300 dues-paying members.

CIC's mission is to advance and support the development, availability and effective use of community indicators for making measurable and sustainable improvements in quality of community life. CIC works to fulfill its mission by hosting an annual international conference, organizing educational and networking events, providing on-line classes, and sharing information in a timely and dependable way. CIC built and maintains a comprehensive online database of past and active community indicator projects all over the world (www.communityindicators.net/projects). In addition, over the dozen years of its existence, CIC has taken on several special projects, led by the interests and opportunities identified by members. One notable project dealt with the intersection of community indicator projects and the use of systems of performance measures in organizations, including local governments. This work resulted in a set of guidelines for the integration of performance measures and community indicators, and the development of a community indicator-performance measurement maturity model which puts these guidelines to the test of practice.

1.3 What Are "Community Indicators"?

The definition of 'community indicators' is often in the eye of the beholder. Breaking the term into its two component parts, it involves indicators, metrics that represent a level or a condition and that often can be expressed as a rate or a count. Just as importantly, it involves 'community', a grouping of people based on a geographic, demographic or social criterion, such as a neighborhood, ethnicity, income level, etc. As a social movement, community indicators groups are often expected to function with some input or leadership from the community, acting outside of or in parallel with formal local government, and to include a process for reporting to the community in a format that is public and accessible to non-experts.

Community indicator projects are developed to serve as a map to guide priority and agenda-setting for the work of multiple responsible groups in improving community-level conditions across the full spectrum of challenges affecting a community. The indicator format allows for progress on each measure of significance to be tracked over time and compared to conditions experienced by comparator communities. Sometimes, an additional step taken within community indicators work is to set numeric targets for indicators, where the intent is to motivate interventions toward achieving a community goal. Targets may be chosen by decision-makers or the community, and can be drawn from science or policy (e.g. acceptable levels of air pollutants established by the World Health Organization), based on the best practices of other communities (e.g. to achieve the same rate of persons with a family doctor as community "x"), or based on the aspirations of the community (e.g. to be the first greenhouse gas neutral community). A city may work to decrease the ground level particulates in the air based on a reference to scientific research that shows at what level that pollutant will impact the health of the most vulnerable, or threaten community health generally; or it may compare the poverty level to that of peer cities or that of the state, province or country, with a view either to addressing inequities in conditions or to building capacity to address poverty overall.

In addition to individual indicators or frameworks, several **indices** have been proposed to summarize a portfolio of measures. When a portfolio of indicators is needed to tell the full story of a community, indices offer an easy to understand solution, hence the popularity of a summarizing index such as the Dow Jones Industrial Average, for example. Interactive indices such as the Ecological Footprint (Wackernagel and Rees 1996), the Walk Score (walkscore.org) and the Livability Index (AARP) have captured the popular imagination because they distil complex ecological or social-economic considerations into a single digit that allows for manipulation and comparisons based on changes in locations or aspirations. The Prosperity Index of the Legatum Institute (http://www.prosperity.com/#!/) is a high-level index of well-being indicators. Its eight dimensions overlap in good part with the Stiglitz et al. (2009) model for measurement of well-being: economy, entrepreneurship and opportunity, governance, education, health, safety and security, personal freedom, and social capital.

Barrington-Leigh and Escande (2016) lament the fact that existing indices with many components often lack transparency as to how the index is formed and thus lack staying power as they may fail to persuade those who will not simply accept the wisdom of the choices implicit within an index.

1.4 Framing Community Indicators Projects

Community indicators span a wide range of dimensions, levels of generality and precision, geography and time series depth. Applicability to the community as a whole or to specific interests and identities, and those that indicate objectively measurable phenomena as well as those that reflect subjective perceptions all may feature together in the indicator system. Some community indicator systems scale their focus at the postal or zip code level, others at the level of the neighborhood or block group, others around the landscape scale such as a watershed or a geopolitical construct, such as a metropolitan region. Many are designed as multipurpose data-rich tools for local understanding and community work, which can be tailored according to different geographies, time periods, interest groups, policy areas of focus, or other specificities.

Just as in performance measurement, it often helps to have an organizing framework for a portfolio of indicators in a given community. Many projects organize community priorities as "domains" and populate each domain with indicators. One of the more popular frameworks groups indicators into environment, economy and equity. The term "triple bottom line" was first coined in 1994 and has been used extensively not only in the community indicator field but beyond (Hindle 2012). Based on Putnam's seminal work, the four basic types of capital—human, social, built, and natural—provide another useful framework well adapted to tracking well-being at the community level. Cultural, political and financial capitals were added by Flora and Flora (2004) to constitute their community capitals framework. Other frameworks employed, particularly in the public sector, are known as the balanced scorecard approach (Kaplan and Norton 1996), the social return on investment (Millar 2012), and results-based accountability (Friedman 1997).

1.5 Situating Community Indicators Work

The work of designing, framing, reporting on and implementing action from a basis of community indicators today is conducted by people from a range of different professions. Over the history of the movement, as different groups of professionals have recognized value in community indicators work, they have also adapted the work involved in creating and using community indicators to suit their own professional norms and capacities. This has added to the richness of debate and diversity in the field. Figure 1.1 presents a diagrammatic understanding of the major professional fields currently engaged in community indicators work, from our perspective within the Community Indicators Consortium. Each field's different engagement with community indicators will be discussed in turn.

Public Administration and Performance Management. Public administration is the implementation of government policy and also an academic discipline that studies this implementation and prepares civil servants for work in the public service. Heavily influenced by organizational management as well as policy analysis theory, indicators within public administration appeal with their promise of reconciling values and high level goals of public service with the instrumental demands of implementation and measuring results. That is, within a typical public administration frame, an indicators initiative, theoretically speaking, can be broken down into four sequential stages of work and pursued in a systematic, efficient manner. Namely, these stages consist of:

Fig. 1.1 The intersection of professional fields involved in the work of community indicators

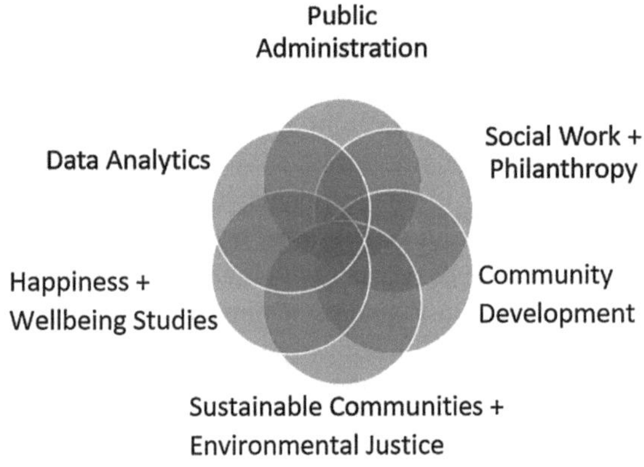

- Selecting indicators to meet the need to measure progress toward particular goals;
- Measuring indicators based upon existing or new data;
- Analyzing and reporting on indicators to communicate trends; and
- Designing actions to improve deteriorating trends in communities.

In the field of public administration, indicators find considerable resonance with the practice of performance measurement, which emerged as an initiative to make more systematic the evaluation of government and public service work. The use of indicators within a performance measurement approach to public administration has not been without its critics, who have pointed out that modelling public and community work based upon private sector models is not always suitable for meeting community goals (e.g. Hartley 2010). Different iterations of new frameworks have evolved, as have understandings of how to attribute value to relationships between the observed conditions, the actions taken, and the outcomes that have transpired.

CIC, with the support of the Alfred P. Sloan Foundation, identified benefits, barriers and strategies for better community indicator/performance measure (CI-PM) integration, highlighting the importance of integration and collaboration to improve citizen engagement in using information for better community decision-making. CI-PM integration leads to better assessment of communities' quality of life and to better engagement of community members and other key stakeholders in the development and use of community indicators and performance measures. The work of CI-PM engages both governmental and non-profit organizations, along with community members.

According to one of the leaders of the field of performance measurement, Harry Hatry (2014) of the Urban Institute, "performance measurement" is a process in which a governmental or non-governmental public service organization undertakes regular collection of outcome and/or output data (preferably both) throughout the year (not only at the end of the year) for its programs and services. One emerging theory within public administration is that of the "public value". Moore and Khagram (2004) coined the term "public value" as the public sector equivalent of shareholder value in the business sector. The goal is to produce socially desirable outcomes for a community. Community indicators are one way to track such progress.

Social Work and Philanthropy. Not far removed from the interests and objectives of public administration, social work and philanthropy sectors use indicators as means to better track and measure success in interventions in communities. Indicators work within this sector emphasizes tracking the success of efforts to improve conditions in poor and marginalized communities, and to learn from the results of interventions. Compared to the domain of public administration, this work is less tied to notions of efficiency, and has demonstrated exciting innovations in recent years related to finding better frameworks for understanding and measuring "collective impact" rather than insisting upon strictly statistical models of causation (Kania and Kramer 2011). Much work is being conducted within private as well as community foundations and social organizations working to redress inequities around the world. The work of the community foundation Jacksonville Community Council (www.jcci.org) is widely recognized as the longest running contemporary community indicators initiative.

Community Development. Community development work can be distinguished from the preceding initiatives by its emphasis on the need for engagement and empowerment of non-expert community members to diagnose and address their own problems. Indicators initiatives have proven a valuable tool for numerous groups, particularly in making a case for the change that they advocate based upon comparing trends with other communities. There are also intersections between the work of community development organizations working with indicators and the public administration strain of indicators work, as these groups too need to prove the method, efficiency, and impact within their work with public and other grant funds.

Sustainable Communities and Environmental Justice. Indicators for sustainable communities and environmental justice groups can be thought of as a special case of community development-based indicators. Emerging from the internationalization of a sustainable development agenda in the early 1990s, many community-based groups took up an indicators approach as a means of coming to terms locally with the meaning and implications of this new frame for thinking about human progress and environmental protection. Like the work of community development organizations more broadly, sustainability and environmental justice indicators efforts have placed a strong emphasis on the process of orienting, framing, selecting, and presenting the indicators. For the community indicators field as a whole, this has brought to light the social learning as well as communicative roles played by indicators, recognizing the limits of the expectation that good data "speak for themselves." The environmental justice movement, sometimes more oriented toward a rights-based argument for action as opposed to one of demonstrating indicators and trends, has found particular utility in indicators work where indicators can be used to visualize and map stark inequities that go unaddressed in policy and practice.

Happiness and Wellbeing Studies. US President John F. Kennedy is often remembered for raising questions about the utility of the single indicator of the Gross National Product or Gross Domestic Product to refer generally to the progress of society. In addition to being taken up as a mantra within many community indicators efforts aiming to diversify and qualify arguments about conditions and trends in local communities, the field of happiness and wellbeing studies has taken off with a key goal being to find better ways to characterize, communicate and support human progress.

Famously, the Kingdom of Bhutan prioritized Gross National Happiness as a national policy priority in the early 1970s, and since this time a growing number of nations and local communities have invested in thinking harder about how to promote what makes people happy and well, rather than or in addition to what makes them rich, or safe, or less vulnerable. In this field, key debates flow around questions of how best to measure subjective concepts such as happiness and wellbeing, how to compare these measurements, and how to interpret differences.

Data Analytics. Analysis and display of data in ways that effectively communicate the story behind a trend in data have always been key to good community indicators work, of any variety. Although community indicators work began well before the use of internet and mobile technologies had become a daily necessity, the field has been part of the evolution of better approaches to data visualization and display as informatics and geographic information systems technologies have evolved.

The field of data analytics has emerged as information and internet technologies have greatly increased the velocity and volume of so-called "big data" available in cities and communities (IBM 2015). At the same time, this has increased the opportunities for data entrepreneurs to create new means to collect data, often via mobile and internet-of-things technologies. With this technological shift, the private sector has become interested in the indicators field in a major way, with information technology companies such as IBM, Siemens and Cisco now promoting "smart cities" and the benefits of living environments that are embedded with sensors and means to collect and track data at every turn, promising to use this data to create a more efficient, comfortable life.

The rise of the big data and the smart city concepts may present opportunities within community indicators, but also present a stark contrast and challenge to the way in which the community indicators movement has traditionally operated in a context of data scarcity, not data overabundance. Community indicators projects have long emphasized the need to collect new and better data to reflect more acutely upon on-the-ground conditions in overlooked communities and trends. Big data promoters promise that, with interconnected networks of continuous flows of data swirling all around our communities, this need for communities to collect their own data will become obsolete, replaced by the need to acquire the technology and expertise to mine the abundant digital data for patterns that matter. As such, trends in big data and data analytics raise many significant questions for the community indicators movement.

In addition to this basic question about whether the work of community indicators needs to change its overall orientation and approach in order to work with abundant, fast data, are other questions about the work of ensuring the openness, transparency, and public nature of data, questions about protection of personal privacy, and questions about whether the flows of big data do anything, in fact, to address data scarcity when it comes to the measures that matter to communities.

1.6 New Research in the Field of Community Indicators

Across this diverse field of interests and approaches in community indicators work, these efforts share a common belief that transparency about specific community trends and their impacts on overall community conditions will lead to positive change that will improve outcomes overall. This belief has been put to the test time and time again within political battles waged by indicators initiatives, in which the superior data and the superior argument do not always hold sway. Through a classical, rational lens of thinking about information and policy change, making a community and its elected decision-makers aware of negative trends and inequities should be sufficient to motivate and mobilize action to turn these trends and inequities around. History tells a different story.

Not unlike the story in other realms of voluntary and community work, efforts in community indicators have been plagued by the short lifespan of many initiatives. All too often, the cycle is one of a burst of investment of enthusiasm, dedication, skill, and resources, a hard slog to establish an initial reputation and reporting system, some small triumphs of media, community, and perhaps even political attention, followed by a series of disappointments in efforts to repeat, accelerate, or institutionalize the work, and ultimately by the decline or disappearance of the initiative. From a capacity-building, social capital and social learning approach, this cycle is not a condemnation of community indicators work, because it serves to launch new careers, political and justice agendas and plant new ideas in community—this is seeding work. From a perspective of institutional change and the development of better habits around the use of data in decision making and community action, this is an unfortunate state of affairs, holding community indicators efforts back from attaining their most significant impacts through a lack of time to measure and argue for the needs that arise from observed trends over time.

Different perspectives exist on the reasons for this cycle, and how it might be broken to produce more stability in the community indicators field. In his chapter in this book, Barrington-Leigh (2017) takes a longitudinal view of community indicators initiatives since the 1970s, and asks what factors may have played the biggest role in determining the resilience of those that have survived to date. His message is one of caution about rushing to generate indices from key indicators and data, because it is the unaggregated and subjectively-oriented indicators initiatives that seem to have out-survived composite indicators work. Grounded within the field of happiness and wellbeing studies, Barrington-Leigh makes a case for subjective measures of life satisfaction, drawing from new understandings of how collective well-being in community can be derived from individual survey responses to questions about individual life satisfaction.

Latching on to the work within the realms of philanthropy and social work, as well as the community development realm of indicators work, a more realistic story about how better information can guide better decisions involves the recognition that additional phases of work are needed to mobilize action. Momentum is growing around the notion that the most effective action is collective—that is, based upon partnerships of different kinds of organizations that agree to join forces in a targeted way around a particular trend, or the need for more information in decision-making more broadly (Kania and Kramer 2011).

The account that Ridzi (2017) provides in his chapter, Community Indicators and the Collective Goods Criterion for Impact, is an account of the power of collective thinking and action. He argues that, although it would be impossible to prove that the community indicators project CNY.vitals itself is the cause of seven years of positive change in the four-year high school graduation rate in Syracuse, New York, the work within this indicators project helped to develop a "measurement mentality" which in and of itself is a collective good in favor of positive change in this community. Drawing the notion of the collective good criterion from the social movement literature, Ridzi argues that the positioning of the community indicator project CNY.vitals in the middle of many social initiatives, with the ability to contribute something to diverse agendas, meant that this project has more power to offer community change agents, in all their diversity, than if it had been the kind of specific, targeted, structured policy change initiative to which impact is typically attributed. This is a story of a community indicator initiative that worked effectively to encourage collaboration and movement-building around an inclusive ideal of desired change as it opened the black box of measures of social progress in the community and how these measures can be leveraged for action in the longer term.

Helmstetter et al. (2017), working on the community indicators initiative Minnesota Compass, provide an account of what it has meant for their work in community indicators to initiate and maintain partnerships. They offer practical reflections on what they have seen to be key to making partnerships work in this field, so that their efforts maintain their focus and build impact as they stay involved with the work of attempting to "move the needle" on the dashboard in the direction of progress. This case from the philanthropic sector in Minnesota is followed by another case for partnership formation from Northeast Ohio, provided by Emily Garr Pacetti, working within the community and economic development sector.

Pacetti's (2017) chapter, Aligning Local and Regional Data to Achieve a More Inclusive Economy: A Northeast Ohio Model, focuses on the importance of laying out the common substantive basis for partnership to align the economic development priorities of different interested groups working in Northeast Ohio, in the metropolitan Cleveland area. This partnership-based approach found its success through the convening of partners across sectors and geographies to build a common understanding of competitive economic development that can benefit the region and that "matters to metros".

An important claim by the author is that the pursuit of racial inclusion and income equality can enhance metropolitan regional economic growth. She draws upon a five-part definition of an inclusive economy, along with evidence that shows how reducing economic disparities can benefit job growth, while simply increasing per capita income may not. Northeast Ohio took these two elements to produce the notion that to sustain growth, communities must invest in opportunities for residents that have often been left behind.

Holden's (2017) chapter, Getting to Groundbreaking But Not Build Out, provides a cautionary tale of partnerships in creating new community indicators projects around housing development that can break down as political gaps are revealed between the partners. While this new community indicators initiative showed a great deal of promise in its initial years of work toward a partnership-based approach to information sharing and reporting related to the creation of new housing in metropolitan Vancouver, Canada, ultimately the shared model of control over the outcomes and messaging, in the context of a yawning political divide amongst the partners, led to breakdown. This chapter offers lessons about what every community indicator practitioner knows: that data may present itself as "raw" and politically neutral, but instead it is always "cooked." Community indicators work treads on politically disruptive ground, to the extent that the initiatives represent new groups, partnerships and coalitions seeking to control and create messages from data that advance policy agendas which threaten the status quo.

Part 2 of the book offers a series of four case studies of community indicators projects that are all, in their diverse contexts, seeking to reveal and rectify disparities and injustices. The papers address environmental justice, economic disparities, veterans' needs, gender equity for women and girls, and the potential of a systemic model to determine policy action priorities.

In the first article by Gunn et al. (2017) entitled: Environmental Justice in Australia: Measuring the relationship between industrial odor exposure and community disadvantage, new ground was covered in metropolitan Melbourne, Australia by examining the spatial correlation between odor complaints, polluting facilities and areas of socio-economic disadvantage. The research sets out to discover the extent of odor exposure from facilities and to help identify if communities affected by odor have different socioeconomic characteristics. The potential benefits are improved pollution mitigation strategies and better understanding of needed separation distances between industrial and residential areas particularly in the context of growing metropolitan areas, that may be increasing the proximity of mixed land uses.

Measurement of odor impact and of socioeconomic status showed indeed that a disproportionate number of vulnerable community members were affected across the region. Residents affected by odor impacts were near polluting facilities located in areas of greater socioeconomic disadvantage with low incomes and poor English language proficiency. The suggestion was made to use smaller, more granular geographic measurement areas to avoid averaging out impacts over larger geographic areas. The authors suggest that the findings of the study be used to facilitate dialogue among policy makers, researchers and communities to inform land use planning and policy. The findings should be used to avoid encroachment between residential areas, new developments and industrial zones going forward.

In the next chapter by Green and Espino (2017) entitled: Addressing Disparities and Improving the System of Care for Veterans through the Community Assessment Process, the authors describe a San Mateo County veterans' needs assessment as part of a strategy to end homelessness among veterans in that county. Green and Espino start with the chilling statistic that veterans represent 7% of the overall population but 11% of those experiencing homelessness.

The authors cite the power of community indicator projects to build on community level data to spur regional partnerships to serve all veterans and to move from a reactive crisis response system to a more proactive system to produce wellbeing. They describe the use of a five step community assessment process to address the challenges of engaging in a veterans' indicator project to bring about social change from the identification of veterans, to developing a set of indicators, building relationships among programs and agencies, improving data systems and outcomes for veterans and sharing findings and suggestions for improving the service delivery system. The authors describe a community veterans summit and formation of a veterans' commission relating to the community indicators project that built on the awareness of the need to develop a more coordinated system to serve veterans.

Next, in the chapter by Lee and Deviney (2017) entitled: Economic Issues for Women in Texas, the authors present a variety of important trends through disaggregation of data in community indicators through gender as an example of a key factors or lens with which to address community indicators. The authors set out to encourage others to learn more about the economic challenges and opportunities faced by women and girls in Texas. The hope is to increase the economic security of women by sharing information with community leaders, elected and appointed officials, non-profit organizations, businesses and foundations. The article gives strength to the principle that is often makes sense to disaggregate data into more refined slices to gain a clearer and more nuanced view of an issue. This is clearly true in the case of the gender lens for women and girls as presented for the state of Texas.

Women and girls in Texas are presented as a young, diverse and growing population. Thirty-seven percent of women and girls are Hispanic or Latina, for example. Women are 1.2 times as likely to be in poverty as a man. Sixty-seven percent of two parent households have both parents working out of the home. Average wages for women are about one quarter less than men. Women are making gains in post-secondary education but economic barriers remain to increasing higher education rates. Child care costs and lack of pre-kindergarten programs are important challenges. Issues of health insurance access and housing affordability also negatively impact women.

By disaggregating data across a number of areas, the paper shows the challenges faced by women and girls and offers support for addressing the critical need to invest in building blocks for economic security for women and girls to the betterment of the state of Texas as a whole.

Finally, King (2017) lays out the framework followed in Houston to develop a comprehensive sustainability indicators program that relies on the power of objective data over that of subjective understandings and preferences. The systematic model pursued in the case of the Houston project is explained, demonstrating the value of geographic information systems and statistical principal components analysis to define clusters of indicator relationships that in turn can help inform strategic priority setting for sustainable development investment with impact. This last case brings the volume full circle back to a similar sense of what community indicators projects are for to that of Barrington-Leigh (2017). That is, that these measurement systems ought to be designed to provide information that will empower others to aggregate it in different ways and make value judgments to inform priorities and actions, across the community and over the long term. Even across the diversity of approaches to community indicators today, widespread agreement exists that this provision of clear, valuable, timely information to non-expert audiences is key to the success of the indicator movement. Where significant difference continues to exist is on the question of what *else* community indicators projects need to do to gain and maintain an audience and institutional presence, remain relevant as other sources of information proliferate, and as conditions may continue to worsen despite the most valiant efforts to bring injustices, deterioration, and failed policy outcomes to light.

As an aggregate, these chapters reveal community indicator projects to be relevant, dynamic and adaptive. Whether applied to a single issue or the wellbeing of a whole community, indicators have the power to inform, convene, unite, and ultimately improve community conditions. The field of community indicators has undergone a rapid evolution in only a few decades, and this evolution is ongoing. Across the field we continue to see a search for balance between the role of subjective well-being and more objective indicators of community well-being, and between more collaborative and values-based and more expert-led approaches. Community indicators projects today operate within a need to amplify the voice of disadvantaged communities, seriously explore the increasing use of information technology, and a continuing struggle to produce positive community change and to sustain these efforts over time.

References

Barrington-Leigh, C. (2017). The role of subjective well-being as an organizing concept for community indicators. In M. Holden, R. Phillips, & C. Stevens (Eds.), *Community quality-of-life indicators: Best cases VII* (pp. 19–34). New York: Springer.

Barrington-Leigh, C., & Escande, A. (2016). Measuring progress and well-being: A comparative review of indicators. *Social Indicators Research*. Forthcoming.

Flora, J. L., & Flora, C. B. (2004). Building community in rural areas of the Andes. In R. Atria & M. Siles (Eds.), *Social capital and poverty reduction in Latin America and the Caribbean: Towards a new paradigm* (pp. 523–542). Santiago, Chile: Economic Commission for Latin America and the Caribbean and Michigan State University.

Friedman, M. (1997). *A guide to developing and using performance measures in results-based budgeting*. Washington, D.C.: Finance Project.

Green, S., & Espino, M. (2017). Addressing disparities and improving the system of care for veterans through the community assessment process. In M. Holden, R. Phillips, & C. Stevens (Eds.), *Community quality-of-life indicators: Best Cases VII* (pp. 135–147). New York: Springer.

Gunn, L., Greenham, B., Davern, M., Mavoa, S., Taylor, E.J., & Bannister, M. (2017). Environmental justice in Australia: Measuring the relationship between industrial odour exposure and community disadvantage. In M. Holden, R. Phillips, & C. Stevens (Eds.), *Community quality-of-life indicators: Best cases VII* (pp. 113–133). New York: Springer.

Hartley, J. (2010). Innovation in governance and public services: past and present. *Public Money and Management, 25*(1), 27–34.

Hatry, H. P. (2014). *Transforming performance measurement for the 21st century*. Washington, D.C.: Urban Institute.

Helmstetter, C., Mattessich, P., Hamberg, R., & Hartzler, N. (2017). Collaboration to promote use of community indicators: Communication is key. In M. Holden, R. Phillips, & C. Stevens (Eds.), *Community quality-of-life indicators: Best cases VII* (pp. 53–68). New York: Springer.

Hindle, T. (2012). *Guide to management ideas and gurus*. London: The Economist.

Holden, M. (2017). Getting to groundbreaking, but not build out: From formation to failure in a regional housing indicators collaborative. In M. Holden, R. Phillips, & C. Stevens (Eds.), *Community quality-of-life indicators: Best cases VII* (pp. 87–110). New York: Springer.

IBM. (2015). *The four v's of big data*. Available online: http://www.ibmbigdatahub.com/sites/default/files/infographic_file/4-Vs-of-big-data.jpg?cm_mc_uid=43829480861414795860187&cm_mc_sid_50200000=1479586018

Kania, J., & Kramer, M. (2011, Winter). Collective impact. *Stanford Social Innovation Review*. 36–41.

Kaplan, R. S., & Norton, D. P. (1996). *The balanced scorecard: Translating strategy into action*. Cambridge, MA: Harvard Business Review Press.

King, L. (2017). Comprehensive sustainability indicators: The Houston sustainability indicators program. In M. Holden, R. Phillips, & C. Stevens (Eds.), *Community quality-of-life indicators: Best cases VII* (pp. 167–184). New York: Springer.

Lee, J., & Deviney, F. (2017). Economic issues for women in texas. In M. Holden, R. Phillips, & C. Stevens (Eds.), *Community quality-of-life indicators: Best cases VII* (pp. 149–165). New York: Springer.

Millar, H. (2012). Social Return on Investment (SROI) and performance measurement. *Public Management Review, 15*, 923–941.

Moore, M., & Khagram, S. (2004). On creating public value: What business might learn from government about strategic management. A Working Paper of the Corporate Social Responsibility Initiative. Cambridge, Mass: Harvard University. https://www.hks.harvard.edu/m-rcbg/CSRI/research/publications/workingpaper_3_moore_khagram.pdf

Pacetti, E. (2017). Aligning local and regional data to achieve a more inclusive economy: A Northeast Ohio model. In M. Holden, R. Phillips, & C. Stevens (Eds.), *Community quality-of-life indicators: Best cases VII* (pp. 69–86). New York: Springer.

Ridzi, F. (2017). Community indicators and the collective goods criterion for impact. In M. Holden, R. Phillips, & C. Stevens (Eds.), *Community quality-of-life indicators: Best cases VII* (pp. 35–52). New York: Springer.

Stiglitz, J., Sen, A., & Fitoussi, J.-P. (2009). *Report by the commission on the measurement of economic performance and social progress*. Paris: Commission on the Measurement of Economic Performance and Social Progress.

Wackernagel, M., & Rees, W. (1996). *Our ecological footprint: Reducing human impact on the earth*. Gabriola Island: New Society.

Author Biographies

Lyle Wray, Ph.D. serves as Executive Director of the Capitol Region Council of Governments based in Hartford, Connecticut that serves one million residents. He has been involved in community indicator projects in California and Connecticut most recently with the www.metrohartfordprogresspoints.org project. He serves as Vice-President of the Community Indicator Consortium. His published work has focused on citizen engagement in community performance measurement projects. He earned a BA, MA and Ph.D. in Psychology from the University of Manitoba, Winnipeg, Canada.

Chantal Stevens is the Executive Director of the Community Indicators Consortium, an open learning network and global community of practice among persons interested or engaged in the field of indicators development and application. Her interests and expertise in sustainability, community indicators, public engagement and performance management were honed over a 25-year career as the Executive Director of Sustainable Seattle, a pioneer in the field of community-generated indicators, and People for Salmon, a state-wide public engagement initiative, as well as Performance Management Analyst and Legislative Auditor with King County, Environmental Division Manager with the Muckleshoot Indian Tribe, and several terms on the Issaquah Planning Commission and many position and diverse boards or commissions. She holds a Master's Degree in Marine Affairs from the University of Washington.

Meg Holden, Ph.D. is a social scientist whose research investigates the promises and results of sustainability planning in cities around the world. She is an Associate Professor of urban studies and geography at Simon Fraser University in Vancouver, Canada. Meg served as a board member of the Community Indicators Consortium from 2011 to 2016 and she currently serves as editorial board member of the journal *Applied Research in Quality of Life* as well as the Springer book series on Community Quality of Life and Wellbeing. Meg is the author of *Pragmatic Justifications for the Sustainable City: Acting in the common place* (Routledge, 2017). Meg obtained the Ph.D. in Public and Urban Policy from the New School for Social Research.

Part I
Organizing Concepts and Collaboration in Community Indicators

Chapter 2
The Role of Subjective Well-Being as an Organizing Concept for Community Indicators

Christopher Barrington-Leigh

Abstract One important objective of community indicator initiatives, often explicit in their title or mandate, is to assess overall well-being, life quality, or social progress. These concepts are increasingly becoming accountable to the evaluation survey respondents give when asked about how their life feels, overall. Such quantitative, subjective data are not directly useful for guiding policy, but statistical analysis based on these subjective well-being data can now be used to guide the choice of indicators in a community indicator system, and can even provide weights to use in calculating a summary index for a set of seemingly unrelated indicator measures. This chapter uses a database of 82 indicator initiatives implemented since the 1970s from 30 countries, and at all geographic scales, to assess trends in the structure, content, and success of attempts to measure human flourishing or life quality. Based on a taxonomy that encompasses unaggregated dashboards of indicators, money-denominated accounts, other indices (composite indicators), and measures oriented around subjective well-being, the database suggests that unaggregated and subjective-well-being-oriented indicator initiatives are more successful in terms of their longevity. Moreover, in the interest of accessibility, transparency, accountability, and the assurance of relevance, the construction of indices should only be carried out when quantitatively guided by the analysis of subjective well-being data. Relying on subjective well-being in this way provides an intuitive, compelling headline indicator or synthetic index, supported by a set of policy-amenable indicators whose inclusion is accountable to the actual experience of citizens.

This chapter is adapted from a longer review to be published in *Social Indicators Research*, and benefits from some additional research assistance carried out by Julianne Skarha. I am grateful for feedback from the editors and from participants of the 2016 CIC Impact Summit. The work was supported by funding from the Social Science and Humanities Research Council of Canada grant 435-2016-0531.

C. Barrington-Leigh (✉)
McGill University, Montreal, Canada
e-mail: chris.barrington-leigh@mcgill.ca

M. Holden et al. (eds.), *Community Quality-of-Life Indicators: Best Cases VII*, Community Quality-of-Life and Well-Being,
DOI 10.1007/978-3-319-54618-6_2

Keywords Human flourishing · Life quality · Composite indicators · Subjective well-being · Genuine progress indicators

2.1 Introduction

While often initiated or led by the civil society sector, community indicators are effective when they capture the attention of the public and government. Considerable benefits may flow from public engagement in the process of deliberation and creation of indicators (Hall and Rickard 2013), but typically the ultimate goal is to build sufficient consensus about measurable objectives for society, and for that consensus to have sufficient duration, that those objectives drive policy and are used to hold decision makers to account.

In order to shed some light on which features in indicator initiatives might be most conducive to achieving this sort of *acceptance, authority,* and *staying power,* this chapter provides a community-indicator-oriented summary of a longer review published in *Social Indicators Research* (Barrington-Leigh and Escande 2016, hereafter: *MPWB*). The review is based on a database of indicator initiatives of well-being and progress at all levels of government and geography. In some sense, the cutting edge of innovation in thinking how to measure progress and well-being happens at the smallest and largest of these, i.e., in local community indicator initiatives and in international organizations, while intermediate levels such as national governments tend to be more tied to conventional metrics, due to larger political stakes and institutional inertia.

In any case, we collected quantitative and qualitative information on 82 different indicator projects, classified them, and analyzed the patterns and trends in what we found. Our sample was not made to be representative, nor was it meant to be all-inclusive. Indicator initiatives were considered eligible for inclusion in the database only if the title or stated objective of the effort relates to some concept of overall well-being or progress. This excludes indicator initiatives focused on a particular issue or demographic component of the population. For instance, indicator projects with scopes limited to "child well-being" or "economic progress" were excluded. It also excludes plenty of efforts which act more as a centralized clearinghouse of policy-relevant statistics. These criteria rule out a significant fraction of the longer list in the Community Indicators Consortium's database of Indicator Projects.

Below I outline some different ways we classified the indicator initiatives.

Geographic scale We included indicator initiatives which encompass a "**local**" or "community" scale, which mostly applies to towns or cities; those which span a "**regional**" scale, i.e, a sub-national province or state; those with "**national**"

coverage; and "**international**" ones which span multiple countries or are even calculated for most or all countries. Usually, the spatial resolution is finer than the geographic scale of coverage.

Responsible agency Within each of those scales, there are several possibilities for who designs or leads the indicator project. These we classified into "**government and inter-government**," "**nongovernment**" for any civil society, non-profit, or for-profit organization, and "**academic**" for systems defined by researchers and which typically can be implemented using existing data.

Rationale In principle, the structure of an indicator system can be chosen "**top-down**", i.e., decided by a small group of experts or representatives, or be derived directly from some theoretical idea; or it can be "**bottom-up**," which could mean either driven by a democratic or broadly consultative process, or derived from some data-driven process able to choose and organize constituent elements of an indicator system.

Structure Much of our emphasis lies in differentiating indicator systems based on how they take many numbers and aggregate them together to produce one, or a few, summary values. We call the different options "**Sets of indicators**," "**Indices**," "**Accounts**," and "**Subjective measures**."

Inclusion of subjective well-being Indicator initiatives can choose to incorporate or eschew individuals' subjective reports of their overall well-being.

Several bits of relevant terminology are ambiguous. The usage in this chapter is as follows. "Well-being" and "progress" are used in their most general senses, in order to encompass the full range of metrics in our database. "Subjective well-being" (SWB) refers to any of a range of questions eliciting different aspects of subjective psychological experience (but not subjective assessments of objective facts), while "life satisfaction" refers to a single question, discussed later, which captures a cognitive evaluation of life. "Measure" and "indicator" are often used interchangeably to refer to any individual quantitative metric, while I use "indicator initiative," "indicator project," or "indicator system" to refer an entry in our database, regardless of which kind of *structure* it has. On the other hand, "sets of indicators" is a category of *structure*, above, and means a collection of measures that are not combined into a summary value in any way. These sets of indicators are sometimes called "dashboards" by others.

Table 2.1 shows a subset of indicator projects, taken from the database of *MPWB*, which are classified as being calculated at the community level. The sample of local projects is, for reasons of practical convenience, biased towards English-speaking regions and North America in particular. The larger database includes projects from 30 different countries. As can be seen in the small sample of Table 2.1, many initiatives have not survived. One line of inquiry is to determine which characteristics of indicator initiatives are associated with better chances of surviving. Of course, those which are no longer active but which made it into our database are only the ones with sufficient prominence or impact in their time in order to come to our attention. The analysis in the rest of this chapter is based on the full database of 82 initiatives.

Table 2.1 "Local" indicator initiatives

Name	Country	Year	Alive	Who	What	How	Pop
Subjective QOL in the City of Flint, and Genesee County, Michigan	USA	1979	N	NG	SWB		420k
The Indices of Community Well-Being for Calgary Community Districts	Canada	1985	N	Gov	Idx	T	1M
Jacksonville Community Council QoL progress report	USA	1985	Y	NG	Set	T/B	840k
Oregon Benchmarks	USA	1989	N	Gov	Set	T/B	
Truckee Meadows Tomorrow —Quality of Life Compact program	USA	1994	Y	NG	Set	T/B	320k
Santa Cruz County California Community Assessment Project	USA	1994	N	NG	Set	T	63k
Ontario SDC, Quality of Life Index	Canada	1997	N	NG	Idx	T/B	14M
GPI Atlantic, Nova Scotia	Canada	1998	N	NG	A/S	T	940k
BC regional Socio-economic Profiles and Index	Canada	1998	N	Gov	Idx	T	4.6k
Federation of Canadian Municipalities QOLRS	Canada	1999	N	Gov	Set	T/B	2.6M
Social Development Index	China	2000	Y	Gov/Acd	Idx	T	7M
Boston Foundation's Boston indicators Project	USA	2000	Y	NG	Set		1M
Zurich sustainability indicator set	Switzerland	2000	Y	Gov	Set	T	400k
Buffalo City 2001 QOL survey	South Africa	2001	N	Gov	Set	T	750k
Porto Monitoring System on Urban Quality of Life	Portugal	2001	Y	Gov/Acd	Set	T	1.7M
GPI, Alberta, Pembina Institute	Canada	2001	N	NG	Act	T/B	4.1M
Tasmania Together Project	Australia	2001	N	Gov	Set	T/B	520k
Newfoundland community accounts	Canada	2002	Y	Gov	Set	T	530k
Peterborough Quality of Life Report	Canada	2002	Y	NG	Set	B	120k
Hennepin County 2002 Community Indicators Report	USA	2002	N	Gov	Set	T	1.2M
City of Florence QOL	Italy	2003	N	Gov/Acd	Set	B	360k

(continued)

Table 2.1 (continued)

Name	Country	Year	Alive	Who	What	How	Pop
Community Foundations of Canada's Vital Signs Program	Canada	2007	Y	NG	Set		30M
Khaveh Shomali QOL	Iran	2009	N	Acd	S/I	T	
The Glasgow Indicators Project	Scotland	2009	Y	Gov/Acd	Set	T	590k
Winnipeg Peg report	Canada	2010	Y	NG	Set	T/B	660k

Indicator initiatives in the database of Barrington-Leigh and Escande (2016) classified as "local," meaning that the geographic precision or scope of the indicators is at the municipality or metro scale. *Year* is the founding year; *Alive* records whether or not the indicator project is still in production; *Who* classifies its creator as government or non-government (there are none of academic origin in this subset); *What* describes its *structure* as a Set of Indicators, an Index, or a set of Accounts, or a combination; and *How* specifies whether it was designed with a top-down, bottom-up, or hybrid approach. *Pop* is the population of the region or regions covered

The goal in what follows is (1) to understand some trends in how indicator initiatives are being constructed, (2) to assess which classes of indicator initiatives best survive the test of time, and (3) to suggest how subjective and objective measures can be used together in order to construct accountable, accessible, and authoritative community indicator systems. I conclude by recommending that subjective well-being can play a central role in measures of human outcomes, but that in order to do them justice most long-term environmental indicators must be separated from those focused on current human well-being.

2.2 Statistical and Cultural Trends of Indicator Initiatives

To begin with, it is interesting to look at broader trends in the fashion of language surrounding progress and well-being. The upper panel of Fig. 2.1 shows a history from 1975 to 2008 of how often different words were used in printed books. It shows some patterns we might expect from the history of social indicators. First, the term "social indicator," popular in the late 1970s, is in decline. The use of terms "gross domestic product" (GDP) and "gross national product" (GNP) is also on the decline, after having peaked in the 1990s. By contrast, reference to modern augmented GDP measures, often referred to as "genuine progress indicators" (GPIs) is on the rise, as are the terms "beyond GDP," "well-being," "happiness," and "sustainability." One may interpret these trends as indicative of overall interest in these concepts, and reflective therefore of the importance English-speaking societies place on them. During this same period, there has been an even stronger trend in writing by academic economists, as judged by their publications. The number of articles appearing in economics journals and referring to "life satisfaction" or "happiness" or "subjective well-being" grew from three in 1991 to >300 per year

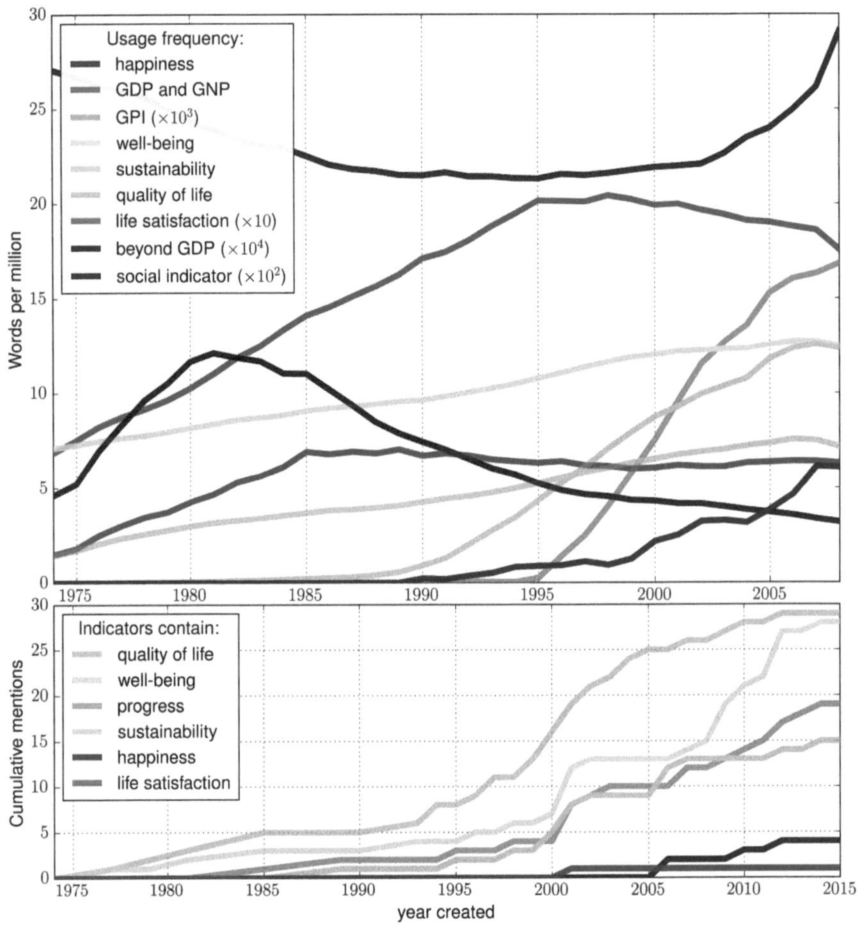

Fig. 2.1 Usage of progress and well-being terminology over time. *Upper panel* Historical incidences of some relevant terms in printed books, taken from Google's n-grams (see http://ngram.google.com for more information). "Life satisfaction" represents the sum of incidences of "life satisfaction" and "satisfaction with life" and is scaled up by a factor of 10 for better visibility. "Social indicator" is scaled up by a factor of 100, and GPI, short for "genuine progress indicator," is scaled up by 1000. Use of the term "sustainable development" shows a similar pattern over time as "sustainability." The Google N-gram database ends in 2008. *Lower panel* the (rescaled) cumulative number of mentions of different terms (labeled by *color* in *top panel*) in the stated name or purpose of those measures

last year (MPWB). To some extent, the growth in indicator initiatives using more human-based measures of progress may have much to do with the idea that we can now measure happiness quantitatively. Advances in research have provided specific

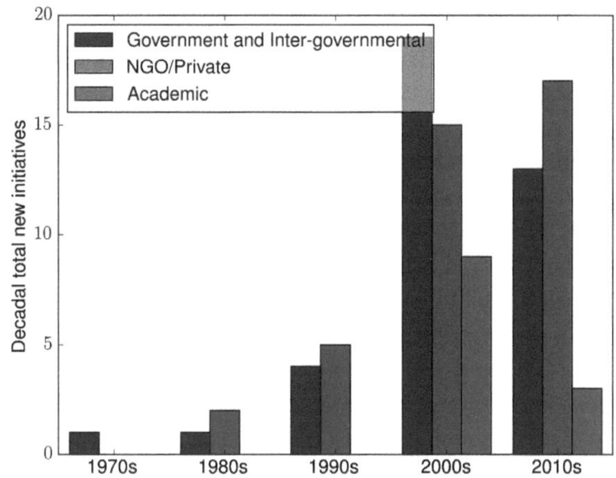

Fig. 2.2 Government and non-government designers. *Bars* show the number of new indicator initiatives in our database by decade. Two indicator initiatives fall simultaneously into the *non-government* and *academia* categories; the rest are in only one

insights about the importance of social links and other life conditions in fostering a satisfying life.

Carrying out a similar analysis on the language used in the names or stated purpose of indicator systems in our database shows consistent trends. The lower panel in Fig. 2.1 shows the cumulative number of mentions of several of these terms. In recent years, "well-being" and "progress" are used more often than "quality of life" or "sustainability" in explaining the essence or objective of new indicator initiatives. "Happiness" is a relatively new term to appear prominently in the name or objective of indicator initiatives.

Figure 2.2 portrays the breakdown of *who* was responsible for leading each effort. In both the full database and the smaller (local) list shown in Table 2.1, the indicator initiatives have been founded by a fairly constant and even mix of government and non-government/private actors. *MPWB* discusses the advantages and challenges particular to each category, but clearly—and particularly for local initiatives—a broad and cross-cutting alliance of stakeholders is the most promising, because it can best ensure ongoing demand for the product, collective accountability for continued efforts to produce it, a robustness of funding in some cases, and of course the legitimacy of a broad base of support for the structure and content.

2.3 Quantitative, Qualitative, Objective, and Subjective

I now turn to the classification of *structure*, mentioned earlier, and outlined by *MPWB*. Indicator initiatives' types have been described and classified in different ways by various authors. Our categories distinguish, first, whether a set of indicators is combined into summary statistics of some kind. Nearly all community indicator initiatives are comprised of a panel of measures, and in many cases this is as far as the quantitative contribution goes. For instance, an initiative focused on child well-being may include an estimate of attendance at primary school, expressed as a fraction of the appropriately-aged child population. It may also present rates of change for this indicator, for instance as the measured change over ten years. Beyond that, a published form of the initiative may go on to provide qualitative evidence in the form of a discussion of associated observations, policy changes, or anecdotes, or may provide normative evaluations of whether the levels and trends are good or bad. For instance, the Boston Indicators project and Canada's Vital Signs projects have considerable and strong emphases, respectively, on such qualitative accounts.

In the example above, the initiative remains a *set of indicators* if its contribution is to collate a series of statistics, relevant to some topic or objective, and accompanying discussion. However, it becomes an *index* if some aggregate measure, for instance named overall child well-being, is constructed to summarize the performance of multiple other measures. Unlike the individual constituent indicators which have natural units such as fraction of children, calories per day, or average reading level (grade) at age 12, indices often have contrived scales and no units. For instance, they may be a number which is scaled so that its value in a base year was 100. A prominent example is the Human Development Index (Human Development Report Office 2013), which is simply a combination of life expectancy, income per capita, and two measures of population education levels. There is no obvious or natural way to combine these, so the method is somewhat arbitrary. A more complex example is the Canadian Index of Wellbeing, which blends 64 individual measures into a summary index (Michalos et al. 2011, p. 6). Clearly, someone else using the same data might choose to combine them in a different way and therefore come up with a different value for the index.

This problem with indices is a serious challenge when they become subject to public scrutiny. The Stiglitz-Sen-Fitoussi Commission, appointed by the French Presidency, wrote in its 2009 report that statistical offices should provide information to empower others to aggregate across dimensions of life quality in various ways, to create a variety of indices (Stiglitz et al. 2009), rather than make the value judgments necessary to settle on and promote a single index. In our database, 52% of indicator initiatives which fit purely into the "index" category have become defunct, as compared with 40% of the collections of indicators which have chosen not to aggregate their components (*MPWB*).

Two kinds of indices appear to have a more accountable rationale for their method. We defer discussion of one of them for later, but the first is those which are summing up things with monetary values, referred to above as *Accounts*. The GDP is such an index, as are many of the "Genuine Progress Indicators" (GPI) which aim to partly "correct" the GDP by including missing components such as the degradation of natural capital. However, even though these indices may be denominated in units of currency, they are not simple sums. Expressing GDP in terms comparable across years is a complex calculation because it must take into account the year-to-year changing market prices of countless goods whose real values have presumably not changed. GPIs have an even harder challenge, since they aim to put financial values onto components of provision, investment, and disinvestment or harm, without having any direct price evaluations to work from. This requires higher levels of judgment and extrapolation in order to quantify the contributions. In fact, the inevitable omissions in these methods leave their indices also lacking in transparency and objectivity.

2.3.1 Subjective Well-Being

So far, the focus has been on objective indicators. The rate of attendance at primary school, life expectancy, and volume of a good produced are all values which, in principle, someone else could re-measure if they had access to the same population, and they should come up with the same answer. By contrast, the use of *subjective* data to assess well-being and progress is on the rise in economics and in indicator design, but relies on an individual's evaluation which cannot be verified by a second or outside authority.

It is worthwhile to consider a certain single survey question which has a somewhat central role in this field:

> Overall, how satisfied are you with life as a whole these days, on a scale from 0 to 10, where zero means you feel "not at all satisfied' and 10 means you feel "completely satisfied"?

While clearly highly subjective, this life satisfaction (LS) question solicits a numeric response, and the data from fielding it are therefore quantitative. This fact has facilitated an extensive and rapidly growing body of research (alluded to earlier) which quantitatively analyzes variations in LS across individuals, communities, and countries, at a point in time as well as using changes over time. The body of evidence shows that LS exhibits reasonable stability within individuals, sensitivity to life conditions and changes, the ability to predict behavior, reasonable variation with material and other circumstances across the entire range of global national development levels, and international and intercultural comparability (Helliwell et al. 2010; Exton et al. 2015). More broadly, SWB reports for an individual are consistent with those predicted on their behalf by family and close friends (Diener 1984; Sandvik et al. 1993), and SWB reports correlate with objective physiological signs of mood and well-being. While an individual's answer is subjective, average responses from a population are a reproducible measurement.

Upon acceptance of the idea that individuals can aggregate their experience in accordance with their own priorities and values in a way that no one else can, the advantages of having access to such measurements become apparent. The aforementioned Stiglitz-Sen-Fitoussi report points out that it is difficult to compare income over time in the face of technological change, for reasons already given above, and it is also a great challenge to value publicly-provided individual services, as well as numerous other experiences which are not a result of choices. By contrast, individuals' own cognitive evaluations of life accommodate in principle all these experiences and changes with the appropriate psychological weights.

The understanding of these measures has advanced rapidly in recent years due to the increasing abundance of empirical data. Efforts by the U.S. National Academies (Stone and Mackie 2014) and in particular the OECD (OECD 2013) have led to a standardization of SWB measurement, in which LS is identified as the primary measure for policy analysis. Politically, too, such "happiness" metrics have gained traction and, increasingly, investment and policy accountability. High-level examples include Prime Minister Cameron's initiative in the U.K. (Cameron 2010; UK Office of National Statistics 2011; Dolan et al. 2011); President Sarkozy's rationale for the Stiglitz-Sen-Fitoussi report (Stiglitz et al. 2009); the OECD's Better Life initiative (OECD 2015, 2016); the World Happiness Reports (Helliwell et al. 2012, and nearly annually since); and the U.S. Federal Reserve chair Bernanke's speech on well-being (Bernanke 2010).

Accordingly, there has arisen our fourth category of indicator system *structure*, the "Subjective measures." These are indicator initiatives consisting entirely of subjective reports, for instance satisfaction with various aspects of a local government's performance, or which are otherwise oriented around subjective well-being. One of the indicator projects listed in Table 2.1, in Genesee County, fits this description. Figure 2.3 shows the distribution of our four categories over time. According to this limited sample, there was a peak of interest in monetary-denominated accounts (GPIs and the like) in the previous decade, but there is a continued growth in the role of indicator initiatives focused on subjective

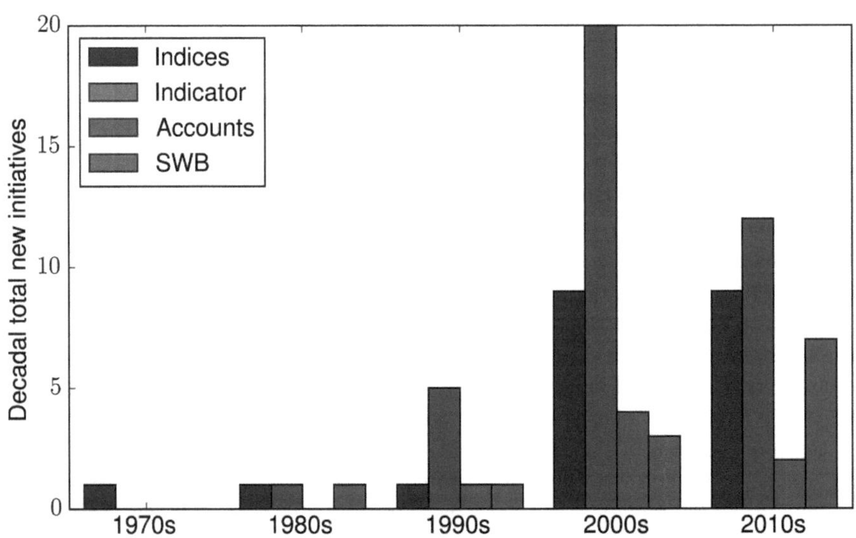

Fig. 2.3 Indicator sets, Indices, Accounts, and Subjective measures. *Bars* show the classification of new measures in our database by decade. The "Indicators" category refers to sets of indicators that are not rolled into an index. The subjective well-being (SWB) category includes measures exclusively composed of subjective assessments, as well as indices aggregated according to weights derived from empirical models of life satisfaction. Excluded from "Index" are those indices which also fit in the SWB category

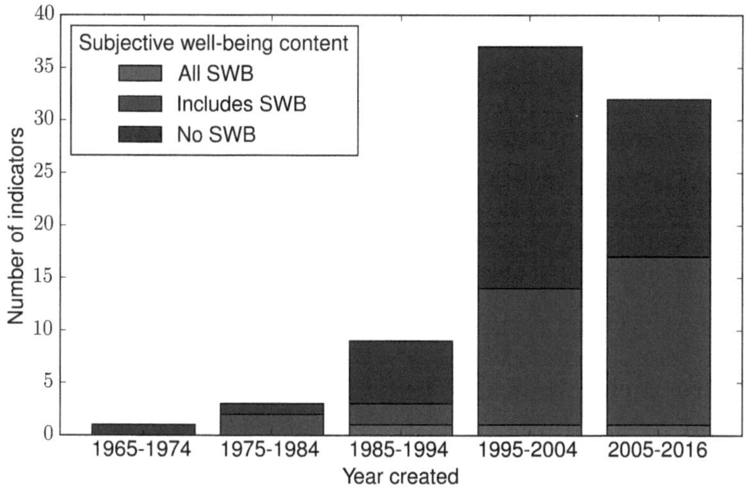

Fig. 2.4 Incorporation of subjective responses into measures of progress. From *MPWB*

well-being. Figure 2.4 provides even stronger evidence of this trend. A number of indicator systems include at least one subjective response measure in their panel of indicators, even if they do not privilege SWB as a focus or guide. In the last decade, fully half of the new indicator initiatives have incorporated subjective responses in one way or another, which is nearly double the rate of the previous decade.

Possibly the most interesting development in the measurement of general-purpose well-being indicator systems is the rise of indices which are built from a set of objective indicators but which use SWB to guide their aggregation. In our classification, these fall both into the "Index category" and the "Subjective measure" category. Earlier I referred to two kinds of indices which appear to be more accountable because of their transparent method of creating an index out of a collection of relatively unrelated indicators; however, I explained why the first, the money-denominated accounts, is in fact plagued by transparency problems.

By contrast, the SWB-based indices may pose a paradigm in which the recipe for building an index from a set of (typically) objective measures is more accountable. Our database includes three examples. The Legatum Prosperity Index (Lind 2014) uses a model explaining variation in responses to Gallup World Poll's life evaluation question to determine weights for building an index out of eight domains. Similarly, a regional analysis in France uses the answer to the question, "In your current life, do you feel happy: never, occasionally, quite often, very often?" along with the same statistical technique to find weights for aggregating 11 indicator dimensions (Bigot et al. 2012). Thirdly, the Economist's *Quality of Life Index* is generated using weights derived from a similar model of life satisfaction data (The Economist Intelligence Unit 2005).

In each case, an objective, reproducible method is used to determine how to build an index out of a set of available measures which may be thought to pertain to quality of life, progress, or well-being.

The method essentially evaluates the importance of each item for explaining variation in SWB, and then uses the measured importance as a corresponding weight. In fact, the resulting index is like a synthetic measure of SWB, as it statistically reproduces the measured subjective indicator using only the set of more objective indicators. In the next section, I discuss the advantages of this approach, and explain some of its limitations.

2.4 Structuring Indicator Initiatives to Be Meaningful and Accountable

Indicator systems meant to reflect policy success, or to capture overall well-being or a broad—if not comprehensive—measure of progress, require several attributes to support their adoption, persistence, and ability to influence. These include accountability, accessibility, and relevance. Being accountable relates to at least two things about the indicator project, corresponding to our categories of *rationale* and *structure*. First, the conception and design of the indicator system must have legitimacy, in its ultimate form but usually also in the process of devising it. In "bottom-up" design processes, for instance, there is a sufficient level of atheoretical input from the population being monitored. Secondly, an accountable structure is one with sufficient transparency in order that others can both reproduce it and understand it.

This last point relates to accessibility, also. Not only must the indicator system structure be feasibly understood by others, but the presentation format of the indicator system should also be appealing. For this reason indicator initiatives sometimes choose to build an index as a summary measure; it acts as a headline feature as well as an organizing concept which can encourage further exploration of the more detailed, disaggregated components which constitute it.

In order to be relevant, of course, the metrics included in an indicator system must in fact help to differentiate good experience from less good experience and ultimately good policy from bad. Ideally, the metrics would also be concise: i.e., they would be the best and smallest available set which address the relevant dimensions, and no more.

My focus on LS reflects two advantages in regards to the criteria described above. First, LS can serve as an organizing concept and headline measure for human welfare or quality of life. Even if is reported in its raw form and a remaining set of indicators is not aggregated into any index, featuring LS as the headline indicator communicates the overall intent of an indicator system. It also conveys a particular approach, in which it is the experience of the target population that is privileged with the ultimate voice and priority. This portrays one kind of accountability in the measurement system simply because the designers are not deciding which policies, departments, or domains are the most important.

Secondly, LS can serve as a statistical tool to provide guidance on weights for an index, and even on what social and economic variables to incorporate in an indicator system. How might one achieve the best and smallest set of indicators in a panel of indicators, and how might one evaluate the relevance of a particular indicator when deciding whether or not to record, include, or publish it? Using LS data as a guide allows exactly this, in principle. Although the process is not completely devoid of judgment, the statistical calculations referred to earlier (typically, these are linear regressions) provide measures of importance for LS for each of an array of indicators that one might propose as jointly relevant for well-being. This process not only provides weights that can be used in building an index out of a set of indicators; it also can suggest which indicators to drop entirely. If an indicator is not deemed important by such models, then it is not currently useful in differentiating between those experiencing high quality of life and those experiencing low quality of life, overall.

One drawback of such data-driven weights in an index is that if a new or better set of indicators arises, for instance because a new, improved measure of social capital becomes available in a survey, it has implications for past assessments of the index. That is, one could then calculate trends over time in two ways—with or without the new value included. Moreover, even with the same set of indicators, the weights could change just with updated values of the data or with newer external science informing the weights. This means that there is not a single possible version of the index, but rather that it remains to some extent a work in progress. In fact, this is not so different from the ever-evolving detailed definition of GDP, or the GPIs which are limited in their inclusiveness only by what data and methods are available at any point.

A second caution is that an indicator system for well-being does not encompass all community indicator objectives. There is no reason to believe that SWB measures like life satisfaction incorporate full assessments of future risks or unseen damage to the environment or to public resource stocks. As a result, well-being indicator initiatives are best separated from complementary ones addressing long-term sustainability (Neumayer 1999; Hall et al. 2011). *MPWB* also articulates deep concerns with treating environmental or sustainability assessments in an analogous way to what is advocated here for well-being, i.e., folding them into a single index. While use of improved accounting systems like GPI and augmented GDPs still has a role for evaluating trade-offs between one asset and another, the task of ensuring environmental integrity is much more complex and lends itself more to tracking a set of indicators which cannot sensibly be combined. Most likely, in this realm policy should be in the form of enforcement of limits (e.g. quotas) on most of those indicators, rather than trying to optimize a single outcome.

Despite these limitations, because LS-based weighting schemes as described above do not rely on arbitrary choice, but are constrained to follow whatever the data say, and because even the set of included factors (indicators) is ultimately chosen by the data itself, the schemes do not suffer as much as other indices from the drawbacks related to accountability and theoretical foundation. When the public and policy makers trust that the weights of an index are meaningful, they may also be more likely to feel interested to investigate and take seriously the more specific indicators that comprise the index.

2.5 Conclusion

Well-being is a bit of a weasel-word, in that it can be used to refer to whatever priorities a given advocate wishes to promote as important. However, subjective well-being, and life satisfaction in particular, is becoming the measure to which other definitions of well-being are accountable.

One new option in the menu of strategies for devising, organizing, and communicating community indicator projects is to use life satisfaction responses as a way to give privilege to a collective voice for defining what is important. Rather than asking citizens explicitly what they believe is important to measure and to pursue, recording life satisfaction allows for the choice to be an implicit one because modern methods are established to infer what matters based only on how people judge their lives, overall, when asked for a cognitive evaluation. That is, when large data sets on individual life satisfaction and an array of more objective life circumstances are brought together, the circumstances can be used to statistically "explain" life satisfaction, and this tells us which life conditions deserve the most focus, and in what proportion. This has the nice property of separating, as much as possible, objective measures from subjective ones, while recognizing that ultimately the selection and pursuit of objective measures are all accountable to our subjective assessment of life quality.

Use of SWB in this way can in principle (1) guide and test the choice of indicators in an indicator initiative; (2) provide objective, empirically-based weights for creating an index measure out of a set of indicators; (3) provide a headline indicator to succinctly communicate the overall goal of pursuing life quality to those who might otherwise be put off by a rather technical array of detailed quantitative indicators; and indeed (4) keep the effort, and therefore policy, accountable above all to a purely human centered and experience-based metric of well-being.

References

Barrington-Leigh, C., & Escande, A. (2016). Measuring progress and well-being: A comparative review of indicators. Social Indicators Research. doi:10.1007/s11205-016-1505-0

Bernanke, B. S. (2010). *The economics of happiness*. www.federalreserve.gov/newsevents/speech/bernanke20100508a.htm. Visited on December 2011.

Bigot, R., Croutte, P., Daudey, E., Hoibian, S., & Müller, J. (2012). L'évolution du bien-être en France depuis 30 ans.
Cameron, D. (2010). *A transcript of a speech given by the Prime Minister on wellbeing on 25 November*. http://www.number10.gov.uk/news/pm-speech-on-well-being (visited on 12/2011).
Diener, E. (1984). Subjective well-being. *Psychological Bulletin, 95*(3), 542–575.
Dolan, P., Layard, R., & Metcalfe, R. (2011). Measuring subjective well-being for public policy. *Office for National Statistics Paper*.
Exton, C., Smith, C., & Vandendriessche, D. (2015). Comparing happiness across the world: Does culture matter? *OECD Statistics Working Papers*. doi:10.1787/5jrqppzd9bs2-en
Hall, J., Barrington-Leigh, C., & Helliwell, J. (2011). Cutting through the clutter: Searching for an over-arching measure of well-being. *CESifo DICE Report, 8*(4), 8–12.
Hall, J., & Rickard, L. (2013). *People, progress and participation: How initiatives measuring social progress yield benefits beyond better metrics*. Gütersloh: Bertelsmann Stiftung.
Helliwell, J. F., et al. (2010). International evidence on the social context of well-being. In E. Diener, J. F. Helliwell, & D. Kahneman (Eds.), *International differences in well-being* (pp. 213–229). Oxford University Press.
Helliwell, J., Layard, R., & Sachs, J. (2012). *World happiness report*. http://worldhappiness.report/ed/2012/
Human Development Report Office. (2013). *Human Development Report 2013: Technical Notes*. Technical Report, pp. 1–8.
Lind, N. (2014). Legatum Prosperity Index. In: *Encyclopedia of quality of life and well-being research* (pp. 3529–3530). Springer.
Michalos, A., et al. (2011). *Technical Report 1.0*. Waterloo, ON: The Canadian Index of Wellbeing and University of Waterloo.
Neumayer, E. (1999). The ISEW—Not an index of sustainable economic welfare. *Social Indicators Research, 48*(1), 77–101. issn: 0303-8300. doi:10.1023/A:1006914023227
OECD. (2013). *OECD guidelines on measuring subjective well-being*.
OECD. (2015). *How's life?: Measuring well-being*. OECD Publishing.
OECD. (2016). *Better life initiative: Measuring well-being and progress*. http://www.oecd.org/progress. Visited on March 2016.
Sandvik, E., Diener, E., Seidlitz, L. (1993). Subjective well-being: The convergence and stability of self-report and non-self-report measures. *Journal of Personality*, 61(3), 317–342. issn: 1467-6494. doi: 10.1111/j.1467-6494.1993.tb00283.x
Stiglitz, J. E., Sen, A., & Fitoussi, J.-P. (2009). *Report by the commission on the measurement of economic performance and social progress*. Paris: commission on the Measurement of Economic Performance and Social Progress.
Stone, A. A, Mackie, C., et al. (2014). *Subjective well-being: Measuring happiness, suffering, and other dimensions of experience*. National Academies Press.
The Economist Intelligence Unit. (2005). The Economist Intelligence Unit quality-of-life index. *The Economist*.
UK Office of National Statistics. (2011). *National statistician's reflections on the national Debate on measuring national well-being*. eprint: www.ons.gov.uk. http://www.ons.gov.uk/ons/guide-method/user-guidance/well-being/wellbeing-knowledgebank/understanding-wellbeing/measuring-what-matters–national-statistician-sreflections-on-the-national-debate-on-measuring-national-well-being.pdf. Visited on December 2011.

Author Biography

Christopher Barrington-Leigh is an Assistant Professor at McGill University, jointly appointed at the Institute for Health and Social Policy and the School of Environment, and is an associate member in McGill's Department of Economics. Originally trained in upper atmospheric and space plasma physics at M.I.T., Stanford, and Berkeley, Chris subsequently received a Ph.D. in Economics at UBC. Chris' research interests lie in two fields. One is focused on empirical and quantitative assessments of human well-being, and their implications for economic, social, and environmental policy, including the pursuit of overall economic growth and material consumption expansion. In particular, his research makes use of subjective well-being reports to address the relative importance of social and community-oriented aspects of life along with material consumption. He uses large international as well as national surveys, experiments, and economic theoretical modeling to understand individual and aggregate consumption benefits, and their implications for policy. His other research pursuit addresses issues in environmental economics, including the structure of urban road networks and their implication for climate policy. Chris was a Global Scholar of the Canadian Institute for Advanced Research (2009–2014).

Chapter 3
Community Indicators and the Collective Goods Criterion for Impact

Frank Ridzi

Abstract Common wisdom holds that communities can accomplish more when people find ways to work together. However, such nuanced sensibilities can be difficult to measure. This is true in the field of community indicators as well as its allied fields of social movements, collective impact, catalytic philanthropy and community coalitions. Due to the elusiveness of evaluation techniques some in the social movements field have argued for a definition of success based on the collective goods criterion (CGC). In this chapter we explore the case of Syracuse, New York on the occasion of its achievement of seven years of positive change in its key community indicator of the four year graduation rate. Though it would be difficult to claim that Syracuse's community indicators project, CNY.vitals, caused this change, we explore how a CGC approach can be used to examine how the measurement mentality that accompanied the community indicators project is associated with collective benefits that have accrued to members of the community in terms of cultural capital, philanthropic investment and governmental policy change.

Keywords Syracuse · CNY vitals · Collective goods · Literacy rate · Catalytic philanthropy · Collective impact · Philanthropy

3.1 Introduction

In this chapter, we focus on the challenge of measuring the success of Community Indicator Projects (CIPs) that aspire to bring about positive community change. The first part of this chapter examines what can be learned from the wisdom of the social movement literature's collective goods criterion. The second part of the chapter provides an overview of a specific case study, CNY Vitals, describing how this criterion can be useful.

F. Ridzi (✉)
Central New York Community Foundation and Le Moyne College,
Syracuse, NY, USA
e-mail: FrankRidzi@gmail.com

M. Holden et al. (eds.), *Community Quality-of-Life Indicators: Best Cases VII*, Community Quality-of-Life and Well-Being,
DOI 10.1007/978-3-319-54618-6_3

3.2 Why the Collective Goods Criterion?

Community Indicators projects (CIPs) seldom limit their ambitions to simply measuring local data. Whether explicitly or implicitly stated, the end game for most CIPs is to help bring about a noticeable improvement in the quality of life that residents experience (Holden and Phillips 2010; Wood 2016). Consequently, CIPs that begin by measuring community well-being often evolve into a follow up phase of mobilizing community stakeholders to attempt to bring about changes in policy, resources and social capital that, it is hoped, will make the community indicators that people have rallied around change for the better (Wood 2016). For instance, if a CIP began by bringing attention to high community obesity rates, the next steps might involve rallying stakeholders to this issue, articulating strategies for community change (such as raising issue awareness and launching exercise and healthy eating programs for youth), and maintaining constant lines of communication about how pre-existing strategies can better coordinate to reinforce the broader initiative. Communities that set out to make this transition from problem identification to taking action toward remediation often turn to implementation structures such as community coalitions (Butterfoss 2007; Ridzi et al. 2011) or other variants of the collective impact approach (Kania and Kramer 2011). These approaches offer frameworks for how to structure collaborative community initiatives that incorporate and coordinate the efforts of groups that, under business as usual, typically carry out their missions in isolation (or silos) from each other. In essence by adopting one of these structures communities do not have to reinvent the wheel while setting out to increase coordination among residents, governments, schools, businesses and others.

While a variety of models exist for the formation of coalitions or other collective impact structures (Butterfoss 2007; Kania and Kramer 2011; Ridzi et al. 2011), there has been remarkably little effort to connect these structures with another type of community mobilization literature—that of social movements. There are likely numerous reasons for this. Most notably, collective impact or coalition movements are a distinctive type of social movement from those that dominate the social movement literature. Social movements and collective impact approaches differ in distinctive ways. While social movements tend to emphasize grassroots resident-led efforts to change community power dynamics, collective impact approaches tend to be more "grass-tips" (Butterfoss 2007: 10) and led by community leaders. Nevertheless, they also have many commonalities; most notably that they both seek to transform the institutions in place to make life better for the constituents of their communities. While exploring the similarities and differences are beyond the scope of this paper, it is nevertheless helpful to explore some of these contrasts when it comes to the issue of measuring the success of their efforts because it helps to elucidate how the common good criterion that has been utilized in social movement literature can also be of use within the CIP/collective impact realm.

Community Indicators projects that evolve into collective impact have sought to measure impact most often by hoping for positive change in the numbers that are spotlighted (Hatry and Morley 2008; Ridzi 2012; Zimmerman 2012; Wood 2016). This is the premise behind numerous projects that have been launched as well as recent software packages that have been developed within the framework of results based accountability (Carlson et al. 2011, see also Results Scorecard 2016). However, there has long been a noted difficulty, even when positive change is brought about, in the actual attribution of credit for such changes. Community Indicators are not alone here. The kindred literature on community coalitions (health focused and otherwise) suggests that, though a vast amount is known about their organization, their ability to mobilize support to achieve policy change, and their regard as effective institutions within the communities they serve, there is little ability to prove that they actually make a community better off. Collective Impact and Catalytic Philanthropy (Kramer 2009) models too often cannot point to improvements in large scale community indicators such as graduation rates based on their work (Henig et al. 2016). Rather they must often look to their successes in rallying people and their governments to bring about policy change as the evidence of their success. So while seeking to enact more expansive medical coverage policies or enroll a greater number of children in healthcare might be pointed to as evidence of effectiveness, we fall short of being able to attribute declines in child mortality in a community to such efforts, even if the two co-occur. The problem is that correlation does not prove causation, especially within the complex ecosystems of communities large enough to warrant community indicator projects. This type of problematic reasoning was made famous in large scale community indicator forays into analysis such as popularized by Freakonomics (Levitt and Dubner 2005). These authors made great sweeping proclamations such as about how legalized abortion has led to a decades later reduction in crime (since unwanted children that would later become thugs were prevented from being born). While plausible, few would say that this correlation actually proves that the noted policy change of abortion caused the outcome of reduced crime, since reality is likely much more complex. The same is true in the case of efforts related to community indicators. These initiatives simply take place in an ecosystem too complex to prove cause and effect. In this respect, community indicators/collective impact efforts and social movements find themselves on similar footing. As Amenta and Young assert, "important developments sometimes happen in the wake of social movements and the collective action of challengers. But it is premature to call these developments the outcomes or results of challenges because events that happen during or after a challenge may be due to forces other than the challenge" (p. 23).

Because it predates the collective impact and coalition craze, the social movements literature has had longer to reflect on this dilemma. Though typically focused on the power struggles of different classes of people, often in a Marxian historical materialist vein, this area of study also sought to understand how community mobilization (not entirely unlike that encouraged by indicators movements) could bring about change for the better. Perhaps in part due to the fact that social movements often materialize out of disenfranchisement (or perceived disenfranchisement), social movements have not been associated with community indicators. Indeed, it is not hard to see why since in a conflict perspective it is those in power who control the means and apparatus of the state and the measurement systems that govern everyday lives (Smith 1999). Hence, it would not behoove a social movement that is seeking to disrupt the power of a ruling class to embrace the same measures that are controlled by a ruling class as its standard for success. While at some level it would appear that social movement literature is at odds with community indicators, it is perhaps this isolation from the control of enumerating apparatus that has led the field of social movements to develop other measures for success, in line with an effort to drive change from the status quo. While there is, of course, the blunt instrument of examining whether a government was overthrown, an allegedly unjust law overturned, or a political party ousted from power, there are also more subtle nuances to success within the social movements literature. The collective goods criterion helps to make this visible since it has been used to conceptualize what constitutes an important result of a social movement effort (Amenta and Young 1999: 22).

The social movement literature asserts that coalitions have three dimensions for measuring impact: "they last long enough to achieve goals or concessions, they consistently carry out collective action, and they manage to influence their targets in desired ways" (Suzanne Staggenborg as seen in Reese 2011). While on first glance this might look very similar to what one might articulate as a goal of CIPs that evolve into collective impact coalition formation, there is a key difference brought about in the phrasing of the outcome. To "influence their targets in desired ways" is, on further analysis, much broader, and much more forgiving than a comparative goal of a CIP effort to for instance "move the needle on a specific targeted community indicator." This broader perspective on what success could look like is not an accident. Ever since William Gamson's 1975 work, *The Strategy of Social Protest*, (2nd edition in 1990) the field has wrestled with the reality that there is often wide disagreement among activists and even between activists and scholars about the official goals of social movements. As might be anticipated, disagreement about the purposes of movements might lead to a bit of a challenge when it comes time to determine if it succeeded. While collective impact may seem to be on different footing since it insists upon shared measures of success from the beginning (Kania and Kramer 2011), in practice, the selection of such measures can be intensely political and may, more often than not, involve settling for what measures are available, or expedient, rather than what the majority of participants would see as a true measure of success. For instance, even though a room full of highly trained professionals may agree to use a specific measure, the majority of these same professionals may readily concede that the agreed upon measure falls far short of capturing the true goal of the initiative. Given this similarity of disagreement in both social movements and CIP/collective impact efforts it may be helpful to resort to the collective goods criterion that allows for the fact that collective action may often result in impacts that, though positive and desirable, were not anticipated by anyone.

Hence, in short the "collective goods criterion" of social movements is much more generous, perhaps because it is born of recognition that activists seldom achieve the goals that they set out to achieve. Furthermore, because of this lack of linearity, the social movement thinkers in this area tend to shy away from using terms such as "success," "failure" or "outcomes" of social movements, but rather focus on the "impact" of such movements (Amenta and Young 1999). This approach sees such movements as impactful if they secure any significant positive movement for the groups on whose behalf they advocate. This could include improvement on the political, individual, institutional, international or cultural realms. It would also include direct and indirect as well as unanticipated and latent effects.

So what types of wisdom might CIPs with collective impact aspirations draw from a collective goods criterion? For starters, a collective good criterion suggests that collective movements should be wary of drawing lines in the sand and insisting that they will be the ultimate measures of the initiative's success. The litany of social movements case studies suggest that collective action can often lead to positive change, but that it is often in ways that were not initially predicted. Groups that draw a line in the sand at the outset risk having a mostly successful effort labeled a failure because it failed to meet one measurable criterion.

Second the collective goods criterion suggests that it is worthwhile to take an inductive approach to identifying indicators of success rather than a deductive approach. A deductive approach picks a measure from the outset and says: if the initiative is a success, the needle will move. An inductive approach, on the other hand, is much more holistic and qualitative. It would look more like a retrospective analysis of all of the positive changes that have occurred following from the initiative with an open minded readiness to be on the lookout for unanticipated positive outcomes. These might take such forms as community investment, governmental policy change and increases in recognition of the importance or validity of the cause.

Finally, the collective good criterion's broad perspective on impact warns against singling out specific members of the community, or programs that they run. To do so would be antithetical to the notion of a movement based on collective action. Not only would focusing on one outcome be too limiting based on the inductive approach of the criterion but it could potentially undercut the core of solidarity that is the heart of what makes collective action a success. This is consistent with advocates of collective impact who have argued that the movement needs to avoid looking for silver bullets to solve our problems and instead look for silver buckshot (Kania et al. 2014):

> Achieving population-level change requires stakeholders to abandon the search for a single silver bullet solution. Instead, they must shift their mindset and recognize that success comes from the combination of many interventions. For practitioners, this shift means thinking about their work as part of a larger context, and considering how their efforts fit into the larger puzzle of activities. Funders and policymakers similarly must shift from investing in individual, single-point interventions toward investing in processes and relationships that enable multiple organizations to work together. It is important to note that this shift toward silver buckshot solutions does not minimize the importance of high quality individual programs, interventions, and policies. Rather, it emphasizes that each of these programs and policies is necessary, but not sufficient, for success. Rather than isolating individual programs and trying to scale them up, collective impact works best when it

focuses on the ways that strong individual interventions or policies fit together and reinforce each other to solve a complex problem.

Taking this metaphor further, the main advantage of using it is that it helps us increase our chances of hitting a target even when it is in motion or when we are trying to hit multiple targets simultaneously. In that regard, it takes into account the imprecision with which we are able to measure our social lives and the constantly changing factors that cause and sustain such intractable social problems as poverty, illiteracy and pollution.

If we were to launch a broad initiative with a single identified goal and then celebrate only one champion from within the larger cohort of collaborators that we identified as causing the change we seek, we would not only be overlooking all of the accomplishments of the various members of the initiative that were not able to be well measured but we would also risk ostracizing the others who participated. Indeed Helmstetter et al. (this volume) assert that overcoming competitive orientations is critical to success. To use another metaphor, singling out a key partner over the collective group of collaborators is akin to asking which battle won the United States' revolutionary war. The answer, from a common good criterion perspective, is "all of them." Every battle fought drew resources and efforts away from others that, if the initial battle had not been fought, might have turned out differently. This is not to say some of the battles themselves were not failures or could not have been implemented more effectively—certainly that is true and (as Kania et al. 2014 suggest) we should not cease to rigorously evaluate the many programs and activities of a collective impact initiative to figure out which seem to be gaining us the most traction so that we can devote more resources to them. This approach simply suggests that the success of the initiative must be the success of all —all flags flying at the same height. It is in the essence of the word collective and the ethos of social movements not to single out some above others. To do so would be to undermine the collective part of collective impact and to diminish the social capital or what David Laird has called the "civic muscle" that enables the movement to continue. This is critical since, as some have argued, the true success of such movements is not the numbers at all but rather the ability to continue collaborating moving into the future. In the words of Aldrich et al. "Interventions come and go; sustaining the capacity to collaborate means the community will always have a durable resource with which to address common concerns" (Aldrich et al. 2009, p. 147).

Thinking still more broadly, the collective good criterion and its emphasis on the value of collective buckshot over emphasizing silver bullets makes the models to which it is applied more likely to be generalizable to other communities. As we know from numerous failed attempts to bring collaborative efforts to scale in other communities, we cannot overlook the diversity that will lead to success in one location and failure in another. The collective good criterion leaves the definitions of success open broadly enough to account for different types of success as the same coalition or collective impact model is applied in multiple diverse communities. In the following pages we explore this robustness that the collective good criterion offers by applying it within a case study of Syracuse New York.

3.3 Community Context

It is hard to think of a more rustbelt city than Syracuse, New York. Like most "legacy cities" in the northeastern United States, it was one of the powerhouse manufacturing hubs that helped the United States climb to prominence by utilizing such superhighways of their day as the Erie Canal and the railway system. However, as global economic shifts have de-centered the former economic centers of the world, key industries have shifted from rust belt to sun belt and then to developing nations. Cities such as Syracuse have persisted and developed rugged community pride and visions of future greatness that comingle with nostalgia for the past. As one of the top three communities for refugee resettlement in the United States (Baker 2016), the central New York region has stemmed the tide of outward migration and sought to build a new future based on embracing diversity and leveraging the many natural resources and key economic engines (such as institutions of higher education and healthcare) that are abundant in the community. Indeed, to many, Central New York offers unparalleled quality of life. Suburbs boast some of the best schools in the nation and a very affordable cost of living, along with proximity to both abundant natural beauty and world class urban destinations such as New York City and Toronto. Unfortunately, as is common in cities across the nation, prosperity has not been evenly shared. Inner cities across the nation have been left behind as jobs and opportunity move to the suburbs. The result is an increase in concentrated poverty, which has affected Syracuse as much as anyone, and led to its ranking as having the highest concentration of poverty for certain racial groups among the nation's largest 100 metro areas (Semuels 2015; Jargowsky 2015). It is in this context that we explore the current triumph of community indicator progress in high school graduation rates and turn to the collective goods criterion to explore how we might share credit among all of the region's community indicators and collective impact efforts.

3.4 An Evolving History of Community Indicators in CNY

The birth of the CNY vitals community indicators project can be traced back to 1997 when a group called FOCUS Greater Syracuse (FOCUS, stands for Forging Our Community's United Strength) convened to lead a community-wide visioning process (Wood 2012). Ultimately collecting input from over 4000 community members, there was a sense that the community's concerns could be grouped into a set of indicator areas and there was a developing desire to be able to measure progress toward meeting community goals. As a result, in 2000 FOCUS gathered approximately 30 content experts and began developing a set of community indicators, looking to the National Civic League for guidance (Wood 2012).

Since that time, however, the community's efforts grew through partnerships with Syracuse University's Community Benchmarks Program and the Central New York Community Foundation from a report of less than 15 pages in 2000 through another follow up report in 2005 to the launch of a website in 2011. At the same time the project expanded from 89 goals to nearly 400 indicators and the involvement of over 80 community leaders (FOCUS 2016a, CNYvitals.org). Furthermore, the indicators project, still very much a product of local sweat equity, has grown to include such tools as "dataZoa" and Results Scorecard.[1]

Today CNY Vitals is a unique community indicators website developed by many partners dedicated to improving the quality of life for those who live and work in Central New York. Within subject areas users will find a robust set of data and indicators concerning Onondaga County and the region. This dynamic and interactive website provides a central clearinghouse for data from a multitude of sources, many of which were not previously available online. Indicator teams, made up of volunteers from many disciplines across the region, work to improve and update indicators at regular intervals.

The purpose of CNY Vitals is to provide timely, accurate data and information on the trends and issues facing Central New York's residents. The hope is that this information will generate discussion, inform plans, inspire collaboration and spur action. The vision is that community leaders will use the information available through CNY Vitals to construct informed plans and secure additional financial resources to address community needs. Furthermore, the community will be well-equipped with the information necessary to see if shared efforts are making a difference and creating positive and lasting change.

3.4.1 Using a Measurement Mentality to Set the Community's Sight on Literacy and Education

With the emergence of Kania and Kramer's seminal article on collective impact in the *Stanford Social Innovation Review* in 2011, there has been recent interest in how community indicator programs can incorporate this new framework to catalyze collective impact initiatives that help to develop approaches to facilitate change (Zimmerman 2012; Wood 2016). Though collective impact is new as a concept, it can also be seen as a re-framing of the vision that was present in the initial FOCUS

[1]dataZoa is a web based tool that automates data updates for community indicators websites (https://www.datazoa.com/about/about.asp) and Results Scorecard (now renamed Clear Impact) is web based platform for setting goals and tracking progress toward movement of indicators in desired directions (http://resultsscorecard.com/).

greater Syracuse convening that led to the group developing a set of indicators guided by the following criteria:

1. The indicator measures something that can be changed by community effort.
2. The information comes from a reliable source.
3. The indicator is clear and understandable.
4. Most people would agree on whether the indicator should move up or down (Wood 2012: 81–82).

Hence, with this introduction of community indicators in Syracuse, New York there was a clear intention to produce measurable change that is the hallmark of a collective impact movement. From the beginning, the education of youth was a major focus of community concern. Nowhere is this more apparent than in the fact the first 11 of the 87 "GOALS-From the People As presented at the FOCUS Greater Syracuse Vision Fair" pertained to an improved educational pipeline:

1. Open schools weekends, nights, and holidays
2. Provide equal, quality, education for all children
3. Increase the number of school days
4. Teach students to be good citizens
5. Keep training teachers and make them accountable
6. Combine city and county schools
7. Increase technology in all classrooms
8. Establish community scholarships
9. Improve services for all children, ages 0-6
10. Provide affordable, quality childcare
11. Organize more programs for teens (FOCUS 2016b).

The interests in improving educational outcomes were not limited to children alone. Syracuse is sometimes referred to as the birthplace of the modern adult literacy movement. This is largely due to the fact that two of the world's largest literacy education groups, Literacy Volunteers of America and Laubach Literacy, were founded in Syracuse. These organizations, respectively, have rich histories of training community volunteers to tutor their neighbors and producing a wealth of reading materials appropriate to developing adult readers. Despite this tradition, however, the focus on literacy did not receive concrete attention until numbers could be put to the nature and extent of the problem. Perhaps most notable was a billboard that was posted announcing that 61,000 adults in the community could not read it (see Ridzi 2012). This helped to launch some philanthropic investment in 2003 that included myriad catalytic philanthropy style interventions. There were banners, media blitzes, professional development opportunities, and a series of community events (Ridzi et al. 2011).

Picking up the torch, in 2005, Syracuse 20/20, another civic group created a "Toward A Competitive City Agenda Score Card For The City Of Syracuse" listing high school graduations as a key area of assessment and tracking whether it was going up. Among its other recommendations, the commission recommended a focus on dropout prevention (Syracuse 20/20 2016).

3.4.2 *Assessing Impact by TheAccrual of Collective Goods in Response to Noted Community Need*

Practitioners of collective impact have noted that "identifying shared measurements is one of the most challenging aspects of the approach" (Wood 2016: 1). Though the above narrative shares that a multitude of community groups coalesced around the goals of improved educational outcomes, it would be difficult, to say the least, to identify any one of these groups as being primarily responsible for the triumphant feeling when, on January 12th 2016, the Syracuse City School District proudly proclaimed that graduation rates again this year, "continued to climb."[2] The school district and the community were celebrating a drop-out rate that decreased from 26% in 2008 to 16% in 2015. Furthermore, they looked forward to an anticipated eight year high in graduations in 2016.[3]

Some groups had articulated, years before, a need to address the indicator of dropouts, others had articulated a series of goals that would lead to increased graduation rates (some of which, like instituting a community scholarship, had been implemented, and others had set to work developing a pipeline to graduation that began with better services to children at birth. Was it the early childhood efforts of the "read ahead" initiative that began focusing on preparing children for kindergarten in 2003? Those children graduating in 2015 would have been kindergarten age in 2003. Or was it the calls from civic groups for the city to take action that resulted in new approaches within the school system? Or was it the launch of a literacy coalition, the community's joining of the campaign for grade level reading and the creation of myriad new afterschool, summer and other programs? The collective good criterion would seem to suggest that this is the wrong line of questioning.

Rather, the collective good criterion would encourage us to look beyond simply the attainment of goals such as the increased graduation rate and to celebrate any and all significant advancements in a positive direction that the CNY community indicators advocates had sought to advance. Furthermore, rather than seek to credit any one component of the community's educational improvement movement, we might do as Haworth and Graham (2007, 128 in Sirgy et al. 2013) have asserted by

---

[2]Graduation Rates in the Syracuse City School District Continue to Climb Published on January 12, 2016 http://www.syracusecityschools.com/districtpage.cfm?pageid=3243.

[3]Syracuse graduation rate reaches 55% for 1st time in 8 years. Published January 14, 2016. Syracuse Post Standard. http://www.syracuse.com/schools/index.ssf/2016/01/syracuse_graduation_rate_reaches_55_percent_highest_in_8_years.html.

seeing, "Well-being is something that we do together, not something that we each possess."

So, how was it that the CNY community has come to this new level of well-being? The collective good criterion might encourage us to look at such things as community investment, governmental policy change and recognition that have accrued as the result of community efforts writ large. In the case of CNY we find an abundance of success here. When it comes to community investment local foundations and national philanthropy teamed up to create a pipeline for children from birth through careers. It begins with the Literacy Coalition of Onondaga County's dissemination of books to all children from birth to age five through the Dolly Parton's Imagination Library Program. This began in a quadrant of the city identified using community indicators of need and then received further support to expand to half of the city, then the entire city, and now the county. At each step in the trajectory an inter-organizational team of collaborators worked to measure the efficacy of the program. During these years children are also invited, along with their parents and caregivers in many cases, to participate in family literacy events and trainings. From there children enter kindergarten and receive remedial help with reading from programs such as the Book Buddies and other community groups. Once in school children are also eligible for summer enrichment programs that are part of the city's Say Yes to Education program. As the nation's first city-wide implementation of this program, Say Yes also offers additional after school supports and the promise of free college tuition to all city graduates that are admitted to any of a growing number of private and public colleges. There to assist students at this next transition is a corps of college and career access organizations that seek to help those students persist through graduation. For those that do not head off to college or who need additional assistance, the community has instituted literacy zones and has worked to better coordinate adult education offerings.

The above description constitutes not a full accounting of community activities all building toward collective impact, but rather some illustrative examples of how the community can count as successes the investments of local donors, volunteers and local and national foundations in the creation of systems change (a more extensive list of community activities building toward collective impact in the Central New York Area is included as an appendix). Though community indicators projects vary considerably, as Holden and Philips have pointed out, "what they share is a commitment to developing a systems-oriented understanding of the path from current trends to the change in our communities that we want to see, a participatory approach to defining and mobilizing change in that direction, and a significant role for high quality information in guiding this change" (Holden and Phillips 2010: 262).

Notably, the above types of changes have not been limited to philanthropy but have included governmental co-leadership and co-investment. This amounts to local governmental policy changes that have done such things as funded the expansion of the book distribution program from just the city to include the entire county and infusion of literacy programming throughout county caseworker home visits and the work of program partners that the county funds. Involved from the beginning, the county took part in active recruitment of at risk youth to programming, strategic planning and the ongoing evaluation work. Being part of this ongoing measurement work has led the county to feel confident expanding its support for the programming. Furthermore, collaboration with the county and state government has led to the recent securing (from state government) of the remaining $20 million needed to endow permanent college scholarships for the children of Syracuse schools (CNYcentral 2016), thus achieving a goal the community set for itself in 1997.

In addition to community investment and governmental policy change, a third form of impact that has occurred following from Syracuse's indicator to collective impact efforts is the increasing recognition of education as a critical local issue. This comes in several ways. First, as Gamson (1990) has pointed out, social movements can achieve a degree of success by either moving their agenda forward in their challenges of the status quo or by becoming recognized as the legitimated mouthpiece for the constituents and issue they represent. This has certainly occurred on multiple levels. Syracuse has been recognized on multiple occasions as a pacesetter community by the Annie E. Casey Foundation-led Campaign for Grade Level Reading. This has brought attention and credibility to local leaders in this area. In addition, local efforts are now routinely mentioned in state of the city and state of the county addresses. It is not uncommon for Community Indicator projects to serve as a facilitator of what Forester (1987 in Wood 2016: 2) calls "attention shaping" by working to bring attention to local issues and foster political will toward action. Similarly, among collective impact efforts one strategy for the use of community-level data is to use it to catalyze discussion about the current state of affairs and what can be done to address its deficiencies (Zimmerman 2012). Given that another way noted to make impact is through transforming culture such as belief systems, ideologies and collective identities (Amenta and Young 1999), this can also perhaps be counted as one of the ways the Central New York movement for educational improvement has been impactful.

3.4.3 National Patterns

While the above reflections on the common good criterion can be seen to extoll the values of a more qualitative and inductive approach to assessing the success of community indicators/collective impact efforts, it should not be mis-construed to suggest that social movements theory is counter to quantitative or numerical analysis. Rather, such approaches are not as common as they could be mostly because of their methodological difficulties. Indeed, as Amenta and Young (1999) assert, "To ascertain or demonstrate the impact of a challenge, researchers must ascertain what might have happened in its absence" (p. 23). This is difficult, they admit because the "basic methodological task, generic to all forms of causal analysis, is a difficult one for this subject matter, because the conditions that influence the rise of challengers may also independently influence both the goals sought by the challengers and occurrences that might benefit those whom the challengers seek to represent" (p. 23).

It is useful to reflect upon the noted methodological challenges of measuring the impact of social movements since they are often similar to those faced when trying to measure CIP/Collective Impact efforts. First of all, collective actions are rarely alone in pressing for changes (Amenta and Young 1999: 36). This can be seen clearly in the above case study, in which multiple efforts emerged with similar goals over time. The result is that it is very difficult to determine if any particular effort brought about a positive change. Given such challenges, social movement analysts have had little choice but to confer an assessment of "impactful" within very generous parameters. Though far from proving causation, some such as Gamson (1990) have considered a movement a success as long as its agenda was mainly accomplished within 15 years of the movement's demise, without needing to demonstrate that the movement was actually what brought that outcome about. Others have just assumed that co-occurring events could be attributed to contemporaneous movements (Burstein 1993 in Amenta and Young 1999). Under this standard, we could without a doubt declare Central New York's indicator-influenced movement a success.

However, much of the challenge to more rigorous claims of impact of social movements is akin to the same challenge among CIP/CI's. For the most part, the literature is dominated with single case studies. In such cases it is very difficult to control for anything. The best solution to date has been to use historical comparisons and to increase the sample of study to include as many communities as possible (Amenta and Young 1999). There also needs to be some variability in the communities included in a study; this is a perennial challenge since evaluators often have data only on communities that are implementing an initiative and so do not have comparison data from communities that are not implementing such efforts. Ideally, statistics can be used with data on performance and impact collected over time. To further illustrate how this might be done, we have used the County Health Rankings, a collaboration between the Robert Wood Johnson Foundation and the University of Wisconsin Population Health Institute (UWPHI). These data were created and made available publically "to build a culture of health by raising awareness of the multiple factors that influence health and stimulating and supporting local action to improve health by addressing these factors" (Catlin 2014: 61). Most specifically, we have looked at high school graduation rates for all counties across the nation, which is available in this dataset. We then compared the graduation rates for communities with literacy coalitions (a form of collective impact structure). What we can see in the chart is that such communities seem to start out in 2010 with graduation rates much lower than the national average. Between 2010 and 2014 the national average for graduations increased, but the communities with coalitions seem to have made more gain overall. As we see, both groups see fairly consistent improvement, up to a point, after which both sets lose their efficacy. Nevertheless, in this time period the gap between the groups diminishes from 5.1 to 2.2% (a nearly 57% decline in the gap).

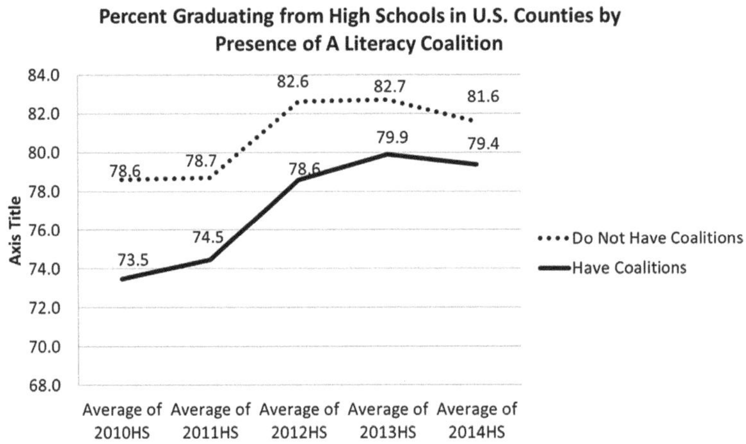

While we do not take this as proof that collective impact efforts indeed have an impact, this is nevertheless meant to display that an approach to assessing social movements and measurable aspects of collective good, can also be applied to community indicators projects and the collective impact approaches they gestate.

3.5 Conclusion

As we have seen in the literature on CIPs, communities "do not just want to help identify local problems; they want to improve decisions and accountability and improve their ability to organize resources to respond to local problems" (Wood 2016: 1). In the pages above we have explored how the collective good criterion can help communities better conceptualize the types of successes they may encounter and to plan accordingly. Because it stresses a broad definition of success, beyond just the indicators identified at the outset as problematic, it encourages communities to avoid drawing lines in the sand. While the collective impact approach that has been gaining momentum across the nation suggests that no positive change can occur without shared measurement, selecting a measure can also be a double edged sword. Groups that gather to start a movement often have ideas about what types of things they assume are measured, and what they feel ought to be measured, but are ignorant of whether these data points are in fact measured. Furthermore, it may avoid problematic retreats in the future if organizations avoid publically announcing specific goals and rather announce areas of focus from which measures of progress will evolve. This approach can be facilitated by taking an inductive approach to identifying indicators of success, and being open to a variety of forms of impact including community investment, governmental policy change and transformation of culture that comes with new recognition of the issues that CIP/CIs embrace. Finally, communities can avoid singling out individuals within the collective impact approach since this is counter to the collective action ethos. While communities that consider the collective good criterion may ultimately decide not to use it, familiarity with this standard that has developed within the social movements literature can contribute to building the repertoire of community indicator proponents.

Appendix: Community Activities Building Toward Collective Impact in the Central New York Area

Arts, culture, and recreation	
IDEAS Arts Collaborative	http://weare.cnyarts.org/programs/ideas-collaborative/
CNY ARTS	http://weare.cnyarts.org/
Engage CNY	http://weare.cnyarts.org/programs/engagecny/
Civic engagement	
Consensus CNY: The Commission on Government Modernization	https://www.facebook.com/ConsensusCNY/
Demographics	
Syracuse refugee alliance	http://www.myhopeprint.org/refugee-alliance/
Alliance of Communities Transforming Syracuse (ACTS)	http://www.acts-syracuse.org/
Economy	
CNY employment consortium (supported employment)	https://www.destinyusa.com/press-releases/cny-employment-consortium-sponsors-abilities-fair-at-destiny-usa/
Upstate revitalization initiative	http://www.syracuse.com/business-news/index.ssf/2015/12/central_new_york_a_winner_in_cuomos_15_billion_upstate_revival_initiative.html
Greater syracuse HOPE—Healing, Opportunity, Prosperity and Empowerment (anti-poverty initiative)	http://www.syracuse.com/crime/index.ssf/2016/01/new_anti-proverty_group_forms_in_syracuse.html
Greater Syracuse Works (GSW)	http://www.greatersyracuseworks.org/
Education	
Literacy Coalition of Onondaga County	http://onliteracy.org/
early childhood alliance	http://www.nyfunders.org/Tools/BroadCaster/Upload/Project111/Docs/ECA_Coordinator.pdf
literacy zones	http://198.36.22.200/about/curriculum/AdultEducation/literacyZones
Success by six	http://unitedway-cny.org/success-by-6/
Environment, transportation, and planning	
Green & healthy homes	

(continued)

(continued)

	http://www.greenandhealthyhomes.org/get-help/find-ghhi-site
Interstate 81 challenge	http://thei81challenge.org/
Housing	
Housing and Homeless Coalition of Syracuse and Onondaga County	https://www.facebook.com/hhccny
Human services and health	
Syracuse area domestic & sexual violence coalition	http://www.verahouse.org/coalition
Human services leadership coalition	http://hslccny.org/
Public safety	
Cuse cares	http://www.localsyr.com/news/cuse-cares-shares-progress-and-struggles-with-violence-prevention
Trauma response team	http://www.ncbi.nlm.nih.gov/pubmed/26282564
In this together	http://falk.syr.edu/MarriageFamilyTherapy/documents/2015/TraumaFlyer.pdf
syracuse truce	http://www.syracusetruce.com/syracusetruce/
Fight crime invest in kids	http://www.fightcrime.org/syracuse-area-police-chiefs-visit-preschool-back-early-education-cut-crime-d1566/

References

Aldrich, L., Silva, D., Marable, D., Sandman, E., & Abraham, M. (2009). Using community-based participatory evaluation methods as a tool to sustain a community health coalition. *Foundation Review, 1*(1), 146–157.

Amenta, E., & Young, M. P. (1999). Making an impact: Conceptual and methodological implications of the collective goods criterion. In M. Giugni, D. McAdam, & C. Tilly (Eds.), *How social movements matter*. Minneapolis: University of Minnesota Press.

Baker, C. (2016). Refugees in Syracuse: Benefit or burden? Here's what the numbers say. *The Post Standard*. Updated March 14, 2016 at 10:42 AM http://www.syracuse.com/poverty/2016/03/refugees_in_syracuse_benefit_burden.html

Butterfoss, Frances Dunn. (2007). Coalitions and Partnerships in Community Health. San Francisco: Jossey−Bass.

Carlson, N. E., Hernández, E., Edmond-Verley, C., Rotondaro, G., Feliz-Santana, E., & Heynig, S. (2011). Developing a master data sharing agreement: Seeking student-level evidence to support a collaborative community effort in education. *The Foundation Review, 3*(4), Article 3. doi: http://dx.doi.org/10.4087/FOUNDATIONREVIEW-D-11-00024

Catlin, B. (2014). The county health rankings: "A Treasure Trove of Data" transforming data into policy-relevant information. In Federal Reserve Bank of San Francisco and Urban Institute (Ed.), *What counts: Harnessing data for america's communities* (pp. 59–73). Available online http://www.communityindicators.net/system/publication_pdfs/90/original/What-Counts-11.25.14.pdf?1417830842

CNYcentral. (2016). Mahoney announces $20 million for Syracuse Say Yes, preserving free tuition program. Tuesday, March 1, 2016. http://cnycentral.com/news/local/say-yes-tuition-program-needs-20-million-in-15-months. Accessed online Marh 23, 2016.

FOCUS. (2016a). *About F.O.C.U.S.* http://www.focussyracuse.org/about-f-o-c-u-s/about-f-o-c-u-s/. Accessed online March 17, 2016.

FOCUS. (2016b). *The 87 GOALS-from the people as presented at the FOCUS Greater Syracuse Vision Fair.* http://www.focussyracuse.org/about-f-o-c-u-s/our-87-goals/. Accessed online March 18, 2016.

Gamson, W. (1975 and reprinted 1990). *Strategy of social protest.* Belmont: Wadsworth Publishing Company.

Hatry, H., & Morley, E. (2008). Guide to performance management for community literacy coalitions. *Urban Institute and National Institute for Literacy.* https://lincs.ed.gov/publications/pdf/NIFLCommunityLiteracyReport.pdf. Accessed online March 23, 2016.

Henig, J. R., Riehl, C. J., Houston, D. M., Rebell, M. A., & Wolff, J. R. (2016). *Collective impact and the new generation of cross-sector collaborations for education: A nationwide scan.* New York, NY: Teachers College, Columbia University, Department of Education Policy and Social Analysis. http://www.wallacefoundation.org/knowledge-center/Documents/Collective-Impact-and-the-New-Generation-of-Cross-Sector-Collaboration-for-Education.pdf

Holden, M., & Phillips, R. (2010). Best research from the Community Indicators Consortium 2009: Introduction to the special issue. *Applied Research in Quality of Life, 5*(4), 261–272.

Jargowsky, P. (2015). *Architecture of segregation: Civil unrest, the concentration of poverty, and public policy.* The century foundation issue brief August 7, 2015. https://tcf.org/content/report/architecture-of-segregation/

Kania, J., & Kramer, M. (2011, Winter). Collective impact. *Stanford Social Innovation Review,* 36–41.

Kania, J., Hanleybrown, F., & Splansky Juster, J. (2014). Essential mindset shifts for collective impact. *Collective Impact Forum Blog.* Posted Tuesday, September 2, 2014 At 3:14 PM. https://collectiveimpactforum.org/blogs/1806/essential-mindset-shifts-collective-impact. Accessed online March 23, 2016.

Kramer, M. R. (2009, Fall). Catalytic philanthropy. *Stanford Social Innovation Review,* 29–35.

Levitt, S., & Dubner, S. J. (2005). *Freakonomics: A rogue economist explores the hidden side of everything.* New York: William Morrow/HarperCollins. ISBN 0-06-073132-X.

Reese, E. (2011). They say cutback, we say fight back!: Welfare activism in an era of retrenchment. *Russell Sage Foundation,* p. 17.

Results Scorecard. (2016). "Case Studies." http://resultsscorecard.com/case-studies/. Accessed online March 23, 2016.

Ridzi, F. (2012). Managing expectations when measuring philanthropic impact: A framework based on experience. *The Foundation Review, 4*(4), Article 8. doi:http://dx.doi.org/10.4087/FOUNDATIONREVIEW-D-12-00007.1

Ridzi, F., Carmody, V., & Byrnes, K. (2011, Spring). From rRead ahead to literacy coalition: The leadership role of the Central New York Community Foundation in the creation of a local institution. *Community Literacy Journal, 5*(2), 101–134.

Semuels, A. (2015). The resurrection of America's slums. *The Atlantic.* http://www.theatlantic.com/business/archive/2015/08/more-americans-are-living-in-slums/400832/. Accessed August 9, 2015.

Sirgy, J., Phillips, R., & Rahtz, D. (Eds.). (2013). *Community quality-of-life indicators: Best cases VI.* New York: Springer.

Smith, D. E. (1999). *Writing the social: Critique, theory and investigations.* Toronto: University of Toronto Press.

Syracuse 20/20. (2016). *Toward A Competitive City Agenda, Mayoral Election 2005.* http://www.syracuse2020.org/About2020/tabid/71/Default.aspx. Accessed online March 18, 2016.

Wood, D. M. (2012). *Facilitating change with community indicator programs.* Unpublished dissertation, http://depot.library.wisc.edu/repository/fedora/1711.dl:RYEBK2GT2JBWT9A/datastreams/REF/content. Accessed online March 17, 2016.

Wood, D. M. (2016). Community indicators and collective impact: Facilitating change. *Community Development*. Published Online 01 Feb 2016. doi:10.1080/15575330.2015.1133685

Zimmerman, G. (2012). *Using Community-Level Data To Drive Efforts For Collective Impact*. http://www.marketsforgood.org/using-community-level-data-to-drive-efforts-for-collective-impact/. Online Accessed March 17, 2016.

Author Biography

Frank Ridzi is Vice President for Community Investment at the Central New York Community Foundation, Associate Professor of Sociology at Le Moyne College and President of the Literacy Funders Network, an affinity group of the Council on Foundations. Frank has conducted research and written in the areas of literacy coalitions, sociology of work, and student affairs. His writings have appeared in such places as the Foundation Review, the Community Literacy Journal, the Journal of Organizational Change Management, and Review of Policy Research. Frank oversees and monitors the grantmaking process, conducts research on issues or concerns of importance to the foundation, shares expertise with donors and manages special projects for the foundation. He has worked for the Community Foundation since 2008, where he previously served as Program Officer for Community Initiatives and Director of Research and Community Initiatives. Frank holds a Masters Degree in Public Administration and a Ph.D. in Sociology from Syracuse University's Maxwell School. He also carries a Certificate of Advanced Study in Women's Studies. Prior to joining the Community Foundation, he served as Director for the Center of Urban and Regional Applied Research at Le Moyne College, where he still serves as Associate Professor of Sociology.

Chapter 4
Collaboration to Promote Use of Community Indicators: Communication Is Key

Craig Helmstetter, Paul Mattessich, Ruth Hamberg and Nancy Hartzler

Abstract To play a meaningful role in quality-of-life efforts, organizations managing indicators initiatives must collaborate with others. After summarizing evidence-based factors that influence the success of collaboration, the chapter highlights factors of greatest potential interest to community indicators initiatives: Mutual understanding and trust, members see the collaboration as in their self-interest, multiple layers of participation, appropriate cross-section of members, and open and frequent communication. These factors are then explored through a case study of the community indicators project that we operate, Minnesota Compass. Finally, we end by outlining a tactical approach to communications and outreach that reinforces collaboration—and helps to ensure the use of indicators toward the broader goal of increasing overall quality of life.

Keywords Minnesota Compass · Collaboration · Quality of life · Communication

4.1 Introduction

In this chapter, we focus on the strengthening of collaboration as a means to enhance the use of community indicators. Because of the complexity of our modern communities, the improvement of the quality of life in a city or region requires the employment of a variety of tools, including collaboration when appropriate, in order to integrate the efforts of multiple organizations, adapt to constant change, customize problem-solving approaches, and thereby succeed.[1] To play a meaningful role in quality-of-life efforts, organizations managing indicators initiatives must collaborate with others.

[1]See, for example, Auspos and Cabaj (2014), Kania and Kramer (2011).

C. Helmstetter (✉) · P. Mattessich · R. Hamberg · N. Hartzler
Wilder Foundation, St Paul, MN, USA
e-mail: craig.helmstetter@wilder.org

M. Holden et al. (eds.), *Community Quality-of-Life Indicators: Best Cases VII*, Community Quality-of-Life and Well-Being,
DOI 10.1007/978-3-319-54618-6_4

The first part of this chapter summarizes evidence-based factors that influence the success of collaboration. We highlight the factors of greatest potential interest to community indicators initiatives. The second part of the chapter provides an overview of a specific case study, Minnesota Compass, describing how it has woven the ingredients for collaborative success into its strategy and operations. The chapter describes, for example, how the extensive use of advisory committees and a governance consortium creates community ownership for the project, ensures the relevance of the indicators for current policy and programmatic priorities, and solidifies a financial base. In the third part, we focus on how to nurture collaboration with a thorough communications and outreach plan, including the use of technology and social media for regular engagement with stakeholders.

4.2 Key Ingredients for Successful Collaboration

Collaboration refers to a mutually beneficial and well-defined relationship entered into by two or more organizations to achieve common goals. A meta-analysis of research literature on collaboration (Mattessich et al. 2001) has identified 20 factors which increase the likelihood of success in collaborative relationships.[2] These factors appear in Table 4.1.

All of these factors have importance for community indicators initiatives. Such initiatives typically require collaboration among organizations of varied types: research organizations, government entities, nonprofit organizations, grantmaking foundations, news media, higher education institutions, database providers, and others. We have limited space in this article, but based on our experience in a highly collaborative social indicators initiative, and our observation of other indicators initiatives, five of these factors merit special attention.

Mutual understanding and trust

> Members of the collaborative group share an understanding and respect for each other and their respective organizations: how they operate, their cultural norms and values, their limitations, and their expectations (Mattessich et al. 2001: 14).

Trust constitutes a significant element of any relationship. Sometimes, the organizations involved in an indicators initiative already know and trust one another; other times, they must build their relationships from scratch. In a situation where

---

[2]See Mattessich et al. (2001) for a description of the meta-analytic procedures used to identify the factors. Note also that Wilder Research is currently updating the meta-analysis of research on collaboration, with the intent to publish updated findings during 2016. The new edition includes expanded content describing how to apply the research-based factors in increasingly diverse 21st Century communities.

Table 4.1 Factors influencing the success of collaboration

1. Factors related to the ENVIRONMENT
A. History of collaboration or cooperation in the community
A history of collaboration or cooperation exists in the community and offers the potential collaborative partners an understanding of the roles and expectations required in collaboration and enables them to trust the process
B. Collaborative group seen as a legitimate leader in the community
The collaborative group (and, by implication, the agencies in the group) is perceived within the community as reliable and competent—at least related to the goals and activities it intends to accomplish
C. Favorable political and social climate
Political leaders, opinion-makers, persons who control resources, and the general public support (or at least do not oppose) the mission of the collaborative group
2. Factors Related to MEMBERSHIP CHARACTERISTICS
A. Mutual respect, understanding, and trust
Members of the collaborative group share an understanding and respect for each other and their respective organizations: how they operate, their cultural norms and values, their limitations, and their expectations
B. Appropriate cross section of members
The collaborative group includes representatives from each segment of the community who will be affected by its activities. It engages members at the appropriate time and at an appropriate level of involvement
C. Members see collaboration as in their self-interest
Collaborating partners believe that they will benefit from their involvement in the collaboration and that the advantages of membership will offset costs such as slower decision making processes
D. Ability to compromise
Collaborating partners are able to compromise, since the many decisions within a collaborative effort cannot possibly fit the preferences of every member perfectly
3. Factors Related to PROCESS AND STRUCTURE
A. Members share a stake in both process and outcome
Members of a collaborative group feel "ownership" of both the way the group works and the results or products of its work
B. Multiple layers of participation
Every level (upper management, middle management, front line) within each partner organization has involvement in the collaborative initiative. Each layer brings different assets to the collaboration and may need to be involved to different degrees and at different stages of development
C. Flexibility
The collaborative group remains open to varied ways of shifting its internal structure, organizing itself, and performing activities to accomplish its work
D. Development of clear roles and guidelines
The collaborating partners jointly develop a set of shared operating principles. They clearly understand their roles and responsibilities and are committed to carrying them out
E. Adaptability to changing conditions
The collaborative group has the ability to make changes, even to major goals, members, etc., in order to deal with changing conditions in the external environment
F. Appropriate pace of development
The structure, resources, and activities of the collaborative group change over time to meet the needs of the collaborative group without overwhelming its capacity, at each point throughout the initiative

(continued)

Table 4.1 (continued)

4. Factors Related to COMMUNICATION
A. Open and frequent communication
Collaborative group members interact often, update one another, discuss issues openly, create transparency, and convey all necessary information to one another and to people outside of the group
B. Established informal relationships and communication links
In addition to formal channels of communication, members establish personal connections —producing a better, more informed, and cohesive group
5. Factors Related to PURPOSE
A. Concrete, attainable goals and objectives
Goals and objectives of the collaborative group are clear to all partners, and can realistically be attained
B. Shared vision
Collaborating partners have the same vision, with clearly agreed-upon mission, operating principles, objectives, and strategy. The shared vision may exist at the outset of collaboration, or the partners may develop a vision as they work together
C. Unique purpose
The mission and goals, or approach, of the collaborative group differ, at least in part, from the mission and goals, or approach, of the member organizations
6. Factors Related to RESOURCES
A. Sufficient funds, staff, materials, and time
The collaborative group has an adequate, consistent financial base, along with the staff and materials needed to support its operations. It allows sufficient time to achieve its goals and includes time to nurture the collaboration
B. Skilled leadership
The individual who provides leadership for the collaborative group has organizing, facilitation, and interpersonal skills, such as emotional intelligence and cultural competence, and carries out the role with fairness. Thus, the leader is granted respect or "legitimacy" by the collaborative partners
(Mattessich et al. 2001)

acquaintance and trust do not yet exist, participants in a new initiative must devote energy to learning about each other. They should understand one another's specific goals and motivations, in addition to their capacity to play their respective roles in the effort. Building strong relationships takes time; moving quickly into decision-making and task accomplishment, before establishing mutual understanding and trust, can lessen the likelihood of success.

Open and frequent communication

> Collaborative group members interact often, update one another, discuss issues openly, and convey all necessary information to one another and to people outside of the group (Mattessich et al. 2001: 23).

All human interaction requires effective communication. To succeed, collaborative initiatives must establish mechanisms for interaction among the partners.

Some interaction will involve specific tasks, e.g., the delivery of data from one partner to another, or the joint development of a report or website. Other interaction will involve broader tasks, such as developing a strategic plan or identifying the potential consumers of the collaborative's products and services and forming an approach to meeting the consumers' needs.

Multiple layers of participation

> Every level (upper management, middle management, front line) within each partner organization has involvement in the collaborative initiative. Each layer brings different assets to the collaboration and may need to be involved to different degrees and at different stages of development (Mattessich et al. 2001: 19).

Most organizations have some form of hierarchy. Research shows that each significant part of this hierarchy needs representation in a collaborative initiative in order to increase the likelihood of success. Problems develop, for example, if staff at one level go too far in planning with other organizations and making commitments on partnership arrangements without somehow including higher-level management in the discussions. This does not imply that someone at every level of the organizational hierarchy must devote significant time to a collaborative initiative. A board of directors or a CEO might just receive briefings every three or four months, while other staff engage in collaborative work every day. Nonetheless, some amount of involvement from every organizational level should occur.

Members see the collaboration as in their self-interest

> Collaborating partners believe that they will benefit from their involvement in the collaboration and that the advantages of membership will offset costs such as slower decision making processes (Mattessich et al. 2001: 17).

Collaboration requires effort. It requires time and other resources. It sometimes requires risk. Initially, the costs might seem to outweigh the benefits. Sometimes, certain partners might need to overcome competitive orientations they held toward each other prior to forming a new partnership to develop indicators. For these reasons and more, the collaborative must provide avenues for each participating organization to further its own individual mission while simultaneously achieving the collaborative mission.

Appropriate cross-section of members

> The collaborative group includes representatives from each segment of the community who will be affected by its activities. It engages members at the appropriate time and at an appropriate level of involvement (Mattessich et al. 2001: 16).

A collaborative initiative needs to determine the necessary partners for success. Who controls data, for example? Whose networks can most effectively acquire the resources necessary for the collection, compiling, analysis, and reporting of indicators? Who has a strong influence on public opinion? Asking questions such as these enables an initiative to identify and recruit partners who will bring necessary expertise, resources, and connections for the intended work.

4.3 Case Study: Minnesota Compass

Minnesota Compass is an on-going, comprehensive, community indicators project run by a nonprofit social research organization, Wilder Research, on behalf of a collaborative of Minnesota-based foundations. The goal of the project is to actively promote the understanding of important social and economic trends facing communities throughout Minnesota, to help inform productive action. Or, as stated more concisely in the project's tagline: "Measuring progress. Inspiring action."

The project's main vehicle for accomplishing this goal is a website that tracks 39 "key measures" (normative indicators) and four "context measures" (descriptive demographic indicators) across 15 major topics (health, housing, economy, education, etc.; see Fig. 4.1). Additionally, the website provides geographic-based data

Fig. 4.1 Minnesota Compass website. *Source* www.MNCompass.org, homepage as of October 6, 2016

profiles for the state as a whole, seven regions within the state, Minnesota's 87 counties, all cities with populations of at least 1000 (355 in 2017), and over 100 urban neighborhoods, as well as "at-a-glance" data profiles for various immigrant and child populations. The website also includes context and analysis in the form of topic overview pages, blog-like "Insights" articles, and libraries of links to relevant reports and data sources.

Although maintaining a website is among the "core" activities of the initiative, Minnesota Compass engages in many activities beyond maintaining a website. For example, roughly half of the broader enterprise's budget is generated through contractual projects that leverage the skills and infrastructure assembled through the grant-funded core. These projects respond to the community's desire to more deeply and thoroughly understand trends and issues related to specific substantive areas (e.g., Science, Technology, Engineering, and Math) or geographic areas (e.g., a developing light rail corridor). Additionally, Minnesota Compass staff frequently offer presentations and serve as a resource to local media outlets. Finally, as we discuss below, the project is as much a community engagement effort as it is an informational hub.

4.3.1 Collaborative Factors at Work

As noted in the first section of this chapter, all major factors of collaboration found in Mattessich et al.'s research can be relevant to indicators projects. We have found five factors to be particularly relevant, and the remainder of this section illustrates how these factors have played out in the implementation and ongoing operations of Minnesota Compass: Mutual understanding and trust; members see the collaboration as in their self-interest; multiple layers of participation; appropriate cross-section of members; members share a stake in both process and outcome; and open and frequent communication.

4.3.2 Mutual Understanding and Trust

The mutual understanding and trust that exists among those collaborating on Minnesota Compass is, perhaps, best reflected in the project's origins. The project had its origins in a much smaller project which developed in the late 1980s and focused only on four counties in Minnesota. Then, in 2004, several local community leaders traveled to Boston, where they learned about an online community indicators project called the Boston Indicators project. Over the next two years a dozen local foundations formed a collaborative to support the development and implementation of the statewide project, Minnesota Compass.

Early on in that process, local foundations designated Wilder Research as the logical research home for this endeavor, in part due to Wilder's previous experience tracking indicators, and in part due to the credibility that Wilder had established directly with the foundations, and with the broader community, through years of previous research and evaluation projects.

Equally as important was the respect and trust that the foundations had amongst themselves; none of the members attempted to use the project as a way of gaining particular prominence over other members, and no members sought to position the data in such a way as to highlight the importance of their grantmaking programs or other initiatives over and above the work of other collaborative members.

4.3.3 Members See the Collaboration as in Their Self-Interest

Minnesota Compass satisfies the self-interest of the collaborative of local foundations in several ways. First and foremost, though the specific strategy of each foundation is tailored to particular programming and a specific geographic range, each foundation was committed to a broad goal of improving quality of life. They saw the Boston Indicators Project, and other web-based community indicators projects, as providing a significant tool to those trying to improve their communities: credible information available free of charge that is both easily accessible and understandable by the general public.

Second, the foundations recognized that the sort of demographic and socioeconomic data maintained by a community indicators project would help them maintain strategic focus. Some foundations had conducted community needs assessments, and others had been assembling information on a more ad hoc basis, but all could see the benefit of having regular access to a set of data that could answer questions like: What community strengths should we be building on? What are the community's most pressing needs? Where are things improving? How does our local community compare to peers nationwide? Answers to questions like these are necessary to foundation officials, who need to make decisions about how to target their grantmaking.

Third, foundations saw the project as a tool that could help nonprofits strengthen their proposals, and ultimately their programming. Foundations recognized that some nonprofits lack capacity to identify credible data that help them make the case for their programming. Additionally, foundations asked that Compass convey not only data, but also help nonprofits identify relevant research, especially evidence-based practices that have been shown to impact social problems. Finally, foundations were interested in having Compass identify existing initiatives aimed at addressing a given issue, to help nonprofits plug into existing efforts rather than proposing to duplicate efforts.

For these reasons, Compass staff developed a template for each major topic covered by the project that not only includes indicators, but also includes "Ideas at Work," a webpage that lists collaborations and links to evidence-based practices, as well as a library of relevant reports and on-line resources. This package was designed with the collaborative in response to their perceived self-interests.

Although a few members of the original collaborative have left over the years, most have stayed and others have joined. This suggests that the self-interested value proposition remains strong.

4.3.4 Multiple Layers of Participation

Over the years we have developed two ongoing "institutional" committees overseeing the work of Minnesota Compass: Governance and Steering. These groups have separate but overlapping functions related to shaping and evolving the project. They also function to involve two layers of participation, buy-in, and championing within each of the organizations that fund Minnesota Compass.

The Compass Governance committee typically meets in person one time per year. This group provides high-level oversight for overall project direction. It is made up of the first-or second-in-command at each of the foundations that back Minnesota Compass. Originally, this group met quarterly and the group itself was of value to the members as a rare venue to network among top foundation executives. Over time, as more "collective impact" initiatives have formed, the Compass Governance committee has become one of many venues where local foundation executives can meet and interact. Some top executives have delegated the assignment to a second-in-command position. Regardless of the exact position, having executive-level involvement has been instrumental to the project's continued success.

The Compass Steering committee typically meets in person two times per year. This group provides strategic direction: for example, recommending which of our topics are due for a re-convening of advisory group members in the coming months. This group is largely made up of foundation managers in charge of the grant programs most closely aligned with Minnesota Compass, as well as a few others (the State Demographer, the head of Minnesota's Citizens League, an official from Minnesota's State College and University system, and a local media representative or two). These individuals help Minnesota Compass stay connected to the many initiatives in which they are involved, and they provide another layer of buy-in at their home organizations.

This two-tiered committee system has served Minnesota Compass well. In the short life of the project there has been some turn-over in both the executive-level positions that participate in the Governance committee and the program-level positions that are involved in the Steering committee. Whenever such turnover occurs, the additional layer of participation is very helpful in maintaining organizational commitment to Compass.

In addition to the committees, yet another layer of participation is often achieved through the periodic topic advisory groups on which Compass relies for input to refresh and revise our topic-based key measures. The primary function of those groups is to obtain involvement of an appropriate cross-section of members.

4.3.5 Appropriate Cross-Section of Members

Minnesota Compass, like most community indicators projects, seeks to inform a broader audience beyond members of the collaboration that are actively working on the project. To gain legitimacy and buy-in from this broader cross-section, Minnesota Compass established time-limited "topic advisory groups" to help shape each of the major topics represented in the project (education, health, workforce, etc.). From the outset, we intentionally selected participants in these groups who would represent a variety of standpoints on a particular issue. In each group we include people from both for-profit and nonprofit organizations, as well as academia and the public sector. We also look for diversity in political ideology, regional representation, and race and ethnicity. The diversity of these advisory groups not only produces broad-scale buy-in, it also leads to the selection of key measures that are useful to those directly involved in the advisory groups and also to others in the community who hold similar interests to the people actually participating in the advisory groups.

4.3.6 Open and Frequent Communication

Community indicators projects rely on open and frequent communications at least as heavily as other types of collaborations. While data management and analysis are more often the focus of community indicators projects, communications are equally as important. Further, not only is it important to communicate with a broader audience to help accomplish goals related to the dissemination of the information maintained by the indicators project, it is also vitally important to maintain open and frequent communication within the collaboration that works on the project. This factor is so central to Minnesota Compass that we have designated the remainder of this chapter to a discussion of some tactical examples of how we have orchestrated open and frequent communications. The concepts and tactics also lend themselves to several of the other factors of collaboration listed in Table 4.1.

4.4 Communications and Outreach: A Tactical Approach

With the right set of communications and outreach strategies, quality-of-life initiatives can strengthen relationships within the collaboration and with other stakeholders of the project.

Table 4.2 Communications and outreach elements

Element	Guiding questions	Application
Mission	What is the mission of your project? Are there interim goals that you are striving toward in pursuit of your mission?	Minnesota Compass' mission to actively promote the understanding of important social and economic trends facing communities throughout Minnesota, to help inform productive action. In short: *Measuring progress. Inspiring action*
Audience	Who else is interested in the project's mission? Who would like to help it move forward? You will use this to build a contact list and determine where to prioritize communication and engagement efforts	Compass' audience is made up of community leaders and decision-makers, broadly-defined, throughout Minnesota and its regions, cities, and neighborhoods
Collaborators	Of your audience, which individuals, partners or organizations have the capacity and resources to help accomplish the mission? These "key stakeholders" will have some influence on whether or not you reach the goal, and under what conditions. Their resources may include financial support, expertise, human capital, and social capital	Compass' key collaborators include funders and founding organizations, and groups who partner with us for contracted work
Key messages	What information would you like your audience to take from an interaction with your work?	Compass' event and project communications plans include a list of 3–5 key messages to align all of our communications

Before exploring the available strategies and tools to implement them, it will help to define the project's mission, audience, collaborators, and key messages. See Table 4.2 for a description of each of these elements and an example of how Minnesota Compass carries it out.

4.4.1 Strategies and Tools

Two key strategies the Compass project has used to build and maintain relationships through communication are to maintain a master contact list and to develop an outreach calendar. The tools we use to implement the plan include a monthly e-newsletter, in-person meetings, presentations, and social media.

4.4.1.1 Contact List

To maintain open and frequent communication, we created a master contact list that documents who we have engaged with or would like to engage with.

Contact lists can be maintained in a variety of formats (electronic documents, e-mail platforms, client relation management (CRM) databases, etc.). Spreadsheets have typically been sufficient for Minnesota Compass.

A contact list is only as useful as it is up to date. It is important to designate someone to manage the task and to formalize a flow: for example, when staff make new contacts at events, how will they record contact information? Who will take the next step of inviting new contacts to learn more about the project or opt into receiving an e-newsletter? Can we include an e-newsletter prompt in the registration process for our events? When do we remove someone from a contact list?

4.4.1.2 Outreach Calendar

The use of an outreach calendar ensures that members in different roles within the collaboration, as well as other key stakeholders, continue to receive the right level of communication at appropriate intervals. It is important to make sure content is tailored to the interests of each of your stakeholder groups.

Our outreach calendar in Table 4.3 notes standard communications each stakeholder group receives. As opportunities arise, we connect in additional ways with each of these groups. For example, we may offer a webinar highlighting a new section of the website, or inform a group in the community about new content that may be of particular interest to them.

4.4.1.3 Communication Tools

As mentioned earlier, we make the data we track publicly available on the Compass website, along with analysis and resources to promote the understanding of important social and economic trends facing communities throughout Minnesota. As indicated in our Outreach Calendar, we use a variety of ways to engage our partners and stakeholders.

The Compass monthly e-newsletter is the primary way we connect with all of our stakeholders to keep them aware of new and updated content on the website. Figure 4.2 provides an example.

We use one of the widely available email marketing services as the technical platform for our newsletter. This platform allows us to quickly reach stakeholders, to easily share newsletter content on our social media channels, and to measure the open, click-through, and opt-out rates for each issue, and compare them with averages for similar industries. For example, compared with other nonprofit users of

Table 4.3 Outreach calendar

Audience (number of people)	In-person meeting	Email update	Social media
Governance Committee (N = 15)	Annual Governance meeting Annual Meeting Presentation offered to each organization	Quarterly Monthly e-newsletter	Ongoing
Steering Committee (N = 15)	Bi-annual Steering Committee meeting Annual Meeting	Bi-monthly Monthly e-newsletter	Ongoing
Time-limited topic advisory committees (N = 20 to 50)	During time they serve on committee: Two advisory meetings Annual Compass Meeting	Monthly e-newsletter (subscriptions invited during committee process for those not already subscribed)	Ongoing
Community partners (N = 150)	Depending on topic, select individuals are invited to Annual Compass Meeting Presentations are commonly offered to organizations and collaboratives	Monthly e-newsletter	Ongoing
Media		Monthly e-newsletter Media alerts as needed	Ongoing
All stakeholders		Monthly e-newsletter	Ongoing

this service, our "open rate average" is higher (35% compared with 21%), and our click-through rate is significantly higher (31% compared with 8%). By keeping our contact list current, we maintain a low opt-out rate of just 1 percent. Our website analytics show website visits increase 15–20% on the day the newsletter goes out. The service we use also allows us to learn what newsletter content is of most interest to our stakeholders, and test how to most effectively present it.

Social media has become a valuable dissemination tool for us. We use it to share "data bites" and links to articles of interest to our audiences more quickly and frequently than the monthly newsletter. Twitter has been a particularly good way to keep news reporters aware of updated data.

We have found face-to-face interactions continue to be our most effective engagement tool for reaching targeted audiences. Our Annual Meeting has a waiting list within a few days after we send an invitation. Our presentations, advisory meetings, and trainings often result in contracts for related work.

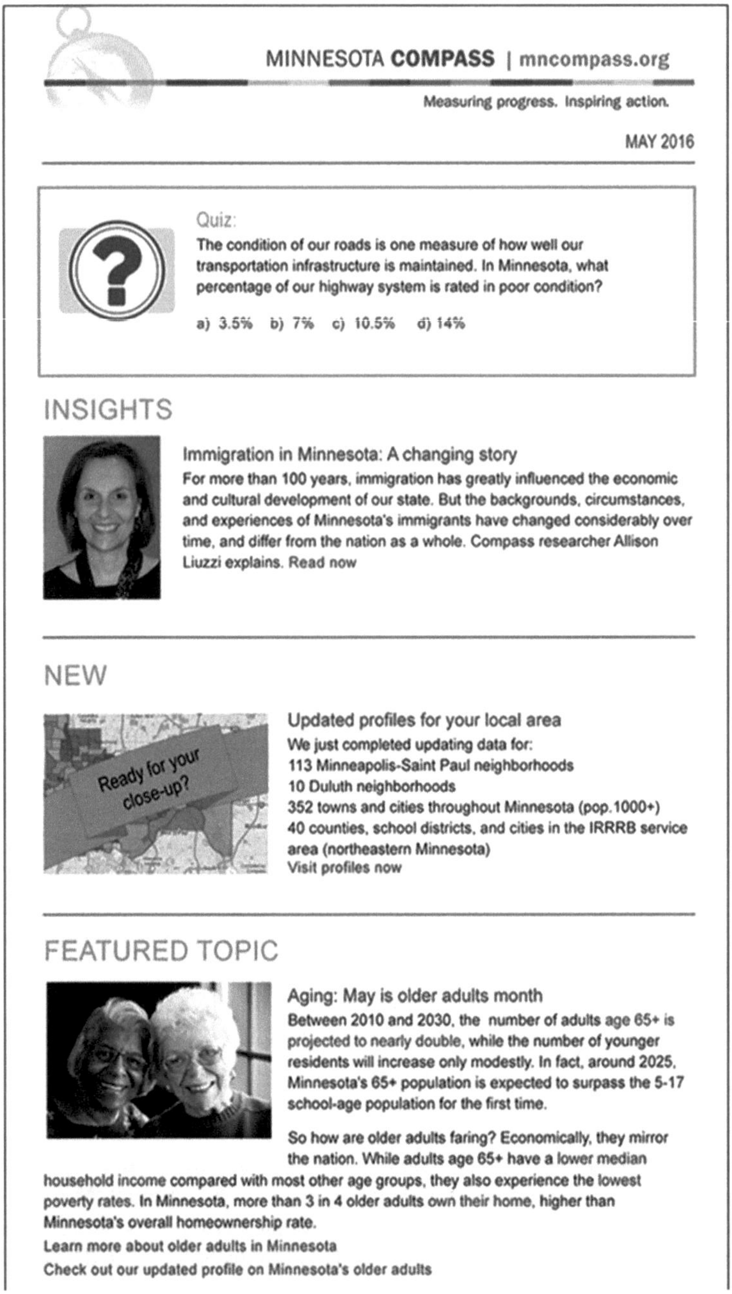

MINNESOTA **COMPASS** | mncompass.org

Measuring progress. Inspiring action.

MAY 2016

Quiz:

The condition of our roads is one measure of how well our transportation infrastructure is maintained. In Minnesota, what percentage of our highway system is rated in poor condition?

a) 3.5% b) 7% c) 10.5% d) 14%

INSIGHTS

Immigration in Minnesota: A changing story

For more than 100 years, immigration has greatly influenced the economic and cultural development of our state. But the backgrounds, circumstances, and experiences of Minnesota's immigrants have changed considerably over time, and differ from the nation as a whole. Compass researcher Allison Liuzzi explains. Read now

NEW

Ready for your close-up?

Updated profiles for your local area

We just completed updating data for:
113 Minneapolis-Saint Paul neighborhoods
10 Duluth neighborhoods
352 towns and cities throughout Minnesota (pop.1000+)
40 counties, school districts, and cities in the IRRRB service area (northeastern Minnesota)
Visit profiles now

FEATURED TOPIC

Aging: May is older adults month

Between 2010 and 2030, the number of adults age 65+ is projected to nearly double, while the number of younger residents will increase only modestly. In fact, around 2025, Minnesota's 65+ population is expected to surpass the 5-17 school-age population for the first time.

So how are older adults faring? Economically, they mirror the nation. While adults age 65+ have a lower median household income compared with most other age groups, they also experience the lowest poverty rates. In Minnesota, more than 3 in 4 older adults own their home, higher than Minnesota's overall homeownership rate.

Learn more about older adults in Minnesota

Check out our updated profile on Minnesota's older adults

Fig. 4.2 Minnesota Compass e-newsletter, May 2016

4.5 Conclusion

Collaboration has comprised an essential dimension of Minnesota Compass. Most other indicators projects will also find collaboration essential—for defining and compiling their constituent indicators, for reporting trends to relevant audiences, and for engaging in community improvement efforts.

This chapter has described evidence-based factors which influence the likelihood that collaborative efforts will succeed. It illustrated ways that indicators projects can operationalize those factors, including very specific, well-established techniques for communication. Indicators professionals of the twenty-first century must possess both scientific proficiency and leadership proficiency. Data science must blend with organizational science. We hope that this chapter has offered insight regarding ways to manage collaboration in order for indicators projects to achieve their maximum potential.

References

Auspos, P., & Cabaj, M. (2014). *Complexity and community change: Managing adaptively to improve effectiveness*. Washington, DC: Aspen Institute.

Kania, J., & Kramer, M. (2011, Winter). Collective impact. *Stanford Social Innovation Review*, 36–41.

Mattessich, P., Murray-Close, M., & Monsey, B. (2001). *Collaboration: What makes it work* (2nd ed.). Chicago: Turner Publishing.

Author Biographies

Craig Helmstetter, Ph.D., is a Senior Research Manager at Wilder Research, a division of the Amherst H. Wilder Foundation in St. Paul; and project director for Minnesota Compass. Craig joined Wilder Research in 2001 after working as a program evaluator for Minnesota's Office of the Legislative Auditor. Prior to that Craig worked as a project director for a survey research center, and in the social services with children, developmentally disabled adults, and people experiencing homelessness. Craig received a master's in Community and Regional Planning and doctorate in Sociology from the University of Oregon. He has taught university-level seminars on quantitative research methods and homelessness, has spoken at several local and national conferences, and currently serves on the board of the Community Indicators Consortium.

Paul Mattessich, Ph.D., has served as the Executive Director of Wilder Research since 1982, and founder of Minnesota Compass. Paul lectures frequently throughout the United States and the United Kingdom, especially on topics of organization and service effectiveness, collaboration/partnerships, and major social trends. He has authored or co-authored more than 300 publications. Since 2000, he has spent several weeks each year in Belfast, Northern Ireland, working with youth development and civic engagement organizations that promote democratic skills to bring communities together and to resolve conflict. He has served on a variety of government and nonprofit boards of directors and special task forces. He currently sits on the boards of the Hamm Memorial Psychiatric Clinic and of Minnesota Community Measurement. He has an appointment as Adjunct Faculty in the Department of Youth Studies, School of Social Work, at the University of Minnesota. He received his doctorate in Sociology from the University of Minnesota.

Ruth Hamberg is an Engagement Specialist at Wilder Research, focusing on Minnesota Compass. She manages development, events, social media, and stakeholder engagement for the project. Ruth also contributes to data processing and analysis. Prior to joining Wilder Research in 2012, Ruth worked in media relations and development operations at Greater Twin Cities United Way. She received her bachelor's degree with honors from the University of Minnesota, Morris, where she studied Spanish, Biology, and Management. Her experience includes research in Ecuador (microfinance) and India (sex ratio) and an internship with a social business in Kolkata, India. Ruth's research interests include migration, sustainable community development, and how nonprofits, businesses and other organizations contribute to social change. She is a leader in the Minnesota Rising network and board member of the Young Nonprofit Professionals Network—Twin Cities.

Nancy Hartzler is Communications Manager for Wilder Research responsible for communications strategy and media relations. She oversees branding; event planning, and print, website, and digital communications. Nancy joined Wilder Research in 2006. Previously she held communications positions at Greater Twin Cities United Way, Minneapolis YWCA, and 3 M Corporation. She has a bachelor's degree in Journalism from the University of Minnesota.

Chapter 5
Aligning Local and Regional Data to Achieve a More Inclusive Economy: A Northeast Ohio Model

Emily Garr Pacetti

Abstract What drives economic growth in our communities and how can we ensure that more people benefit from that growth? While economic growth has been the focus of many U.S. cities and regions since the Great Recession, it is the second question that is gaining much-needed attention in recovery years. Answering either question is complicated by the lack of ability to access, analyze and apply data across diverse stakeholders and geographies. This chapter is for practitioners and policymakers interested in coordinating data across multiple stakeholders and geographies, and is particularly relevant for those interested in addressing inequality through more equitable economic development efforts. The chapter surfaces one example of a model in which cross-sector partners identified ways to improve labor market outcomes for all residents, especially lower income residents, across an 18-county region: first by using data and research to identify economic challenges and opportunities, and second by coordinating a plan of action across diverse sectors and jurisdictions. The chapter discusses the process that Northeast Ohio, and specifically the Fund for Our Economic Future, experienced as one example of cross-sector partners struggling to build—and re-build—a competitive economic base that benefits all people in its various communities. Its lessons have relevance for others trying to do the same in their own local, national or global contexts.

Keywords Northeast Ohio · Fund for our economic future · Economic development · Great recession · Inequality · Partnership · Cleveland

E.G. Pacetti (✉)
The Rockefeller Foundation, New York, USA
e-mail: epacetti@rockfound.org

E.G. Pacetti
Fund for Our Economic Future, Cleveland, OH, USA

M. Holden et al. (eds.), *Community Quality-of-Life Indicators: Best Cases VII*, Community Quality-of-Life and Well-Being,
DOI 10.1007/978-3-319-54618-6_5

5.1 Introduction

Many communities throughout the United States were severely affected by the Great Recession, which began approximately ten years ago.[1] Over that decade, much of the emphasis on recovering from the downturn was placed on regaining jobs lost, without regard to what kind of jobs, what part of the region they went to, or who filled them.

As the national labor market tightens and more people find work (the national unemployment rate was roughly halved in six years, from a high of about 10% in 2009 to about 5% in 2015), local and regional leaders are rightly seeking more comprehensive and lasting solutions to persistent, structural economic development challenges that supersede the next recession, and those that inevitably will follow. These macro-turned-micro challenges are complex and varied. They include the uneven concentration of job growth within certain neighborhoods, regions and industry sectors, rising income inequality, declining shares of the total population that are employed, increasing irregularity and vulnerability with the growth of the independent workforce, mediocre productivity growth and a corresponding loss in wages for the typical worker.[2] At the same time, unemployment is near record low, the pace of job growth is as high as it has been since the 1990s and there is a spirit of optimism, social and environmental responsibility, entrepreneurship and re-invention among new generations entering the workforce.

This chapter features Northeast Ohio as a region that, due largely to the severity of previous recessions, recognizes the long-term nature of economic development, and the need to build on short-term successes to achieve and maintain a healthy economy that works for all residents. In 2006, public, private and non-profit partners in Northeast Ohio came together to support a comprehensive indicator project, *What Matters to Metros* (formerly the *Dashboard of Economic Indicators*) to better understand the drivers of economic growth in American metropolitan areas, and situate local priorities accordingly. *What Matters to Metros* is not remarkable due only to its data-driven approach, but how partners used the data to inform and align action across various geographies and industry sectors. Led by a collaboration of funders called the Fund for Our Economic Future ("the Fund"), partners applied the information to an ongoing strategic process that engaged public, private and non-profit sector leaders in the following: identifying economic

[1]Refers to the 2007–2009 recession as defined by the National Bureau of Economic Research (NBER), available at http://www.nber.org/cycles.html.

[2]The best source I have found for U.S. metro area economic trends is the Brookings Institution's Metropolitan Monitor, from which many of the trends referred to here are derived. In its latest version (Shearer et al. 2016), data are available between 2009 and 2014 for variables related to growth (jobs, gross product (GMP) and aggregate wages), prosperity (averages wages per job, GMP, productivity) and inclusion (share of the population employed, median wages and poverty rates relative to local area income). See also Berube and Holmes (2016) for income inequality; EIG (2016) for spatial inequality across cities and neighborhoods; and Dourado and Koopman (2015) for growth of the independent workforce.

growth goals, agreeing on priority areas like more inclusive entrepreneurship and business growth, establishing accountability and tracking progress. Geographically, the Fund understood the need to identify priorities and data in ways that reflected the realities of an 18-county region, including 4.4 million urban, suburban and rural residents in and around four major metropolitan areas: Cleveland, Akron, Youngstown and Canton, Ohio.

Data are key to knowing whether a region is making progress. Only since 2005 have American cities and regions like Northeast Ohio been able to track progress on broad range of socio-economic related variables, due in large part to the American Community Survey released annually by the U.S. Census Bureau. U.S. localities are therefore in a unique position globally in that they are able to count on reliable, albeit imperfect, local area data to help inform decisions in (close to) real-time. Prior to 2005 for example, we would not have had the ability to track U.S. residents' incomes or poverty rates at the neighborhood, city, county or metro level, from a standardized dataset in more frequent intervals than every ten years.

Despite advances in public data availability at smaller geographies, however, communities struggle with how to access, analyze and apply such data in their work. Data, particularly economic data, often come in inconsistent, unstandardized slices from multiple sources. Challenges loom, like how to affect trends where you may not be able to see changes in one, five, or ten years' time; or how to decipher between trends that one can influence, versus global, national or regional trends that are far more responsible for some of the outcomes that may be in question (see de Souza Briggs et al. 2015). With broader availability, there is also increased risk that data will be mis-managed, misinterpreted and/or misdirected.[3] In order to leverage data to its fullest potential practitioners, policymakers and advocates must be specific about the data gaps in our strategies that inhibit us from achieving a more inclusive economy. We must look toward frameworks and solutions that are strong enough on their own that resonate globally, while still being responsive and adaptable to various social, political, economic and environmental contexts that play out every day in our—very different—local communities.[4]

As more and better data become available to more people, there is an opportunity for communities of every political stripe and growth trajectory to learn from each other on how to improve data gathering for a common purpose. Many communities are doing just that as it pertains to more inclusive economic development. Cross-sector networks such as those in the Living Cities' Integration Initiative, the Federal Reserve Bank of Boston's Working Cities Initiative (currently active in small industrial communities in Massachusetts, Rhode Island and Connecticut) and the Brookings-Rockefeller Project on State and Metropolitan Innovation are such examples. These efforts represent communities that use data to help deliver more

---

[3]See brief reflection by Shepherd (2016) on the potential and risk of big data influence decision-making at both micro and macro levels.

[4]See also Lui (2016), which highlights five principles for "remaking economic development," the first being to set the right goals (pp. 20–21).

sustained economic growth that benefits all residents, but especially low-income residents. Although I have had the privilege of witnessing the pitfalls and the successes in each of these national-scale approaches as both researcher and evaluator, I have been most involved in the efforts of Northeast Ohio. It is this example that I bring forward because I believe the work we did together is truly of consequence to other such efforts to pursue more inclusive economic development.

5.2 Identifying "What Matters": Using Data to Help Set Priorities

Local priorities—be they economic, health, environmental, political or social-must align to the geographic level where change happens. But first, what are those priorities? The process to identify and measure priorities—if there is a process—and who leads and participates in that process, varies substantially by community. The process itself can help or hinder the ability for a small, local community to ultimately connect their intervention to regionally significant outputs and outcomes.[5]

In Northeast Ohio, a top priority has been and remains economic growth. Since the 70s, Northeast Ohio has struggled to gain footing in a new economy given its relative dominance in a declining manufacturing sector and related supply chain. In some way it has succeeded by reinvention and innovation, but it has not been a smooth, easy or necessarily inclusive journey.

Unsurprisingly then, many Northeast Ohioans know that "economic growth" is a long-term aspiration rather than a short-term target. Beginning in the mid-2000s, in order to help determine where forward-looking economic development efforts and investment should be focused, the Fund, in partnership with The Federal Reserve Bank of Cleveland and Cleveland State University, conducted periodic analyses to identify how different indicators perform across the nation's metropolitan areas.[6] The objective was twofold: to understand more about how U.S. metros like those in Northeast Ohio performed on various socioeconomic indicators, and how such performance related to measures of economic growth, be it GDP, per capita income,

---

[5]For more on local consensus building around social and economic inclusion priorities, see de Souza Briggs et al. (2015) and Mallach (2014).

[6]Previous editions can be accessed at www.thefundneo.org/what-matters. *The Dashboard of Economic Indicators* was originally designed by Randall Eberts, George Erickcek, and Jack Kleinhenz in 2006 as a working paper for the Federal Reserve Bank of Cleveland. Subsequent refinements are largely attributable to Ziona Austrian, Iryna Lendel, Afiah Yamoah and Merissa Piazza of the Cleveland State University, with the latest analysis [retitled *What Matters to Metros* (2013)] authored by Emily Garr Pacetti. Deviations from past models include the period of growth, defined here as change over time between 1990 and 2011, in place of a subset of growth years as the dependent variable; and an extended variable list including indicators related to health, the arts, housing, and sustainability that had not been considered in previous iterations. For a detailed methodology, please refer to *The Dashboard of Economic Indicators* (Austrian et al. 2009).

productivity or job growth. Economic inclusion, the process by which all residents regardless of income, race or ethnicity, are connected to the economy, was and still remains at the heart of the research. Similar to what was uncovered in the original *Dashboard* (Eberts et al. 2006), one theme remained true in the most recent version of the rebranded *What Matters to Metros* (Pacetti 2013): the pursuit of social goals like racial inclusion and income equality are likely to help sustain economic growth, not deter it.[7]

The research helped to inform decision-making and investment at a regional scope and scale. Between 2006 and 2015, the research guided over one hundred million dollars of investment in areas such as business growth and innovation, talent development, and economic and racial inclusion.[8] *What Matters to Metros* sought to answer questions such as: What factors characterize economically vibrant communities across the U.S.? What investments should be prioritized? How does Northeast Ohio stack up to other metro areas from year to year on the things that matter most? The research was then substantiated and importantly, challenged by the perceptions of the region's residents.[9] It was also periodically supplemented with the most up-to-date analysis on what the competitive industries are in the region and how they are trending.

The most recent analysis, *What Matters to Metros* (Pacetti 2013) underscores the disconnect between income and job growth, based on data from 115 mid-sized U.S. metro areas between 1990 and 2011. The study found that contrary to popular belief, many metro areas that experienced the most robust job growth over the past two decades were characterized by a high incidence of poverty, inequality, crime, and lower health insurance coverage in the post-Recession era than other metro areas (see Table 5.1, a statistically significant, positive correlation between Employment Growth in column 1 and Economic Polarization in row 2).

The finding challenged a popular assumption that job growth is inevitably associated with residents' income growth. It suggests instead that jobs in many high-growth areas were low quality and/or low-paying jobs, with no clear association with gross metropolitan product or productivity. The findings led key leadership in Northeast Ohio and elsewhere to acknowledge that there are many types of

---

[7]Originally envisioned as a "dashboard" from which to track the region's progress year to year, the research contained many indicators that were, by their nature, slow to change. This prompted the Fund to focus more on its usefulness as a tool to help identify what is important to the economy in a given period of time, i.e. "what matters" to metros.

[8]For examples, see "A Regional Agenda to Advance Northeast Ohio" (The Fund for Our Economic Future 2011) and "Growth and Opportunity: A Call to Action" (Schweitzer et al. 2014).

[9]Initially referred to as "Voices and Choices," this engagement and feedback effort evolved from a broad-based community campaign to understand the public's priorities, to a more targeted outreach exercise with key stakeholders, communities, academics and community leaders, who helped guide the research year-to-year. Note: There was and is no silver-bullet engagement strategy that the Fund employed, and there was broad recognition that engagement activities could always be more robust, more long-term and more directly applied to resulting strategies. Resource constraints tend to complicate this task. For more discussion and examples of failed and successful community engagement efforts, see Barnes and Schmitz (2016).

Table 5.1 Results from *what matters to metros* (Pacetti 2013)

	Growth indicators *(dependent variables)*			
Factor groupings *(independent variables)*	Employment (1990–2011)	Gross metropolitan product (1990–2011)	Productivity (1990–2011)	Per capita income (1990–2010)[a]
Education and innovation		3.73[c]	8.59[c]	6.68[c]
Economic polarization	2.33[b]			−3.40[c]
Self-employment, entrepreneurship and inclusion	6.95[c]	7.49[c]	5.21[c]	2.01[b]
Business costs	−8.60[c]	−8.56[c]	−3.91[c]	
Dynamics of place				
Connectivity			2.16[b]	4.14[c]

[a]Based on logged per capita income and controlled for 1990 levels
[b]95% Significance
[c]99% Significance
Note Numbers displayed as t statistics

"growth"; and in order to sustain growth that ultimately benefits residents' pocketbooks, communities must also invest in and promote good quality employment opportunities, especially those for residents that have historically been left behind.[10]

Subsequent analyses by the Brookings Institution also demonstrate a weak correlation between traditional economic growth measures (e.g. jobs, GDP) and inclusion in U.S. metro areas—be it racial or economic inclusion (Shearer et al. 2016). Economists such as Paul Krugman have emphasized the weakness of the correlation as well, stating that we must be cautious in asserting a relationship between equality and growth where there may in fact be none.[11]

Importantly, new research finds that inequality and social fragmentation has an impact on *how long* growth is sustained, if not growth itself (Benner and Pastor

[10]Through a series of discussion forums, the Fund's research reached more than 800 regional and national civic leaders. The discussions focused on the observation that job growth cannot be a region's only measure of success and led to additional conversations and strategic planning about how to better link economic growth and equitable opportunity. Ultimately, the research led the Fund, in partnership with the Federal Reserve Bank of Cleveland and others, to a "Growth and Opportunity" agenda (Pacetti 2014; Schweitzer et al. 2014), that reinforced connections among workforce and training efforts ("job preparation"), employer demand ("job creation") and the spatial and social disconnect between jobs and workers ("job access"). For more information, see http://www.thefundneo.org/growth-opportunity.

[11]A Conversation between Paul Krugman and Janet Gornick, Equality Indicators Conference, City University of New York (CUNY), Institute for State and Local Governance. October 1, 2015. An alternative vision is offered in Treuhaft et al. (2011).

2013, 2015).[12] To quote one of the authors' original hypotheses: "what if paying attention to equity—building it into economic strategies from the get-go—could actually help prosperity be more sustainable as well as more widespread?" After analyses of employment in 184 largest metro areas in the U.S., they find that the most significant negative impact on the length of growth spells is a metro's initial level of inequality. They suggest that to achieve more inclusive and robust, sustained growth, the first step involves "restoring a sense of common destiny—in which first metros and then the nation become more connected across income, race and place" (Benner and Pastor 2015: 27, 55).

Such research poses questions about how communities might catalyze an era of growth that (if it is not faster) is smarter, shared and more sustainable. Difficult but essential questions for communities include:

- What defines "economic growth" for our community?
- Who benefits from the outcomes of that growth?
- What affects growth trends, and how do we (residents, local, state and federal government, civic, business and philanthropic leaders) adjust our strategies to ensure that growth benefits all members of the community long-term?

Questions about what drives economic growth in our communities and what we can do to ensure that everyone benefits from that growth, are at the center of local economic development planning today, spurred by both structural and cyclical changes in the labor market. During the recovery years, for example, job growth was disproportionately concentrated at the higher and lower ends of the wage spectrum, with fewer in between. Between 2013 and 2015, that trend now seems to be shifting to a growth in middle and high-wage jobs, paying between $12 and $24 per hour, and $46 per hour and higher respectively.[13]

While many communities succeed in identifying common priorities—in this case a more inclusive regional economy—it often remains an elusive goal unless and until they begin to track progress towards them, and establish some basic level of shared accountability. This is as true for small, local, low-budget non-profit

---

[12]Benner and Pastor (2013) conducted an exercise for 184 metro areas with a population of 250,000 or above, and found that the capacity of regions to maintain growth and withstand recessionary shocks was positively associated with various measures of equity (lower racial segregation, lower income inequality and less political fragmentation). The data are backed up by previous empirical investigations (Benner and Pastor 2012; Carlson et al. 2012) and reinforced in their recent book (Benner and Pastor 2015).

[13]Analysis by Shierholz (2016), based on Bureau of Labor Statistics data between 2007 and 2015. The analysis compares job losses and gains during the recession (2007–2009) to those in the recovery (2009–2013) by pay per hour. It finds that during the Recovery period, low wage jobs (jobs that pay $10 per hour or less) and high wage jobs (jobs that pay between $47 and $50 per hour) increased disproportionately to middle wage jobs. The exception was jobs paying $51 per hour or higher.

programs, city mayors' offices and regional economic development efforts as it is for CEOs of large international corporations and international development organizations.[14]

5.3 Pursuing "What Matters": Establishing Shared Goals and Accountability Across Diverse Jurisdictions and Stakeholders

5.3.1 Geography Matters

Once stakeholders collect data and identify priorities, they must ensure that priorities align at the geography where one wants to affect change. For example, if you want to increase labor force participation regionally, you must have a consistent way to measure it locally in order to know whether or not—and where—progress is being made. Unfortunately, the "where" is often overlooked in the national discourse on economic opportunity, despite increasing recognition that geography matters to socioeconomic outcomes.

Central to the data challenges of measuring economic inclusion is a misuse of, if not misunderstanding of, economic geography. Markets are not confined by political boundaries. Regions are often patchworks of rural, urban and suburban neighborhoods that are geographically, politically and socioeconomically distinct; however residents' economic choices are not bounded by where they live. Residents produce, consume and operate in a universe that crosses the political and jurisdictional boundaries of census "block groups," workforce investment boards, municipalities, counties, states and countries. Therefore, a solid understanding of where economic opportunity is located in a region, is essential to understanding who is or is not connected to it.[15]

Northeast Ohio's $229 billion economy depends not on one city, but the network of production and consumption across 18 counties.[16] The region's largest county, Cuyahoga, accounts for about one-third of the region's population yet on its own consists of more than fifty municipalities, each politically distinct but economically interdependent, Cleveland being the largest.

---

[14]See Shepherd (2016) for micro and macro examples.

[15]For this reason, the best proxy we have for economic regions, or market areas, is at the metropolitan level. A metropolitan statistical area ("metro area") is defined by the Office of Management and Budget as a geographical region with a relatively high population density at its core (minimum population of 50,000 in core urban area) and close economic ties throughout its surroundings. It constitutes one or more counties with a high degree of social and economic integration (as measured by commuting to work) with the urban core.

[16]Based on latest estimate from Moodys.com, as reported by Team NEO (2016).

Without strong connections between neighborhoods and the regional economy, the region risks ending up with aggregate growth even while pockets of poverty remain stagnant or in decline.[17] A recent analysis of distressed zip codes, cities and counties between 2010 and 2014 bears this out. The study, conducted by the Economic Innovation Group (EIG), emphasizes spatial inequality across cities and counties, finding that "even the technology-intensive knowledge economy hubs that have charged U.S. economic growth over the past decade-plus have struggled to generate prosperity that is broadly shared across neighborhoods." (EIG 2016: 31) Such metros include places such as Charlotte, Austin and San Diego and even places such as Denver and Minneapolis that on other measures of income inequality metro-wide—may seem more evenly spread.

The interconnection between local and regional economies in the U.S. is perhaps more important now than in any other period in recent history (**see Box** 5.1, **Local Assets, Regional Economies**). If better understood, markets can be leveraged to benefit local communities otherwise systematically disenfranchised from the regional economy. First, jurisdictions must work together to understand and connect trends at both the micro and macro levels. As communities come together around specific priorities and goals, they are then understandably challenged by the question of how to track progress across jurisdictions.

Box 5.1. Local Assets-Regional Economies

"*During the 2000s, the distance between where people live and where people work increased dramatically as jobs spread out from the urban core. In 2010, 43% of jobs in a sample of the nation's largest 100 metropolitan areas were located at least ten miles away from a central business district, compared to 23% within three miles* (Kneebone 2013). *Notably since 2000, the number of poor in the suburbs outpaced —and soon outnumbered—those in the city, spurred by foreclosures, abandonment and cheaper housing stock* (Kneebone 2013; Kneebone & Garr (Pacetti) 2010; Raphael and Stoll 2010). *By 2012, the number of jobs within a typical commute distance fell by seven percent, disproportionately affecting poor and minority residents, for whom that number fell by 17%* (Kneebone and Holmes 2015). *Often, such trends mean higher, long-term infrastructure costs (read: higher taxes), labor market inefficiencies (connecting the 'right' jobs to the 'right' workers) and longer commutes. Just as these challenges are regional, so are the solutions. Unfortunately, too many efforts to address 'opportunity' are isolated from the*

[17]See Pacetti et al. (2015) for a detailed analysis of job growth in Northeast Ohio, highlighting the outward growth of jobs away from city centers over the last two decades and the increasing disconnect between jobs and workers. Such disconnects in cities, as measured by commute times, are associated with a significant decrease in workers' economic mobility (Chetty et al. 2014). For more on the importance of connecting regional and local economic development efforts generally, see Weissbourd (2004), Weissbourd et al. (2009), Carlson et al. (2012), Lynch and Kamins (2012), Pacetti (2013).

regional economy, treating neighborhoods and cities as if they were islands rather than part of a complex web of regional markets and relationships."
—Adapted from Pacetti (2014)

Northeast Ohio exemplifies a community trying to understand (in this case) economic growth, what drives it, who benefits from it, and where those benefits are incurred. We continue with the Northeast Ohio example to illustrate how one community aligned partners with varied but complementary skill sets around common goals, using data tracking systems that would benefit their respective urban, suburban, and rural service areas and constituencies.

5.3.2 *Setting Concrete Goals*

In 2013 private sector and philanthropic leaders from across Northeast Ohio came together to develop a regional economic competitiveness strategy.[18] Key objectives included: understanding the current economic trajectory of the region and potential alternative scenarios, setting short, long, and medium-term goals to improve that trajectory, and developing a strategy to achieve those goals.

Once the economic trajectory of the region was understood by partners, the hard work of goal setting began. What emerged were four, well-defined goals (Fig. 5.1). Due in part to post-recession research that showed job growth alone was insufficient to achieve a healthy economy (discussed above), there was broad acknowledgement that actions must address not only the average prosperity of the region, but also take steps to increase economic opportunity in distressed communities. Consequently, beyond establishing what might be considered standard economic growth goals around aggregate jobs, gross product and per capita income, partners included an additional measure of labor force connectedness: the number of census tracts considered "distressed" across the region. Economically distressed tracts were defined as tracts (a proxy for neighborhoods) where less than 65% of residents between ages 25 and 64 were working or looking for work, and where median household income

[18]The group was made up of representatives of small and large philanthropic organizations, community foundations, hospitals, educational institutions, banks, and leading companies. It included representation from non-profit intermediaries such as NorTech (focused on innovation), JumpStart, Inc. (entrepreneurship), MAGNET (advanced manufacturing), BioEnterprise (biotechnology), Team NEO (business development) and other business development organizations throughout an 18 county region that focused on business retention and attraction. Team NEO worked in parallel with a state-led effort called JobsOhio.

	Short term 1-5 Years 2013-2017	Intermediate term 5-10 Years 2018-2022	Long term 10-20 Years 2023-2033
Employment	Close gap between NEO and US growth rate by 50%	US growth rate	Exceed U.S. growth rate
GRP	Close gap between NEO and US growth rate by 50%	US growth rate	Exceed U.S. growth rate
Per Capita Income	US growth rate		Exceed U.S. growth rate
Labor Force Participation	Increase labor force participation in economically distressed areas[1]		

1 Distressed areas are defined as census tracts where the following are true: less than 65% of residents between 25-64 participate in the labor force and 2) more than 50% of households have low to moderate income.

Fig. 5.1 Goals framework: *example*. *Source* Reproduced with permission from The Fund for Our Future and Team NEO, Regional Strategy Task Force

fell in the bottom quartile regionally.[19] Based on 2008/2012 aggregated census data, approximately 5%, or 200,000 of the 4.4 million residents living in Northeast Ohio, lived in distressed areas, spread across ten counties.[20] It is indicative of poverty trends today that while about half of the distressed population was concentrated in one or two large urban areas, a significant share also lived in suburban and even rural tracts, affecting the majority of counties across the 18-county region and reinforcing this to be "everyone's issue" not just a central-city one.

By including a region-wide labor force participation metric as a topline goal (see Fig. 5.2, Labor Force Connectedness), partners acknowledged that if certain pockets of the region remained disconnected from the economy it was to nobody's benefit, and thus everyone's charge to improve it. This was far more innovative and

---

[19]Population was limited to residents between the ages of 25–64 in order to provide an accurate assessment of those who were working age without confounding them with retirees and/or students. Standard labor force participation rates typically measure the population 16+ and may skew the perception of communities with disproportionately high or low student or elderly populations (the latter of which is the case for Northeast Ohio, which has a disproportionately older population). A notable drawback of this measure is its inability to measure progress year-to-year due to its dependence on smaller geographic data -census blocks or tracts that require an aggregation of (pooled) data over two, three or five years from the American Community Survey. A benefit is that even as residents may "move out" of distressed neighborhoods—presumably moving on to better opportunities, the tracking of "number of distressed areas" would adjust accordingly, as tracts are periodically readjusted based on population—the focus being on the share of the overall population who lives in these places.

[20]Examples of community-specific profiles and maps of economically distressed areas in Northeast Ohio are available at: http://www.thefundneo.org/growth-opportunity/neighborhood-profiles.

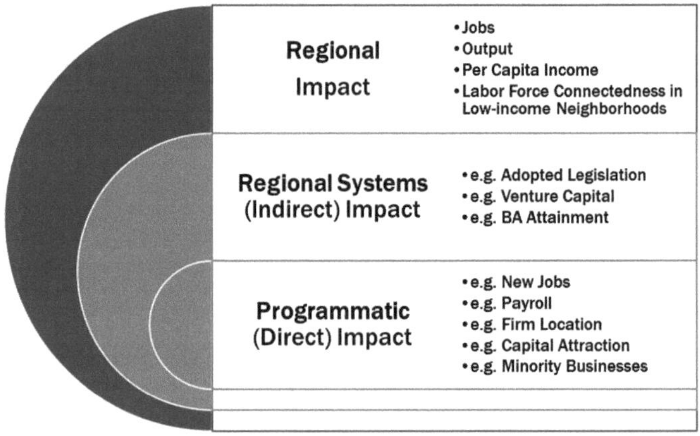

Fig. 5.2 Cascading metrics concept

meaningful than any localized metric such as labor force participation rates in one neighborhood or one city. It was able to be measured both at the regional level through an aggregation of counties and/or metropolitan areas, as well as the city and neighborhood (tract) level through the American Community Survey.

The four goals—jobs, gross regional product, per capita income and labor force connectedness—were ambitious, but painstakingly benchmarked against the U.S. economy to see what was realistically achievable for the region over the short (1–5 years), medium (5–10 years) and long-term (10–20 years). Rather than set specific target levels, which would vary depending on the macro economic climate, partners were careful to set goals relative to the U.S. economy, and translate those into absolute numbers year-to-year (see Fig. 5.1, Goals Framework). Note that specific data points that emerged from these goals are not shared here. Inevitably, however, target levels were more effective than percentage increases as a way convey economic growth goals to the general public (e.g. 200,000 additional jobs by 2020, or 20–30,000 additional jobs per year), albeit less statistically accurate. These targets were subject to revision as economic circumstances shifted either upward or downward year-to-year.

5.3.3 *Tracking Progress*

Once partners established benchmarks for each measure, they used an approach they called "cascading metrics" to determine how their goals connected to their respective programmatic, institutional or jurisdictional purviews (Fig. 5.2). The approach enabled communication across various industry sectors, an understanding of a shared agenda and goals, each actor's role in achieving those goals and their level of accountability.

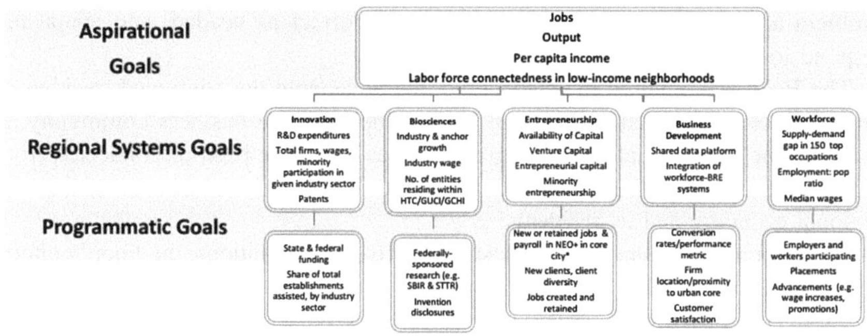

Fig. 5.3 Cascading metrics example

The cascading metrics model is a model which connects the high-level goals that describe **Regional Impact** to various "Systems" (e.g. workforce development, manufacturing, advanced technology), to specific organizations and programs. These enumerated goals are the essential link that enable organizations and initiatives to understand their contribution to the broader goals of any strategy. **Regional Systems Impact**, in this case, represents a small number (3–5) of regional indicators per priority area, that convey how the region is doing in distinct sectors of the economy. The assumption is that together these systems can affect regional outcomes. In Northeast Ohio's case, priority areas included innovation, biosciences, entrepreneurship, business development and workforce (Fig. 5.3). These indicators are those that organizations can put our fingers on but may not be able to attribute to any one organization, network of organizations (referred to here as intermediaries), or initiative. **Programmatic Impact** is more refined, and includes measures of impact that are connected to specific organizations, intermediaries or initiatives, and linked to some level of accountability. This would be the level at which partners heavily engage, in order to understand how they can contribute to the larger Regional Systems goals—and by extension, Regional Impact.

Importantly no one organization, public or private, should be under the illusion that the movement towards or away from a regional goal, such as net job growth or gross metropolitan product (aka output), is attributable to a particular intervention. Rather, progress at this level is the result of many variables, some within and many outside of any one organization's or sector's control. Consistent with the collective impact literature, the theory is that as time progresses the articulation and adaptation of shared goals across organizations will increase the likelihood of achieving them.[21] And if regularly revisited, the approach would enable partners to identify

[21]Collective Impact was first introduced in a 2011 and is based on the premise that large-scale social change requires broad cross-sector coordination, rather than isolated interventions of individual organizations. The article describes five conditions for collective success: a common agenda, shared measurement systems (emphasized here), mutually reinforcing activities, continuous communication, and backbone support organizations. See Kania and Kramer (2011).

problem areas or gaps in the strategy, course-correct as needed, and adapt and respond to unanticipated challenges.

The Fund was integral to establishing and advancing the continued tracking of progress across regional systems, in partnership with the business community. It has used the model to identify geographic areas that have been disconnected from growth, better target interventions and continue pushing on "what matters" to the regional economy and its residents.

However as with many of the most productive collaborations, the Fund's efforts and those of its partners are often hard to sustain. While the partnership has continued to check back on goals and involve partners in the achievement of milestones set forth year-to-year, it has been hard to establish an incentive structure that can be maintained across organizations with any kind of regularity. As it stands and despite its success in bringing diverse actors to the table, Northeast Ohio is far from achieving its four regional strategic (growth) goals, let alone a more inclusive economy. Cleveland, Northeast Ohio's most populous city, was cited as one of the country's most "distressed cities" in the post-recession era according to EIG's recent Distressed Communities Index, underscoring the lack of connectedness between hard-hit areas and broader regional growth.[22]

Nevertheless, the process that took place in Northeast Ohio—of identifying goals and establishing shared measurement across jurisdictions and stakeholders—holds as an impressive model from which other communities can learn from and adapt to their changing environment and needs. In confronting economic trends such as those described above, Northeast Ohio faces many of the same struggles that communities across the country face with regard to the persistent application of data to inform strategy: resource-intensive community engagement, the ability to connect the communities they are trying to serve to broader regional objectives, the ability to keep influential actors at the table over time, and the ability for stakeholders to be held accountable for what they set out to achieve—individually as well as collectively.

Fortunately, regional partners across Northeast Ohio know that economic gains that are both sustained and shared do not happen overnight. This, combined with increasing recognition among residents of the need to connect struggling communities to the regional economic growth objectives (—growth that is in fact, fueling Northeast Ohio's sure yet slow recovery) is a tremendous achievement. Most importantly, the region knows where it stands and it knows where it wants to go.

[22]See Russell (2016). "In An Improving Economy, Places in Distress," *New York Times*. February 24, 2016. The data represents aggregate trends over the 2010–2014 time frame.

5.4 Toward an Inclusive Economy in U.S. Cities & Regions

Of course, an inclusive economy cannot just be measured by economic growth, no matter how you define it (e.g. jobs, GDP, productivity or labor force connectedness). The Rockefeller Foundation asserts that an inclusive economy, whether at a local, regional, state or national scale, exhibits the following five characteristics (of which growth is only one)[23]:

- *equitable* where more opportunities are available to enable upward mobility for more people;
- *participatory* where people can participate fully in economic life and have greater say over their future;
- *growing* where an economy is increasingly producing enough goods and services to enable broad gains in well-being and greater opportunity;
- *sustainable* where economic and social wealth is sustained over time, thus maintaining inter-generational well-being; and
- *stable* where individuals, communities, businesses and governments have a sufficient degree of confidence in the future and an increased ability to predict the outcome of their economic decisions.

By its nature, a more inclusive economy implicates a diversity of actors across sectors and geographies. How to measure progress towards such an economy requires those actors to be honest, diligent and persistent about identifying the goals they want to achieve, tracking their contributions toward those goals, and adjusting strategies accordingly.

In retrospect, Northeast Ohio's efforts to build consensus around a long-term regional agenda are truly remarkable. The use of data to inform strategy and pursue that strategy in a coordinated way—across diverse interests and geographies, is unparalleled among economic development approaches in the U.S. At the same time, no community—Northeast Ohio included—has yet been able to fully translate measurement to the achievement of its long-term objectives. This effort and ones like it are difficult to scale, or don't engage partners from the myriad of sectors necessary to enact change.

As communities across the country look to reframe the economic development conversation from one of "growth" to more comprehensive, meaningful and lasting economic inclusion, communities must be able to understand how to link what they want to achieve locally, to the broader regional economic landscape. This entails trusted partnerships across sectors and geographies, relevant data and a realistic roadmap for success.

---

[23]See Irons and Berube (2016), based on the Rockefeller Foundation framework, currently in development.

References

Austrian, Z., Yamoah, A., & Clouse, C. (2009). *Regional dashboard of economic indicators*. The Cleveland State University. Prepared for the Fund for Our Economic Future. http://www.thefundneo.org/sites/default/files/content-media/Dashboard%20Indicators%202009.pdf. Accessed October 1, 2016.

Barnes, M., & Schmitz, P. (2016). Community engagement matters (now more than ever). *Stanford Social Innovation Review*. https://ssir.org/articles/entry/community_engagement_matters_now_more_than_ever. Accessed October 1, 2016.

Benner, C., & Pastor, M. (2012). *Just growth: Inclusion and prosperity in America's metropolitan regions*. Regional studies association regions and cities series. New York: Routledge.

Benner, C., & Pastor, M. (2013). *Buddy, can you spare some time? Social inclusion and sustained prosperity in America's Metropolitan Regions*. Working Paper. Building Resilient Regions Research Network. http://brr.berkeley.edu/wp-content/uploads/2013/05/Benner-Pastor-Buddy-Spare-Some-Time.pdf. Accessed October 1, 2016.

Benner, C., & Pastor, M. (2015). *Equity, growth and community: What the nation can learn from America's metro areas*. Oakland, CA: University of California Press.

Berube, A., & Holmes, N. (2016). *City and metro inequality on the rise, driven by declining incomes*. The Brookings Institution. https://www.brookings.edu/research/city-and-metropolitan-inequality-on-the-rise-driven-by-declining-incomes/. Accessed October 1, 2016.

Carlson, P., Leiken, S., Michon, S., & Siegel, B. (2012). *Linking growth and opportunity: Findings from the front*. Regional Prosperity Project. http://www.thefundneo.org/sites/default/files/content-media/Linking%20Growth%20and%20Opportunity.pdf. Accessed October 1, 2016.

Chetty, R., Hendren, N., Kline, P., & Saez, E. (2014). *Is the United States still a land of opportunity? Recent trends in intergenerational mobility*. NBER Working Paper No. 19843. The National Bureau of Economic Research. http://www.nber.org/papers/w19843. Accessed October 1, 2016.

de Souza Briggs, X., Pendall, R., & Rubin, V. (2015). *Inclusive economic growth in America's cities: What's the Playbook and the score*. Policy Research Working Paper 7322. The World Bank Group. http://documents.worldbank.org/curated/en/819391468179050671/pdf/WPS7322.pdf. Accessed October 1, 2016.

Dourado, E., & Koopman, C. (2015). *Evaluating the growth of the 1099 workforce*. George Mason University Mercatus Center. https://www.mercatus.org/publication/evaluating-growth-1099-workforce. Accessed October 1, 2016.

Eberts, R., Erickcek, G., & Kleinhenz, J. (2006). *Dashboard indicators for the Northeast Ohio economy*. Working Paper 06-05. Federal Reserve Bank of Cleveland. http://www.thefundneo.org/sites/default/files/content-media/Dashboard%202006%20Report.pdf. Accessed October 1, 2016.

Economic Innovation Group. (2016). *Distressed communities index: An analysis of community well-being across the United States*. http://eig.org/wp-content/uploads/2016/02/2016-Distressed-Communities-Index-Report.pdf. Accessed October 1, 2016.

Fund for Our Economic Future. (2011). *A regional agenda to advance Northeast Ohio*. Northeast Ohio Regional Business Plan prepared in collaboration with The Brookings Institution. http://www.thefundneo.org/sites/default/files/content-media/NEO_Business_Plan%20FINAL.pdf. Accessed October 9, 2016.

Irons, J., & Berube, A. (2016). *Measuring inclusive economies in metropolitan America. The Brookings Institution*. https://www.brookings.edu/blog/the-avenue/2016/05/12/measuring-inclusive-economies-in-metropolitan-america/. Accessed 1 October 2016.

Kania, J., & Kramer, M. (2011). Collective impact. *Stanford Social Innovation Review*. https://ssir.org/articles/entry/collective_impact. Accessed October 1, 2016.

Kneebone, E. (2013). *Job sprawl stalls: The great recession and metropolitan employment location*. The Brookings Institution. https://www.brookings.edu/research/job-sprawl-stalls-the-great-recession-and-metropolitan-employment-location/. Accessed October 1, 2016.

Kneebone, E., & Garr (Pacetti), E. (2010). *The suburbanization of poverty: Trends in metropolitan America, 2000 to 2008*. The Brookings Institution. https://www.brookings.edu/research/the-suburbanization-of-poverty-trends-in-metropolitan-america-2000-to-2008/. Accessed October 1, 2016.

Kneebone, E., & Holmes, N. (2015). *The growing distance between people and jobs in metropolitan America*. The Brookings Institution. https://www.brookings.edu/research/the-growing-distance-between-people-and-jobs-in-metropolitan-america/. Accessed October 1, 2016.

Lui, A. (2016). *Remaking economic development: The markets and civics of continuous growth and prosperity*. The Brookings Institution. https://www.brookings.edu/wp-content/uploads/2016/02/BMPP_RemakingEconomicDevelopment_Feb25LoRes.pdf. Accessed October 1, 2016.

Lynch, T., & Kamins, A. (2012). *Creating equity: Does regionalism have an answer for urban poverty? Can it?* Initiative for a Competitive Inner City.

Mallach, A. (2014). *Out of the Shadow: Strategies for Change in Small Postindustrial Cities*. Federal Reserve Bank of Philadelphia.

Pacetti, E. G. (2013). *What matters to metros: Foundational indicators for economic competitiveness*. The Fund for Our Economic Future. http://www.thefundneo.org/what-matters/what-matters-metros. Accessed October 1, 2016.

Pacetti, E. G. (2014). *Growth and opportunity: A framework for stronger, more equitable local and regional economies*. The Fund for Our Economic Future. http://www.thefundneo.org/our-research-what-matters%E2%84%A2/growth-opportunity-framing-paper. Accessed October 1, 2016.

Pacetti, E. G., Murray, C., & Hartman, S. (2015). *The geography of jobs: The increasing distance between jobs and workers in Northeast Ohio and why it matters for future growth*. The Fund for Our Economic Future. http://www.thefundneo.org/sites/default/files/content-media/Geography%20of%20Jobs.pdf. Accessed October 1, 2016.

Raphael, S., & Stoll, M. (2010). *Job sprawl and the suburbanization of poverty*. The Brookings Institution. https://www.brookings.edu/research/job-sprawl-and-the-suburbanization-of-poverty/. Accessed October 1, 2016.

Russell, K. (2016, February 24). In an improving economy, places in distress. *New York Times*.

Schweitzer, M., Fee, K., Boise, A., Rizika, J., & Segedy, J. (2014). *Growth & opportunity: A call to action to grow Northeast Ohio through job creation, job preparation and job access*. The Fund for Our Economic Future. http://www.thefundneo.org/our-research-what-matters%E2%84%A2/growth-opportunity-call-action. Accessed October 1, 2016.

Shearer, R., Berube, A., Ng, J., & Friedhoff, A. (2016). *Metro monitor: tracking growth, prosperity and inclusion in the 100 largest U.S. metropolitan areas*. The Brookings Institution. https://www.brookings.edu/wp-content/uploads/2016/07/MetroMonitor.pdf. Accessed 1 October 2016.

Shepherd, K. (2016). *How much development data is enough?* World Economic Forum in partnership with Project Syndicate. https://www.weforum.org/agenda/2016/01/how-much-development-data-is-enough/?utm_content=buffer6f6f6&utm_medium=social&utm_source=twitter.com&utm_campaign=buffer. Accessed October 1, 2016.

Shierholz, H. (2016). *The wages of jobs being added*. U.S. Department of Labor. October 29, 2015. https://blog.dol.gov/2015/10/29/the-wages-of-jobs-being-added/. Accessed October 1, 2016.

Team NEO (2016). *Quarterly Economic Review*. June 2016.

Treuhaft, S., Glover Blackwell, A., & Pastor, M. (2011). *America's tomorrow: Equity is the superior growth model*. PolicyLink. http://www.policylink.org/sites/default/files/SUMMIT_FRAMING_SUMMARY_WEB.PDF. Accessed October 1, 2016.

Weissbourd, R. (2004). *The changing dynamics of urban America*. CEOs for Cities. http://rw-ventures.com/publications/downloads/Changing%20Dynamics%20report.pdf. Accessed October 1, 2016.

Weissbourd, R., Bodini, R., & He, M. (2009). *Dynamic neighborhoods: New tools for community and economic development*. Living Cities. http://www.rw-ventures.com/ftp/DNT%20Final%20Report.pdf. Accessed October 1, 2016.

Author Biography

Emily Garr Pacetti is Associate Director at the Rockefeller Foundation in New York City, focused on helping cities and regions build more inclusive economies, particularly in the U.S. Prior to joining the Foundation, she spent four years working with the Fund for Our Economic Future in Cleveland, Ohio, a collaboration of foundations, business and non-profit leaders dedicated to making the region more economically competitive and inclusive. A former Fulbright Fellow, she also brings experience in regional labor market analyses gained at The Brookings Institution Metropolitan Policy Program and The Economic Policy Institute in Washington, D.C., where she tracked the geographic distribution of poverty, income and jobs in the 2007 Recession and slow-growth recovery. Garr Pacetti has a master's in public administration from Harvard Kennedy School of Government, a master's in urban studies from El Colegio de Mexico in Mexico City, and a bachelor's in political communications from Emerson College. She is the author of "Growth and Opportunity: A Framework for Stronger, More Equitable Local and Regional Economies" and "What Matters to Metros™: Foundational Indicators for Economic Competitiveness."

Chapter 6
Getting to Groundbreaking, but not Build Out: From Formation to Failure in a Regional Housing Indicators Collaborative

Meg Holden

Abstract Getting to Groundbreaking (G2G) is a housing indicators project formed in 2013 that brought together home builders, industry associations, municipalities, the regional government, and academic urban researchers around a common interest: to understand what works in housing development regulation and planning across the Metro Vancouver region of British Columbia, Canada. The project aims were to inject new, credible information into the discussion of regulation of land and housing development. The project investigated trends in the provision of housing, surveyed opinions and practices amongst municipalities, homebuilders and the public, and collected information on new innovations in regulating the provision of housing. The G2G 2014 report detailed the cost, timing and regulatory best practices involved in the development approvals process for new town houses, and the G2G 2016 report examined these factors related to woodframe apartment buildings. The Metro Vancouver region is marked by high regulatory costs and long time frames for housing development, with considerable variability at the municipal level. However, G2G data does not indicate any relationship between lower regulatory costs and less time in the regulatory process and a lower cost of housing. In the context of the politically charged debate about the cost and regulation of housing, we detail the collaborative industry-researcher-government multistakeholder partnership approach taken by G2G and discuss the divergent interests in data transparency, and the politics of participation and control that pervaded the G2G project. In 2016, the G2G partnership broke down as a result of these unresolved questions, leaving unclear how much collaboration can be expected to offer the practice of urban indicators work in a heated political terrain.

Keywords Housing · Development charges · Impact fees · Partnership · Metro Vancouver · Housing affordability

M. Holden (✉)
Simon Fraser University, Vancouver, Canada
e-mail: mholden@sfu.ca

M. Holden et al. (eds.), *Community Quality-of-Life Indicators: Best Cases VII*, Community Quality-of-Life and Well-Being,
DOI 10.1007/978-3-319-54618-6_6

6.1 Introduction

This chapter tells the story of an effort to create a regional housing development process indicators reporting system in the Metropolitan Vancouver region of British Columbia, Canada. The community of reference for this effort is a new network of local actors, consisting of unlikely collaborators often seen as sitting on opposite sides of the metaphorical decision making table. This effort emerged in the context of a regional, municipal and development planning system that is one of the strongest in North America (Harcourt et al. 2007), and a metropolitan region facing some of the highest levels of residential development activity and residential development value appreciation on the continent as well. Among the numerous loci of blame for the housing affordability crisis that has ensued is a costly and timely development planning process. Yet the extent to which these costs contribute materially to the end cost of housing, and who bears this cost, is hotly debated in Vancouver (Gordon 2016; for the case of San Francisco, see Ruiz and Smooke 2014).

Home builders and developers, municipal development staff, affordable housing advocates and urban housing researchers all share an interest in better understanding the extent to which the costs incurred within the development approvals process play a material role in unaffordable housing in the Metro Vancouver region. The Getting to Groundbreaking (G2G) project emerged to build a network by which all these actors together could create a collaborative research and indicators reporting system to support this understanding. G2G was founded in 2013, operated for three years, produced two reports, and disbanded in 2016. This chapter provides an account of the genesis, process, results and ultimate network failure of the G2G initiative. In addition, we offer reflections from the signs of distress and conflicting values and priorities of the participants around the collaborative G2G table that created new insights into the challenge and opportunities for the use of indicators in a politically-contentious policy vacuum.

6.2 Background and Context: Housing Development Regulation in Vancouver and the Housing Affordability Crisis

Housing policy in Metro Vancouver has reached a turning point. The benchmark or "typical" price for detached, single family housing in the region is now over $1.5 million; for apartments it is over $500,000. Debate over housing affordability is super-charged with anecdotes and innuendo. Supply and demand side arguments are thrown about, and the heated discussion over regulation of vacant housing and foreign investment has pitted the real estate industry against government, and government against foreign investors, while the media laments the loss of the millennial generation to more affordable regions of the province. With 40,000 new residents arriving each year, lower than average incomes, and the most expensive housing of any Canadian city, new ideas and interventions are needed in order to maintain livability in the region and create sufficient, quality, affordable homes for all residents.

While many macroeconomic and political-economic drivers of housing unaffordability have been posited and tested, revealing the larger context in which housing price escalation is occurring (Hulchanski and Shapcott 2004; Dalton 2009), relatively neglected have been the micro-scale municipal context contributors to housing development activity (housing diversity) and costs (housing affordability). Rising development costs have been clearly linked to the preference among developers to build predominantly for higher income home buyers (Conference Board of Canada 2010)—and even to the justification of these higher end developments as a key means to finance community amenities, infrastructure, and affordable housing alternatives elsewhere. Equally legitimate is the argument that increasing affordable housing options farther away from town centres and rapid transit serves to worsen automobile dependency, traffic congestion, and to threaten quality of life for moderate income households, at the same time as it increases infrastructure cost burden (City of Calgary 2013; Thompson 2013).

Among the factors criticized for the high cost of housing in the Vancouver region are the costs of planning: the time it takes, the cost of charges, compliance with regulations and other process-based measures in the course of development. The role of the municipal housing development policy context, including fees, approval processes and schedules, and institutional relationships and structures for collaboration with the residential development industry, are all pieces of the housing development diversity and housing affordability equation. A sizeable body of research examines the relationships between such factors of planning and housing outcomes, internationally (e.g., Ihlanfelt 2007; Glaeser and Ward 2009; Ruming et al. 2011). For example, in the Australian context, research by Ruming et al. (2011: 258) examines "the experiences and perspectives of individual developers, state and local government planners, regarding housing affordability, funding approaches for local infrastructure, the capacity to pass charges to purchasers, and implications for the design, quantity and location of new housing." They find that planning requirements can affect the cost of housing production and thus the price of completed homes in many ways: from the location and quantity of residential development opportunities in different parts of the city, to the style and density of housing design, to the cost of contributing to local infrastructure and amenities. In Canada, a report from conservative research organization the Fraser Institute posits that a "negative relationship" exists "between regulation and the growth of housing stock" (Green et al. 2016).[1]

The role of these factors becomes particularly significant in regional contexts like that of Vancouver, due to the diversity in approaches to housing development policy amongst the region's 21 municipalities, one electoral area and one treaty

[1]Data on regulation in this study is based upon survey responses from home builders.

First Nation. Recent research conducted by the Metro Vancouver housing policy division reveals that the 15 largest municipalities in the region are, in sum, using a range of over 250 municipal measures to increase affordability, with an additional 30 measures pending adoption (Eberle et al. 2011; Metro Vancouver 2016). While the development and home building industries are quick to point out the constraints that municipal policy and process put on affordable housing supply, municipalities are just as quick to respond that developers continue to profit from development. Indeed, development is currently being approved at historically high levels in Metro Vancouver municipalities (Canadian Press 2016; Connolly 2016).

Following an earlier phase of "roller coaster" growth in Vancouver in the early 1980s, Development Cost Charges (DCCs)[2] were introduced by the Province "to encourage the fair treatment of all firms in the development industry, to reduce uncertainty and to eliminate the appearance of arbitrariness" in the municipal application of fees (Skaburskis 1991: 84). Skaburskis (1990) examined the impact of DCCs on housing cost. The impact of DCCs on housing price at that time was shown to depend upon market conditions; with the kinds of conditions prevalent in Vancouver suggesting that these levies can bring about progressive income redistribution. He notes the secondary effect of these impact fees, namely that they affect different municipalities differently. In a centre-periphery urban growth model, this kind of policy regulatory structure has tended to privilege sprawl and exclusionary development on the urban periphery and density and potentially inclusionary development in the urban core. Metro Vancouver, however, is a polycentric region, in which each of the 21 municipalities has its own growth centre and own planning and development process.

The experience of DCCs gave municipalities confidence in their need for the means to finance growth and ensure a continued quality of life which will maintain demand for new homes. Since the 1990s, municipalities introduced a plethora of new processes, fees and charges to the home development process. Lampert and Denhez (1997: i) found that these costs vary widely across the 26 Canadian municipalities in 10 Provincies and 2 Territories they studied and represent up to $65,000, or close to 20% "of the value of typical modest new single detached and row dwellings in many municipalities." The means by which different municipalities handle the financing and provision of infrastructure varied too; for example, while developers in most parts of Canada install infrastructure within their subdivisions to the municipality's specifications, "there are significant differences among municipalities in the way that developers and municipalities share the costs of financing and installing the required external services" (Lampert and Denhez 1997: i–ii). A study commissioned by CMHC called "Municipal Planning for Affordable

[2]Development Cost Charges (DCCs) (Development Cost Levies within City of Vancouver) are permitted by British Columbia Provincial legislation in order to recuperate the costs incurred in providing new infrastructure in municipal developments. DCCs can be spent on a restricted range of items, specifically water, sewer, drainage, roads and parks. DCCs are a fixed rate charge established by municipal by-law and are levied as part of a subdivision or rezoning on the number of new lots only.

Housing," involved workshops conducted in six urban regions across Canada to compare the utility of six new planning mechanisms aimed at improving affordability of housing (Tomalty et al. 2000). This study found the value of these measures to vary based upon the size and type of housing development, market conditions, surrounding density, and type of policy measure. They found that the mix of approaches used in municipalities often suffered from the lack of an integrated framework to ensure correspondence, coordination and mutual reinforcement of all measures taken.

These studies in the 1980s and 1990s did not include, but noted the additional costs represented by "the important political aspects" (Skaburskis 1990: 175) of charge and policy structures. Such aspects are listed by Lampert and Denhez (1997: v) as: "lengthy land development and approvals process"; "contentious building and land development requirements… including: unnecessary expensive requirements in building codes; requirements for deposits and letters of credit" and "changes in the rules with respect to taxes and charges that apply to the housing industry."

The fuller suite of charges and policy considerations imposed in housing development today includes goals other than efficient land development, paying for growth, and encouraging the private provision of affordable housing. The picture is complicated by changes to the core-periphery model of urban expansion. Typical models of the impact of planning on housing costs are based on a core-periphery view in which land prices decrease with distance from the urban core and price jumps are experienced as agricultural land at the periphery 'flips' to urban uses. What difference does it make to model these effects in a polycentric urban region, with shifting plan and policy priorities as well as diverse resident preferences for low, medium, and high density housing choices? Other goals supported by 15 years of regional land use planning in the Vancouver region include: to promote social mixing and particular ideals of urban design and urban form (though not always well-defined), to encourage energy efficiency and resource conservation, to promote alternatives to the automobile in transportation choices, to preserve green space and heritage, and to support public art and urban 'creativity.' The 'wish list' is growing, but the understanding of how to measure and track our progress toward these goals is lagging behind.

This situation opens up a window for new possibilities to move forward under conditions that no one would claim to be ideal, making the need for accountability, transparency and evaluation, as well as a network-based approach, essential and clear. Private sector housing developers are increasingly being called upon to engage in the provision of more affordable housing in order to contribute to a range of housing options and to meet housing needs of communities. At the same time, municipal development policy and planning structures in place work to ensure quality in developments, incentivize innovation and desirable density and housing forms, and provide enhanced amenity. There is a fine line to be tread here, balancing the values of flexible negotiation versus predictable, clear rules; entrepreneurial municipal governments and regulatory municipal protectors of the long-term public interest; and between the municipal, citizen, private and non-profit sectors in housing provision and housing outcomes. Current research into what is needed to permit the private sector to play a more significant role in the provision of affordable housing in Canadian cities points to the important role of municipalities in "creating a positive planning and policy environment" (Tsenkova and Witwer 2011: 52). A network approach based on an up-to-date and solid foundation of key information can shed light on the complex situation of need in our municipalities and make apparent the different roles that different actors can play most productively toward solutions.

It is in this context that the need for a project like Getting to Groundbreaking emerged. The research questions that launched the G2G project involve investigation of the equity and public value dimensions of the emerging charge, timing and regulatory structure of housing policy approaches in the region. What are the implications of a variable and often unpredictable policy and regulatory context for housing development in the region's municipalities, for the housing type produced, for future investment in housing by the private sector, and for the provision of infrastructure and amenities in our growing region?

6.3 The Inception of Getting to Groundbreaking (G2G)

In 2013, the Greater Vancouver Home Builders Association approached Simon Fraser University Urban Studies researchers for research support in realizing a new project that would compare practices in housing development processing in different municipalities of Metro Vancouver. Initially, the GVHBA thought of this project as a "report card" for municipalities on their performance with respect to the efficiency and cost of their development approval processes. At the same time, the GVHBA recognized the need to engage municipalities as partners in this effort and sought to persuade municipalities of mutual value in doing the work. Creating a network in order to guide the project was the solution decided upon.

The GVHBA describes itself as a member-based residential construction industry representative, offering a liaising role between industry members and municipalities, as well as information transfer, networking, training, and association recognition. The member-composed board structure of GVHBA gives it a strong stake in putting the housing affordability crisis in Metro Vancouver on a path to resolution. In the interests of adding clarity to this debate, and instituting a culture of transparency on both sides of the home building and housing approvals processing equation, the GVHBA recognized the need for an arm's length, research-based review of municipal housing development processing. An additional value of this research partnership for the GVHBA is that its members have a need for this kind of research in order to operate competitively and efficiently in the diverse municipal contexts in the region. SFU Urban Studies entered into Getting to Groundbreaking as research arm and network convenor, with a view to designing a project that could offer objectivity, credibility, and accountability to the experience of housing development processing from both municipal and home builder perspectives.

(i) ***Project Objectives***

The project was designed as a network partnership between the home building industry, represented by both the GVHBA and the Urban Development Institute (UDI),[3] the local authorities of the Metro Vancouver region, and housing researchers. The network structure for this partnership was considered essential due to the political sensitivity of municipal policy and financial sensitivity around private sector residential development economics. On the one hand, this situation called out for an objective third-party approach to the research in the interests of credibility and validity. Confidentiality and integrity could be assured by University-based design and implementation of the survey and associated data collection and analysis accountable to University research ethics regulations (SFU Department of Research Ethics Approval Number 2013s0346). On the other hand, the situation called for personal access, close reading of context, and understanding of relationship dynamics within the development industry in particular, as well as in the relationships between developers and municipal housing policy environments. There was also a need for confidentiality of research findings in the case of the residential development industry data in particular. The network structure engaged the GVHBA and its members on a regular, ongoing basis, via working sessions and formal committee meetings. It also was structured to engage municipalities via presentations to standing committees of the regional government comprised of municipal members, one-on-one engagement with individual municipalities, and regular meetings of the project advisory group.

The specific project objectives of G2G were the following:

- To promote transparency and accountability in the regulation and promotion of a full-spectrum of housing development in the Vancouver region;
- To build a long-term database of the contributions of municipalities and housing developers to a healthy, diverse and adequate housing supply in Metro Vancouver that supports municipal and regional goals;
- To report annually on key indicators, innovations, and areas in need of improvement in municipal housing policy context and conditions, in municipal-development sector relationships, and housing development outcomes;
- To support a culture of predictability and continuous improvement in housing development supply to meet demands and affordability and sustainability aspirations of municipalities and the region; and
- To generate a process in improving housing development information and policy innovation that is scaleable and transferable to other urban regions.

[3]Non-partisan, non-profit development industry and related professions association with a local chapter in Vancouver.

(ii) *The advisory group*

A multistakeholder advisory group was formed as the decision making body for the project. Membership was sought from the diversity of perspectives in key roles related to new housing provision in the Metro Vancouver area. As such, members came from the GVHBA, UDI, private residential development industry, regional and municipal housing policy staff, the non-profit housing sector, and academic housing researchers. Terms of Reference and Data Confidentiality agreements were drafted and reviewed by this group. These included the following items:

1. The specification of intellectual property and data products produced by the study;
2. Information and responsibilities regarding mandatory University Research Ethics guidelines;
3. Access and dissemination rights to research data for board members; and
4. Board member responsibilities and requirements for consent for the publishing of data.

The intent of establishing these agreements with the advisory group was to ensure a collaborative review and decision making process in reporting on project data such that individual members of the project advisory group would be satisfied with the contents of the reports before the reports were published. Additionally, these agreements were intended to ensure that no member of the advisory group could prevent another member from making project data public if they gave notice to the group about their intentions, provided that ethical standards for research were maintained.

(iii) *The project name*

While the GVHBA initially wanted the project to be explicitly named the Report Card, the research team wanted to avoid the perception that the GVHBA was passing judgment on municipalities. Looking for nuance and scope, the research team suggested: From Hammers to Homes, referring to the double meaning of hammers as a necessary tool in home building and also as a particular kind of figurative impact of government regulation. Industry members objected on the practical point that the subject of the analysis was not the hammer-holding stage of home building but instead the preceding period of project planning. Planners on the advisory group suggested the title Planning to Build. This did not meet the approval of members from the industry. A call for anonymous title submissions was made to advisory group members. The winner was ‘Getting to Groundbreaking’, acclaimed by all members as suitable because the portion of the development process being considered was precisely that component that preceded ground-breaking for the initiation of a new home building project. The G2G acronym became the project’s de facto name.

(iv) *Data Collection*

G2G data collection methodology was structured around an annual survey of Metro Vancouver municipal development planners on residential development policies, charges, and approval times. This survey was designed with input from all parties involved in the partnership, via secondary research, and based upon a number of existing partial templates. Additional secondary research was conducted in tandem with survey development, including desk research into the housing stock and development activity and the policy context in each municipality.

The survey included a hypothetical residential development permit application scenario. The first scenario, for the 2014 report, proposed a 22-unit townhome development. The second scenario, reported in 2016, proposed a four-storey 60-unit woodframe apartment building. Both scenarios represent housing forms that are being constructed in considerable numbers in almost every municipality throughout Metro Vancouver. These scenarios were developed as specific and realistic points of reference in the survey in order to standardize interpretation of the survey questions with regard to development charges and timing of the approval process. The survey was piloted with two willing municipalities, presented for vetting by the project advisory group, and then revised and prepared in a web survey format, customized somewhat for the different policy context of the 17 largest municipalities in the Metro Vancouver region.[4]

The research instrument for municipalities consisted of four parts, with the survey designed to elicit objective responses and a follow up interview designed to solicit qualitative perspectives. Part I asked about the housing and planning goals of the municipality and how the regulatory and incentive structure seeks to help meet these goals. Part II asked about the specific design requirements, charges, and processing time associated with three scenario applications, and perceptions of effectiveness and 'bottlenecks' or barriers in this structure. Part III asked about the suite of housing policies and related measures in place and their perceived effectiveness in producing diverse and affordable housing options. Part IV asked for perceptions of the quality of relationships within the system, perceptions of best practices in other municipalities, innovations in-progress, and reflections on the local appetite for greater harmonization.

The survey/interview research instrument for home builders paralleled this structure, asking about the scale and type of home building activity of the firm, the extent to which their activities seek to meet regional housing goals, and the requirements and timing responses of a key municipality in which they work. Home builders also provided their assessment of the effectiveness of the suite of housing policies and related measures in municipalities in which they work, and reflected on their perceptions of the quality of relationships, best practices, desirable innovations, and on their business. The pairwise survey design for this research was key to

---

[4]Vancouver, Surrey, Burnaby, Richmond, Coquitlam, Delta, Langley Township, North Vancouver District, Maple Ridge, New Westminster, Port Coquitlam, City of North Vancouver, West Vancouver, Port Moody, Langley City, White Rock, Pitt Meadows.

permitting the triangulation of municipal responses with responses from the development industry regarding charges, timing, tools and contextual factors at play in housing diversity and affordability results.

For survey respondents, members of the GVHBA were sampled based upon their recent experience with the development scenarios provided, and their experience working in more than one municipality in the region, to provide breadth of perspective.

6.4 Research Results and Reactions

The research resulted in two reports, published in 2014 and 2016. Some key highlights of research findings are presented next.

(i) ***Meeting the region's demand for new homes***

G2G analyzed new housing completion data published for municipalities in the region to determine the change in the mix of new housing being built in recent years. We compared these results against the estimated housing demand modelled in the Regional Growth Strategy (Metro Vancouver 2011). This demonstrated, overall, a slight shortfall of new housing being built compared to regional demand estimates, with Vancouver building far beyond this estimate, other municipalities, notably Surrey, building less, and others building about on target (see Fig. 6.1). Overall, this also showed that the majority of new homes being built region-wide, and in 11 out of 18 local government areas, are apartments rather than ground-oriented homes (see Fig. 6.2).

(ii) ***The impact of fees and charges***

The cost of fees and charges imposed by the development approvals process on new developments was tabulated. We also compared development approvals processing timelines. A challenging, iterative process ensued to determine how to reach an agreeable way to report on this data, because municipal respondents provided best case scenario answers, for those development applications that were able to navigate the complexities of development approvals optimally, whereas developers provided their actual results, which usually were not optimal. Debate also ensued, particularly with respect to the timing of the approvals process, about whether applicants or municipalities typically were responsible for process delays, for a host of reasons.

The results of the fees tabulation (Fig. 6.3) demonstrated a variation between municipalities of over $25,000 per unit. The municipality with the highest fees, Surrey, is experiencing a rapid development rate as it urbanizes from a traditionally suburban municipality with primarily greenfield style tract housing development. The least costly municipality for development fees, Port Moody, is a geographically small municipality predominated by medium density infill development. When we

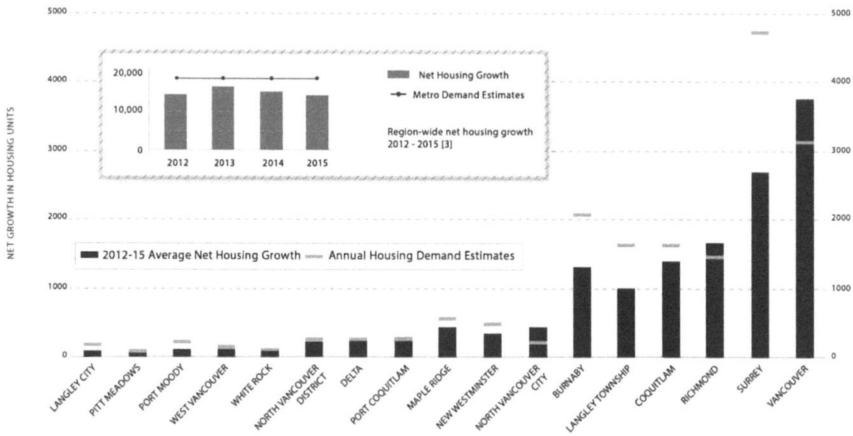

Fig. 6.1 Net housing growth and housing demand estimates in Metro Vancouver, 2012–2015

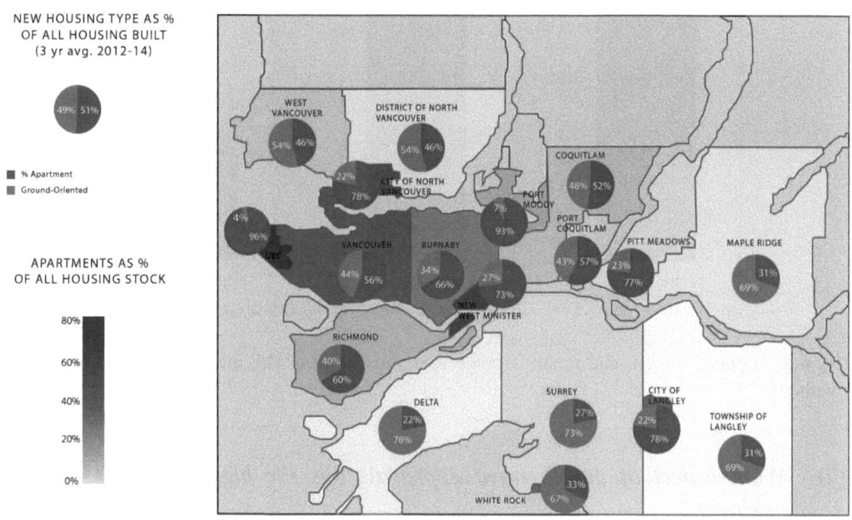

Fig. 6.2 Map of Metro Vancouver showing the proportion of apartments in new housing and in the housing stock

compared the benchmark price of a new home to the cost in fees and charges in each of these municipalities, we found an inverse relationship: in the municipality with the highest fees and charges, home buyers pay lower prices for new town-homes than they do in the municipality with the lowest fees and charges. The difference in median price for a new townhouse was over $136,000 per unit.

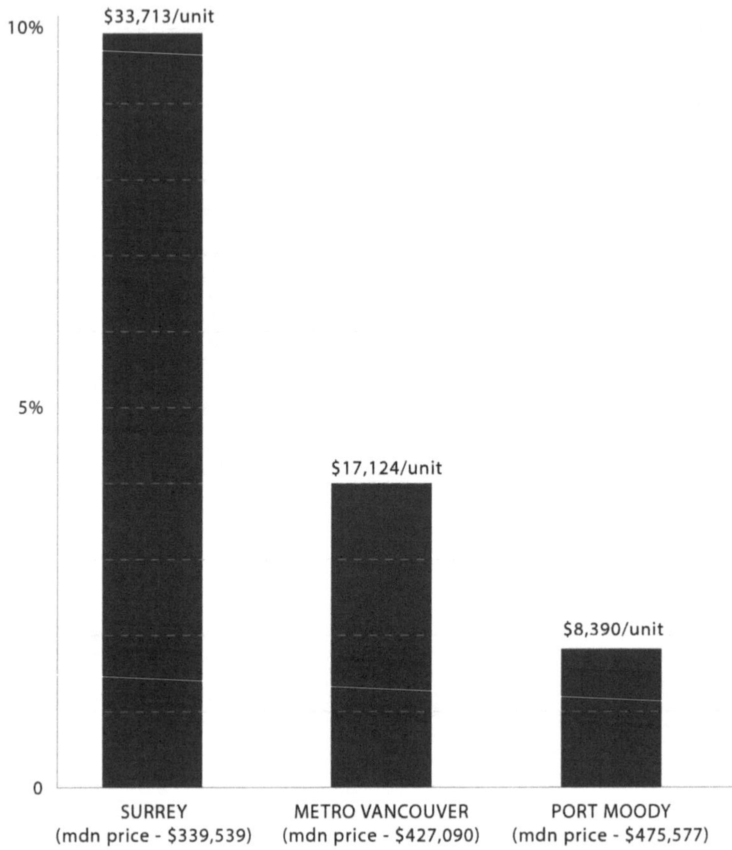

Fig. 6.3 Highest, lowest, and metro average fees and charges, with median selling price of new townhouse

(iii) ***What aspect of development approvals has the biggest impact on your business?***

G2G research demonstrated that when considering the differential impact of higher fees and longer processing time (Figs. 6.4 and 6.5), home builders were more concerned about the impact of long processes on their business. We heard from survey and interview responses that home builders are willing to pay municipal charges for development permitting, but feel that excess time spent in the permitting process is a severe detriment to their ability to supply housing. They responded that extended processing times were causing reduced profit margins, postponing land acquisition, and building less overall.

At the same time, if delays were driving developers as an industry to take their home building activity elsewhere, we would see the queues decreasing in the municipalities with the longest backlogs. This is precisely what is not happening.

Fig. 6.4 Home builder survey responses: In 2011–13, municipal approvals processes timing or fees caused my company to …

What stands out from our research, instead, is that the municipalities with the most development applications are also the municipalities struggling to keep up with the pace of diligent scrutiny and review (Canadian Press 2016). Ergo, without budget or staffing increases, it takes them more time to complete these reviews and grant permits to worthy housing development projects. Moreover, municipal planners emphasized that taking the time to plan for development ensured a successful home building result overall. One planner expressed that rather than an imposition of cost and time to good housing outcomes, "planning is the foundation!"

(iv) ***The Housing Partnership Index***

The desire to construct a report that provided value to both municipal development approvals offices and home builders drove the construction of a Housing Partnership Index for the first round of G2G (Fig. 6.6). Through our process of research and review, the G2G advisory group had developed a shared understanding that what makes a municipality a great place for homebuilding is not a simple formula of low fees and quick processing times. The Housing Partnership Index tried to take this into account through a four point, normalized weighting of scores for (1) total fees

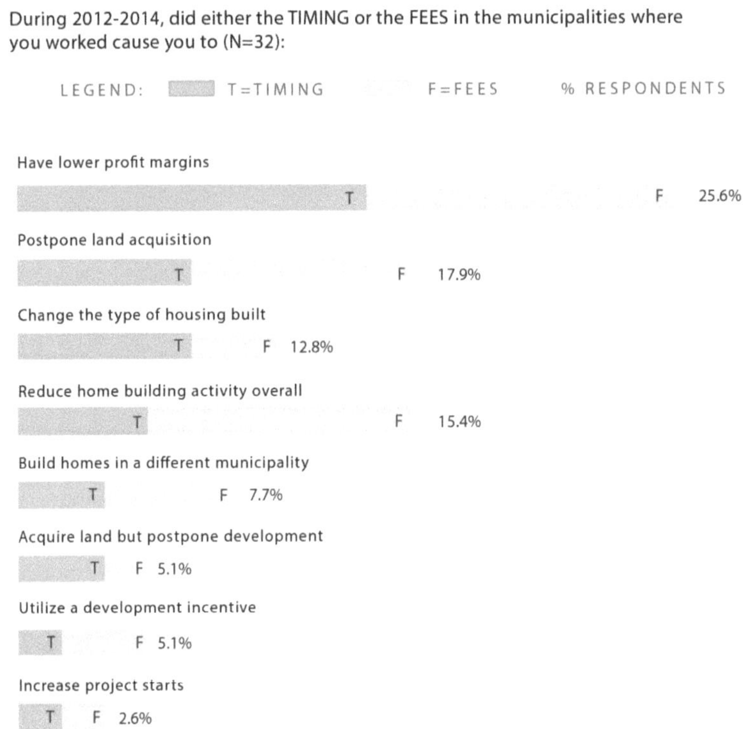

Fig. 6.5 Home builder survey responses: during 2012–2014, did either the TIMING or the FEES in the municipalities where you work cause you to …

and charges, with attention to predictability; (2) overall processing time, with attention to the use of concurrent application processing; (3) estimated score for municipal culture as per qualitative home builder survey response to the request "Describe the culture of the municipalities where you work"; and (4) estimated score for municipal survey response to the question "What factors make your municipality unique when it comes to the residential development approval process?" Because the four items in the index were equally weighted, half of the index score is specific to the housing typology being specifically considered (in this case, townhouses) and half refers to development approvals in general.

The results of this index demonstrated that a municipality's reputation for development processing can come from a number of different efforts specific to different municipal contexts. In Langley Township, for example, a relative abundance of greenfield land and a large number of townhouse development applications in the past three years make the process more streamlined and efficient. Richmond fares well for an effective website and digital communications. Vancouver's good results here were driven by the recognized professionalism and dedication of staff and a high level of clarity of regulations. Port Moody, with very little greenfield land, scored well for lower fees and charges.

Fig. 6.6 Results of the 2014 housing partnership index

HOUSING PARTNERSHIP INDEX

#1 - Langley Township

#2 - Richmond

#3 - Vancouver

#4 - Port Moody

#5 - Coquitlam

#6 - Surrey

#7 - Maple Ridge

#8 - White Rock

#9 - Port Coquitlam

#10 - City of North Vancouver

This construction reflected the expectation and hope of G2G project advisors that participants in building homes and regulating home building, in Metro Vancouver, saw the costs and benefits of this process as a longer term process than a one-shot-deal. The value of a longer-term partnership orientation, even for industry, was clarified well by a comment from a project advisor:

> … many [builders] have longer time horizons. Like planners, they want projects that are livable with good amenities - because that sells. In addition, if they are known as good builders, they are more likely to get a positive response from municipalities and communities when they propose future projects, which may mean faster approval processes. (G2G project advisor)

(v) ***Report Card versus Best Practices***

To take this focus on continuous improvement and engagement one step further, we sought feedback from both municipalities on best practices in the housing development approvals process, as well as ratings of performance on each of these. The best practices that were recommended by both groups included instrumental components of good process, but also elements reflecting a willingness to learn, communicate, reflect on complexities, and attempt to account for some of the intangible values of productive and professional relationships. The additional step of rating municipal performance on these practices demonstrated the places where municipalities and home builders both recognized that improvement was needed, such as improving public engagement and providing clear policy, as well as where there was a mismatch of priorities, such as around the empowerment of municipal staff on specific development files (Fig. 6.7).

Best Practices	How important is it? Municipalities	How are municipalities doing? Home Builders
Improving public engagement	★★★★★★★	👍👍👍
Providing clear policy	★★★★★★★	👍👍👍👍
Providing pre-application meetings	★★★★★★	👍👍👍👍👍👍👍
Providing predictable fees and charges	★★★★★★	👍👍👍👍👍
Building efficient patnerships for development	★★★★★	👍
Having file champions and coordinated teams	★★★★★	👍
Offering concurrent processing	★★★★	👍👍
Enforcing completeness of applications	★★★	👍👍
Empowering municipal staff	★★	👍👍👍👍👍👍
Providing accessible and complete information online	★	👍👍

Fig. 6.7 Recognized best practices and municipal and home builder ratings

6.5 G2G: First Launch to Network Failure

Following the lengthy negotiations around the design of the research instruments and framing of results in the report, the launch of the inaugural report provided the next real test of the strength of the network partnership. It was the test on which the network ultimately failed. The siting, structure and content of the launch event was a matter of considerable negotiation. The ultimate decision was to hold the event early in the morning, downtown, at a University venue. Initially planned as a press conference, the choice was made to stage the event as a panel discussion, followed by a "media scrum." This was done as a compromise between the desire for an event intended to communicate the project and its outcomes and to generate interest in G2G among industry members of the GVHBA and UDI and one intended to communicate the project to the local media. The panel consisted of Holden, whose responsibility was to present a project overview, its outcomes and recommendations, a local government manager, to offer his view of the utility of the project and his own rationale for municipal engagement with G2G, and comments from the CEO of the GVHBA, who also served as moderator of the panel. Rather than provide an opportunity for questions from the public audience of about 200, the decision was made not to engage in any panel or audience discussion following the initial remarks. Instead, reporters were invited up to the stage for more privately fielded questions.

The event itself was successful, in terms of attendance, including a good mix of industry people, municipal people, researchers, elected officials, and some interested members of the public. Most left somewhat confused by the lack of opportunity to discuss the findings of the report at all. It was on the question of how the report was represented in the local media that the major dispute arose. Box 1 provides a vignette of what in retrospect was a critical turning point toward the eventual termination of the project, a year and a half later.

Box 1. Turning point toward network failure

Everything was ready. The GVHBA was staffing the registration table. Urban Studies brought paper copies of the report, slides and notes for presenting the report's findings. Holden was setting her presentation up at the front of the conference room. The Executive Director of the GVHBA approached, anxiously. He asked: "Did you see the cover of the Business Section of the Sun this morning?" referencing the major city newspaper.

The advisory group had discussed an embargo until the day of the launch, and that the GVHBA would focus on the community newspapers, where they had contacts, whereas Urban Studies would focus on the Sun, where they had contacts. Holden had spoken with a Sun reporter in advance of the launch, let him know about the embargo, and encouraged him to come to the launch.

"Oh, is it good?" Holden asked, thinking: All coverage is good coverage for public awareness raising, right?

The man's countenance deepened. "No." He persisted: "How did he get his hands on the report?"

"I spoke to him," Holden replied. "I told him about the embargo."

His eyes became livid. "He broke the embargo?"

Media coverage of the initial G2G report was widespread. The *Vancouver Sun* article that caused such consternation to the GVHBA was entitled: "Housing development approval processes, costs differ greatly across Metro Vancouver" (Constantineau 2014). It led with the line: "Researchers used four measures to produce a Housing Partnership Index that lists the top 10 Metro Vancouver communities for townhouse development."

The *Surrey North Delta Leader* community paper, invited to the launch by the GVHBA, ran the headline: "Report targets high home building fees, red tape" (Nagel 2014). The first line was: "A new study makes the case for reforms to streamline municipal development approvals and restrain fees to help home builders keep pace with housing demand and control prices." The first quote, from the GVHBA President, read: "This is about red tape and getting rid of inefficiencies."

Following the launch of the first G2G report, the research and advisory groups took stock of the project, conducted a limited internal evaluation of their efforts, and renewed the research instruments for round two. The housing typology selected for the second round of research was four-storey woodframe apartments. Resistance to participation from municipalities was higher with this round, and interest in participation from home builders was low. Following numerous delays, the second report was prepared and released.

Media coverage of the second G2G report, released a year and a half after the first report, was muted. In the *Province* newspaper, the GVHBA (De Wit 2016) penned a guest column entitled: "Cut red tape to get new homes built." The subheader read: "MEETING DEMAND: Finding ways to streamline municipal approval process could help bring prices down."

Immediately following the release of this report, the GVHBA informed SFU Urban Studies that the organization was no longer willing to participate in the Getting to Groundbreaking project. With this removal of the founding partner, the project advisory group determined the project itself should be terminated.

G2G, then, after a three year period of intensive collaboration, with productive results and perhaps a needed outlet for considerable tension related to the role of municipal approvals processes in home building activity and outcomes in Metro Vancouver, failed. In the remainder of this chapter, with a view to improving researchers' expectations of multistakeholder partnerships and network approaches to collaborative urban and community indicator efforts, we look into some of the factors that contributed to this failure.

(i) ***Results: Initial excitement, deteriorating support***

G2G received a number of congratulatory comments on the first round of the project. The first report compiled a wealth of diverse data, with a great deal of potential to offer comparability, the identification of best practices across the region, and learning. G2G received the welcome feedback that the report struck a respectful balance in terms of presenting results that did not "take sides" between municipal and home builder perspectives and that thus did not alienate potential future participants. At the same time, the results themselves were seen as little more than the "tip of the iceberg"; that required a good deal more longitudinal support in order to have real value for housing development processing policy and practice in the region.

Comments were collected following the release of the first G2G report in order to inform the revision of the process for follow-up research. As a result, the project advisory group made the following determinations to revise the project:

- The survey was shortened considerably.
- Follow-up interviews with survey participants were determined to present an excessive demand upon participants' time, and were not repeated.
- Communication that this initiative is meant to be a positive learning/sharing experience, not negative comparison, was considered imperative.
- The format of the release event needed changing, to stimulate discussion and consideration.

G2G researchers and project advisors participated in communication work during its start-up phase, in order to garner support and survey and interview completion from a broad base of municipalities and home builders. This work, while successful for an initial round, was not ultimately sustainable. No project advisors were willing to take on this essential, ongoing communications work.

Table 6.1 Divergent interests in goals for the G2G network partnership

Home builder interests in the project	Municipal interests in the project
Are we building sufficient homes to meet expected demand?	Is there demand for this form of housing in this community?
What are the costs of process timing and fees? How are these having an impact on home builders?	Will reduced processing times and/or fees result in any payoffs for municipalities, like increased housing supply and housing affordability?
What is the variation in processing times and fees & charges in municipalities?	What are the legitimate causes of these variations?
Do home builders' and municipal objectives conflict or align on matters of municipal and regional interest?	How is home builder concern for e.g. design, quality, and equity reflected in this report?
How can efficiency (certainty, transparency) be achieved in this process?	How does the process add value to projects and to overall planning goals?
What elements are most time consuming?	What legislated and ethical requirements do municipalities have to meet in this process?
What are best practices that both municipalities and home builders can agree to?	How can municipalities learn from peers in terms of innovation in this area?

Without widespread and continuous commitment to this communications effort, municipal support for further iterations of the project, which was never high, dwindled further. It was rumoured that municipalities that participated in the first round would not do so again, because it was too time consuming and did not benefit them. It was also not clear that the survey was collecting high quality information in all cases, or that the people with the best information were receiving the request to participate. The ultimate goal of the project was not clear; in fact, what the interim evaluation made clear was that there was no agreement on a single goal for the project (Table 6.1). Identification of best practices was seen to be a laudable goal that could receive more emphasis in the continuation of the project, but it was not clear how to turn these results into advice suitable for implementation across the diversity of municipalities and home building companies. The real value of comparing conditions and contexts in different municipalities of the region was called into question.

Without a regulatory or other kind of incentive to continue on the path to partnership, this deeper understanding of the divergence in goals for the project between industry and municipalities suggested it would be difficult to sustain the work.

(ii) ***Results: The Politics of Participation in Indicator Projects***

G2G called into play a distinct politics of participation in research into indicators of performance on development processing. Participation in the G2G effort drew out strongly divergent senses of the motivations and drawbacks for this kind of work, from both home builders and municipalities. The consensus from home builders and industry representatives was that municipalities had no standing to refuse to participate in G2G because of the need for transparency among public bodies and also the sense among those in the industry that there were obvious improvements to development approvals processes that could be made, with just a bit more scrutiny. From this view, to fail to participate in this politically-neutral, information-seeking effort would be to solicit embarrassment. To industry, municipalities ought to recognize that development activity was key to the quality of life they could offer, and seek to minimize their expenditures of tax dollars on things that would inhibit this activity.

From the municipal perspective, by contrast, the G2G effort was extremely political and, in fact, ran the risk of simply pitting municipalities against one another in a zero sum game for faster and cheaper processes that might lower the bar for the quality of outcomes over all. Regardless of what municipalities might do to improve their work, it was the nature of the development industry to always seek for it to be done faster and more cheaply, so there was no way for municipalities to "win" via participation. Indeed, the results of the first round of research did appear to have a "backfiring" impact on the industry, as one of the municipalities, White Rock, determined from the results that their fees were too far below the regional average, and increased them. There was political capital to be gained in this direction, too, because this demonstrated the confidence of the municipality to capture the windfall from development in order to help pay for the infrastructure and amenities needed locally in the public interest.

One municipality, Maple Ridge, responded to the release of the first report in the way the G2G advisory committee had hoped: it struck a new development advisory committee of both industry and municipal representatives and made progress on the practices identified in the G2G report (Fig. 6.7) the committee's agenda for its first year.

6.6 Discussion and Conclusion

The G2G effort was an innovative and collaborative effort in generating new indicators via a network partnership, that shed new light on a complex and highly politicized debate about planning, housing development, affordability, and quality of life in the Metro Vancouver region. In its first three years, the project generated considerable excitement among partners, as well as consternation and a desire to control the results. It generated useful data, some of which contradicted widely-held views about the relationship between the cost of fees and charges and the cost of housing. It drove some changes in policy amongst the Metro Vancouver municipalities, although not always in expected ways. It generated a better informed debate about the role of housing development approvals processes in housing activity outcomes.

Everyone involved in G2G recognized the project as contentious from its outset. No one on the G2G advisory group table held illusions about any neutral status of the data being collected. It was the presentation, juxtaposition, and interpretation that was the stuff of negotiation from the start. The checks and balances provided by the diverse perspectives of different members of the partnership network were the way in which this indicators effort sought to guard against different "cooking" methods of data that could never be "raw" (Bowker 2005). The research team, in this politicized domain, played not so much the neutral moderator's role as the role of "poultice" for the festering frustrations of both municipalities and home builders. The project and its research provided a focal place to air frustrations about this set of tangled issues, which had not previously had a public outlet. We cannot say, following the failure of the network and the project after its first three years, that the project successfully persuaded anyone that a collaborative approach could be an effective and productive means to improve the governance of housing planning and development, nor that the possibility of consensus might exist between industry and municipal perspectives.

From a research perspective, our work provides ample evidence that, in the Metro Vancouver region, residents' quality of life benefits from the existence of a robust regulatory and planning framework. Regional planning, official community planning, neighbourhood planning, and long-term policy processes work to meet increasing expectations and provide opportunities for municipalities, residents and home builders to engage in big picture, long term thinking. The residential development approvals process fits within this larger structure to navigate the layers of expectations for an individual development approval process. Notably, the research demonstrated that the efficiency and cost of the impacts of municipal housing development processes and policy cannot be considered to pertain automatically to affordability. There are no guarantees that cost savings from reduced expenses in the development process are passed on to home buyers (Sherlock 2013). G2G research demonstrated, if anything, an inverse relationship. At the heart of the question of good regulatory process for homebuilding is the distribution of risks and rewards between the public (local government) and the private sector (the home building industry).

In efforts such as G2G, which crack open politically-fraught questions with the promise of neutral data and collaborative analysis, it is important to keep in mind Donald Campbell's Law (1979): "The more any quantitative social indicator is used for social decision-making, the more subject it will be to corruption pressures and the more apt it will be to distort and corrupt the social processes it is intended to monitor." The call for better indicators and more data can be a call to exert control and standardization over a situation that needs something other than more discipline in order to improve. Some enter into indicators partnerships in order to attempt to manage complex processes from afar, by disciplining under-performance as determined by quantitative, though still subjective, targets (Craglia et al. 2004). This kind of new managerial approach flies in the face of the real work of collaboration in a partnership of equals, which demands a sense of willingness to seek new knowledge and understandings that may threaten existing ones, and to forego the will to control outcomes completely.

6.7 Coda: The Network, Post-failure

Following the termination of the project, the GVHBA approached SFU researchers with the idea of nominating the project for a Land Award, a competitive award given by the Real Estate Foundation of BC, an early project funder. An application was prepared collaboratively and submitted, nominating the GVHBA as the project initiator. Following its deliberations, the Real Estate Foundation of BC decided not to award the project the prize. They provided the following reason:

> The Land Awards were created to celebrate projects that demonstrate leadership, innovation and collaboration in sustainable land use. The Getting to Groundbreaking series demonstrates each of these qualities and the committee was particularly impressed by the depth and detail of the reports, and the connections drawn between development, sustainability and affordability. Ultimately, the judges felt that the reports were excellent examples of best practices, but fit very closely with GVHBA's portfolio of work.

There is a clear irony in the divergent perception of this project as, from the GVHBA perspective, too risky and beyond direct control, and from an external perspective, too overtly self-serving of this industry association's goals.

Acknowledgements The author gratefully acknowledges funding support provided for the G2G project by the federal MITACS internship program, the Real Estate Foundation of BC, and the GVHBA. Research assistance was provided by Terry Sidhu, Sébastien Froment, Jacint Simon, Sophie Fung, Daniel Sturgeon and Julia Hulbert. Finally, thanks go to all project advisors and municipal and industry participants.

References

Bowker, G. C. (2005). *Memory practices in the sciences*. Cambridge: MIT Press.

Campbell, D. T. (1979). Assessing the impact of planned social change. *Evaluation and Program Planning, 2*(1), 67–90.

Canadian Press. (2016). *Record number of building permits issued amid Vancouver construction boom*. http://www.ctvnews.ca/business/record-number-of-building-permits-issued-amid-vancouver-construction-boom-1.2736007. Accessed January 13, 2016.

City of Calgary. (2013). *Cost of growth: The Calgary experience*. Ottawa: FCM Sustainable Communities Conference. https://www.fcm.ca/Documents/presentations/2013/SCC2013/Implications_of_Alternative_Growth_Patterns_on_Infrastructure_Cost_EN.pdf. Accessed February 28, 2013.

Conference Board of Canada. (2010). *Building from the ground up: Enhancing affordable housing in Canada*. Ottawa.

Connolly, J. (2016). *Residential building starts and permits continue to soar: CMHC, StatCan*. REW.ca news. http://www.rew.ca/news/residential-building-starts-and-permits-continue-to-soar-cmhc-statcan-1.2192937. Accessed March 8, 2016.

Constantineau, B. (2014). *Housing development approval processes costs differ greatly across Metro Vancouver*. Vancouver Sun. http://www.vancouversun.com/business/affordability/Housing+development+approval+processes+costs+differ+greatly+across+Metro/10437736/story.html. Accessed December 2, 2014.

Craglia, M., Leontidou, L., Nuvolati, G., & Schweikart, J. (2004). Towards the development of quality of life indicators in the 'digital' city. *Environment and Planning B, 31*(1), 51–64.

Dalton, T. (2009). Housing policy retrenchment: Australia and Canada compared. *Urban Studies, 46*(1), 63–91.

De Wit, B. (2016). *Cut red tape to get new homes built.* The Province. http://www.pressreader.com/canada/the-province/20160421/281754153500949. Accessed April 21, 2016.

Eberle, M., Woodward, J., Thomson, M. & Kraus, D. (2011, June). *Municipal measures for housing affordability and diversity in metro Vancouver.* Burnaby: CMHC External Research Program.

Glaeser, E. L., & Ward, B. A. (2009). The causes and consequences of land use regulation: Evidence from Greater Boston. *Journal of Urban Economics, 65*(3), 265–278.

Gordon, J. (2016). *Vancouver's housing affordability crisis causes, consequences and solutions.* Vancouver: SFU Centre for Public Policy Research. https://www.sfu.ca/content/dam/sfu/mpp/pdfs/Vancouver%27s%20Housing%20Affordability%20Crisis%20Report%202016%20Final%20Version.pdf. Accessed September 28, 2016.

Green, K. P., Filipowicz, J., Lafleur, S., & Herzog, I. (2016). *The impact of land-use regulation on housing supply in Canada.* Vancouver: Fraser Institute. https://www.fraserinstitute.org/sites/default/files/impact-of-land-use-regulation-on-housing-supply-in-canada.pdf. Accessed September 28, 2016.

Harcourt, M., Cameron, K., & Rossiter, S. (2007). *City making in paradise: Nine decisions that saved Vancouver.* Vancouver: Douglas & MacIntyre.

Hulchanski, D., & Shapcott M., (Eds). (2004). *Finding room: Policy options for a Canadian rental housing strategy.* University of Toronto, Centre for Urban and Community Studies.

Ihlanfelt, K. (2007). The effect of land use regulation on housing and land prices. *Journal of Urban Economics, 61*(3), 420–435.

Lampert, G., & Denhez, M. (1997). *Levies, fees, charges, taxes and transaction costs on new housing.* Ottawa: Canada Mortgage and Housing Corporation and Canadian Home Builders' Association.

Metro Vancouver Regional District. (2011). *Regional growth strategy.* Burnaby.

Metro Vancouver Regional District. (2016). *Regional affordable housing strategy.* Burnaby. http://www.metrovancouver.org/services/regional-planning/PlanningPublications/RegionalAffordableHousingStrategy2016.pdf. Accessed May 27, 2016.

Nagel, J. (2014). *Report targets high home building fees, red tape.* Surrey Leader. http://www.surreyleader.com/news/284773541.html. Accessed December 4, 2014.

Ruiz, D., & Smooke, J. (2014). *Developers aren't going to solve the housing crisis in San Francisco.* Truthout Media. http://www.truth-out.org/news/item/26656-developers-aren-t-going-to-solve-the-housing-crisis-in-san-francisco-the-definitive-response-to-supply-side-solutionists. Accessed October 8, 2014.

Ruming, K., Gurran, N., & Randolph, B. (2011). Housing affordability and development contributions: New perspectives from industry and local government in New South Wales, Victoria and Queensland. *Urban Policy and Research, 29*(3), 257–274.

Sherlock, T. (2013). *City fees add to Metro Vancouver's housing-cost disparity.* Vancouver Sun. Online: http://www.vancouversun.com/business/affordability/City+fees+Metro+housing+cost+disparity+Vancouver/8363876/story.htm. Accessed May 10, 2013.

Skaburskis, A. (1990). The burden of development impact fees. *Land Development Studies, 7*(3), 173–185.

Skaburskis, A. (1991). The design of development cost charge schedules. *Journal of Property Research, 8*(1), 83–98.

Thompson, D. (2013). *Suburban Sprawl: Exposing Hidden Costs, Identifying Innovations.* Ottawa: Sustainable Prosperity, University of Ottawa. Retrieved from: http://thecostofsprawl.com/report/SP_SuburbanSprawl_Oct2013_opt.pdf. Accessed October 31, 2013.

Tomalty, R., Hertz, A., & Spurr, P. (2000). Municipal planning for affordable housing. *Research Highlights, 63,* 00–42.
Tsenkova, S., & Witwer, M. (2011). Bridging the gap: Policy instruments to encourage private sector provision of affordable rental housing in Alberta. *Canadian Journal of Urban Research, 20*(1), 52–80.

Author Biography

Meg Holden, Ph.D. is a social scientist whose research investigates the promises and results of sustainability planning in cities around the world. She is an Associate Professor of urban studies and geography at Simon Fraser University in Vancouver, Canada. Meg served as a board member of the Community Indicators Consortium from 2011 to 2016 and she currently serves as editorial board member of the journal *Applied Research in Quality of Life* as well as the Springer book series on Community Quality of Life and Wellbeing. Meg is the author of *Pragmatic Justifications for the Sustainable City: Acting in the common place* (Routledge, 2017). Meg obtained the Ph.D. in Public and Urban Policy from the New School for Social Research.

Part II
Community Indicators Identifying Different Types of Disadvantage

Chapter 7
Environmental Justice in Australia: Measuring the Relationship Between Industrial Odour Exposure and Community Disadvantage

Lucy Dubrelle Gunn, Billy Greenham, Melanie Davern, Suzanne Mavoa, Elizabeth Jean Taylor and Mark Bannister

Abstract Community impact and environmental justice issues are examined across metropolitan Melbourne, Australia, using 2008–2011 self-reported odour complaint data as a direct measure of odour pollution exposure. Differences in pollution exposure and indicators of socio-economic disadvantage were compared across areas using spatial clustering and statistical analyses. Results found that odour affected areas have greater socio-economic disadvantage supporting the existence of environmental justice issues in metropolitan Melbourne. Commonly used buffers of 1 km surrounding polluting facilities under-represent odour affected areas. Findings have implications for urban planning and policy in establishing separation distances between residential and industrial zones in new and existing developments where guidelines are lacking.

L.D. Gunn (✉) · B. Greenham · M. Davern · S. Mavoa
McCaughey VicHealth Community Wellbeing Unit, Melbourne School of Population and Global Health, The University of Melbourne, Melbourne, VIC 3010, Australia
e-mail: lucy.gunn@unimelb.edu.au

B. Greenham
e-mail: billyg@pgrad.unimelb.edu.au

M. Davern
e-mail: mdavern@unimelb.edu.au

S. Mavoa
e-mail: suzanne.mavoa@unimelb.edu.au

E.J. Taylor
Centre for Urban Research, Royal Melbourne Institute of Technology, Melbourne, VIC, Australia
e-mail: elizabeth.taylor@rmit.edu.au

M. Bannister
Environment Protection Authority Victoria, Melbourne, VIC, Australia
e-mail: mark.bannister@epa.vic.gov.au

M. Holden et al. (eds.), *Community Quality-of-Life Indicators: Best Cases VII*, Community Quality-of-Life and Well-Being,
DOI 10.1007/978-3-319-54618-6_7

Keywords Indicators · Environmental justice · Socioeconomic disadvantage · Odour pollution

7.1 Introduction

7.1.1 Background

The environmental justice movement is a response to the disproportionate burden of pollution and environmental hazards affecting the health and wellbeing of poor and minority populations, and the lack of voice and protection afforded to them through legal and political systems (Mohai et al. 2009). Early research examined the location of polluting facilities in African-American and Hispanic communities (USGAO 1983) which was later expanded to a national study by the United Church of Christ's Commission for Racial Justice investigating race, ethnicity, and income (Chavis and Lee 1987). Since then descriptive, spatial, and regression analyses have been used to test for correlations between polluting facilities and socio-economically disadvantaged areas in the US and other countries (Maantay 2002; Schlosberg and Carruthers 2010). Much research has used air inventory data as measures of air pollution with no focus on odour. Furthermore, little research exists using odour complaint data, although many countries collect and use these data for determining odour issues (RDWI Air Inc. 2005; Kaye and Jiang 2000; Nicell 2009; Schauberger et al. 2006).

7.1.2 Existing Environmental Justice Methods: Advancements and Limitations

Spatial coincidence is a form of proximity-based analysis using the location of polluting facilities based on administrative boundaries such as census tract, municipality boundary, or postal/zip code area as a measure for exposure (Chakraborty et al. 2011). Spatial coincidence has a number of limitations: it assumes polluting facilities have equal effect; ignores the type and quantity of polluting facilities present; and does not account for cross-boundary exposure or "edge effect problems," which over-simplifies results (Bolin et al. 2002).

Proximity-based analysis uses a buffer around a polluting facility and negates the edge effect problem of buffers crossing into administrative boundaries without polluting facilities (Mohai et al. 2009). Proximity-based analyses also have limitations, mainly because true pollution exposure from proximity is complex and difficult to measure (Maantay 2002). Nevertheless, buffer zones are commonly set at 1 mile or a range of values from 500 m up to 5 km (Chakraborty et al. 2011). Buffer zones of different sizes can also lead to different exposures and research results, therefore it is important to evaluate the sensitivity of buffer distances

(Sheppard et al. 1999). Furthermore, exposure to pollution might be unequally distributed or influenced by a range of factors including: meteorological conditions; such as wind speed and direction; the type and quantity of facility and pollution being emitted; and site conditions such as the height of smoke stacks affecting the measurement of exposure (Maantay 2002).

Risk-based analysis is another approach that measures the dispersion of pollution with plume based methods being an example (Chakraborty and Armstrong 1997; Mohai et al. 2009). Limitations associated with risk based analysis are difficulties in sourcing data and the use of complex methodology which can make them challenging to use. Hence, even though the approach has provided methodological advancements, it can be difficult to establish a causal link between pollution exposure and health outcomes (Maantay 2007).

7.1.3 Odour Pollution Exposure

Although difficult, the measurement of odour pollution is important as odour is understood to be a stressor of wellbeing even though long term physical effects remain unclear (EPAV 2015a). Odour is pervasive and can lead to headaches, nausea, stress, and can restrict the daily activities of people to such an extent as to warrant regulation (Nicell 2009; Shusterman 1999). Furthermore, half of all air pollution complaints in the US are related to odour (Henshaw et al. 2006). Odour can be measured objectively through the use of field assessments, portable olfactometers or scentometers that are used to detect and measure odour dilution. A complexity of odour monitoring and measurement is that odour is subjectively observable and can be construed as a nuisance or annoyance by some people and not concern others. Consequently, the health risk presented by odour is determined by a detectable threshold – this means that when it is noticeable, it is having an impact. This provides a rationale for using odour complaints as a strong proxy measure of odour exposure that circumnavigates issues of objective measurement, which do not account for the true spatial extent or offensiveness of odour which can be perceived to be more or less offensive by different people (Nicell 2009). Consistent with this understanding, this study employs the use of georeferenced individual level odour complaints as a direct measure of odour pollution exposure in the Australian context.

7.1.4 Spatial Correlation Between Polluting Facilities and Odour Pollution Exposure

The spatial distribution of odour complaints can be used to define an estimated buffer zone for odour pollution exposure. This allows the buffer to be data driven and implicitly accounts for long term meteorological, topographical and site conditions. Many residential areas in Australia are co-located with industrial zones releasing noxious gases and odour from industries such as tanneries, wool scouring, blubber rendering, meat processing, timber and paper mills, paint manufacturing, and petroleum refineries among others (Byrne and MacCallum 2013). In many locations, close proximity of residential areas to several odour polluting facilities makes establishing the cause of the odour difficult. However, the number of odour complaints surrounding industrial zones yields a clear indicator of odour pollution exposure useful for measuring environmental justice issues within and across different communities.

In Australia, previous research into environmental justice issues has focused on lead emissions from mining in Mt Isa (Mackay et al. 2013) and the metal smelters at Port Pirie (Taylor and Schniering 2010) while more recent research has used national pollution inventory data (Chakraborty and Green 2014a, b). However, Australian research has not examined the spatial correlation between odour complaints, polluting facilities and socio-economic disadvantage.

Analysing the spatial distribution of odour complaints could reveal the extent of odour exposure and identify whether odour-affected communities differ from the rest of the population based on socio-economic characteristics. Furthermore, greater understanding about the spatial distribution of odour could be used to devise future pollution mitigation strategies and inform urban planning and policy about separation distances between industrial and residential zones. This is particularly important for urban development areas where encroachment occurs between industrial and residential zones in response to increased population growth and urban sprawl development.

7.1.5 Study Objective

This study examines the distribution of odour exposure measures using georeferenced individual level odour complaint data, indicators of socio-economic disadvantage, and the location of polluting facilities within metropolitan Melbourne, Australia. Results are used to evaluate the extent of environmental justice issues in the Australian context and provide recommendations for urban planning policy.

7.2 Data and Methods

7.2.1 Odour Complaint Data and Pollution Data

The Environment Protection Agency Victoria (EPAV) is a statutory authority established in 1971 under the *Environment Protection Act 1970*. It makes regulatory decisions under the Act and is responsible for concordant compliance and enforcement (EPAV 2015b). The EPAV provided self-reported data on odour complaints and the location of polluting facilities from 2008 to 2011. The EPAV provides a 24-hour hotline with complaints of noise and odour recorded with georeferenced location across the State of Victoria, Australia. 9215 odour complaints were reported across the 3 year period, and for 4517 of these reports, the polluting facility causing the odour was confirmed by an EPAV field trip.

Polluting facilities data included georeferenced locations of 117 scheduled and 29 problem premises. Scheduled premises are large facilities requiring EPAV licenses and work permits aligned to activities that potentially cause adverse environmental impacts while problem premises have previously been issued a pollution abatement notice by the EPAV. Eleven smaller premises that were non-scheduled or not problem premises were also included in the polluting facilities dataset. Industries of the 157 polluting facilities included landfills, sewerage treatment, composting, food and other animal intensive activities, with a smaller number relating to petroleum, chemicals and aerosols.

7.2.2 Indicators of Socio-economic Disadvantage

Six indicators of socio-economic disadvantage were used to understand the characteristics of communities affected by odour pollution. These included vulnerable age, which was defined as people aged less than 15 or greater than 65 years of age to represent people most susceptible to negative health impacts from pollution (Medina-Ramón and Schwartz 2008).

Household income determines the economic status of a household and influences quality of life and provides the resources to cover basic necessities such as food, shelter and health care. Vulnerable income was defined as the percentage of household incomes in the lowest 3 deciles for Victoria corresponding to between $A400 ($A20,800 annually) and $A799 per week ($A41,599 annually).

English proficiency describes an individual's ability to use a common language for communication. Being unable to communicate is a barrier to completing everyday activities and can lead to social isolation. Being able to communicate is particularly important for self-reported pollution monitoring. Poor English proficiency was defined as the percentage of total respondents from the 2011 ABS Census indicating their standard of spoken English was "Not well" or "Not at all."

The Socio Economic Indexes for Areas (SEIFA) are compiled by the Australian Bureau of Statistics (ABS). SEIFA are area level indexes that rank areas on the basis of relative socio-economic advantage or disadvantage. Area level indexes aid comparisons between areas based on disadvantage and are useful in determining the existence of environmental justice issues. Area level socio-economic disadvantage indicators were derived from the 2011 ABS *Census of Population and Housing 2011* (ABS 2011) at the Statistical Area Level 1 (SA1) for metropolitan Melbourne.

SA1 is the smallest unit for Census data and includes between 200 and 800 people with an average of 400 people and an average size of 1 km^2. It is also the geographic level on which SEIFA data are recommended for use in contextual analyses such as this (ABS 2013). To minimize bias, 288 SA1s with population counts less than 20 or missing SEIFA data were removed (Chakraborty and Green 2014a). Analyses were conducted using 8781 remaining SA1s. SEIFA included in analyses are the Index for Relative Social Disadvantage (IRSD), Index for Economic Resources (IER) and Index for Educational Opportunities (IEO) (ABS 2013).

7.2.3 *Methods*

7.2.3.1 Clustering Methods

Odour complaints were spatially mapped then clustered using two common techniques: K-Means and Nearest Neighbour Hierarchical (NNH) clustering (Levine 2010). The NNH technique clusters data on a pre-set minimum number of data-points with clusters formed based on a threshold distance parameter between data-points. The K-Means technique clusters data into groups based on a pre-set number of clusters determined a priori. The main drawback of this technique is that determining the number of clusters is arbitrary and often unknown. Both techniques were used, however the NNH technique was preferred as it does not require the number of clusters to be specified a priori. Visual inspection and preliminary cluster formation on the odour complaint data confirmed that this approach fitted the location of odour complaints well (Fig. 7.1).

Initially, NNH clusters were examined based on a minimum number of data-points including: 10; 20; 50 and 100 odour complaints. These values were trialled because the optimal number of odour complaints needed to determine clusters was unknown. Visual inspection of clusters formed using 10 odour complaints revealed that these clusters were too small to be representative of a community affected by odour. In comparison, clusters formed using a minimum of 100 odour complaints covered an area that was too large and didn't capture the localized issue of odour. Convex hull clusters formed using a minimum of 20 and 50 odour complaints appeared to visually fit the data well. Convex hull clusters describe polygons representing all odour complaints contained within a cluster. Once these clusters were identified cluster analysis was completed using Crimestat IV software with distance parameters tested across the full range of settings (Levine 2010).

7.2.3.2 Statistical Approach

Three statistical tests were completed to determine whether people exposed to odour were more socio-economically disadvantaged than people living in areas less

Fig. 7.1 **a** Clayton South, metropolitan Melbourne, Australia: Nearest Neighbour Hierarchical clusters based on a minimum of 20 odour complaints, Clayton South, metropolitan Melbourne. **b** Clayton South, metropolitan Melbourne, Australia

exposed to odour. Tests included: the Spearman rank correlation test; t-tests comparing communities with and without exposure to odour; and t-tests comparing the number of odour complaints within communities.

Relationships between the number of odour complaints, polluting facilities and the socio-economic disadvantage indicators were examined using the Spearman rank correlation test (Chakraborty and Green 2014b). In these analyses, the number of polluting facilities impacting on SA1s within a 1 km boundary were included to adjust for the "edge effect problem" (Chakraborty and Green 2014a).

The use of t-tests to compare means in areas with and without odour exposure follows established methods used previously (Chakraborty and Green 2014a). SA1s intersecting with NNH clusters were selected using polygon containment and used to represent odour exposed areas (Chakraborty et al. 2011) with remaining SA1s representing areas less exposed to odour.

T-tests were also used to compare differences in the number of odour complaints (odour intensity) and socio-economic disadvantage indicators. Odour intensity is measured using three groups: SA1s with no odour complaints; SA1s with ≤ 20 odour complaints; and a high exposure group containing SA1s with >20 odour complaints. An absolute threshold value of 20 was chosen as a reasonable number of minimum influence particularly when percentiles can change between samples making it harder to translate into policy contexts (Lamb and White 2015).

7.3 Results

7.3.1 Clustering of Odour Complaint Data

GIS analysis revealed single odour complaints made from unique residential locations. However for some residential locations, multiple complaints were made suggesting that some households are more engaged in reporting odour offences than others. The impact of multiple complaints from single residential locations on the formation of clusters was also examined. Slightly larger clusters were formed when using unique odour complaints than clusters based on all available data including multiple complaints. This is consistent with the requirement for a cluster to grow to satisfy the NNH clustering criteria. Due to the similarity in clusters, only clusters associated with all available odour complaint data, including multiple complaints, were considered further.

A case study from the Clayton South area is presented in Fig. 7.1. This area is characterized by landfills, market gardens, compost areas and industrial zones known to cause odour problems. Convex hull clusters based on a minimum of 20 odour complaints with a R5 = 0.75 distance threshold setting in Crimestat IV yielded the best clusters visually. However, clusters based on a minimum of 50 odour complaints with a L5 = 0.05 distance threshold setting were also appropriate. The clusters based on a minimum of 20 odour complaints shown in Fig. 7.1a cover more odour complaints and area than clusters based on a minimum of 50 odour complaints, shown in Fig. 7.1b.

Figure 7.1 reveals a greater intensity of odour complaints in the north and south east residential areas surrounding the Clayton South industrial zone corresponding to the suburbs of Clarinda, Clayton South and Dingley Village. There are few odour complaints in the south west area, due to it being non-residential and zoned as 'other land uses,' which include golf courses and market gardens.

The maps and odour clusters indicate the extent of odour exposure and the separation distances potentially required to mitigate odour impacts. Figure 7.1 shows that a 1 km buffer around polluting facilities does not fully capture odour clusters. However, for some polluting facilities a 1 km buffer can be sufficient and appears to be related to the size and type of the polluting facility as shown in Fig. 7.2. Figure 7.2a shows odour complaints and clusters associated with the Hallam Road Landfill. Figure 7.2b shows several facilities in the Alphington area relating to the Amcor paper processing plant which closed in late 2012. In the Bellfield area shown in Fig. 7.2b, odour complaints relate to a food packaging manufacturer.

Separation distances may be more difficult to determine for large industrial zones with multiple polluting facilities, as the source of odour pollution is likely to come from multiple sources. Nevertheless, odour complaint clusters offer insight into the areas and distances from the source that are exposed to odour. For the Clayton South area, the odour complaint clusters are better captured using a 2 km buffer from the centre of the polluting facilities as shown in Fig. 7.3.

7.3.2 Maps of Socio-Economic Disadvantage Indicators

Figure 7.4a–c shows that residents in Clarinda and Clayton South have greater disadvantage compared to the south eastern suburb of Dingley Village. Communities affected by odour have unique socio-economic disadvantage characteristics and this is evident in other industrials zones across metropolitan Melbourne including Hobson's Bay and Dandenong South (not presented).

Vulnerable income shown in Fig. 7.4d is proximally related to the industrial zone and surrounding odour complaint clusters. Figure 7.4e shows that the Clarinda and Clayton South areas have higher proportions of poor English proficiency compared to areas in Dingley Village. However, vulnerable age has a greater range of values across the SA1 areas shown in Fig. 7.4f and it is not clear whether disadvantage exists for this indicator.

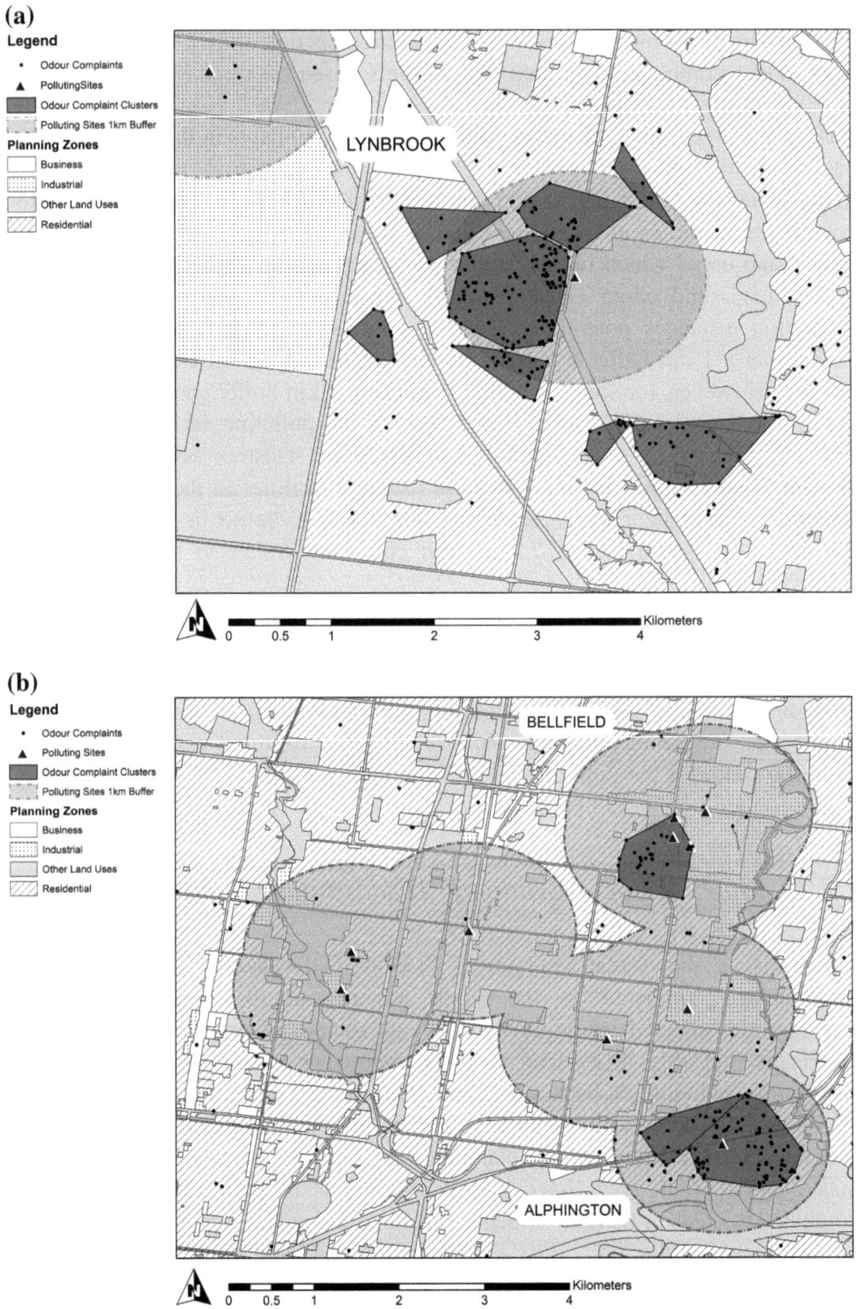

Fig. 7.2 **a** Hallam Road landfill in Lynbrook, metropolitan Melbourne, Australia. **b** Amcor site in Alphington, metropolitan Melbourne, Australia

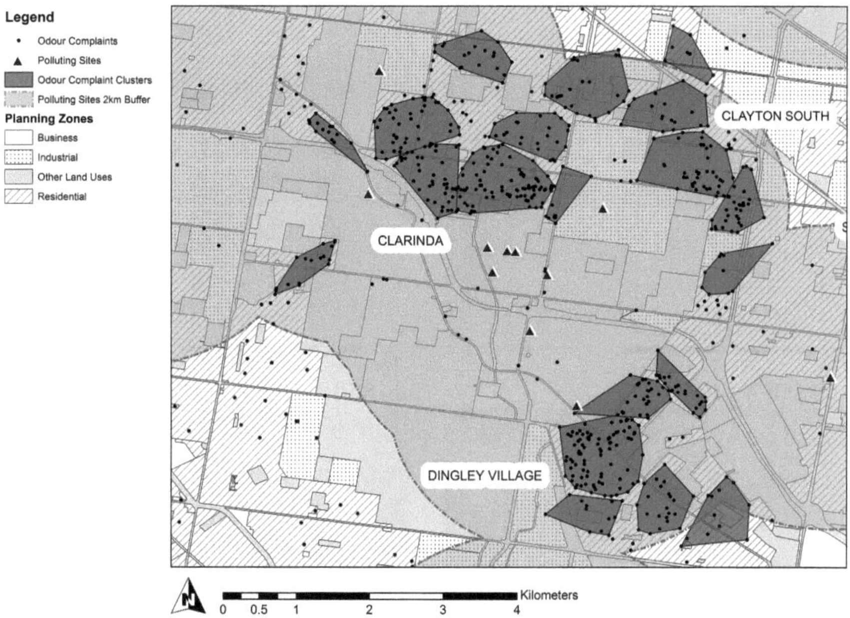

Fig. 7.3 2 km circular buffers surrounding polluting facilities, Clayton South, metropolitan Melbourne, Australia

7.3.3 Correlations of Odour Complaints, Polluting Facilities and Socio-Demographic Disadvantage Data

Table 7.1 provides results for the Spearman's rank correlation tests. Significantly negative correlations are present between the number of odour complaints, the number of polluting facilities and the 3 SEIFA indexes. Remaining results suggest higher percentages of people with low incomes or poor English proficiency live in areas with large numbers of odour complaints or polluting facilities. The correlation between the number of odour complaints and vulnerable age is significantly negative (r = −0.030) indicating that the proportion of people aged below 15 and greater than 65 years is lower in areas where odour complaints were made. However, the correlation between vulnerable age and the number of polluting facilities (r = 0.010) was not significant.

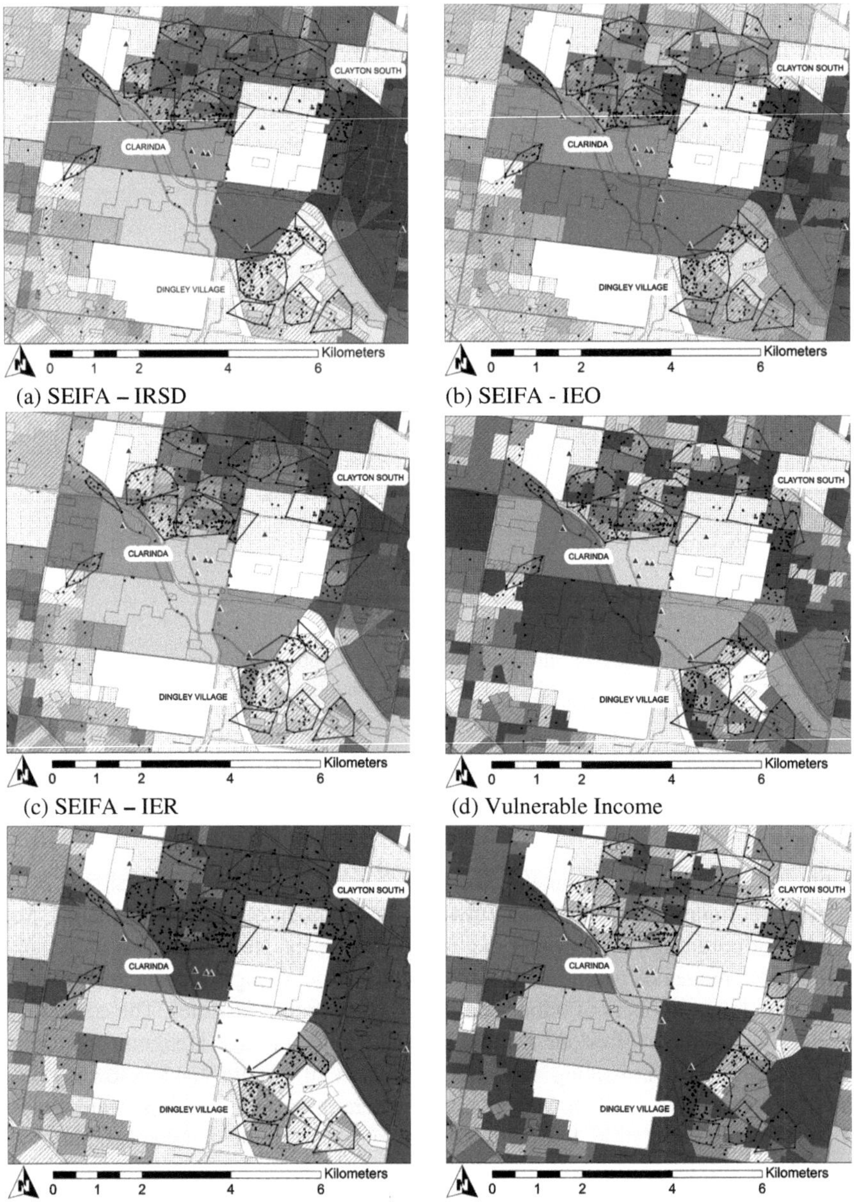

(a) SEIFA – IRSD

(b) SEIFA - IEO

(c) SEIFA – IER

(d) Vulnerable Income

(e) Poor English Proficiency

(f) Vulnerable Age

Fig. 7.4 Maps of socio-economic disadvantage indicators, Clayton South, metropolitan Melbourne, Australia

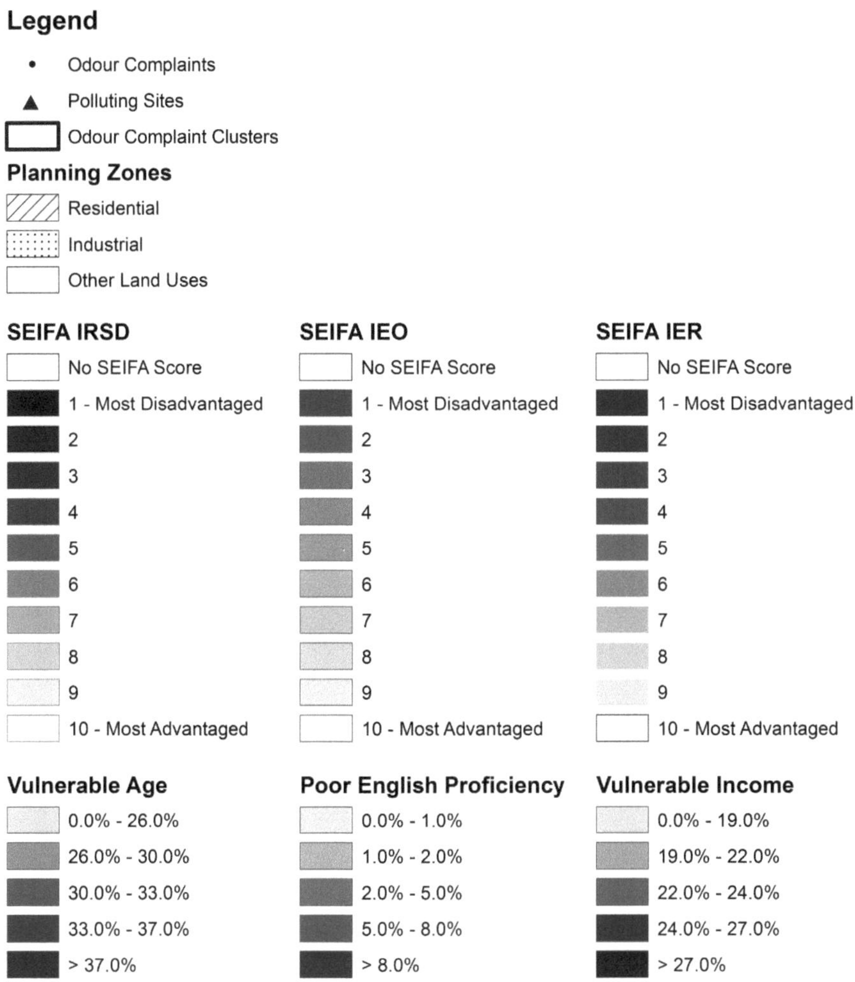

Fig. 7.4 (continued)

7.3.4 Comparison of Means t-Test for Areas with and Without Odour Exposure

Table 7.2 shows that mean values for the SEIFA indexes are significantly lower for the SA1 areas associated with odour complaints and significantly higher for vulnerable income and poor English proficiency. These results indicate that odour complaints are correlated with areas with low household income, and poor English language skills. No significant differences were found for vulnerable age and areas affected by odour and those that are not.

Table 7.1 Spearman rank correlation test of odour, pollution and socio-economic disadvantage indicators

	Number of odour complaints	Number of polluting facilities
Number of polluting facilities	0.144**	–
SEIFA-IRSD	−0.071**	−0.082**
SEIFA-IEO	−0.064**	−0.092**
SEIFA-IER	−0.049**	−0.029**
Vulnerable income	0.029**	0.053**
Vulnerable age	−0.030**	0.010
Poor English proficiency	0.076**	0.087**

**p-value < 0.01; N = 8781

Table 7.2 Comparison of means using t-test for areas with and without exposure to odour

Variables	Melbourne	Outside odour cluster	Within odour cluster	Mean difference	t-test: p-value
Panel (a) Clusters based on a minimum of 20 odour complaints with a distance threshold of R5 = 0.75					
SEIFA-IRSD	1020.12	1020.96	997.29	23.66	0.000
SEIFA-IEO	1033.71	1034.71	1006.52	28.19	0.000
SEIFA-IER	1007.30	1007.76	994.57	13.19	0.006
Vulnerable income	22.79	22.75	23.88	−1.13	0.000
Vulnerable age	31.66	31.65	31.91	−0.26	0.593
Poor English proficiency	0.05	0.05	0.08	−0.02	0.000
Number of SA1s (n)	8781	8423	358	–	–
Panel (b) Clusters based on a minimum of 50 odour complaints with a distance threshold of L5 = 0.05					
SEIFA-IRSD	1020.12	1020.55	997.66	22.88	0.004
SEIFA-IEO	1033.71	1034.29	1003.20	31.08	0.000
SEIFA-IER	1007.30	1007.52	995.74	11.78	0.086
Vulnerable income	22.79	22.77	24.05	−1.28	0.000
Vulnerable age	31.66	31.65	32.10	−0.45	0.495
Poor English proficiency	0.05	0.05	0.07	−0.02	0.000
Number of SA1s (n)	8781	8602	179	–	–

Table 7.3 Comparison of means using t-tests by number of odour complaints

Variables	No exposure group 1	Medium exposure group 2	High exposure group 3	Trend[a] *p*-value
Threshold for the number of odour complaints	0	<20	≥ 20	
SEIFA-IRSD	1022.61	1005.09	989.29	<0.0001
SEIFA-IEO	1009.43	993.34	996.31	<0.0001
SEIFA-IER	1035.64	1023.42	990.46	<0.0001
Vulnerable income	22.74	22.97	24.72	0.008
Vulnerable age	31.71	31.34	31.61	0.307
Poor English proficiency	0.05	0.06	0.07	<0.0001
SA1s (n)	7605	1100	76	–

[a]Trend *p*-values calculated using STATA 13 and the nptrend command for testing linear trend across groups

7.3.5 Comparison of Means t-Test by Number of Odour Complaints

Table 7.3 shows significant differences between the means of all socio-economic disadvantage indicators except for vulnerable age. The mean values for the SEIFA-IRSD and SEIFA-IER are higher for SA1s with no odour complaints, but decline for SA1s with ≤ 20 odour complaints and decline further for SA1s with the highest intensity of >20 odour complaints. These results suggest that socio-economic disadvantage is associated with more odour complaints.

The reverse pattern occurs for the indicators of vulnerable age and poor English proficiency. As odour complaint intensity increases, so too does the proportion of people with vulnerable income and poor English proficiency. For the SEIFA-IEO, there are significant differences between groups. Areas with no exposure have higher mean SEIFA-IEO values (Group 1 mean = 1009.43) relative to the two remaining groups of ≤ 20 and >20 odour complaints, where mean differences are marginal (Group 2 mean = 993.34 and Group 3 mean = 996.31). There are no significant differences between groups for the mean values for vulnerable age.

7.4 Discussion

This research confirms the disproportionate distribution of vulnerable community members in areas affected by odour pollution within metropolitan Melbourne. Residents affected by odour pollution were co-located with polluting facilities in areas of greater socio-economic disadvantage, with low household income and poor

English proficiency. Furthermore, this research confirms that odour complaint data provides a useful proxy measure of odour pollution exposure, with spatial clustering using the NNH clustering technique a useful method for identifying areas and residents affected by odorous facilities.

Two sets of clusters based on a minimum number of 20 and up to 50 odour complaints were found to fit the odour complaint data well. The cluster results established odour-affected areas and demonstrated that they are co-located with polluting facilities and industrial zones. Both sets of clusters were associated with greater socio-economic disadvantage in the Clarinda and Clayton South areas compared to Dingley Village for all indicators except for vulnerable age. Results also indicated that for some polluting facilities, a buffer of 1 km was sufficient for measuring the extent of odour exposure, but could be insufficient in the presence of multiple odour polluting facilities. Instead a 2 km buffer offered better coverage for the Clayton South area. This finding supports the use of variable separation distances based on the quantity, type and magnitude of the pollution problems co-located with residential areas.

Environmental justice issues were confirmed using three statistical tests confirming significant correlations between the location of polluting facilities, odour complaint clusters and socio-economic disadvantage indicators. Statistical differences in socio-economic disadvantage indicators were also confirmed for areas affected by odour compared to those without. The final test confirmed the presence of a trend based on the intensity of odour complaints. Statistical testing consistently demonstrated that areas impacted by odour have greater socio-economic disadvantage for all 3 SEIFA indexes, vulnerable income and poor English proficiency. Notably, the relationship with vulnerable age was not consistent reflecting a more even distribution across metropolitan Melbourne for this indicator.

Areas with the greatest levels of socio-economic disadvantage were associated with more than 20 odour complaints. However, a lack of monotonic trend in vulnerable income was similar to the findings of Pastor et al. (2005) who suggested these income results could be a function of the denser urban environment. In support of this, maps demonstrated clear differences between specific areas (i.e. Clayton South and Dingley Village) for the indicators of vulnerable income and SEIFA-IER, with less disadvantage evident in Dingley Village. These results are consistent with previous findings where socioeconomic status was a significant indicator of disproportionate proximity and exposure to environmental hazards and polluting sources in vulnerable communities (Chakraborty et al. 2011). However, results also provide evidence that socio-economic disadvantage differences between small areas can be averaged out when using larger administrative area data confounding results for environmental justice studies. Consequently, these results support the use of data visualisation techniques and emphasise the importance of scale in assessing environmental justice issues, particularly with localized problems such as odour.

7.5 Limitations

This research provides evidence that environmental odour pollution disproportionately affects people from lower socio-economic backgrounds and with poor English proficiency. However, there are limitations to the research. It is possible that self-reported odour complaint data might not accurately represent exposed odour areas despite providing insight into the spatial scale and dispersion of odour. The objective extent of odour remains unknown and complicated by the complexities of measuring and characterizing odour (Nicell 2009) particularly when combining spatial phenomena with data measured using administrative boundaries. These issues are covered in discussions of the modifiable area unit problem previously raised by Baden et al. (2007). In this study, and to assist with simplicity, the polygon containment method was used for selecting small areas while areal apportionment has been considered superior by others (Mohai and Saha 2006). Furthermore, the distribution and number of odour complaints included in this study are related to a 3 year timeframe and we recommend shorter timeframes be examined to uncover the relationship between pollution releases, meteorological conditions, odour complaints and other relevant factors (Schauberger et al. 2006).

7.6 Conclusions and Implications

Using clusters to represent communities affected by odour is a novel approach to measuring pollution exposure and could be expanded in future research to include alternate clustering methodologies such as Ripley's K or DBScan to assist in the identification of the best scale for measurement. Furthermore, other techniques such as spatial regression could negate issues of discretely differentiating odour affected communities, recognizing that odour exposure might decline gradually according to distance from the source (Chakraborty et al. 2011).

Longitudinal analyses are also recommended in future research. These analyses could help measure the impact of planning decisions on residential and industrial areas given that polluting facilities have been shown to move over time, with increasing scale and concentration escalating amenity impacts and decreasing land values in addition to impacting health and wellbeing (Taylor 2013). Such research could provide empirical evidence for commonly adopted regulations such as those in Canada where 5 written complaints from separate households over a 90 day period is considered representative of an odour problem (Nicell 2009).

Complementary analysis techniques and the use of differing types of odour data could also lead to more robust results in defining separation distances between polluting facilities and residential areas (Nicell 2009). Our results suggest that the spatial extent of odour exposure may be related to the size, type and quantity of polluting facilities which warrants further investigation for developing regulations.

In summary, this study provides evidence of the existence of environmental justice issues in metropolitan Melbourne demonstrated through clustering techniques and the applied use of socio-economic and community indicators. Odour exposure measured using odour complaints were associated with indicators of socio-economic disadvantage in communities affected by odour pollution. The findings of this study should be used to facilitate dialogue between policy makers, researchers and communities to inform land use planning and policy development towards avoiding future co-location and encroachment between residential areas, new developments and industrial zones.

Acknowledgements This project was supported by Community Indicators Victoria at The University of Melbourne. B. Greenham is supported by The University of Melbourne 2013 Vice-Chancellor's Engagement Award. M. Bannister provided in-kind support via The University of Melbourne-Environment Protection Authority Victoria Partnership. Special thanks to Rebecca Roberts for GIS mapping assistance.

The authors declare they have no actual or potential competing financial interests.

References

Australian Bureau of Statistics. (2011). *Census of population and housing*. Canberra: ABS.

Australian Bureau of Statistics. (2013). *Socio-economic indexes for areas, cat. no. 2033.0.55.001.* Canberra: ABS.

Baden, B. M., Noonan, D. S., & Turaga, R. M. R. (2007). Scales of justice: Is there a geographic bias in environmental equity analysis? *Journal of Environmental Planning and Management, 50*(2), 163–185. doi:10.1080/09640560601156433

Bolin, B., Pijawaka, K., Scott Smith, C., Sicotte, D., Sadalla, E., Matranga, E., et al. (2002). The ecology of technological risk in a Sunbelt city. *Environment and Planning A, 34,* 317–339.

Byrne, J., & MacCallum, D. (2013). Bordering on neglect: 'Environmental justice' in Australian planning. *Australian Planner, 50*(2), 164–173. doi:10.1080/07293682.2013.776984

Chakraborty, J., & Armstrong, M. P. (1997). Exploring the use of buffer analysis for the identification of impacted areas in environmental equity assessment. *Cartography and Geographic Information Systems,* 24(3), 145–157.

Chakraborty, J., & Green, D. (2014a). Australia's first national level quantitative environmental justice assessment of industrial air pollution. *Environmental Research Letters, 9*(4), 1.

Chakraborty, J., & Green, D. (2014b). The relationship between industrial air pollution and social disadvantage in Australia: National and regional inequities. *Air Quality and Climate Change, 48*(4), 35–38.

Chakraborty, J., Maantay, J. A., & Brender, J. D. (2011). Disproportionate proximity to environmental health hazards: Methods, models, and measurement. *American Journal of Public Health, 101*(S1), S27–S36.

Chavis, B. F., & Lee, C. (1987). *Toxic wastes and race in the United States: A national report on the racial and socioeconomic characteristics of communities with hazardous waste sites.* New York: United Church of Christ.

Environment Protection Authority Victoria. (2015a). *EPAV (environment protection authority Victoria) your environment—Odour.* http://www.epa.vic.gov.au/your-environment/odour. Accessed April 30, 2015.

Environment Protection Authority Victoria. (2015b). EPAV (environment protection authority Victoria) about us—Who we are. http://www.epa.vic.gov.au/about-us/who-we-are. Retrieved April 21, 2015.

Henshaw, P., Nicell, J., & Sikdar, A. (2006). Parameters for the assessment of odour impacts on communities. *Atmospheric Environment, 40,* 1016–1029. doi:10.1016/j.atmosenv.2005.11.014

Kaye, R., & Jiang, K. (2000). Development of odour impact criteria for sewage treatment plants using odour complaint history. *Water Science and Technology, 41*(6), 57–64.

Lamb, K. E., & White, S. R. (2015). Categorisation of built environment characteristics: The trouble with tertiles. *International Journal of Behavioral Nutrition and Physical Activity, 12*(1), 1–8. doi:10.1186/s12966-015-0181-9

Levine, N. (2010). *Crimestat: A spatial statistics program for the analysis of crime incident locations (Version IV).* Washington, DC: Ned Levine & Associates, Houston, TX, and the National Institute of Justice.

Maantay, J. (2002). Mapping environmental injustices: Pitfalls and potential of geographic information systems in assessing environmental health and equity. *Environmental Health Perspectives,* 110(Suppl 2), 161–171.

Maantay, J. (2007). Asthma and air pollution in the Bronx: Methodological and data considerations in using GIS for environmental justice and health research. *Health and Place, 13,* 32–56. doi:10.1016/j.healthplace.2005.09.009

Mackay, A. K., Taylor, M. P., Munksgaard, N. C., Hudson-Edwards, K. A., & Burn-Nunes, L. (2013). Identification of environmental lead sources and pathways in a mining and smelting town: Mount Isa, Australia. *Environmental Pollution, 180,* 304–311. doi:10.1016/j.envpol.2013.05.007 [Article].

Medina-Ramón, M., & Schwartz, J. (2008). Who is more vulnerable to die from ozone air pollution? *Epidemiology, 19*(5), 672–679. [research article].

Mohai, P., Pellow, D., & Roberts, J. T. (2009). Environmental justice. *Annual Review of Environment and Resources, 29,* 405–430.

Mohai, P., & Saha, R. (2006). Reassessing racial and socioeconomic disparities in environmental justice research. *Demography, 43*(2), 383–399.

Nicell, J. A. (2009). Assessment and regulation of odour impacts. *Atmospheric Environment, 43,* 196–206. doi:10.1016/j.atmosenv.2008.09.033

Pastor, M., Jr., Morello-Frosch, R., & Sadd, J. L. (2005). The air is always cleaner on the other side: Race, space, and ambient air toxics exposures in California. *Journal of Urban Affairs, 27* (2), 127–148. doi:10.1111/j.0735-2166.2005.00228.x

RDWI Air Inc. (2005). *Final report odour management in British Columbia: Review and recommendations.* British Columbia: Ministry of Water, Land and Air Protection.

Schauberger, G., Piringer, M., & Petz, E. (2006). Odour episodes in the vicinity of livestock buildings: A qualitative comparison of odour complaint statistics with model calculations. *Agriculture, Ecosystems & Environment, 114,* 185–194.

Schlosberg, D., & Carruthers, D. (2010). Indigenous struggles, environmental justice, and community capabilities. *Global Environmental Politics, 10*(4), 12–35. http://www.mitpressjournals.org/loi/glep

Sheppard, E., Leitner, H., McMaster, R. B., & Tian, H. (1999). GIS-based measures of environmental equity: Exploring their sensitivity and significance. *Journal of Exposure Analysis and Environmental Epidemiology, 9*(1), 18–28.

Shusterman, D. (1999). The health significance of environmental odour pollution: Revisited. *Journal of Environmental Medicine, 1*(4), 249–258.

Taylor, E. J. (2013). *'Tipped off': Residential amenity and the changing distribution of household waste disposal in Melbourne.* Paper presented at the State of Australian Cities Conference, November, Sydney.

Taylor, M. P., & Schniering, C. (2010). The public minimization of the risks associated with environmental lead exposure and elevated blood lead levels in children, Mount Isa, Queensland, Australia. *Archives of Environmental & Occupational Health, 65*(1), 45–48.

US Government Accountability Office. (1983). *Siting of hazardous waste landfills and their correlation with racial and economic status of surrounding communities.* Washington: U.S. Government Print Office.

Author Biographies

Lucy Gunn, Ph.D. is a Research Fellow at The McCaughey VicHealth Community Wellbeing Unit, The University of Melbourne. Her role covers research and consultancy projects with a focus on using statistical and spatial methods to evaluate the impact of built environments on the health and wellbeing of people and communities. As a researcher and consultant with Community Indicators Victoria, Lucy has worked with a range of government and community partners, including the Environment Protection Authority Victoria. Lucy's remaining role is with the Centre for Research Excellence in Healthy, Liveable, Communities where she provides policy related evidence for understanding which built environments are supportive of health in designing healthy cities. Lucy's current research interest focuses on exploring nonlinear relationships between the built environment and health, with knowledge on this to be used in the development of hypothetical built environment interventions and economic evaluations.

Billy Greenham is an Urban Planner with a strong belief in sustainable development and the positive impact planning can have. Billy completed the Masters of Urban Planning at the University of Melbourne. His thesis on the topic of Environmental Justice lead to this further work in the field. Billy maintained his research role with the University of Melbourne while returning to his home region to work as a planner in Local Government.

Dr. Melanie Davern is Director of Community Indicators Victoria and Senior Research Fellow at the McCaughey VicHealth Community Wellbeing Unit within the School of Population & Global Health, University of Melbourne. Her research interests focus on community and individual wellbeing with specific expertise in policy focused research, the development and use of community wellbeing indicators as a measurement tool for policy development, program evaluation, knowledge translation and community engagement. Melanie has extensive expertise in the development and construction of community wellbeing indicators, worked closely with a range of government and community partners and is passionate about using data as a catalyst for action.

Suzanne Mavoa, Ph.D. is a Senior Research Fellow and geographic information systems (GIS) team lead in the McCaughey VicHealth Community Wellbeing Unit at the University of Melbourne. She also holds a part-time appointment at the SHORE and Whariki Research Centre, Massey University, New Zealand. Her research focuses on improved geospatial methods to measure the environment and people's exposure to the environment. These research and methods have been applied across a number of areas of public health, geography, transport and urban planning.

Elizabeth Taylor, Ph.D. is a Vice Chancellor's Post-Doctoral Research Fellow in the Centre for Urban Research at RMIT University. Her interests are in policy-focused research across urban planning, housing markets, property rights and locational conflict and her research often makes use of Geographical Information Systems (GIS). An increasing research focus is car parking policy. Elizabeth's publications have explored the housing market implications of urban containment policies; the contested role of research in planning practice; and the 'Not in My Back Yard' (NIMBY) phenomenon. The latter includes food, waste and animal-based land uses that expose contradictions in the distribution of rights associated with production and consumption.

Mark Bannister, M Environ Sci. is a Senior Analyst at Environment Protection Authority Victoria. His work has involved regional scale and long term air quality modelling, understanding hazardous waste markets and the impact of regulation and the application of environmental justice principles through the use of demographic data, pollution reporting and air quality data. More recent work has focussed on supporting policy and analytical approaches to regulation reform.

Chapter 8
Addressing Disparities and Improving the System of Care for Veterans Through the Community Assessment Process

Samantha Green and Melanie Espino

Abstract A disproportionate number of U.S. military veterans experience homelessness and housing instability. It is estimated that more than 47,000 U.S. veterans are homeless on any given night, and while veterans represent 7% of the overall population, they represent 11% of those experiencing homelessness (HUD 2015). The City of New Orleans has effectively ended homelessness among veterans and many communities including Houston, Phoenix and Salt Lake City are not far behind. These communities have addressed the issue by providing permanent supportive housing and building partnerships between the United States Department of Veterans Affairs (VA) and the homeless services system. Yet ensuring all veterans in the community remain housed requires knowledge, coordination and partnerships beyond the VA and the homeless service providers. Community indicator projects have the potential to gather community-level data and build regional partnerships in an effort to serve all veterans, address disparities, and help communities move away from a crisis response system toward a system of prevention and improved community wellbeing. The San Mateo County Veterans Needs Assessment was developed in an effort to address the growing need of ageing veterans and the high proportion of veterans experiencing homelessness. Developing a veteran's indicator project for social change is challenging in the current climate. There are barriers to identifying veterans in the general population and developing common indicators across programs and systems. Yet there is the potential for communities to improve mainstream and civilian data systems, and enhance services and outcomes for veterans through community assessment.

Keywords Veterans needs assessment · Homelessness · Community assessment · Applied survey research

---

S. Green (✉)
Applied Survey Research, Watsonville, CA, USA
e-mail: samantha@appliedsurveyresearch.org

M. Espino
Actionable Insights, LLC, San Jose, CA, USA

M. Holden et al. (eds.), *Community Quality-of-Life Indicators: Best Cases VII*, Community Quality-of-Life and Well-Being,
DOI 10.1007/978-3-319-54618-6_8

8.1 Introduction

It is estimated that more than 47,000 U.S. veterans are homeless on any given night and while veterans represent 7% of the overall population, they represent 11% of those experiencing homelessness (HUD 2015). On average, homeless veterans have served their country for more than three years and yet they are without a place to call home.

Since 2008 a primary focus of the Obama Administration has been the goal of ending veteran homelessness. Since that time, nearly 79,000 HUD-VASH housing vouchers have been provided to over 400 Public Housing Authorities (PHAs) nationwide (HUD 2015). President Obama's recent budget includes a total of $674 million for VA programs that prevent or end homelessness among veterans, including $300 million for Supportive Services for Veterans Families (SSVF). Using resources like these, the City of New Orleans has effectively ended homelessness among veterans and many communities including Houston, Phoenix and Salt Lake City are not far behind. These communities have addressed homelessness among veterans by providing permanent supportive housing and by building partnerships between the VA and the homeless services system.

Preventing and ending veteran homelessness requires knowledge and partnerships beyond the VA and the homeless continuum of care. Community indicator projects have the potential to gather community level data and build regional partnerships in an effort to serve all veterans, address disparities, and help communities move away from a crisis response system.

The San Mateo County Veterans Needs Assessment was developed in an effort to address the growing need of aging veterans and the high proportion of veterans experiencing homelessness. For many, the project began with a single indicator: veterans represent 12% of the population experiencing homelessness, yet less than 6% of the overall county population. Embedded in this one indicator was a story about the challenges facing a heroic group of individuals, the strain of local service providers and gaps in a dedicated system of care. The San Mateo County Veterans Needs Assessment tells the story of county veterans and identifies ways in which the county can strengthen the safety net and provide services before veterans find themselves in shelters, hospitals, and county jails.

This chapter details the challenges of engaging in a veteran indicator project for social change, including barriers to identifying veterans in the general population, developing common indicators across programs and systems to help understand local veteran populations, the need for interim proxy measures and methods for developing relationships between community programs, local, state, and federal agencies. It explores the potential for communities to improve mainstream and civilian data systems, enhance services and outcomes for veterans and share findings and suggestions collected from service providers, veterans and veteran family members through the community assessment process.

8.2 Background

San Mateo County is located in the heart of Silicon Valley, just south of San Francisco and north of San Jose. It has a large coastal region, bordering both the Pacific and San Francisco Bay. While the county has escaped some of the challenges other Bay Area communities have experienced since the Tech Boom, the cost of living is still incredibly high.

The county is home to roughly 740,000 residents (U.S. Census Bureau 2014). At the time of the assessment, veterans represented roughly 6% of the county population (U.S. Census Bureau 2014). While a small percentage of the overall population, there were clear indications the veteran population was in need of additional support. Veterans represented 12% of the population experiencing homelessness in the county and were frequently presenting in community hospitals and county courts.

In 2014 San Mateo's County Manager's Office and Human Services Agency partnered with Applied Survey Research (ASR), a social research firm, to conduct the San Mateo County Veterans Needs Assessment. In 2013, the County Manager's Office had worked with county supervisors to recommend setting aside $100,000 a

Fig. 8.1 Applied Survey Research's community assessment process

year in Measure A sales tax revenue to improve local veterans services. The Veterans Needs Assessment was developed to determine how best to use the allocated funding. The assessment was designed for action, defining the current state of county veterans, assessing the existing system of services, determining areas of unmet need and developing steps for future action.

The needs assessment process was based on Applied Survey Research's five-step community assessment model (see Fig. 8.1). The following sections outline the process undertaken in each of the five steps.

8.3 Collaboration

The San Mateo County Veterans Needs Assessment began with the development of a steering committee of community stakeholders. Developing a diverse group of committed community members is essential for moving data to action. The steering committee included representatives from various state and county agencies, area non-profits and community groups. Members included individuals from the Veterans Administration, the California Department of Veterans Affairs, various veteran advocacy groups and veteran serving agencies. Members represented each of ASR's six identified domains of community wellbeing: education, health, economy, physical environment, public safety, and social environment. Many members were themselves veterans who resided in San Mateo County. The steering committee met to develop key indicators, and prioritize primary data collection opportunities. They also oversaw the community convening once data collection was underway.

For many of the service providers who participated in the steering committee, the meetings were the first opportunities to meet and interact with one another. Meetings were not only used to develop the Needs Assessment but to strengthen partnerships and the existing system of care. Committee members had the opportunity to discuss the system of care in an open setting, not only identifying their current challenges but working in interdisciplinary teams to address those challenges within the current system.

8.4 Data Collection

Objective and subjective measures are essential to community assessment. This is particularly true of projects dedicated to community improvement as it is people's perceptions that drive action (Hall 2013). Essential to the San Mateo Veterans Needs Assessment project was assessing and developing a system of care that worked for people. A perfectly designed system that isn't useful or sensitive to those it is intended to serve would be useless. Therefore, data collection included both quantitative and qualitative methods.

8.4.1 Primary Data

Focus groups and key informant interviews with veterans and stakeholders were included in the study in order to better understand their perspectives on veterans' needs, the services and supports available to veterans, and their suggestions on addressing veterans' needs. Key informants were identified based on their broad perspective on veterans' needs with a focus on the systems-level issues that impact access to services. Focus group participants included veterans and their family members. Participants represented veterans from the Korean War, Vietnam War, Operation Enduring Freedom (OEF), Operation Iraqi Freedom (OIF) and Operation New Dawn (OND) as well as those who served in peacetime. The age range of participants was broad and nine out of the thirty-six veterans who participated were female. The research questions that guided both the interviews and focus groups were simple, and included:

- In your opinion, what are the biggest issues facing veterans in San Mateo County?
- What are the biggest or most important gaps in the support/services available to veterans in San Mateo County?
- What are barriers to veterans accessing support/services? What would it take to eliminate those barriers?
- Are there any groups or subpopulations who may not be taking advantages of supports/services?
- What do you think are the biggest issues that need to be addressed at the systems level?
- What are the issues for individuals connecting to services or navigating the system of care?
- Have you seen good examples/models in other places that address veterans' services that you feel would work in San Mateo County?

8.4.2 Secondary Data

Secondary data collection included data and indicators familiar to most community assessment projects. Data were collected on population demographics, housing, employment, education, health, and public safety. While "big data" and access to public databases have made data collection on special populations attainable, gathering reliable data on populations which are statically rare remains challenging.

- Population and Demographic Data: The U.S. Census Bureau is the primary source of data on veteran populations in the United States. Indeed, the VA also relies on these data. Census and ACS data are available on veterans and Public Use Microdata Sample (PUMS) make regional analysis possible. However, detailed information on the population are limited to age, gender, service era, employment, income and disability status. Information on household status, sexual identity, and other basic demographics are not available from the US Census for this subpopulations. Due to the small population of veterans in San Mateo County, data smaller than the county level have a significant margin error, often larger than the data estimates. Therefore, these data are not reliable for service planning.

At the time of the report, the County of San Mateo and CalVet (California Department of Veterans Affairs) did not have access to the number of veterans exiting the military and reentering the county as veterans. Basic information on residency of those leaving the military is maintained by the Department of Defense. While these data have their limitations, in that the place of discharge may not correspond to where each veteran will ultimately reside, having consistent data on the number of new veterans in the county can help to better define the population and support local outreach and prevention efforts.

- Housing: Data regarding the housing of veterans is limited. According to the VA, fewer than 13% of veterans have used housing benefits. Housing benefits for veterans include home loans for veterans (regardless of disability status), service members and surviving spouses for purchasing homes without a down payment and refinancing of home mortgages. It also provides loans and grants to those with service-connected disabilities for building adapted homes, purchasing adaptive equipment and making home modifications. However, a high percentage of San Mateo County residents are not homeowners but renters and data on veterans rentals, including those accessing housing support, were limited.
- Homelessness: Data on local homeless veterans were more readily available. The recent focus and available funding for homeless veterans has driven not only service but data collection. Data from the county Homeless Management Information System (HMIS) was collected and analyzed for the project. Data collection was inconsistent across all programs entering data in HMIS, particularly those that did not target services to the population.
- Employment and Education: Employment and education data relied heavily on U.S. Census and ACS data. Regional education and employment programs working with veterans were unable to report on the number and characteristics of those they served.
- Health and Social Support (Including Veterans Benefits): Veteran health and benefit data were gathered from the VA using a Freedom of Information Act request (FOIA). The FOIA provides that any person has a right of access to federal agency records, except to the extent that such records are protected from release by a FOIA exemption or a special law enforcement record exclusion. It is VA's policy to release information to the fullest extent under the law. The VA has a decentralized system for handling FOIA requests, therefore the FOIA requests were addressed directly to the VA medical and benefits offices serving San Mateo County.

Information on both county and VA benefits are limited. While the VA was able to provide information on the health of county veterans, the request for information on residents' VA claims was unfulfilled at the time of this report. Additional information on the number of residents' receiving assistance, by type, and the demographics of those with benefits may help to address some of the kinds of assistance the county and community organizations can or should provide. Additionally, data on pending claims may help those working locally to understand the challenges veterans face in seeking those services and help them to outreach to those who are not currently receiving assistance from the VA. Information on veterans receiving mainstream support services did not exist at the time of the study. This lack of data made it impossible to assess whether or not the needs of the community are being addressed and what proportion of the population is already connected to county services.

- Public Safety and Criminal Justice Systems: San Mateo County benefited from a Veterans Treatment Court, one of 20 that existed in the country at the time. The program was able to report the number of veterans served by the program in the two years it had been operating but was unable to report on program outcomes. Data from the county jail and state prisons were not available at the time of this report. Additionally, information from the Probation Department and Department of Children and Family Services are not collected for veterans. Therefore, levels of local legal and criminal justice involvement are unknown.

8.5 Reporting and Primary Findings

In the end, the San Mateo County Veterans Needs Assessment included 87 pages of primary and secondary data, community resources, and identified best practices. The Assessment and the future work of the community present an interesting challenge. The focus on a relatively rare population presented challenges to current data collection but provided an immediate opportunity for improvements in outreach, education, data collection, and community understanding. Additionally, while San Mateo County's overall population continues to grow, the veteran population is declining. The Department of Veterans Affairs (VA) estimates that the veteran population of San Mateo County will drop more than 50% by 2025, similar to nationwide projections. At the national level, the number of military veterans has declined gradually since its surge at the end of World War II. During World War II an estimated 12% of the U.S. population was in the armed forces. As of 2004, less than 1% of the U.S. population was in military service (Population Reference Bureau 2004). The assessment process and system improvements must be targeted not only to a small population but also to a population that will decrease with time. This has major implications to staffing and resource allocation.

Participants in the project recognized the need to quantify the number of veterans in the community by the type and scale of needs. In addition to this, they sought to know what benefits or assets these individuals were accessing. However, based on the available data, such estimates remain unknown. Therefore, the greatest need identified was the need for additional data and improved tracking of services and requests for assistance.

That being the case, available data identified four broad needs within the community, which were seen through both qualitative and quantitative measures. These included identification and outreach, housing and homelessness, behavioral health services, and cultural competency—especially as it related to new and returning veterans and women.

From the data collected, it became clear that not all veterans wished to be identified and many do not know whether or not they qualified as veterans due to different definitions and program participation criteria. While the Veterans Needs Assessment project stemmed out of the known issue of homelessness for veterans, housing was expressed as an issue for all community members involved in the project. Veterans and service providers reported the need for additional supports and services for veterans with behavioral health needs. Veterans who were reached in high-end service programs, including homeless shelters, housing programs and court diversion programs, reported that their paths began with unmet mental and behavioral health needs. Finally, while quantitative data suggested they veterans were similar to the overall population in diversity of makeup and even along most outcomes, they reported that they felt different and services needed to recognize that difference.

Based on the secondary quantitative data and primary qualitative data that were available, the County of San Mateo identified a list of existing needs of the community, including:

- Education and Outreach
  - Education and anti-stigma campaigns
  - Outreach and information about services and benefits
- Improved Access to Benefits
  - VA claims assistance
  - Improved timeliness of VA medical and mental health appointments
- Incarceration and Justice System
  - Criminal record expungement (such as through Veterans Treatment Court)
  - Training on veteran informed service and trauma informed care for law enforcement
- Education and Employment Training
  - Assistance for veterans seeking to access/utilize GI Bill
  - Increased support for veteran students
  - Assistance transferring military skills and experience into civilian careers
  - Assistance with reintegration into work settings after service or disabling events

- Housing and Economic Supports
  - Assistance for veterans with housing vouchers looking for homes
  - Increase affordable housing stock dedicated to veterans and all community members
  - Supportive group housing environments for veterans
- Behavioral Health Care
  - Specific information about VA mental/behavioral health services and benefits
  - Supportive services for the reintegration into civilian life for returning veterans
  - Increased access and availability of PTSD services
  - Increased access and availability of alcohol and drug treatment
  - Targeted Behavioral Health Services for depression and suicide
- Female Veterans Needs
  - Outreach and services specific to the needs of women veterans
  - Services tailored to and sensitive to Military Sexual Trauma (MST).

8.6 Action

8.6.1 Community Convening

San Mateo County held the Veterans Summit prior the release of the full report. The purpose of the summit was to convene stakeholders from across the County, present them with the preliminary findings of the report, and collect information about their perception of the existing needs of local veterans. San Mateo County invited known stakeholders from veteran-serving agencies and also welcomed the general public. One hundred and seven guests from various sectors participated, including elected officials and their representatives, representatives from County and state government, non-profit leaders, Veterans Affairs staff, and interested community members. Participants were presented with preliminary findings, heard from a panel of veteran community members, and met in small working groups to discuss quality of life domains. At the end of the session, participants were asked to consider the top two most pressing needs requiring community action. Participants were also asked how they would like to engage in the process for improving quality of life for veterans in their community.

8.6.2 Veterans Commission Formation

In November of 2015 the San Mateo Veterans Commission was formed. The commission was developed to monitor the needs of the population and the system of care, and move from data to action. As of 2016 the commission had begun work to increase partnership and collaboration with veteran-serving agencies and departments, improve the outreach with County Veterans Service Officers reaching into the community, and improve education and identification of veterans through posters, flyers and the "If you served, you earned" campaign. The have also worked toward focused outreach to female veterans, increased trainings to community providers on role of Veterans Service Officers in assisting veterans in the community, and improving data collection across all county departments. As part of the improved data collection and outreach, the county implemented the veterans ID project, issuing 115 veteran IDs in one month.

8.7 Conclusions and Lessons Learned

The Veterans Needs Assessment was developed to determine how best to use the allocated funding. The assessment was designed for action, defining the current state of county veterans, assessing the existing system of services, determining areas of unmet need, and developing steps for future action.

8.7.1 Coordination

Through the process of needs assessment, it became clear that both service providers and focus group participants were aware of the disjointed nature of services offered to veterans in San Mateo County. Focus group participants reported that they were often unaware of services and veteran-serving organizations in the County, and many reported obtaining information on existing programs and supports from other veterans rather than service providers. Participants spoke of the difficulty of navigating their way through services because there was no single point of entry or connection between programs. Also, while service providers knew that they were serving veterans, many did not know how many or who those veterans were, due to inconsistent data collection and reporting.

Coordinated systems of care that aim to serve the needs of the target population will operate at two levels, the system level (which will provide coordination) and the program level (which will interact directly with veteran clients). The system would integrate both public and private organizations and provide services effectively and with equity. Such coordination requires a common goal of serving the identified population and leadership to guide the process. Coordinated systems often rely upon an organizing body that represents service providers as well as those it seeks to serve.

8.7.2 Leadership

Through the efforts of the Needs Assessment, the County of San Mateo has established its role within the emerging system, developing a new group of community stakeholders and building leadership. Furthermore, support from state and county agencies, elected, and local advocacy organizations provide the group with authority and legitimacy needed for systems change.

This leadership is needed to help facilitate the process of integrating independent programs into one service network. Such leadership helps to build partnerships and assist organizations in learning about services and systems and builds relationships with professionals in the broader community. Developing a strong partnership with the VA, the primary service providers for veterans in the nation, is essential. The VA has a significant role to play but by their own statutes do not service everyone who identifies as a veteran. Coordination between local service providers and mainstream support systems will help veterans with connecting the benefits and services they need. This will increase the overall capacity of the system, and perhaps help to alleviate the strain on mainstream benefit systems with budgets that are continuing to be cut.

8.7.3 Program Measures

A coordinated system requires that the services provided are targeted to the needs of the community. The system must have the potential to assess whether or not those needs are met through the services provided and determine if those needs are changing over time. Indicators, and a system for regular monitoring of progress, are an integral tool to improving long-term outcomes for the population.

Through the process of this Veterans Needs Assessment, it became clear that many services and organizations providing services to veterans did not have a consistent or effective way of tracking the number of veterans they served and many were unable to assess the number of clients who identify as veterans in San Mateo County. Departments within the County, such as Health, Behavioral Health and Recovery Services, Human Services Agency, and Superior Court were among the organizations that had limited data on the veterans in their care. However, this is true in most communities. State agencies like the California Department of Veterans Affairs were unable to obtain information on the number of services members exiting the military and entering the County. While the VA is developing their system of care and increasing transparency, gathering local data from the national agency was still difficult and required a FOIA request.

8.7.4 Communty Assessment

Future indicator projects should understand the time that is needed to map a system of services that is not yet integrated, building timelines that not only allow for the system of care to reveal itself but also for data requests from disparate local, state and national agencies to be processed. These requests take time and the persistence of leadership to follow up and advocate for their needs.

It is essential that communities have regular access to data on the entire veteran population in order to be able to regularly monitor the system of care and the strategies used to increase wellbeing. Common measures across agencies are essential for communitywide understanding and to help bring meaning to the data. Meaningful, timely data is essential to addressing needs with the nuances necessary to effectively help individuals while providing services in a systematic and cost-effective way. Community indicator projects have the potential to address this need. However, they cannot be seen as data reports but projects intended for action.

8.7.5 Relevance

It is essential to recognize that homelessness and unstable housing place individuals' physical and emotional health at risk. Individuals experiencing homelessness experience higher rates of preventable illnesses, have longer hospitalization stays, and die much earlier than those with stable housing. It is estimated that those experiencing homelessness stay four days (or 36%) longer per hospital admission than non-homeless patients (Hwang et al. 2011). A study conducted by the National Health Care for the Homeless Council found that the average life expectancy for a person without permanent housing was between 42 and 52 years, more than 25 years less than the average person in the United States (O'Connell 2005). We have a duty to improve the system of care and end homelessness in our communities.

The San Mateo County Veterans Needs Assessment is unique in a number of ways. While it was developed with a focus of addressing the disproportionate number of individuals experiencing homelessness who were veterans, it focused on the broader population of veterans in the community. This perspective is essential to the work. The current amount of federal funding targeted to those who are homeless or at risk of homelessness presents communities with an opportunity to address the needs of local veterans in a meaningful way, especially when the funding is focused on prevention. Identifying veterans among those served by general human services agencies and connecting them to veteran-specific services means less strain on mainstream systems, and it also means improved assessment, evaluation, and provision of services.

References

Hall, J. (2013). From capabilities to contentment: Testing the links between human development and life satisfaction. *World Happiness Report*. United Nations, Sustainable Development Solutions Network. New York: NY.

Hwang, S. W., Weaver, J., Aubry, T. D., & Hoch, J. S. (2011). Hospital costs and length of stay among homeless patients admitted to medical, surgical and psychiatric services. *Medical Care, 49*(4), 350–54. doi:10.1097/MLR.0b013e318206c50d

O'Connell, J. J. (2005). Premature mortality in homeless populations: A review of the literature. *National Health Care for the Homeless Council, Inc.*

Population Reference Bureau. (2004). *America's Military Population*. Retrieved 2014 from http://www.prb.org/source/acf1396.pdf

U.S. Census Bureau. (2014). *ACS demographics and housing estimates*. Retrieved 2016 from http://factfinder.census.gov/faces/tableservices/jsf/pages/productview.xhtml?src=CF\

U.S. Department of Housing and Urban Development. (2015). *HUD-VASH vouchers*. Retrieved 2015 from https://portal.hud.gov/hudportal/HUD?src%2520=/program_offices/public_indian_housing/program

Author Biographies

Samantha Green is a Project Manager with Applied Survey Research, a Bay Area research firm dedicated to helping build better communities through data. Her work links program performance and population outcomes in an effort to improve community wellbeing. Interest areas include social disparities affecting health, housing and education. She has worked throughout California on the issue of homelessness among children, youth and young families. She has most recently engaged in a collaborative study of youth homelessness in America with Chapin Hall at the University of Chicago. She previously taught a course on homelessness at the University of California at Santa Cruz, engaging youth in data and community action.

Melanie Espino is co-founder and principal of Actionable Insights, LLC in San Jose, California. Ms. Espino leads strategic planning efforts, program evaluations, and assessment projects concerning community health, school wellness, Latinos, children 0–5, and youth. Ms. Espino's recent work includes data collection and qualitative research for Community Health Needs Assessments on behalf of several Bay Area consortiums of non-profit hospitals, and strategic planning and reporting for member hospitals. In addition to leading community assessment projects such as the 2014 Veterans Needs Assessments in San Mateo County, she does evaluation planning for non-profit and government organizations seeking to measure their impact and make data-driven decisions.

Chapter 9
Economic Issues for Women in Texas

Jennifer Lee and Frances Deviney

Abstract As opportunities have opened for women, they have made strides in many societal domains. However, women remain more financially insecure than men by many measures. The greater likelihood of living in poverty and lower incomes creates insecurity not only for women, but for an increasingly large share of families that depend on their incomes. Texas is one of the largest states in the United States with a population of over 26 million. Analyzing Census and state agency data, the article identifies four "building blocks" of economic security for women: child care as a work support, education as a pathway to greater opportunities, health insurance as a critical protection, and housing as a financial anchor. Educational attainment and health insurance rates have improved for women, while housing and child care continue to be financial challenges. The analysis points to areas of investment that can help communities strengthen the economic security of women, and by extension, their families.

Keywords Texas · Women · Poverty · Economic security · Educational attainment · Housing · Gender inequity

9.1 Using Data to Address Community Challenges

Community indicator projects can use data in multiple ways, including analyzing data to identify or prioritize problems, setting common targets or goals across a community, and measuring progress. One particularly powerful use of data lies in the disaggregation of data by a relevant characteristic (e.g., age, race/ethnicity, gender) to focus attention on s particular demographic group of interest (e.g. seniors, Latinos, women). Disaggregating data and observing disparate outcomes can help to identify barriers for specific populations and provide more meaningful

J. Lee · F. Deviney (✉)
Center for Public Policy Priorities (Austin, TX),
on behalf of Texas Women's Foundation, Dallas, TX, USA
e-mail: deviney@cppp.org

M. Holden et al. (eds.), *Community Quality-of-Life Indicators: Best Cases VII*, Community Quality-of-Life and Well-Being,
DOI 10.1007/978-3-319-54618-6_9

information that can be used to refine policies, programs and practices so that they are more targeted, efficient, responsive to community needs, and ultimately more effective. This report is part of an ongoing project focused on the economic security of women and girls in Texas, which uses data to identify key issues, provide a common language and metrics for policy change, and engages communities across Texas around changing both policies and resources available to improve the economic security of women and girls.

9.2 The Women and Girls of Texas

The story of Texas women mirrors the story of Texas—dynamism, fierce independence and growing influence. In the past 40 years, the population of women and girls in Texas has more than doubled, reaching 12.6 million (U.S. Census Bureau 2012s) Women and girls are a critical part of Texas' success, and securing a bright future for women and girls is important not only for their sake, but for our families, our communities and our state.

Most women in Texas live in cities, the engines of the Texas economy. Texas claims three of the 10 largest cities in the United States, (U.S. Census Bureau 2012s) and five of the 10 fastest growing cities (U.S. Census Bureau 2012u). Eighty-five percent of the women and girls of Texas live in urban areas, (U.S. Census Bureau 2012b, Table B01002; U.S. Census Bureau 2012q, Table S0101) and half live in just three metropolitan areas: Dallas, Fort Worth and Houston (U.S. Census Bureau 2010, 2012a, Table B01001). Women in Texas are also younger than women in the nation as a whole. Slightly more than half of women and girls in Texas are under the age of 35, compared to age 39 in the U.S (U.S. Census Bureau 2012b, Table B01002). In Texas' urban areas, the median age is younger than 33 (U.S. Census Bureau 2012p, Table GCT0101).

Texas has long been a magnet for women and men from all over the country and world seeking economic opportunities and a better future. Opportunity and openness to newcomers has led to Texas boasting one of the most diverse populations in the nation. About 17% of women and girls who call the state home were not born in the United States (U.S. Census Bureau 2012c, Table B05003). Of these, almost 40 percent are U.S. citizens (U.S. Census Bureau 2012c, Table B05003). An additional 22 percent of women and girls were born in another state in the U.S. but, as the saying goes, "got here at fast as they could" (U.S. Census Bureau 2012d, Table B06003). Forty-five percent of women and girls in Texas are non-Hispanic white; 12% black or African-American; 5% Asian; and 1% some other race. Thirty-seven percent of women and girls are Hispanic or Latina[1] (U.S. Census Bureau 2012t). A young, diverse, and growing population of girls and women is a powerful asset for Texas if we commit resources to help them reach their highest potential.

[1]Hispanics may be of any race.

9.2.1 *The Female Face of Poverty*

Texas women are 1.2 times more likely to live in poverty than a man (U.S. Census Bureau 2012h, Table B17001). For a family of one parent and two children, that means living with an income below $18,769 a year (U.S. Census Bureau 2012j)—far below what's necessary to live a comfortable life, enjoy a feeling of security from day to day, and have confidence that you can provide your children with the opportunities they deserve. Poverty affects girls and women throughout their lives. Girls who live in poverty are less likely to complete high school and more likely to have children when unmarried (Magnuson and Votruba-Drzal 2009). Women and girls who live in poverty are more likely to experience health problems, such as asthma, diabetes and heart disease (Magnuson and Votruba-Drzal 2009). And many women in Texas who are not "officially poor"—a mom with two kids whose income is above $19,000 a year—still struggle to make ends meet.

Women are more likely to live in poverty because they tend to work in industries that are historically underpaid, while at the same time are more likely to shoulder the responsibilities of raising children. Women raising children alone are especially vulnerable. Single parents are almost twice as likely to be women, and a single mother is almost twice as likely as a single father to live in poverty (U.S. Census Bureau 2012j, Table B17012). More than half of households in Texas who live in poverty are headed by single women (U.S. Census Bureau 2012j, Table B17012). And it's not that single moms aren't working—61% of single moms work at least 30 h per week (Ruggles et al. 2010). Furthermore, more women and girls of color in Texas live in poverty. Although Hispanic females make up 37% of women and girls in Texas, they make up 56% of women and girls living in poverty (U.S. Census Bureau 2012h, Table B17001).

Many existing policies and programs were designed assuming that one adult could earn enough income to support an entire family, and one adult could bear the full-time responsibility of raising children. Now, most families require two adults to both work and raise children, but many families still rely on a single adult for support. New policies and programs are needed to reflect the reality of the Texas economy and the families we have in the state. All families have the same need for economic security and the same high hopes for their children. Texas can and should be a place that works for every one of our families—single-mother families included (Tables 9.1 and 9.2).

Table 9.1 2013 Federal poverty thresholds

Family size	One person	Two people	One adult and two children	Two adults and two children
Max. yearly income for household (or less)	$12,119	$15,600	$18,769	$23,624

Note Family size of one assumes person is under 65 years old; family size of two assumes two adults under 65; family size of three assumes one adult and two children; family size of four assumes two adults and two children
Source U.S. Census Bureau, Poverty Thresholds for 2013

Table 9.2 2012 Texas poverty rate by family type

Family type	Two-parent (%)	Single father (%)	Single mother (%)
Poverty rate	11	22	41

Note CPPP analysis of American Community Survey, 2012 ACS 5-Year Estimates. Table B17012

9.3 Working Women, Working Families

Working women are not a new phenomenon that arose in the latter part of the 20th century. Women in Texas have always worked—whether at home, in the field or in a business. But the shift of more Texas women working outside the home for pay has been substantial in recent years. Forty years ago, only 40% of Texas' married-couple families with children had both parents in the labor force. Today, that percentage has grown to 67% of married-couple families (Glynn 2010).

9.3.1 Women and Wages in Texas

Women make up 63% of low-wage workers, earning minimum wage or less in Texas, largely because jobs with a high concentration of women tend to be among the lowest-paying jobs, such as home health aides and child care workers (U.S. Bureau of Labor Statistics 2013a, b). The wage gap persists in all occupations, from traditionally lower-wage jobs, such as nursing aides (85 cents to a dollar) to higher-wage jobs like engineering (84 cents to a dollar) (U.S. Census Bureau 2012r, Table S2402). More than half of Texas families have women as either the primary or co-breadwinner in Texas families (Glynn 2010) and that rate is growing. When women earn less, the financial security of Texas families is negatively impacted.

9.3.2 Women's Earnings Critical Part of Families' Earnings

In 2010, 39% of mothers in Texas were "breadwinners"—that is, they earned half or more of their family income. An additional 20% of mothers were "co-breadwinners," meaning they earned 25 to 49% of a family's income (Glynn 2010). Although these women do not earn the majority of a family's income, co-breadwinners contribute a critical portion of a family's economic resources, without which a family's well-being would suffer significantly. The percentage of families with breadwinning or co-breadwinning mothers has increased in the past 40 years from 34 to 59% of all Texas families with children (Glynn 2010). Co-breadwinning women have long been important contributors to family incomes in Texas. The greatest increases are seen in married-couple families, where the percentage of female breadwinners has almost quadrupled in the past 40 years (Glynn 2010). Single breadwinners have also increased in importance, and today half of breadwinning women are single (Glynn 2010).

The increasing role of women as breadwinners is driven by several important factors, including: (1) stagnating wages for men (Greenstone and Looney 2011); (2) the increasing cost of living; and (3) an increase in single-mother families (now at one out of every four Texas families with children (U.S. Census Bureau 2012e, Table B11003). That makes the types of jobs women have and the wages they are paid more important for Texas' overall family financial security than ever before.

9.3.3 The Wage Gap Between Men and Women

Unfortunately for women and their families, working women still do not earn as much as men, a circumstance known as the "wage gap." Lower earnings for women contribute to higher poverty rates and impede women's ability to build economic security, from saving for retirement or emergencies, to accessing health care and providing basic enrichment opportunities for their children (such as books in the home). In Texas, media earnings for full-time workers in 2012 are $44,521 for men and $35,363 for women separately, indicating the wage gap for full-time workers amounts to a $9,158 difference in earnings per year (U.S. Census Bureau 2012l, Table B20017).[2] Another way to think about the wage gap is that women typically earn 79 cents for every dollar that men earn. Women would have to work more than 10 extra hours per week to "catch up." When you include both full-time and part-time workers, the gap grows even wider, (U.S. Census Bureau 2012m, Table B20002) as women are more likely to work part-time because of child rearing or other caregiving responsibilities.

9.3.4 Why Does the Wage Gap Exist?

Many women work in traditionally low-paying jobs (U.S. Government Accountability Office 2011). Women are overrepresented on the lowest end of the pay scale—in Texas, 63% of the 452,000 workers earning minimum wage or less are women (U.S. Bureau of Labor Statistics 2013a). Jobs with a high concentration of women also tend to be among the lowest-paying jobs. For example, home health and personal care aides in Texas earn an average annual wage of $17,430, and the vast majority of these aides are women (U.S. Bureau of Labor Statistics 2013a).

[2]Earnings are defined as the sum of wages, salary income and net income from self-employment.

Many women leave paid work for unpaid work and family care, reducing their earning potential long-term. Both single and married women are more likely than men to take time off work to care for sick children, elderly parents or a new baby. Even if the choice to temporarily leave work is a positive choice for the family, time off from work in order to take time at home typically results in reduced earnings, and negatively impacts future employment and social security pay (Budig and England 2001).

Only a portion of the wage gap is explained by type of job or women temporarily leaving the workforce. Even taking into account differences in occupations, work experience and educational attainment, some of the wage gap remains unexplained (Blau and Kahn 2007). Recent research shows that unconscious biases by both male and female hiring managers may in fact contribute to women's lower salaries (Moss-Racusin et al. 2012).

9.3.5 Why Does It Matter?

Women's earnings are increasingly critical for their family's economic security. And for many families, when women's earnings don't cover basic expenses, they must make tough choices about what kind of care their child will receive, the food they put on the table, and the safety of the home and neighborhood they live in. Financially secure women make financially secure families and communities-and that makes for a financially secure Texas.

9.4 Education: A Pathway to Economic Security

Education is the primary pathway to better-paying jobs and economic security. When women can access education, the return on investment is high: with each step up in their education, women in Texas tend to earn more (U.S. Census Bureau 2012n, Table B20004). Texas women with bachelor's degrees earn nearly twice what women with high school diplomas earn (U.S. Census Bureau 2012n, Table B20004). Women have made large gains, and now out-perform men on many measures of educational achievement. More girls are graduating from high school than boys, more women are enrolling in college, and more women are getting college degrees (Texas Education Agency 2012). In the past 40 years, the percentage of women in Texas with a college degree has more than tripled, and similar percentages of women and men now have college degrees (U.S. Census Bureau. 1970 Census of Population and Housing, Texas; U.S. Census Bureau 2012g, Table B15002).

9.4.1 Texas Women in College

The majority of women in public higher education in Texas enroll in two-year colleges. Sixty-three percent of female students enroll in two-year colleges, compared to 59% of male students, representing almost 117,000 more women who depend on public, two-year colleges. (Texas Higher Education Coordinating Board 2013). Due to the wage gap, education debt leaves women with additional financial hardship. Women who attend public colleges borrow on average $13,110, slightly more than men ($12,784) (U.S. Department of Education, 2008).[3] Because women earn less than men after college, student loan repayments are a larger part of earnings, hurting their ability to build assets and economic security. The biggest "leak" in the education pipeline happens between enrolling in college and competing a degree. Fewer than half of women in Texas who enroll in college complete a credential within six years. (Texas Higher Education Coordinating Board and Texas Education Agency 2014). One promising practice is for women to take high school and college-level courses at the same time, so the transition to higher education is more seamless. South Texas College in McAllen has been a leader in this strategy, more than tripling the number of degrees and certificates earned by women in the last 10 years (Texas Higher Education Coordinating Board).

9.4.2 If Women Are Making Gains in Education, Why Aren't They Doing Better Overall?

For all the progress that women have made, there are still many barriers. Texas is losing far too many students—both female and male—in a phenomenon called the "leaky pipeline." Tracking students over time, only 23% of eighth-grade female students in Texas completed a higher education credential within 11 years (Texas Higher Education Coordinating Board and Texas Education Agency 2014).

We know that a woman with an associate's degree, bachelor's degree or other higher education credential is much less likely to live in poverty, (U.S. Census Bureau 2012i, Table B17003) so it's critical for girls and women to move successfully through the education pipeline. Supporting girls' education and unlocking their potential is a smart strategy for Texas, and no one should be satisfied until all our students—women and men—attain the skills they need to achieve economic security.

Even with more women getting degrees, women in Texas today tend to earn less than men, even when they have similar levels of education. In fact, women with higher levels of education often earn less than men with lower levels of education. Working women with an associate's degree or some college coursework earn $2020

[3]Averages include all amounts greater than zero.

Table 9.3 Pipeline to college

Timeline	Fall 2001	2005–2007	2006–2011	2012
	Begin in 8th grade	Graduate high school	Enrolled in TX higher Ed.	Achieved TX higher Ed. credential
Female	100%	71%	56%	23%
Male	100%	67%	47%	16%

Note. Texas Higher Education Coordinating Board and Texas Education Agency (2014)

Table 9.4 Median earnings by gender and educational attainment

Educational attainment	Less than high school	High school diploma only	Some college or associate's degree	Bachelor's, graduate or professional degree
Female	$18,891	$27,276	$34,347	$52,531
Male	$26,265	$36,367	$46,470	$75,766

Note Median earnings for full-time, year-round workers ages 25 and over in 2012
Source Compares full-time, year-round workers ages 25 and over. Population Reference Bureau analysis of data from U.S. Census Bureau, 2012 American Community Survey, Public Use Microdata Sample

less than men with only high school diplomas (Population Reference Bureau 2012a) (Tables 9.3 and 9.4).[4]

A variety of factors, including low-paying jobs and family demands that fall more heavily on women, are behind this disparity. But as women's earnings become increasingly important to Texas families, it's critical that education's return-on-investment remains high for both men and women. In one in five married-couple families with children, the woman contributed an equal or greater amount to the family's income (Glynn 2010). And for the 750,000 single moms in Texas, (U.S. Census Bureau 2012e, Table B11003) earnings are imperative because they are the only reliable source of income for the family.

9.4.3 Increases in College Costs Have Made the Education Pathway Steeper for Women

From fall 2003 to fall 2012, the total cost of college in Texas doubled (Texas Higher Education Coordinating Board, Overview).

To help pay for their education, many female students in Texas get jobs and borrow money. Both men and women worked an average of 20 h per week while attending four-year colleges and 28 h per week while attending two-year colleges[5] (U.S. Department of Education 2008). But women in both public four-year and

[4]Compares full-time, year-round workers ages 25 and over.
[5]Averages include all amounts greater than zero.

two-year colleges tend to borrow larger amounts than men to finance their education (U.S. Department of Education 2008).

Working and borrowing can strain students' resources and create challenges for women who want to reach the next step in their education. Although jobs can provide valuable experience and skills, too many working hours contributes to poor academic performance and a decreased likelihood of finishing a degree (The Forum for Youth Investment 2011).

Borrowing to pay for education can lead to a personal debt burden that hinders the beginning of students' working lives. In Texas, 17% of all students default on their student loans within three years of entering repayment. (US Department of Education 2013). Because more women enroll in college than men, borrow larger amounts for their education, and tend to earn less after college, the ability to pay off student loans is a critical issue for the women of Texas.

9.5 Child Care: A Critical Work Support for Women

All women should be able to take the steps they want to move up the economic ladder. But without reliable and affordable child care, applying and interviewing for jobs, working or furthering an education present challenges. With access to child care, women have one of the basic building blocks in place to strengthen the economic security of their families.

9.5.1 Women and Child Care

There is a lack of access to financial assistance for child care in Texas. Child care subsidies increase the ability of low-income mothers to work. Procedural problems can cause eligible families to lose assistance, so simplified processes and longer eligibility periods would improve stability of child care (Adams and Matthews 2013). When women have access to child care, they are more likely to work, stay employed for longer periods of time and increase their wages. Women who are consistently employed over time are more likely to increase their wages and move up the economic ladder. Tracking women's work experience over time, single mothers were twice as likely to remain employed over a two-year period if they used child care centers. Women who had a high school degree or less were almost three times more likely to still be employed after two years if they used center-based child care (Boushey 2002). Reducing child care costs would lift more people out of poverty. The "poverty line" does not currently measure the effects of expensive family budget items such as child care. If work expenses such as child care and transportation were included in the poverty calculation, the U.S. poverty rate would increase by almost two percent (Short 2013).

9.5.2 *Women Face Difficult Trade-Offs Between What They Earn and the Cost of Child Care*

The rising cost of child care creates difficulties for working families. Earnings from paid work outside the home may immediately be eaten up by child care costs, effectively making work unaffordable. The lack of affordable child care can force women out of the job market, including those who want or need to work. The burden of costly child care is especially heavy for single mothers in Texas. Costs vary depending on multiple factors, including the age of a child, the type of child care provider and whether or not the care is part-day or full-day. Taking these variations into account, the typical cost of child care for a full-time, working parent in Texas is about $5000 per year per child. (Ray Marshall Center 2012)[6] A typical single mom in Texas earns slightly less than $24,000 per year, meaning that care for one child represents 21% of a single mom's income. (Ray Marshall Center calculations; U.S. Census Bureau 2012k, Table B19126).

9.5.3 *Child Care Subsidies and Pre-K Programs*

Programs that support the child care needs of working, low-income mothers are often limited and fail to reach many Texas women who would benefit from them. One example is the Texas Workforce Commission's subsidized child care program for low-income, working parents. Low-income families pay a reduced amount for child care, dependent on their income, and the state reimburses child care providers at a set rate. Parents can then work, attend school or participate in job training (Texas Workforce Commission 2013). However, many more families need assistance than state and federal funds can currently support. Only eight percent of families in Texas that need the support actually receive financial assistance through subsidized child care.[7] (Ray Marshall Center 2010).

Lack of funding is an issue, but simplifying and streamlining eligibility policies would support access (Adams and Matthews 2013).

Public pre-kindergarten programs decrease child care expenses, with the added benefit of providing critical early learning opportunities for young children. But more children could benefit from access to pre-K programs. Many families with

---

[6]A "typical" median rate was derived by weighting rates for the age of child, full/part-day care and type of child care facility, by representation in the state. Yearly cost is based on child care needs for 250 days per year.

[7]Subsidy eligibility varies by workforce board. To estimate statewide subsidy receipt, the average monthly number of children receiving subsidies for early care was compared to the number of children under 5 living at less than 185 percent of the federal poverty guidelines (FPG). Out of the 28 workforce boards, 24 set their basic eligibility higher than 185% FPG, three set eligibility at 185% FPG, and one set eligibility lower than 185% FPG. Therefore, this is a conservative state estimate.

eligible young children are not aware of pre-K programs or live in a school district where public pre-K is not available. Scheduling and transportation challenges for half-day pre-K also act as barriers to enrollment. The Texas Education Agency estimates that more than 31,000 children who are eligible for pre-K programs are not currently served.[8]

9.6 Health Insurance: A Financial Shield for the Unexpected

In Texas, one in every four females lacks health insurance (U.S. Census Bureau 2012m, Table B2700n). Uninsured women and girls are no less likely to get an ear infection, have a car accident, develop breast cancer or decide to start a family than an insured individual. And when life throws a curveball, difficult situations can escalate to financial catastrophes.

When the uninsured need doctors, health care costs more, both for the individual and the community. Uninsured women and girls are less likely to receive the care that can detect something like cervical cancer or a problematic pregnancy at an early stage than those with insurance. Catching health problems at a later stage is more dangerous for women and more costly to treat. On average, the uninsured end up paying at least a third of the full cost of care out of their own pockets, but the remainder that would typically be covered by an insurance company results in higher insurance premiums or taxes for everyone (Families USA 2009).

9.6.1 Women and Health Insurance

98% of Texas women over 65 are insured. Senior women are the most likely age group to have health insurance. Medicare protects most individuals over age 65 from living without health insurance (U.S. Census Bureau 2012o, Table B27001). Almost 500,000 girls under 18 do not have health insurance in Texas. However, the percentage of uninsured children has gone down over the past 10 years because of programs like Medicaid and the Children's Health Insurance Program (CHIP). The percentage of girls under 18 who are uninsured (15%) is less than half the percentage for women age 18 to 34 (36 percent uninsured) (U.S. Census Bureau 2012o, Table B27001). Women between the ages of 18–34 are the least likely to have health insurance in Texas. 36% of women lack health insurance during the primary childbearing years when good health and access to prenatal care are important for babies' health (U.S. Census Bureau 2012o, Table B27001). Many

[8]See footnote 7 above. TEA estimates the percentage of eligible pre-K students not served by comparing enrolled, low-income kindergartners to pre-kindergartners.

women work in jobs in which health insurance is not available as a benefit, or they are paid too little to purchase insurance on their own. However, subsidies offered through the Affordable Care Act should help more women in Texas purchase private health insurance coverage.

9.7 Housing: The Anchor of Economic Security

Stable housing serves as an anchor for families, while a lack of stable housing leads to negative health and educational outcomes for children (Cunningham and MacDonald 2012). Because housing is the single largest expense in most families' budgets, the cost of housing directly impacts economic stability. When housing costs increase faster than incomes, the rest of a family's budget is affected, and for Texas women in particular, this forces tough choices between paying the rent, buying food or paying for safe child care. Families that spend 30% or more of their income on housing are considered "housing-cost burdened." This threshold is widely used as a measure of hardship by housing assistance programs and of risk by mortgage lenders (Schwartz and Wilson 2007). Single mothers who rent or own their homes are more likely to be burdened by housing costs than single fathers and married couples (Population Reference Bureau 2012b).[9]

9.7.1 Women and Housing

Texas women are more likely than men to rent their homes. 53% of single women rent their homes, and 47% own them. The rate is flipped for single men-53% own their homes, and 47% rent. 80% of married-couple families in Texas own their homes. (U.S. Census Bureau 2012f, Table B11012). Housing costs are especially burdensome for single mothers in Texas. Families that spend 30% or more of their income on housing lack the security of knowing they can pay for other necessities. Based on this measure, 35% of single mothers who own their homes are burdened with housing costs. 63% of single-mother renters spend 30% or more of their income on rent (Population Reference Bureau 2012b). For many women, the home they own is their largest financial asset, but more Texas women than men live in "asset poverty." Assets give families a financial cushion to get through unexpected events, and are an important source of collateral for loans. However, women in general have fewer financial assets than men. Single female-headed families are less likely to own their homes than male-headed families, and they tend to earn less money. (U.S. Census Bureau 2012f, Table B11012). Therefore, more women live

---

[9]Housing costs for homeowners include mortgage payments, real estate taxes, various insurances, utilities, fuels, mobile home costs, and condominium fees.

Table 9.5 Homeowner status by family type

Family type homeowner status	Married-couple families (%)	Single-father families (%)	Single-mother families (%)
Renters	36.7	41.8	63.3
Homeowners	17.1	24.8	35

Note Population Reference Bureau analysis of American Community Survey data, 2012. Housing costs for homeowners include mortgage payments, real estate taxes, various insurances, utilities, fuels, mobile home costs, and condominium fees

in "asset poverty," meaning they do not have a financial cushion to live for three months at the poverty level with a sudden loss in income. One in three single female-headed households in Texas lives in asset poverty (Bay Area Council Economic Institute 2012) (Table 9.5).

9.8 Conclusion

We hope this report serves as a catalyst to learn more about the economic challenges and opportunities that Texas women face. By sharing this information with community leaders and working with elected and appointed officials, nonprofit organizations, businesses and foundations, the economic security of women across the state can be strengthened.

Texas Women's Foundation believes that strong women make a better world. Texas women are already a vital part of what makes Texas great, but as we've seen in this report, many women, especially single women with children, are more likely to encounter barriers on their road to achieving and building economic security. This struggle is not due to women not working hard enough, but to barriers to success that continue across our communities and state.

Supporting women's educational success is highly important. Women have taken advantage of educational opportunities opened to them, and they have made significant gains. But it's clear that barriers still exist beyond school that reduce the financial benefits of education for women. We can do more to support women as they advance through education and the workplace to ensure that working women are not penalized for having children.

Other building blocks of women's economic security match common items in a family budget: child care, health insurance and housing. Health insurance helps to protect women's financial security when a health emergency strikes. Younger, working-age women who are trying to start careers, families and post-school lives on secure financial footing are the least likely to have health insurance. The lack of affordable child care prohibits more women than men from reaching their full earning potential. And the rising cost of housing eats up a larger share of the family budget from year to year, and is especially burdensome for single mothers.

Each community of women in Texas faces its unique challenges, but there are many common issues that impact women across the state. Whether or not these building blocks are in place affects not only women's ability to be economically stable, but to move up the economic ladder.

When working on a community indicators project focused on a specific demographic group, such as women and girls, it is important to highlight indicators that can be affected by policy and practice. Other data may be useful to provide context around a specific issue, but the key indicators should be those that can be improved through a community's efforts.

Although the project described here includes data at the statewide level, the comprehensive project also included nine reports with data produced at the metropolitan level, reflecting the size of Texas and the desire of communities for local data. Connecting local data to a larger geographic area can be an effective strategy for community engagement, especially when policy change is required at multiple administrative levels, but it requires a balancing of the availability and comparability of data at multiple geographic levels, as well as the capacity to analyze additional data. Investing in the building blocks of economic security helps Texas women be economically secure and magnifies the ripple effect that benefits families and communities. We hope this report will spark a desire to learn more about issues affecting women, encourage you to share what you've learned, and motivate you to act to improve the economic security of women in your community. Breaking down data by gender or other demographic factors (e.g. age, race/ethnicity) can illuminate the specific challenges or opportunities that exist and provide information that policymakers and community organizations can use to better meet the needs of all in their communities.

References

Adams, G., & Matthews, H. (2013). *Confronting the child care eligibility maze: Simplifying and aligning with other work supports*. Washington: Urban Institute. Retrieved from file:///C:/Users/Blasohn/Downloads/WSS-CC-Paper.pdf.

Bay Area Council Economic Institute. (2012). Analysis of U.S. Census Bureau, CFED Scorecard. Survey of income and program participation, 2008 Panel, Wave 7. Washington, DC: U.S. Department of Commerce.

Blau, F. D., & Kahn, L. M. (2007). The gender pay gap: Have women gone as far as they can? *Academy of Management Perspectives, 21,* 843–860.

Boushey, H. (2002). *Staying employed after welfare: Work supports and job quality vital to employment tenure and wage growth* (EPI Briefing Paper 128). Retrieved from http://www.epi.org/publication/briefingpapers_bp128/

Budig, M. J., & England, P. (2001). The wage penalty for motherhood. *American Sociological Review, 66,* 204–225.

Cunningham, M., & MacDonald, G. (2012). *Housing as a platform for improving education outcomes among low-income children.* Urban Institute. Retrieved from http://www.urban.org/sites/default/files/alfresco/publication-pdfs/412554-Housing-as-a-Platform-for-Improving-Education-Outcomes-among-Low-Income-Children.PDF

Families USA. (2009). *Hidden health tax: Americans pay a premium. Family USA.* Retrieved from http://familiesusa.org/sites/default/files/product_documents/hidden-health-tax.pdf

Glynn, S. J. (2010). Analysis of King, M., et al., *Integrated public use microdata series, Current Population Survey: Version 3.0.* [Machine-readable database]. Minneapolis: University of Minnesota.

Greenstone, M., & Looney, A. (2011). Trends: Reduced earnings for men in America. *The Milken Institute Review.* Retrieved from http://www.brookings.edu/~/media/research/files/papers/2011/7/men-earnings-greenstone-looney/07_milken_greenstone_looney.pdf

Magnuson, K., & Votruba-Drzal, E. (2009). Enduring influences of childhood poverty. *Focus, 26* (2), 32–37.

Moss-Racusin, C. A., Dovidio, J. F., Brescoll, V. L., Graham, M. J., & Handelsman, J. (2012). Science faculty's subtle gender biases favor male students. *PNAS, 109*(41), 16474–16479.

Population Reference Bureau. (2012a). Analysis of data from U.S. Census Bureau, American Community Survey, public use microdata sample.

Population Reference Bureau. (2012b). Analysis of American Community Survey data.

Ray Marshall Center. (2010). Calculations using 2010 Child Care subsidy and Census data.

Ray Marshall Center. (2012). Calculations using 2011 and 2012 Child Care Market Rate Survey data.

Ruggles, S., Alexander, J. T., Genadek, K., Goeken, R., Schroeder, M.B., & Sobek, M. (2010). *Integrated public use microdata series: Version 5.0* [Machine-readable database]. Minneapolis: University of Minnesota, 2010.

Schwartz, M., & Wilson, E. (2007). *Who can afford to live in a home? A look at the data from the 2006 American Community Survey.* U.S. Census Bureau. Retrieved from http://www.census.gov/housing/census/publications/who-can-afford.pdf

Short, K. (2013). *The research: Supplemental poverty measure: 2012.* Washington, DC: U.S. Department of Commerce, Economics, and Statistics Administration, U.S. Census Bureau. Retrieved from https://www.census.gov/prod/2013pubs/p60-247.pdf

Texas Higher Education Coordinating Board. (2011, March). *Overview: Tuition Deregulation.* Retrieved from http://www.thecb.state.tx.us/reports/PDF/3013.PDF?CFID=6390271&CFTOKEN=88291295

The Forum for Youth Investment. (2011, November). Ready by 21, Credentialed by 26 Series, #4: When working works: Employment and postsecondary success. Washington, D.C. Retrieved from http://forumfyi.org/files/CB26_Issue%20_Brief4.pdf

Texas Education Agency. (2012). Grade 9 longitudinal graduation and dropout Rates, by race/ethnicity, economic status, and gender, Texas public schools, class of 2012.

Texas Higher Education Coordinating Board. (2013). *Fall 2013 enrollment data.* Retrieved from texas higher education accountability System: http://www.txhighereddata.org/Interactive/Accountability/

Texas Higher Education Coordinating Board and Texas Education Agency. (2014). *FY2002 8th grade cohort tracked through FY 2012 higher education—11*-year study [Data file]. Retrieved from http://www.texastribune.org/education/publiceducation/8th-grade-cohorts/

Texas Workforce Commission. (2013, January 15). *Evaluation of effectiveness of subsidized child care program. Report to the 83rd Texas legislature.* Retrieved from http://www.twc.state.tx.us/files/twc/evaluation-effectiveness-child-care-program-83-legislature-twc.pdf

U.S. Bureau of Labor Statistics. (2013a). *Minimum wage workers in Texas.* Retrieved from http://www.bls.gov/ro6/fax/minwage_tx.htm

U.S. Bureau of Labor Statistics. (2013b). *Occupational employment and wages.* Retrieved from http://www.bls.gov/oes/current/oes399021.htm

U.S. Census Bureau. (2010). *Census urban and rural classification and urban area criteria*. Retrieved from http://www.census.gov/geo/reference/ua/urban-rural-2010.html
U.S. Census Bureau. (2012a). American Community Survey, 5-Year Estimates, Table B01001.
U.S. Census Bureau. (2012b). American Community Survey, 5-Year Estimates, Table B01002.
U.S. Census Bureau. (2012c). American Community Survey, 5-Year Estimates, Table B05003.
U.S. Census Bureau. (2012d). American Community Survey, 5-Year Estimates. Table B06003.
U.S. Census Bureau. (2012e). American Community Survey, 5-Year Estimates, Table B11003.
U.S. Census Bureau. (2012f). American Community Survey, 5-Year Estimates, Table B11012.
U.S. Census Bureau. (2012g). American Community Survey, 1-Year Estimates, Table B15002.
U.S. Census Bureau. (2012h). American Community Survey, 5-Year Estimates. Table B17001.
U.S. Census Bureau. (2012i). American Community Survey, 5-Year Estimates, Table B17003.
U.S. Census Bureau. (2012j). American Community Survey, 5-Year Estimates. Table B17012.
U.S. Census Bureau. (2012k). American Community Survey, 5-Year Estimates, Table B19126.
U.S. Census Bureau. (2012l). American Community Survey, 5-Year Estimates, Table B20017.
U.S. Census Bureau. (2012m). American Community Survey, 5-Year Estimates, Table B20002.
U.S. Census Bureau. (2012n). American Community Survey, 5-Year Estimates, Table B20004.
U.S. Census Bureau. (2012o). American Community Survey, 5-Year Estimates, Table B27001.
U.S. Census Bureau. (2012p). American Community Survey, 1-Year Estimates. Table GCT0101.
U.S. Census Bureau. (2012q). American Community Survey, 5-Year Estimates, Table S0101.
U.S. Census Bureau. (2012r). American Community Survey, 5-Year Estimates, Table S2402.
U.S. Census Bureau. (2012s). Population division. Annual estimates of the resident population for incorporated places over 50,000, ranked by July 1, 2012 Population: April 1, 2010 to July 1, 2012.
U.S. Census Bureau. (2012t). Population division. Annual estimates of the resident population by sex, race alone or in combination, and Hispanic origin for the United States, states, and counties: April 1, 2010 to July 1, 2012.
U.S. Census Bureau. (2012u). Population division. Cumulative estimates of resident population change for incorporated places over 50,000, ranked by percent change: April 1, 2010 to July 1, 2012.
U.S. Census Bureau. (2013). *Poverty thresholds*. Retrieved from http://www.census.gov/hhes/www/poverty/data/threshld/index.html
U.S. Department of Education. (2008). National Center for Education Statistics. 2007–08 National Postsecondary Student Aid Study (NPSAS:08).
U.S. Department of Education. (2013). *Three-year official cohort default rates for schools*. Retrieved from http://www2.ed.gov/offices/OSFAP/defaultmanagement/cdr.html
U.S. Government Accountability Office. (2011, October). *Gender pay differences: Progress made but women remain overrepresented among low-wage workers*. Retrieved from http://www.gao.gov/assets/590/585721.pdf

Author Biographies

Jennifer Lee is a Research Associate at the Center for Public Policy Priorities (CPPP), an independent public policy organization that uses data and analysis to advocate for solutions that enable Texans of all backgrounds to reach their full potential. Lee joined CPPP in 2013. Before coming to CPPP, she was an Education Pioneers Fellow with The New Teacher Project and Houston ISD. She earned a Bachelor of Arts in History from Wellesley College in 2007 and a Master of Public Affairs from the LBJ School of Public Affairs, University of Texas at Austin in 2013. Before returning to graduate school, Lee was the Associate Editor at the educational publisher Eye On Education. Her co-authored report "Economic Issues for Women in Texas" was produced by CPPP on behalf of the Texas Women's Foundation, the research and advocacy arm of Dallas Women's Foundation. Texas Women's Foundation focuses on issues that impact women across Texas, produces research studies and reports, and coordinates collective action.

Frances Deviney, Ph.D., is an Associate Director and Program Director of the Research and Planning team at the Center for Public Policy Priorities (CPPP), an independent public policy organization that uses data and analysis to advocate for solutions that enable Texans of all backgrounds to reach their full potential. As an Associate Director, Dr. Frances Deviney coordinates the Organizational Development work and oversees many of CPPP's data-based advocacy projects, including the Texas KIDS COUNT project and the Better Texas Family Budgets tool. Before coming to the Center in 2005, she conducted education research at the Southwest Educational Development Laboratory and was Legislative Director for a Texas State Representative. She earned her BA in Psychology from Vanderbilt University and Doctorate in Developmental Psychology from The University of Utah. Her co-authored report "Economic Issues for Women in Texas" was produced by CPPP on behalf of the Texas Women's Foundation, the research and advocacy arm of Dallas Women's Foundation. Texas Women's Foundation focuses on issues that impact women across Texas, produces research studies and reports, and coordinates collective action.

Chapter 10
Comprehensive Sustainability Indicators: The Houston Sustainability Indicators Program

Lester O. King

Abstract The goal of the Houston Sustainability Indicators (HSI) program is to develop a system of indicators best suited to monitor development in the City of Houston. Considered as a process model, HSI was developed to cover the following four objectives: (1) Prioritizing issues (2) Examining interrelatedness in urban development (3) Conducting spatial analysis through the use of Geographic Information Systems (GIS) and (4) Public education, stakeholder participation and public policy development.

Keywords Houston · Houston sustainability indicators · GIS · Principal components analysis · Comprehensive sustainability indicators · Distressed neighbourhoods · Policy indicators

10.1 Introduction

This article presents the process for the development of sustainability indicators for the City of Houston. The resulting indicators derived from this process were used to report urban sustainability performance at three (3) different spatial levels within the City: the municipality, district level and community level. Additionally an exploratory research procedure was applied to the indicators at the community level to make comparisons between communities. This research addresses some of the problems, in the practice of developing indicators. These are: (1) the development of a more systematic procedure to choose indicators and subsequently explore their usefulness beyond serving as a gauge (Dalal-Clayton and Bass 2002); (2) The lack of comprehensiveness of indicators making coverage of the complexity of urban areas possible (Wiek and Binder 2005); and (3) The lack of agreement on the benefits of utilizing indicators (Holden 2006a). Specifically, the discord between

L.O. King (✉)
Rice University, Houston, USA
e-mail: lok1@rice.edu

M. Holden et al. (eds.), *Community Quality-of-Life Indicators: Best Cases VII*, Community Quality-of-Life and Well-Being,
DOI 10.1007/978-3-319-54618-6_10

policy impact and knowledge offered to a variety of stakeholders (Brugmann 1997a, b; Pinfield 1997).

The Houston Sustainability Indicators Project (HSI), is the case study examined in this article. Following this introduction, we present an assessment of the systematic nature of the model procedure employed by HSI. Then we review the comprehensive nature of the HSI model, presenting the final list of indicators chosen for the case study of Houston. The next section reviews the importance of utilizing indicators by demonstrating three important uses of indicators. These are: (1) indicators serving as a tool for *public communication and public participation*; (2) indicators serving a more *technical and managerial* role, and (3) indicators serving to achieve *political objectives* (Pinfield 1997). It is important to point out that although this chapter highlights three uses of indicators, sustainability indicators can also serve other important functions to achieve the goals of development within human settlements such as: problem recognition and awareness; justificatory function; as well as providing normative guidance (King 2016; Neuman 2005).

Data used in HSI is primarily managed within a Geographic Information System (GIS). The benefits of utilizing this software include the ability to create applications to manage data; design maps for visual communication; and consolidation of spatial[1] and attribute[2] data. The HSI project currently consists of 25 indicators in 9 thematic areas. Reporting is conducted at three different levels of analysis (City level, where n = 1; District level, where n = 11; Community level, where n = 88). Data was collected from 1990 to present and will be collected annually into the future. The HSI indicators data includes a mixture of demographic, economic, cadastral and environmental types of data. This project integrates data from several sources including: federal data sources—US Decennial Census, US Geological Survey (USGS); state data sources—Texas Commission on Environmental Quality (TCEQ), Texas Education Agency (TEA); regional data sources—Houston-Galveston Area Council (HGAC); local data sources—City of Houston (COH), Harris County; and private data sources—InfoGroup. Data is collected in several different formats, not necessarily conforming to our preferred levels of analysis, which is the smallest level available. For example data may be collected at the parcel, block-group, census tract or county level. To manage the myriad data formats, the HSI team developed separate geodatabases roughly corresponding to the year each report is produced (2012–2015). Separate GIS applications are then developed for each year and each theme in HSI.

In reflecting on the details of constructing the HSI project, this chapter presents a model to develop sustainability indicators, which goes beyond linear measurement reporting. The HSI model can be used to identify underlying structures between sustainability indicators, which in turn helps to explain interactions in the complexity of the built environment (Moussiopoulos et al. 2010).

[1]Spatial data refer to measures such as distance, location, area measures etc.

[2]Attribute data refers to measures such as population counts, median housing value etc.

10.2 Systematic Procedure

The systematic procedure to develop the HSI project was conducted in 3 steps (Table 10.1). The model includes a normative operational component to integrate stakeholders; a systematic procedure to bridge the ecosystem elements of complex urban environments; and a function to evaluate the effectiveness of the indicators (Wiek and Binder 2005).

The uniqueness of each locale therefore can be reflected in the goals and objectives reached by all of the stakeholders in that system (Normative component). After indicators are chosen a virtual system is created, which has objective evaluation criteria based on applied statistical methodologies (Systematic component). Of course it is essential that the goals and objectives be periodically reviewed and the value of the indicators assessed (Evaluation component). The HSI model procedure ensures that the efforts of stakeholders are integrated and protected, since the Delphi methodology, described below, allows for joint decision making with the possibility that participants may change their opinion based on feedback from the opinions of others in the group. This generates equity in and amongst the suite of indicators within the system. The HSI procedure may be used as a model for other cities to follow. There exist other indicator project models, which present specific indicators for municipalities to follow such as ISO 37120 (2014). However the important contribution HSI presents is procedural. HSI is a procedural model, which allows for unique indicators to be developed by each locale since it is important to support local stakeholders to achieve their own goals, aspirations and needs according to the original definition of sustainable development (WCED 1987).

10.2.1 Normative Component

First we developed a *Draft Indicator Set* based on consolidation of two informational sources. The first source was a review of a meta-analysis study to identify the

Table 10.1 Three step HSI model procedure for sustainability indicators development

HSI model	
Components	Procedure
Normative component	**Step 1**: Define Indicators—Integrate Stakeholders
	Methodology: Decision management technique—Delphi exercises
Systematic component	**Step 2**: Explore interrelatedness between indicators
	Methodology: Exploratory research technique—Components analysis
Evaluation component	**Step 3**: Reporting and evaluating city and community performance to understand and explain urban complexity
	Methodology: Stakeholder feedback—Communicate findings through diverse media outlets and presentations to stakeholders

25 most frequently used indicators in a random sample of varying sized indicator projects in North America (SCS 2011, see Table 10.2). The second source was a review of indicators developed by the UN Commission on Sustainable Development (UNCSD).

There were 100 indicators in the UNCSD (2007) set. In comparison, the SCS national survey identified 27 most commonly used indicators. From these two sources 22 of the indicators were listed in both sources.

Three expert panels were convened for three separate half-day workshops to review and come to consensus on the most pressing sustainability priorities, policies and strategies appropriate for the City of Houston. Using the Delphi[3] methodology as the decision management technique, participants were supplied with the *Draft HSI Indicator List* along with data on development patterns using the *Draft HSI Indicators*. Experts were led in this exercise to form consensus on the ideal themes/topics that should be utilized to represent the most pressing sustainability priorities. The results from the expert panel workshops were consolidated to determine the *Final HSI Indicator Set*. Nine of the *Final HSI indicators* can be attributed to both the UNCSD (2007) indicators and the (SCS 2011) national survey.

Two different indicators frameworks were combined to develop the HSI indicators. These are the *Theme-SubTheme* framework and the *Category* framework. Both themes were chosen to ensure comprehensiveness of the final indicators. The *Theme-SubTheme* framework assists with comprehensiveness from a more normative perspective. This is achieved through the capability of allowing for recognition of sub layers within themes, which means stakeholders can identify indicators to monitor the progress of various strategies within one theme (UNCED 1992). This framework allows for the integration of multiple themes. Themes are representative of the most important aspirations of Houstonians and issues facing the city. The *Category* framework also achieves comprehensiveness, but from a more structural perspective. This is achieved in the HSI project by striving to balance the numbers of indicators identified within the sustainable development pillars of economic development, social development and environmental development. Table 10.3 presents the indicators selected for the HSI project.

10.2.2 Systematic Component

The majority of indicator studies display simple descriptive statistics to show each indicator's performance in the target city or country. Indexes are also a commonly

[3]Delphi methodology starts by first collecting and then consolidating participant responses to questions or a decision making challenge. The next stage is to present these responses back to participants showing divergence and convergence of opinions. Participants are then given another opportunity to amend their choices based on feedback from the opinions of the entire group. This procedure is continued iteratively for 3–4 iterations.

Table 10.2 Most frequently cited indicators from 20 city-regions in the US, Canada and the UK (SCS 2011)

Categories	Boston	Bay Area Alliance	Issaquah	Tuscon	Santa Monica	Missoula	Calvert-Henderson	Fraser Basin	Seattle	Calgary	Baltimore
City Count	23	21	20	20	20	19	19	19	18	16	16
Educational Achievement and Performance	X	X	X	X	X	X	X	X	X	X	X
Community Engagement	X	X	X	X	X		X	X	X	X	X
Employment/Unemployment	X	X	X	X			X	X	X	X	X
Land Use	X	X	X	X	X	X	X	X	X		X
Water Conservation	X	X	X	X	X		X	X	X	X	X
Affordable Housing	X	X	X	X	X	X			X	X	X
Crime	X	X	X	X		X	X	X	X	X	X
Air Quality—PM	X	X		X	X	X	X	X	X		
Cost of Living	X	X	X	X	X	X	X			X	X
Health Care: Access	X	X	X	X	X	X	X	X	X	X	X
Homelessness/Poverty	X	X	X		X	X	X	X		X	X
Waste Production		X	X		X		X	X	X	X	
Commuting		X	X	X	X	X			X	X	
Ecological Footprint	X		X	X	X		X	X	X	X	
Income Distribution	X	X		X		X	X	X	X	X	
Public Transportation	X	X	X	X	X	X		X			X
Air Quality—Ozone	X	X		X	X	X					X
Ecological Health	X		X	X	X	X	X	X	X	X	
Green Space	X	X	X	X		X		X	X		X
Recreation Area	X		X	X	X	X		X			X
Air Quality—Toxics	X	X			X	X	X		X		
Demographics	X	X			X	X	X	X	X	X	X

(continued)

Table 10.2 (continued)

Categories	Boston	Bay Area Alliance	Issaquah	Tuscon	Santa Monica	Missoula	Calvert-Henderson	Fraser Basin	Seattle	Calgary	Baltimore
Economic Diversification	X	X	X	X			X	X		X	X
Health Care: Affordability	X	X	X	X	X	X	X	X	X		
Obesity/Weight	X		X		X	X	X				

Categories	Chicago	Pasadena	Hamilton	Cincinnati	Minneapolis	NRDC—Smarter Cities	Ontario	FOF—British Cities	SustainLane	Total
City Count	15	14	13	11	11	10	10	8	8	
Educational Achievement and Performance	X			X	X		X	X		16
Community Engagement	X		X	X	X	X				15
Employment/Unemployment	X	X	X		X		X	X		15
Land Use	X	X	X	X			X			15
Water Conservation		X	X		X	X			X	15
Affordable Housing	X		X		X		X		X	14
Crime	X		X	X	X					14
Air Quality—PM		X	X			X	X		X	13
Cost of Living	X			X	X	X				13
Health Care: Access	X			X						13
Homelessness/Poverty	X	X			X	X				13
Waste Production		X	X	X		X		X	X	13
Commuting		X				X	X	X	X	12
Ecological Footprint		X			X	X		X		12
Income Distribution	X		X	X			X			12
Public Transportation	X	X		X					X	12
Air Quality—Ozone	X	X	X			X			X	11

(continued)

Table 10.2 (continued)

Categories	Chicago	Pasadena	Hamilton	Cincinnati	Minneapolis	NRDC—Smarter Cities	Ontario	FOF—British Cities	SustainLane	Total
Ecological Health					X			X		11
Green Space		X				X		X		11
Recreation Area		X	X				X		X	11
Air Quality—Toxics	X	X	X					X		10
Demographics	X									10
Economic Diversification	X						X			10
Health Care: Affordability				X						10
Obesity/Weight		X	X	X	X		X			10

Table 10.3 Houston sustainability indicators Final Indicator Set

Social indicators					
Theme	SubTheme	Indicator	National Survey	UN (2007)	Livability Literature
(I) Social Demography	Population Growth	(1) Population growth rate		x	
	Education	(2) Graduate degree attainment rate	x	x	
	Community Involvement	(3) Voter Participation	x		
(II) Poverty	Income Inequality	(4) Ratio of share in income of highest to lowest quintile	x	x	x
	Income Poverty	(5) Proportion of population living below poverty line	x	x	
	Healthcare Delivery	(6) Percent of population with health insurance	x	x	
(III) Livability	Cost of Living	(7) Proportion of persons spending more than 30% income on housing costs	x		x
	Quality of Life	(8) Proportion of persons living within ¼ mile to a public park			x
	Health and Nutrition	(9) Proportion of persons living more than 1 mile from large supermarket			x

(continued)

Table 10.3 (continued)

Social indicators					
Theme	SubTheme	Indicator	National Survey	UN (2007)	Livability Literature
Economic Indicators					
Theme	**SubTheme**	**Indicator**			
(IV) Economic Development	Employment	(10) Employment—population ratio	x	x	
	Macroeconomic Performance	(11) Primary Jobs/Green Jobs			
	Earnings	(12) Median income	x		
(V) Consumption and Production	Waste Generation and Management	(13) Generation of waste	x	x	
	Energy Use	(14) Annual energy consumption, total and by main user category		x	
(VI) Transportation	Access	(15) Proportion of population living within ¼ mile to transit stop	x		x
	Demand	(16) Total Vehicle Miles Travelled	x		
	Mode	(17) Modal split of passenger transportation		x	x
Environmental Indicators					
Theme	**SubTheme**	**Indicator**			
(VII) Atmosphere	Air Quality	(18) Ambient concentration of air pollutants	x	x	
	Climate Change	(19) Emissions of greenhouse gasses	x	x	

(continued)

Table 10.3 (continued)

Social indicators					
Theme	SubTheme	Indicator	National Survey	UN (2007)	Livability Literature
(VIII) Fresh Water	Water Quality	(20) Presence of faecal coliforms in freshwater		x	
	Water Demand	(21) Water use intensity by economic activity		x	
	Water Resources	(22) Proportion of total water resources used		x	
(IX) Land	Flooding	(23) Percentage of population living in the floodplain		x	
	Land Cover	(24) Land use change	x	x	
	Classification	(25) Jobs/Housing Balance			x

utilized strategy to simplify reporting. The use of indexes requires employing normative weights to the different indicators to construct the index. Weights are a normative construct and hence may not meet the demands of a rationally objective systematic procedure. The HSI model does not make use of normative weightings, but utilizes an exploratory research technique called *principal components analysis* to objectively assess interrelatedness among the indicators in the study. This produces a more systematic and objective system for index weights. The importance of understanding interrelatedness between the indicators in this study gives further insight into important phenomena existing between the 88 distinct communities in the study city. This HSI procedure ensures the integrity and reliability of an objective system by separating between normative contributions and systematic findings.

Principal components analysis was used to group the large number of indicators into clusters showing commonalities among the data. These clusters were given names by the research team to describe the unique ranking of indicators in each cluster and what the indicators with the highest weights in each group can tell us about the communities. Findings from the components analysis (Table 10.4) revealed five (5) distinct clusters of data. The clusters were titled: Wealthy Areas, Inner City Areas, Growth Areas, African American Areas, and Single Land Use Areas. The first cluster 'Wealthy Areas' is described here. Table 10.4 shows the cluster of nine high ranking indicators, which included Median Income (+), Health

Table 10.4 Components analysis

Indicators	Components/ Clusters				
	Wealth Areas	Inner City	Growth Areas	African American	Single Land Use Areas
MedianIncome	**.947**	.054	.100	.056	.016
HealthSpending	**.934**	.040	.046	.185	-.014
BelowPoverty	**-.893**	.118	-.073	.071	-.119
House+TransCosts	**.871**	-.314	.017	.098	.078
MedianValueHouse	**.834**	.324	-.037	.193	.007
WhitePersons	**.831**	-.023	.109	-.066	.016
MastersDegree	**.802**	.366	.065	.323	.086
Unemployment	**-.690**	-.297	-.137	.203	-.098
TransitUse	**-.534**	.406	.011	.505	-.106
VMT	-.133	**-.889**	.027	-.239	-.041
TransitAccess	-.108	**.826**	-.067	.324	-.066
OpenSpace	-.044	**-.772**	-.018	.039	.135
IntersectionDensity	-.011	**.738**	-.138	.108	.053
FoodDesertPersons	-.110	**-.722**	-.073	.075	.014
HighDevelopment	-.137	**.716**	.043	-.223	-.157
DistanceToCBD	.226	**-.671**	.440	-.217	.250
HousingInCenters	.404	**.635**	-.030	-.004	.123
ParkAccess	.155	**.617**	-.163	.076	.007
WaterUsePerHouse	.208	.052	**.867**	.083	.088
PopGrowth90-10	.190	-.203	**.815**	-.033	-.029
PopDensity	-.026	-.023	**.809**	-.017	-.102
PopClosetoWaste	-.207	.064	**.397**	-.093	-.048
HispanicPersons	-.305	-.240	-.107	**-.783**	-.154
Voting	.336	.090	-.122	**.688**	-.157
BlackPersons	-.455	-.421	-.112	**.545**	.184
LandUseMix	.028	-.227	-.223	.014	**.767**
PoorStreets	.207	.446	.182	.098	**.535**
HouseCost>30%Incom	-.182	.066	-.206	.000	**-.485**

Notes

Indicators Not shown due to low component clustering: %Jobs Primary; Other Races; Air Exceedances; Low-Mid Dev; Population Flooded; Adequate Storm Sewers

Components Analysis: PCA with Varimax orthogonal rotation. Explained Variance: @60%. KMO: 0.707

Care Spending (+), Poverty (−), Housing + Transportation costs (+), Median Housing Value (+), Concentration of White Persons (+), Masters Degrees (+), Unemployment (−), Transit Use (−). This cluster can be used to identify 'Wealthy' communities or their, their antithesis, 'Distressed' communities. These findings show that 'Wealthy' or 'Distressed' communities in Houston should be defined by more than simply *Median Income* alone, since eight other indicators correlate strongly with *Median Income* when analyzing all the measures across all the communities in Houston. Further it can be stated that when compared to the entire set of indicators measured across all the communities in Houston, this cluster of nine indicators are the strongest predictors to identify concentrations of Wealth and concentrations of Distressed communities.

To understand how the 88 communities in Houston ranked according to the 'Wealthy Areas' cluster, in terms of the continuum from most Wealthy to most Distressed, we ran another analysis to build a rationally objective index. We calculated *component scores* for each of the 88 communities. To determine the component score for a community, the community's measure on each indicator is multiplied by the component weight for that indicator. The sum of these weight-times-data products for all the variables yields the component score in the Wealthy/Distressed Index ranking shown below in Table 10.5 and Map 10.1.

Table 10.5 Factor scores

Component 1—Wealthy Areas		Wealthy Index Ranking of Communities	
Median Income	0.95	Rank	Communities (#1-Most Wealthy to #88-Most Distressed)
Average Spent Healthcare	0.93	1	AFTON OAKS/RIVER OAKS AREA
Per Below Poverty	−0.89	2	UNIVERSITY PLACE
Housing + Transportation Costs	0.87	3	LAKE HOUSTON
Median Value Houses	0.83	4	MEMORIAL
% White	0.83	5	KINGWOOD AREA
% Masters Degrees	0.8	6	GREENWAY/UPPER KIRBY AREA
% Unemployed	−0.69	7	GREATER UPTOWN
% Using Transit	−0.53	8	BRAESWOOD PLACE
		9	CLEAR LAKE
		10	WASHINGTON AVENUE COALITION/MEMORIAL
		79	SUNNYSIDE PARK
		80	GREATER GREENSPOINT
		81	GULFTON
		82	SETTEGAST
		83	INDEPENDENCE HEIGHTS
		84	OST/SOUTH UNION
		85	GREATER THIRD WARD
		86	WESTWOOD
		87	GREATER FIFTH WARD
		88	KASHMERE GARDENS

Neighborhoods were ranked according to the Data clusters

Cluster score for community j and cluster k: $Fij = \sum_{k=1}^{p} WjkXik$

where F—community score; *i*—community; *j*—cluster; W—component score coefficient; *k*—variable; X—standardized score; *p*—number of items in correlation matrix

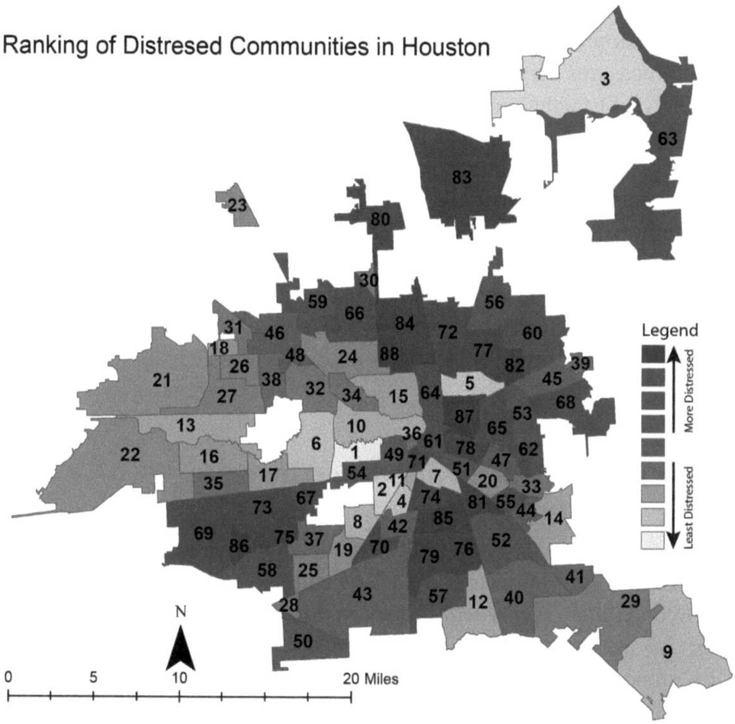

Map 10.1 Ranking of Distressed communities in Houston

10.2.3 Evaluation Component

To determine the value of HSI and its contribution to sustainable development in Houston, feedback from stakeholders is critically important. We presented the outcomes to stakeholders during a workshop, which was also open to the general public. Stakeholders were invited to review performance measures and re-evaluate the effectiveness of the indicators. The HSI team served as support staff only during this workshop. The goal of the workshop was to empower stakeholders to take ownership of the system of indicators; and to educate stakeholders and the general public using the performance results of their communities relative to the indicators. At the end of the session stakeholders presented their findings to the general public who attended the workshop. Some of the feedback we received included: several participants appreciated the comprehensiveness of the sustainability indicators; participants also appreciated the comparisons between communities.

The HSI team also reported results to several city departments and to elected officials. We were invited to participate in developing indicators to monitor the first General Plan in Houston, which is still under development. Several of the HSI indicators were adopted in the Houston General Plan. We were also invited to serve as external reviewers to the Parks Department and the development of District Park plans. The Houston Parks Board has invited us to support their efforts to review performance measures for the planning and development of largest park and trail system in the city to date.

The HSI project is communicated to the general public using a variety of strategies including: a web-based data visualization portal; presentations at community meetings; radio (Houston Public Media 2015); television (KPRC 2013) and newspaper reports and articles (Sarnoff 2013; Rudick 2013). In short, the strategy here is to prepare reports bi-annually on the various themes within the indicators database. Subsequent to new reports published, findings are communicated in as many different media as possible. Although data is updated annually, the indicators are scheduled for update with stakeholder review and participation every five years.

10.3 Policy Impact and Knowledge Increase

The Houston case study is an ideal example demonstrating the many different functions sustainability indicators programs can serve: *Political and Operational*; *Problem Recognition and Awareness*; *Justificatory*; *Monitoring Control and Reporting*; *Normative Guidance*; *Communication and Opinion Forming* (King 2016). It is important to state that the success of indicator programs should not be measured by direct contribution to policy making alone. Research exists to suggest that today's policy making is primarily influenced by economic elites and business lobbies when compared to other groups (Gilens and Page 2014). A more appropriate evaluation for indicator programs may consider the following roles:

(1) The *Public communication and Participation* role of educating stakeholders.
(2) The *Technical and Managerial* role of assessment of existing conditions and evaluation tool to focus actions.
(3) The *Political objective* role of performance measurement for accountability to planning decisions and goals (Pinfield 1997).

In this section we review the success of the HSI project in meeting its own stated objectives, which are (1) Prioritizing issues (2) Examining interrelatedness in urban development (3) Conducting spatial analysis through the use of Geographic Information Systems (GIS) (4) Public education, stakeholder participation and public policy development.

Sustainability indicators are an ideal format to communicate the prioritization of issues in an urban area. HSI utilized a combination of convening stakeholders to contribute to a decision management workshop to decide on ideal indicators. Then through a systematic and very objective methodology, we were able to demonstrate the most important issues and how they relate and compare to other also important issues. Last but not least, through social media, traditional media, workshop presentations, and neighborhood group meetings, we were able to communicate findings on major issues facing Houstonians. An important take-away form the HSI project is that urban areas exhibit a complex relationship between several internally complicated forces, therefore a simple index rating of 'Most sustainable', or 'Most Green' should be carefully justified by purveyors of such titles. HSI successfully utilized a more objective approach to ranking communities according to issues. Again, the HSI model does not make use of normative weightings, but utilizes an exploratory research technique called *principal components analysis* to objectively assess interrelatedness among the indicators in the study. Thereby producing a more systematic and objective system for index weights. This methodology for data mining lends itself to produce results that are more reliable.

Robust scientific methodologies were employed to explore the interrelatedness of the HSI indicators. The HSI project was the first and currently only comprehensive report developed in the City of Houston to address the state of development within and between electoral districts (King 2013). HSI is also the only source for reporting comprehensive development patterns between the 88 communities in Houston (King 2014a). These reports have facilitated a major gap in providing intelligence within and between communities in Houston. There now exists a comprehensive scientific methodology to assess communities according to demographics, economics, public services and the state of development. Many studies focus on individual indicators or thematic studies built around a few discrete measures, however HSI presents a methodology to demonstrate interrelatedness of indicators and thereby increase knowledge of connected phenomena in urban management and how this in turn affects individual communities.

Building the data into a GIS system to manage the indicators allows for efficient visual depiction of communities and study areas (Ghose and Huxhold 2002). It also allows for the efficient creation and extraction of data at the neighborhood level, which is difficult to obtain from many sources. The National Neighborhood Indicators Partnership (NNIP) is an umbrella organization that has organized indicator programs around the US and strives to encourage programs to make data available to the benefit of the general public. HSI is collaborating with NNIP to this end, for the city of Houston. This relationship is expected to further leverage the ability for HSI to more efficiently support local groups with access to data and intelligence of community dynamics.

Public participation, education and policy development are all difficult to measure since direct and indirect opportunities grow organically from indicator programs (Holden 2006b). Communication using several varied media outlets is a good strategy not just to publicize data, but seizing the opportunity to educate the general public on the epistemology of sustainable development. The Houston Planning Department invited the HSI team to assist with the development of indicators for the first Houston General Plan in 2015. Many of the indicators identified as part of the HSI project were adopted by the planning staff to be used directly in the General Plan. Although this is clear evidence of linear policy uptake, it should be stated once more that there are several other important functions, roles and purposes indicators can perform in addition to direct linear policy impacts. For example, the HSI team collaborated with the World Business Council for

Sustainable Development (WBCSD) to identify ideal indicators to monitor alternative energy usage and management among various classes of buildings in Houston (King 2014b).

10.4 Conclusion

This research demonstrates a few important contributions to the literature on sustainability indicators. The most important contribution is the applied methodology to separate between normative contributions and objective, empirical findings. Normative contributions tend to be heavily political and biased within many urban areas. It is important for stakeholders who are politically active to participate, but less so for these participants to manipulate findings based on normative pre-conceived notions. The benefit of utilizing a large number of indicators is the possibility of generating wider knowledge of the comprehensive performance of an urban area (Science for Environment Policy 2015). This is further buttressed by employing methodologies to understand interrelatedness between different themes represented by indicators. HSI demonstrates a methodology to accomplish this goal of soliciting new understandings of connections and interrelated processes within and between our communities.

Urban sustainability has matured into a very complex system of management of social, physical, institutional and policy environments. In our society the three competing interests of social, market and environmental perspectives, each have a stake in these changing diverse environments and as such should be the gauge by which to balance the environments. Using social, market and environmental perspectives as the gauge for balance we can apply community discourse to achieve that goal. However we should keep in mind that the process itself would be dependent on the distribution of power and organized interests (Kaiser et al. 1995).

The benefits of utilizing the HSI procedure as a model for sustainability indicators development are clearly demonstrated in the preceding research analysis. Relationships in urban development measures can be combined in a systematic format under the rubric of sustainability. The publication and wide dissemination of these results is part of the ideal procedure for the HSI model. This supports the empowerment of citizens to better enable analysis of urban development patterns.

References

Brugmann, J. (1997a). Is there a method in our measurement? The use of indicators in local sustainable development planning. *Local Environment, 2*(1), 59–72.

Brugmann, J. (1997b). Sustainability indicators revisited: Getting from political objectives to performance outcomes—A response to Graham Pinfield. *Local Environment, 2*(3), 299–302.

Dalal-Clayton, B., & Bass, S. (2002). *Sustainable development strategies*. London, UK: Earthscan Publications.
Ghose, R., & Huxhold, W. E. (2002). The role of multi-scalar GIS-based indicator studies in formulating neighborhood planning policy. *URISA Journal, 14*(2), 6–17.
Gilens, M., & Page, B. (2014). Testing theories of American politics: Elites, interest groups, and average citizens. *Perspectives on Politics, 12*(3), 564–581.
Holden, M. (2006a). Revisiting the local impact of community indicators projects: Sustainable Seattle as prophet in its own land. *Applied Research in Quality of Life, 1*(3), 253–277.
Holden, M. (2006b). Urban indicators and the integrative ideal of cities. *Cities, 23*(3), 170–183.
Houston Public Media. (2015). *Is it about race or income? How we define gentrification in Houston,* Houston, TX, October 8.
ISO. (2014). *ISO 37120: Sustainable development of communities—Indicators for city services and quality of life*. Geneva, Switzerland: International Standards Organization.
Kaiser, E. J., Godschalk, D. R., & Chapin, F. S. (1995). *Urban land use planning* (Vol. 4). Chicago, IL: University of Illinois Press.
King, L. (2014a). *Houston Community Sustainability: The quality of life Atlas*. Houston, TX: Shell Center for Sustainability, Rice University.
King, L. (2014b). *Energy efficiency in buildings: Market review*. Washington, DC: World Business Council for Sustainable Development.
King, L. (2016). Functional sustainability indicators. *Ecological Indicators, 66,* 121–131.
King, L. (2013). *The sustainable development of Houston Districts: The Health of the City Report*. Houston, TX: Shell Center for Sustainability.
KPRC. (2013). *Houston's sustainability*. TX: Houston.
Moussiopoulos, N., Achillas, C., Vlachokostas, C., & Spyridi, D. (2010). Environmental, social and economic information management for the evaluation of sustainable areas: A system of indicators for Thessaloniki Greece. *Cities* 377–384.
Neuman, M. (2005). Notes on the uses and scope of city planning theory. *Planning Theory, 4*(2), 123–145.
Pinfield, G. (1997). The use of indicators in local sustainable development planning: A response to Jeb Brugmann. *Local Environment, 2*(2), 185–188.
Rudick, T. (2013). Houston's not so affordable anymore: New study ranks it on 26th among major U.S. cities. *CultureMap*, September 25: 1.
Sarnoff, N. (2013). Housing costs put hurt on incomes. *Houston Chronicle*, September 24: 1.
Science for Environment Policy. (2015). *Indicators for sustainable cities*. Bristol, UK: European Commission DG Environment.
SCS. (2011). *Measuring city sustainability: Project Houston*. Houston: Shell Center for Sustainability, Rice University.
UNCSD. (2007). *Indicators of sustainable development: Guidelines and methodologies* (3rd ed.). New York, NY: United Nations.
UNCED. (1992). Agenda 21, Program of Action for Sustainable Development. *United Nations Conference on Environment and Development.* Rio de Janeiro, Brazil: United Nations.
WCED. (1987). *Our common future*. Oxford, UK: Oxford University Press.
Wiek, A., & Binder, C. (2005). Solution spaces for decision-making: A sustainability assessment tool for city-regions. *Environmental Impact Assessment Review, 25,* 589–608.

Author Biography

Dr. Lester King is a scholar of urban studies and environmental policy, specializing in urban sustainable development planning. His research interests focus on community sustainability with specific expertise in strategic planning and the development and use of community sustainability indicators as a measurement tool for development planning, program evaluation and community engagement. Dr. King has extensive expertise in the development and construction of community wellbeing indicators, has developed partnerships with a range of government, community partners and business partners and is passionate about using comprehensive data to fully understand community and urban dynamics.

MIX
Papier aus verantwortungsvollen Quellen
Paper from responsible sources
FSC® C105338
FSC
www.fsc.org

If you have any concerns about our products,
you can contact us on
ProductSafety@springernature.com

In case Publisher is established outside the EU,
the EU authorized representative is:
Springer Nature Customer Service Center GmbH
Europaplatz 3, 69115 Heidelberg, Germany

Printed by Libri Plureos GmbH
in Hamburg, Germany